D0463131

Effective
School
Interventions

Evidence-Based Strategies
for Improving Student Outcomes

second edition

Natalie Rathvon

THE GUILFORD PRESS
New York   London

Library of Congress Cataloging-in-Publication Data

Rathvon, Natalie.
  Effective school interventions : evidence-based strategies for improving student outcomes / Natalie Rathvon. — 2nd ed.
    p. cm.
  Includes bibliographical references and index.
  ISBN 978-1-57230-967-8 (hardcover : alk. paper)
  1. Inclusive education—United States. 2. Classroom management—United States. 3. Behavior modification—United States. 4. Academic achievement—United States. 5. Social skills—Study and teaching—United States. I. Title.
  LC1201.R38 2008
  371.9′046—dc22

                                                                        2008019958

*For Ryan Fraser Getgood
and Erin Ramsey Getgood—
Two natural interventions*

About the Author

Natalie Rathvon, PhD, earned a doctorate in education from George Mason University and a doctorate in clinical psychology from The George Washington University, where she is Assistant Clinical Professor of Psychology. A former teacher, guidance director, special education coordinator, and counselor educator, she provides consultation and professional development to schools and agencies in the areas of assessment and accountability, reading, problem-solving teams, and school-based interventions. She has been a trainer for Reading First, trainer and peer reviewer for Early Reading First, and member of the U.S. Department of Education technical workgroup reviewing Even Start state accountability systems. Dr. Rathvon is a member of the board of directors of SchoolTalk, Inc., a nonprofit corporation in the District of Columbia that develops models and provides training for dispute resolution and home–school collaboration in special education service delivery. She is the author of the first edition of *Effective School Interventions*, subtitled *Strategies for Enhancing Academic Achievement and Social Competence* (1999, Guilford Press); *Early Reading Assessment: A Practitioner's Handbook* (2004, Guilford Press); and *The Unmotivated Child: Helping Your Underachiever Become a Successful Student* (1996, Simon & Schuster).

Preface

Since the first edition of this book was published in 1999, the field of school-based interventions has undergone a remarkable expansion. The mandates of the No Child Left Behind Act of 2001 (NCLB; 2001) and the Individuals with Disabilities Education Improvement Act (IDEA; 2004) to support students in general education with scientifically based instructional practices have focused attention as never before on the critical importance of implementing classroom strategies that can meet the needs of today's increasingly diverse student population. Schools are now explicitly charged with implementing scientifically based interventions and evaluating their effectiveness, using a response-to-intervention (RTI) approach designed to enhance the likelihood that all students will reach the proficiency standards set forth in NCLB. Accompanying these legislative mandates has been unparalleled growth in the knowledge base of empirically validated interventions, most notably in the area of reading (National Reading Panel, 2000; Snow, 2002; Snow, Burns, & Griffin, 1998). Other developments, such as the expansion of school-based problem-solving teams and the use of RTI approaches to special education determination and service delivery, have underscored the need for research-based, practical strategies that can enhance all students' opportunities for success in the regular classroom.

As pressures for improving academic performance and documenting students' progress in meeting proficiency standards have increased, so too have the demands on school consultants. Today's school consultants need more than a few isolated strategies targeting a single low-performing or ineffectively behaving student. They need to be knowledgeable about a broad range of strategies that enhance teachers' capacity to create orderly, productive learning environments and students' capacity to benefit from instruction. In particular, they need to be knowledgeable about interventions that can improve the outcomes for an entire classroom group while still accommodating diverse learners. The importance of considering effectiveness in intervention selection has been underscored by the American Psychological Association Division 16 and the Society for the Study of School Psychology Task Force on Evidence-Based Interventions in School Psychology (Task Force). Formed in 1998 to help bridge the often-cited gap between research and practice and endorsed by the National Association of School Psychologists, the Task Force has developed a framework with specific efficacy criteria for evaluating empirically supported intervention and prevention programs described in the literature (Kratochwill & Stoiber, 2002). Despite these efforts and the growing database of empirically validated interventions, evidence-based interventions have been slow to enter regular classroom practice (Gersten, Chard, & Baker, 2000; Riley-Tillman, Chafouleas, Eckert, & Kelleher, 2005). Many of the intervention studies in the literature have been implemented by researchers in controlled settings rather than in typical contexts by natural intervention agents, such as teachers and parents, and are impractical for general education classrooms (Stichter, Clarke, & Dunlap, 2004). Unless interventions can be translated into the day-to-day realities of the classroom, teachers will be reluctant to implement them and maintain them over time, regardless of the quantity and quality of the evidence base.

Moreover, busy practitioners have limited time to sift through the ever expanding array of intervention-oriented journals, books, and web-based resources to locate a strategy that matches the problem they are trying to address. Even if practitioners are able to locate an intervention targeting the referral problem, other barriers to implementation remain. Because of space limitations in journals and books, interventions are seldom described in sufficient detail to permit accurate and effective implementation. Many interventions described in the literature or available from commercial publishers are too costly, time-consuming, and/or complex to be implemented by regular classroom teachers. Consultants seeking to assist teachers of struggling students must first identify a suitable strategy for the identified problem within the limits of their resources and then attempt to adapt it to the exigencies of the classroom environment. Given these constraints, it is a small wonder that even when pre-referral interventions are attempted, consultants tend to rely on a narrow range of strategies, and teachers often report that the referral problem remains unsolved.

PURPOSE

This text is designed to bridge the gap between research and the practical realities of consulting in today's schools by providing a handbook of empirically validated interventions that have been translated from the original source or sources and adapted for implementation in the regular classroom environment. Each of the 70 interventions is presented in a standardized format that provides step-by-step implementation procedures to facilitate treatment integrity and successful outcomes. Designed specifically for use within a consultation framework, the format has been developed and refined in the context of numerous consultations, *in vivo* coaching sessions, intervention assistance team meetings, and professional development programs. To meet the increasing demand for accountability and data-driven decision making in educational programming, each intervention includes an evaluation component that describes several different methods of assessing its effects on the targeted area of concern. This book is also designed as a resource guide to the rapidly expanding field of evidence-based school interventions. In addition to the citations for each intervention, each chapter includes an annotated list of print and web-based resources to assist consultants in locating other useful materials.

AUDIENCE

This book is written for practitioners in school psychology, child and adolescent clinical psychology, regular and special education, counseling, educational administration, and school social work, and for graduate or preservice students in those disciplines. It should be especially useful to school psychologists and consultants, special education coordinators, regular and special education teachers, and other practitioners involved in intervention-based service delivery. It is also intended to serve as a resource for practitioners who conduct psychological and psychoeducational assessments with school-age children. Using this book, they can locate strategies targeting a wide variety of referral problems and include them in the recommendation sections of their reports to help link assessment results to intervention. Examples of this application are provided in Chapter 2.

ORGANIZATION OF THE TEXT

The text consists of two parts. Beginning with two case examples, Part I reviews the challenges faced by today's educators in addressing the needs of an increasingly diverse student population and recently developed approaches to meeting those challenges, including the evidence-based intervention movement, intervention assistance programs, and RTI approaches. Chapter 1 also presents the criteria for intervention selection, intervention format, targets of intervention, and suggestions for using the book. Chapter 2 describes best practices for maximizing the success of an intervention-based approach to improving student outcomes, steps in the intervention assistance process, legal and ethical considerations, issues in the selection and use of reinforcers in contingency-based interventions, and strategies for evaluating intervention effectiveness. Two case examples are presented to illustrate how several strategies can be combined to create a comprehensive intervention plan for an individual student or an entire class.

Part II presents the 70 interventions and is divided into four chapters. In keeping with the book's ecological perspective, the chapters follow a logical progression from proactive classroom management strategies to academic enhancement interventions to behavior management strategies. Chapter 3 presents 16 proactive strategies designed to create a motivating, disruption-free classroom environment. The proactive interventions target seven key classroom management tasks: (1) organizing a productive classroom environment, (2) establishing classroom rules and procedures, (3) managing transitions, (4) managing small-group instruction and independent seatwork, (5) communicating competently with students, (6) teaching prosocial behaviors, and (7) building positive relationships in the classroom. Because these strategies promote high levels of student engagement and motivation, they should reduce the need for subsequent interventions targeting poor academic performance and disruptive behavior, which often result from ineffective instructional and behavior management systems.

Chapter 4 presents 34 interventions designed to improve academic performance. Also included is an introduction to curriculum-based measurement (CBM), an assessment technology ideally suited to monitoring student progress and evaluating intervention effectiveness. Intervention targets include academic productivity (classwork and independent seatwork); homework; and performance in four academic domains (reading, mathematics, writing, and the content areas of social studies and science). The reading section is further divided into three sections, based on the subskill targeted: (1) decoding and word recognition, (2) fluency, and (3) vocabulary and comprehension. The writing section is divided into two sections: (1) spelling and (2) written expression. Chapter 5 presents 13 interventions targeting student behavior and social competence, divided into two sections: (1) strategies for increasing on-task behavior and reducing disruptive behavior in the classroom and (2) strategies for improving behavior in nonclassroom settings, such as lunchrooms, playgrounds, and hallways. Chapter 6 presents seven interventions for preschoolers, divided into three sections: (1) proactive classroom management strategies, (2) strategies to enhance language and early literacy skills, and (3) strategies to improve behavior and social competence.

NEW TO THIS EDITION

Although this revision retains the same basic structure and intervention categories as the previous edition, the two introductory chapters have been substantially modified to incorporate recent research and developments in the field of school-based interventions, including RTI approaches to intervention design and delivery. Other changes designed to reflect best practices and enhance usability are described below.

Updated and Expanded Intervention Coverage

• Of the 70 interventions, 42 are new to this edition: 8 proactive interventions, 24 academic interventions, and 10 behavior interventions. In the field of school-based interventions, recency is not always synonymous with efficacy and usability, however. The text retains a core group of keystone strategies, especially in the area of proactive classroom management. Field testing and research alike attest to the crucial role these interventions play in creating optimal learning environments for both teachers and students. In addition, based on data obtained during field testing, one strategy (*Countdown to Free Time: Improving Productivity during Small-Group Instruction*) has been moved from the Behavior Interventions chapter to the Proactive Classroom Management Interventions chapter.

• A seventh category of proactive interventions targeting positive relationships in the classroom has been added to reflect a growing body of research documenting the powerful and long-lasting contribution of teacher–student relationships to children's academic and social outcomes and the role of peer influence in shaping classroom and school norms. The category on managing independent seatwork has also been expanded to include strategies for managing small-group instruction to reflect the current emphasis on differentiated instruction and the fact that independent seatwork often occurs in conjunction with teacher-delivered small-group activities.

• In keeping with the increasing use of positive behavior support (PBS) models designed to enhance social competency for all students, several schoolwide interventions are included in the section of behavior strategies targeting nonclassroom settings. The title of this section has also been changed from "Interventions to Improve Behavior in Special Classes and Less Structured Situations" to "Interventions to Improve Behavior in Nonclassroom Settings" to clarify the difference between settings.

• Academic interventions that can be applied across a variety of curricular domains are now presented in the Academic Productivity section of the Academic Interventions chapter rather than in the subject-area sections. This modification not only conserves space but also increases usability by demonstrating how the same basic strategy can be implemented in several academic subjects.

• Consistent with the increasing focus on early intervention in federal and state initiatives, a chapter with interventions for preschoolers has been added. Although these interventions also have utility for primary-grade children, they were originally designed and validated in preschool settings. The three sections in the chapter reflect the three intervention categories in the rest of the text: (1) proactive classroom management strategies, (2) language enhancement strategies, and (3) behavior strategies.

• Based on field testing and feedback from practitioners using the first edition, intervention procedures have been expanded to clarify key aspects of implementation. Additional tables and figures have also been included to enhance users' understanding of the procedures and thus increase treatment fidelity. Similarly, a larger number of intervention variations are presented to help practitioners tailor strategies to the needs of their own student populations.

To help accommodate this expanded coverage, the total number of interventions has been slightly reduced (from 76 to 70 strategies).

Updated and Expanded Coverage of Curriculum-Based Measurement Procedures

• Descriptions of CBM procedures now include a recently developed version for the content areas (*Vocabulary Matching*). Procedures for the other four subject areas (reading, mathematics, spelling, and writing) have been extensively revised to reflect the expanding CBM knowledge base and the increasing use of generic materials rather than CBMs constructed from students' own curricula.

New Features and Resources

• In response to reader requests and changes in federal laws and regulations since the previous edition, the section on legal issues and ethics considerations in Chapter 2 has been expanded to provide additional guidance to practitioners, especially those participating in team-based intervention assistance programs.

• Each intervention section now includes a *cross-reference box* to help readers locate strategies in other sections or chapters with similar components but different targets and/or other strategies with potential utility for improving outcomes in the targeted area.

• *Special topics sections* throughout the text highlight key concepts, critical issues, and best practices in areas such as evaluation, intervention scripts, motivation, academic engagement, brief experimental analysis, and functional behavioral assessment.

• An appendix is provided at the end of each of the four intervention chapters to assist readers in rapidly locating appropriate strategies and comparing strategies within the same domain (i.e., proactive, academic, behavioral, and preschool interventions).

A NOTE OF THANKS

I would like to express my appreciation to the many readers and field-test participants who have provided feedback on the first edition of this book. I welcome your suggestions for improving future editions of *Effective School Interventions: Evidence-Based Strategies for Improving Student Outcomes* and invite you to contact me at *nrathvon@natalierathvon. com.*

Acknowledgments

I would like to express my sincere appreciation to the authors, publishers, and journal board members for permitting me to adapt their work into the intervention format and to all of the authors cited in this book for their contributions to the field of evidence-based interventions. I would also like to thank the teachers, administrators, psychologists, consultants, graduate students, parents, and students who participated in the field testing. A special note of thanks goes to the staff of the AppleTree Institute for Education Innovation, especially Mary Anne Lesiak, Director of Education, and Heather Benson, Early Intervention Coordinator.

I also would like to thank Craig Thomas, Editor for School Psychology at The Guilford Press, for his assistance and support during the preparation of this book, and Chris Jennison, Publisher for Education at Guilford, with whom this revision was first undertaken, and who has been an unwavering source of encouragement throughout my happy association with Guilford.

This book would not have been possible without the assistance of The George Washington University Gelman Library staff, including Glenn Canner, Manager of Resource Sharing; Michael Pounds of the Interlibrary Loan Service; Kim To and Michelle Stewart of the Consortium Loan Service; Debbie Bezanson, Coordinator of Electronic Resources; Caroline Crouse, Reference and Electronic Resources Librarian; Gale Etschmaier, Assistant University Librarian for Public Services; Randy Hertzler, Collection Development Librarian for the Social Sciences; Joyce Whitmore, Periodicals Manager; and Wendell Kellar, Periodicals Desk Manager. My thanks also go to the faculty and students of The George Washington University Department of Psychology, especially Dr. Rolf Peterson and Dr. Risa Brody.

As always, I happily acknowledge my gratitude to my husband, James, my dearest companion and collaborator.

Contents

EFFECTIVE SCHOOL INTERVENTIONS

PART I

The Intervention Assistance Approach to Improving Student Outcomes

CHAPTER 1

Introduction

Toby is an engaging 8-year-old second grader whose broad smile is seldom evident in the classroom these days. Over the course of the year, Toby has become increasingly inattentive, unproductive, and uncooperative, especially during reading instruction and independent seatwork. He often fails to begin assigned tasks promptly or to complete them on time, complains that school is "boring," and bothers his classmates when they are trying to work. Toby's problems are beginning to spill over onto the playground, and Mrs. Melloy notices that the other students are now avoiding him at recess. Because he is older than many of his classmates, Mrs. Melloy is reluctant to recommend him for retention, but she worries that he will be unable to cope with the academic and behavioral demands of third grade.

The students in Mr. Garrison's seventh-grade English class have always been talkative, but recently they have become noisier and more unruly. Every day it takes them several minutes to settle down before Mr. Garrison can begin the lesson, and even then some students continue talking and joking among themselves while he is speaking. When he tells them to be quiet, they either protest that they weren't talking, offer some excuse as to why they were talking, or complain that he is picking on them. Mr. Garrison also worries that the class as a whole is becoming less productive. Many students turn in their homework late or fail to complete it at all, and their grades are slipping. Although Mr. Garrison has talked with the class several times about the importance of behaving appropriately and completing homework, these conversations have had little impact on behavior or academic performance. Referring the most disruptive students to in-school suspension has also failed to solve the problem.

CHALLENGES TO TODAY'S EDUCATORS

As school consultants know only too well, today's teachers are encountering increasing numbers of students who, like Toby and those in Mr. Garrison's class, have problems with academic performance, behavior, or both. The last few decades have seen a dramatic rise in the diversity and intensity of student needs, coupled with greater demands for accountability and a school curriculum linking student performance to high-stakes testing. America's classrooms are now home to a highly diverse student population in terms of achievement levels, ethnic and linguistic backgrounds, socioeconomic status, and disability status, including an increasing number of students from families living below the poverty level and/or from homes in which English is not the primary language. Between 1972 and 2004, the percentage of students from minority backgrounds enrolled in public schools increased from 22 to 42%, with the largest increase among Hispanic students (from 6 to 20%). Moreover, between 1979 and 2005, the percentage of students speaking a language other than English at home rose from 9 to 20% (National Center for Education Statistics, 2007a).

The need for effective school-based interventions has been underscored by reports from the National Assessment of Educational Progress (NAEP) indicating that only about one-third of U.S. fourth, eighth, and twelfth graders are performing at proficient levels in reading and less than one-third are proficient in mathematics (National Center for Education Statistics, 2005, 2007b). U.S. students also score lower in mathematics and science on international assessments compared with their counterparts in other industrialized nations (National Center for Education Statistics, 2004a). Moreover, despite efforts to reduce the numbers of students in special education programs, the number and percentage of students receiving special education services has risen steadily, from 3.7 million students (8% of total public school enrollment) in the period 1976–1977 to 6.7 million students (14% of total public school enrollment) in the period 2005–2006 (National Center for Education Statistics, 2007a). In response to this achievement crisis, recent federal legislation, including the 2004 reauthorization of the Individuals with Disabilities Education Improvement Act (IDEA; 2004), which promotes early intervention and the use of evidence-based interventions prior to referral for special education, and the No Child Left Behind Act of 2001 (NCLB; 2001), with its mandates for scientifically validated practices, have highlighted the importance of classroom strategies that can enhance the capacity of teachers to meet student needs and the capacity of students to respond to instruction. At the same time, there has been a growing recognition of the critical influence of school experiences on children's long-term outcomes, especially for children from high-poverty and diverse backgrounds (Hamre & Pianta, 2001; Klingner & Artiles, 2006; La Paro & Pianta, 2000; Rimm-Kaufman, Fan, Chiu, & You, 2007). To meet these challenges, school consultants will need expertise in helping teachers create classroom environments that promote academic productivity and appropriate social behavior for an increasingly diverse student population. In particular, they will need information about a broad range of strategies that are not only effective in enhancing outcomes for individual students but that can also be applied on a group basis to help all the students in a classroom become successful learners. Consultants will also need information about the *intervention assistance process*—the process of designing, implementing, and evaluating interventions—whether that process is implemented by an individual consultant or, as is rapidly becoming standard practice, within a team-based framework.

THE EVIDENCE-BASED INTERVENTION AND PRACTICE MOVEMENT

In the not too distant past, consultants and teachers tended to rely on interventions based primarily on familiarity. Under NCLB mandates, however, schools are required to use scientifically validated practices in order to bring all students to proficiency by the year 2017. There have also been numerous calls in the field urging school psychologists and consultants to implement evidence-based strategies and practices at the classroom and building level to assist students with learning and behavioral problems (e.g., Christenson, Carlson, & Valdez, 2002; Kratochwill & Shernoff, 2004; Kratochwill & Stoiber, 2000a, 2000b). In 1998, Division 16 of the American Psychological Association and the Society for the Study of School Psychology collaborated to form the Task Force on Evidence-Based Interventions in School Psychology with the mission of bridging the research-to-practice gap by identifying prevention and intervention programs, using rigorous criteria to review them, and providing ratings reflecting that review (Kratochwill & Stoiber, 2002; Stoiber & Kratochwill, 2000). In a related effort, the Institute of Education Sciences at the U.S. Department of Education established the What Works Clearing House (*http://www.whatworks.org*) in 2002 to develop standards for reviewing and synthesizing educational research and to provide educators, policymakers, researchers, and the public with a central independent source of scientific evidence of effective educational interventions.

Evidence-Based Interventions

Evidence-based interventions (EBIs) are strategies, practices, and programs for which research is available documenting their effectiveness. Although NCLB refers on numerous occasions to evidence-based practices, it offers no specific definition as to what constitutes an evidence-based intervention or practice. It does, however, provide a definition of scientifically based reading research:

> The term "scientifically based reading research" means research that—
>
> (A) applies rigorous, systematic, and objective procedures to obtain valid knowledge relevant to reading development, reading instruction, and reading difficulties; and
> (B) includes research that—
>   (i)   employs systematic, empirical methods that draw on observation or experiment;
>   (ii) involves rigorous data analyses that are adequate to test the stated hypotheses and justify the general conclusions drawn;
>   (iii) relies on measurements or observational methods that provide valid data across evaluators and observers and across multiple measurements and observations; and
>   (iv) has been accepted by a peer-reviewed journal or approved by a panel of independent experts through a comparably rigorous, objective, and scientific review. (20 U.S.C. § 6368[6])

Moreover, there is no consensus regarding the quantity or quality of evidence needed to identify a specific intervention as evidence-based. Dunst, Trivette, and Cutspec (2002) have offered this useful operational definition of evidence-based practices: "Practices that are informed by research, in which the characteristics and consequences of environmental variables are empirically established and the relationship directly informs what a practitioner can do to produce a desired outcome" (p. 3).

The Need for a New Paradigm in Special Education Systems

The emphasis on evidence-based practices and intervention-oriented service delivery in NCLB and IDEA 2004 arose in response to concerns regarding numerous serious problems associated with traditional special education practices, including overidentification and misidentification of students, overrepresentation of students from minority backgrounds, wide variations in identification and eligibility procedures, and the failure of the process to produce positive outcomes for children (Bentum & Aaron, 2003; Donovan & Cross, 2002; Fletcher et al., 2002; Kavale & Forness, 1999; Reschly & Ysseldyke, 2002). In the past several years, increasing concern has also been expressed by professional organizations, researchers, and practitioners regarding definitions and procedures for identifying students under the category of specific learning disability (e.g., Fletcher, Coulter, Reschly, & Vaughn, 2004; Learning Disabilities Roundtable, 2002). When the Education for All Handicapped Children Act (Public Law 94-142) took effect in 1975, it did not mandate a specific approach for states and local school districts to use in identifying and classifying students as learning disabled

(LD). Moreover, at that early point in research on learning disabilities, there was no consensus on the specific cognitive and linguistic markers for LD. By default, diagnosis became an *exclusionary process*—that is, IQ tests were administered to rule out the possibility that a child's academic problems resulted from low intelligence, based on the assumptions that the problems of children with average intelligence differed from those of children with low intelligence, arose from a different set of cognitive deficits, required different interventions, and had a different (i.e., better) prognosis (Torgesen, 2000). The necessity of demonstrating a severe discrepancy between cognitive ability and achievement meant that help was delayed until the student's achievement level was low enough to meet the criterion. As a result, most students were not formally identified as LD until third grade or later, well after the time when assistance could have been most effective (Torgesen et al., 2001). Given this "wait and fail" model, it was not surprising that many students made minimal academic gains after placement and that few were able to exit special education programming (Donovan & Cross, 2002; Lyon et al., 2001).

All of these assumptions underlying the IQ–achievement discrepancy model have recently been challenged, however, with the vast majority of researchers arguing that the discrepancy model should be abandoned in favor of alternative models of identification (e.g., Fletcher et al., 2004; Meyer, 2000; Sternberg & Grigorenko, 2002). Similarly, recent syntheses of empirical research have concluded that ability–achievement discrepancy models are ineffective in identifying LD, provide no useful information for designing services to address children's learning needs, and fail to predict outcomes (Bradley, Danielson, & Hallahan, 2002; Donovan & Cross, 2002; Lyon et al., 2001). These conclusions have been supported by the report of the President's Commission on Excellence in Special Education (U.S. Department of Education, Office of Special Education and Rehabilitative Services, 2002), which recommended abandoning the discrepancy model for identifying specific learning disabilities and other high-incidence disabilities in favor of a model based on response to evidence-based instruction and interventions.

RESPONSE TO INTERVENTION

An intervention-oriented approach to service delivery has been incorporated in the reauthorization of the Individuals with Disabilities Education Improvement Act of 2004 (IDEA; 2004), which focuses on consultation and intervention services rather than on traditional assessments to identify students' needs and to monitor progress. IDEA 2004 permits local education agencies to use up to 15% of federal funds for early intervening services for students in kindergarten through grade 12, with a special focus on students in grades K–3 who have not been identified as needing special education or related services but who require additional academic and behavioral support to succeed in a general education environment (20 U.S.C. § 1413[f][1]). In addition, IDEA 2004 permits local education agencies to identify children with specific learning disabilities by means of a process that measures response to scientific, research-based interventions as a substitute for or supplement to ability–achievement discrepancy models of eligibility determination (20 U.S.C. 1414 [b][6]; 34 C.F.R. 300.307[a] [2]). Although the term is not specifically used in IDEA 2004, this process is referred to as *response to intervention* (RTI).

RTI Models

In contrast to the "wait and fail" model of identification and service delivery, RTI is a proactive approach designed to identify students with academic or behavioral difficulties *as soon as they begin to struggle* (Barnett, Daly, Jones, & Lentz, 2004; Yell, Shriner, & Katsiyannis, 2006). In RTI models, students receive evidence-based instructional practices and interventions, with the level of service matched to their level of need and frequent monitoring to determine response. Progress monitoring results are used to make decisions about the need for additional interventions or levels and types of services in general and/or special education. Although there are several variations of the RTI approach, they all have several components in common: (1) the use of increasingly intensive levels ("tiers") of intervention, (2) a reliance on research-based instruction and interventions, (3) a problem-solving approach for matching interventions to student needs and making educational decisions, and (4) systematic data collection and monitoring to determine if students are making sufficient progress.

In a three-tier model, Tier 1 consists of universal screening, evidence-based instruction, and progress monitoring for all students in the general education program. Students who fail to make adequate process in Tier 1 receive a second level of support in Tier 2, usually called "targeted or strategic interventions," that are typically delivered in small-group settings in addition to the regular curriculum. At this point, two methods for providing Tier 2 support have been developed. In the "standard protocol" approach, research-based interventions are provided in a small-group setting three or four times a week for a specified time period, typically 8–12 weeks (e.g., Fuchs, Mock, Morgan, & Young, 2003; Rashotte, MacPhee, & Torgesen, 2001; Vaughn, Linan-Thompson, & Hickman, 2003). In the second approach, individualized interventions are designed and implemented via a school-based problem-solving team. In either approach, students who demonstrate insufficient progress are referred for more intensive interventions and/or additional services. In three-tier models, students failing to respond to Tier 2 interventions are considered for eligibility or deemed eligible for special education services, and special education programming serves as Tier 3. In some models, this level is divided into two separate tiers, with intensive individualized interventions as Tier 3 and special education services as Tier 4. Although RTI is a promising framework for providing early intervention and for addressing many of the concerns associated with ability–achievement discrepancy models, many unanswered questions about implementation remain. To date, RTI approaches have primarily targeted students with academic rather than behavioral problems, and there is little empirical evidence for the utility of RTI in areas other than reading or for students beyond the early elementary grades. As the effectiveness and practicality of RTI approaches continue to be debated (Case, Speece, & Molloy, 2003; Fletcher et al., 2004; Fuchs & Deshler, 2007; Vaughn & Fuchs, 2003), however, states and districts across the country are moving rapidly to implement RTI systems, typically in the context of school-based intervention assistance teams (IATs).

INTERVENTION ASSISTANCE TEAMS

Origins and Development of IATs

Although RTI is new as a legal construct, models for early identification and intervention prior to special education referral have been operating for more than 2 decades in the form of school-based teams. School-based IATs originated in the 1980s as part of special education reform efforts. IAT models fall into two general categories, depending on team composition. Teacher assistance teams (Chalfant, Pysh, & Moultrie, 1979; Hayeck, 1987), which were developed as an alternative to traditional inservice training programs, do not include non-teaching staff, such as administrators or special education personnel, and function primarily as peer support and self-help groups for teachers. The second category of problem-solving teams, which originated in the work of Graden and her associates at the University of Minnesota (Graden, Casey, & Bonstrom, 1985; Graden, Casey, & Christenson, 1985), emphasizes a more formal, data-based consultative process. In these IATs, special educators or other resource personnel serve as individual consultants to classroom teachers or as members of a multidisciplinary team to design, implement, and evaluate interventions for students with learning or behavior problems. The primary goal of these IATs is to increase teachers' ability to deal effectively with struggling students in general education and thus prevent inappropriate special education referrals and placements. These IATs have been called a variety of names, including "instructional consultation teams" (Rosenfield & Gravois, 1996), "mainstream assistance teams" (Fuchs, Fuchs, & Bahr, 1990), "prereferral intervention teams" (Graden et al., 1985), "instructional support teams" (Kovaleski, Tucker, & Stevens, 1996), "intervention assistance teams" (Graden, 1989; Whitten & Dieker, 1995), and "problem-solving teams" (Bahr & Kovaleski, 2006b). This book uses the term *intervention assistance team* (IAT) to emphasize that consultative assistance is not confined to the instructional domain and to counter the notion that interventions occur only in conjunction with referrals to special education. When intervention services are provided by an individual consultant rather than by a team, this book uses the term *intervention assistance program* (IAP).

Core Characteristics of IATs

Despite differences in titles, IATs share a set of core characteristics. First, they create a collaborative problem-solving process at the school level designed to provide consultative help to teachers of students with learning and/or behavior problems. Second, they are aligned with federal mandates to provide evidence-based interventions in the general education setting to improve outcomes for struggling students rather than labeling children and removing them from the regular classroom. Third, IATs serve both remedial and preventive functions. In addition to providing interventions on behalf of students already experiencing academic or behavior problems, they have the potential to prevent future problems and improve outcomes for all students by enhancing teachers' ability to implement effective instructional and behavior management systems. Fourth, in contrast to the internal deficit attributions implicit in traditional special education assessment and decision-making practices, IATs are based on an ecological perspective that views student problems as related to the variables in the classroom and school environments in addition to the characteristics of the child and the home environment. As a result, IATs emphasize the importance of analyzing classroom, school, and home ecologies not only to determine the effects of these settings on student performance, but also to assess their capacity to improve performance targets (Sheridan & Gutkin, 2000). Consistent with this perspective, IATs have the potential to shift the focus of teachers and other educators from identifying deficits in individual students to implementing environmentally based strategies that can improve the functioning of entire classroom groups.

Fifth, IATs emphasize finding solutions rather than diagnosing problems. In the traditional special education paradigm, when a student experienced difficulty in the classroom, efforts were directed toward answering the question "Is this student handicapped and if so, by what condition?" With the intervention assistance approach, the question becomes "What can be done to help teachers improve the performance of this student in regular education?" (Flugum & Reschly, 1994). Assessment therefore focuses on gathering information for use in designing interventions and monitoring student response, not classifying student problems as falling into one of a group of categories eligible for special education services. Finally, rather than requiring a lengthy referral and assessment process, IATs provide immediate assistance to teachers of struggling students. As soon as teachers make a referral, assistance can be offered, strengthening the preventive aspects of IATs.

Changes in the Focus and Function of IATs

In recent years, IATs have become standard practice in states and districts across the nation (Buck, Polloway, Smith-Thomas, & Cook, 2003; Truscott, Cohen, Sams, Sanborn, & Frank, 2005). A survey of 51 state education departments, including the District of Columbia (Truscott et al., 2005), found that 69% of states currently mandate prereferral intervention, with 86% requiring or recommending prereferral intervention teams. Under the influence of NCLB mandates that schools demonstrate annual improvements in the numbers of students reaching proficiency and IDEA 2004's emphasis on early intervention and the use of general education interventions prior to referral for special education, however, the conceptualization and role of IATs are undergoing a transformation. Although IATs first arose as part of the effort to reduce unnecessary referrals to special education, school-based teams are moving away from a prereferral model, in which team activities are primarily focused on documenting interventions for use in determining special education eligibility, to a collaborative problem-solving model that provides support to teachers in improving outcomes for all students, regardless of whether a student is suspected of having a disability. As Bahr and Kovaleski (2006b) have stated, "It is now time for these teams to focus not merely on preventing referral to special education, but on supporting teachers in their use of evidence-based practices that are targeted to foster the proficiency of all students" (p. 3). It is in this respect that the greatest potential of IATs lies—that is, in their ability to assist not just individual students who are struggling but to improve outcomes for every student in a classroom by building teacher capacity.

Research on the Effectiveness of IATs

Despite the expansion of IATs, the body of empirical research evaluating their effectiveness is still relatively small. Until quite recently, most studies evaluated IAT success in terms of systemic outcomes, such as reducing the number of inappropriate special education referrals and placements and the number of students retained in grade, reducing the disproportionate referral and placement of minority students in special education, and improving teachers' attitudes toward diverse learners (e.g., Chalfant & Pysh, 1989; Fuchs et al., 1990; Gravois & Rosenfield, 2006; Gutkin, Henning-Stout, & Piersel, 1988; Kovaleski, Gickling, Morrow, & Swank, 1999; McDougal, Clonan, & Martens, 2000; McNamara & Hollinger, 1997). With the shift in focus from a prereferral orientation toward improving outcomes for all students, however, more recent research has attempted to document the degree to which IATs produce measurable gains in student performance. To date, however, relatively few studies have demonstrated that IATs are effective in enhancing student achievement or behavior. Moreover, many of the investigations documenting improvement for referred students suffer from methodological problems, such as small sample sizes, lack of randomization, or lack of control groups, or rely on the perceptions of teachers or team members for judgments of effectiveness.

The problems associated with efforts to evaluate IAT effectiveness are illustrated in a recent meta-analysis of IAT studies examining both systemic and student outcomes (Burns & Symington, 2002). The authors reported positive results for both outcome categories, with a mean effect size (ES) of 0.90 for systemic outcomes, such as referrals to special education, new placements in special education, and number of students retained in a grade, and an ES of 1.15 for student outcomes, such as time on task, task completion rates, and other performance-based measures. Unfortunately, however, only 9 of the 72 relevant articles located were included in the review after the authors applied their selection criteria, and even those articles did not meet the authors' initial standards. Moreover, the mean ES for studies in which IATs were implemented by university-based teams was more than twice as large as that for studies involving field-based teams (ES = 1.32 vs. 0.54), supporting Safran and Safran's (1996) earlier contention that positive results are much more likely to occur in the case of university-based teams, whereas field-based teams report inconsistent results.

EFFECT SIZE: HOW MUCH DIFFERENCE DOES AN INTERVENTION MAKE?

In analyzing experimental and quasi-experimental research to determine which interventions are effective, researchers commonly use the method of meta-analysis. In a *meta-analysis,* the results from each study are converted into a common unit of measurement called an *effect size* (ES) that expresses the difference in outcomes between the experimental (intervention) group and the control (nonintervention) group in standard deviation units. The results of several studies evaluating the same intervention or instructional practice can then be combined to determine the average effect of that strategy. A positive ES indicates that the intervention group outperformed the control group, whereas a negative ES indicates that the intervention group performed less well than the comparison group. In addition to determining the average overall ES for an intervention, researchers can use statistical analyses to determine whether greater ES's are associated with various characteristics of the students receiving the intervention (e.g., grade, initial vocabulary skills, behavior) and/or various forms or intensities of the intervention (e.g., researcher- vs. teacher-delivered, less vs. more intensive, individual vs. small-group format).

In the most common method of deriving ES, termed *d,* the mean of the control group is subtracted from the mean of the experimental group or, in the case of a one-group study, the mean of the pretest is subtracted from the mean of the posttest. That product is then divided by the pooled (average) standard deviation of the two groups ($[SD_1 + SD_2]/2$) to obtain a common standard deviation that represents the difference between the measurements. For example, an ES of +0.50 means that students in the experimental group scored, on average, one-half of a standard deviation higher on the outcome measure than did students in the control group (Cooper, Valentine, & Charlton, 2000).

Interpreting Effect Size

Cohen's (1988) guidelines are commonly used to interpret effect size, with an ES of 0.20 indicating a small or mild effect, an ES of 0.50 indicating a medium or moderate effect, and an ES of 0.80 indicating a large or strong effect. According to the What Works Clearinghouse Intervention Rating Scheme (*http://www.whatworks.ed.gov/reviewprocess/essig.pdf*), a minimum ES of +0.25 is the smallest positive value at which the effect is "substantively important." ES's can also be translated into percentile gains for use in interpreting the impact of an intervention. For example, an ES of +0.25 represents a percentile gain of 10 points for the average student in the intervention group, meaning that the typical treated student scored higher than 60% of untreated students. An ES of 0.80 (large effect) indicates that the typical student in the intervention group scored higher than 79% of untreated students. Marzano, Pickering, and Pollock (2001) provide an appendix with a conversion table for transforming effect sizes to percentile gains or losses.

Problems with IATs

Evaluating the effectiveness of IATs in improving student outcomes is also complicated by the diversity of models and practices. In the absence of federal guidelines for specific prereferral or intervention assistance practices, IATs have been implemented in a wide variety of ways across and within states. As Buck and his colleagues (2003) have observed, "prereferral is one of the most inconsistently applied processes in education" (p. 350). Under these circumstances, it is not surprising that research also indicates that IATs often fail to achieve their goals of improving teacher effectiveness and student functioning. Several factors appear to contribute to the frequent failure of teams to realize their potential. First, the interventions provided by IATs are often simplistic and low quality (Flugum & Reschly, 1994; Telzrow, McNamara, & Hollinger, 2000; Truscott et al., 2005). Rather than targeting the classroom environment and making recommendations that require teachers to make substantive changes in their instructional or behavior management practices, IATs tend to emphasize recommendations that focus on factors outside of the classroom, such as counseling and after-school tutoring (McNamara & Hollinger, 2003; Meyers, Valentino, Meyers, Boretti, & Brent, 1996; Truscott et al., 2005).

Second, IATs are often unable to assist teachers in solving the referral problem, especially in the case of students with behavioral difficulties. Teams rarely consider the function of ineffective behavior or the influence of classroom environmental factors on student behavior and tend to select punitive and exclusionary strategies rather than strategies that help students learn acceptable replacement behaviors (Scott et al., 2005). Under these circumstances, the likelihood of a successful outcome is greatly diminished. In one survey, nearly half of the special education teachers and one-third of the general education teachers responding reported that management modifications suggested by teams were either "ineffective" or "very ineffective" for students with behavior problems (Myles, Simpson, & Ormsbee, 1996).

Third, teachers often make little or no effort to implement team recommendations, especially at the secondary level (Rubinson, 2002). As Sindelar, Griffin, Smith, and Watanabe (1992) have aptly observed, "Regardless of the quality of the plan that the team develops, its implementation by the classroom teacher remains the most crucial step of the process" (p. 255). Teachers' failure to implement recommendations may be related to the frequent failure by teams to provide adequate follow-up and support to teachers after recommending interventions (Bahr, Whitten, Dieker, Kocarek, & Manson, 1999; Doll, Haack, Kosse, Osterloh, & Seimers, 2005), as well as to teachers' perception that teams ignore or devalue their input during the problem-solving process (Slonski-Fowler & Truscott, 2004).

Fourth, IATs often fail to implement a systematic data collection and progress monitoring system to generate information for problem solving or to assess intervention effectiveness (Truscott, Cosgrove, Meyers, & Eidle-Barkman, 2000). Teams typically devote too little time to gathering and reviewing information to help define problems and move too rapidly to discussing intervention alternatives (Meyers et al., 1996). Once interventions have been implemented, teams and teachers alike often fail to employ objective evaluation procedures to determine whether the intervention has been implemented as planned (i.e., to assess treatment integrity) or to assess changes in student performance (Bahr, 1994; Bahr et al., 1999; Flugum & Reschly, 1994; Meyers et al., 1996). Even when some form of follow-up is provided, teams seldom use direct measures of student outcomes, such as curriculum-based assessments or classroom behavioral observations. Instead, teams typically rely on verbal contacts for follow-up and teacher judgment for evaluating intervention effectiveness (Bahr et al., 1999; Truscott et al., 2005). Data-based evaluation methods, such as graphing intervention results, comparing pre- and postintervention data, and conducting systematic classroom observations, are rarely used (Bahr et al., 1999). Without collecting and analyzing data to document intervention effects, however, consultants and teachers cannot determine which, if any, strategies result in improved student performance.

Finally, virtually all of the studies evaluating IAT effectiveness have been conducted in elementary or middle schools with general education students. At the time this book went to press, no empirical studies could be located assessing the effectiveness of IATs in improving outcomes for secondary level students or students with identified disabilities being served in general education settings. Empirical studies assessing the effectiveness of IATs with students from diverse cultural and linguistic backgrounds are also lacking.

Many of the problems associated with IATs appear to be a function of lack of knowledge of evidence-based interventions and effective problem-solving processes by team members. In a recent survey of school psychologists' knowledge of evidence-based techniques in reading assessment and interventions (Nelson & Machek, 2007), self-reported knowledge of interventions was low, with over 90% of respondents indicating that more training in interventions would benefit them as practitioners. Although training increases the chances of successful team outcomes (Kovaleski et al., 1999; Meyers et al., 1996), states often fail to provide systematic training in the intervention assistance process or in specific strategies for the professionals responsible for developing and implementing those strategies, and district-level professional development efforts are highly variable (Buck et al., 2003; Truscott et al., 2005). Similarly, despite evidence that students referred to teams that include special educators are significantly less likely to be retained or referred for special education evaluations (Burns, 1999), educational specialists, such as reading teachers or speech–language pathologists, are often not included on teams, limiting teams' ability to design effective interventions, especially strategies targeting academic performance (Slonski-Fowler & Truscott, 2004; Truscott et al., 2005).

To help meet the need for information in these critical competencies, this book includes 70 empirically validated interventions that have been adapted to the exigencies of the regular classroom environment. Each strategy is presented in a standardized teachable format specifically designed for use in consultation sessions, professional development workshops, and IAT meetings. In addition, Chapter 2 presents a set of best practices to assist school-based problem-solving teams in developing and implementing effective team processes. By using these strategies and best practice guidelines, practitioners have the tools they need to meet the major goal of IATs: enhancing educational outcomes for all students.

CRITERIA USED TO SELECT INTERVENTIONS

The interventions included in this text were located by searching online databases, peer-reviewed journals, and books in the consultation, behavioral sciences, and teacher effectiveness literature. The strategies have been adapted from the original sources as needed to facilitate implementation in general education settings. In cases in which an intervention has been modified and validated in one or more subsequent studies, two or more sources have been cited, and the most effective and practical features of each version have been retained. In several cases, the components evaluated in two or more studies have been combined to create a single intervention (e.g., *Delivering Effective Reprimands*; *Delivering Effective Commands: The Precision Request Program*). The seven criteria used to select interventions for inclusion in this book are described below.

Criterion 1: Documented Evidence of Effectiveness

Only interventions with empirical evidence of effectiveness in improving the behaviors they were designed to address were considered for inclusion. This meant that the original source had to include some systematic, objective method of documenting observable changes in student performance. Many studies employed single-subject designs, such as A-B-A-B or withdrawal, reversal, alternating treatments, or multiple baseline methods, using data from observations of classroom behavior, or academic measures, such as percent-correct scores on classroom tasks. A sizable number of the interventions have been validated across different grades, academic subjects, settings (e.g., resource room, inclusive classroom, general education classroom), formats (e.g., individual, small-group, whole-class), and student populations (students without identified disabilities, students with disabilities, English language learners, etc.), providing additional evidence of their effectiveness in improving student outcomes.

Criterion 2: Consistent with an Ecological Perspective

Focusing on internal child deficits as the sole cause of students' school problems provides little information or direction for designing school-based interventions. In contrast, an ecological approach views student problems as arising not only from child characteristics but also from mismatches between student needs and environmental variables, including classroom management and instructional practices. Adopting an ecological perspective to academic and behavior problems not only expands the analysis of factors that may be contributing to those problems, but also yields a broader range of targets for school-based interventions (Barnett, Bell, & Carey, 2002; Truscott et al., 2005). Also in keeping with an ecological perspective, the interventions are designed to be minimally intrusive so that they can be implemented in general classroom settings without singling out individual students or unduly disrupting teachers' typical instructional and behavior management systems. Interventions that require major alterations in classroom ecologies are unlikely to become integrated into teachers' routines or to have the desired effects on student performance (Elliott, Witt, Kratochwill, & Stoiber, 2002; Lentz, Allen, & Ehrhardt, 1996). Several interventions designed for parent delivery are also included, but these too require minimal training and supervision by school personnel and minimal alterations in family routines.

Criterion 3: Emphasis on a Proactive Approach to Classroom Problems

Priority has been placed on strategies that help teachers create learning environments that prevent problem behavior from occurring rather than on strategies that are applied after problem behavior has already occurred. Many of the classroom interventions that have appeared in the literature are *contingency-based,* that is, they involve manipulating *consequences* to shape behavior. In contrast, proactive strategies emphasize manipulating *antecedents,* that is, modifying the classroom environment to promote high levels of student engagement and thus prevent academic failure and disruptive behavior. An entire chapter is devoted to proactive management strategies drawn from the teacher effectiveness literature and interventions with proactive features that have been adapted from research in the behavioral sciences. Two additional proactive interventions designed specifically for preschoolers are included in Chapter 6. Moreover, although the strategies in Chapter 4 target academic performance, they also have the potential to reduce inappropriate behavior arising from student frustration at lack of success with classroom tasks.

Criterion 4: Capable of Classwide Application

Traditional intervention assistance approaches directed at a single low-performing or ineffectively behaving student are of limited utility in helping teachers become more effective instructional managers or behavioral problem solvers. On the contrary, given the growing needs and diversity of the student population and federal mandates for improving outcomes for all students, teachers need strategies that can enhance the academic performance and social competence of all of the students in a classroom. Moreover, when a teacher refers an individual student because of some learning or behavior problem, consultants often discover that the problem extends beyond the referred child to several students or to the class as a whole. Although the teacher is focusing on one student, the referred child's dysfunctional behavior is embedded within an ineffective organizational, instructional, or behavior management system that is interfering with the optimal performance of several or all of the students in that classroom. In keeping with this universal perspective, interventions have been selected that were either originally designed to be implemented on a classwide basis or could be readily adapted to that format while at the same time accommodating students with special needs within that group.

This edition also includes several behavioral interventions that were originally designed to be implemented on a schoolwide basis. Schoolwide interventions are increasingly being used to improve behavior and social competence for an entire student body and are especially valuable in targeting problem behaviors that occur in nonclassroom settings, such as hallways, cafeterias, and the playground (Scott, 2001; Serna, Nielson, Lambros, & Forness, 2002; Sugai, Horner, & Gresham, 2002).

Criterion 5: Capable of Being Easily Taught through a Consultation Format

Interventions that place high demands on consultant or teacher time to ensure accurate implementation are unlikely to find their way into consultants' repertoires or teachers' routines, regardless of their documented effectiveness in solving the target problem (Boardman, Arguelles, Vaughn, Hughes, & Klingner, 2005; Gersten, Chard, & Baker, 2000). For this reason, only interventions that can be easily taught to educators in individual or group-oriented consultative settings have been included. Similarly, strategies with complex implementation or evaluation procedures as presented in the original sources have been modified to increase their practicality and to facilitate a high degree of treatment integrity. The standardized format used for all of the assessments and interventions in this book has been designed specifically for use in consultation settings, including consultant–teacher sessions, professional development programs, and IAPs. Strategies that were judged to be so complex that modifications to accommodate the realities of the regular classroom would have reduced intervention effectiveness were excluded from consideration.

Criterion 6: Capable of Implementation Using Regular Classroom Resources

This criterion reflects the goal of IAPs of enhancing the capacity of general education teachers to meet the needs of diverse learners rather than relying on special education programming. All the interventions in this book can be delivered using resources that are already present in the typical classroom or can be prepared or obtained with minimal cost and effort. Interventions have been selected that capitalize on the human and material resources already present in general education settings, including teachers, peers, the regular curriculum, and typically available classroom resources. Strategies requiring substantial additional human or material resources, such as extra staff, special services personnel, supplementary curricular materials, and special equipment, or requiring the removal of students from the regular classroom, were modified or excluded from consideration. This eliminated individual and small-group social skills training or counseling programs, as well as the ever increasing array of commercially published curricula targeting academic performance or social competence. For similar reasons, most interventions with a home-based component had to be excluded. Although numerous strategies involving parents as intervention agents have appeared in the literature, the majority require a substantial investment of teacher, consultant, and/or parent time for accurate implementation, target a single student or a small group, and even then sometimes fail to achieve meaningful changes in student achievement or behavior (e.g., Callahan, Rademacher, & Hildreth, 1998; Kahle & Kelley, 1994). Here, only the simplest school–home interventions that require minimal parent training and teacher or consultant involvement and that can be applied to an entire classroom group have been selected.

Criterion 7: Capable of Being Evaluated by Reliable, Valid, and Practical Methods

Consistent with the evidence-based intervention movement, federal mandates, and ethical practice (American Psychological Association, 2002; National Association of School Psychologists, 2000), the interventions in this book target concrete, observable student behaviors that can be objectively measured over time. In addition to the evaluation procedures described in Chapter 2 and the curriculum-based measurement (CBM) procedures presented in Chapter 4, each intervention includes at least two and as many as four methods of gathering information on preintervention performance and evaluating performance changes subsequent to intervention. Observational and evaluation measures are designed to be as practical as possible so that they can be easily implemented by regular classroom teachers, consultants, or other personnel participating in IAPs. Although efforts have been made to match the methodology of the original sources, evaluation procedures have been modified for many interventions to accommodate the exigencies of the regular classroom setting and to approximate more closely the typical data collection methods of classroom teachers and school-based consultants. Moreover, because many of the interventions originally targeted only one student or a small group of students, observational and evaluation methods suitable for classwide application have been substituted for or added to the original individually focused procedures.

INTERVENTION FORMAT

The 70 interventions are grouped into four chapters that present proactive, academic, behavioral, and preschool strategies, in that order. Each intervention has been adapted from the original source or sources into a standardized format designed to be as succinct and nontechnical as possible while still including sufficient detail for accurate implementation and reliable evaluation. Samples of materials required for implementation, such as charts and student handouts, are included for many of the interventions. The format is designed to facilitate the intervention assistance process in individual and group-oriented consultative settings and has been extensively field-tested in professional development workshops, individual and group consultations with teachers, and IAT meetings. The 11 sections of the intervention format (10 core sections, 1 supplementary section) are described below.

Overview

The overview provides a brief description of the intervention, its target, a rationale for its use, and a summary of the anticipated results. Also included is information about the original setting and student participants and the results obtained in the original study or studies. For schoolwide strategies, a brief description of school demographics and other relevant characteristics of the original intervention site is included.

Purpose

This section presents the specific purpose or purposes of the intervention in terms of concrete, observable student academic and/or social behaviors.

Materials

This section lists all of the materials required for successful implementation. Many interventions require minimal materials, such as posterboard for charts, and some require no material resources at all. For contingency-based strategies, suggestions for tangible, activity, or social reinforcers are included in this section.

Observation

The observation section presents methods of obtaining baseline measures of the target behavior(s) for use in analyzing the nature and extent of the problem. For each intervention, at least two and as many as four different data-gathering strategies are included, varying along a continuum of complexity from naturally occurring classroom assessments, such as grades on tests and quizzes, to observational methods using special recording forms, examples of which are provided in Chapter 2. Although emphasis is placed on measures that gather information about target behaviors for an entire classroom, methods for documenting the behavior of a single student or a small group of students are also included for most interventions.

Intervention Steps

This section provides comprehensive step-by-step implementation procedures. In many cases, procedures have been amplified or modified from those presented in the original studies for the sake of clarity and practicality. Every effort has been made to accommodate the realities of the regular classroom environment without sacrificing effectiveness and fidelity to the original strategy. Because teaching students a specific set of procedures is a key component for many of the strategies, two subsections—*Introduction and Training* and *Implementation*—have been added to those interventions to enhance usability. Similarly, a *Preparation* subsection has been added for several strategies requiring additional planning steps prior to implementation.

Evaluation

The evaluation component describes a variety of measures that are linked to the baseline assessments described in the observation component. Teachers or consultants can use one or more of these methods to obtain reliable, objective information for assessing the effectiveness of the interventions that have been implemented. As in the observation component, measures are primarily designed to evaluate the impact of interventions on the entire classroom, although options suitable for assessing changes in the behavior of an individual student or a small group of target students are included for most strategies.

Variations

This component describes one or more intervention variations. Some of these variations were developed during field testing, whereas others are derived from additional experiments presented in the original article or from other studies implementing modifications of the original intervention. By providing additional intervention alternatives for consultants to offer to teachers, these variations increase the likelihood that teachers will find some of the suggested strategies acceptable and implement them with fidelity.

Notes

The notes component presents additional information designed to enhance implementation, such as tips on training students in the procedures. Also cited here are implementation issues and problems, if any, reported by the original authors or observed during field testing, along with suggestions for overcoming those problems.

Sources

The sources section provides a complete citation for the article(s) or book(s) from which the intervention was adapted. In the case of interventions drawing on more than one source, all of the relevant references are cited.

Additional Resources

This additional section, which is included for several strategies, describes print and electronic resources that can facilitate implementation, such as commercially available versions of the intervention or websites with relevant materials.

TARGETS OF INTERVENTION

The organization of the intervention chapters—presenting proactive strategies first, followed by academic interventions, and finally behavioral interventions—is intended to underscore the book's ecological perspective that views inadequate classroom management, lack of success with academic tasks, or both, as contributing to students' ineffective behavior. This arrangement is replicated in the chapter on strategies for preschoolers. Because of the interrelated nature of human behaviors, however, the categorization of interventions is necessarily artificial. Every proactive intervention is designed to set the conditions for high academic engagement rates, which are incompatible with off-task and disruptive behavior. Similarly, academic interventions have the potential to promote positive social behavior because active responding to academic material is incompatible with misbehavior. Moreover, increasing academic competence is likely to reduce student frustration and foster cooperation with teachers and classroom peers and positive attitudes toward school. Finally, behavioral interventions designed to reduce classroom disruptions can increase instructional time and make students more available for learning.

HOW TO USE THIS BOOK

From the perspective of this book, school-based interventions should focus on enhancing students' academic and social competence rather than on simply reducing unwanted behavior. Moreover, interventions should target the learning context within which inappropriate behavior is occurring. Readers are therefore encouraged first to consider the proactive strategies presented in Chapter 2 when selecting interventions to address problems. When implemented with high fidelity, these strategies help create a classroom environment that maximizes students' opportunities to respond to academic material within a supportive, motivating atmosphere, thus minimizing the need for interventions to remediate learning or behavior deficits. Readers may also use the table of contents and index to locate strategies for specific targets, such as homework completion, reading vocabulary, or disruptive behavior in nonclassroom situations. Cross-references in each section direct readers to related interventions in other chapters or other sections in the same chapter, and a table summarizing the key features of the strategies is appended to each intervention chapter.

Cautions

As school consultants know only too well, no intervention is equally effective with every student, with every teacher, or in every situation. Intervention selection should be a collaborative effort between consultant and teacher, or, in the case of IATs, among team members and referring teachers. Parent involvement is also a critical element in enhancing intervention effectiveness. In contrast to traditional school–home communications that simply provide parents with information—often negative—about children's performance, the intervention assistance approach actively encourages parents' participation in analyzing and solving their children's school problems. Finally, whether consultants are working with individual teachers, school-based teams, or parents, they can enhance their own effectiveness by offering a variety of empirically based intervention alternatives for consideration and facilitating the decision-making process rather than advocating a particular strategy.

PRINT RESOURCES

Bahr, M. W., & Kovaleski, J. F. (Eds.). (2006a). Current status of problem-solving consultation teams [Special series]. *Remedial and Special Education, 27*(1 & 3).

   The six articles in this special series address a variety of issues relevant to problem-solving teams, including applications of federal legislation to intervention delivery systems, practices to improve outcomes for students from diverse cultural backgrounds, and models to help administrators improve team functioning. Also included are two outcome studies evaluating team problem-solving processes and statewide implementation of instructional support teams.

Gutkin, T. B. (Ed.). (2002). Evidence-based interventions in school psychology: The state of the art and future directions [Special issue]. *School Psychology Quarterly, 17*(4).

   The 12 articles in this special issue review accomplishments and controversies related to the evidence-based intervention movement. Articles present a detailed overview of the Procedural and Coding Manual developed by the Task Force on Evidence-Based Interventions in School Psychology, examples applying Task Force coding criteria to single-participant and group-based design intervention studies, and methods for evaluating the evidence in research-based practices.

Fuchs, D., & Fuchs, L. S. (Eds.). (2007). Responsiveness to intervention [Special issue]. *Teaching Exceptional Children, 39*(5).

   The eight articles in this special issue provide a comprehensive review of RTI approaches and practices in the academic domain. Articles address RTI as an approach to preventing school failure and identifying students with learning disabilities, RTI models, the historical foundations of RTI, best practices in Tier 1 screening and reading instruction, and examples of secondary and tertiary interventions and progress monitoring.

WEBSITES

National Center for Learning Disabilities
http://www.ncld.org

The website for the National Center for Learning Disabilities provides numerous resources on RTI, including a parent advocacy brief with case examples of two students (both with early reading problems) illustrating the RTI implementation process.

National Research Center on Learning Disabilities
http://www.nrcld.org

The National Research Center on Learning Disabilities conducts research designed to help the learning disabilities field understand policies, practices, and prevalence of LD identification as well as to identify best practices for its components. Among the resources offered on the website is a learning disabilities toolkit to assist practitioners in understanding changes related to specific learning disabilities (SLD) determination and RTI.

Promising Practices Network for Children, Families and Communities
http://www.promisingpractices.net

Sponsored by the RAND Corporation, this website features summaries of programs and practices that have been empirically demonstrated to improve outcomes for children, youth, and families. Program information can be viewed according to four major outcome areas: (1) healthy and safe children, (2) strong families, (3) children ready for school, and (4) children succeeding in school.

Task Force on Evidence-Based Interventions in School Psychology
http://www.sp-ebi.org

Formed in 1998 and supported by Division 16 of the American Psychological Association and the National Association of School Psychologists, the Task Force's mission is to examine and disseminate the knowledge base on empirically supported prevention/intervention programs in five domains: (1) academic intervention programs, (2) comprehensive school health care programs, (3) family intervention programs, (4) schoolwide and classroom-based programs, and (5) school-based programs for social behavior problems.

What Works Clearinghouse
http://www.whatworks.ed.gov

Established in 2002 and sponsored by the U.S. Department of Education, the What Works Clearinghouse (WWC) is designed to provide educators, policymakers, and the public with an independent source of scientific evidence of effective educational programs and practices. The frequently updated site provides intervention and topic reports for strategies targeting elementary, middle, and high school students. Among the new features is an "intervention finder" to assist users in locating WWC-reviewed interventions based on topic and rating.

CHAPTER 2

The Intervention-Oriented Approach to Improving Student Outcomes

"I did what you suggested, and it didn't make any difference."

"I can't do all that for just one child! What about the other 24 students in my classroom?"

"I've already tried everything, and nothing works. He needs to be in special ed!"

How many times have school consultants heard these kinds of comments as they attempt to help teachers meet the needs of struggling students? How can consultants maximize the likelihood that teachers will implement evidence-based interventions to improve students' opportunities for success, and do so with fidelity? To help teachers create productive, disruption-free classrooms and enhance student outcomes, today's school consultants must be familiar with a wide variety of strategies with documented effectiveness in improving learning environments and students' academic achievement and social competence. At the same time, however, knowledge of empirically validated interventions is a necessary but insufficient component of the complex process of creating positive change in school settings. Indeed, it is only one of a broad range of skills that school consultants must possess if they are to be able to use their expertise in ways that are genuinely helpful to teachers, students, and parents.

Zins and Erchul (2002) identified five sets of competencies needed for effective consultation practice: (1) self-awareness, including awareness of one's own interpersonal style, values, and theoretical bases and their influence in the consultation and problem-solving process; (2) good interpersonal and communication skills, including the ability to establish warm, caring relationships with consultees; (3) knowledge of intervention technology, including knowledge of research-based strategies and skills in problem solving and applied behavior analysis; (4) understanding of the influence of school climate, norms, and values in the consultation process; and (5) sensitivity to cultural diversity and awareness of the impact of sociocultural factors on the consultative process. Although the emphasis in this book is on knowledge of intervention technology (i.e., content expertise), even consultants armed with an array of scientifically based interventions will be unsuccessful if they cannot use their skills to address everyday classroom problems; communicate with teachers, administrators, parents, and students; and negotiate among the interrelated systems of classroom, school, home, and community. The importance of communication and interpersonal skills in the intervention assistance process cannot be underestimated. Because the personality of the consultant is inevitably the medium for interactions between the consultant and other individuals in the intervention assistance process, a teacher may reject an intervention offered by one consultant but accept the identical strategy when it is suggested by a different consultant. Consultants can also enhance their effectiveness by following the best practice guidelines presented below, which are based on the consultation and intervention research literature, field-testing observations, and the author's experiences as a consultant and school practitioner.

BEST PRACTICES FOR MAXIMIZING THE SUCCESS OF IATS

Best Practice 1: Understanding Teachers' Perspectives on Classroom Problems.

Much has been written about teacher resistance to consultation in general and to classroom-based interventions in particular (e.g., Fairbanks & Stinnett, 1997; Nastasi & Truscott, 2000; Wickstrom & Witt, 1993; Wilson, Gutkin, Hagen, & Oats, 1998). Dealing effectively with so-called teacher resistance begins with understanding teachers' perspectives on student problems and their experiences with special education service delivery. Despite abundant evidence that classroom variables, such as the nature and pacing of instruction, teachers' management and relational styles, and behavioral contingencies, have a powerful effect on students' academic achievement and social behavior (Barth, Dunlap, Dane, Lochman, & Wells, 2004; Perry, Donohue, & Weinstein, 2007; Wang, Haertel, & Walberg, 1993), teachers tend to attribute student problems to internal dispositional causes or home factors over which they believe they have no control, especially in the case of behavior problems (Athanasiou, Geil, Hazel, & Copeland, 2002; Goyette, Dore, & Dion, 2000; Truscott et al., 2000; Wilson et al., 1998). If teachers view problems as arising from the characteristics of the student or the student's home environment, they have little incentive to modify their instructional or behavior management practices in an effort to improve the student's chances for success. Instead, it is more logical from the teacher's perspective to seek assistance in removing the "sick" student from the "healthy" classroom. Teachers are therefore likely to refer students with the goal of removing them from the classroom or accessing treatments delivered outside of the classroom, such as tutoring and counseling, rather than implementing interventions that require alterations in their own routines.

A second factor contributing to teacher resistance to the intervention assistance process relates to teachers' expectations based on traditional special education service delivery. Prior to the inclusion movement and IDEA's emphasis on serving students in the least restrictive environment, teachers developed the expectation that the vast majority of the students they referred would be tested, found eligible for services, and placed in special education programs for some or all of the school day. Despite the widespread implementation of IATs, many teachers continue to view them from a *prereferral* perspective—that is, as a time-consuming step on the way to obtaining special services for students (Klingner & Harry, 2006; Slonski-Fowler & Truscott, 2004). It is also important to remember that when teachers refer a student to a consultant or an IAT, they are likely to feel that they have already tried everything possible to help that student. As a result, they may resist implementing strategies requiring them to modify their current instructional or management practices, or they may fail to implement the strategies as planned and then declare them unsuccessful (Gutkin & Curtis, 1999). In addition, because of school psychologists' traditional role as assessors of individual students, teachers tend to view them as the gatekeepers for special education services. If consultants offer classroom-based interventions rather than individual psycho-educational evaluations as possible solutions to student problems, teachers may regard the intervention assistance process as preventing students from accessing needed services, at least initially (Doll et al., 2005; Rubinson, 2002; Truscott et al., 2000).

Consultants may also inadvertently contribute to teacher resistance by failing to acknowledge teachers' previous efforts to support struggling students. Armed with information about evidence-based interventions and the desire to be helpful, consultants may initiate the problem-solving process too soon, making recommendations prematurely to overwhelmed teachers and unwittingly increasing their feelings of ineffectiveness. This is especially likely to occur in the context of an IAT meeting, during which referring teachers must discuss their inability to help a student succeed academically or behaviorally in front of their own colleagues (Doll et al., 2005). Such an experience can be humbling for any teacher, but can be particularly difficult for experienced teachers, who are accustomed to being able to solve their own problems without assistance from others. Sometimes listening empathically to a frustrated teacher's concerns and validating the teacher's attempts to help a low-performing or misbehaving student is the most helpful intervention that consultants can offer.

A key strategy for addressing teacher resistance to an intervention-oriented approach to student problems is to educate teachers and other stakeholders, including administrators and parents, about the purpose of IATs and the manner in which they function, a process that is likely to extend over the first several years of implementation. Before teachers can fully invest in the intervention assistance process, they are likely to have to experience its effectiveness in increasing their capacity to help their own students. Because success reduces resistance, consultants participating in IATs should make every effort to work first with teachers who request assistance and to focus on problems that appear solvable. Teachers who have positive results with IATs are likely to share their experiences with their fellow teachers, thus increasing program acceptability. On the other hand, no news spreads faster than a failed consultation, and even a single failure can solidify teacher resistance (Conoley & Conoley, 1992).

Despite the obstacles to teacher acceptance of IATs, adopting an ecological approach to student problems can be empowering for consultants and teachers alike. When problems are ascribed not solely to the student's characteristics but to mismatches between the student's needs and the characteristics of the learning environment, the consultant's role is no longer that of helping an ineffective teacher obtain an out-of-class placement for a dysfunctional child with a teacher with greater expertise (i.e., the special education teacher). Instead, the consultant's task is to enhance the referring teacher's professional skills by helping that teacher create a more effective learning environment not only for the target student, but for all of the students in the classroom.

Best Practice 2: Be Creative in Finding Time for Consultation.

Finding time to consult with teachers is a perennial problem for practitioners (Doll et al., 2005; Erchul & Martens, 2002). In many elementary schools, teachers do not have daily planning periods when they are free from the responsibility of supervising students. More often, teachers have several free periods a week on different days while their students participate in physical education, art, or other "specials." Finding time to consult with teachers at the middle and high school levels can be even more difficult. Although most secondary level teachers have one regular planning period per day, it can take days or even weeks to find a time when all of the staff responsible for a particular student or, at a minimum, all those who have concerns about a student, can meet. Carving out time for IAT meetings can be even more difficult (Myers & Kline, 2002; Rubinson, 2002). Although many teams schedule their activities at the end of the school day when teachers do not have classroom duties, teachers often have other responsibilities, such as attending other meetings and sponsoring after-school activities. Nevertheless, finding a regular time for team meetings and sticking to it is critical to team functioning and effectiveness. The more regular team meetings can be, the more likely is the team to become integrated into the school culture (Iverson, 2002).

Collaborating with administrators to find time for teacher consultation is essential to the success of individual consultants and team-based IATs alike. If a teacher is experiencing problems with a student or classroom group, however, the building administrator also has a problem. Principals are often willing to arrange for support staff to cover classes or to cover classes themselves to permit teachers to meet with a consultant. Eating lunch with teachers can create opportunities for consultation, but problems of confidentiality arise if conversations about students can be overheard by other staff or pupils (Marks, 1995). Arranging to join teachers for lunch in their classrooms on a day when they do not have cafeteria duty is a better alternative and can help create an informal collegial atmosphere conducive to problem solving. Groups of teachers who are having difficulty with a particular class or student are often willing and eager to meet during their lunch period to discuss the problem, especially if they believe that the consultant will be available for follow-up assistance.

Other strategies include doubling classes to free teachers for consultation time. For example, two classes can meet in the auditorium or media center for a presentation by a resource speaker or to view an educational video or DVD. Paraprofessionals or substitute teachers can also be used to cover classes so that teachers can meet with the consultant or attend IAT meetings. In some schools, principals arrange for a permanent substitute one day a week throughout the year who rotates through classes so that teachers can join the IAT. Effective consultation takes time—time to observe in classrooms, to talk with teachers, to design intervention plans, to assist with implementation and progress monitoring, and to provide follow-up support. Regardless of the time constraints that beset all consultants, their personal receptiveness and availability to help teachers are crucial to the success of the intervention assistance process. Consultants who appear overly busy or preoccupied may inadvertently communicate the message that they are not genuinely interested in listening to teachers' concerns and are therefore unlikely to be approached for assistance. Similarly, consultants who merely suggest strategies without taking time to provide concrete help with implementation can undermine teachers' sense of self-efficacy, contribute to teacher resistance, and reinforce the notion that only "experts" can deal with difficult-to-teach students.

On the other hand, teachers can be tremendously creative in carving out time from a busy school day to talk with a consultant who appears to be genuinely interested in helping them solve classroom problems. Provided that the teacher and the consultant can talk together without being overheard, productive consultations can be conducted on the playground, in the hall during class changes and restroom breaks, outside of the building at dismissal time, and in the classroom while students are having snack breaks, resting, doing independent seatwork, or working in cooperative learning groups. When teachers and administrators believe that consultation is valuable, they will find time to consult where no time seemed available before.

Best Practice 3: Offer Interventions That Balance Treatment Effectiveness with Treatment Acceptability.

Although consultants are ethically bound to offer evidence-based strategies, even an intervention with a documented history of effectiveness in solving the referral problem will be unsuccessful in improving student functioning unless the teacher implements it. Assessing treatment acceptability is therefore an important aspect of intervention selection. *Treatment acceptability* refers to judgments made by intervention consumers, such as teachers, students, and parents, regarding the degree to which they believe a planned intervention is reasonable, appropriate, and likely to be effective (Eckert & Hintze, 2000; Elliott et al., 2002). There is considerable evidence that teachers do not select interventions based on whether or not the strategies have been empirically validated but instead on whether they themselves believe that the strategies can enhance learning for all students, are feasible, and are easy to implement (Boardman et al., 2005; Gersten et al., 2000; Klingner, Vaughn, Hughes, & Arguelles, 1999). Although acceptability is positively related to implementation accuracy and intervention effectiveness (Allinder & Oates, 1997; Eckert & Hintze, 2000), it is important to note that teacher satisfaction with interventions is not sufficient to ensure accurate implementation or successful outcomes (Cowan & Sheridan, 2003; Noell et al., 2005). Moreover, even when interventions are effective in improving the target behavior, teachers often discontinue them after the researchers have departed (Armendariz & Umbreit, 1999; Carlos et al., 2004; Fuchs & Fuchs, 1996), indicating that other factors are critical to maintenance.

In general, positive strategies, such as praise, differential reinforcement, and token economies, are more acceptable to teachers and other intervention consumers than reductive strategies, such as ignoring, response cost, and time-out (Alderman & Nix, 1997; Cowan & Sheridan, 2003; Fairbanks & Stinnett, 1997). Not surprisingly, teachers tend to prefer interventions that are less complex, less time-consuming, and fit easily into the classroom ecology (Elliott et al., 2002; Lentz et al., 1996). There is also an inverse relationship between treatment acceptability and years of teaching experience, such that more experienced teachers rate *all* interventions as less acceptable than do less experienced teachers (Elliott, 1988; Witt & Robbins, 1985). On the other hand, the more severe a student's problem, the more likely it is that any intervention will be considered acceptable, especially if teachers are able to access on-site technical assistance (Northup et al., 1994).

Assessing Intervention Acceptability

In matching interventions to teacher preferences and classroom ecological systems, consultants may wish to assess intervention acceptability using a formal measure. Several scales have been developed for this purpose, including the *Behavior Intervention Rating Scale* (BIRS; VonBrock & Elliott, 1987), a 24-item, 6-point Likert scale assessing teacher or parent perceptions of intervention acceptability and effectiveness. The BIRS has been used frequently to assess intervention acceptability in analogue investigations (Elliott & Treuting, 1991; VonBrock & Elliott, 1987) and treatment programs (Cowan & Sheridan, 2003; Olive & Liu, 2005; Sheridan, Eagle, & Doll, 2006; Weiner, Sheridan, & Jenson, 1998). Consultants may also wish to measure students' reactions to school-based interventions. The most widely used measure of children's judgments of intervention acceptability is the *Children's Intervention Rating Profile* (CIRP; Witt & Elliott, 1985). Written at a fifth-grade readability level, the CIRP is a seven-item, 6-point Likert scale assessing children's perceptions of the acceptability of behavioral interventions. The CIRP has been validated on more than 1,000 students in grades 5 through 10 and used in numerous investigations of behavioral treatments (Elliott, Turco, & Gresham, 1987; Lane, 1999; Lane, Mahdavi, & Borthwick-Duffy, 2003; Turco & Elliott, 1986). Both the BIRS and the CIRP are reproduced in Elliott et al. (2002).

In addition to using these generic scales, consultants can develop and administer intervention-specific acceptability scales for teachers or students prior to implementation to evaluate acceptability or after implementation as consumer satisfaction surveys. Figure 2.1 presents an example of a Student Intervention Acceptability Scale designed to measure student reaction to the *Good Behavior Game Plus Merit*, a team-based intervention targeting disruptive behavior. This version is intended for use with elementary school students, but it can be modified for use with older students by including additional items and/or increasing

How I feel about the *Good Behavior Game Plus Merit*	Yes	Not Sure	No
1. I liked playing the *Good Behavior Game Plus Merit*.			
2. The *Good Behavior Game Plus Merit* was fair for everyone.			
3. The *Good Behavior Game Plus Merit* helped our class follow the rules and behave better.			
4. Other teachers should use the *Good Behavior Game Plus Merit*.			
5. I would tell my friends to participate in the *Good Behavior Game Plus Merit*.			

FIGURE 2.1. Student Intervention Acceptability Scale for the *Good Behavior Game Plus Merit*.

From *Effective School Interventions: Evidence-Based Strategies for Improving Student Outcomes* (2nd ed.) by Natalie Rathvon. Copyright 2008 by The Guilford Press. Permission to photocopy this figure is granted to purchasers of the book for personal use only (see copyright page for details).

the number of ratings from three to five (i.e., from strongly disagree to strongly agree) to enhance measurement sensitivity.

Strategies for Enhancing Intervention Acceptability

Because ecological intrusiveness is a major factor in teacher resistance to interventions, consultants can enhance acceptability by matching interventions to teachers' current classroom routines and procedures as closely as possible (Elliott, 1988; Lentz et al., 1996). For very overwhelmed teachers, interventions should be as simple as possible and require minimal modifications in instructional and behavior management routines. Suggesting that a teacher with severe classroom management problems begin by implementing *Collaborative Strategic Reading*—an intervention that involves dividing the class into groups that engage in a sequence of self-managed reading and writing activities—is likely to increase rather than solve those problems, at least initially. Moreover, the teacher would be likely to resist such a recommendation out of fear of losing control of the class. Consultants can also increase the acceptability of an intervention by taking the time to explain not just the procedures for implementation but also the rationale for the strategy, its theoretical basis, and the anticipated outcomes. The more knowledge teachers have regarding the purpose of an intervention and its potential effect on student learning and behavior, the more likely they are to implement interventions as planned and to sustain them over time (Klingner, Vaughn, Hughes, et al., 1999).

Best Practice 4: Emphasize Strategies That Enhance the Functioning of the Entire Classroom Group Rather Than Merely the Target Student.

Although teachers typically refer individual students rather than groups of students for intervention assistance, consultants following up a referral with a classroom observation often discover that some, many, or all of the other students in the classroom have similar problems. This is especially likely to be true for referrals for inappropriate behavior. As Kartub, Taylor-Greene, March, and Horner (2000) have observed, if more than one or two students in a classroom exhibit the same disruptive behavior, the environment—not the students—needs to change. Even when a single student is the focus of intervention, priority should be given to strategies that can be implemented with the entire class rather than just with the target individual. Group-focused strategies have many advantages over interventions targeting a single student. First, they are efficient in terms of time and labor, especially in classrooms with more than one low-performing or ineffectively behaving student. Second, they avoid the problem of singling out individual students, which may be embarrassing for students, especially those beyond the early primary grades. Third, class-wide strategies are more acceptable to teachers, who often complain that it is unfair to allocate special attention to one student at the expense of others (Gersten, Fuchs, Williams, & Baker, 2001). Fourth, by incorporating peer influence as a core intervention component, group-oriented strategies can be especially effective in encouraging academic productivity and prosocial behavior (Hoff & Robinson, 2002). Fifth, shifting the focus of intervention assistance from one low-performing or misbehaving student to the classroom system as a whole has the potential to have a positive impact on the functioning of the other students in that system (Elliott et al., 2002).

Best Practice 5: Be Prepared to Support Teachers throughout the Intervention Assistance Process.

Until quite recently, consultants primarily depended on oral instructions as the primary vehicle for change within the consultation framework (Witt, 1997). Contrary to this "talk and hope" strategy, there is abundant evidence that verbal instructions are insufficient to ensure that teachers will implement an intervention accurately or continue it after consultation contacts have ended (e.g., Noell & Witt, 1999; Witt, Noell, LaFleur, & Mortenson, 1997). Even when verbal instructions are supplemented with access to printed materials, implementation often does not occur as planned (Vadasy, Jenkins, Antil, Phillips, & Pool, 1993). On the contrary, it is now clear that teachers require much more training and support than was previously thought if they are to implement the interventions to which they have agreed and maintain them accurately over time (Jones, Wickstrom, & Friman, 1997; Noell, Witt, Gilbertson, Ranier, & Freeland, 1997; Witt et al., 1997).

During the initial implementation phase, consultants should be available to provide hands-on assistance in the form of modeling, coaching, and performance feedback. Classroom-based technical assistance, such as *in vivo* modeling and coaching, is especially important for interventions that involve major changes in classroom organizational and instructional structures, such as collaborative learning formats (e.g., *ClassWide Peer Tutoring*; *Reciprocal Peer Tutoring in Math*) and strategies that require misbehaving students to move to a different location (e.g., *Sit and Watch: Teaching Prosocial Behaviors*). In-class assistance also ensures that consultants are available to provide support with behavior management if it is needed. Research (e.g., Klingner, Ahwee, Pilonieta, & Menendez, 2003; Klingner, Vaughn, Arguelles, Hughes, & Leftwich, 1999) and field testing alike attest that low levels of treatment integrity or failure to sustain an intervention are often related to classroom management issues rather than to dissatisfaction with the intervention.

Although classroom-based technical assistance may be a new role for some practitioners, it is an essential competency for today's school consultants. An increasing body of research documents the importance of providing *in vivo* technical assistance as an integral part of professional development and the process of introducing evidence-based practices into classrooms (Abbott, Walton, Tapia, & Greenwood, 1999; Fuchs, Fuchs, Mathes, & Simmons, 1997; Lane & Menzies, 2003). Not only does classroom-based support increase intervention acceptability and enhance the consultant's credibility with teachers, it also provides an opportunity to obtain valuable insights about the classroom ecology, including teacher–student and student–student interactions, teachers' behavior management skills, and the nature and pacing of instruction. It is also a powerful relationship-building practice. A teacher who observes a consultant struggling to implement *Sit and Watch: Teaching Prosocial Behaviors* (a strategy that requires a misbehaving child to sit quietly in a chair at the classroom periphery and watch his classmates engaging in an activity from which he has just been removed) with a very oppositional student is likely to feel supported in an entirely different way than a teacher who receives only a verbal or written description of the same intervention. Just as importantly, classroom-based assistance increases the consultant's ability to empathize with the teacher and understand the teacher's perspective regarding the nature of the problem and the possible barriers to successful implementation.

Consultants should also be available to help teachers collect and analyze data for use in monitoring students' response to interventions. Although the observation and evaluation methods for the interventions in this book have been designed to be as simple as possible without sacrificing reliability and validity, even the simplest observation can be more easily performed by someone other than the teacher, who must be continually responding to the demands of daily classroom life. For this reason, consultants are encouraged to offer assistance in gathering baseline data, monitoring student progress, and evaluating intervention effectiveness, especially when initiating a consultative relationship.

COACHING: KEY TRAINING TOOL FOR INTERVENTION SUCCESS

Coaching refers to the process in which a consultant provides direct assistance to a teacher in learning a specific intervention or using the intervention as planned. An outgrowth of direct behavior consultation (Watson & Robinson, 1996; Witt, Gresham, & Noell, 1996), coaching comprises a variety of activities, including observation, demonstration, modeling, guided practice, and performance feedback, to assist teachers with accurate implementation. Often used in teacher preparation programs to support preservice teachers and improve their instructional effectiveness (Hasbrouck, 1997; Scheeler, Ruhl, & McAfee, 2004), coaching is increasingly serving as a tool to bring evidence-based practices into the classroom (Hasbrouck & Christen, 1997; Neufeld & Roper, 2003; Poglinco et al., 2003) and is an essential aspect of professional development under Reading First. In an intervention assistance context, coaching may occur in several settings and formats. The consultant can model the use of the intervention in the classroom while the teacher observes, after which the teacher implements the intervention while the consultant observes, providing reinforcement for accurate implementation and immediate feedback as needed (e.g., LaFleur, Witt, Naquin, Harwell, & Gilbertson, 1998). In-class coaching may also include prompting the teacher to perform the next step in the strategy or to perform a procedure more effectively. Coaching can also take place in a demonstration setting prior to classroom implementation to enhance teachers' feelings of comfort prior to attempting to apply the intervention in the target context.

For classroom-based coaching, immediate performance feedback can be delivered in several ways. In the least intrusive method, the consultant observes from the back of the classroom (or some other convenient place) and signals to the teacher to take an action when it is needed. A high-tech version of this involves a wireless transmitter system that permits the coach to prompt or provide immediate corrective feedback to the teacher without interrupting instruction (Giebelhaus, 1994). Teacher training programs have successfully used this "bug in the ear" (BIE) technology to improve teacher use of appropriate instructional practices (Scheeler & Lee, 2002). In the absence of this technology, the consultant can simply walk up to the teacher and give a quiet prompt that cannot be heard by nearby students. Coaching that includes direct observation with immediate performance feedback and, if necessary, additional *in vivo* modeling and support, is especially important in helping teachers to implement interventions targeting disruptive behavior. Field testing and intervention studies alike reveal that teachers often fail to provide consistent consequences for inappropriate behavior when implementing behavioral strategies (e.g., Proctor & Morgan, 1991). A growing body of evidence (e.g., Filcheck, McNeil, Greco, & Bernard, 2004; LaFleur et al., 1998) demonstrates that coaching that includes in-class observation and immediate performance feedback can enhance treatment integrity and positive outcomes for behavioral interventions. Moreover, teachers themselves endorse in-class demonstrations of interventions proposed by problem-solving teams (Lane et al., 2003).

Best Practice 6: Assess and Maximize Treatment Integrity.

Treatment integrity, also called *treatment fidelity,* refers to the degree to which a planned intervention is implemented as it was intended (Allen & Blackston, 2003; Yeaton & Sechrest, 1981). Treatment integrity is affected by a wide range of factors, including (1) intervention complexity, (2) the time and material resources required for implementation, (3) the number of intervention agents, (4) efficacy (actual and as perceived by the intervention agents and stakeholders), and (5) the motivation of the intervention agents and stakeholders (Gresham, MacMillan, Beebe-Frankenberger, & Bocian, 2000; Gresham, Gansle, Noell, Cohen, & Rosenblum, 1993). Assessing treatment integrity is essential to help distinguish between interventions that are ineffective in addressing the target behaviors and those that are potentially effective but are inaccurately implemented (Gresham, 1989; Gresham et al., 1993). Numerous studies (e.g., Mortenson & Witt, 1998; Noell et al., 2000; Noell, Duhon, Gatti, & Connell, 2002; Noell et al., 2005; Witt et al., 1997) have documented the fact that treatment integrity for classroom interventions deteriorates rapidly over time, with teachers typically implementing interventions as planned for a few days, after which they fail to implement them accurately or discontinue using them altogether. Although 100% treatment integrity is not necessary to produce successful results (Allen & Blackston, 2003; Wickstrom, Jones, LaFleur, & Witt, 1998), most studies have found a positive relationship between treatment integrity and intervention effectiveness (e.g., Gresham, Gansle, & Noell, 1993; Gresham, Gansle, Noell, et al., 1993).

Unfortunately, consultants and IATs alike often fail to assess treatment integrity. Even when treatment integrity is assessed, measures are often confined to teacher verbal reports. In studies that included both direct observations and teacher self-reports of intervention integrity, the two sources of data have often yielded conflicting results (Allen & Blackston, 2003; Little, Hudson, & Wilks, 2002; Robbins & Gutkin, 1994; Wickstrom et al., 1998). In one investigation targeting disruptive behavior (Wickstrom et al., 1998), teachers reported that they implemented the strategy as planned 54% of the time, whereas direct observation found that teachers implemented the intervention as planned only 4% of the time! Treatment integrity can be assessed using a variety of methods, including direct observation, teacher self-reports or logs, teacher and student interviews, permanent products (e.g., score cards for a math intervention or a poster listing strategy steps for a writing intervention), or checklists documenting the completion of each intervention component or step (see Figure 2.2).

Strategies for Maximizing Treatment Integrity

The following recommendations for maximizing treatment integrity are drawn from observations made during field testing and from the literature as noted.

Implementation Checklist: *Sit and Watch*

Class/student name: _____   Teacher: _____

Activity observed: _____   Observer: _____

Observation time: ____ to ____

Check to indicate completed intervention components.

Date of observation:	_____	_____	_____	_____	_____
Sit and Watch component 1. Teacher describes student's inappropriate behavior.					
2. Teacher identifies acceptable replacement behavior(s) for the situation.					
3. Teacher escorts student to Sit and Watch chair.					
4. Teacher directs student to observe the appropriate behaviors of other students.					
5. After student has been sitting quietly for 1 minute, teacher asks student if ready to rejoin the activity and display the appropriate behavior.					
6. If student responds positively, teacher permits student to return to the activity. If student responds negatively, teacher tells student to continue to sit and watch and then asks again in a few minutes.					
7. When student returns to group, teacher provides positive attention for appropriate behavior as soon as possible.					
Quiet Place component 1. If student continues to be disruptive, teacher escorts student to classroom Quiet Place and indicates reason for the removal.					
2. When the student is calm and sitting quietly, teacher asks student if ready to sit quietly and watch in Sit and Watch chair.					
3. If student responds positively, teacher returns student to Sit and Watch chair and continues from Step 4. If student responds negatively, teacher tells student to continue to sit and watch in the Quiet Place and then asks again in a few minutes.					
4. When student returns to group, teacher provides positive attention for appropriate behavior.					
Number of procedures accurately implemented (total of seven for *Sit and Watch* only; total of 11 with Quiet Place backup)	____ /7 ____ /11	____ /7 ____ /11	____ /7 ____ /11	____ /7 ____ /11	____ /7 ____ /11

FIGURE 2.2. Sample implementation checklist.

1. Avoid complex ecologically intrusive strategies that unduly disrupt current instructional and behavior management routines. Treatment integrity is inversely related to the complexity of an intervention and the time and material resources required for implementation (Gresham, 1989; Lentz et al., 1996). The goal of any intervention is to increase teachers' professional effectiveness in meeting student needs, not to increase their burden in the classroom.

2. Develop a written intervention plan that specifies implementation procedures, responsibilities for intervention agents, strategies for monitoring progress, and dates for reviewing the plan. As part of the plan, detailed descriptions of interventions should be provided and reviewed with intervention agents to ensure that they understand the intervention goals, procedures, and anticipated outcomes (Barnett et al., 1999; Zins & Erchul, 2002).

3. Supplement indirect training (i.e., didactic training and printed materials) with direct training in intervention procedures, including modeling, guided practice, coaching, and performance feedback (Sterling-Turner, Watson, Wildmon, Watkins, & Little, 2001; Watson & Kramer, 1995; Witt et al., 1997). Optimally, direct training should not only involve demonstrations of intervention procedures outside of the target context but also modeling and coaching in the intervention setting (e.g., classroom, hallway, playground) so that the consultant can help the teacher integrate the strategy into established classroom routines (Kovaleski, 2002).

4. Build a follow-up observation component into the intervention plan. Follow-up observations provide an opportunity to assess treatment integrity, modify the intervention as needed, and evaluate the effectiveness of the intervention plan (Bahr et al., 1999). Data from follow-up observations should be in written form so that the consultant can review the information with the teacher and/or the IAT. Implementation checklists are one type of measure that can be used in the follow-up process (see Figure 2.2).

INTERVENTION SCRIPTS AND IMPLEMENTATION CHECKLISTS: TOOLS FOR PROMOTING AND ASSESSING TREATMENT INTEGRITY

An intervention script consists of a set of guidelines or prompts outlining each step of a strategy or set of strategies (i.e., an "intervention package") in observable terms (Allen & Blackston, 2003). Written in the language of the intervention agent, scripts promote treatment integrity by ensuring that teachers and other intervention agents, such as parents, have access to complete descriptions of implementation procedures. Scripts are especially helpful in enhancing treatment integrity when interventions will be implemented in more than one setting or by more than one agent, such as in several classrooms, in the classroom and on the playground, or at home and at school (Barnett, 2002). The Intervention Steps component for the strategies in this text has been specifically designed to serve as a script to increase teachers' ability to implement the planned intervention with integrity and consultants' ability to support teachers in the implementation process.

Scripts are also valuable tools in the technical assistance process. The consultant can use the script to role-play the intervention with the teacher to anticipate implementation problems and clarify any misunderstandings. After the consultant has role-played the entire intervention, the consultant and the teacher can collaborate to modify the script as needed (Barnett et al., 1999). Similarly, scripts serve as supports for *in vivo* demonstrations during which the consultant implements the intervention in the target setting while the teacher follows along with the script. The use of scripts with teachers as intervention agents is associated with high levels of treatment integrity and positive outcomes for students (Allen & Blackston, 2003; Ehrhardt, Barnett, Lentz, Stollar, & Reifen, 1996; Hiralall & Martens, 1998; Martens & Hiralall, 1997).

Moreover, both teachers and parents rate intervention scripts as highly acceptable (Barnett et al., 1997; Barnett et al., 1999), especially when scripts are developed collaboratively (Allen & Blackston, 2003; Ehrhardt et al., 1996).

An intervention script can be converted into an *implementation checklist* for use in assessing treatment integrity and providing performance feedback to teachers. Also called a *procedural checklist* or *treatment integrity checklist,* an implementation checklist is a direct observation recording form that documents the completion of each intervention step (De Martini-Scully, Bray, & Kehle, 2000; Jones & Wickstrom, 2002). Implementation checklists can be completed by teachers, consultants, or IAT members during initial implementation or at periodic intervals to monitor treatment integrity over time. Figure 2.2 displays an implementation checklist for *Sit and Watch: Teaching Prosocial Behaviors* that can be used by a teacher or an observer for up to five observation sessions. With this type of checklist, treatment integrity can be operationalized as the percentage of steps in the intervention procedures that are completed correctly.

Best Practice 7: Use a Variety of Training Formats to Expand Teachers' and Team Members' Knowledge of Interventions and the Intervention Assistance Process.

Lack of training for teachers and team members in effective interventions has been repeatedly identified as a major barrier to successful implementation of school-based problem-solving teams (Bahr, 1994; Bahr et al., 1999; McDougal et al., 2000; Meyers et al., 1996; Truscott et al., 2005). Given the time constraints of typical consultation sessions and IAT meetings, consultants need to explore a variety of formats for helping teachers and team members learn about evidence-based interventions for solving common referral problems, as well as effective procedures and processes related to the intervention assistance process. For teacher training, options include preservice and inservice professional development programs, small-group workshops, and individual consultation. Training during preservice days is a particularly good alternative because teachers have not yet established classroom routines and behavioral expectations. Workshops that include small-group activities not only provide opportunities for teachers to share effective strategies for enhancing student achievement and behavior with their colleagues, but can also increase staff cohesion and encourage a collaborative approach to problem solving. Providing opportunities for collaboration among regular and special education personnel is especially important because their schedules often give them little time to interact during the school day.

Field testing indicates that preservice training in a core group of keystone interventions targeting critical management targets is much more effective than attempting to train teachers in a large repertoire of alternative strategies for managing behavior. Moreover, implementing the same strategies across classrooms and nonclassroom settings (e.g., hallways, the lunchroom) can have a powerful positive effect on schoolwide student behavior and overall school climate. At the same time, however, follow-up training is essential once school has begun, with beginning teachers especially likely to need additional *in vivo* technical assistance. The full complement of professional development components, including initial training, guided practice, and follow-up observations and feedback, should be provided to all faculty and staff involved in implementation. For example, for an intervention targeting transitions in a classroom that regularly includes aides or assistants, all classroom staff should participate in training and receive periodic performance feedback. Similarly, for interventions that potentially involve other teaching or office staff (e.g., *Sit and Watch: Teaching Prosocial Behaviors; Debriefing: Helping Students Solve Their Own Problems*), including all intervention agents in all aspects of training is crucial to success. Of course, for schoolwide interventions (e.g., *Reducing Hallway Noise with Sound Level Monitoring and Group Contingencies: A Schoolwide Intervention*; *Improving Bus-Riding Behavior with a Schoolwide Intervention*), training and follow-up technical assistance should be provided to all faculty and staff with implementation responsibilities, not just classroom teachers.

An effective but often neglected training format in expanding teachers' knowledge and use of evidence-based practices is peer mentoring, in which a teacher who has mastered an intervention provides direct assistance and support to another teacher in using the same strategy. Although peer observations take time and effort to arrange, the opportunity to watch a colleague implementing an intervention is a powerful learning tool and can diminish resistance to a particular strategy. Peer mentoring has been successful in expanding the use of research-based interventions in schools and is much preferred by teachers to traditional professional development formats (Vaughn & Coleman, 2004). Moreover, teachers are more likely to sustain innovative instructional practices if they have an opportunity to interact with their fellow teachers who are also implementing those practices (Klingner, Vaughn, Hughes, et al., 1999).

When IATs serve as the delivery system for intervention assistance programs, the consultant's role in professional development becomes more complex. The consultant can meet with the team to provide information about a variety of interventions targeting common referral problems, demonstrate specific strategies, and conduct workshops on topics identified by the team as priorities based on student and teacher needs. Training for team members in team-based consultation practices, including observations, data collection and analysis, the problem-solving process, team building, and outcome evaluation, will also need to be provided. Although comprehensive training for all team members in the technical skills and competencies required in the intervention assistance process is optimal, it may be very difficult for every member to participate in the full range of professional development activities provided at the building, district, and/or state level. One approach is to provide comprehensive training in one or more specific areas or skills (e.g., data collection and analysis, consultation, intervention design) to a single team member, who can then train the other team members or serve as the resident expert on that team in those areas (Doll et al., 2005; McDougal et al., 2000).

Finding effective and practical forums for training parents presents another set of challenges when parents serve as the primary intervention agent (e.g., *Parents as Reading Tutors*; *Paired Reading*) or participate in interventions with a home component (e.g., *Reciprocal Peer Tutoring in Mathematics*). Training can be provided on an individual basis, through group-oriented parent education programs, or through parent participation on an IAT. When students receive psychological or psychoeducational assessments as part of the problem-solving process or for special education eligibility determination, information on specific interventions can be provided to parents and teachers in the recommendations sections of the reports, as described below.

INTERVENTION-ORIENTED TEST REPORTS

Until quite recently, psychological and psychoeducational evaluations tended to focus on classification for categorical decision making rather than on providing clinically and instructionally relevant information to improve children's functioning (Rathvon, 1999). The following examples illustrate how the interventions in this book can be included in the recommendation sections of test reports to help teachers and parents implement evidence-based strategies targeting the areas of need that have been identified by the evaluation. The examples, based on data from actual test reports, are grouped according to the target domain.

Recommendations for Improving Academic Productivity and Homework

1. To encourage Juanita to complete her class assignments in a timely manner, have her monitor her own attentiveness and task completion using *Self-Monitoring of Academic Productivity*. This involves having her record her academic behaviors on a 10-item form for her teacher to review. The intervention can be implemented on a classwide basis if her teacher so desires. A sample of the self-monitoring form is attached to this report.

2. To promote independent work habits and task persistence, Stuart's teacher may wish to use the *Coupon System,* in which a predetermined number of coupons are taped on Stuart's desk and removed for unnecessary requests for help. If Stuart has at least one coupon left at the end of the designated period, he earns a reward. This strategy can also be used on a whole-class basis.

3. Marcia would benefit from direct instruction in effective homework strategies, using *Project Best: Seven Steps to Homework Completion*. In this intervention, students learn a seven-step strategy for managing homework assignments, as well as a set of effective study habits. Marcia's mother is encouraged to attend the training session so that she can support her daughter in practicing positive homework habits at home.

Recommendations for Improving Reading

1. To build Antonio's decoding skills, use the *Word Building* strategy. In the word building activity, students learn letter–sound relationships by changing a single letter in a target word to form a new word. A sample word building sequence is attached to this report.

2. Ryan would benefit from additional opportunities to read aloud and receive immediate feedback for oral reading errors. In the easy-to-use *Paired Reading* procedure, parent and child read aloud together until the child indicates that he or she is ready to read independently, after which the parent provides support with any mistakes. Ryan's parents are encouraged to use *Paired Reading* for 10–15 minutes four times a week. His teacher will be able to recommend reading material at an appropriate level.

3. Lakeisha should be taught strategies for organizing and remembering the material in her textbooks, such as using *Critical Thinking Maps,* which provide a visual framework for organizing text. She can complete maps during or after reading to enhance her learning and then use the completed maps as study aids. An example of a critical thinking map is attached to this report.

Recommendations for Improving Written Language

1. Jeffrey would benefit from *Peer Editing,* an intervention that teaches students a structured procedure for revising their written productions within a peer tutoring format. Peer editing can be conducted during writers' workshop or as part of the language arts period.

2. To increase Renardo's spelling skills, use *Word Boxes,* an activity that teaches students to make connections among the sounds and letters in a word. Word box activities can be conducted on a one-to-one basis, during small-group reading instruction, or with the entire class. A sample word box sequence is attached to this report.

Recommendations for Improving Behavior and Social Competence

1. To encourage Abby to follow teacher directions promptly, *Precision Requests and a Time-Out Ribbon* is recommended. This strategy combines a structured request sequence with incentives for compliance. At the beginning of each activity, Abby receives a happy face sticker, which she can wear as long as she follows directions. If she still has the sticker at the end of the activity, she receives a small reward or puts a sticker on a Good Behavior Chart. Using precision requests at home as well as at school enhances the effectiveness of the strategy.

2. Josiah would benefit from the opportunity to monitor his own classroom productivity and behavior using the *Three Steps to Self-Managed Behavior* intervention. In this strategy, Josiah records his behavior on a checklist that is reviewed by his teacher at the end of each period. His teacher awards points for accurate self-ratings and positive behavior and talks briefly with him about acceptable alternative behaviors if needed. When Josiah earns a specific number of points on 4 out of 5 days, he receives a reward. Josiah should take his checklist home every day so that his parents can encourage his efforts to work productively.

Recommendations for Monitoring Progress

1. Weekly *Curriculum-Based Measurements in Reading* (R-CBMs) are recommended to monitor Damian's progress in reading and to modify interventions as needed. R-CBMs involve having Damian read aloud for 1 minute, counting the number of words read correctly, and graphing the results. R-CBMs can be conducted by his teacher, a tutor, or his parents. Involving Damian in graphing his scores and monitoring his own progress is strongly recommended as a confidence-building strategy. A sample graph is attached to this report.

Note: Step-by-step procedures for implementing the italicized interventions may be found in *Effective School Interventions: Evidence-Based Strategies for Improving Student Outcomes* (2nd ed.) in the [name of school/agency] professional library. The examiner is available to demonstrate the interventions and provide assistance during implementation.

Best Practice 8: Foster Relationships with Key Participants in the Intervention Assistance Process.

The intervention assistance process is embedded in a set of complex relationships involving consultants, teachers, team members, administrators, students, and parents. Because consultation is an indirect service delivery model, its ultimate success depends upon the cooperation of the consultee in implementing the agreed-upon intervention (Gutkin & Curtis, 1999). In other words, the most carefully designed intervention plan won't enhance a student's chances for success unless the teacher takes action. Because school consultants rarely have direct line authority over teachers, consultants' ability to build trusting relationships with teachers is fundamental to teachers' investment in the intervention assistance process and the extent to which they implement the interventions to which they have agreed (Erchul & Martens, 2002). If teachers believe that their input is not valued or that they have not received sufficient follow-up and support after implementation, they are likely to disengage from the intervention assistance process by failing to implement the recommended strategies or failing to refer other students (Slonski-Fowler & Truscott, 2004).

The Role of the Principal in IAT Success

Research has consistently identified administrator support as critical to the success of consultation in general and of IATs in particular (Doll et al., 2005; Kovaleski, 2002; Kruger, Struzziero, Watts, & Vacca, 1995; Rafoth & Foriska, 2006; Rubinson, 2002). In a study by Kruger and colleagues (1995), administrator support accounted for more than 50% of the variance in teacher satisfaction with school-based teams. In fact, a teacher's failure to use an intervention may reflect a perceived lack of support from administrators or the community rather than teacher discomfort with the intervention itself (Broughton & Hester, 1993). Although it is not clear whether direct participation by administrators in team meetings is essential to the success of school-based teams or whether more general support is sufficient, a recent national survey of teams in 200 elementary schools (four teams per state) found that 75% of teams included general education administrators as regular members (Truscott et al., 2005). Principals play a crucial role in supporting the intervention assistance process by helping to ensure that team members and faculty receive sufficient training for effective participation, allocating resources to support evidence-based practices recommended by IATs, and conveying to teachers the message that they are responsible for implementing classroom interventions with integrity and monitoring students' response to intervention before special education services can be considered (Kovaleski, 2002). Administrator involvement is also necessary to schedule space and times for meetings, facilitate contacts with other teams and specialists within the building and district, and integrate IATs with other projects and initiatives being simultaneously implemented at the building and district level. Just as importantly, principals play an indirect but vital role in creating a school culture that values a collaborative, intervention-oriented approach to student problems and in which IATs are likely to succeed (Gutkin & Nemeth, 1997). In schools in which principals are uninvolved in or resistant to IATs, failure is virtually inevitable (Rubinson, 2002).

Consultants should make every effort to encourage the building principal to participate in IAT planning and to become a regular member of the school-based team. Principal participation in IAT-related professional development, especially during initial implementation of a school-based problem-solving team, can be critical to success. In addition to demonstrating support for teachers and team members, principal involvement in training activities ensures that administrators are exposed to the same set of learning experiences as the rest of the staff and thus are able to reinforce teachers' efforts to apply what they have learned. Consultants can also promote administrators' investment in IATs by expanding their role in intervention delivery. Involving the principal as an intervention agent not only capitalizes on the influence of the most powerful individual in the school but can also increase administrator commitment to IATs by providing opportunities for the principal to encourage positive student behavior rather than merely to impose consequences for problem behavior. One of the keystone proactive interventions in this text—*Debriefing: Helping Students Solve Their Own Behavior Problems*—was originally designed to be delivered by administrators rather than teachers. *Sit and Watch: Teaching Prosocial Behaviors*, another core proactive strategy, includes a backup component that requires office staff involvement. Of course, administrator involvement is essential to the implementation of any schoolwide strategy, such as interventions targeting nonclassroom settings (e.g., *Improving Behavior in Transition Settings with Active Supervision and Precorrection: A Schoolwide Intervention*; *Loop the Loop: A Schoolwide Group Contingency Program to Improve Playground Behavior*).

Building Collaborative Relationships with Parents

Unfortunately, collaborating with parents is one of the most neglected aspects of IATs. Although there is considerable evidence that interventions that involve both parents and teachers can significantly enhance children's academic performance and school-related behavior (e.g., Bates, 2005; Cox, 2005; Heller & Fantuzzo, 1995), very few studies have evaluated the extent or effects of parent participation in IATs. In a study of parents' satisfaction with their involvement with school-based teams (McNamara, Telzrow, & DeLamatre, 1999), parents rated the problem-solving model positively, but parent membership on teams from the initiation of the intervention process failed to predict either parent ratings of effectiveness or student attainment of intervention goals. Parent report of home support for interventions was a significant predictor of goal attainment, however, supporting the inclusion of parents in the intervention assistance process. Unfortunately, parent participation in the intervention assistance process is typically minimal. In a recent national survey of school-based problem-solving teams (Truscott et al., 2005), less than a third (28%) of surveyed teams included parents as members. Moreover, only about 9% of reported interventions involved working with parents or increasing communication between school and home, and only 4% of the interventions were designed to be delivered by parents.

The failure to promote the meaningful participation of parents in the intervention assistance process is especially ironic in view of the fact that teachers and team members overwhelmingly attribute the source of student problems to within-student or within-family factors (Rubinson, 2002; Truscott et al., 2000). It has been this author's experience that many interventions fail because parents are not involved or only nominally involved in the problem-solving process. Chronic behavior problems and lack of academic productivity are especially resistant to classroom interventions without some meaningful form of home–school collaboration. Although involving parents in the intervention assistance process can be difficult because of cultural or linguistic differences, family stressors, work and health issues, and a host of other factors, school consultants must make every effort to solicit the assistance of the individuals who have the greatest investment in the referred student and his or her success. Two of the interventions in this text specify parents as the primary intervention agents (*Paired Reading*; *Parents as Reading Tutors*), and several other strategies were originally developed for parent delivery (*Delivering Effective Commands: The Precision Request Program*; *Banking Time*; *Enhancing Emergent Literacy Skills with Dialogic Reading*). Moreover, many other interventions in this book can be delivered by parents who receive training in the procedures and follow-up support. Strategies that are appropriate for parent delivery or involvement are identified in the comments section of the appendix at the end of each of the four intervention chapters.

Best Practice 9: Be Sensitive to Cultural Diversity in the Consultation and Intervention Assistance Process.

Given the rapidly changing demographics in the United States, one of the greatest challenges facing today's consultants and educators is designing interventions that are acceptable and effective across different cultural and linguistic groups. Despite the current emphasis on providing evidence-based interventions in the regular classroom to improve student outcomes and reduce unnecessary referrals to special education, there is still a dearth of empirical data on the relative acceptability or effectiveness of school-based interventions with students from culturally and linguistically diverse backgrounds (Lindo, 2006). Similarly, despite the widespread implementation of school-based problem-solving teams, there is virtually no research specifically evaluating the effectiveness of IATs with students from diverse backgrounds. In the absence of a well-defined research base, two research-based consultative frameworks can be especially useful to practitioners as they strive to develop and maintain a culturally and linguistically responsive intervention assistance process: (1) an ecological perspective and (2) an ethnic validity model. Although an ecological approach is important in problem analysis and intervention design for all students, it is especially important in the case of culturally and linguistically diverse learners. When considering factors contributing to problems displayed by students from culturally and linguistically diverse backgrounds, consultants and educators must be sensitive to the ways in which cultural and linguistic factors influence learning and behavior at school (Ortiz & Flanagan, 2002; Ortiz, Wilkinson, Robertson-Courtney, & Kushner, 2006). Data obtained during the problem-solving process must be interpreted in the context of the student's cultural, linguistic, and racial/ethnic background in order to distinguish between background differences that may be contributing to school problems and learning or behavior deficits that warrant intervention (Garcia & Ortiz, 2002; Wilkinson, Ortiz, Robertson, & Kushner, 2006). Childrearing and socialization practices, communication styles, norms for behavior, and attitudes toward education are all embedded in a cultural context (Sheridan, 2000). In the case of English language learners, differentiating between genuine disabilities and problems related to limited English proficiency and educational histories characterized by frequent disruptions of schooling and inadequate instructional opportunities can be especially difficult (Figueroa & Newsome, 2006).

A second framework that can assist consultants in considering the effects of cultural differences on the intervention assistance process and evaluating the appropriateness of interventions with students from diverse backgrounds is the ethnic validity model (Barnett et al., 1995). An extension of the concept of social validity, *ethnic validity* refers to the degree to which intervention goals, assistance processes, and outcomes are acceptable to intervention recipients and stakeholders with respect to their cultural/ethnic beliefs and value systems. In the context of a problem-solving model, three key components are involved in establishing ethnic validity: (1) the problem-solving process, (2) intervention acceptability, and (3) teaming strategies. During the problem-solving process, consultants must consider the possible impact of cultural and linguistic differences on the tasks involved in each stage. For example, individuals from different ethnic groups may view student problems from very different perspectives. Cultural differences also have an influence on the acceptability of interventions. For example, interventions that provide tangible rewards for academic performance or positive behavior may be unacceptable to individuals from certain cultures. Consultants must be especially sensitive to cultural beliefs and value systems in designing home-based interventions or interventions with a parent component. In the absence of this sensitivity, intervention failure or low levels of treatment integrity may reflect a mismatch between intervention design and family values (Sheridan, 2000). To enhance ethnic validity, consultants can design interventions that are sensitive to the values of students and their families and offer a range of interventions from which to choose.

Consultants can also increase ethnic validity through teaming strategies by adopting a collaborative approach to problem solving that respects the family's cultural values and norms. One way of enhancing ethnic validity relative to this component is to include school staff or community individuals from the same cultural/ethnic/linguistic background as the referred student in the intervention assistance process (Barnett et al., 1999). Ethnically valid teaming also requires taking the time to establish rapport and build trust rather than moving rapidly to discussing interventions. It is important to listen respectfully to the parents' perspective on the nature and origin of the problem, their past efforts to deal with the problem, and their perspectives on the most appropriate interventions (Ortiz & Flanagan, 2002). Including family members throughout the problem-solving process is essential to help distinguish between behaviors that reflect academic or social competence deficits and behaviors that are appropriate in light of students' cultural and linguistic backgrounds (Ortiz et al., 2006). Moreover, when consultants communicate to families that they respect their cultural values and educational goals for their child, families are more likely to become active participants in the intervention assistance process (Ortiz & Flanagan, 2002).

Bias in the Intervention Assistance Process

Awareness of one's own cultural values and biases and those of others involved in the intervention assistance process is especially important in view of evidence that students' racial/ethnic and/or linguistic backgrounds may influence teachers' referral patterns, the assessment process, eligibility decisions made by teams, and the interventions that students receive. In a recent synthesis of the research literature on referral rates for assessment or intervention for three racial groups (African American, Caucasian, and Hispanic), Hosp and Reschly (2003) found that African American students were significantly more likely to be referred than Caucasian students. Research also indicates that special education eligibility teams often fail to consider the potential impact of contextual factors, such as prior schooling, language proficiency, and home variables, on learning or behavior problems and have difficulty distinguishing between cultural and linguistic differences and specific disabilities (Figueroa & Newsome, 2006; Ortiz et al., 2006). In a study by Wilkinson and colleagues (2006) examining the eligibility decisions for 21 Spanish-speaking English language learners identified as having reading-related learning disabilities by school multidisciplinary teams, determinations by an expert panel differed significantly from those of the school teams. Although the panel agreed that 5 of the 21 students had reading-related learning disabilities, they questioned whether that was the appropriate classification for 6 other students and judged that the achievement problems of the remaining 10 students were attributable to factors other than specific disabilities, such as interrupted schooling or lack of prereferral interventions.

Students' racial and linguistic backgrounds may also have an influence on the intervention assistance process and the types of interventions students receive. When English language learners are referred for academic or behavioral difficulties, teams often give only perfunctory attention to prereferral strategies and move rapidly to recommend testing for special education services (Klingner & Harry, 2006). Moreover, when English language learners are identified with disabilities, traditional special education delivery systems, such as resource room placements, rather than classroom-based strategies, are typically recommended (McCloskey & Athanasiou, 2000). Teachers' intervention preferences also vary by racial/ethnic group. In a survey of 600 regular and 600 special educators (Ishii-Jordan, 2000), teachers selected punitive and exclusionary interventions most frequently for Asian American students and least often for Hispanic students.

If IATs are to serve as effective delivery systems for improving the performance of diverse students, consultants must ensure that the intervention assistance process is culturally and linguistically responsive. By maintaining an awareness of their own cultural and ethnic values and encouraging an open dialogue throughout the problem-solving stages, consultants will be better prepared to adjust the intervention assistance process, intervention plans, and specific strategies to address the needs of culturally diverse students and their families. As part of this effort, consultants can help to organize professional development activities to increase their own knowledge of culturally competent practices and that of others involved in IATs. As Ortiz and Flanagan (2002) have aptly observed, however, developing cultural competency is a lifelong process.

STEPS IN THE INTERVENTION ASSISTANCE PROCESS

The 10-step intervention assistance process described below is based on procedures developed during field testing, the author's experiences with problem-solving teams, and resources in the literature (Barnett et al., 1999; Iverson, 2002; Kratochwill, Elliott, & Callan-Stoiber, 2002; Tilly, 2002). The process is intended to apply to intervention-oriented assistance provided by individual consultants as well as to team-based IATs.

Stage 1: Problem Definition

Step 1: Initial Referral

The intervention assistance process begins with a request for help from a teacher to the consultant or a referral from a teacher, faculty member, or parent to the IAT. In the case of IATs, referrals are reviewed by the team chairperson to determine if all the necessary information has been included. Teachers and staff members who have relevant information about the referred student are asked to complete a data collection form prior to the meeting so that their input can be considered even if they are unable to attend the meeting. Field testing indicates that it is extremely helpful if the consultant or a team member conducts an observation in the classroom or problem setting prior to the first meeting to "see what the teacher is seeing" and help identify the nature of the problem.

A record is maintained of the initial referral and subsequent parent contacts, consultation sessions, and/or IAT meetings. In the case of a referral by a teacher, the teacher should have contacted the parent prior to the referral to review the concerns, obtain the parent's perception of the problem, and engage in informal problem solving. At this point, the team chairperson contacts the parent to inform him or her of the referral and invites the parent (and the student, if appropriate) to participate in a meeting to discuss the problem and generate solutions. Written notification of the referral is also sent to the parent at this time.

Step 2: Clarifying the Problem

The teacher and consultant or the teacher and IAT members collaborate to clarify the problem and define it in observable and measurable terms. At the IAT meeting, members review the referral information and the strategies the teacher has previously tried to resolve the problem. Members then reach a consensus regarding the nature of the problem, the specific skills the student needs to acquire or use in order to be successful, and the desired outcomes of intervention. Focusing on only one or two target behaviors at a time is strongly recommended to avoid overwhelming the teacher and team members alike. Defining the problem in observable behavioral terms also helps the team identify methods of assessing the student's current level of performance. A case manager is assigned at this point to serve as the major resource for the referring teacher for the remainder of the process and to assist with implementation and progress monitoring. A staff member may also be assigned to serve as an advocate for the parent and/or student and to support the parent and student during IAT meetings.

Step 3: Obtaining Baseline Data

The referring teacher, consultant, and/or IAT members obtain additional direct measures of the target behaviors to identify preintervention performance levels and help clarify the discrepancy between the student's current and desired level of performance. Data gathering may include classroom observations by the consultant or an IAT member, teacher observations of the student, parent and student interviews, and/or direct assessments (i.e., curriculum-based measurements in the target area). In the case of behavioral concerns, this includes a functional behavioral assessment to develop hypotheses about the purpose of the ineffective behavior.

Stage 2: Problem Analysis

Step 4: Conducting an Ecological Analysis of the Problem

The teacher and consultant and/or IAT members review the data that has been collected to identify the factors that may be contributing to the problem, including student, peer group, classroom, curriculum, and home variables. Parents are also involved in analyzing the problem, as are students, as developmentally appropriate. Field testing indicates that data obtained from parent and student interviews, especially for students beyond the early primary grades, and from classroom observations can be critical in developing hypotheses about factors contributing to problems, especially chronic disruptive behavior and lack of academic productivity.

Step 5: Exploring Alternative Intervention Strategies

The teacher and consultant and/or IAT members discuss intervention strategies that may help reduce the discrepancy between the current and the desired performance. Students and parents are also involved in generating possible school- and home-based interventions. Strategies are evaluated for acceptability, effectiveness, cost in terms of human and material resources, feasibility in terms of the skills and styles of intervention agents, and closeness of match to classroom and home ecologies.

Step 6: Selecting Interventions

One or more strategies are selected. Final intervention selection rests with the teacher(s) and/ or parent who will be responsible for implementing the strategies. In a team situation, several team members or other personnel may be implementing strategies.

Step 7: Developing the Intervention Plan

A written intervention plan is developed that describes the selected strategy or strategies and timelines for implementation. The plan also clarifies the roles and responsibilities of the individuals involved in implementation, including teacher, parent, and/or student roles; assistance to be provided by the consultant, IAT members, and/or school staff; and strategies for monitoring progress. The plan includes a date for reviewing the effectiveness of the plan in reducing the discrepancy between the current and the desired performance. Ideally, the interval between initial implementation and plan review should be based on data generalized from published studies of the intervention. Field testing indicates that the time period between initial implementation and plan review should be no more than 2 weeks for behavior problems (and considerably less if problems are severe). For academic problems, a time period of 8 to 10 weeks or a full grading period is often necessary to evaluate students' response to supplementary instruction or other interventions.

Stage 3: Plan Implementation

Step 8: Implementing the Intervention Plan

The teacher or other intervention agent implements the agreed-upon plan with the support of the consultant or IAT case manager. Support for teachers may include in-class coaching, demonstrations, modeling, and performance feedback, depending on the complexity of the intervention, teacher skills and experience, and the severity of the problem. Support for parents may include direct training, indirect training (i.e., didactic training), follow-up telephone contacts and conferences, and other means of assistance. Progress is monitored by the intervention agent with the assistance of the consultant or IAT case manager. Another classroom observation occurs at this point to assess treatment integrity and provide feedback and support for the teacher.

Stage 4: Plan Evaluation

Step 9: Evaluating Intervention Plan Effectiveness

The teacher and consultant and/or IAT analyze the student's rate of progress and performance relative to the goals specified in Step 7. Additional evaluation data are obtained from the parent and student (as appropriate) for use in comparing baseline and current performance. If the student is making insufficient progress toward the goals defined in the plan in Step 7, the parent and student (as appropriate) are invited to another meeting to collaborate in identifying barriers to progress and modifying the intervention plan. If the student is making sufficient progress toward meeting the goals defined in the plan, the strategies are continued, with periodic reviews to monitor progress. If the goals of the plan have been achieved and no further assistance is needed, the case is closed, with follow-up consultation as needed. Records are kept to document outcomes and provide information for evaluating the effectiveness of the intervention assistance team.

Step 10: Continued Problem Solving, Plan Revision, and Possible Referral

If the student has not made sufficient progress toward achieving the goals in the plan, additional data for use in understanding and solving the problem may be obtained, and a revised plan developed. When the teacher and consultant or IAT members agree that the interventions have been appropriate and that the problem is still not solved, the student is referred for a special education evaluation or other more individualized and intensive forms of assistance. Data obtained from Stages 1 through 4 should be used in the special education eligibility determination process, and, if the student is found eligible for services, to develop the Individualized Education Plan (IEP).

LEGAL ISSUES AND ETHICAL CONSIDERATIONS
IN THE INTERVENTION ASSISTANCE PROCESS

Careful attention to legal and ethical issues relative to selecting, implementing, and evaluating interventions is a key component of the intervention assistance process. Practitioners must ensure that the interventions they recommend through IATs, case-centered consultation, professional development, and other forms of service delivery are aligned with federal and state laws and regulations, district guidelines, and the ethical principles and practice standards of professional groups, including the American Psychological Association (APA; 2002) and the National Association of School Psychologists (NASP; 2000). The major issues in this area include (1) intervention targets, (2) intervention effectiveness, (3) possible undesirable side effects and outcomes, (4) parent involvement, (5) student involvement, (6) documentation, (7) evaluation, (8) consultant competence, and (9) provisions for referral for additional services if interventions are unsuccessful.

Intervention Targets

Ethical practice mandates that interventions focus on enhancing academic and social competencies rather than on reducing unwanted behavior or what Conoley and Conoley (1992) have termed "dead-person targets," that is, behaviors best performed by dead people, such as sitting still and being quiet. Moreover, an ecological perspective requires that intervention targets include not only student behaviors but also environmental variables that may be influencing student performance. The sequence of interventions in this book—beginning with strategies targeting the classroom environment, followed by interventions designed to enhance academic performance, and finally by interventions designed to reduce inappropriate behavior and improve social competence—is intended to emphasize the order in which targets should be considered. One promising approach to intervention target selection is to focus on *keystone behaviors* (Barnett, Bauer, Ehrhardt, Lentz, & Stollar, 1996; Barnett et al., 1999), defined as behaviors that are likely to have the greatest impact in terms of the desired outcomes and/or that lay the foundation for improved functioning in the student's current or future environment. For example, cooperation and self-regulation, which have been repeatedly identified as keystone behaviors for children (Barnett et al., 1999; Lane, Givner, & Pierson, 2005; Pelco & Reed-Victor, 2007), constitute the primary or secondary targets of many of the proactive and behavioral interventions in this text.

Intervention targets should also be reviewed in terms of their *social validity*. Social validation is concerned with three basic issues central to the intervention process: (1) the *social significance* of intervention goals, (2) the *social acceptability* of the intervention procedures designed to achieve those goals, and (3) the *social importance* of the effects of the intervention (Gresham & Lopez, 1997; Wolf, 1978). For example, increasing on-task behavior is less socially significant as an intervention goal than increasing academic responding because increases in on-task behavior do not necessarily result in higher student achievement, whereas providing students with additional opportunities to respond to academic material can have positive effects on behavior as well as achievement (Lalli, Kates, & Casey, 1999; Lane, O'Shaughnessy, Lambros, Gresham, & Beebe-Frankenberger, 2000). Similarly, strategies that teach positive alternative behaviors and enhance students' capacity to manage their own behavior are preferable to strategies that merely impose negative consequences for undesired behavior. Finally, under IDEA, IEP teams must consider positive behavioral interventions and supports in developing plans to address the problem behavior of students with disabilities (34 C.F.R. § 300.324[a][2][i]).

Intervention Effectiveness

Early in the history of school interventions, consultants had limited access to resources on empirically validated strategies and often relied on their own subjective judgment or personal repertoire of interventions. Given the growing database of empirically validated interventions, however, and the mandates of NCLB and IDEA to implement scientifically based practices, consultants have a responsibility to recommend strategies with demonstrated effectiveness in addressing the referral problem, that is, strategies "that the profession considers to be responsible, research-based practice" (NASP Principles for Professional Ethics [NASP-PPE], IV, C, #4). Indeed, part of their ethical responsibility is to keep informed about interventions that have empirical support of effectiveness and relevance for their student populations (NASP-PPE, II, A, #4 & IV, C, #7). All of the interventions in this text have a research base documenting their effectiveness in addressing the referral problem. In addition, each intervention includes at least two and as many as four measures for monitoring progress so that intervention plans can be modified when data indicate that the student is not responding to the intervention or that the response is insufficient to achieve the specified goal.

Possible Undesirable Side Effects and Outcomes

Consultants are ethically obligated to select procedures that maintain the dignity of students and minimize the risk of adverse side effects, while simultaneously balancing these considerations with considerations of effectiveness (NASP-PPE, III, B, #1 & IV, C, #1a). Many of the interventions in this text include interdependent group contingencies, in which access to reinforcement depends on some aspect of performance for the entire group. Although group contingencies can have powerful effects on student behavior and performance (Stage & Quiroz, 1997) and are much more efficient than individually based contingency programs, consultants should be aware of the potentially negative social consequences that may occur under these systems. Although interdependent group contingencies are designed to capitalize on positive peer pressure, with group members encouraging each other to work toward the reward, peer harassment can occur if students perceive that some individuals are performing poorly or are deliberately trying to sabotage the group's chances of earning the reward. Consultants who recommend strategies involving interdependent group contingencies should therefore advise teachers of this possibility and help them take preventive measures, such as modeling appropriate behavior if the group fails to earn the reward for a particular intervention period, selecting interventions with built-in opportunities to earn back lost points (e.g., the *Good Behavior Game Plus Merit*), and placing uncooperative students in a separate group so that their behavior does not reduce their classmates' chances to obtain reinforcement. Observations during initial implementation can also help detect any undesirable side effects or negative outcomes that may not have been anticipated during the planning process.

Parental Involvement

Parental involvement in the intervention assistance process is not only an essential component of best practice but also an integral aspect of an ecological approach to problem solving. Regardless of the level of commitment and dedication among consultants and IAT members, no one is more invested in the child's success than the parent. As noted in Step 1 of the problem-solving process, the parent should be contacted by the classroom teacher as soon as a concern has been identified, rather than waiting until a referral for intervention assistance is imminent. That is, when parents learn that their child is being referred to an IAT, communications between the referring teacher and parents, including efforts to resolve the problem, should have already taken place, so that the referral simply constitutes another phase in the intervention assistance process. Once the referral has been made, parental involvement can take many forms, including sharing information during problem identification and analysis, helping to develop the intervention plan, and helping to monitor the student's response to the intervention. One effective but underutilized form of parent involvement consists of training parents in the same academic or behavioral strategies being implemented by the teacher in the classroom. Many of the interventions in this text can be taught to parents in one-to-one training sessions or as part of group-oriented parent education programs. Interventions suitable for parental involvement are identified as such in the comments section of the appendix at the end of each intervention chapter.

Involving parents as collaborative partners throughout the intervention assistance process is not only consistent with ethical standards requiring consultants to encourage parental participation in designing services for their children, including "linking interventions between home and school, tailoring parental involvement to the skills of the family, and helping parents gain the skills needed to help their children" (NASP-PPE, III, C, #3), but also with IDEA mandates to inform parents about the strategies designed to increase their child's rate of learning (34 C.F.R. § 300.311[a][7]), receive progress monitoring data (34 C.F.R. § 300.309[b][2]), and participate in meetings relating to their child's identification, evaluation, and placement (34 C.F.R. § 300.501). In designing intervention plans, consultants should also be mindful that they are ethically obligated to offer alternatives regarding the services to be provided that take into account parental values and capabilities and show respect for the family's ethnic/cultural values (NASP-PPE, III, C, #1, #5). Moreover, if parents object to school-based services, consultants are ethically bound to respect those wishes and direct parents to alternative resources in the community (NASP-PPE, III, C, #4).

With the widespread implementation of IATs, most school districts have developed policies requiring parental notification for referrals to team-based IATs, although formal policies relating to the need for notification in the case of individual consultants are less common. When the consultant is a regular school employee, such as a school psychologist, written parental permission is generally not necessary to consult with teachers regarding strategies for enhancing a student's opportunities to learn in the regular classroom setting, as long as those strategies do not involve unusual or out-of-classroom treatments. When a nonschool employee, such as an external consultant, will be providing consultation or intervention assistance services, however, parents should be notified in writing. Moreover, when the consultant is not a school employee, written parental permission must be obtained for school staff to provide the consultant with personally identifying student information. Parental permission is generally not required for interventions that affect all students in a class equally unless those interventions involve some unusual contingency or departure from daily routines, such as a field trip occurring off school grounds. Written parental consent should *always* be obtained for assessments and interventions that involve providing additional services to an individual student, such as a behavioral assessment, individual or small-group social skills training, or a major change in the student's educational program, especially if it involves removing the student from the classroom or treating the student differently from his or her classmates in some way. Even with classwide interventions, however, informing parents and inviting their input and support can enhance both acceptability and effectiveness (Brantley & Webster, 1993; Heller & Fantuzzo, 1993).

Student Involvement

At a minimum, students should be informed about the nature of a planned intervention, the intervention agents involved, and the anticipated outcomes (NASP-PPE, III, B, #2, #3). Explaining the essential components of an intervention plan to the target student and soliciting assent can be an empowering experience that encourages investment by the key stakeholder in the intervention assistance process. Although many students in the upper elementary grades and above can benefit from participating in consultation sessions and IAT meetings, the degree of benefit and the optimal level of involvement depend on several factors, including the nature of the referral problem, the student's capacity to participate positively in the problem-solving process, and the parents' views regarding the desirability of their child's involvement. Although there is virtually no research on the nature, extent, and results of student participation in IATs, there is some evidence that student monitoring of response to intervention is as effective as teacher monitoring, if not more so (Bahr, Fuchs, Fuchs, Fernstrom, & Stecker, 1993). Field testing indicates that involving the referred student in analyzing the problem, generating possible solutions, affirming intervention goals and strategies, and evaluating progress can be essential to the success of the plan, especially in the case of chronic lack of productivity and/or problem behavior. Of course, consultants must take care that the discussions in meetings attended by the student focus on developing solutions and affirming the student's capacity to participate positively in the intervention assistance process rather than on rehearsing the student's deficits. Finally, in strategies that involve another student as an intervention agent, such as peer tutoring or peer behavior monitoring, and that will not be implemented on a classwide basis, permission for the peer intervention agent to participate should be obtained in writing from his or her parents, as well as assent from the peer agent.

Intervention Assistance Documentation

Documenting the intervention assistance process is important not only to monitor the progress of the students being served but also to provide accountability data regarding the intervention assistance activities (Kovaleski, 2002). Intervention plans for individual students should be documented in the student's school record. If interventions are delivered through a team-based format, they should also be documented in team records. One advantage of maintaining a master set of IAT records is that all the data are together and readily available for use in program evaluation. Consultants and IAT members should bear in mind that under the 1974 Family Educational Rights and Privacy Act (FERPA; Public Law 93-380), also known as the Buckley Amendment, parents have access to essentially all of their child's school records, including records of classroom observations, intervention-related assessments, consultations, and intervention plans, as well as the right to challenge the accuracy of those records and the right to a hearing regarding their accuracy (34 C.F.R. § 99.10). Exempted from this requirement are so-called sole possession notes, defined in FERPA as "records that are kept in the sole possession of the maker, are used only as a personal memory aid, and are not accessible or revealed to any other person except a temporary substitute for the maker of the record" (34 C.F.R. § 99.3). If consultants share their notes with others, such as teachers, administrators, or IAT members, however, these notes are reclassified as educational records and become accessible to parents. Moreover, under IDEA's procedural safeguards, parents have the right to examine any records that have been collected as part of the special education decision-making process for their child (34 C.F.R. § 300.501).

If interventions target an entire class of students and do not involve major changes in educational programming or single out any students for differential treatment, documentation in IAP or IAT records is sufficient, although providing written notification to parents is recommended. *Reciprocal Peer Tutoring in Math* in Chapter 4 includes a sample letter informing parents about a classwide intervention that can be easily adapted for use with other strategies. Examples of forms for documenting IAT activities are available on the NASP website (*http://www.nasponline.org* (search under *problem-solving model*), at Intervention Central (*http://www.interventioncentral.org*), and on numerous district and state department of education websites.

Evaluating Intervention Effectiveness

Ethical practice requires that consultants provide targeted, data-based interventions and "modify or terminate the treatment plan when data indicate the plan is not achieving the desired goals" (NASP-PPE, IV, C, #6). Although consultants and teachers alike often fail systematically to collect accountability data in the intervention assistance process, especially data directly related to student outcomes (Bahr et al., 1999; Doll et al., 2005), failure to do so means that there is no objective basis for determining the effectiveness of the interventions that have been implemented. As noted above, plans should specify the time period for evaluating students' response to interventions, as well as the specific measures that will be used for progress monitoring. Frequent progress monitoring helps to ensure that interventions that are inappropriate, inadequate in intensity, or less than optimal in some other way can be modified in a timely manner so that students are not deprived of the right to learn (Heron, Martz, & Margolis, 1996). To facilitate progress monitoring and accountability, all the interventions in this book include at least two and as many as four methods for evaluating their effectiveness, ranging from measures already in place in regular education classrooms, such as homework completion rates and report card grades, to direct observational methods for measuring the productivity or behavior of an entire classroom group. Additional information on intervention evaluation is provided in a separate section below.

Consultant Competence

Consultants are ethically obligated to be aware of the limits of their own competence and to offer services only within those boundaries (NASP-PPE II, A, #1; APA *Ethical Principles of Psychologists and Code of Conduct* [APA-EP] 2.01a). Given an increasingly diverse student population and legislative mandates for evidence-based practices and data-based decision making, demands on consultant competence are greater than ever. In practice, it can be difficult for consultants to determine the degree to which they possess an acceptable level of competency in each of the many domains in which they are providing services (intervention design, team-based consultation, professional development, data collection and analysis, etc.). As part of the process of evaluating their own competence, consultants involved in IATs should ask themselves the following questions:

1. Am I offering a broad enough range of research-based interventions to intervention agents and consumers?
2. Do I understand the theoretical basis, rationale, and the likely outcomes for the interventions I recommend?
3. Am I aware of the amount and quality of the evidence base for the interventions in terms of the target student population?
4. Can I provide a comprehensive written description of intervention procedures?
5. Can I demonstrate the strategies to intervention agents and provide them with hands-on technical assistance so that they can implement them with fidelity?
6. Can I help intervention agents to evaluate the effectiveness of the strategies in the setting(s) in which they will be implemented?
7. Do I understand the possible side effects or potential negative consequences of the strategies with the target student population?

As the student population becomes increasing diverse, consultants must continually evaluate their competence to provide services to students and families from culturally diverse backgrounds, a task complicated by the paucity of empirically based intervention studies with students from ethnic and linguistic minorities (Artiles, Trent, & Kuan, 1997; Gersten & Baker, 2000a, 2000b). As stated in the most recent APA guidelines, psychologists are required "to consider client characteristics such as cultural background, disability, native language, or other diversity factors when assessing their own competence to provide services" (APA-EP 2.01b). Similarly, NASP guidelines underscore the fact that consultants are ethically obligated to provide services to students and families that respect cultural diversity and family ethical and cultural values (NASP-PPE, III, C, #5). A collaborative approach to problem solving can help to meet this standard and is aligned with ethical guidelines requiring practitioners to "enlist the assistance of other specialists in supervisory, consultative, or referral roles as appropriate in providing services" (NASP-PPE, II, A, #1). Moreover, consultants are required to maintain and enhance their competency by participating in professional development experiences that enhance their knowledge and skills (NASP-PPE, II, A, #1, #4). Keeping abreast of ethical and legal issues in school-based consultation and IATs is a challenging but critical aspect of continuing professional development for consultants.

Provisions for Referral

Consultants and IATs must ensure that the problem-solving process does not abrogate parents' rights under IDEA. The intervention assistance process described above includes provisions for referring students for special education evaluations or other services if interventions are unsuccessful or if the student's response is insufficient. Documenting interventions is important not only for assessing the student's response to scientifically based interventions, but also for maintaining a record of the strategies that have been implemented prior to referral for additional services. Because, under IDEA, parents have the right to request that their child be evaluated at any time if they suspect the presence of a disability (34 C.F.R. § 300.301[b]), consultants should inform parents of their right to a free comprehensive evaluation for their child while also informing them of the benefits potentially available through the intervention assistance process. A review of district and state procedural manuals for IATs reveals a wide variation in guidelines for the time period during which interventions are attempted before teams move to a referral for special education services. Kovaleski (2002) has suggested that a period of 50 school days from the initial referral by a parent or teacher to the completion of the IAT process, including an evaluation of intervention effectiveness, is sufficient to ensure that an intervention has had time to work without unduly delaying an assessment, if appropriate. Including parents as collaborators from the beginning of the intervention assistance process, including analyzing the problem, planning strategies, and assessing intervention effectiveness, not only facilitates home–school communication about the student's response or the lack thereof but also ensures that parents are cognizant of each aspect of the problem-solving process in the event that an individual evaluation is recommended at a later date.

ISSUES IN SELECTING AND DELIVERING REINFORCERS

For many low-performing and disruptive students, the usual rewards available in the classroom environment, such as grades and teacher praise, are insufficient to maintain appropriate behavior. As a result, many of the interventions in this book are *contingency-based*, that is, they include some form of incentive to encourage academic productivity and prosocial behavior, such as public recognition, opportunities to participate in team-based competitions, and material and activity rewards. Although these contingency-based strategies have been documented to have positive effects on the target behaviors, the use of external rewards in schools continues to be a matter of controversy. In recent years, the growth of schoolwide incentive programs that offer tokens or "dollars" for positive academic and/or social behavior that can be redeemed for items in a school store has fueled the long-running debate as to whether external rewards undermine motivation and achievement (e.g., Martens & Witt, 2004; Witzel & Mercer, 2003).

REWARDS AND MOTIVATION: WHAT DOES THE RESEARCH SAY?

The use of rewards in school settings to promote student performance and motivation has long been a controversial issue among researchers and educators alike (Akin-Little, Eckert, Lovett, & Little, 2004). Despite the numerous studies attesting to the effectiveness of rewarding students for academic achievement and appropriate behavior, including the voluminous literature on functional behavioral analysis (see Reitman, 1998), some authors have charged that rewards undermine creativity, impair performance quality, and cause children to lose interest in tasks once rewards are withdrawn (e.g., Deci & Ryan, 1987; Deci, Koestner, & Ryan, 1999; Kohn, 1993, 1996; Lepper, Keavney, & Drake, 1996). Contrary to this contention, empirical studies evaluating the effects of rewards on performance and motivation (Cameron & Pierce, 1996; Cameron, Pierce, Banko, & Gear, 2005; Eisenberger, Rhoades, & Cameron, 1999), including a meta-analysis of nearly 100 studies of intrinsic motivation (Cameron & Pierce, 1994), have consistently found that extrinsic rewards not only do not undermine performance or motivation but actually increase task interest and engagement. In these studies, negative effects are confined to situations in which external rewards are offered simply for engaging in a task and without regard to task completion or performance quality, and even in these cases the impact on intrinsic motivation is minimal. Moreover, many of today's students lack the motivational resources needed to sustain effort on their school assignments, and even the most effective classrooms include some activities, such as drill-and-practice tasks, that students often find boring (Rathvon, 1996). Finally, the strategies in this book that incorporate incentives as intervention components have been empirically demonstrated to be effective in enhancing academic productivity, achievement, and/or social behavior.

Noncontingent Reinforcement as an Intervention for Challenging Behavior

Among reward-based interventions, *noncontingent reinforcement* (NCR), also called *fixed-time reinforcement* or *timed positives,* has been reported as an effective treatment for challenging behavior among individuals with developmental disabilities. Most frequently implemented by trained therapists in controlled settings, NCR involves delivering reinforcement on a fixed-time schedule independent of the target individual's behavior (for reviews, see Carr et al., 2000, and Tucker, Sigafoos, & Bushell, 1998). The stimulus delivered is typically the stimulus that has been demonstrated in a functional analysis to maintain the problem behavior, such as attention or access to preferred tangible items. For example, a child exhibiting severe tantrums might receive teacher attention every 30 seconds, regardless of his or her behavior during the interval. After the tantrums have been reduced, the schedule of reinforcement is gradually faded to a level that is more ecologically viable. Because NCR does not result in increases in appropriate alternative behaviors, it is often combined with educationally oriented interventions to promote the development of positive skills (Doughty & Anderson, 2006; Marcus & Vollmer, 1996).

Potential Pitfalls of Contingency-Based Strategies

Despite the efficacy of rewards in promoting academic productivity and appropriate social behavior, consultants should be aware of several potential pitfalls in implementing contingency-based interventions. These include (1) teacher resistance to the use of rewards, (2) reward satiation, and (3) delivery in situations in which only a subset of students in a classroom earns the reward.

Dealing with Teacher Resistance to Rewards

Although teachers have long used social reinforcers such as public recognition and praise to encourage academic productivity and appropriate behavior, some teachers are reluctant to implement interventions that involve delivering material rewards in the belief that such rewards constitute bribes for behaviors students should exhibit naturally. Resistance is especially likely if teachers are asked to implement strategies that offer incentives to only one or a few unproductive or disruptive students while their appropriately behaving classmates have no access to the reward. The interventions in this book avoid this problem because all the strategies are designed to be applied to an entire classroom group rather than to one student or to a small group. Even for interventions that create intraclass team competitions, the procedures permit all teams to win and obtain the reward. Another concern frequently expressed by teachers regarding the use of material reinforcers is the amount of time and effort required to dispense rewards. To address this concern, the reinforcement procedures for the interventions in this book were either originally designed or have been adapted to permit maximum ease of delivery and minimum disruption to ongoing instruction. In addition, a variety of tangible, social, and activity-based rewards are suggested for contingency-based strategies, permitting teachers to select reinforcers best matching their own preferences and classroom ecologies.

Reducing Satiation Effects

A second potential pitfall for contingency-based interventions is *reward satiation,* which refers to a situation in which rewards lose their ability to motivate behavior with continued use. There are several strategies that can reduce satiation effects. First, students can be involved in selecting the rewards or privileges. Many of the contingency-based strategies in this book include the use of a *reinforcement menu*—a list of possible rewards—to assess student preferences. In view of evidence that students may favor different kinds of rewards than those preferred by teachers, parents, and administrators (Berkowitz & Martens, 2001; Gray, Gutkin, & Riley, 2001), involving students in reward selection can be critical to intervention success. Moreover, because reinforcement surveys may be more accurate in identifying rewards that *lack* motivating properties for students than those that can enhance performance (Northup, 2000; Northup, George, Jones, Broussard, & Vollmer, 1996), developing a reinforcement menu that identifies as many rewards as possible that are not only appealing to students but also acceptable to teachers is highly recommended (see Figure 2.3 for an example).

Reward satiation can also be mitigated by incorporating unpredictability into the reinforcement structure. For example, the teacher can invite students to draw from a grab bag or "surprise box" containing a variety of small rewards, such as colorful pencils and erasers, inexpensive toys, and wrapped candy. A popular reward in this format is the "homework pass," a note exempting the student from homework in a particular subject for that day. The surprise box can also contain numbered slips of paper, with each number designating a reward listed on the reinforcement menu. Another strategy involves conducting a classroom raffle, with eligibility to participate in the raffle based on satisfactory performance of the target behaviors. At the end of the day or week, the names of all students achieving the criterion are placed in a box, one name is drawn, and the student whose name is drawn receives the reward. This strategy not only limits expenditures on rewards but is especially appropriate for incentives that involve reducing academic tasks, such as homework passes, because teachers are usually reluctant to permit large groups of students to skip assignments. The *Response Cost Raffle* in Chapter 5 is based on this type of contingency system.

A growing body of research indicates that making the rewards in contingency-based interventions unpredictable can significantly enhance the power of the contingency. Two of the interventions in this book (*Promoting Homework Completion and Accuracy with Mystery Motivators; A Multicomponent Intervention to Reduce Disruptive Behavior*) make use of the "mystery motivator" strategy (Rhode, Jenson, & Reavis, 1992), which involves displaying an envelope containing a reward or description of a reward in a prominent place in the classroom. Viewing a concealed and uncertain reward, as with a wrapped gift, increases anticipation and the motivating capacity of the reward. Another strategy is to randomize reinforcement criteria so that students cannot predict which set of performance standards will be applied to the target behaviors (see *The Rewards Box: Enhancing Academic Performance with Randomized Group Contingencies* in Chapter 5). Interventions randomizing group contingency components can produce immediate and dramatic improvement in academic performance (Popkin & Skinner, 2003; Sharp & Skinner, 2004) and classroom behav-

REINFORCEMENT MENU

Directions: Below is a list of possible rewards our class could earn. Please put a check in the column that matches your level of interest in each reward. Your ratings will be used to help select the rewards for our class.

Possible reward	Level of interest		
	Low	Medium	High
30 minutes of computer time			
Class video or DVD			
Visit another grade to read aloud to students			
10 minutes of classroom basketball			
15 minutes of card or board games			
Permission to take the class pet home for the weekend			
15 minutes of silent ball			
10 minutes extra lunch time			
15 minutes of a math computer game			
Trip to computer lab			
One game of fruit-basket turnover			
Homework pass			
10 minutes of extra recess			
10 minutes of music			
Class field trip			
Class party			
Group games in gym			
Free time			
15 minutes of reading with a classmate			
Good note home			

FIGURE 2.3. Reinforcement menu.

ior (Kelshaw-Levering, Sterling-Turner, Henry, & Skinner, 2000; Theodore, Bray, Kehle, & Jenson, 2001).

Finally, using social reinforcers, such as public recognition and positive teacher attention, rather than tangible rewards can help minimize satiation. Many of the interventions in this text include public recognition of academic performance or positive social behavior as a motivational component (e.g., *ClassWide Peer Tutoring*; *Tootling: Enhancing Student Relationships with Peer Reporting, Public Posting, and Group Contingencies*). Relationship-based rewards that provide opportunities for students to interact with valued adults or peers are also likely to be less subject to satiation effects. These rewards can include eating lunch with the teacher, reading to other students, participating in school service projects, or coming early or staying after school to help the teacher with a special project.

Managing Reinforcement Delivery

Because all of the interventions in this book have been designed or adapted for use with entire classes rather than individual students, all students have an equal opportunity to earn rewards under the contingency-based strategies. As a result, most of the problems associated with delivering a reward to a few students while others remain unrewarded have been eliminated. Even with classwide interventions, however, reinforcement delivery problems can occur with interventions that involve competition among teams. In some investigations of team-based strategies, nonwinning teams were required to continue performing school tasks, often in the same classroom as their victorious peers. Field testing and research alike (e.g., Wolfe, Boyd, & Wolfe, 1983) indicate that students may become disgruntled and disruptive if they must watch their classmates enjoying a reward or privilege they have failed to earn. Supervising a group of nonrewarded students under these circumstances can be especially problematic for teachers with poor classroom management skills and can increase resistance to the intervention assistance process. Although the team-based interventions in this book permit all students to win and receive the reward if each team meets the criterion, every team may not meet the criterion on a particular day or on enough days to earn a weekly reward. Moreover, teachers may occasionally wish to use a contingency-based intervention with a single student or a small group of students rather than with the entire class.

There are several methods of managing reinforcement delivery when some students in the classroom will not receive a reward. One strategy is to send the students who have earned the reward to another teacher or staff member to receive the reinforcement. For example, the reward can consist of viewing a video or DVD in another classroom or extra time in the gym, media center, or computer lab. Teachers implementing the same intervention can collaborate in supervising students, with winners from the two classrooms going to one room to receive the reward while students who did not earn the reward go to the other room to continue working on their assignments or to participate in some less preferred activity. A second strategy is to replace activity rewards with small tangible rewards that can be delivered unobtrusively to individual students, such as positive school–home notes, stickers, or miniature candy bars. Delivering these reinforcers at the very end of the school day minimizes opportunities for disruptive and unproductive behavior among students not receiving the rewards (see the *Response Cost Raffle,* Variation 1, in Chapter 5). Third, reinforcement for appropriate academic or social behavior can be provided at home rather than in the classroom. Teachers and consultants can collaborate with parents and students to develop home-based social or material incentives for academic or behavior goals (see *Reciprocal Peer Tutoring in Math,* Variation 2, in Chapter 4).

EVALUATING INTERVENTION EFFECTIVENESS

The importance of documenting changes in student outcomes during the intervention assistance process cannot be overemphasized. After intervention implementation, consultants may hear teachers report, "I tried what you [or the team] recommended, and it didn't work," only to discover that no objective assessment of the effects of the intervention on student performance has been conducted. Systematically evaluating changes in performance or behavior not only provides information for assessing intervention effectiveness so that strategies can be modified as needed, but also contributes to teachers' maintenance of interventions by demonstrating that positive change is indeed occurring. Specifying objective measures of changes in student performance is even more critical for interventions targeting social behavior than for strategies targeting academic achievement. Because grades and measures of academic productivity, such as homework completion rates, are part of the regular data-gathering process in classrooms, teachers can readily monitor changes in academic performance. In contrast, teachers are much less likely to use objective methods of monitoring social behaviors, such as checklists documenting the frequency of desired and undesired target behaviors, and thus may fail to detect small positive changes and abandon an intervention prematurely.

Barriers to Evaluation in the IAT Process

Despite the increasing emphasis on data-based decision making in education and frequent calls in the professional literature to document intervention effects (e.g., Elliott et al., 2002; Steege, Brown-Chidsey, & Mace, 2002), evaluation continues to be the most neglected aspect of the intervention assistance process. In a recent survey of school psychologists (Bramlett, Murphy, Johnson, & Wallingford, 2002), only 40% of respondents reported that they conducted some type of evaluation to assess the effectiveness of their consultation and intervention practice. Moreover, when evaluations were conducted, teacher verbal report was the most common form (55%). Similarly, studies of IATs have consistently reported that teams fail to conduct adequate assessments of target behaviors prior to intervention and changes in those behaviors after implementation and that the data typically collected are subjective in nature (Burns & Symington, 2002; Flugum & Reschly, 1994; Kovaleski, 2002; Safran & Safran, 1996; Wilkinson, 2005).

Several factors contribute to the frequent failure of participants in the intervention assistance process to evaluate intervention effects. First, given the constraints on consultant and teacher time, the pressure to create changes in the performance of a low-performing or disruptive student or classroom group often takes precedence over systematically evaluating student response to those efforts. As a result, teacher and consultant time tends to be allocated to implementation rather than to evaluation, and evaluation often consists of the subjective impressions of the teacher and consultant, which may not coincide with each other or with observable changes in student behavior (e.g., Jones et al., 1997; Noell et al., 1997; Witt et al., 1997). Teachers' resistance to evaluation is also related to the increased demands placed on them by the intervention assistance process. Teachers who refer students to IATs are typically asked first to provide data on the student's current level of performance, then to alter their instructional and/or management routines by implementing one or more interventions, and then to collect additional data documenting the student's response to the interventions. If the interventions appear to be successful in solving the referral problem from the teacher's perspective, documenting changes in student outcomes may seem even less of a priority. On the other hand, if student achievement or behavior does not appear to be improving, teachers may become discouraged or frustrated with the intervention assistance process and may fail to collect data systematically, especially if the evaluation methods do not fit into the classroom ecology.

Finally, lack of training plays a major role in practitioners' failure to evaluate intervention effectiveness, with school-based teams reporting that they lack training in monitoring student progress and evaluating the effectiveness of intervention plans (McDougal et al., 2000; Telzrow et al., 2000; Welch, Brownell, & Sheridan, 1999). This is not a surprising finding, given that many consultants and educators received their training before the current emphasis on data-based decision making, which requires a broad range of technical skills and competencies in areas such as observational recording, curriculum-based measurement, functional behavioral assessment, and data analysis. Moreover, because many states leave IAT training to local districts, the quantity and quality of the training that consultants and participants receive varies considerably (Buck et al., 2003).

Rationale for Evaluating Intervention Effectiveness

Despite these obstacles, integrating accountability into the intervention assistance process is an essential aspect of best practice for several reasons. First, evaluation is needed to assess changes in the target behavior of referred individual students or classroom groups. Without systematic accountability methods, consultants and teachers will be unable to determine which interventions are effective with which types of problems and with which types of student populations, and interventions will continue to be delivered primarily on the basis of familiarity or ease of implementation rather than effectiveness. Second, accountability data can encourage participants to remain engaged in the intervention assistance process (Slonski-Fowler & Truscott, 2004). When teachers and team members have objective data indicating that a student is responding positively to an intervention, they are more likely to be supportive of that strategy and the intervention assistance process in general. Feedback to students is probably the most neglected aspect of the evaluation process, despite accumulating evidence that providing students with explicit information about their own progress can significantly enhance their performance (Eckert, Dunn, & Ardoin, 2006; Whinnery & Fuchs, 1993). Many of the interventions in this book include student-focused feedback components, such as public posting (e.g., *ClassWide Peer Tutoring, Red Light/Green Light*), contingent teacher praise (e.g., *Delivering Effective Praise*), and systematic error correction (e.g., *Using Response Cards to Increase Academic Engagement and Achievement*). Moreover, several strategies involve training students to monitor their own performance (e.g., *Self-Monitoring of Academic Productivity*; *Three Steps to Self-Managed Behavior*). Finally, as noted above, ethical practice requires that consultants assess the effectiveness of planned interventions in terms of student outcomes. Conducting a systematic evaluation of intervention effectiveness may be time-consuming, but it is essential to ensure that IATs will achieve the purpose for which they have been developed: enhancing the quality of education for all students.

Selecting Evaluation Measures

Researchers have used a wide variety of measures to assess intervention effectiveness, ranging from a single-item scale rating the behavior of one student on a 5-point continuum from completely unmanageable to completely manageable (Filcheck et al., 2004) to computer-facilitated observational systems that can record information about dozens of teacher and student variables (Greenwood, Carta, Kamps, Terry, & Delquadri, 1994; Carta, Atwater, Schwartz, & Miller, 1990). In this book, evaluation of changes in student performance is an integral component of every strategy, but pre- and postintervention measures have been designed from an ecological perspective. That is, the focus is on assessing changes in target behaviors in the context of the regular classroom environment, using measures designed to be as unobtrusive and practical as possible without sacrificing reliability and validity. Just as importantly, measurement targets and data collected must be directly related to observable student behaviors rather than perceptions of other stakeholders, such as teachers or parents. Although teacher and parent judgments of changes in student performance and behavior provide valuable consumer satisfaction data, evaluation measures must also include direct assessments of student behavior because the ultimate goal of school-based interventions is improvement in student functioning (Durlak, 2002).

The observation–evaluation component of each intervention in this book describes at least two and as many as four assessment strategies for documenting changes in classroom environmental variables, academic performance, or behavior. In keeping with the group-oriented nature of the interventions, evaluation measures are primarily designed to assess aspects of student engagement, academic achievement, or social behavior for an entire classroom, but most can be easily adapted for use with individual students or small groups of target students. To encourage the regular collection of accountability data, many evaluation measures rely on naturally gathered information, such as report card grades, scores on quizzes and tests, or homework accuracy rates. Naturalistic evaluation procedures that fit readily into current classroom routines are not only less ecologically intrusive but are also more acceptable to teachers, who typically bear the dual responsibilities of intervention implementation and progress monitoring.

Evaluating Changes in Academic Performance

Assessing changes in academic achievement is especially important because students' success is defined by the degree to which they are able to master the "business" of school: learning. Evaluation strategies for many of the academic interventions rely on *curriculum-based measurement* (CBM), a method of direct assessment that can be used to measure student growth over time with any type of instructional method or curriculum. Because CBMs can be administered frequently, they yield a pattern of scores that indicate if the student is making adequate progress relative to intervention goals, classroom peers, and/or grade-level expectations. Moreover, CBMs in mathematics, spelling, written expression, and the content areas can easily be administered to groups. Chapter 3 presents an overview of this type of assessment and provides step-by-step procedures for conducting CBMs in reading, mathematics, spelling, writing, and the content areas. Two other methods with utility for assessing response to academic interventions—*brief experimental analysis* and *percentage gain*—are described below.

BRIEF EXPERIMENTAL ANALYSIS: APPLYING CBM TO IDENTIFY EFFECTIVE ACADEMIC INTERVENTIONS

Brief experimental analysis (BEA) is an assessment technology that uses curriculum-based measurement (CBM) within a response-to-intervention (RTI) model to identify effective strategies for academic problems, especially reading problems. An experimental form of functional assessment, BEA directly tests the effects of several interventions within a short time frame by comparing baseline performance on CBMs in reading (R-CBM) with R-CBM performance subsequent to the introduction of one or more interventions. Interventions are selected based on hypotheses regarding the factors that may be contributing to poor performance, such as lack of motivation, low skill levels, insufficient practice, or a mismatch between student skills and instructional materials (Daly, Andersen, Gortmaker, & Turner, 2006). Current approaches to BEA include three different methods. In the first approach, intervention components are applied and evaluated one by one, beginning with the easiest and least complex (Daly, Martens, Dool, & Hintze, 1998; Jones & Wickstrom, 2002). For example, contingent rewards, repeated reading, and listening previewing are introduced sequentially, performance under each intervention condition is compared with the baseline, and the most effective intervention is selected. In the second approach, an intervention is introduced, after which additional strategies are implemented one by one until the desired results are obtained (Daly, Martens, Hamler, Dool, & Eckert, 1999; Daly, Murdoch, Lillenstein, Webber, & Lentz, 2002). In the third approach, an intervention "package" consisting of several components is applied simultaneously, after which the package is dismantled one component at a time until the simplest intervention capable of producing the desired results is identified (Daly, Persampieri, McCurdy, & Gortmaker, 2005). Although this approach requires more resources initially than the first two approaches, it may ultimately enhance usability because a simpler intervention can be selected if it produces the same results as the package (Daly et al., 2006). A growing body of research documents BEA's utility in selecting effective interventions for students with reading problems (Daly et al., 2005; Noell, Freeland, Witt, & Gansle, 2001; VanAuken, Chafouleas, Bradley, & Martens, 2002). BEA has also been validated for use in selecting components for parent–child tutoring interventions (Persampieri, Gortmaker, Daly, Sheridan, & McCurdy, 2006; Valleley, Evans, & Allen, 2002).

PERCENTAGE GAIN: ASSESSING RESPONSE TO ACADEMIC INTERVENTIONS

A useful method for assessing changes in student academic performance subsequent to the introduction of academic interventions involves calculating *percentage gain* (Menlo & Johnson, 1971). Originally designed to measure change for individuals, percentage gain scores can be combined to yield group averages so that the progress of an entire class can be monitored in targeted academic areas. Percentage gain scores have several advantages over simple change scores. They correlate more highly with posttest scores and, unlike simple change scores, do not place initially high-scoring individuals at a disadvantage by reducing their gains below those of initially low scorers. In cases in which the final score exceeds the initial score, the percentage gain score is defined as

$$\text{Percentage gain} = \frac{X_2 - X_1}{R_p} \times 100$$

where X_2 is the final score, X_1 is the initial score, and R_p is the highest possible score minus the initial score (i.e., the maximum possible gain). In cases in which the final score is less than the initial score, the percentage gain score (which will be negative) is defined as

$$\text{Percentage gain} = \frac{X_2 - X_1}{R_n} \times 100$$

where R_n is the initial score minus the lowest possible score (i.e., the maximum possible loss).

For example, if Marissa's average score on vocabulary quizzes was 65 out of a possible 100 prior to implementing *Peer Tutoring in Vocabulary* and 75 after implementation, her percentage gain is 28.5% ([(75 – 65)/35] × 100 = 28.5%). A classwide average percentage gain score can be calculated by summing percentage gain scores for each student and dividing by the number of students in the class. Comparing the percentage gain score for an individual target student with the class average percentage gain score provides useful information on the target student's response to the intervention compared with that of class peers. If the average percentage gain score for Marissa's class is 45% after classwide implementation of *Peer Tutoring in Vocabulary,* this indicates that she is not responding to the intervention in the same way as her classmates and that additional targeted interventions are in order.

Evaluating Changes in Student Behavior

In assessing the effectiveness of interventions targeting social competence, it is important to select measures that are capable of detecting small changes in student behavior. Although numerous teacher rating scales have been developed to assess student behavior, most of these measures are designed to screen for emotional and behavioral disorders rather than to detect changes in classroom behavior subsequent to school-based interventions. Similarly, although a wide variety of methods have been developed for observing student behavior in classrooms and nonclassroom settings, such as the playground, many of the published scales require extensive training for observers and even then may not reach acceptable psychometric standards for reliability (for reviews, see Leff & Lakin, 2005, and Volpe, DiPerna, Hintze, & Shapiro, 2005). In recent years, researchers have developed a variety of computerized systems to collect and analyze real-time classroom observational data, some of which can be delivered using personal digital assistant (PDA) software (see Kahng & Iwata, 1998, for a review). Although this trend is likely to continue, many consultants and teachers do not have access to these systems, and they can be quite complex to implement. This section describes observational recording methods that are both practical and reliable. A useful metric for assessing response to behavioral interventions—*percentage reduction*—is also described below.

PERCENTAGE REDUCTION: ASSESSING RESPONSE TO BEHAVIORAL INTERVENTIONS

The *percentage reduction measure* is used to document the impact of behavioral interventions in reducing problem behavior (Carr et al., 1999). Also called a *suppression index,* the percentage reduction measure is ideally suited for evaluating interventions targeting problem behavior because it takes into account research designs and functional analysis applications in which more than one intervention is implemented sequentially, or reversal designs, in which an intervention is applied and then removed several times. Because sequentially added interventions often produce a downward trend in problem behavior levels, the overall mean for intervention conditions may underestimate the final effect of the intervention. To minimize this possibility, the percentage reduction measure compares the mean of the last three sessions of the final intervention condition with the last three baseline sessions to assess the overall degree of improvement at the end of the intervention period (i.e., percentage reduction from baseline).

To calculate percentage reduction, subtract the mean of the last three data points ($\bar{X}_{interv3}$) in the intervention phase from the mean of the last three data points in the baseline phase ($\bar{X}_{base3}$). Then divide the difference by the mean of the last three baseline data points ($\bar{X}_{base3}$), and multiply the resulting quotient by 100, as follows:

$$\text{Percentage reduction} = \frac{\bar{X}_{base3} - \bar{X}_{interv3}}{\bar{X}_{base3}} \times 100$$

For example, Nathan's baseline frequency of aggressive behavior was 10, 15, and 8 aggressive acts (baseline mean = 11 aggressive acts) and his frequency during the intervention period (based on the last three data points) was 2, 4, and 0 aggressive acts (intervention mean = 2 aggressive acts). His percentage reduction score is 81.8% ([11 – 2]/11 = 81.8 × 100 = 81.8%). Percentage reduction can be calculated for data reported as a frequency, as in event recording, or as a percentage of time samples, as in interval recording.

Observational Recording Methods

The observational strategies included in the interventions in this book are designed to be as user-friendly as possible while still yielding reliable and valid measures of relevant student behaviors. Many of the strategies make use of one or more of four observational coding methods: (1) group event recording, (2) group interval recording, (3) classwide scanning, and (4) group time sampling. These four methods are versions of two basic observational procedures: (1) event recording and (2) momentary time sampling.

Event recording consists of tallying the number of times one or more target behaviors occurs. The *Group Event Recording Form* (see Figure 2.4) is designed to monitor the frequency of occurrence of one to five positive and/or negative target behaviors for an entire class for up to 7 days or observation periods. *Discrete behaviors*—behaviors with identifiable beginnings and endings, such as call-outs, out-of-seats, or hand raises—are most appropriate for monitoring with event recording. The data yielded by this method are frequency counts of the target behaviors displayed by a class or group.

Momentary time sampling consists of observing a student at predetermined intervals and recording whether or not the student is exhibiting a target behavior at the moment of observation. The *Group Interval Recording Form* is designed for consecutively recording the behavior of every student in a class or group at predetermined intervals, such as every 5, 10, or 15 seconds (see Figure 2.5). The observer records whether each student is displaying one of several mutually exclusive behaviors, such as on-task, off-task, or disruptive behavior, at the moment of observation. The data collected by this method are classwide or group-wide rates of each of the target behavior categories. Because observation is continuous, this method must be conducted by some individual other than the classroom teacher, at least while the teacher is delivering instruction. Although the emphasis in this book is on classwide observation methods, the *Group Event Recording Form* and the *Group Interval Recording Form* can also be used to monitor the behavior of an individual student or a small group of target students.

Classwide scanning, a version of momentary time sampling, involves rapidly surveying an entire class and tallying the number of students in each of several mutually exclusive behavior categories at the moment of observation. Classwide scanning differs from the standard momentary time sampling procedure in that student behavior is monitored at longer intervals rather than coded sequentially every few seconds. Using the *Classwide Scanning Form,* the observer records whether students are on-task, off-task, or disruptive at predetermined intervals, such as every 3, 5, 10, or 15 minutes (see Figure 2.6). Although shorter intervals yield more reliable data, longer intervals permit teachers to monitor student behavior systematically without unduly interrupting ongoing instruction. When classwide scanning is conducted by individuals not involved in delivering instruction, shorter intervals can be used. The data collected by classwide scanning consist of the percentages of students falling into each of the behavior categories.

In *quadrant sampling,* a variation of classwide scanning, the observer divides the class into four groups by eye and sequentially records the behavior of each quadrant as either on-task or off-task in an all-or-nothing judgment. If all of the students in the group being observed are on-task, the interval is scored as on-task, whereas if one or more students in the group are off-task, the interval is scored as off-task. The *Group Time Sampling Form* (see Figure 2.7) is designed to sample student behavior at predetermined intervals, such as every 3 or 5 minutes. Because student groups are identified on the form by number, the observer can determine whether some groups are more off-task than others and use that information to modify classroom organization and instructional routines. The data yielded by quadrant sampling consist of the percentage of students in each group and in a class as a whole with on-task (and off-task) behavior.

(text continues on p. 62)

GROUP EVENT RECORDING FORM

Teacher: _____ School: _____

Description of class or group: _____

Number of students in class or group: _____

Dates of observation: _____ Time(s) of observation: _____

Observer: _____ Class activity: _____

Directions: Select one or more target behaviors (desired or undesired) to monitor and list them in the first column. Place a check or tally in the box for each occurrence of each target behavior during the observation session or day.

Target behavior	Session 1	Session 2	Session 3	Session 4	Session 5	Session 6	Session 7

Behavior 1 occurrences: _____

Behavior 2 occurrences: _____

Behavior 3 occurrences: _____

Behavior 4 occurrences: _____

Behavior 5 occurrences: _____

FIGURE 2.4. *Group Event Recording Form.*

GROUP INTERVAL RECORDING FORM

Teacher: _____   School: _____

Description of class or group: _____

Number of students in class or group: _____   Class activity: _____

Date of observation: _____   Time of observation: _____ to _____

Observer: _____   Length of observation interval: _____

Directions: Beginning at the left side of the room, glance at each student at the designated interval (e.g., 5, 10, or 15 seconds) and code that student's behavior as on-task (+), off-task (–), or disruptive (×) at the moment of observation. Record behavior for each student in turn and then begin again with the first student.

1	2	3	4	5	6	7	8	9	10	11	12	13	14	15	16	17	18	19	20
21	22	23	24	25	26	27	28	29	30	31	32	33	34	35	36	37	38	39	40
41	42	43	44	45	46	47	48	49	50	51	52	53	54	55	56	57	58	59	60
61	62	63	64	65	66	67	68	69	70	71	72	73	74	75	76	77	78	79	80
81	82	83	84	85	86	87	88	89	90	91	92	93	94	95	96	97	98	99	100
101	102	103	104	105	106	107	108	109	110	111	112	113	114	115	116	117	118	119	120
121	122	123	124	125	126	127	128	129	130	131	132	133	134	135	136	137	138	139	140
141	142	143	144	145	146	147	148	149	150	151	152	153	154	155	156	157	158	159	160
161	162	163	164	165	166	167	168	169	170	171	172	173	174	175	176	177	178	179	180

$$\text{Percentage of target behavior} = \frac{\text{Number of intervals per category}}{\text{Total number of observation intervals}} \times 100$$

Percentage of on-task behavior   = _____

Percentage of off-task behavior   = _____

Percentage of disruptive behavior   = _____

FIGURE 2.5. *Group Interval Recording Form.*

CLASSWIDE SCANNING FORM

Teacher: _____   School: _____

Description of class or group: _____

Number of students in class or group: ____ Class activity: _____

Date of observation: _____   Time of observation: _____ to _____

Observer: _____   Length of observation interval: _____

Directions: Scan the class at the designated interval (e.g., every 3, 5, 10, or 15 minutes) and tally the number of students in each behavior category. Tally marks for each interval should sum to the number of students in the entire group. Sum the tallies for each behavior category and divide by the number of intervals coded times the total number of students to obtain the percentage of students in each category.

Interval	On-Task	Off-Task	Disruptive	Totals
1				
2				
3				
4				
5				
6				
7				
8				
9				
10				
11				
12				

$$\text{Percentage of students per category} = \frac{\text{Total number of students per category}}{\text{Number of intervals} \times \text{total number of students}} \times 100$$

Percentage of on-task students   = _____

Percentage of off-task students   = _____

Percentage of disruptive students = _____

FIGURE 2.6. *Classwide Scanning Form.*

GROUP TIME SAMPLING FORM

Teacher: _____ School: _____

Description of class or group: _____

Number of students in class or group: ____ Class activity: _____

Date of observation: _____ Time of observation: _____ to _____

Observer: _____ Length of observation interval: _____

Directions: With your eye, divide the class into four groups of approximately equal numbers of students. If desired, write the names of the students in each group in the corresponding blanks at the bottom of the form. Beginning at the left side of the room, glance at each quadrant at the selected interval (1-, 3-, or 5-minute interval). If all of the students in the group are on-task at the moment of observation, record a plus (+) for the observed quadrant. If any of the students in the quadrant being observed are not on task, record a minus (–). During the next interval, observe the next group, and so forth until you have observed all of the groups. Then begin again with the first group.

Group 1	Group 2	Group 3	Group 4	Group 1	Group 2	Group 3	Group 4
Group 1	Group 2	Group 3	Group 4	Group 1	Group 2	Group 3	Group 4
Group 1	Group 2	Group 3	Group 4	Group 1	Group 2	Group 3	Group 4
Group 1	Group 2	Group 3	Group 4	Group 1	Group 2	Group 3	Group 4

$$\text{Group percentage of on-task intervals} = \frac{\text{Number of plus intervals per group}}{\text{Number of intervals per group}} \times 100$$

$$\text{Classwide percentage of on-task intervals} = \frac{\text{Total number of plus intervals}}{\text{Total number of observation intervals}} \times 100$$

Group 1 percentage of on-task behavior = ____% Students: _____

Group 2 percentage of on-task behavior = ____% Students: _____

Group 3 percentage of on-task behavior = ____% Students: _____

Group 4 percentage of on-task behavior = ____% Students: _____

Classwide percentage of on-task behavior = ____%

FIGURE 2.7. *Group Time Sampling Form.*

From *Effective School Interventions: Evidence-Based Strategies for Improving Student Outcomes* (2nd ed.) by Natalie Rathvon. Copyright 2008 by The Guilford Press. Permission to photocopy this figure is granted to purchasers of the book for personal use only (see copyright page for details).

SELECTING AN OBSERVATIONAL METHOD

In considering which observational procedure to recommend, consultants should keep in mind the demands on teacher time and the degree of expertise required by the different methodologies. Classwide scanning methods are especially suitable for teacher use because observations can be distributed at wide intervals. Event recording methods, which monitor discrete behaviors, are also relatively easy for classroom teachers to use. Momentary time sampling methods, which involve rating student behavior several times per minute, are more feasible for an observer other than the teacher. Consultants should also involve teachers in selecting observational methods and data collection procedures. Collaborating with teachers in selecting data collection measures as well as interventions not only conveys respect for teachers' perspectives but also affirms teachers as active participants in documenting improvement in students' academic or social competence. In addition, consultants should be prepared to demonstrate the selected methods, observe the teacher using them, and help analyze and interpret the results. Finally, consultants should be prepared to conduct some of the observations themselves. Although the observation and evaluation methods for the interventions in this book have been designed to be as simple as possible without sacrificing reliability and validity, even the simplest observation can be more easily performed by someone other than the teacher, who must be continually responding to the demands of daily classroom life. Assisting with data collection not only supports teachers in the intervention assistance process, it also provides consultants with invaluable information regarding the classroom environment that can be used to design and modify interventions.

ASSESSING THE RELIABILITY OF BEHAVIORAL OBSERVATIONS

Given the realities of the typical school environment, a single individual will conduct classroom observations in most cases. Using two or more observers yields more reliable information, however, and is necessary to obtain interrater reliability data. The two observers can consist of the referring teacher and the consultant, two IAT members, or pairs of trained student interns or paraprofessionals. A common formula for calculating interrater reliability for two observers that can be used for event recording and time sampling procedures is as follows:

$$\text{Interobserver agreement} = \frac{\text{Number of agreements}}{(\text{Number of agreements} + \text{Number of disagreements})} \times 100\%$$

This percentage agreement index represents the percentage of occasions on which two observers agree that a behavior did or did not occur. Interobserver percentage agreement should be 80% or higher in order to conclude that measurements of behavior are reliable and valid (Steege et al., 2002).

GRAPHING: AN ESSENTIAL TOOL
FOR EVALUATING INTERVENTION EFFECTIVENESS

Detecting changes in student performance or behavior can be difficult and time-consuming when reviewing lists of numbers, a series of observational forms or anecdotal records, and other types of data. Graphs provide a way of organizing data collected during baseline and intervention phases into easy-to-read visual displays that permit teachers, team members, parents, students, and others involved in the intervention process to determine whether the intervention plan is having the desired effect on the target behavior. The graph most commonly used to analyze behavioral data is a *time-series graph,* which depicts changes in one or more target behaviors over time. Frequency, percent score, or some other metric is plotted on the vertical axis (*y* axis) and time is plotted on the horizontal axis (*x* axis). A line connects the individual data points, creating a path that reveals the pattern and trend of the target behavior. To denote the change from baseline to intervention phrase or from one intervention to another, a *condition line*—a vertical line drawn parallel to the *y* axis and separating the data points in the various phases—can be added.

Graphs also serve as key tools in demonstrating the need for special services in RTI eligibility decision making. Graphs can be used to display not only the student's response to intervention but also the intensity of the intervention supports that have been implemented, such as the frequency of teacher contacts. Moreover, by plotting comparison peer performance on the same graph, the discrepancy between the performance of the referred student and that of typical students in the same educational context can be easily evaluated (Barnett, Daly, Jones, & Lentz, 2004; Bell & Barnett, 1999).

Figure 2.8 displays baseline and intervention conditions for Anthony, a kindergarten student referred for high rates of aggressive behavior, including pushing, hitting, and throwing toys and other objects. Also plotted on the graph are median aggressive behaviors for three typical classroom peers selected by the teacher. An inspection of the graph reveals not only that the frequency of Anthony's aggressive behaviors has decreased markedly during the intervention phase compared with baseline, but also that his aggressive behavior has stabilized at approximately the level of typical classroom peers.

Graphing resources are available on the Intervention Central website (*www.intervention-central.org*), including ChartDog, an on-line application for generating time-series graphs for academic performance data, and a link to a site permitting users to create Excel time-series

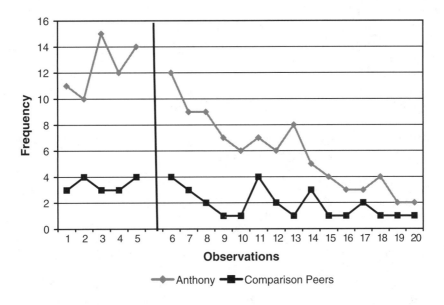

FIGURE 2.8. Frequency of aggressive behaviors during baseline and intervention phases for Anthony and three comparison peers.

graphs for common academic measures (curriculum-based measurement [CBM] and Dynamic Indicators of Basic Early Literacy Skills [DIBELS]) and behavioral measures (frequency, time-on-task, and the *Behavioral Observation of Students in Schools* [BOSS; discussed in Chapter 4]).

Evaluating IAT Outcomes

In addition to evaluating changes in the performance of individual students and groups of students, school-based teams should assess the overall effectiveness of their IATs. Frequently used measures of IAT effectiveness include the following: (1) number of students referred for special education who are actually placed in special education programs (i.e., appropriate referrals for special education services); (2) proportion of students from minority backgrounds placed in special education programs (i.e., checks for the disproportionate placement of students from certain racial/ethnic/linguistic minority groups); (3) changes in the achievement and behavior of referred students; (4) teacher, parent, and student satisfaction with IAT activities and interventions; (5) changes in teachers' instructional and behavior management practices; and (6) number of requests for intervention assistance. Gathering information on outcomes of referred students is essential not only for data-based decision making but also for evaluating overall team effectiveness. Moreover, student outcomes should be evaluated not only in terms of whether or not referred students have met the goals specified in their intervention assistance plans, but also in terms of the degree to which the discrepancy between their level of performance and grade-level standards has been reduced. Data for discrepancy-based evaluation methods can be gathered from norm-referenced and criterion-referenced achievement tests, curriculum-based measures, report card grades, office disciplinary referrals, behavior rating scales, and other objective measures. For example, a review of IAT data may reveal that 85% of students referred for academic problems attained their individual goals, but that only 50% were reading on grade level at the end of the intervention period, as measured by criterion-referenced reading assessments, or scored within the average range on end-of-year standardized tests.

Self-evaluation of team procedures and processes is also a critical accountability component for team-based IATs. Bahr and his colleagues (1999) have developed a 10-item scale to assess the effectiveness of school-based intervention teams from the perspective of the team members themselves (see Figure 2.9). The scale has evidence of content validity, based on judgments by school consultation experts, has an overall reliability of .95, and has been used in several large-scale IAT evaluation studies (Bahr et al., 1999; Bahr et al., 2006). Scales for evaluating IAT effectiveness from the perspective of intervention consumers, including teachers and parents, are available on numerous district and state department of education websites and at Intervention Central (*http://www.interventioncentral.org*).

INTERVENTION CASE EXAMPLES

Although in some cases a single intervention will be sufficient to solve a classroom problem, consultants often discover that individual students and classroom groups referred to IATs have not one but multiple problems that interfere with their ability to benefit from instruction. In such cases, implementing an *intervention package* consisting of several strategies targeting the set of problem behaviors enhances the likelihood of success. The following case examples illustrate the use of intervention packages to improve student outcomes, the first for an individual student and the second for an entire class.

TEAM EFFECTIVENESS SCALE

1. Our team develops appropriate interventions regarding the student's needs.						
Strongly Agree						Strongly Disagree
1	2	3	4	5	6	7
2. Our team develops manageable interventions for teachers and students.						
Strongly Agree						Strongly Disagree
1	2	3	4	5	6	7
3. Our team uses a shared decision-making process.						
Strongly Agree						Strongly Disagree
1	2	3	4	5	6	7
4. Our team clearly defines the role every member has in working on a specific student concern.						
Strongly Agree						Strongly Disagree
1	2	3	4	5	6	7
5. I encourage fellow educators to use our team when they have a specific student concern.						
Strongly Agree						Strongly Disagree
1	2	3	4	5	6	7
6. I am satisfied with our intervention team process.						
Strongly Agree						Strongly Disagree
1	2	3	4	5	6	7
7. Our team is effective in meeting the needs of the problem identifier (e.g., teacher).						
Strongly Agree						Strongly Disagree
1	2	3	4	5	6	7
8. Our team is effective in meeting the needs of the student.						
Strongly Agree						Strongly Disagree
1	2	3	4	5	6	7
9. Team members communicate clearly with one another.						
Strongly Agree						Strongly Disagree
1	2	3	4	5	6	7
10. Overall, I think our team is effective.						
Strongly Agree						Strongly Disagree
1	2	3	4	5	6	7

FIGURE 2.9. Team Effectiveness Scale. Adapted from Bahr, Whitten, Dieker, Kocarek, and Manson (1999, p. 72). Copyright 1999 by the Council for Exceptional Children. Adapted by permission.

Case Example 1: Aggressive and Noncompliant Preschooler

Four-year-old Kelvin was a constant disruption in his prekindergarten classroom. He frequently grabbed toys from other children, had difficulty completing activities without the constant support of the teacher or classroom assistant, and often failed to comply with adult directions. His behavior was especially problematic during transitions and nap time. He had trouble waiting in line and would push or bother the children standing near him, and during nap time he would wander around the room rather than resting. When his teacher or the classroom assistant would attempt to redirect or correct him, he would put his hands over his ears, pull away from them, or attempt to kick or hit them. Screening measures indicated that his receptive and expressive language skills were in the average range, but he had so much difficulty attending to instructional activities that his early literacy skills were beginning to lag behind those of his classmates. Although his teacher had talked with Kelvin about his behavior and offered numerous incentives for positive behavior, these strategies were only occasionally effective, and Kelvin's aggressive and noncompliant behaviors were increasing as the school year continued.

Intervention Targets and Components

Results of a functional behavioral assessment (FBA; see Chapter 6) that included several classroom observations and interviews with Kelvin's teacher and mother, suggested that adult and peer attention for inappropriate behavior, along with the desire to escape from less preferred activities, might be fueling the problem behavior. Moreover, during the FBA interview, Kelvin's mother noted that because of her work situation, he spent much of his time outside of school with her own mother, who set few limits on Kelvin's behavior. Intervention targets were as follows: (1) increasing compliance with adult directions, (2) reducing aggressive behavior and increasing cooperative behavior, and (3) encouraging use of verbal rather than physical means to communicate needs. An intervention package consisting of three strategies selected from the proactive and behavioral categories was implemented. To address Kelvin's noncompliant and aggressive behavior, *Delivering Effective Commands: The Precision Request Program,* which integrates several dimensions of effective reprimands into a structured instructional sequence, was implemented. A second proactive intervention, *Sit and Watch: Teaching Prosocial Behaviors,* which combines a classroom time-out with contingent observation and incidental teaching, was implemented to help Kelvin acquire more socially appropriate behaviors. Because transitions were the most frequent settings for aggressive behavior, *Promoting Independent In-Class Transitions with Self-Assessment and Contingent Praise* was also applied, an intervention that teaches children to monitor their own transition behaviors.

Interventions were taught via a series of professional development workshops attended by the entire prekindergarten faculty, followed by classroom-based technical assistance. *In vivo* support included modeling, guided practice, and performance feedback, with the consultant prompting and providing direct assistance to the teacher and classroom assistant in using the strategies as they were needed. For example, if Kelvin failed to comply with teacher instructions and the teacher did not immediately take action, the consultant would quietly prompt the teacher to follow through to ensure that inappropriate behavior was consistently consequated. Similarly, if Kelvin resisted going to the Sit and Watch chair, the consultant would demonstrate the procedures and provide support as needed. All three of the interventions were implemented on a classwide basis.

Although implementation of these strategies was associated with decreases in disruptive and aggressive behavior, Kelvin's teacher did not feel that his response to the intervention package sufficiently reduced the discrepancy between his behavior and her behavioral expectations for the class. *Banking Time*—a strategy in which a teacher provides brief sessions of nondirective, relationship-building interactions to target students—was therefore added to the package. After group and individualized training, the teacher began providing 5-minute Banking Time sessions for Kelvin three times a week at the beginning of nap time. Not only did the sessions help Kelvin relax prior to what was often a difficult period for him, but they also provided an opportunity for him and his teacher to relate to each other in a new and more rewarding way. Kelvin's mother attended a Banking Time session to observe the procedures and agreed to implement the strategy at home several times a week. By the end of the year, Kelvin's behavior had improved dramatically, and his teacher and mother were hopeful that he would be able to transition successfully to kindergarten.

Case Example 2: Unproductive and Disruptive Sixth-Grade Social Studies Class

The teacher of this sixth-grade social studies class was in her second year at an inner-city middle school in which the majority of students were from minority low-income backgrounds. Although she was experiencing management problems with most of her classes, her social studies class was especially disruptive and unproductive. The students also had very diverse academic skills, with many students reading 2 or more years below grade level. Results of schoolwide language and reading screening assessments indicated that many students also had low vocabulary and comprehension skills, making it difficult for them to understand their textbooks or to follow ongoing classroom instruction. At the time that consultation was initiated, more than half the class had failing grades, and the teacher and principal were extremely concerned.

Intervention Targets and Components

A series of classroom observations revealed that most students were displaying low levels of academic engagement and high rates of off-task and disruptive behavior and that the teacher was failing to scan the entire room on a regular basis. During one observation, the teacher was so focused on interacting with a student seated on one side of the room that she failed to notice when two other students sitting on the other side of the room got up and wandered out into the hall. Interventions were taught by means of a year-long schoolwide professional development program focusing on proactive classroom management and reading enhancement for middle school students, supplemented by classroom observations, individual teacher consultations, and in-class coaching. Because of concerns about poor student achievement and recurring discipline problems across all three grades, the school also initiated an IAT that met twice a month to provide consultative help to teachers and design professional development activities targeting common problems. Intervention targets included the following: (1) increasing opportunities to respond to academic material, (2) increasing classwork and homework completion rates, (3) building comprehension skills in the context of content area instruction, and (4) encouraging more positive attitudes toward learning. Because reviews of students' grades and screening data indicated that the most inattentive and disruptive students also had the most severe reading problems, emphasis was placed on enhancing vocabulary and comprehension while simultaneously increasing opportunities to respond to academic material.

A package consisting of four interventions—two proactive strategies, one academic strategy, and one behavioral strategy—was implemented. First, to increase available instructional time and to reduce opportunities for off-task and disruptive behavior, the teacher implemented *Active Teaching of Classroom Rules,* which provides direct instruction in classroom procedures and contingent teacher praise for following the rules. For students with chronic disruptive behavior, *Debriefing: Helping Students Solve Their Own Behavior Problems*—a strategy that helps students cope more effectively with situations that have been the setting for inappropriate behavior—was implemented with the support of the assistant principal. This intervention was implemented on a schoolwide basis to promote consistency across settings. To encourage peer support for following classroom rules, the teacher also implemented the *Good Behavior Game Plus Merit,* a team-based strategy that provides rewards for appropriate behavior. Field testing has demonstrated that this and other interventions that divide students into teams that compete to earn rewards based on prosocial behaviors are particularly helpful in combating negative peer group attitudes and behaviors. In this case, the variation that provides bonuses for academic productivity was implemented (see Chapter 5). As disruptive behavior diminished, *Admirals and Generals: Improving Content Area Performance with Strategy Instruction and Peer Tutoring*—an intervention in which pairs of students work together to read and summarize textual material—was added twice a week.

As the semester continued, the frequency and intensity of disruptive behavior diminished. Students also became more actively engaged in class discussions and their academic tasks and looked forward to the opportunity to work with a partner for part of the class period. Two of the students with the most serious behavior problems were referred to the school's IAT and began receiving intensive individualized assistance that included targeted reading assessments, after-school tutoring, and regular conferences that included family members and the school counselor. At the end of the semester, most of the students' grades and attitudes had improved substantially, and the teacher reported that although she had considered not returning to the school the following year, she now looked forward to continuing in her current position.

PRINT RESOURCES

Jacob, S., & Hartshorne, T. S. (2006). *Ethics and law for school psychologists* (5th ed.). New York: Wiley.

This comprehensive sourcebook on ethics, law, and professional standards is specifically designed for school psychologists. Two chapters with particular relevance to IATs review ethical and legal issues in school counseling and therapeutic interventions and in teacher and parent collaboration. Numerous case examples—some from case law, some fictitious—illustrate core principles.

National Association of School Psychologists. (2000). *Professional conduct manual.* Bethesda, MD: Author.

This publication contains the NASP *Principles for Professional Ethics* and *Guidelines for the Provision of School Psychological Services.* The association reviews the manual every 5 years to ensure that the principles and standards reflect current conditions. The manual is available for free download at *http://www.naspweb.org.*

Shinn, M. R., Walker, H. M., & Stoner, G. (2002). *Interventions for academic and behavior problems: II. Preventive and remedial approaches.* Bethesda, MD: National Association of School Psychologists.

This is a one-volume, state-of-the-art guide to intervention-oriented school psychological services. The 38 chapters review evidence-based strategies in areas such as school safety and violence prevention; prevention and management of behavior problems for secondary students; self-monitoring procedures; social skills training; and reading, mathematics, and writing instruction. The chapter by Elliott, Witt, Kratochwill, and Stoiber on intervention selection and evaluation will be of particular interest to readers of this text.

WEBSITES

Intervention Central
http://www.interventioncentral.org

Created by Jim Wright, a school psychologist from Syracuse, N.Y., this website offers a wealth of free tools for promoting positive classroom behavior and effective learning, including extensive resources on IATs, RTI approaches, and curriculum-based measurement.

National Center for Culturally Responsive Systems (NCCRESt)
http://www.nccrest.org

Funded by the U.S. Department of Education's Office of Special Education Programs, NCCRESt provides technical assistance and professional development to close the achievement gap between students from culturally and linguistically diverse backgrounds and their peers and to reduce inappropriate referrals to special education. The site offers an extensive library of practitioner briefs, assessment tools, and research reports in the areas of culturally responsive practices, early intervention, literacy, and positive behavior support.

Wrights Law
http://www.wrightslaw.com

The Wrights Law website includes thousands of articles and resources about special education and advocacy, including the full text of IDEA 2004 and documents comparing IDEA 1997 and 2004. Available for purchase is the second edition of *Special Education Law* by Peter Wright and Pamela Wright, which includes the full text of IDEA 2004, IDEA 2004 regulations, the full text of FERPA, and other federal statutes, with analysis and commentary.

PART II

Evidence-Based School Interventions

CHAPTER 3

Proactive Interventions

Strategies That Create a Productive, Disruption-Free Classroom Environment

Proactive classroom management refers to an approach to classroom management that simultaneously promotes high levels of academic engagement while also preventing off-task and disruptive behavior. Proactive classroom management is distinguished from other management models by three characteristics. First, it is designed to be *preventive* rather than *reactive* by establishing an instructional program that minimizes opportunities for inappropriate behavior (Darch & Kame'enui, 2004; Gettinger, 1988). Research has documented that effective and ineffective classroom managers do not differ in terms of how they respond to misbehavior but in terms of their ability to maintain student engagement in academic tasks and prevent problem behaviors from occurring (Evertson, Emmer, & Worsham, 2006; LaFleur et al., 1998; Lewis & Sugai, 1999). Studies also attest to the fact that once teachers lose control of their classes, it becomes increasingly difficult for them to regain it (Nelson & Roberts, 2000). Second, rather than treating instruction and management as separate domains, proactive classroom management integrates both into a comprehensive classroom system. With a proactive classroom management approach, teachers not only deliver instruction in academic subjects but also provide explicit instruction, guided practice, and performance feedback in classroom rules and routines to enhance students' chances for academic and social success (Gettinger & Seibert, 2002; McGinnis, Frederick, & Edwards, 1995). Third, proactive management focuses on group aspects of classroom management rather than on individual student behavior (Doyle, 2006; Gettinger, 1988). Interventions that apply consequences to the behavior of a single student or a few students in the context of a disorderly, poorly managed classroom are inefficient and unlikely to be effective. Consultants who receive several behavioral referrals from the same classroom are likely to find an ineffective classroom management plan in place (McGinnis et al., 1995).

Proactive Classroom Management and Student Outcomes

A large body of evidence attests to the critical influence of classroom management and organization on students' academic performance and behavior (Barth et al., 2004; Beyda, Zentall,

& Ferko, 2002; Cameron, Connor, & Morrison, 2005; Evertson & Weinstein, 2006; Pianta, La Paro, Payne, Cox, & Bradley, 2002; Wang et al., 1993). The more time teachers devote to orienting students to classroom procedures and practices at the beginning of the year, the more students are engaged in their academic tasks throughout the rest of the year (Cameron et al., 2005; Evertson & Emmer, 1982). Proactive interventions also help to maximize the amount of time available for learning. Academic achievement is significantly related to the amount of time allotted for instruction and to *academic engagement rates,* the proportion of instructional time in which students are engaged in learning, as demonstrated by behaviors such as paying attention, working on assignments, and participating in class discussions (Gettinger & Seibert, 2002). Effective teachers are able to maximize the amount of time students are actively engaged in responding to academic material and to minimize the amount of time students spend transitioning or waiting for learning activities to occur. The importance of increasing instructional time and academic engagement rates is underscored by studies indicating that only about two-thirds of the school day is actually devoted to instruction. According to a recent study of time usage in a national sample of more than 500 elementary classrooms (Roth, Brooks-Gunn, Linver, & Hofferth, 2003), students spent an average of 2 hours and 10 minutes each day engaging in nonacademic activities. Observational studies have also documented wide variations across classrooms in the amount of time devoted to instruction and in academic engagement rates during instructional periods (Greenwood, 1991; Greenwood, Arreaga-Mayer, & Carta, 1994; Greenwood, Horton, & Utley, 2002). In one study of nine first-grade classrooms of teachers who had been nominated as outstanding literacy instructors, students in most of the classrooms were typically engaged in learning 80 to 90% of the time, but engagement rates were as low as 50% in some classrooms (Wharton-McDonald, Pressley, & Hampston, 1998). In another observational study targeting 122 students with and without disabilities in 10 urban and suburban schools (Muyskens & Ysseldyke, 1998), students typically spent only 65 minutes a day responding to instructional material and spent 37 minutes a day behaving inappropriately!

STANDARDS FOR ACADEMIC ENGAGEMENT RATES: WHAT LEVEL OF ON-TASK BEHAVIOR IS NEEDED FOR MAXIMUM LEARNING?

When consultants conduct classroom observations to collect data on target students or to collaborate with teachers to design proactive interventions, they may be unsure concerning the rate of on-task behavior that is required for optimal student learning. Observational studies (Mitchem, Young, West, & Benyo, 2001; Wharton-McDonald et al., 1998) have identified a rate of 80% simultaneous on-task behavior or higher as the goal for an effectively managed classroom. Consultants can assess simultaneous on-task behavior rates using one or more of three measures described in Chapter 2: (1) the *Group Time Sampling Form,* which involves dividing the class into four quadrants and recording the behavior of each quadrant in turn as on-task or off-task; (2) the *Classwide Scanning Form,* which involves rapidly surveying the entire classroom and tallying the number of students who are on-task, off-task, or disruptive; and (3) the *Group Interval Recording Form,* which involves consecutively coding every student in the class as on-task, off-task, or disruptive. The following guidelines for evaluating pre- and postintervention engagement rates are recommended: *low engagement* = fewer than 60% of students are on task; *moderate engagement* = 60–79% of students are on-task; *high engagement* = 80% or more of the students are on-task.

In keeping with a proactive approach to classroom management, the interventions in this chapter are designed to set the conditions for high levels of academic engagement and appropriate behavior for an entire classroom group. Strategies have been drawn from the effective teaching literature as well as from the behavioral sciences literature. As Evertson (1989) has noted, however, creating and maintaining an effective classroom environment requires more than a collection of isolated techniques, such as token economies or time-out. Fortunately, research has identified a core set of effective strategies that target critical areas of classroom management and can be taught within a consultative framework. From the perspective of this text, a proactive approach to classroom management also encompasses strategies that promote positive teacher–student and student–student relationships. A voluminous body of research attests to the importance of helping students, especially at-risk students, to develop positive attachments to adults and peers at school (e.g., Pianta, 1999, 2006; Pianta, Hamre, & Stuhlman, 2003). Students with supportive interpersonal relationships at school have more positive attitudes toward school and higher levels of academic achievement, whereas students lacking such relationships are at risk for a host of negative educational and social outcomes, including disruptive classroom behavior, poor achievement, dropping out of school, violence, and substance abuse (see Blum & Libbey, 2004, for a recent review).

PROACTIVE STRATEGIES AND DIVERSE LEARNERS

Although all students profit from proactive strategies that increase instructional time and maximize learning opportunities, proactive interventions are especially important for students at risk for academic failure, including low-performing students, students with disabilities, and students living in poverty (Gettinger & Seibert, 2002). Observational studies (Greenwood, 1991; Greenwood et al., 2002; Greenwood, Delquadri, & Hall, 1989) have consistently documented significant differences in instructional time and academic engagement between students in impoverished urban settings and their more advantaged counterparts in suburban schools. Classwide interventions that increase instructional time and academic engagement rates are also important for students with learning disabilities, who not only display lower rates of attending in the regular classroom versus resource room settings, but are significantly affected by group behavior, with engagement rates significantly higher when the engagement of the entire class is high (Friedman, Cancelli, & Yoshida, 1988).

Providing professional development in proactive classroom management interventions is most helpful during the preservice days before teachers have encountered their students and established expectations for academic and social performance. Practitioners and researchers alike (Bohn, Roehrig, & Pressley, 2004; Evertson, 1989; Evertson & Emmer, 1982) underscore the critical importance of teachers' very first contacts with students in establishing effective behavior for the rest of the year. As Brooks (1985) has aptly observed, "There is only *one* first day of school" (p. 69; emphasis in the original). It is especially important to help beginning teachers acquire a set of core proactive strategies during preservice training and to provide follow-up assistance and support during the first few weeks of the year. New and experienced teachers alike consistently report that their training in classroom management during their teacher preparation programs was both inadequate and impractical (Jones, 2006; Stough, 2006). Moreover, field testing strongly indicates that first-year teachers who experience classroom management problems during the first few weeks of school and do not receive classroom-based assistance very shortly after problems have been identified are likely to struggle for the rest of the year.

Evaluating the Effectiveness
of Proactive Interventions

Evaluation methods for the interventions in this chapter include a variety of assessments of the classroom environment and student performance that have been designed to be as practical as possible and still yield reliable and valid information. Although many of the evaluation strategies can be adapted to assess the performance of a single student or small groups of students rather than an entire class, documenting classwide behavior is essential in planning and evaluating interventions that target the learning environment as a whole. In addition to measures assessing the impact of interventions on academic engagement and achievement, measures are included that target learning-related behaviors, such as the number of student contributions during class discussions, and task-management behaviors, such as rates of compliance and time spent in transitions. Measures of relevant teacher behaviors, such as the number of reprimands delivered during classroom routines or instructional periods, are also included.

In recent years, numerous paper-and-pencil measures, as well as computer-assisted tools, have been developed to assess academic engagement and other aspects of student and teacher behavior and the classroom ecology (Kahng & Iwata, 1998; Vaughn & Briggs, 2003). Greenwood and his colleagues at the Juniper Gardens Children's Project at the University of Kansas have developed several instruments to gather information about classroom variables or "events" affecting learning, including the *Mainstream Version of the Code for Instructional Structure and Student Academic Response* (MS-CISSAR; Kamps, Greenwood, & Leonard, 1991). The MS-CISSAR is a classroom observation system assessing five categories of classroom ecological variables (Setting, Activity, Task, Physical Arrangement, and Instructional Structure), four categories of teacher events (Teacher Definition, Teacher Behavior, Teacher Approval, and Teacher Focus), and three categories of student events (Academic Responding, Task Management, and Inappropriate Behavior). MS-CISSAR observations can be completed using portable notebook computers and a software system: the Ecobehavioral Assessment Software System (EBASS: Greenwood et al., 1997). The MS-CISSAR has been used to identify classroom settings that facilitate engagement for students with disabilities (Logan, Bakeman, & Keefe, 1997), to evaluate the effects of academic interventions on student engagement and competing behaviors (McDonnell, Thorson, Allen, & Mathot-Buckner, 2000), to assess engagement rates in inclusive classrooms (Wallace, Anderson, Bartholomay, & Hupp, 2002), to compare the effectiveness of reading strategies for students with disabilities (Marston, Deno, Kim, Diment, & Rogers, 1995), and to gather data on class and schoolwide engagement rates for use in instructional decision making (Greenwood et al., 2002).

More practical for many consultants is the *Behavioral Observation of Students in Schools* (BOSS; Shapiro, 2004a, 2004b), an observational code that assesses two categories of engagement (active engaged time [AET] and passive engaged time [PET]) and three categories of nonengagement (off-task motor, off-task verbal, and off-task passive). The code includes an additional category examining the type of instructional setting (e.g., student in independent seatwork, teacher in small group not including target student). Although the BOSS is designed to assess the academic performance of a single student, data are collected on classroom peers as well as on the target pupil. On every fifth interval, observations are conducted on a different randomly selected peer, and the data are combined to derive a peer comparison score for the behaviors sampled. Teacher-directed instruction is also coded every fifth interval to provide a sampling of the time during which the teacher is engaged in instructing individual students or the class. Data from the BOSS provide information about on- and off-task behavior rates, academic engagement rates in different instructional settings, and opportunities to respond (AET level vs. PET level), as well as the extent to which the target student's behavior differs from classroom norms. A software program with desktop and personal digital assistant (PDA) applications is available to facilitate data collection and analysis (*http://www.harcourtassessment.com*).

Proactive Classroom Management Interventions

The interventions in this chapter have been organized according to seven tasks identified in the literature (e.g., Evertson et al., 2006; Emmer, Evertson, & Worsham, 2006; Pianta et al., 2003) as critical to successful classroom management and a positive classroom climate: (1) organizing a productive classroom environment, (2) establishing classroom rules and procedures, (3) managing transitions, (4) managing small-group instruction and independent seatwork, (5) communicating competently with students, (6) teaching prosocial behaviors, and (7) building positive relationships in the classroom. Taken together, the 16 interventions targeting these seven tasks form the basis of a comprehensive classroom management system that can help teachers establish and maintain an orderly, productive, and positive learning environment.

TASK 1: ORGANIZING A PRODUCTIVE CLASSROOM ENVIRONMENT

Although the impact of classroom environments on student performance and behavior has long been recognized (Davis & Fox, 1999; Jones, 1990; McEnvoy, Fox, & Rosenberg, 1991; Rosenfield, Lambert, & Black, 1985), surprisingly little research has examined the effects of specific seating arrangements on achievement or learning-related variables, such as attention and participation, especially in recent years. Observational studies (Evertson, 1985, 1989) of elementary and secondary classrooms reveal that effective teachers design classroom arrangements that permit all students to view instruction, provide ready access to frequently used materials and equipment, keep high-traffic areas free of congestion, and facilitate monitoring student work and behavior. Some authors (e.g., Paine, Radicchi, Rosellini, Deutchman, & Darch, 1983) advocate arranging desks in rows facing the chalkboard to promote attention to teacher-directed instruction and reduce opportunities for inappropriate student interaction. In support of this view, studies comparing desk arrangements have consistently found that row-and-column arrangements are associated with higher on-task behavior rates for students with and without disabilities (Wheldall & Lam, 1987; Wheldall, Morris, Vaughan, & Ng, 1981), as well as higher levels in terms of the quantity and quality of academic work (Bennett & Blundell, 1983), compared with arrangements that place students in closer proximity to each other, such as table seating or desk clusters.

Another arrangement that has been demonstrated in field testing to have positive effects on academic engagement consists of rows of paired desks facing the chalkboard (or the main site of teacher-delivered instruction) with a larger space between the rows in the center of the room. With this arrangement, the teacher can not only see all students to monitor behavior and evaluate responses to instruction, but also move rapidly to any area of the room to prevent disruptive behavior from spreading or escalating. Such an arrangement also facilitates the implementation of interventions involving student dyads, such as *ClassWide Peer Tutoring* or *Partner Reading*. New teachers and teachers with less well developed classroom management skills are advised to avoid desk clusters or other types of face-to-face seating at the beginning of the year, when instructional routines and behavioral expectations are being established. During field testing, first-year teachers who had studied collaborative learning strategies in their teacher preparation programs or had observed veteran teachers using these strategies during their practicum training often began the year by arranging their classrooms in desk clusters of four to six students, only to experience difficulty maintaining student attention and productivity.

Although row-and-column arrangements have been demonstrated to have a positive impact on students' on-task behavior, they have also been associated with lower rates of student participation and student–teacher interaction. In an observational study of 56 physical science and chemistry classes (Jones, 1990), class interactions were dominated by a small proportion of students who received the majority of direct questions, teacher conversation, and feedback. During the observed class period, nearly 30% of all students were completely silent, and in some classrooms as many as 64% of students were silent! Given the importance of increasing academic engagement and response rates for all students and especially for at-risk learners, teachers should consider seating arrangements that promote equal participation opportunities for all students in the classroom. The intervention in this section—*Increasing Student Participation with a Semicircular Desk Arrangement*—is designed to facilitate on-task behavior and group discussion by means of a circular seating arrangement and is especially useful in subjects in which discussion is a key instructional feature, such as social studies, history, and literature. Other useful seating arrangements are depicted in Colvin and Lazar (1997) and Evertson et al. (2006) for elementary classrooms and in Emmer et al. (2006), Weinstein (2003), and Wolfgang (2005) for secondary classrooms.

INCREASING STUDENT PARTICIPATION
WITH A SEMICIRCULAR DESK ARRANGEMENT

Overview

Classroom desk arrangements can have significant effects on students' behavior and academic performance. The traditional arrangement of desks in rows and columns may reduce unwanted peer interaction but may also increase withdrawal responses during instruction and independent work periods for students seated farther away from the teacher. Similarly, arranging desks in clusters facilitates collaborative learning activities but increases the likelihood of off-task behavior because of greater opportunities for unsanctioned peer interaction. In this intervention, student desks are arranged in two parallel semicircles to promote active attention and participation during instructional and discussion periods. In the original study, implemented in a fourth-grade classroom, question-asking rates were significantly higher when students were seated in a semicircle compared with the traditional row-and-column arrangement. Semicircular arrangements may be especially important for lower performing students and English language learners, who benefit from increased opportunities to respond to instructional material.

Purpose

To increase active student engagement and participation during instructional periods by arranging classroom desks in two parallel semicircles.

Materials

None.

Observation (Select One or More)

Option 1

1. Select an instructional period during which you wish to increase student engagement and participation rates.
2. Using a *Classwide Scanning Form* with a 5-minute interval, tally the number of students in each of the categories below, beginning with the left side of the room and continuing for 30 minutes or the entire period:
   a. *On-task behavior,* defined as orientation toward the teacher or a participating peer, working on assigned tasks, responding to questions or raising hands to participate, or engaging in any other lesson-related behavior.
   b. *Off-task behavior,* defined as detachment from the lesson, including failing to attend to the teacher, participating peers, or instructional materials; looking at or playing with nonlesson materials; or any other passive nonlesson behavior.
   c. *Disruptive behavior,* defined as behavior interfering with one's own learning or that of others, such as calling out, making noises, tapping pencils, getting out of seat, or verbal or physical aggression.
3. Conduct these observations for 4 to 7 days.

Option 2

1. Using a *Group Event Recording Form*, tally the frequency of discussion comments for the entire class during a selected instructional period for 4 to 7 days. *Discussion comments* are defined as student verbal contributions that are related to teacher questions and/or lesson content.

Option 3

1. Select a group of target students with low rates of participation in class discussions.
2. Using a *Group Event Recording Form*, record the number of discussion comments, questions, and hand raises made by target students during class discussions in a selected instructional period for 4 to 7 days.

Intervention Steps

Introduction and Training

1. Select one or more subjects, such as social studies, literature, or creative writing, during which you wish to promote broad class participation. Explain to the students that you will be using a new seating arrangement for the instructional period(s) that will help everyone focus on and participate in the lesson.
2. Using *Say Show Check: Teaching Classroom Procedures*, demonstrate how students should move their desks quickly and quietly to form two semicircles, one behind the other. Alternately, arrange the desks yourself prior to the target instructional period. To the extent possible, seat the students with the lowest participation rates in the inside semicircle.
3. Place the teacher's chair or lectern at the front and center of the two semicircles.
4. Again using *Say Show Check*, review appropriate behavior during class discussions (e.g., raising one's hand and waiting to be called upon before talking, looking at and listening to others who are speaking, waiting to raise one's hand until the other person has finished speaking, using polite and appropriate language, staying on the topic).

Implementation

1. Conduct the lesson as usual with the semicircular arrangement. Acknowledge and encourage student contributions, provide praise for appropriate behavior during discussions, and give corrective feedback as needed.

Evaluation (Select One or More)

Option 1

1. Compare the percentages of students displaying on-task, off-task, and disruptive behavior during the selected instructional period before and after implementation.

Option 2

1. Compare the frequency of discussion comments for the entire class during the selected instructional period before and after implementation.

Option 3

1. Compare the frequency of discussion comments, questions, and hand raises for target students during the selected instructional period before and after implementation.

Notes

1. In the original study, students seated in central positions in the row-and-column arrangement (the "action zone") displayed higher question-asking rates compared with their classmates in other positions. These action zone effects were not observed in the semicircle seating arrangement, however.
2. If students sit at tables rather than at individual desks, have them push the tables against the wall and arrange their chairs in two semicircles in the center of the classroom at the beginning of the target period.

Source

Marx, A., Fuhrer, U., & Hartig, T. (1999). Effects of classroom seating arrangements on children's question-asking. *Learning Environments Research, 2,* 249–263. Copyright 1999 by Springer Science and Business Media. Adapted by permission.

TASK 2: ESTABLISHING CLASSROOM RULES AND PROCEDURES

Classroom rules play a critical role in creating a learning environment that promotes student engagement, cooperation, and productivity (Malone & Tietjens, 2000; Rademacher, Callahan, & Pederson-Seelye, 1998). Without guidelines for expected classroom behavior, it is impossible for teachers to deliver instruction effectively or for students to learn. Rules and procedures communicate to students the expectations for acceptable classroom behavior. *Rules* identify general standards or expectations for behavior, whereas *procedures* refer to the steps necessary to accomplish a specific task or activity (Evertson et al., 2006). Compared with ineffective teachers, effective teachers spend more time establishing classroom rules and procedures for student behavior at the beginning of the year and reviewing them periodically during the course of the year (Bohn et al., 2004). Explicit teaching of classroom rules early in the year not only facilitates a smoother school beginning but also has long-term positive effects on student behavior and performance. In classes in which teachers establish routines on the first day of school, students are more engaged in academic activities and make more academic progress during the rest of the year (Bohn et al., 2004; Evertson, 1989; Evertson & Emmer, 1982).

At the same time, however, rules in and of themselves are insufficient to promote academic productivity or to maintain appropriate student behavior. Instead, teachers must implement rules in the context of a comprehensive instructional and behavior management system that includes careful planning to meet individual and group needs, learning activities that promote active student responding, and consistent consequences for rule infractions (McGinnis et al., 1995). Rules should also be consistent with the school's culture and fit within the structure of the school's code of conduct (Malone & Tietjens, 2000). Similarly, simply telling students what the rules for behavior are is not sufficient. Instead, rules must be explicitly taught, just as other skills and concepts are taught, and monitored for compliance (Darch & Kame'enui, 2004; Rademacher et al., 1998). In addition to general classroom rules, rules are needed for numerous classroom routines and activities, such as transitioning, collaborative learning activities, independent seatwork, and class discussions. This section includes two interventions designed to enhance the effectiveness of classroom rules. *Say Show Check: Teaching Classroom Procedures* is a keystone strategy with a model–lead–practice format that can be used not only to teach classroom rules and routines but also to introduce any of the interventions in this book. *Active Teaching of Classroom Rules* provides a systematic procedure for teaching and rehearsing rules that is ideal for implementation at the beginning of the school year. Following the initial direct teaching of rules, even a brief daily rule review can enhance managerial and instructional effectiveness by reducing off-task behavior and increasing opportunities to respond (Rosenberg, 1986). The ultimate goal of this kind of rule training is self-regulation, with students internalizing classroom rules and procedures so that the maximum amount of time can be spent on instruction and learning.

CROSS-REFERENCE: Several other strategies in this chapter include direct instruction in classroom rules as a key intervention component (e.g., *Countdown to Free Time: Encouraging Productivity during Small-Group Instruction*; *Delivering Effective Commands: The Precision Request Program*). In addition, numerous strategies in Chapters 5 and 6 include rule training as part of an intervention package targeting behavior (e.g., the *Good Behavior Game*; *Loop the Loop: A Schoolwide Intervention to Reduce Problem Behavior on the Playground*; *Improving Compliance with Precision Requests and a Time-Out Ribbon*).

SAY SHOW CHECK: TEACHING CLASSROOM PROCEDURES

Overview

Socializing students to the rule-based environment of the school is a critical component of proactive classroom management. This keystone strategy maximizes instructional time and minimizes opportunities for disruptive behavior by providing direct instruction in how students should behave during classroom routines and activities. Using a three-step lesson format, the teacher shows the rule visually, checks student understanding by exhibiting the incorrect action, and then models the correct behavior again. Knowledge of procedural and motor rules builds students' sense of security in the classroom, permits them to be available for instruction, and prevents them from having to discover the rules by accidentally misbehaving and being reprimanded. Originally developed for preschoolers, this intervention can be adapted for any grade and any classroom procedure.

Purpose

To teach classroom rules and procedures through explicit instruction, guided practice, and performance feedback.

Materials

None.

Observation (Select One or Both)

1. Using a sheet of paper attached to a clipboard, record the number of reprimands you deliver during selected classroom routines, such as class discussions, lining up for lunch and specials, or cooperative learning activities, for 4 to 7 days.
2. Using a *Group Event Recording Form*, tally the number of inappropriate behaviors during one or more classroom routines for 4 to 7 days. *Inappropriate behaviors* are defined as any behaviors that interfere with the completion of classroom routines, such as dawdling, failing to follow directions, and verbal or physical aggression.

Intervention Steps

Step 1: Say

1. Introduce the rule to be taught and the rationale for its use:

   > "Today we are going to learn how to participate in class discussions. Following the rules for class discussions makes it easier for everyone to have a chance to take part."

2. Use words to verbally encode the motor or procedural rule.

   > "We raise our hands when we want to participate in class discussions."

Step 2: Show

1. Show the rule visually by having a student model the correct behavior or do it yourself.

   > "Serena, show the class how we raise our hands and wait to be called on to participate in discussions." After the student demonstrates, say, "That's right!"

Step 3: Check

1. Check students' understanding by exhibiting the incorrect behavior while asking them to watch for a mistake:

   > Call out, "I know, I know!" while wildly waving your hand. Then ask, "Class, did I ask to participate correctly?"

2. Demonstrate the correct behavior or ask a student to demonstrate it, and have students respond as to the correctness of the behavior.

   > "Randy, show us how we raise our hands and wait to be called on to participate." After the student demonstrates, ask, "Was that correct, class?"

3. Praise the student for demonstrating the behavior correctly and the rest of the class for watching attentively.

Evaluation (Select One or Both)

1. Compare the number of reprimands delivered during selected classroom routines before and after implementation.
2. Compare the number of inappropriate behaviors during selected classroom routines before and after implementation.

Variation: Small-Group Demonstration with Classwide Feedback

1. To reinforce learning, add a small-group practice component to the *Show* and *Check* stages. After you guide an individual student through a role play of the correct behavior, invite a group of students seated in a row or at a desk cluster or table to show the appropriate behavior and have the rest of the class evaluate the correctness of the demonstration.

Notes

1. When using this strategy with upper elementary or middle school groups, demonstrate the incorrect behavior (see Step 3) cautiously, if at all. Demonstrating the incorrect behavior or having a student demonstrate it can result in temporary increases in incorrect responding in an effort to attract peer attention.
2. Teachers report that this is one of the most useful strategies in the entire book in helping to establish and maintain an orderly classroom environment.

Source

Wolfgang, C. H., & Wolfgang, M. E. (1995). *The three faces of discipline for early childhood: Empowering teachers and students* (pp. 223–225). Boston: Allyn & Bacon. Copyright 1995 by Pearson Education. Adapted by permission of the publisher.

ACTIVE TEACHING OF CLASSROOM RULES

Overview

Simply listing classroom rules on a chart or the chalkboard is not sufficient to develop and maintain appropriate student behavior. In contrast, actively teaching classroom rules not only communicates to students exactly what is expected but also provides teachers with opportunities to reinforce behavior consistent with the rules. This proactive intervention teaches classroom rules as a lesson with feedback and examples and includes a brief daily review and rehearsal to reinforce learning. In the original study, conducted in a seventh-grade mathematics class referred as a group for problem behavior, active rule teaching and review resulted in a significant reduction in disruptive behavior and a corresponding increase in academic engagement. Moreover, the rules strategy was more effective than two other interventions implemented with the same group of students in two other classes: a self-monitoring intervention implemented in reading class and an intervention consisting of a weekly class syllabus and individual student conferences implemented in language arts class. A variation with a parent involvement component is also presented.

Purpose

To help create and maintain a productive, disruption-free classroom by explicitly teaching and regularly reviewing classroom rules.

Materials

1. Posterboard chart with a list of classroom rules, such as:
   a. Be prepared for class every day.
   b. Be considerate of others.
   c. Be on time to class.
   d. Do what you are asked to do the first time you are asked.
   e. Follow directions.
2. 8½″ × 11″ sheets of paper listing the rules, one per student.

Observation (Select One or Both)

Option 1

1. Using a *Classwide Scanning Form* with a 5-minute interval, scan the room beginning with the left side and tally the number of students displaying each of the three categories of behavior listed below:
   a. *Disruptive behavior,* defined as behavior that produces observable physical changes in the classroom environment and interferes with assignment completion for oneself or other students (e.g., talking without permission, making noises, throwing paper).
   b. *Inappropriately engaged behavior,* defined as directing attention toward or engaging in nonlesson activities or materials (e.g., writing and passing notes, gazing into space, looking at unengaged classmates, playing with nonlesson materials).
   c. *Appropriately engaged behavior,* defined as directing attention toward or engaging in assigned tasks and activities (e.g., raising hand, participating in class discussions, writing on worksheets).
2. Conduct these observations for 30 to 45 minutes during a selected instructional period for 4 to 7 days.

Option 2

1. Using a *Group Event Recording Form,* record the number of disruptive behaviors as defined above during a selected instructional period for 4 to 7 days.

Intervention Steps

Introduction and Training

1. During the selected instructional period, display the classroom rules on the chart and give each student a handout listing the rules.
2. Spend about 10 minutes discussing the rules, the rationale for each rule, and the importance of rules in creating a classroom environment in which every student feels free to learn. Provide specific examples for each rule and invite students to offer their own examples.
3. Tell students that you will be observing them at various times during the lesson to see if they are following the rules.

Implementation

1. During the lesson, provide behavior-specific praise and feedback at least three times for individual students and groups of students who are following one or more of the rules.

   Example: "I appreciate how Row 3 students are following directions."
2. After the first day, spend about 3 minutes reteaching one or two rules at the beginning of each class period. During the lesson, deliver specific praise to students as individuals and groups for following the rules.

Evaluation (Select One or Both)

Option 1

1. Compare the percentages of students displaying disruptive behavior, inappropriately engaged behavior, and appropriately engaged behavior during the selected instructional period before and after implementation.

Option 2

1. Compare the frequency of disruptive behavior during the selected instructional period before and after implementation.

Variation: Rule Review with Parent Involvement

1. Have students take home their copies of the classroom rules, discuss them with their parents, and return them signed.

Note

1. This intervention was originally implemented with an intact group of students who were taught by different teachers in different classrooms. For self-contained classroom groups, reteach the rules at the beginning of the school day.

Source

Johnson, T. C., Stoner, G., & Green, S. K. (1996). Demonstrating the experimenting society model with classwide behavior management interventions. *School Psychology Review, 25,* 199–214. Copyright 1996 by the National Association of School Psychologists. Adapted by permission.

TASK 3: MANAGING TRANSITIONS

The typical school day includes 8 to 15 transitions (Paine et al., 1983; LaFleur et al., 1998). Teachers must deal with several types of transitions. *In-class transitions* involve changing from one activity to another within the same room, such as switching from one subject to another or moving from a whole-class to a small-group instructional format. *Room-to-room transitions* are involved when students move from the classroom to another part of the building, such as another classroom, the cafeteria, or the playground. Transition times vary widely from teacher to teacher, even within the same building. In a recent study of 827 first-grade classrooms (Cameron, Connor, & Morrison, 2005), 17% of classroom activities on average consisted of transitions, such as lining up for recess and waiting for a lesson to begin, with an average of nearly 1 hour per day (54 minutes) over the school year. At the same time, however, there were striking differences in average daily transition times across classrooms (14 minutes to more than 2 hours), indicating that some teachers were able to manage transitions much more efficiently than others.

A key characteristic of effective teachers is their ability to minimize classroom interruptions and make quick, orderly transitions between activities (Nowacek, McKinney, & Hallahan, 1990; Wharton et al., 1998). Inappropriately structured transitions not only reduce instructional time but also provide opportunities for inappropriate behavior that can quickly escalate (Colvin, Sugai, Good, & Young-Yon, 1997). Smooth, rapid transitions protect learning time not only by reducing the time needed to change from one activity to another, but also by minimizing the time needed to regain control lost after ineffective transitions. Moreover, because disruptive behavior is much more likely to occur in the context of transitions, establishing effective transition procedures decreases the likelihood that students will behave inappropriately (Colvin et al., 1997; LaFleur et al., 1998). Keeping transitions as rapid as possible is especially important for diverse learners and students with disabilities, who are already at risk for lower engagement rates and need additional opportunities to master academic material (Connell, Carta, Lutz, Randall, & Wilson, 1993; Davis & Reichle, 2002).

This section presents three interventions designed to promote rapid, disruption-free transitions: one targeting in-class transitions, one targeting room-to-room transitions, and one that can facilitate either type of transition. Although all three strategies were originally designed for use by individual teachers with intact classroom groups, they are ideal for implementation on a gradewide or a schoolwide basis. *Teaching Transition Time* is a scripted strategy that provides direct instruction, choral responding, guided practice, and performance feedback in a lesson format. It can be used for any type of transition and is especially helpful at the beginning of the year as part of a comprehensive classroom management system. *Six Steps to Speedy Transitions* promotes rapid in-class transitions by means of an instructional sequence that includes explicit timing, guided practice, and performance feedback in a game-like format. A preschool version with simplified directions is included as a variation. Critical elements in both interventions include preparing students for transitions, closely monitoring compliance, and providing immediate corrective feedback if needed.

Designed to facilitate transitions that require students to move from the classroom to another area in the building, the *Timely Transitions Game: Reducing Room-to-Room Transition Time* combines three empirically validated intervention components: (1) overt timing, (2) publicly posted feedback, and (3) interdependent group contingencies with randomly selected transitions and criteria. *Interdependent group contingencies*, in which all or none of the students receive a reward, based on whether or not the entire class meets a group-oriented criterion, are especially appropriate for room-to-room transitions because each student's transition rate is dependent on the behavior of his or her classmates. A unique aspect of this intervention is the use of randomly selected transition and criteria contingencies so that students cannot predict which transition or time limit will be selected for reinforcement.

CROSS-REFERENCE: For schoolwide strategies targeting inappropriate behavior during room-to-room transitions, see *Reducing Hallway Noise with Sound Level Monitoring and Group Contingencies: A Schoolwide Intervention* and *Improving Transition Behavior with Active Supervision and Precorrection: A Schoolwide Intervention* in Chapter 5. For a transition intervention designed especially for preschoolers, see *Promoting Independent In-Class Transitions with Self-Assessment and Contingent Praise* in Chapter 6.

TEACHING TRANSITION TIME

Overview

Because teachers must guide students from one activity to another several times every day, transition routines should be taught systematically at the beginning of the school year. The importance of a structured procedure for teaching transitions is underscored by the fact that the average elementary school classroom loses nearly an hour a day to transitions. Reducing transition time between activities not only increases instructional time but also contributes to a positive classroom climate by limiting opportunities for inappropriate behavior. In this intervention, which combines direct instruction, guided practice, and performance feedback, transition time procedures are taught as a lesson, with classwide choral responding to reinforce learning. Although the original strategy did not provide for backup contingencies, a variation with classwide incentives is included.

Purpose

To increase available instructional time by systematically teaching procedures for quick, orderly transitions between classroom tasks and activities.

Materials

1. Timer with an audible bell, stopwatch, or watch with second hand (optional).
2. Posterboard chart listing the transition rules:
    a. Move quietly.
    b. Put your materials away and get what you need for the next activity.
    c. Keep your hands and feet to yourself.
    d. Use your inside voice.

Observation (Select One or More)

Option 1

1. Using a stopwatch or watch with a second hand and a sheet of paper attached to a clipboard, record the number of minutes required for students to complete one or more transitions for 5 days, preferably Monday through Friday.
2. If desired, calculate a weekly average time for each of the targeted transitions by summing the total number of minutes per transition and dividing by 5.

Option 2

1. Using a stopwatch or watch with a second hand and a sheet of paper attached to a clipboard, record the number of minutes required for students to complete every major transition during the school day, such as entering the classroom at the beginning of the day and getting ready for instruction, going to and from specials, going to and from the cafeteria, going to and from recess, and exiting the classroom at the end of the day.
2. Conduct these observations for 5 days, preferably Monday through Friday, and calculate a total weekly transition time by summing the number of minutes per day spent making the targeted transitions.

Option 3

1. Using a sheet of paper attached to a clipboard, record the number of reprimands you deliver during one or more transitions for a week.

Intervention Steps

Step 1: Review the transition rules and the transition signal.

1. Display the chart with the four transition rules on it and say:

> "Transition time is the time it takes to change what you are doing. What is transition time?" [Have students respond as a group.]

"It is important that transition time be quick and quiet. What is important about transition time?" [Have students respond as a group.]

"That's right! I'm going to tell you four ways to make transition time quick and quiet. *Move quietly.* What is one way for transition time to be quick and quiet?" [Have students respond as a group.]

"Good. Now I'm going to tell you some more ways." [Repeat the procedure for all four rules.]

"Let's say all four ways to make transition time quick and quiet." [Point to the chart and have students respond as a group.]

2. Teach students the signal for transition time as follows:

"When we are ready to make a transition, I will let you know by saying, 'It's transition time. Get ready for _____. You need [describe the materials needed for the next activity or give additional directions for that transition] _____.' What will I say?" [Have students respond as a group.] If desired, include a nonverbal signal to focus attention that the transition is beginning, such as switching off the light or clapping your hands.

Step 2: Demonstrate appropriate transition behaviors.

1. Place a student desk and chair at the front of the classroom and say:

"Now I'm going to show you what I mean. Watch while I change activities at my desk." [Sit at the desk, put one book away, get out another book, have pencil and paper ready, and sit quietly.]

"What did I do during this transition time?" [Call on individual students to review the first two rules.]

"Good, you're really watching! Now watch again as I show you a different kind of transition." [Put the book in the desk, get out another book, stand up, quietly push in your chair, walk to the reading table, sit down, open the book, and wait quietly.]

"What did I do during this transition time?" [Call on individual students to review all four rules.] Demonstrate other transitions as appropriate.

Step 3: Guide students in practicing appropriate transition behaviors.

1. Return to the front of the classroom and say:

"Great! Now *I'm* going to watch. I know you can change what you're doing by moving quietly, getting the proper materials ready, moving your chairs quietly, and keeping your hands and feet to yourself." [Lead students through several practice transitions while you monitor performance, giving praise and reminders as needed.]

2. Using this three-step lesson format, teach procedures for all major transitions, including in-class transitions between activities and transitions that involve moving to other areas of the building.

Evaluation (Select One or More)

Option 1

1. Compare the number of minutes required to complete one or more transitions or the weekly average number of minutes required to complete one or more transitions before and after implementation.

Option 2

1. Compare the total weekly transition time before and after implementation.

Option 3

1. Compare the number of reprimands you deliver to students during one or more transitions before and after implementation.

Variation: Transitioning with Classwide Incentives

1. Using data collected during the observational period, set a criterion time for transitions that are especially problematic, such as returning to the classroom after lunch and beginning the afternoon work period. Add 5 extra minutes of recess or free time for each 1 minute under the criterion. Gradually increase the requirement for meeting the criterion from daily to weekly as transition behaviors improve.

Notes

1. For maximum benefit, teach the transition time lesson during the first week of school and review it at the beginning of each week for several weeks thereafter. Reteach the lesson after vacation breaks or whenever transitions are becoming lengthy or disruptive.
2. Setting a criterion and providing an incentive for meeting it, as in the variation, is especially helpful if the intervention is introduced after the school year has begun and students have already developed poor transition habits.

Source

Paine, S. C., Radicchi, J., Rosellini, L. C., Deutchman, L., & Darch, C. B. (1983). *Structuring your classroom for academic success* (pp. 84–88). Champaign, IL: Research Press. Copyright 1983 by the authors. Adapted by permission.

SIX STEPS TO EFFECTIVE CLASSROOM TRANSITIONS

Overview

Rapid, orderly transitions are an essential component of proactive classroom management. Because transitions occur frequently during the school day, teachers have multiple opportunities to increase academic learning time and promote prosocial behaviors by managing transitions efficiently. This multicomponent intervention targets transitions with a combination of explicit instruction, active supervision, goal setting, timing, and performance feedback in a game-like format. In the original study, implemented in four elementary school classrooms, transition times were reduced to 4 minutes or less across all four classrooms. Three variations are included: one for preschoolers, one with a response cost contingency, and one with a classwide incentive.

Purpose

To promote quick, orderly transitions using a six-step instructional sequence in a game-like format.

Materials

1. Timer with audible bell or stopwatch with audible signal.

Observation (Select One or Both)

1. Using a sheet of paper attached to a clipboard, record the number of minutes required for students to complete one or more transitions for 4 to 7 days.
2. Using a sheet of paper attached to a clipboard, tally the number of disruptive behaviors that occur during one or more transitions for 4 to 7 days. *Disruptive behaviors* are defined as behaviors that interfere with the orderly completion of a transition, such as dawdling, failing to follow directions, getting out of line, pushing, and arguing.

Intervention Steps

Introduction and Training

1. Explain to the students that they will be learning to make faster transitions so that you have more time to teach and they have more time to learn and have fun at school.
2. Demonstrate the signal that you will use to indicate that the transition is beginning (e.g., clapping hands, switching off the lights, executing a clapping pattern that students must repeat).
3. Guide students through the six-step transition process, as described below.

STEP 1: SIGNAL TO OBTAIN STUDENT ATTENTION.

   a. Give the transition signal to focus student attention on you.

   Example: Clap your hands three times.

STEP 2: COMMUNICATE YOUR EXPECTATIONS FOR ACADEMIC AND SOCIAL BEHAVIOR.

   a. Give academic directions: tell students what they need to do to get ready for the next activity.

   Example: "Put your social studies books away and get out your math homework."

   b. Give behavior directions: remind students how they should behave during transitions and how they should look so you know they are ready to begin the next activity.

   Example: "Remember, change your materials without making too much noise with them and without talking. Then show me you're ready for math by sitting quietly with your math homework on your desk."

STEP 3: SPECIFY THE TIME LIMIT FOR THE TRANSITION.

   a. Tell students the amount of time they have to get ready for the next activity, set the timer for that amount of time, and encourage them to "beat the buzzer."

   Example: "You have 2 minutes to get ready for math. [Display the timer or stopwatch.] Ready? Try to beat the buzzer!" [Set the timer or stopwatch for the specified time.]

STEP 4: MONITOR FOR COMPLIANCE.

   a. Walk around the room and observe students as they perform the transition.
   b. Praise students who are following the academic and behavior directions and redirect or give a specific prompt for noncompliant students.

STEP 5: SIGNAL THE END OF THE TRANSITION BY BEGINNING THE NEXT ACTIVITY.

   a. Begin the next lesson promptly.

STEP 6: PROVIDE PERFORMANCE FEEDBACK ON THE SUCCESS OF THE TRANSITION.

a. Tell the students if they beat the buzzer or if the time required for the transition exceeded the criterion. Remind them that every student must have completed the transition within the time limit for the criterion to be met.

b. Praise the class if they met the criterion. If the time exceeded the criterion, tell the students that you are disappointed they did not beat the buzzer but that they will have another opportunity to beat the buzzer later that day.

Implementation

1. Use the timer or stopwatch to monitor times for targeted transitions throughout the day.
2. Provide praise and corrective feedback as needed after each transition.

Evaluation (Select One or Both)

1. Compare the number of minutes required for students to complete one or more transitions before and after implementation.
2. Compare the frequency of disruptive behaviors during one or more transitions before and after implementation.

Variations

Variation 1: Beat the Buzzer

1. For preschoolers or early primary grade students, modify the directions as follows:

> "Boys and girls, today we are going to play a game. I am going to give you ___ minutes on this timer, and I want to see if you can [move from first activity to second activity] before the time is up. All your materials from [first activity] must be put away, and you must be ready for [second activity] when the time is up. [Hold up the stopwatch or display the timer.] Get ready to beat the buzzer! … Go!"

2. As students become more successful in making rapid transitions, gradually reduce the number of minutes permitted for the targeted transitions.

Variation 2: Transitioning with Response Cost

1. Write the permitted amount of time for the target transition(s) on the chalkboard and take away 5 minutes of recess that day or the next day for each 1 minute over the criterion.

Variation 3: All-Day Transitioning with Incentives

1. Select two to five key transitions throughout the school day. Draw bar graphs on the chalkboard to represent the number of minutes required for students to complete each of these transitions and label each graph (e.g., "Getting Ready for Lunch," "Preparing for Dismissal").
2. Using data collected during the observation period, set a criterion for the total time permitted to complete all of the targeted transitions.
3. Time each targeted transition as it occurs and record the number of minutes required for completion on the appropriate graph. Near the end of the day, sum the total number of minutes spent in transitioning and announce whether the class has met the criterion. If the criterion has been met, provide an end-of-day activity reward, such as extra outdoor recess or a classroom game session. As the class becomes more successful in meeting the daily criterion, require students to meet the criterion on 4 out of 5 days in order to earn the reward.

Notes

1. Using a stopwatch rather than a timer does not appear to reduce the effectiveness of the strategy and is more acceptable to older students.
2. In the study by LaFleur and her colleagues (1998), the authors set a criterion of 4 minutes for transitions, based on earlier evidence that the average classroom transition lasts 8 minutes (Paine et al., 1983). Because other studies have demonstrated that in-class transitions can be completed in less than 4 minutes (e.g., Campbell & Skinner, 2004; Yarbrough, Skinner, Lee, & Lemmons, 2004), teachers should adjust criterion times to reflect baseline data and their goals for student performance.

Sources

LaFleur, L., Witt, J. C., Naquin, G., Harwell, V., & Gilbertson, D. M. (1998). Use of coaching to enhance proactive classroom management by improvement of student transitioning between classroom activities. *Effective School Practices, 17*, 70–82. Copyright 1998 by the Association for Direct Instruction. Adapted by permission.

Wurtele, S. K., & Drabman, R. S. (1984). "Beat the buzzer" for classroom dawdling: A one-year trial. *Behavior Therapy, 15*, 403–409. Copyright 1984 by the Association for Behavioral and Cognitive Therapies. Adapted by permission.

THE TIMELY TRANSITIONS GAME: REDUCING ROOM-TO-ROOM TRANSITION TIME

Overview

Although room-to-room transitions are a necessary part of the school day, they take up time that could be available for learning. Room-to-room transitions are also likely scenarios for inappropriate and disruptive behavior because students are physically closer to each other, the situation is less structured, and teachers have more difficulty monitoring behavior. Attempts to address student misbehavior can further extend transition time, such as when the teacher requires the entire class to wait in the hall until every student is quiet before entering the classroom. This game-like intervention encourages students to make rapid, disruption-free transitions with a combination of overt timing, publicly posted feedback, and an interdependent group contingency with randomly selected transitions and time criteria. Randomizing transitions and time criteria provides a powerful incentive for appropriate behavior because the class can still earn a reward after a poor transition, given that any of the targeted transitions may be selected at the end of the day and used to determine if the randomly selected criterion has been met. In two investigations, the first with a second-grade classroom and the second with a sixth-grade classroom, the *Timely Transitions Game* produced immediate, large, and sustained decreases in transition times, with the average weekly transition time reduced by approximately 2 hours in the first study and by 1.5 hours in the second study. Teachers also reported that inappropriate transition behaviors decreased in frequency and intensity. A variation targeting a single transition rather than multiple transitions is also presented.

Purpose

To facilitate rapid, disruption-free room-to-room transitions by means of a transition game combining explicit timing, public posting, and a group contingency with randomized elements.

Materials

1. Stopwatch or watch with second hand.

2. Two plastic containers, with press-on paper labels and slips of paper, as follows:
   a. Label the first container "Transitions." Place in the container six slips of paper with one of the following phrases written on each slip: "Going to recess," "Returning from recess," "Going to lunch," "Returning from lunch," "Going to specials," "Returning from specials." (Modify the descriptions to reflect the targeted transitions. Skip this step if you are implementing Variation 2.)
   b. Label the second container "What It Takes to Win." Place in the container 13 slips of paper with a range of acceptable transition times, using data obtained during the observation period (see Observation, Option 1) to help select the time criteria.
3. "Timely Transitions Feedback Chart," consisting of a posterboard chart or section of the chalkboard with nine columns, as follows:
   a. Label the first column "Date," the next six columns for each of the targeted transitions, the eighth column "Randomly Selected Time," and the ninth column "P–A–R–T–Y" (see Figure 3.1 on p. 96).
4. Brightly colored construction paper letters (optional).
5. Materials for a class party, such as popcorn, videos, DVDs, or music CDs.

Observation (Select One or Both)

Option 1

1. Select one or more room-to-room transitions, such as to and from recess, to and from the cafeteria, and to and from specials. Using a stopwatch or watch with a second hand and a sheet of paper attached to a clipboard, record the number of seconds required for students to complete the selected transitions for 4 to 7 days.
2. For transitions that involve leaving the classroom, begin timing when you give the signal to line up and stop timing when the last student exits the classroom.
3. For transitions that involve returning to class, begin timing when students cross the threshold of the classroom and stop timing when all students have been seated quietly for 5 seconds.

Option 2

1. Using a sheet of paper attached to a clipboard, tally the number of inappropriate behaviors that occur during one or more room-to-room transitions for 4 to 7 days. *Inappropriate behaviors* are defined as talking without permission, touching or pushing other students, getting out of line, and failing to follow directions.

Intervention Steps

Introduction and Training

1. Explain to the students that they will be learning a game that will help them get to recess, lunch, and specials faster and will give them a chance to earn a class party for appropriate behavior.
2. Guide students through the transition procedures, as described below.

STEP 1: REVIEW APPROPRIATE TRANSITION BEHAVIOR.

   a. Review appropriate ready-to-line-up behavior as follows: (1) clear your desk, (2) sit in your seat quietly, and (3) wait for your row or table to be called.
   b. Review appropriate in-line behavior as follows: (1) get in line promptly when your row or table is called; (2) stand quietly, facing forward; (3) keep your hands and feet to yourself; and (4) wait for directions.

STEP 2: DEMONSTRATE THE TIMING PROCEDURE AND CONDUCT A PRACTICE TRANSITION.

    a. Tell the students that they will have a chance to practice making effective transitions by going to and from the specials room (or some other destination).

    b. Display the stopwatch and tell the students that you will start it when the transition begins and let it run until they are ready to leave the classroom.

    c. Say, "It is time to line up now to go to the specials room," and start the stopwatch. When all of the students are displaying ready-to-line-up behavior, have them line up by rows, tables, or some other arrangement. When all of the students are exhibiting appropriate in-line behavior, stop the stopwatch and direct them to file out of the classroom and walk toward the destination room.

    d. If students misbehave at any time while they are in the hallway during the transition, stop the class and start the stopwatch again. When students are again displaying appropriate in-line behavior, stop the stopwatch and instruct them to continue transitioning. The transition is over when the last student crosses the threshold of the destination room. Record the transition time on a slip of paper or a sheet of paper attached to a clipboard.

    e. Conduct another practice transition back to the classroom. As before, start the stopwatch after you direct students to line up and stop it when they are exhibiting appropriate in-line behavior. If students exhibit inappropriate behavior during the transition, stop the class and start the stopwatch. When students are behaving appropriately again, stop the stopwatch and resume the transition.

    f. When you reach the classroom, start the stopwatch again when the first student crosses the threshold and stop it when all students are in their seats and have been sitting quietly for 5 seconds.

    g. Tell students what their transition times were going to and from the destination room and record those times on the chalkboard.

STEP 3: EXPLAIN THE GROUP REWARD PROCEDURE.

    a. Display the "Transitions" and "What It Takes to Win" containers. Explain that you will write the date and each targeted transition time on the Timely Transitions Feedback Chart each day. At the end of the day, you will draw a transition from the "Transitions" container to select the transition time that will be used to determine whether the class meets the criterion for earning the reward.

    b. Show the students the slips of paper with the criterion times and list the times on the chalkboard. To ensure that students understand the times, write times over 1 minute in minutes and seconds.

    c. Explain that you will select a criterion time from the "What It Takes to Win" container and compare it with the students' actual time for the transition you have drawn. The class will earn a letter in the word P–A–R–T–Y if their time is less than the criterion time drawn from the container. If the actual time is greater than the criterion, you will put a dash on the chart to indicate that no letter was earned. After the word *party* is spelled, the class will celebrate with a popcorn party (or some other type of party).

Implementation

1. Remind students about the Timely Transitions Game at the start of each school day.
2. Using the stopwatch or watch with a second hand, record transition times for each targeted transition. When students return from a destination room or area, announce the number of seconds required to go to and return from the destination and record the two transition times on the Timely Transitions Feedback Chart. Repeat this process throughout the school day.

3. At the end of the day, draw a slip of paper from the "Transition" container to indicate the selected transition and put a star beside that time on the chart (or have a student do this).

4. Then draw or have another student draw a slip of paper from the "What It Takes to Win" container and record the selected time in the eighth column on the chart. If the actual time for the selected transition is less than the criterion, record a letter in the last column and praise the class. If desired, tape a large construction paper letter (e.g., "P," "A") to the top of the chalkboard each day that the class met the criterion.

5. If the actual time is greater than the criterion, enter a dash in the last column on the chart and encourage the class to do better the next day.

6. Deliver the group reward when the word *party* is spelled out on the chart.

Evaluation (Select One or Both)

Option 1

1. Compare the number of seconds required for students to complete one or more transitions before and after implementation.

Option 2

1. Compare the frequency of disruptive behaviors during one or more transitions before and after implementation.

Variation: Single-Transition Version

1. Select a single problematic transition, such as entering the classroom and settling down after lunch or recess. Prepare a "What It Takes to Win" container containing slips of paper with a range of acceptable times. Record the amount of time needed to complete the selected transition and write it on the chalkboard. At the end of the day, draw a slip of paper from the container and record a letter on the Timely Transitions Feedback Chart if the class time beats the time you have drawn.

Notes

1. To maintain student motivation, vary the reinforcers after the class earns each reward. Other rewards used in the original studies included listening to music during independent seatwork (*M–U–S–I–C*), going outside for lunch (*P–I–C–N–I–C*), watching a brief video (*M–O–V–I–E*), and eating treats brought by students (*C–U–P–C–A–K–E–S*).

2. As students become more successful in making rapid transitions, use longer words or phrases to represent rewards, such as *F–I–E–L–D–T–R–I–P–T–O–Z–O–O*, and replace longer times in the time criteria pool with shorter times.

Sources

Campbell, S., & Skinner, C. H. (2004). Combining explicit timing with an interdependent group contingency program to decrease transition times: An investigation of the timely transitions game. *Journal of Applied School Psychology, 20,* 11–27. Copyright 2004 by The Haworth Press. Adapted by permission.

Yarbrough, J. L., Skinner, C. H., Lee, Y. J., & Lemmons, C. (2004). Decreasing transition times in a second grade classroom: Scientific support for the timely transitions game. *Journal of Applied School Psychology, 20,* 85–107. Copyright 2004 by The Haworth Press. Adapted by permission.

Date	To Recess	From Recess	To Lunch	From Lunch	To Specials	From Specials	Randomly Selected Time	P-A-R-T-Y
10/23	380	125*	118	134	236	345	140	P
10/24	220	112	164	148*	220	300	120	—
10/25	150	99	105*	139	218	278	151	A
10/26	88	101	98	112	224*	250	99	—
10/27	91	79	101	108	199	100*	100	R

FIGURE 3.1. Example of the Timely Transitions Feedback Chart. Times are in seconds. An asterisk indicates the transition that was selected for that day. Time criteria vary from day to day. Adapted from Campbell and Skinner (2004, p. 16). Copyright 2004 by The Haworth Press, Inc. Adapted by permission.

TASK 4: MANAGING SMALL-GROUP INSTRUCTION AND INDEPENDENT SEATWORK

Managing Small-Group Instruction

Teacher-directed small-group instruction plays a key role in improving the academic outcomes of at-risk learners, including struggling readers (Foorman & Torgesen, 2001; Rashotte et al., 2001; Torgesen et al., 2001), students with disabilities (Elbaum, Vaughn, Hughes, & Moody, 1999; Elbaum, Vaughn, Hughes, Moody, & Schumm, 2000; Vaughn & Schumm, 1996), and English language learners (Gerber et al., 2004; Taylor, Pearson, Clark, & Walpole, 2000). Small-group instruction is especially effective when teachers differentiate instruction and materials based on the needs of the students in each group (Lou, Abrami, & Spence, 2000). Unfortunately, many teachers fail to use this instructional format or use it ineffectively. Although teachers report that they occasionally implement small-group instruction, observational studies indicate that this actually rarely occurs, even in resource room settings (Moody, Vaughn, & Schumm, 1997; Schumm, Moody, & Vaughn, 2000). A major factor contributing to teachers' failure to use small-group instruction is difficulty ensuring that all students are productively engaged, not merely those in the teacher-directed small group (Elbaum et al., 1999; Moody et al., 1997). Teachers themselves report that they receive little or no training in strategies for implementing instructional groups and that they find managing small-group instruction one of their most challenging tasks (Morrow, Reutzel, & Casey, 2006). If grouping formats are to have beneficial effects on student outcomes, however, effective classroom management is essential (Invernizzi & Hayes, 2004; Pressley et al., 2001).

Managing Seatwork

Seatwork is an instructional context in which students work without direct teacher supervision on assigned tasks. Although seatwork enables teachers to provide individual or small-group instruction, grade papers, and deal with myriad daily classroom tasks, seatwork settings are accompanied by an array of instructional and behavior management challenges. First, teachers assisting individual students or small groups must deliver instruction while simultaneously ensuring that seatwork students perform their assigned tasks and do not disrupt teacher-directed activities. Second, although seatwork is intended to enhance students' academic skills by providing additional practice opportunities, most studies have failed to confirm that typical seatwork activities improve achievement. On the contrary, the excessive use of seatwork activities is associated not only with lower achievement and lower rates of task-appropriate behavior compared with teacher-directed instruction (Beyda et al., 2002; Helmke & Schrader, 1988), but also with negative student affect (Prawat & Anderson, 1994) and an increased risk of placement in special education (Cooper & Speece, 1990). Independent seatwork is an especially problematic instructional context for students with learning disabilities, who display significantly lower engagement rates and achievement during seatwork periods compared with teacher-directed instruction in both regular classroom and resource room settings (Cancelli, Harris, Friedman, & Yoshida, 1993; Friedman et al., 1988).

Interventions for Managing Small-Group Instruction and Independent Seatwork

The three strategies in this section are designed to promote academic productivity and decrease off-task and disruptive behavior during instructional periods that include small-group instruction and independent seatwork. For maximum effectiveness, they should be implemented in the context of a seatwork structure characterized by clear explanations of the goals to be achieved by seatwork tasks, specific instructions for completing assignments, frequent teacher monitoring, and immediate intervention when disruptions occur (Hemlke & Schrader, 1988). In *Checking Stations,* students learn a self-managed error correction procedure that eliminates the need to wait for teacher assistance when they complete seatwork assignments. *The Coupon System: Decreasing Inappropriate Requests for Teacher Assistance* uses a peer-monitored response cost system to encourage independent effort and reduce interruptions of teacher-directed small-group instruction. This strategy, which ranks high in acceptability to both teachers and students, can also be used to target disruptive behaviors, such as inappropriate verbalizations. *Countdown to Free Time: Encouraging Productivity during Small-Group Instruction* targets academic productivity among students not in the small-group setting with a combination of several empirically validated components, including a response cost contingency and an innovative visual cuing device to signal access to reinforcement.

CROSS-REFERENCE: Chapter 4 includes several interventions that are designed to replace independent seatwork with collaborative peer practice, including *ClassWide Peer Tutoring, Cover Copy Compare, Reciprocal Peer Tutoring in Math,* and *Add-A-Word Spelling.* Chapter 4 also presents several performance-based strategies that can be used to target seatwork, such as *The Rewards Box: Enhancing Academic Performance with Randomized Group Contingencies* and *Self-Monitoring of Academic Productivity. Six Steps to Effective Small-Group Instruction*—a strategy consisting of a validated managerial sequence for conducting small-group instruction with preschoolers—is presented in Chapter 6.

CHECKING STATIONS

Overview

Providing students with immediate feedback about their performance not only enhances learning but also prevents mistakes from being perpetuated. Unfortunately, the demands of the classroom make it difficult for teachers to deliver feedback to individual students immediately upon assignment completion, especially if they are combining small-group instruction with independent seatwork. This intervention teaches students to correct some of their own papers at "checking stations," classroom centers equipped with teacher-prepared answer keys. Checking stations decrease downtime and increase academic productivity during independent seatwork periods because students do not need to wait to receive feedback on their written work. Moreover, checking stations reduce the burden of grading papers for teachers because students have completed the initial evaluation process themselves. Especially useful in classrooms with a differentiated small-group instructional format, the strategy has been implemented successfully with students as young as first graders. A variation with classwide incentives for accurate self-checking is also presented.

Purpose

To improve academic productivity and learning by teaching students a self-managed procedure for evaluating their own seatwork assignments.

Materials

1. Two or more checking stations, consisting of a small table and chair or two adjacent desks and chairs, with a separate station for each targeted subject area (approximately one station per 8 to 10 students).
2. Teacher-prepared answer keys, one per assignment to be checked.
3. Red pen or marker, one per station.
4. Box, tray, or folder for corrected work, one per station.
5. Posterboard chart at each checking station listing the following rules:
   a. Only one person uses each checking station at a time.
   b. Leave your own pens and pencils at your desk.
   c. Check your work quietly.
   d. Place your corrected work in the box.
6. Stickers, homework passes, and/or other small reinforcers.

Observation (Select One or Both)

1. Calculate the percentage of papers completed with 80% accuracy or above by the entire class during an independent seatwork period for 4 to 7 days.
2. Using a sheet of paper attached to a clipboard, record the number of student requests for assistance during an independent seatwork period for 4 to 7 days.

Intervention Steps

Introduction and Training

1. Tell the students that they are going to be learning a new way of correcting their own papers.
2. Using the posterboard chart, review the checking station rules as follows:
   a. If someone is already using a checking station, go to another station or stay at your desk until that station is clear.
   b. Leave pencils and pens at your desk and take your paper to the checking station.
   c. Using the answer key, check each answer carefully.
   d. Circle incorrect answers with the red pen or marker.
   e. Go back to your seat, cross out the wrong answers, and write in the correct answers.
   f. Return to the checking station and check your paper again with the answer key.
   g. Put the corrected paper in the box.

3. Tell students that you expect them to be honest and that you will look at some of the papers each day to make sure they have been checked correctly. If the students whose papers you check have found and corrected all their mistakes, everyone in the class will earn a reward (e.g., sticker, homework pass, or special classroom privilege).
4. Using *Say Show Check: Teaching Classroom Procedures,* model correct use of the checking stations and then select one or two students to demonstrate the procedures. Provide praise and corrective feedback as appropriate.

Implementation

1. Spotcheck some of the papers at each checking station every day to review accuracy. Provide praise and a small reward if students have found all of their mistakes.
2. If cheating occurs, talk with the student privately and administer an individual consequence as soon as you detect it, such as requiring the student to redo the paper and deducting 10 minutes from recess. Follow up with a classwide review of checking stations procedures, including a discussion of the purpose of checking stations and the importance of honest, accurate self-correction.
3. Phase out the rewards as students become accustomed to using the checking stations.

Evaluation (Select One or Both)

1. Compare the classwide percentage of papers completed with at least 80% accuracy during the independent seatwork period before and after implementation.
2. Compare the frequency of student requests for help during the independent seatwork period before and after implementation.

Variation: Checking Stations with Classwide Rewards

1. Keep a running tally of consecutive days on which students use the checking stations correctly, including refraining from cheating. Deliver a classwide reward, such as a 15-minute free period, when the class meets a specified criterion for correct checking station use, such as 5 consecutive days of correct use. Gradually increase the criterion required to earn the reward as students become more successful with the procedures.

Notes

1. Begin with a checking station in only one subject. Mathematics is recommended as the easiest subject for initial implementation. As students become more familiar with the procedure, add another subject.
2. For implementation in the early primary grades, illustrate the checking station rules chart with pictures and review the procedures frequently.

Source

Paine, S. C., Radicchi, J., Rosellini, L. C., Deutchman, L., & Darch, C. B. (1983). *Structuring your classroom for academic success* (pp. 123–127). Champaign, IL: Research Press. Copyright 1983 by the authors. Adapted by permission.

THE COUPON SYSTEM:
DECREASING INAPPROPRIATE REQUESTS FOR TEACHER ASSISTANCE

Overview

Students' excessive or inappropriate requests for teacher assistance can disrupt ongoing instruction and reduce opportunities for learning in both whole-class and small-group settings. This simple, cost-effective intervention uses a response cost token system to encourage independent effort and reduce unnecessary requests for help. Originally implemented with a second grader with learning disabilities in a regular education classroom, the strategy produced an immediate, marked decrease in inappropriate attention-seeking behaviors. Adapted here for classwide application by using peer monitoring and a group contingency within a team format, it is especially useful when the teacher is delivering small-group instruction while the rest of the class is performing independent seatwork. Two variations are included: (1) a classwide teacher-mediated response cost system and (2) the original individualized format.

Purpose

To decrease inappropriate requests for teacher assistance with a peer-monitored response cost token system.

Materials

1. Coupons, consisting of 1″ × 2″ strips of colored construction paper, a specific number per team or target student, with different colors for each team.
2. Paper or plastic cups, one per team.
3. Tape (optional, see Variation 2).
4. Small material rewards, such as stickers, school supplies, and wrapped candy (optional).

Observation (Select One or Both)

1. Select an instructional period that includes independent seatwork. Using a sheet of paper attached to a clipboard, tally the number of requests for assistance that is not really needed made by the entire class or a group of target students for 4 to 7 days. These data will help you determine how many requests for assistance to permit at the beginning of the intervention (see Intervention Step #5).
2. Using a sheet of paper attached to a clipboard, record the frequency of disruptive behaviors displayed by the entire class or a group of target students during a selected instructional period for 4 to 7 days. *Disruptive behaviors* are defined as any student behaviors that interfere with ongoing instruction or the on-task behavior of another student, such as calling out, being out of seat without permission, or talking loudly.

Intervention Steps

Introduction and Training

1. Explain to the students that they will be playing a game to help them learn to work more independently during the selected instructional period.
2. Using *Say Show Check: Teaching Classroom Procedures*, discuss and demonstrate appropriate and inappropriate requests for assistance. Explain that asking for help when it is not really needed reduces the amount of time you have to teach and students have to learn.
3. Divide the class into teams according to rows, tables, or desk clusters and assign a "team captain" for the week.

4. Place a paper or plastic cup containing the predetermined number of strips of construction paper on the captain's desk or in the center of the table or cluster. Distribute one more coupon per team than the permitted number of requests for assistance (e.g., six coupons for five requests).
5. Explain that the strips of paper are "coupons" that can be redeemed for various privileges, such as lunch with the teacher, computer time, a special art activity, or extra recess time, or for small material rewards, such as stickers, school supplies, and wrapped candy.
6. Explain that each time a student requests your help during the target period, you will assess the student's ability to understand and complete the task. If the student again seeks assistance after you have informed him or her not to do so by saying, "I think you understand what to do," you will instruct the captain of that student's team to remove one coupon and return it to you.
7. At the end of the period, the captains will count and report the number of remaining coupons. All teams with at least one coupon left at the end of the period will receive the reward.
8. Using a group of students seated at a row, table, or desk cluster, demonstrate the procedures, including responding appropriately to the removal of a coupon, counting the remaining coupons, and reporting the results.

Implementation

1. At the beginning of the intervention period, distribute the specified number of coupons to each team. Be sure to use different colored strips for each team to prevent students from supplementing their coupons with coupons taken from other teams. Have captains remove coupons for inappropriate requests for help at your direction as described above.
2. At the end of the period, have the captains report the number of coupons remaining for their teams. Deliver the reward immediately or at the end of the school day to all members of winning teams. Encourage losing teams to try harder the next day. If all teams are winners, provide a bonus group activity reward, if desired.
3. As students make fewer inappropriate requests for help, decrease the number of coupons distributed per team or increase the length of the intervention period.

Evaluation (Select One or Both)

1. Compare the frequency of unnecessary requests for assistance made by the entire class or the target students during the selected instructional period before and after implementation.
2. Compare the frequency of disruptive behaviors displayed by the entire class or the target students during the selected instructional period before and after implementation.

Variations

Variation 1: Classwide Coupon System

1. For implementation as a whole-class rather than a team-based strategy, place a predetermined number of coupons in a plastic or paper cup on your desk or at the table where you are conducting small-group instruction.
2. When a student makes an inappropriate request for help, remove a coupon and announce your action, as well as the number of remaining coupons.

> *Example:* "Tamira, I think you understand what to do. That's one coupon lost. Class, you have four coupons left."

3. If at least one coupon remains at the end of the period, deliver the reward to the entire class.

Variation 2: Single-Student or Small-Group Coupon System

1. For implementation with a single student or a small group of target students, tape a predetermined number of coupons on the desk of each target student and remove them for inappropriate requests for help (or instruct the student to bring them to you). Deliver a reward if the student has at least one coupon remaining at the end of the period.

Notes

1. If the intervention targets only a few students rather than the entire class, it is important to use social and activity reinforcers (e.g., eating lunch with the teacher, helping the teacher prepare materials, positive school–home notes) rather than material reinforcers so that the rest of the class is not deprived of the opportunity to earn tangible rewards.
2. Because asking for assistance is appropriate when students do not understand their assignments or lack the skills necessary to complete them, providing explicit instructions for completing seatwork assignments and assessing students' competence to perform the assigned tasks are essential to the success of this strategy.
3. This intervention can also be used to reduce disruptive behavior, such as inappropriate verbalizations (e.g., calling out without permission, talking to other students who are trying to work). In the original investigation, a second experiment produced an immediate and substantial reduction in the inappropriate verbalizations of a fifth grader with learning disabilities during the reading instructional period in a regular classroom.

Source

Salend, S. J., & Henry, K. (1981). Response cost in mainstreamed settings. *Journal of School Psychology, 19*, 242–249. Copyright 1981 by Elsevier Science Ltd., Oxford, England. Adapted by permission.

COUNTDOWN TO FREE TIME: ENCOURAGING PRODUCTIVITY DURING SMALL-GROUP INSTRUCTION

Overview

Maintaining an orderly and productive classroom environment during small-group instruction is a perennial classroom management problem. Although behavior among students in the teacher-directed group is typically appropriate, students assigned to perform seatwork activities on their own have many opportunities to be off-task or disruptive. Moreover, teachers' efforts to manage the behavior of seatwork students can interfere with small-group instruction, reducing academic productivity and opportunities to learn for students in both settings. This multicomponent intervention combines performance feedback with self-monitoring and response cost to improve on-task behavior during seatwork. In the original study, implemented in regular education classes with one second grader and one third grader with attention-deficit/hyperactivity disorder (ADHD), one target student monitored his behavior with a small flipchart similar to a ratings chart managed by the teacher, while the second target student viewed a desktop electronic counter with a digital display activated by the teacher. In this classwide adaptation, students use index cards to match teacher ratings displayed on a flipchart and earn rewards based on an interdependent group contingency. Three variations for this highly usable intervention are also presented.

Purpose

To increase on-task behavior and reduce disruptive behavior during small-group instruction and seatwork using classwide self-monitoring and response cost procedures.

Materials

1. Flipchart on stand or easel with 21 tagboard cards or large sheets of paper, as follows:
   a. Using a black marker, number the cards or sheets of paper from 20 to 0 with numerals large enough to be visible to all students.
   b. Punch holes in the cards or sheets, and hang them on the flipchart, with the 20 on top.
2. 4″ × 6″ index cards, one per student.
3. Tape.
4. Posterboard chart listing the classroom rules, such as:
   a. Stay in your seat unless you have permission to get up.
   b. Talk only when you are called on.
   c. Work quietly on your assignments during seatwork time.
   d. Follow directions the first time they are given.
5. Paper bag, basket, or box containing slips of paper with descriptions of a variety of group activity rewards written on them, such as "Reading to First Graders," "Classroom Basketball," "Music Time," "Partner Reading Time," and "Trip to Special Playground" (optional).

Observation (Select One or More)

Option 1

1. Calculate percent-correct scores on seatwork assignments during a small-group instructional period for the entire class or a group of target students for 5 to 10 days or for the previous grading period.

Option 2

1. Using a *Group Event Recording Form*, record the frequencies of the following behaviors during a small-group instructional period for the entire class or a group of target students:
   a. *Out-of-seat behavior*, defined as not sitting firmly in one's seat unless permission to be elsewhere has been granted.
   b. *Talk-out behavior*, defined as talking to a classmate, calling out, or making an audible vocalization, such as laughing or humming.
2. Conduct these observations for 4 to 7 days.

Option 3

1. Using a sheet of paper attached to a clipboard, record the number of reprimands you deliver to the entire class or a group of target students during a small-group instructional period for 4 to 7 days.

Intervention Steps

1. Display the flipchart with the number 20 showing and tell students that they can earn up to 20 minutes of free time (or extra recess or some other time-based privilege) for working hard during the selected instructional period.
2. Explain that you will be looking around the room at regular intervals while you are working with the small groups. If you see that all students are working on their assignments, you will not deduct any time. If one or more students are not working, however, you will flip a card over on the chart to indicate that 1 minute of free time has been lost.
3. Distribute the index cards and have students tape the cards to the top of their desks, with the longer side of the card as the vertical.

4. Demonstrate on the chalkboard how to print the numerals from 20 to 0 in descending order on the cards. Move around the room to help students number their cards.

5. Tell students that they should occasionally look at the number displayed on the flipchart during the instructional period and cross off numbers on their own charts to match the class chart.

6. Demonstrate how to check the class chart and mark student cards.

7. Review rules and procedures for the free-time period. For example, students may read books brought from home on their own or with a partner, listen to books on tape, listen to music, work in centers or on the classroom computers, or play classroom games.

8. Conduct the instructional period as usual. Place the flipchart next to the small-group instructional area so that you can flip cards without having to walk to the front of the room. If you move from group to group, take the flipchart with you. Alternatively, leave the flipchart at the front of the classroom where all students can see it and assign a student seated nearby to flip the cards at your direction.

9. At the end of the instructional period, praise the class for working hard and award the amount of free time corresponding to the number displayed on the chart. Alternately, select a student to draw a slip from the grab bag and permit the entire class to engage in the activity described on the slip for the amount of time they have earned.

Evaluation (Select One or More)

Option 1

1. Compare percent-correct scores on seatwork assignments during the small-group instructional period for the entire class or the target group before and after implementation.

Option 2

1. Compare the frequency of out-of-seats and talk-outs during the small-group instructional period for the entire class or the target group before and after implementation.

Option 3

1. Compare the frequency of reprimands delivered to the entire class or the target group during the small-group instructional period before and after implementation.

Variations

Variation 1: Chalkboard Countdown

1. Instead of using a flipchart, list numbers from 20 to 0 on the chalkboard, and cross off a number in descending order each time you deliver a reprimand for unproductive or disruptive behavior during the instructional period. Having a designated student cross off numbers permits you to remain with the small groups rather than having to go to the front of the room for each rule infraction.

2. Award the number of minutes of free time corresponding to the highest number remaining on the board at the end of the period.

Variation 2: Countdown with Recess Contingency

1. List numbers from 20 to 0 on the chalkboard, with the highest number corresponding to the minutes usually allowed for the recess period.

2. Cross off a number (or instruct a student to cross off a number) each time you deliver a reprimand for unproductive or disruptive behavior during the instructional period.

3. Award the number of minutes of recess corresponding to the highest number remaining on the board at the end of the period.

Notes

1. In the original study, response cost was superior to Ritalin in increasing on-task behavior and improving academic performance for both target students.

2. During field testing, teachers consistently preferred Variation 2 over the original version because of its greater usability.

Source

Rapport, M. D., Murphy, H. A., & Bailey, J. S. (1982). Ritalin vs. response cost in the control of hyperactive children: A within-subject comparison. *Journal of Applied Behavior Analysis*, *15*, 205–216. Copyright 1982 by the Society for the Experimental Analysis of Behavior. Adapted by permission.

TASK 5: COMMUNICATING COMPETENTLY WITH STUDENTS

One of the most important aspects of classroom management is the ability to communicate effectively with students (Cothran, Kulinna, & Garrahy, 2003; Evertson et al., 2006). Although teachers primarily use verbal statements to maintain appropriate classroom academic and social behavior (Abramowitz, O'Leary, & Futtersak, 1988; McIntyre & Brulle, 1989; Rosén, Taylor, O'Leary, & Sanderson, 1990), teachers' communications with students sometimes fail to achieve the desired result and at times they have the opposite effect to that which is intended (Lewis, 2001; Shores, Gunter, & Jack, 1993). This section presents strategies targeting three key teacher–student communications: (1) praise, (2) reprimands, and (3) commands. Although the strategies are presented separately, they are not intended to be implemented as stand-alone interventions but as components in a comprehensive classroom management system. In particular, reprimands should always be used in the context of praise and positive attention, not only because positive teacher communications are essential to a warm, supportive classroom environment, but also because a combination of praise and reprimands is much more effective in improving on-task behavior and increasing academic productivity than either type of communication alone (Houghton, Wheldall, Jukes, & Sharpe, 1990). Systematic delivery of praise, reprimands, and/or commands is also a frequent component in intervention packages targeting academic achievement or social competence (e.g., Connell, Carta, Lutz, et al., 1993; De Martini-Scully et al., 2000; Hiralall & Martens, 1998).

Delivering Effective Praise

Teacher praise has been documented to be effective in shaping achievement, behavior, and attitudes for students at every level, including preschoolers (Connell, Carta, Lutz, et al., 1993), elementary students (Martens, Hiralall, & Bradley, 1997; Sutherland, Wehby, & Copeland, 2000), and middle and high school students (Alber, Heward, & Hippler, 1999; Houghton et al., 1990). Compared with less effective teachers, more effective teachers use a more enthusiastic tone and deliver praise more frequently—behaviors that communicate teacher competence and interest in student learning (Bohn et al., 2004; Brigham, Scruggs, & Mastropieri, 1992; Nowacek et al., 1990). Teacher-delivered praise and positive affect, such as enthusiasm, are especially important for encouraging low-achieving students and students with disabilities (Brigham et al., 1992; Heward, 2003). Despite the effectiveness of praise and teachers' reported preference for positive interventions such as praise over negative strategies such as reprimands (Martens, Witt, Elliott, & Darveaux, 1986; Whinnery, Fuchs, & Fuchs, 1991), teachers' natural rates of praise are quite low in general education classrooms (Beaman & Wheldall, 2000; Craft, Alber, & Heward, 1998; Matheson & Shriver, 2005) and classrooms serving students with disabilities (Alber et al., 1999; Shores et al., 1993; Wehby, Symons, Canale, & Go, 1998). Praise for prosocial behavior is even more infrequent (Beaman & Wheldall, 2000), especially in classrooms serving students with emotional and behavioral disorders (Shores et al., 1993; Shores & Wehby, 1999; Wehby et al., 1998). Moreover, when teachers praise students, their praise often fails to shape behavior in the desired direction because it does not function as an effective reinforcer. Although behavior-specific praise is the most effective form of praise, it makes up only a small percentage of the total amount of praise teachers deliver in regular or special education settings (Matheson & Shriver, 2005; Sutherland et al., 2000). Instead, teachers tend to deliver nonspecific praise, such as "You're such a good boy!" or the ubiquitous "Good job!" (Martens & Hiralall, 1997; Rathvon, 1996).

There is also abundant evidence that praise alone is insufficient to effect behavior change or maintain acceptable levels of on-task behavior and academic productivity (Acker & O'Leary, 1987; Agran, Blanchard, Wehmeyer, & Hughes, 2001; Pfiffner, Rosén, & O'Leary, 1985; Sullivan & O'Leary, 1990). Although many teachers have been taught to praise positive behavior and ignore negative behavior, this praise-and-ignore strategy is likely to result in an escalation of misbehavior because of the reinforcement provided by peer attention and the likelihood that disruptive behavior will spread to other students. In addition, teacher praise can lose value for students, especially after the early primary grades, whereas peer attention for disruptive behavior can be a powerful reinforcer (Broussard & Northup, 1997; Hughes, 2002). Finally, even appropriately delivered praise will have little effect on achievement if students' academic skill deficiencies are not identified and addressed. In other words, social reinforcement in and of itself will not be sufficient to sustain on-task behavior and academic productivity if students are incapable of performing their assigned tasks.

Dimensions of Effective Praise

Studies of motivation and effective teaching have identified four key dimensions of effective praise. First, praise should be *specific*—that is, it should communicate approval of the desired target behavior (Chalk & Bizo, 2004). Second, praise should be *contingent*—that is, it should directly follow the performance of the desired behavior (Houghton et al., 1990). Third, praise should focus on the *effort and strategies* used to perform the task, not on ability (Dweck, 2002). Fourth, praise may be more effective when delivered privately, especially in the case of older students. Although younger students typically enjoy praise that can be overheard by their classmates, secondary-level students tend to prefer *private* praise—that is, praise that is audible only to the target student (Burnett, 2001; Houghton et al., 1990). *Delivering Effective Praise* combines these four empirically validated dimensions into an instructional protocol that maximizes the effectiveness of teacher praise in enhancing student performance and behavior.

PRAISE AND MOTIVATION: A COMPLEX RELATIONSHIP

A fascinating series of studies by Carol Dweck and her colleagues (e.g., Dweck, 2002; Kamins & Dweck, 1999; Mueller & Dweck, 1998) has demonstrated that different kinds of praise exert very different effects on individuals' beliefs about themselves, motivation, and ability to cope with setbacks. Students were first given a set of puzzle-like tasks on which they were able to be very successful. One group received *process praise*—praise focusing on the effort and strategies used to accomplish a task ("You did really well! You must have worked really hard on those problems!" "You discovered a good way to do that!") The second group received *ability praise*—praise focusing on intelligence or skill ("You did really well! You're really good at this!" "You must be smart at these kinds of problems!") After receiving praise, students were given a much more difficult set of problems on which they did much less well. Finally, students received a third set of problems that was equivalent in difficulty to the first set. The performance of the students receiving ability praise declined significantly from the first through the third set of problems. Moreover, the ability-praised students showed significant declines in persistence and task enjoyment, compared with the process-praised students. Despite the fact that they had received praise for their intelligence, they were much more likely to attribute their failure to lack of ability rather than to lack of effort and ultimately selected less challenging tasks in an attempt to obtain a better performance. In contrast, the performance of the process-praised students improved significantly from the first to the third set of problems. In addition, they displayed persistence and appeared to enjoy the challenges, even after experiencing setbacks.

Why did the two different kinds of praise produce such different results? According to Dweck and her colleagues, different types of praise orient students toward different views of intelligence. Ability praise implies that a positive evaluation is based on a fixed, innate set of abilities, so failure means low intelligence. Thus, persistence in the face of challenges will only lead to more failure. Over time, ability praise leads students to value performance rather than learning and undermines persistence and enjoyment when they encounter difficult tasks. In contrast, process praise implies that skills are malleable, so failure means low effort, not low ability. When setbacks occur, skills can be expanded through effort and the application of effective strategies, so persistence pays off. In other words, process praise leads students to value learning opportunities and to sustain effort, even in the face of setbacks, whereas ability praise leads students to attempt to protect their self-esteem by avoiding challenging tasks.

CROSS-REFERENCE: In Chapter 6, *Promoting Independent In-Class Transitions with Self-Assessment and Contingent Praise* targets transitions in preschool classrooms with a combination of direct instruction, teacher praise, and self-monitoring.

DELIVERING EFFECTIVE PRAISE

Overview

Teacher-delivered praise is an integral part of a comprehensive classroom management program and a key component in many intervention packages targeting academic achievement or behavior. Praise also helps to create a positive classroom climate and can enhance student motivation and persistence with challenging tasks. Despite its potentially positive impact, however, praise is often ineffective in improving academic performance or social behavior because it lacks specificity and contingency. Similarly, praise that emphasizes ability can lead to impaired performance and reduced motivation and resilience in the face of setbacks, whereas praise that focuses on the processes students use when performing a task, including effort and strategies, enhances performance, task persistence, and interest in learning. In this intervention, these three dimensions—specificity, contingency, and process-focus—are combined to maximize the impact of teacher-delivered positive attention. Privacy is included as an optional component for older students because of evidence that middle school and high school students respond more positively to praise delivered privately rather than publicly.

Purpose

To improve on-task behavior, academic achievement, and motivation with systematic teacher-delivered praise.

Materials

None.

Observation (Select One or More)

Option 1

1. Using a *Classwide Scanning Form* with a 5-minute interval, tally the number of students in each of the categories below during the selected instructional period, beginning with the left side of the room:
   a. *On-task behavior,* defined as looking at the textbook or lesson materials, writing on worksheets, raising one's hand to ask task-related questions, and looking at the teacher during instruction.
   b. *Off-task behavior,* defined as sitting without appropriate materials, looking at or playing with nonlesson materials, gazing around the room after assignments have been made, or failing to attend to the teacher during instruction.
   c. *Disruptive behavior,* defined as behavior that interferes with the learning of others, such as making noises, calling out, or verbal or physical aggression.
2. Conduct these observations for 30 to 45 minutes for 4 to 7 days.

Option 2

1. Select an instructional period during which students are especially unproductive or disruptive. Divide the class by eye into four groups of approximately equal numbers of students. Using a *Group Time Sampling Form,* observe the students in the first group for 4 seconds. If all of the students in the group are on-task for all 4 seconds, code that group as on-task. If any of the students are off-task for any of the 4 seconds, code the group as off-task. Repeat these observations for the second and third group and then return to the first group.
2. Calculate the classwide percentage of on-task behavior by summing the number of on-task intervals and dividing by the total number of observations. Conduct these observations for 30 to 45 minutes for 4 to 7 days.

Option 3

1. Select a small group of students who are frequently unproductive or disruptive during instruction or independent seatwork.
2. For each student, calculate the percent-accuracy-and-completion rate on one or more class assignments during the selected period by dividing the number of correctly completed problems by the total number of problems assigned.
3. Conduct these observations for 4 to 7 days.

Intervention Steps

1. Select an instructional period during which students are especially off-task and unproductive.
2. When a student performs a desired behavior, move close to the student, obtain eye contact if possible, and deliver a specific, contingent, and process-focused praise statement as follows:
   a. *Specific.* Using the student's name, describe the approved behavior in specific terms.

   > *Example:* "Joshua, you're really working hard on those math problems today," not "Good job!" or "That's nice."

   b. *Contingent.* Deliver the praise as soon as possible after you observe the desired behavior.
   c. *Process-oriented.* Focus the praise on the student's effort and/or strategies, rather than on his or her ability or the outcome.

   > *Effort example:* "Wow, Joshua, you did really well on your spelling! You must have studied really hard!" not "Wow, Joshua, you did really well on your spelling! You're so smart!"

   > *Strategy example:* "Joshua, it looks like you've figured out how to set up equations with two unknowns! That's really using your head," not "See, Joshua, you can do it if you try!"

   d. *Private.* For middle and high school students, move close to the student, obtain eye contact if possible, and deliver the praise so quietly that it is audible only to the target student.
3. Try to deliver at least 10 to 15 praise statements per instructional period. Also try to deliver at least five classwide praise statements per instructional period.

   > *Example:* "Seventh grade, you are really working hard on your group projects! I'm so proud of your efforts!"
4. Remember to provide praise contingent upon prosocial as well as academic behavior.

   > *Public example:* "Class, I'm really impressed with the way you're working so well together as teams on your history timelines!"

   > *Private example:* "Stephanie, I've been noticing how kind you've been to Tamara today and how you've been showing her how we do things. It's not easy to be a new student, and you're being a big help."

Evaluation (Select One or More)

Option 1

1. Compare classwide on-task, off-task, and disruptive behavior rates during the selected instructional period before and after implementation.

Option 2

1. Compare the classwide percentage of on-task behavior during the selected instructional period before and after implementation.

Option 3

1. Compare percent-accuracy-and-completion rates for the group of target students on classwork assignments during the selected instructional period before and after implementation.

Note

1. Delivering private praise can be difficult during whole-class instruction if teachers spend most of their time in one area of the classroom. Circulating periodically around the room during

whole-class instruction not only facilitates praise delivery but also helps to prevent minor incidents of inappropriate behavior from escalating.

Sources

Houghton, S., Wheldall, K., Jukes, R., & Sharpe, A. (1990). The effects of limited private reprimands and increased private praise on classroom behaviour in four British secondary school classes. *British Journal of Educational Psychology, 60,* 255–265. Copyright 1990 by the *British Journal of Educational Psychology.* © The British Psychological Society. Adapted by permission.

Kamins, M. L., & Dweck, C. S. (1999). Person versus process praise and criticism: Implications for contingent self-worth and coping. *Developmental Psychology, 35,* 835–847. Copyright 1999 by the American Psychological Association. Adapted by permission.

Sutherland, K. S., Wehby, J. H., & Copeland, S. R. (2000). Effect of varying rates of behavior-specific praise on the on-task behavior of students with EBD. *Journal of Emotional and Behavioral Disorders, 8,* 2–8, 26. Copyright 2000 by PRO-ED, Inc. Adapted by permission.

Delivering Effective Reprimands

Teachers use reprimands more frequently than any other behavior management strategy and much more often than praise in both regular and special education classrooms (Van Acker & Grant, 1996; Wehby, Dodge, & Valente, 1993; Wehby, Symons, & Shores, 1995). Although reprimands can help to reduce inappropriate behavior (Abramowitz & O'Leary, 1990; Acker & O'Leary, 1987) and, in some cases, improve academic productivity as well (Abramowitz et al., 1988), there are several problems associated with the use—or rather, the overuse and misuse—of reprimands. First, reprimands can be highly disruptive to ongoing instruction, especially when they are long, loud, and delivered at a distance from the misbehaving student. Second, although reprimands may temporarily suppress inappropriate behavior, they lose their effectiveness if they are used excessively. Students rapidly habituate to frequent reprimands, so that teachers must increase the frequency and volume of their reprimands to obtain the same results, leading to an escalating cycle of student misbehavior followed by teacher reprimands of greater intensity but diminishing effectiveness. Third, peer attention can sustain student misbehavior, even in the context of teacher reprimands. In fact, by providing teacher attention for misbehavior, frequent reprimands can actually reinforce the very behaviors they are designed to reduce, especially for students who are at risk for aggression (Maag, 2001; Van Acker & Grant, 1996).

Dimensions of Effective Reprimands

Research on teacher–student communications has identified seven dimensions that enhance reprimand effectiveness: (1) promptness, (2) brevity, (3) softness, (4) proximity, (5) calmness, (6) eye contact, and (7) touch. *Promptness* is the single most important parameter in reprimand delivery. To be effective, reprimands should be delivered as soon as possible after the inappropriate behavior has occurred. Because peer attention serves as a competing reinforcer for misbehavior, even a 2-minute delay after the onset of off-task behavior can render reprimands ineffective (Abramowitz, Eckstrand, O'Leary, & Dulcan, 1992; Abramowitz & O'Leary, 1990). Second, short reprimands consisting of the student's name and no more than two other words are more effective than long reprimands, probably because short reprimands provide less attention for inappropriate behavior and are less likely to elicit arguments from misbehaving students (Abramowitz et al., 1988). Third, soft, private reprimands that are audible only to the target student can have a dramatic positive effect on behavior (Houghton et al., 1990), whereas loud, public reprimands are not only ineffective but can precipitate a cycle of misbehavior, followed by louder reprimands, followed by more disruptive behavior (Rosén, O'Leary, Joyce, Conway, & Pfiffner, 1984). Fourth, reprimands have little effect when delivered from a distance but produce a marked reduction in disruptive behavior when delivered close to (within 1 meter of) the misbehaving student (Van Houten, Nau, MacKenzie-Keating, Sameoto, & Colavecchia, 1982). Fifth, maintaining a calm, consistent tone of voice and keeping from becoming emotionally upset are critical to reprimand effectiveness (Rosén et al., 1984). Finally, the effectiveness of verbal reprimands is enhanced by eye contact (Everett, Olmi, Edwards, & Tingstrom, 2005; Hamlet, Axelrod, & Kuerschener, 1984), as well as by physical contact, such as a firm grasp of the student's shoulder (Van Houten et al., 1982). *Delivering Effective Reprimands* combines the first six dimensions to maximize the effectiveness of this form of teacher–student communication as a classroom management strategy. Because some students may misinterpret or respond negatively to any type of physical contact, touch is included only as a variation.

DELIVERING EFFECTIVE REPRIMANDS

Overview

Teachers use reprimands more often than any other strategy to control problem behavior. Despite their frequent use, reprimands are often ineffective in increasing on-task behavior or academic productivity and, when overused, can contribute to a negative classroom environment and actually intensify disruptive behavior. This intervention combines six elements that have been empirically demonstrated to enhance reprimand effectiveness: (1) promptness, (2) brevity, (3) softness, (4) proximity, (5) calmness, and (6) eye contact. Short, soft reprimands delivered with a calm demeanor and in close proximity to misbehaving or unproductive students are less embarrassing for students, and are thus less likely to provoke a confrontation or damage teacher–student relationships. Moreover, they interfere less with ongoing instruction, reduce teacher attention for inappropriate behavior, and elicit less peer attention that might reinforce the undesired behavior. The addition of touch has also been found to enhance the effectiveness of reprimands, at least for elementary grade students. Because many teachers are reluctant to use even positive touch because of concerns that it may be misinterpreted, however, the use of touch is included as a variation.

Purpose

To reduce off-task and disruptive behavior with systematic teacher-delivered reprimands.

Materials.

None.

Observation (Select One or More)

Option 1

1. Select an instructional period during which students are most disruptive and unproductive. Using a *Classwide Scanning Form,* scan the room every 3 to 5 minutes from left to right and tally the number of students in each of the following behavior categories:
   a. *On-task behavior,* defined as answering or asking lesson-oriented questions, looking at the teacher during instruction, sitting quietly and waiting for directions, or any other behavior consistent with the ongoing lesson or activity.

   b. *Off-task behavior,* defined as sitting without appropriate materials, looking at nonlesson materials, or looking around the room after assignments have been made.

   c. *Disruptive behavior,* defined as any behavior that disrupts the academic performance of another student, including making noises, calling out, and physical aggression.

2. Record these behaviors for 30 to 45 minutes for 4 to 7 days.

Option 2

1. Select a small group of students who frequently exhibit off-task or disruptive behavior during a selected instructional period. Using a *Group Interval Recording Form,* glance at a target student every 5 seconds and record the student's behavior at that instant as on-task, off-task, or disruptive as defined above.

2. Record behavior for each target student in turn for 30 to 45 minutes for 4 to 7 days.

Option 3

1. Calculate the class average percent-correct score for classwork during the selected instructional period for 5 to 10 days by summing individual student percent-correct scores and dividing by the total number of students.

Option 4

1. Using a sheet of paper attached to a clipboard, record the number of reprimands you deliver to the entire class or a target group of students during a selected instructional period for 4 to 7 days.

Intervention Steps

1. If this intervention is primarily directed toward a small group of students, move them near the front of the classroom or to an area that you can reach rapidly.

2. When a student exhibits an undesired behavior, immediately move to within touching distance, obtain eye contact if possible, and deliver a reprimand as described below.

   a. *Prompt:* Deliver the reprimand as soon as possible after you observe the inappropriate behavior.

   b. *Short:* Use a firm tone and deliver the reprimand in statement form with as few words as possible in addition to the student's name.

      Example: "Sam, stop talking!"

   c. *Soft:* Deliver the reprimand so that it is audible only to the student being reprimanded.

   d. *Close:* Deliver the reprimand near enough to the student to be able to obtain eye contact and within touching distance.

   e. *Calm:* Maintain emotional control. Use a calm, consistent tone of voice.

3. Try to catch the reprimanded student behaving appropriately within the next few minutes so you can provide praise for positive academic or social behavior.

Evaluation (Select One or More)

Option 1

1. Compare the percentages of on-task, off-task, and disruptive students during the selected instructional period before and after implementation.

Option 2

1. Compare on-task, off-task, and disruptive behavior rates for the target students during the selected instructional period before and after implementation.

Option 3

1. Compare the class average percent-correct score for daily classwork during the selected instructional period before and after implementation.

Option 4

1. Compare the number of reprimands delivered to the entire class or the target students during the selected instructional period before and after implementation.

Variation: Reprimands with Touch

1. If the student is off-task, gently lay a hand on the student's upper arm or shoulder for the duration of the reprimand (3 to 4 seconds). Do not use this variation if the student is exhibiting disruptive or aggressive behavior, if the student has a history of negative responses to physical touch, or if school policy discourages or forbids any form of physical contact with students.

Notes

1. Even if this intervention is directed primarily at one student or a small group of unproductive or disruptive students, effective reprimands should be used with all of the students in the class because of evidence of positive "spillover" effects. That is, class peers seated near target students receiving effective reprimands also show improvement in on-task behavior and productivity (Van Houten et al., 1982).
2. Because reprimand efficacy is most strongly related to promptness, this procedure requires frequent scanning of the room to detect potential problems.
3. Attempt to obtain eye contact when delivering reprimands, but do not force the student to look at you. Forcing eye contact may be shaming for some students and may provoke a confrontation. Moreover, if obtaining eye contact prolongs the length of the reprimand, the reprimand will be less effective.
4. Although maintaining emotional control can be very difficult when dealing with a provocative or chronically disruptive student, a calm demeanor and an even, consistent tone of voice are critical to reprimand effectiveness. Managing one's emotions prevents a power struggle, provides a model of self-control, and avoids damaging the teacher–student relationship. Moreover, field testing indicates that the ability to evoke a negative emotional reaction from a teacher can be highly reinforcing for certain students.

Sources

Abramowitz, A. J., O'Leary, S. G., & Futtersak, M. W. (1988). The relative impact of long and short reprimands on children's off-task behavior in the classroom. *Behavior Therapy, 19,* 243–247. Copyright 1988 by the Association for Behavioral and Cognitive Therapies. Adapted by permission.

Houghton, S., Wheldall, K., Jukes, R., & Sharpe, A. (1990). The effects of limited private reprimands and increased private praise on classroom behaviour in four British secondary school classes. *British Journal of Educational Psychology, 60,* 255–265. Copyright 1990 by the *British Journal of Educational Psychology.* © The British Psychological Society. Adapted by permission.

Rosén, L. A., O'Leary, S. G., Joyce, S. A., Conway, G., & Pfiffner, L. J. (1984). The importance of prudent negative consequences for maintaining the appropriate behavior of hyperactive students. *Journal of Abnormal Child Psychology, 12,* 581–604. Copyright 1984 by Springer Science and Business Media. Adapted by permission.

Van Houten, R., Nau, P. A., MacKenzie-Keating, S. E., Sameoto, D., & Colavecchia, B. (1982). An analysis of some variables influencing the effectiveness of reprimands. *Journal of Applied Behavior Analysis, 15,* 65–83. Copyright 1982 by the Society for the Experimental Analysis of Behavior. Adapted by permission.

Delivering Effective Commands

Prompt student compliance with teacher commands is essential to maintain an orderly learning environment and to maximize instructional time. Unfortunately, teacher requests and commands are not always effective in obtaining compliance and sometimes have little effect on student behavior (Ford, Olmi, Edwards, & Tingstrom, 2001; Matheson & Shriver, 2005; McIntyre & Brulle, 1989). These negative results are due in part to the ineffective and inconsistent manner in which teachers deliver commands. Teachers often phrase commands as rhetorical questions ("Marsha, why are you out of your seat?" "Timmy, what do you think you're doing?") that can lead to unproductive teacher–student exchanges and contribute to a negative classroom climate (Rathvon, 1996). Moreover, teachers often repeat commands, even when students are in the process of complying, and seldom follow compliance with either verbal or nonverbal positive social consequences (Shores et al., 1993). Delivering effective commands and following through with consequences if commands do not achieve compliance is especially important for students who display oppositional and defiant behavior patterns or are at risk for aggression (Arnold, McWilliams, & Arnold, 1998).

Dimensions of Effective Commands

Research on teacher–student communication and parent–child compliance training has identified six dimensions that maximize command effectiveness: (1) specificity, (2) positive statement commands, (3) a firm but calm and unemotional tone of voice, (4) proximity, (5) eye contact, and (6) praise for compliance. As with praise statements, commands should be *specific* to ensure that the student understands exactly what the teacher wants him or her to do (LaFleur et al., 1998). Delivering a command as a "do" versus a "don't" request (Houlihan & Jones, 1990; Neef, Shafer, Engel, Cataldo, & Parrish, 1983) while using a calm unemotional tone of voice (Ford et al., 2001; Rosén et al., 1984) is also associated with higher rates of compliance. Delivering the command in close proximity to the target student (Van Houten et al., 1982) and establishing and maintaining eye contact during command delivery also enhance effectiveness (Everett et al., 2005; Hamlet et al., 1984). Finally, a command should be followed by praise when the student complies (Ford et al., 2001).

The intervention in this section—*Delivering Effective Commands: The Precision Request Program*—is designed to achieve rapid compliance to teacher commands, especially in the case of chronically oppositional and defiant students, by means of the precision request procedure, a managerial sequence that incorporates these six dimensions. Originally developed as part of a parent training program for noncompliant children (Forehand & McMahon, 1981), *precision requests* consist of explicit directives, positive social reinforcement for compliance, and reductive techniques if compliance is not obtained (Neville & Jenson, 1984). The words "please" and "need" are used in the first and second requests, respectively, and serve as discriminative stimuli for the desired response. Precision requests increase the effectiveness of other reductive behavior strategies, such as time-out (Mackay, McLaughlin, Weber,

& Derby, 2001; Yeager & McLaughlin, 1995), and have been included in intervention packages targeting disruptive behavior in general education classrooms (De Martini-Scully et al., 2000) and special education settings (Musser, Bray, Kehle, & Jenson, 2001).

CROSS-REFERENCE: For an intervention that combines precision commands with a backup time-out system to improve compliance and on-task behavior in preschoolers, see *Improving Compliance with Precision Requests and a Time-Out Ribbon Procedure* in Chapter 6.

DELIVERING EFFECTIVE COMMANDS: THE PRECISION REQUEST PROGRAM

Overview

Obtaining rapid student compliance to teacher requests is critical in maintaining an orderly classroom and ensuring a high proportion of time for instruction. Unfortunately, teachers often use ineffective methods of attempting to gain compliance, such as asking questions rather than giving directives ("Why are you out of your seat?"), issuing several commands at the same time ("Alonso, stop bothering Maria, get back in your seat, and get going on those spelling sentences!"), or failing to wait long enough for students to comply with an initial request. As a result, valuable instructional time is lost in repeating commands and waiting for student compliance. Ineffective commands also provide opportunities for students to argue with the teacher, further reducing academic learning time and damaging teacher–student relationships. First developed as part of a parent training program for noncompliant children, the precision request program enhances command effectiveness with a structured sequence of instructions using specific words (*please* and *need*), positive social reinforcement, and backup consequences for noncompliance. Although precision requests can be used to obtain prompt compliance from all students, they are especially helpful with chronically oppositional students who resist teacher directives and become argumentative. A variation with a simple response cost group contingency is also presented.

Purpose

To obtain prompt student compliance with teacher directives by means of a structured command sequence.

Materials

1. Posterboard chart listing the classroom rules, such as:
   a. Do what the teacher asks you to do the first time you are asked.
   b. Raise your hand when you wish to speak.
   c. Keep your attention on the teacher or your own work.
   d. Stay in your seat unless you have permission to get out of it.
   e. Use kind and respectful language to everyone.

Observation (Select One or More)

Option 1

1. Using a sheet of paper attached to a clipboard, record the number of times the entire class or a group of target students fail to comply with an initial teacher request during a selected instructional period for 4 to 7 days.

2. If desired, calculate an average daily noncompliance rate for the class or group by dividing the number of compliance failures by the number of days observed.

Option 2

1. Using a sheet of paper with two columns attached to a clipboard, place a check in the first column (headed "Teacher Requests") each time you deliver a command to any student in the class or a group of target students during a selected instructional period. Place a check in the second column (headed "Student Compliance") each time the student complies with the command in the first 5 seconds.
2. Calculate the prompt compliance rate for the class or group by dividing the number of compliance acts by the total number of commands and multiplying the obtained value by 100. For example, if you deliver 30 commands during the period and students comply promptly to 12 of those commands, the prompt compliance rate is 40%.
3. Conduct these observations for 4 to 7 days.

Option 3

1. Using a *Group Interval Recording Form* with a 15-second interval and beginning at the left side of the room, glance at each student in turn and record a plus (+) if the student displays disruptive behavior at any time during the interval. *Disruptive behavior* is defined as failure to respond to teacher requests within 5 seconds, making noises, talking out of turn, being out of seat, or any other behavior interfering with one's own learning or that of other students.
2. Conduct these observations for 4 to 7 days.

Intervention Steps

1. To deliver a command, move to within 3 feet of the student, obtain eye contact, and make the request, beginning with the word *please*.

    Example: "Arthur, please get in line." Make the request in the form of a statement rather than a question and use a firm, calm, unemotional tone.

2. Make the request as specific as possible so that the student understands exactly what he or she is supposed to do without unduly lengthening the request.

    Example: "Kim, please sign off on the computer and join us at the reading table."

3. After making the request, wait approximately 5 seconds but do not interact with the student during the wait time. If the student complies with the request, provide praise, referring to the act of compliance or the specific requested behavior.

    Example: "Very good, Arthur, you got in line quickly," or "Kim, thank you for helping us start our reading circle on time."

4. If the student does not comply within the 5 seconds, repeat the request, using the word *need*.

    Example: "Arthur, you need to put away the markers and get in line," or "Kim, you need to log off the computer and come to the reading table."

    Use the same distance, eye contact, and tone of voice as in the first request.

5. After making the second request, wait an additional 5 seconds without interacting with the student. If the student complies with the second request, provide praise as in the first situation.

6. If the student still does not comply within 5 to 10 seconds after your second request, deliver the regular consequence for a rule infraction. Then repeat the second request, using the word *need*. If the student complies, praise the student's behavior. If the student does not comply, implement the next consequence in the classroom behavior management system.

Evaluation (Select One or More)

Option 1

1. Compare average noncompliance rates for the class or the group of target students during the selected instructional period before and after implementation.

Option 2

1. Compare prompt compliance rates for the entire class or the group of target students during the selected instructional period before and after implementation.

Option 3

1. Compare classwide disruptive behavior rates during the selected instructional period before and after implementation.

Variation: Precision Requests with Classwide Response Cost

1. List numerals in descending order from 20 to 0 on the chalkboard, with the highest number corresponding to the number of minutes available for recess. Explain that you will cross off a number each time you must repeat a direction more than once and that the class will spend that many minutes reviewing the rules in the classroom before going to recess for whatever minutes are remaining.
2. Each time that a student fails to comply with a request within 5 seconds, cross off a number in descending order or direct a nearby student to do so.
3. At the end of the intervention period, use *Active Teaching of Classroom Rules* to conduct a rule review for as many minutes as numbers are crossed off. Provide recess for whatever minutes are remaining in the regular recess period.

Notes

1. Field testing indicates that this intervention is especially useful for beginning teachers, who often have difficulty delivering effective commands.
2. As Step 6 indicates, be sure to deliver another request, even after administering the consequence. This gives students the message that they cannot avoid complying with teacher commands.
3. Having a backup plan is essential if students continue to be noncompliant after the second request. The next section of this chapter includes two interventions that are appropriate for this purpose: (a) *Sit and Watch: Teaching Prosocial Behaviors*, a nonexclusionary time-out procedure designed for preschool and primary grade students, and (b) *Debriefing: Helping Students Solve Their Own Behavior Problems*, a collaborative problem-solving strategy designed for older students.

Source

De Martini-Scully, D., Bray, M. A., & Kehle, T. J. (2000). A packaged intervention to reduce disruptive behaviors in general education students. *Psychology in the Schools, 37,* 149–156. Copyright 2000 by John Wiley & Sons, Inc. Adapted by permission.

TASK 6: TEACHING PROSOCIAL BEHAVIORS

Helping students learn and practice socially responsible behavior has long been a goal of the American educational system (Gresham, 2002b; Wentzel, 1991). Moreover, because of the declining influence of other traditional socializing agents such as the family, the community, and religious institutions, today's schools are assuming a larger role in children's prosocial development (Sharpe & Crider, 1996). The importance of implementing school-based prosocial interventions is underscored by research indicating that social skills, such as cooperation and self-control, are powerful predictors of academic success, beginning as early as kindergarten (Agostin & Bain, 1997; Malecki & Elliott, 2002; McClelland, Morrison, & Holmes, 2000). In a 17-year prospective longitudinal study, Teo, Carlson, Mathieu, Egeland, and Sroufe (1996) found that socioemotional adjustment in school was a reliable predictor of academic achievement at grades 1, 3, 6, and again at age 16, even after controlling for cognitive ability and prior achievement. Although the exact nature of the relationship between social skills and achievement is unclear, prosocial behavior appears to create an interpersonal context characterized by self-regulation, cooperation, and adaptive responses to conflict that is conducive to the development of positive academic and social goals (Wentzel, 1991, 1993).

Interventions designed to help students acquire key social competencies have often produced only modest effects, with limited evidence that trained students go on to apply those skills in their natural social environments or maintain them over time (Lane, 1999; Mathur & Rutherford, 1996). Empirical support is especially limited for the efficacy of social skills interventions with high-risk students, including students with aggressive and antisocial behavior patterns and students with disabilities (Bullis, Walker, & Sprague, 2001; Mathur, Kavale, Quinn, Forness, & Rutherford, 1998; Quinn, Kavale, Mathur, Rutherford, & Forness, 1999). The failure to achieve generalization may be related to the fact that the majority of social skills intervention studies have been conducted in settings outside of general education classrooms and by researchers or specially trained personnel rather than by teachers. For maximum generalization and maintenance, however, training should be delivered in natural contexts, such as classrooms and playgrounds, to encourage skill use and facilitate reinforcement opportunities arising from positive teacher and peer responses (Gresham, 1998; Sheridan, Hungelmann, & Maughan, 1999). Moreover, it is critical to involve teachers as intervention agents because of their ability to prompt and reinforce socially responsible behaviors during the course of everyday school activities (Lo, Loe, & Cartledge, 2002). At the same time, however, teachers cannot interrupt instruction to conduct a social skills lesson whenever inappropriate behavior occurs. Instead, teachers can help students acquire and practice critical prosocial skills by means of strategies that incorporate *incidental teaching,* an instructional practice that capitalizes on naturally occurring events in teacher–student interactions and daily routines to teach socially responsible behavior (Barnett et al., 1999; Gresham, 2002b).

Interventions for Teaching Prosocial Behaviors

The two interventions in this section incorporate incidental teaching procedures to help students learn critical prosocial behaviors in naturalistic contexts—the first in the form of a structured observation that can be conducted in the classroom or in other school areas, such as the playground or the cafeteria, and the second in the form of a problem-solving interview that can be conducted in the classroom, hallway, or an administrative office. *Sit and Watch: Teaching Prosocial Behaviors* is based on *contingent observation,* a strategy that combines a nonexclusionary time-out with incidental teaching and choice making. Unlike the typical time-out, in which the target student is removed from the setting in which the misbehavior occurred, here the misbehaving student is briefly removed to the classroom periphery and prompted to observe his or her appropriately behaving peers. *Sit and Watch* is a keystone strategy in a comprehensive classroom management system because it teaches social competencies critical to school success, such as compliance and self-control, while also preventing misbehavior from escalating into a major disturbance and damaging teacher–student relationships. Moreover, it minimizes interruptions to instruction, especially if the variation with a self-management component is implemented. The strategy has been demonstrated to be highly effective in reducing disruptive behavior and increasing appropriate social behaviors for preschoolers in day care settings (Porterfield, Herbert-Jackson, & Risley, 1976), primary grade students in regular education (Fleece, O'Brien, & Drabman, 1981), and students with developmental disabilities in special education settings (Mace & Heller, 1990). A variation has also been validated for use in recess and physical education classes (White & Bailey, 1990).

Debriefing: Helping Students Solve Their Own Behavior Problems consists of a structured protocol for prompting or teaching prosocial behaviors in specific situations to disruptive or noncompliant students and preparing them to transition successfully back into the classroom. Based on the Life Space Interviewing procedures often implemented with students with behavior disorders (Gardner, 1990; Wood, 1990), debriefing is intended to be used when group-oriented interventions have been unsuccessful in improving behavior and in the context of an overall classroom management program. Although debriefing is delivered after misbehavior has occurred, it is included in this section because it can prevent future behavior problems by helping students acquire positive alternative strategies for coping with stressful situations.

SIT AND WATCH: TEACHING PROSOCIAL BEHAVIORS

Overview

Children often misbehave because they have not learned the appropriate skills in social situations or have not been held accountable for their behavior. This keystone intervention uses *contingent observation*, which combines instruction with a brief time-out, to teach students prosocial behaviors they are not presently displaying. As a proactive classroom management strategy, it not only increases instructional opportunities for disruptive students and their classmates by minimizing the time needed for behavior sanctioning, but also helps to prevent inappropriate behavior from escalating by avoiding punitive strategies that can provoke arguments and confrontations. Originally implemented with preschool children in a day care setting, the procedure has also been validated with elementary grade students in regular and special education classrooms. Teachers in the preschool and early primary grades indicate that successful use of this strategy is critical in creating an orderly classroom. Two variations are included: one with a self-management component that reduces the amount of teacher monitoring needed and one for physical education classes and/or the playground.

Purpose

To teach children appropriate social behaviors with guided observation and a brief time-out.

Materials

1. "Sit and Watch chair," placed on the edge of classroom activities (e.g., in a corner but facing the class rather than the wall) with or without a "Sit and Watch Chair" label affixed to it.

2. "Quiet Place" in the classroom, consisting of a comfortable chair or pillow on a rug placed as far away as possible from the center of classroom activity.
3. Backup "Quiet Place" in another classroom or the school office, consisting of a comfortable chair placed as far away as possible from the center of activity but still observable.
4. Posterboard chart listing the classroom rules, such as:
   a. Follow the teacher's directions.
   b. Be polite and kind to others.
   c. Finish all your work.
   d. Respect others and their property.

Materials for Variation 2

1. Posterboard chart listing the rules for physical education or recess, such as:
   a. Follow the teacher's and aide's directions.
   b. Line up promptly when you are called.
   c. Use equipment safely.
   d. Play so that everyone can have fun.
2. Two or three kitchen timers (optional).

Observation (Select One or Both)

1. Using a *Group Event Recording Form*, tally the number of disruptive behaviors for the entire class or a group of target students during a selected instructional period or interval, such as the first 2 hours of the day, for 4 to 7 days. *Disruptive behaviors* are defined as aggression, crying or whining, having tantrums, damaging toys or classroom materials, and interfering with the task-related behavior of other students.
2. Using a sheet of paper attached to a clipboard, record the number of reprimands you deliver to the entire class or to one or more target students during a selected instructional period or interval for 4 to 7 days.

Intervention Steps

Introduction and Training

1. Display the chart with the classroom rules and discuss the rationale for each rule. For young students, use a chart with pictured rules.
2. Point out the Sit and Watch chair and explain that you will be telling students who forget to follow the classroom rules to sit in the chair for a short time and watch the other students behaving appropriately.
3. Also point out the Quiet Place and explain that this is a place for students who have trouble sitting in the Sit and Watch chair.
4. Teach the Sit and Watch procedures as described below, using *Say Show Check: Teaching Classroom Procedures*.
5. Then guide a student who typically displays appropriate behavior through a role play of the procedures while the other students observe. Select a second student and include a visit to the Quiet Place as part of the role play.

Implementation

1. When inappropriate behavior occurs, first describe it to the misbehaving student:
   "Andy, don't hit other children at your table."
2. Then describe what would have been appropriate behavior in the situation:

"Keep your hands to yourself when you are doing your work."

3. Tell the student to go to the Sit and Watch chair and observe the appropriate social behavior of the other students.

"Go to the Sit and Watch chair and watch how the other children work without hitting." (Escort preschoolers to the chair until they are accustomed to the routine.)

4. When the student has been watching quietly for a brief period (about 1 minute for preschoolers, 3 minutes for older children), ask if he or she is ready to rejoin the activity and display the appropriate behavior:

"Do you know how to work without hitting now?"

5. If the student indicates by nodding or verbalizing readiness to return, allow him or her to do so. If the student does not respond or responds negatively, tell him or her to sit and watch until ready to perform the appropriate behavior:

"Sit here and watch the children until you think you can do your work without hitting others."

6. When the student has been sitting quietly for another brief period, return to the student and repeat Steps 4 and 5.

7. When the student returns to the group, give positive attention for appropriate behavior as soon as possible:

"Good, you're doing your work without hitting others."

8. If the student cries for more than a few minutes or refuses to sit quietly so that other children's activities are disturbed, take him or her to the Quiet Place in the classroom. Explain the reason for the removal by saying:

"Since you can't sit quietly here, you need to go to the Quiet Place and practice sitting quietly."

9. When the student is calm and is sitting quietly in the Quiet Place, ask if he or she is ready to sit quietly and watch. Return the student to the Sit and Watch chair after a positive response and continue from Step 3. If the student continues to be disruptive or gives a negative response, tell him or her to continue to sit quietly.

"Practice sitting quietly and I will ask you again in a few minutes if you're ready to return to the group."

10. If the student continues to be very distressed or disruptive after another query, implement the backup Quiet Place as described above.

Evaluation (Select One or Both)

1. Compare the frequency of disruptive behaviors for the entire class or for the target students during the selected instructional period or interval before and after implementation.

2. Compare the frequency of reprimands delivered to the entire class or the target students during the selected instructional period or interval before and after implementation.

Variations

Variation 1: Sit and Watch with Self-Management Component

1. Instead of approaching students in the Sit and Watch chair and asking them if they are ready to return to the group, teach them to raise their hands to indicate their readiness to return. With this variation, the teacher does not need to interrupt instruction to interact with the student.

Variation 2: Sit and Watch in Physical Education Classes or on the Playground

1. At the beginning of the physical education period or in the classroom before recess, explain to students that they will be learning a new way of helping everyone have more fun during physical education or recess.
2. Display the chart with the rules for physical education or recess and discuss the purpose of each rule.
3. Designate a Sit and Watch location, such as against one wall of the gymnasium or on one side of the playground.
4. Demonstrate the Sit and Watch procedures, and have several students role-play going to the Sit and Watch area. If you will be using timers, teach students how to set them for 3 minutes.
5. When a student breaks a rule or engages in unsafe or inappropriate behavior, send the student to the Sit and Watch area. If you are using timers, the student must sit down, set the timer to ring in 3 minutes, and stay in the area until the timer has rung. Otherwise, the student must sit down in the Sit and Watch area until you signal that he or she may rejoin the group. Release the student after he or she has been sitting quietly for about 3 minutes. Continue to observe the student so that you can provide praise for appropriate behavior as soon as possible.
6. Be sure to monitor the student in the Sit and Watch area and not to place children too closely together when more than one child is removed from the group.
7. Students who are sent to Sit and Watch twice in one period must remain in the Sit and Watch area for 6 minutes on the second occasion.
8. If students are sent to Sit and Watch three times in one period, they must remain in the Sit and Watch location for the rest of the physical education or recess period.
9. Students who tattle on others or talk to a student in Sit and Watch must go to Sit and Watch.

Notes

1. Field testing indicates that additional positive behavior support may be needed to help very defiant and/or undercontrolled young children respond appropriately to the Sit and Watch procedures. Conduct an individual role play with the target student prior to implementation and praise the student for compliance during the rehearsal. If the student is subsequently sent to Sit and Watch and either resists going to the chair or attempts to get out of it before being released, deliver a *Precision Command* at eye level (e.g., "You need to sit in the Sit and Watch chair and watch the other students playing without hitting until I tell you that you can get up"). Then stand near the chair so that you can return the student promptly to the chair if needed.
2. Providing a backup Quiet Place in another location, such as a nearby classroom or the principal's office, is essential to the success of this strategy. In these cases, arrange for the student to be escorted to the other classroom or the office by a teacher's aide or another staff member. Practice the entire procedure with the target student and the participating staff members and discuss it with the student's parents. Ask staff members to interact with the student as little as possible during the Quiet Place time. These out-of-class time-outs should last no longer than 15 minutes, depending on the age of the child, and should be followed in the classroom by returning the child to the Quiet Place and continuing from Step 8.

Sources

Porterfield, J. K., Herbert-Jackson, E., & Risley, T. R. (1976). Contingent observation: An effective and acceptable procedure for reducing disruptive behavior of young children in a group setting. *Journal of Applied Behavior Analysis, 9*, 55–64. Copyright 1976 by the Society for the Experimental Analysis of Behavior. Adapted by permission.

White, A. G., & Bailey, J. S. (1990). Reducing disruptive behaviors of elementary physical education students with sit and watch. *Journal of Applied Behavior Analysis, 23*, 353–359.

DEBRIEFING: HELPING STUDENTS
SOLVE THEIR OWN BEHAVIOR PROBLEMS

Overview

When problem behavior occurs, the consequences typically available to teachers may be only temporarily effective in modifying the inappropriate behavior, especially in the case of chronically unproductive or noncompliant students. If a student persists in behaving ineffectively, teachers are likely to deliver more punitive consequences, creating an escalating cycle of problem behavior and negative teacher response that damages the teacher–student relationship and reduces learning opportunities for all students. Debriefing consists of a set of structured teacher–student interactions that follow the application of consequences for problem behavior and are designed to help students identify and use socially acceptable behaviors when they confront challenging situations. Debriefing has three basic steps: (1) identifying the circumstances triggering the problem behavior, (2) reminding the student of a socially acceptable replacement response (or teaching it if the behavior has not been acquired), and (3) preparing the student to resume the classroom routine. As part of the debriefing strategy, the student completes a written form that serves as a plan for the alternative prosocial behavior. Debriefing not only reduces misbehavior by teaching appropriate replacement behaviors, but it also improves the teacher–student relationship by interrupting the misbehavior–punishment cycle. Often implemented in special education settings and by school disciplinary staff in the context of an office referral, debriefing can also be conducted by regular classroom teachers in one-to-one or small-group formats. Three variations are included: (1) a teacher-delivered version with a delayed debriefing session, (2) a teacher-delivered version without a writing component for minor rule infractions, and (3) a version for implementation by office disciplinary personnel.

Purpose

To help chronically disruptive or unproductive students develop and use positive alternative behaviors by means of structured problem-solving conferences.

Materials

1. Debriefing form (see Figure 3.2 on p. 126).

Observation (Select One or More)

1. Using a *Group Event Recording Form,* record the frequency of one or more problem behaviors for one or more target students during a selected instructional period. For example, tally the number of call-outs, out-of-seats, or acts of noncompliance for 4 to 7 days.
2. On a sheet of paper attached to a clipboard, record the number of reprimands you deliver to one or more target students during a selected instructional period for 4 to 7 days.
3. Calculate the number of office disciplinary referrals for a target student, a group of target students, or the entire class for the previous month.

Intervention Steps

1. When an incident of problem behavior occurs, call the student displaying the problem behavior to your desk or an area of the classroom where conversation can be as private as possible.

Quickly and quietly administer or assign the usual consequence for the rule infraction (e.g., points lost from behavior chart, office referral, lunchtime detention).

2. After the student has completed the consequence, talk with the student briefly about the factors that may have contributed to the problem and how the student might manage the situation more appropriately next time (see Figure 3.3 for a sample debriefing session).

3. Give the student a debriefing form (see Figure 3.2), and allow time for the student to complete it at his or her desk. If time does not permit, have the student return the completed form the following day and review it with him or her as described below.

4. When the student has completed the form, ask him or her to read it aloud and elaborate upon the written response. Praise efforts to identify alternative prosocial behaviors and provide corrective feedback and suggestions as needed. Make sure the form is legible.

5. To underscore the importance of the debriefing form and problem-solving process, have the student sign the form. Make copies of the form for the student, office disciplinary staff, and yourself, and send a copy home for the parent/guardian to sign and return with the student.

6. To help determine whether the student is prepared to cooperate with adult directives and participate appropriately in the normal classroom routine, ask the student what he or she is expected to do at this time and whether he or she is ready to rejoin the class activity. If time and circumstances permit, have the student role-play more appropriate ways of responding.

7. If the student does not appear ready to resume the normal classroom routine, administer a modified time-out (e.g., sitting quietly with or without head down on the desk for 2 minutes), and then visit with the student again to assess readiness for a successful transition.

8. Arrange for the student to experience success as soon as possible in the classroom and provide positive attention for prosocial behaviors.

9. Talk with the student again in the next few days to review his or her progress in responding appropriately to the problem situation and other circumstances previously associated with ineffective behavior and provide support for acceptable alternative responses.

Evaluation (Select One or More)

1. Compare the frequency of the problem behavior(s) displayed by the target student(s) during the selected instructional period before and after implementation.

2. Compare the frequency of reprimands delivered to the target student(s) during the selected instructional period before and after implementation.

3. Compare the number of office disciplinary referrals for problem behavior for a target student, a group of target students, or the entire class before and after implementation.

Variations

Variation 1: Delayed Debriefing

1. Although debriefing is most effective when it is conducted immediately after the student has served the consequence and before he or she resumes the regular classroom routine, teacher-conducted sessions must sometimes be postponed until there is an opportunity for conferencing (e.g., lunchtime, recess, packing up to go home, homeroom advisory period). In this event, give the debriefing form to the student after the consequence has been served, have the student complete the form and return it, and conduct the debriefing session as soon as circumstances permit.

Variation 2: Debriefing Without a Written Plan

1. In situations in which the problem behavior is less serious, administer an in-seat time-out and omit the writing requirement. For example, if a student crumples up a paper and throws it on

the floor when told to correct the paper, quietly direct the student to fold his or her arms and put his or her head down on the desk for 30 seconds. Tell the student that you will talk with him or her later about solving the problem.

2. After the student has completed the time-out and after an interval of about 10 minutes, move to the student's desk and in a quiet, calm tone of voice, indicate the following: (a) a more appropriate manner of responding in the same situation and (b) the consequence if the behavior continues (e.g., the student will have to miss recess or have an office disciplinary referral). Also provide support for successfully resuming the classroom routine (e.g., indicate how to get started in correcting the paper).

3. Be sure to praise the student when he or she begins displaying the appropriate behavior.

Variation 3: Debriefing by Office Disciplinary Staff

1. For implementation by office staff, conduct the debriefing session as described above but outside of the classroom. Give a copy of the completed debriefing form to the student's teacher and ask the teacher to review it within 24 hours and talk with the student about what he or she will do differently the next time the problem circumstances arise. Teachers should avoid dwelling on the misbehavior in favor of reintegrating the student into the classroom and arranging success experiences as soon as possible.

Notes

1. The key to successful implementation of this strategy is maintaining the focus on helping the student to acquire appropriate prosocial behaviors rather than using the debriefing session to recall previous rule infractions. Role playing with a colleague or consultant prior to implementation can be very helpful in avoiding a resumption of the misbehavior–punishment cycle.

2. Have students complete the debriefing form themselves only if they are willing to do so and have the necessary writing skills. For students who are very distressed, are young, or have limited reading or writing skills, completing the form may be difficult or aversive and may lead to an escalation of the inappropriate behavior. In that case, the teacher or staff member should read the questions to the student and write in the responses. Alternately, implement Variation 2, especially if the problem behavior is not severe.

3. If a small group of students displays a pattern of disruptive behaviors in the classroom (e.g., excessive socializing, arguing), conducting a debriefing session with the entire group can both be productive and time-efficient. Debriefing interviews with groups of more than three students are not recommended, however, because of the possibility of peer reinforcement for negative behaviors.

4. The debriefing form can serve as a written record of the behavior incident for inclusion in the student's file or for use in a teacher–parent–student conference. As in the debriefing session, the conference should focus on encouraging home support for prosocial alternative behaviors rather than simply discussing previous incidents of inappropriate behavior. If the problem persists, a functional behavioral assessment (FBA) should be conducted to develop an individualized behavior support plan that specifies an acceptable replacement response for the problem behavior and arranges the classroom environment to maximize opportunities for the student to display the prosocial rather than the problem behavior.

Source

Sugai, G., & Colvin, G. (1997). Debriefing: A transition step for promoting acceptable behavior. *Education and Treatment of Children, 20*, 209–221. Copyright 1997 by West Virginia University Press. Adapted by permission.

CHOOSING BETTER BEHAVIOR

Student name: _____   Grade: _____

Teacher name: _____   Date: _____

1. What problem behavior did you have?
2. When, where, and why did the problem behavior happen?
3. What will you do next time instead of having the problem behavior?
4. What do you need to do after you complete this form?
5. Do you need any help after you complete this form? If so, what?

Student signature: _____

Teacher/staff member signature: _____

Parent/guardian signature: _____

Copies to: _____ student _____ teacher _____ principal _____ parent/guardian

FIGURE 3.2. Sample debriefing form. Adapted from Sugai and Colvin (1997, p. 215). Copyright 1997 by West Virginia University Press. Adapted by permission.

SAMPLE DEBRIEFING SESSION

CASEY: [balling up math paper and throwing it on the floor]: Dumb old stuff!

TEACHER: [approaching the student's desk and using a quiet tone] Casey, crumpling up your paper and throwing it on the floor when you're asked to redo a math problem is not acceptable. You will need to serve a lunchtime detention today. I'll talk with you after that to see what we can do to prevent this problem from happening again.

> [After the student has completed the consequence] TEACHER: Casey, I'd like to understand what made you upset in algebra class so we can make a plan to solve the problem.

CASEY: I just don't get this new stuff with two unknowns. You go too fast! And if I flunk algebra, I'll have to go to summer school and then my mom won't let me get a job.

TEACHER: I'm hearing that you got upset because you weren't sure how to do your classwork and because you're worried about your grade. Getting comfortable with algebra can take a while. Can you think of a better way to handle this if you run into this situation again?

CASEY: I guess I could ask for help or something.

TEACHER: Right. When you ask a question in class, that lets me know you don't understand something. Now, I'd like you to use this form to write down your ideas about solving the problem. Raise your hand to let me know if you need any help with the form. I'll check back with you in a few minutes after everyone gets started on the assignment. [Student completes form and returns it to the teacher]

TEACHER: [reading over the form]: Asking for help when you don't understand sounds like a good strategy. What about staying after school on math Tuesdays for some extra practice?

CASEY: I guess I could do that if my mom will pick me up.

TEACHER: That's great! Extra practice in algebra really makes a difference, especially when you're learning a new type of equation. Let's add that to your plan. [Student writes in additional suggestions] OK, you've got some good ideas here. I'll look forward to seeing you at 3:00 tomorrow, then. Be sure to bring a note so I know you have a ride home. Now we'll sign the form, and I'll get a copy for you to take home before you leave school today. I'd like you to go over it with your mom and bring it back to me signed tomorrow. And how about if we visit again in a couple of days to make sure everything's back on track?

CASEY: OK.

TEACHER: Good. Now, what do you need to do for the rest of class?

CASEY: Ask if I need help and don't mess up my papers.

TEACHER: That's right. Are you ready to join the class?

CASEY: Yeah, I guess so.

TEACHER: Great!

FIGURE 3.3. Sample debriefing session. Adapted from Sugai and Colvin (1997). Copyright 1997 by West Virginia University Press. Adapted by permission.

TASK 7: BUILDING POSITIVE RELATIONSHIPS IN THE CLASSROOM

In recent years, there has been an increasing recognition of the importance of the social aspects of classroom management in developing and maintaining effective learning environments (Carter & Doyle, 2006; Nucci, 2006; Pianta, 2006). An accumulating body of evidence attests to the critical role of teacher–student relationships in students' academic success or failure (Birch & Ladd, 1997; Hamre & Pianta, 2001; Pianta, Steinberg, & Rollins, 1995), relationships with classroom peers (Birch & Ladd, 1998; Howes, 2000; Hughes, Cavell, & Willson, 2001), and development or acceleration of disruptive and aggressive behavior patterns (Hamre & Pianta, 2001; Hughes, Cavell, & Jackson, 1999; Ladd & Burgess, 2001). The significant associations between teacher–student relationships measured early in elementary school and children's subsequent academic and social outcomes hold even after controlling for children's initial levels of achievement and adjustment (Hamre & Pianta, 2001; Hughes et al., 1999; Meehan, Hughes, & Cavell, 2003). Similarly, students' feelings of relatedness to teachers are key predictors of classroom behavior and academic motivation and performance for elementary grade students (Furrer & Skinner, 2003) as well as middle school students (Bru, Stephens, & Torsheim, 2002; Klem & Connell, 2004).

Relationship-enhancing interventions are especially important for students who are at risk for academic failure and conflictual teacher–student relationships, including boys (Birch & Ladd, 1997; Hamre & Pianta, 2001), students living in poverty (Silver, Measelle, Armstrong, & Essex, 2005), students with disabilities (Murray & Greenberg, 2001), students from minority backgrounds (Meehan et al., 2003; Saft & Pianta, 2001), and students with problem behavior (Decker, Dona, & Christenson, 2007; Silver et al., 2005). Close, supportive teacher–student relationships appear to serve as a protective factor for children who are at risk for academic or social failure. Children at risk for retention or referral to special education who have positive relationships with their teachers are less likely to be retained or referred than are children who have conflictual relationships with their teachers (Pianta et al., 1995). In addition, conflictual teacher–student relationships in kindergarten are harbingers of an acceleration in externalizing behavior problems across the early primary grades, whereas close teacher–student relationships are associated with significant declines in externalizing behavior problems, with the effects especially strong for children with the highest levels of behavior problems at school entry (Silver et al., 2005). Supportive relationships with teachers may be especially important at transition points, such as the transition to kindergarten (Silver et al., 2005), the transition to elementary school (Birch & Ladd, 1997; Hamre & Pianta, 2001), and the transition from elementary to middle school (Wentzel, 1998).

Teacher–Student Relationships and Classroom Management

A growing body of evidence documents that interventions designed to enhance the quality of teacher–student relationships are also associated with improvements in key indicators of well-managed classrooms (see Pianta, 2006, for a review). Especially after the early primary grades, positive teacher–student relationships play a crucial role in successful classroom management because student cooperation with established rules and routines is essential if teachers are to create and maintain an orderly learning environment. Research has demonstrated that perceptions of teacher emotional support strongly influence students' motivation to cooperate, follow classroom rules, and adopt prosocial values and goals (Bru et al., 2002; Cothran et al., 2003; Wentzel, 1998, 2002). Moreover, relationship-based interventions have potential benefits for teachers as well as students. Interventions that enhance the quality of teacher–student relationships are associated not only with improvements in student outcomes and classroom climate but also with increases in teachers' job satisfaction, sense of self-efficacy, and emotional well-being (Battistich, Solomon, Watson, & Schaps, 1997; Pianta, 1999, 2006).

Promoting Positive Peer Relationships in the Classroom

Positive peer relationships also play a crucial role in fostering a sense of community in the classroom and encouraging academic productivity and prosocial behavior for all students (Elias & Dilworth, 2003; Wang et al., 1993). Numerous studies have documented that student–student interactions and peer influence processes have as much or more impact on the quality of school and classroom climate than adult–student interactions (Emmer & Gerwels, 2006; Horner et al., 2004) and are especially important in orienting students toward academic learning and academic effort (Furrer & Skinner, 2003; Wentzel, 1998, 1999). Consultants often receive referrals from teachers struggling to cope with students who display peer-to-peer aggression, including arguing, bullying, and teasing. This kind of peer-directed aggression is not only highly disruptive to instruction but is likely to spread and escalate because peer attention reinforces the inappropriate behavior. Over time, classroom social norms may come to support negative behavior and discourage positive behavior because of the influence of peer models for inappropriate behavior and the operation of *deviancy training* (Emmer & Gerwels, 2006). Strategies enhancing positive peer relationships are especially important to academic outcomes in classrooms in which teachers use collaborative learning structures. With collaborative instructional formats, the success of each group and the learning activity as a whole depends in large part on students' peer-related social skills and interactions, including the willingness to listen to each other, work toward a common goal, and solve conflicts adaptively (Carter & Doyle, 2006).

DEVIANCY TRAINING: PEER TEACHING OF ANTISOCIAL BELIEFS AND BEHAVIORS

School-based interventions designed to shape peer influence processes in positive directions are especially important in classrooms with high percentages of students with low academic skills and problem behaviors. In these settings, peers are likely to model and reinforce antisocial behaviors, leading to the establishment of peer norms that reject teacher authority and school achievement, a process that has been termed *deviancy training* (Dishion, Patterson, Stoolmiller, & Skinner, 1991; Dishion, Spracklen, Andrews, & Patterson, 1996). These negative peer influence processes contribute to classroom and school climates in which students with antisocial attitudes reject academic achievement and prosocial behaviors displayed by their peers and reinforce inappropriate behavior and antiauthoritarian attitudes (Hughes, 2002). Over time, antisocial and antiachievement beliefs and behaviors become the norm, with students rejecting typical school rewards, such as teacher praise and good grades, in favor of peer attention and reinforcement for deviant behavior. Moreover, contrary to the usual link between aggression and peer rejection, peer acceptance is positively related to aggression in these high-aggression settings (Stormshak et al., 1999). Although children may be most vulnerable to deviancy training in adolescence, when peers have powerful effects on each other's attitudes, values, and aspirations and when exposure to peer antisocial behavior is associated with rapid increases in problem behavior, the phenomenon has been documented as early as kindergarten (Snyder et al., 2005). Especially in view of evidence that peer-related social skills taught in artificial environments do not generalize to natural settings and have minimal effects on peer relationships (DuPaul & Eckert, 1994; Mathur et al., 1998), interventions that target the classroom socialization context have far greater potential to combat negative peer influence processes (Hughes, 2002).

Interventions Promoting Positive Classroom Relationships

With the increasing awareness of the critical importance of supportive relationships for students in the school setting, empirically based interventions directly targeting school relationship processes are now appearing in the literature (Anderson, Christenson, Sinclair, & Lehr, 2004; Burchinal, Peisner-Feinberg, Pianta, & Howes, 2002; Conduct Problems Prevention Research Group, 2002; Hughes et al., 2001; Rimm-Kaufman et al., 2007). Although the outcomes of these efforts have been encouraging, many relationship-enhancing programs are designed for schoolwide rather than classroom implementation and require special curricular materials, extensive training for intervention agents, supplementary services for students and parents, and other resources not available to classroom teachers. This section includes two validated and highly usable interventions that focus on classroom relationships, one targeting teacher–student relationships and the other targeting student–student relationships. Based on procedures in Barkley's (1987) parent training program for defiant children, *Banking Time* involves teachers in providing regular brief sessions of nondirective, relationship-building interactions with individual target students, small groups of target students, or the entire class in a small-group format. During these sessions, teachers offer nonevaluative messages of safety, predictability, and support for learning rather than evaluation of skills or performance. The strategy is called "Banking Time" because it is designed to "save up" positive experiences that teachers and students can "draw on" during times of stress, so the teacher–student relationship can survive conflict without resuming the negative cycle of interactions. Strengthening teacher–student relationships in this manner not only enhances teachers' effectiveness as classroom managers by reducing relational conflict but also serves as a protective factor for children at risk for severe behavior problems (Pianta et al., 1995; Pianta et al., 2003).

The second intervention targets peer–peer relationships with structured classwide praise sessions. *Tootling: Enhancing Student Relationships with Peer Reporting, Public Posting, and Group Contingencies* is based on the assumption that reinforcement in the classroom context is essential if students are to learn and practice appropriate social behaviors. Under typical punishment-based classroom disciplinary systems, students may spend so much time monitoring their peers' socially inappropriate behavior that they fail to observe or reinforce instances of incidental peer prosocial behavior. To counteract this tendency, *Tootling* uses public posting and an interdependent group contingency to encourage students to report each other's positive behaviors that occur during the course of the school day, with the goal of building a sense of community in the classroom. Studies in elementary classrooms have demonstrated that students can easily learn the tootling procedure and that public posting and group rewards increase tootling rates, with students observing and reporting many instances of their classmates' prosocial behavior (Cashwell, Skinner, & Smith, 2001; Skinner, Cashwell, & Skinner, 2000).

CROSS-REFERENCE: For a version of *Tootling* that specifically targets socially rejected or isolated students, see *Positive Peer Reporting* in Chapter 5.

BUILDING POSITIVE TEACHER–STUDENT RELATIONSHIPS WITH BANKING TIME

Overview

Positive teacher–student relationships are critical not only to children's academic and social development but also to effective classroom management because student cooperation is essential to a productive, disruption-free classroom. In the *Banking Time* (BT) intervention, teachers provide brief sessions of focused, nondirective interactions that convey messages of safety, predictability, and support for exploration rather than evaluation of performance. First developed to improve teachers' relationships with individual children at risk for behavior disorders and to help prevent teacher burnout, the strategy is called "Banking Time" because the sessions are designed to help teachers and students "invest" positive interactions to "draw on" during stressful times, so that the teacher–child relationship can survive conflict without resuming the negative cycle of interactions. BT has also been validated as a classroom-level intervention by incorporating sessions into a small-group activity format. By rotating through groups of five or six students, teachers can conduct BT sessions with each student two or three times a week. The original individual student format is included as a variation.

Purpose

To promote positive teacher–student relationships and create a supportive climate for learning with regular sessions of nondirective teacher–student interactions.

Materials

None.

Observation (Select One or More)

Option 1

1. Using a *Group Event Recording Form*, record the frequency of one or more inappropriate and disruptive behaviors, such as call-outs, making noises, arguing, and out-of-seats, for a target student, a group of target students, or the entire class.
2. Conduct these observations for 30 to 45 minutes during a selected instructional period for 4 to 7 days.

Option 2

1. On a sheet of paper attached to a clipboard, record the number of reprimands you deliver to a target student, a group of target students, or the entire class during a selected instructional period for 4 to 7 days.

Option 3

1. Using a sheet of paper attached to a clipboard, record the frequency of negative student verbalizations made by the entire class or a group of target students. *Negative verbalizations* are defined as teasing, name calling, threatening, or any other unfriendly or aggressive verbalization.
2. Conduct these observations for 30 to 45 minutes during one or more selected instructional periods or transitions for 4 to 7 days.

Intervention Steps

Preparation

1. Select a time during the school day when students are already working in small groups or when small-group activities can be readily implemented so that BT sessions can occur predictably. For example, BT can be included during cooperative learning activities, center time, or end-of-day activities.
2. Decide how long BT sessions can be (between 5 and 15 minutes) during the selected period. For example, if the time allotted for cooperative learning is 40 minutes, you can provide an 8-minute BT session for each of five groups during that period.
3. Identify no more than three primary BT messages that emphasize the caring and helpful aspects of your role as teacher. If possible, select these messages on the basis of observations of current teacher–student relationships made by a consultant (see Note 2). Messages should be designed to disconfirm student negative expectations of or beliefs about the teacher and promote positive expectations of and beliefs about the teacher. Sample BT messages include the following:
   a. I am interested in you.
   b. I accept you.
   c. I am a helper when you need me or ask me.

   d. I will try to be fair and available.

   e. I can help you solve problems.

Introduction and Training

1. Tell the students that you have selected a regular part of the classroom routine (e.g., cooperative learning time, center time) during which you will be spending time with them in a different way.

2. Explain what the small-group activities will be and when they will occur. Write the weekly schedule for BT on the chalkboard where all the students can see it.

3. Explain to students that you will be spending time with them rather than teaching them during that period, but that the rules for behavior are the same as during other classroom time. That is, if a student breaks a classroom rule during a BT session, you will deliver the usual consequence after the session.

Implementation

1. Conduct BT sessions at the appointed time each week. As much as possible, permit students to direct the small-group activities or to be engaged with the learning or play materials within the limits established.

2. During BT sessions for small groups or individual students, keep your behavior and verbalizations as neutral and objective as possible. Observations of student behavior should not focus on skill performance. Try to refrain from teaching, directing, and offering reinforcement during sessions. Instead, use the terms in the selected messages as "relationship themes." Figure 3.4 displays examples of BT statements and non-BT statements.

3. If a student breaks a rule during BT, do not terminate the BT session for that group or child. Instead, try to use the session as a way of understanding the problem behavior and affirming the messages of consistency, helpfulness, and caring. At the conclusion of the session, administer the usual consequence.

4. Between BT sessions, use the same relationship-theme messages to communicate consistency, helpfulness, and caring during routine classroom interactions, such as teacher requests for compliance and student requests for assistance.

> *Examples*: During small-group instruction, say "I need help from everyone in using quiet voices so that I can hear the students in the reading circle." During center time or independent seatwork, say "I wonder if you need help with that. I'm here to help."

Evaluation (Select One or More)

Option 1

1. Compare the frequency of inappropriate and disruptive behaviors for the target student(s) or the entire class during the selected instructional period before and after implementation.

Option 2

1. Compare the frequency of reprimands delivered to the target student(s) or the entire class during the selected instructional period before and after implementation.

Option 3

1. Compare the frequency of negative verbalizations made by the entire class or a group of target students during the selected instructional period(s) or transitions(s) before and after implementation.

Variation: Banking Time with Individual Students

1. To implement BT with one or more individual target students, provide 5-minute one-to-one sessions two or three times a week during independent seatwork, center time, collaborative learning time, or at the end of the day during the "packing up" period. Keep your comments and interactions as low key and unobtrusive as possible while other students continue with the regular classroom routine. Incorporating BT into the last moments of the school day can help mend relationships that have become strained during the course of the day's events.

Notes

1. BT must not be contingent on student behavior (e.g., "Class, you have really earned your Banking Time today" or "Jeremy, I'm sorry, but your behavior has been so bad that you've lost your Banking Time today"). Adhering to this guideline can be very difficult for teachers who believe that paying attention to misbehaving students will reinforce the problem behavior. According to the researcher, this is only the case when teacher attention is contingent on the misbehavior, that is, when it occurs immediately after and in the same situation as the misbehavior. Because BT sessions are scheduled beforehand, teacher attention during BT sessions should not serve as a reinforcer for inappropriate behavior.
2. Having a consultant observe the class to help select specific BT messages is strongly recommended, especially if teacher–student relationships have already deteriorated.
3. Role-playing BT with a consultant or colleague who can provide supportive feedback is a key aspect in successful implementation. This type of adult–child interaction does not come easily to many educators, who are accustomed to delivering instructional and managerial statements rather than nondirective, nonevaluative messages.

Source

Pianta, R. C. (1999). *Enhancing relationships between children and teachers.* Washington, DC: American Psychological Association. Copyright by the American Psychological Association. Adapted by permission.

Additional Resources

BT is a component in *Students, Teachers, and Relationship Support* (STARS), a classroom intervention program developed by Robert Pianta and Bridget Hamre and published by Psychological Assessment Resources (*http://www.parinc.com*). Also available from the same publisher is the *Student–Teacher Relationship Scale* (STRS), a 28-item self-report instrument that measures the

Teachers' Statements to Students

Typical Teacher Statements	Banking Time Statements
• You need to take turns reading.	• You enjoy reading to each other.
• Let me show you how to do that.	• I can help you with that if you want.
• You've done a good job on your social studies project so far.	• Your group made that whole chart together.
• What are you trying to do on this page?	• You have some interesting possibilities here.

FIGURE 3.4. Typical teacher statements versus Banking Time statements. Adapted from Pianta (1999, p. 141). Copyright 1999 by the American Psychological Association. Adapted by permission.

quality of a teacher's relationship with a target student and can be used to identify teacher–student relationships that would benefit from intervention.

TOOTLING: ENHANCING STUDENT RELATIONSHIPS WITH PEER REPORTING, PUBLIC POSTING, AND GROUP CONTINGENCIES

Overview

Many important social skills are acquired and mastered during day-to-day interactions with peers, that is, through incidental learning. Unfortunately, classroom environments are typically structured to prevent incidental negative behavior rather than to encourage incidental prosocial behavior, with rule systems that identify inappropriate behaviors and the aversive consequences that will follow them. Students often participate in these punishment-focused programs by "tattling" (monitoring and reporting their classmates' negative behaviors) and fail to notice their classmates' positive social interactions. In contrast, "tootling" (a combination of "tattling" and "tooting your own horn") is designed to improve the quality of student–student interactions in the classroom by encouraging students to focus on each other's prosocial behaviors. Tootling includes three components: (1) direct instruction in peer monitoring of prosocial behaviors, (2) an interdependent group contingency to reinforce peer reporting of these behaviors, and (3) public posting of the number of tootles. Studies in elementary classrooms demonstrate that students can learn to report peer prosocial rather than antisocial behaviors and that group rewards and publicly posted progress feedback increase positive peer reporting rates. By encouraging students to attend to their classmates' positive rather than negative social behaviors, tootling has the potential not only to increase prosocial behaviors but also to enhance positive peer relationships and the classroom climate. Tootling is especially helpful in classrooms in schools with high student turnover rates and classrooms that include students with emotional or behavior disorders, who are at high risk for social rejection and isolation.

Purpose

To promote positive peer relationships and a warm, collaborative classroom environment with peer reporting of prosocial behaviors, public posting, and group rewards.

Materials

1. 3" × 5" index cards, three to five per student per day.
2. Shoe box with a slot cut in the top and wrapped in bright wrapping paper.
3. "Tootling Progress Chart," consisting of a posterboard chart with a ladder drawn on it and removable cardboard icons to indicate progress, such as a smiley face, foot, or stick figure.
4. Tape (optional).

Observation (Select One or More)

Option 1

1. Using a sheet of paper attached to a clipboard, record the number of tattling behaviors during recess, center time, the cooperative learning period, or the morning instructional period for 4 to 7 days. *Tattling behaviors* are defined as any student complaints about the verbal or physical behavior of a classmate.

Option 2

1. Using a sheet of paper attached to a clipboard, record the frequency of negative verbalizations emitted by the entire class during a selected instructional period or for the morning

instructional period for 4 to 7 days. *Negative verbalizations* are defined as verbalizations with unpleasant content directed toward oneself or peers, such as making self-derogatory comments, teasing or verbally threatening peers, or making inappropriate comments that disrupt instruction.

2. Calculate the number of negative verbalizations per minute by dividing the number of negative verbalizations by the number of minutes in the observation period.

Option 3

1. Using a *Group Event Recording Form*, tally the number of aggressive behaviors displayed by the entire class or a target group of students during recess or the morning instructional period for 4 to 7 days. *Aggressive behaviors* are defined as hitting, pushing, throwing objects at others, verbally or physically attacking others, or verbally or physically interfering with the activities of others.

Intervention Steps

Introduction and Training

1. Tell the class that that they will be playing a "tootling" game that will give them a chance to name a classmate who has been friendly or helpful to them during the school day.
2. Explain the difference between *tattling* and *tootling* as follows: *Tattling* involves telling the teacher when a classmate does something wrong. *Tootling* involves telling the teacher when a classmate does something helpful for you or another classmate.
3. Review the criteria for tootling as follows:
   a. The behavior observed must be that of another classmate (not teacher behavior or behavior of students from other classrooms).
   b. Students can only report instances in which a classmate was friendly to or helped them or other students—not the teacher or other adults.
   c. The behavior has to occur at school.
4. Provide examples of tootling, such as helping others to pick up their books, lending a student a pencil, greeting a new student pleasantly, encouraging another student in a game at recess, and showing a student how to solve a math problem.
5. Invite the students to provide their own examples. Praise the examples that fit the criteria for tootling and provide corrective feedback if students give examples that do not fit the criteria.
6. Demonstrate on the chalkboard how to record tootles, as follows: who (name of classmate) did what (friendly or helpful behavior) and for whom (name of classmate who was the recipient of the prosocial behavior).
7. Give each student an index card and ask everyone to write down one tootle.
8. Collect the cards and read the examples aloud. Commend examples that fit the definition of tootling and offer corrective feedback for examples that do not.
9. Display the Tootling Progress Chart and explain that when the class cumulative total of tootles reaches 100, the entire class will earn a 30-minute extra recess period (or another group activity reward).

Implementation

1. At the beginning of the following day, give each student an index card or, for early primary grade students, tape a card to each desk. Place the shoe box and a stack of index cards on your desk or a table.
2. Ask the students to observe their classmates for friendly and helpful behaviors during the day and write down all the tootles they observe. When students fill out a card, they are to place it in the box and take another index card from the stack next to the shoe box.

3. At the end of each day, open the shoe box and count the number of tootles. Only count tootles in which students identify who, did what, and for whom. If more than one student reports the same instance, count all instances.

4. At the beginning of each day, announce how many tootles the class made the previous day. Read examples that fit the criteria, as well as one or two that do not fit the criteria.

5. Tape the cardboard icon on the ladder at the appropriate rung to indicate the number of tootles earned toward the goal (cumulative total). Praise the students for being good observers and encourage them to continue reporting their peers' prosocial behaviors.

6. When the class meets the goal, praise the students and tell them they have a day off from tootling. Provide the extra recess or group activity reward on the day students reach the goal, if possible.

7. On the following day, set a new, higher goal (e.g., 150 tootles) and indicate a new group activity reinforcer, such as 30 minutes of time in the school gym, access to a special play area, or an opportunity to choose a video or DVD to watch in the classroom.

Evaluation (Select One or More)

Option 1

1. Compare the frequency of tattling behaviors during the selected period before and after the intervention.

Option 2

1. Compare the frequency of negative verbalizations made by the entire class or the group of target students during the selected period before and after implementation.

Variation: Tootling with Verbal Reporting

1. For students with limited writing skills, such as younger students and students with disabilities, tootles can be reported verbally. Schedule a specific time for tootling each day, such as 10 minutes after recess or at the end of the day. Praise students for tootles that meet the criteria and provide feedback when errors are made. Keep a running total of tootles that meet the criteria, announce the total at the end of the tootling session, and tape the icon on the ladder at the appropriate rung, as described above.

Note

1. Some students may engage in a competition to see who can write the most cards, with an emphasis on depositing cards in the box rather than observing prosocial behaviors. In that case, limit students to three to five cards per day and remind them that the purpose of the activity is to notice their peers' positive behaviors, not to write the most cards.

Sources

Cashwell, T. H., Skinner, C. H., & Smith, E. S. (2001). Increasing second-grade students' reports of peers' prosocial behaviors via direct instruction, group reinforcement, and progress feedback: A replication and extension. *Education and Treatment of Children, 24,* 161–175. Copyright 2001 by West Virginia University Press. Adapted by permission.

Skinner, C. H., Cashwell, T. H., & Skinner, A. L. (2000). Increasing tootling: The effects of a peer-monitored group contingency program on students' reports of peers' prosocial behaviors. *Psychology in the Schools, 37,* 263–270. Copyright 2000 by John Wiley & Sons, Inc. Adapted by permission.

PRINT RESOURCES

Emmer, E. T., Evertson, C. M., & Worsham, M. E. (2006). *Classroom management for middle and high school teachers* (7th ed.). Boston: Allyn & Bacon. *http://www.ablongman.com*

Evertson, C. M., Emmer, E. T., & Worsham, M. E. (2006). *Classroom management for elementary teachers* (7th ed.). Boston: Allyn & Bacon.

These companion volumes describe classroom management principles and procedures based on a research program extending nearly 25 years and including observational studies and field experiments involving more than 550 elementary and secondary classrooms. The focus is on preventing problems by developing rules and procedures for instructional and behavioral management systems at the beginning of the year. Available for each volume is a classroom management video that illustrates procedures, planning, communication, and behavior management issues, with scenes taken from actual classroom footage.

Evertson, C. M., & Weinstein, C. S. (Eds.). (2006). *Handbook of classroom management: Research, practice, and contemporary issues*. Mahwah, NJ: Erlbaum.

This landmark volume includes articles on a wide range of issues relating to classroom management, including classroom management in urban settings, management in different instructional formats, school-wide behavior support programs, professional development, and legal and ethical issues related to classroom management.

Rathvon, N. (1996). *The unmotivated child: Helping your underachiever become a successful student*. New York: Simon & Schuster.

Designed for parents and teachers of underperforming students, this book includes a chapter on effective communication strategies, including deconstructing students' verbal communications, managing emotions in confrontational situations, delivering effective praise, and promoting problem solving. Numerous examples of parent–child and teacher–student conversations are provided to illustrate the use of the strategies.

WEBSITES

My Teaching Partner
http://www.MyTeachingPartner.net

Developed by Robert Pianta and his colleagues, this web-based resource is designed to support teachers in management-related classroom interactions and teacher–student relationships. Teachers can access hundreds of video clips of teacher–student classroom interactions that have been rated as high quality using the *Classroom Assessment Scoring System* (CLASS: Pianta, La Paro, & Hamre, 2006) and that are accompanied by text descriptions. Internet-mediated consultation with feedback is also available for teachers who provide videotapes of their own classroom interactions.

The Really Big List of Classroom Management Resources
http://drwilliampmartin.tripod.com/classm.html

Created by Dr. William Martin and members of his online graduate course at Monmouth University in West Long Branch, New Jersey, this site provides hundreds of links to classroom management resources.

APPENDIX 3.1. Summary Characteristics of Proactive Classroom Management Interventions

Intervention	Description	Comments
Organizing a Productive Classroom Environment		
Increasing Student Participation with a Semicircular Desk Arrangement	Desks are arranged in two parallel semicircles to facilitate student participation and on-task behavior during whole-group instruction.	This arrangement is especially useful in classes with a lecture/discussion format, such as social studies, civics, and history classes.
Establishing Rules and Procedures		
Say Show Check: Teaching Classroom Procedures	This instructional sequence consists of a model–guide–practice format for teaching classroom routines.	This highly usable keystone strategy provides a framework for teaching classroom routines and introducing interventions.
Active Teaching of Classroom Rules	Classroom rules are taught in a lesson format, with brief daily reviews to enhance maintenance.	Field testing indicates that providing parents with a written copy of the rules to sign and return to school enhances the likelihood of success.
Managing Transitions		
Teaching Transition Time	In this scripted strategy, students learn and practice four key transition behaviors.	This strategy can be adapted to promote effective in-class or room-to-room transitions for students at any grade level.
Six Steps to Speedy Transitions	Teachers guide students through a transition instructional sequence embedded in a game-like format.	This intervention specifies criterion times for each transition, which can be adjusted based on type of transition and teacher goals.
The Timely Transitions Game: Reducing Room-to-Room Transition Time	This game-like intervention targets transitions with explicit timing, publicly posted feedback, and randomized interdependent group contingencies.	This transition intervention includes a variety of motivational components, including publicly posted feedback and classwide incentives.
Managing Small-Group Instruction and Independent Seatwork		
Checking Stations	Students learn to correct their own seatwork assignments with a self-managed error correction procedure.	Checking stations are especially useful in classrooms using a differentiated instructional model because students can check their own seatwork assignments without disturbing teacher-delivered instruction.
The Coupon System: Decreasing Inappropriate Requests for Teacher Assistance	In this peer-monitored response cost strategy, students lose "coupons" for inappropriate requests for help and earn rewards for retaining a specified number of coupons.	This strategy is also highly effective in reducing attention-seeking behaviors, such as inappropriate verbalizations, during small-group or whole-group instruction.
Countdown to Free Time: Encouraging Productivity during Small-Group Instruction	Students earn free time by matching their self-ratings of academic productivity to teacher ratings displayed on a flipchart.	Observing minutes being incrementally deducted from a free period or recess for rule infractions, combined with self-monitoring of point losses, can have immediate, dramatic effects on off-task and disruptive behavior.

(continued)

Intervention	Description	Comments
Communicating Competently with Students		
Delivering Effective Praise	This instructional protocol combines four empirically validated dimensions to maximize the effectiveness of teacher-delivered praise.	For older students, privately delivered praise may be more effective than publicly delivered positive teacher attention. Parents also benefit from training in effective praise.
Delivering Effective Reprimands	This instructional protocol combines six empirically validated dimensions to maximize the effectiveness of teacher-delivered reprimands.	Field testing indicates that maintaining emotional control is the most difficult aspect of delivering effective reprimands. Parents also benefit from training in effective reprimands.
Delivering Effective Commands: The Precision Request Program	This instructional protocol combines six empirically validated dimensions to maximize the effectiveness of teacher-delivered commands.	First developed as part of a parent training program for oppositional and defiant children, the Precision Request Program is designed for use with chronically noncompliant students in the classroom. This strategy is especially effective when simultaneously implemented at home and at school.
Teaching Prosocial Behaviors		
Sit and Watch: Teaching Prosocial Behaviors	Misbehaving students observe their positively behaving peers during a modified time-out.	Field testing indicates that this intervention can be crucial in maintaining an orderly classroom and helping young children develop self-control. Positive effects are enhanced when it is implemented at home as well as at school.
Debriefing: Helping Students Solve Their Own Behavior Problems	Misbehaving students are guided through a structured protocol that prompts or teaches alternative prosocial behaviors in problematic situations and prepares for a successful transition back into the classroom.	Debriefing sessions can be conducted by administrators, designated office staff, or classroom teachers.
Building Positive Relationships in the Classroom		
Building Positive Relationships with Banking Time	Teachers spend brief, regular nondirective sessions with at-risk or chronically noncompliant students to build a more trusting relationship.	This intervention can be delivered on an individual, small-group, or whole-class basis. Providing sufficient training and support is essential to the success of this strategy because many teachers find it difficult to maintain a nondirective stance with children, especially those with whom they have conflictual relationships. Banking Time is also appropriate as a home-based intervention.
Tootling: Enhancing Student Relationships with Peer Reporting, Public Posting, and Group Contingencies	Students earn group rewards by reporting their classmates' positive behaviors that occur during the course of the school day.	Reinforcing students for focusing on positive peer behaviors rather than peer rule infractions can result in dramatic reductions in tattling behaviors.

CHAPTER 4

Interventions to Improve Academic Performance

The majority of referrals to school psychologists involve students with academic problems (Bramlett et al., 2002; Shapiro, 2004a). Given the increasing diversity of students being served in regular classrooms, including children of poverty, non-native English speakers, and students with disabilities, helping teachers implement instructional practices that can enhance the academic performance of groups of students as well as individual students is a priority for today's consultants. In particular, consultants need information about group-oriented interventions that promote academic productivity and achievement and can be implemented using regular curricular materials. Interventions that improve academic achievement are crucial not only to assist students in meeting learning standards, but also to promote positive social outcomes. Academic achievement is strongly associated with social competence, beginning in the early primary grades (Bennett, Brown, Boyle, Racine, & Offord, 2004; McIntosh, Horner, Chard, Boland, & Good, 2006; Welsh, Parke, Widaman, & O'Neil, 2000). The relationship between academic achievement and social competence is especially strong for reading, with mounting evidence that interventions that enhance reading skills can also have positive effects on behavior (Lane, Beebe-Frankenberger, Lambros, & Pierson, 2002; Lane et al., 2001).

Academically focused interventions have the potential to reduce disruptive behavior by creating a classroom ecology within which all students are productively engaged. The less "down time," the fewer are the opportunities for off-task behavior to escalate into disruption. Moreover, strategies that increase students' ability to respond correctly to instruction are likely to reduce inappropriate behavior arising from students' effort to escape from tasks that they perceive as too difficult (Gunter, Hummel, & Conroy, 1998). In fact, decreases in nontargeted disruptive behavior were observed in several of the original studies for the interventions included in this chapter (Fantuzzo, King, & Heller, 1992; Gardner, Heward, & Grossi, 1994). Academic enhancement interventions are especially critical in combating the development of a "failure identity" among children who are already displaying aggressive and noncompliant behavior (Forehand & Wierson, 1993). Given the well-documented relationship between aggression and school failure (e.g., Dishion et al., 1991; Hinshaw, 1992a, 1992b), interventions that focus only on reducing inappropriate behavior are insufficient to promote positive outcomes in at-risk children.

Targets of Academic Interventions

Although many interventions designed to enhance academic achievement have targeted on-task behavior, improvement in on-task behavior is not always accompanied by improvement in academic performance (e.g., Mitchen et al., 2001; Wood, Murdock, Cronin, Dawson, & Kirby, 1998). Interventions that increase on-task behavior only make students more available for learning. Moreover, improvements in on-task behavior will be short-lived if students do not simultaneously receive help in mastering instructional material. In contrast, interventions targeting rapid, accurate academic responding are associated with improvement in both on-task behavior and achievement for students with and without disabilities (Greenwood et al., 2002; Greenwood, Maheady, & Delquadri, 2002; Randolph, 2007; Sutherland & Wehby, 2001). Strategies that maximize opportunities to respond are especially important for students of diversity, such as English language learners (Gersten & Baker, 2000a, 2000b) and students attending schools in poor urban neighborhoods, who typically receive fewer opportunities to respond to academic material than their counterparts in more advantaged settings (Greenwood, 1991; Greenwood et al., 1989).

TYPES OF ACADEMIC INTERVENTIONS

Academic interventions can be characterized as skill-based, performance-based, or some combination of the two. *Skill-based strategies* enhance learning by means of antecedent procedures, such as direct instruction, modeling, and guided practice, whereas *performance-based strategies* manipulate consequences for academic productivity and achievement by providing reinforcement in the form of feedback and/or contingencies (Rathvon, 2004a). Many of the strategies in this chapter consist of "intervention packages" that include both skill- and performance-based components to enhance effectiveness. The interventions in this chapter are organized into three categories, based on target: (1) academic productivity, including classwork and independent seatwork; (2) homework performance; and (3) specific academic subjects, including reading, mathematics, writing, and the content areas of science and social studies. Reading interventions are subdivided into strategies targeting decoding, fluency, and vocabulary and comprehension, whereas writing interventions are subdivided into strategies targeting spelling and written expression. Most of the interventions also target directly or indirectly what DiPerna and Elliott (2002) have termed *academic enablers*, that is, nonacademic skills, behaviors, and attitudes that contribute to academic competence by encouraging students to become active, motivated learners, often by incorporating incentives or opportunities to collaborate with peers on classroom tasks.

Evaluating the Effectiveness of Academic Interventions

Although investigators have sometimes evaluated the impact of academic interventions on task completion rates without considering the percentage of work completed accurately or the absolute level of achievement (e.g., Wood et al., 1998), the effectiveness of academic interventions must be evaluated in terms of the degree to which they produce educationally meaningful gains in student achievement (Rathvon, 2004a). Similarly, researchers have often measured teachers' and parents' perceptions of changes in student performance to assess the effectiveness of academic interventions (e.g., Carrington, Lehrer, & Wittenstrom, 1997). Although consumers' perceptions are valuable in assessing the social validity of interventions, it is important to document changes in terms of actual student learning outcomes. The evaluation section of each intervention in this chapter therefore includes at least one direct measure of academic achievement. Evaluation methods for the strategies in this chapter rely primarily on assessments used in typical classroom accountability systems, such as report card grades; scores on classwork, quizzes, and tests; and homework accuracy and completion rates. Given that all of the interventions are designed for classwide application, many of the evaluation strategies involve group-oriented academic measures, such as class averages on tests and classwide percentages of homework assignments completed with 80% accuracy or higher. Because interventions targeting academic performance also have the potential to improve behavior by increasing student engagement and success in responding to tasks, several interventions also include measures for assessing changes in on-task behavior.

CURRICULUM-BASED MEASUREMENT

In addition to the evaluation methods built into each intervention, procedures for conducting *curriculum-based measurements* (CBMs) in reading, mathematics, spelling, written expression, and the content areas are presented in the introductory portion of each of these sections, using the same step-by-step intervention format. Developed by Deno, Mirkin, and their colleagues at the University of Minnesota Institute for Research on Learning Disabilities (e.g., Deno, 1985, 1986; Deno & Mirkin, 1977), CBM is a set of standardized, fluency-based measurement procedures that can be used to index academic performance and progress toward intervention goals or grade-level standards. CBM is ideally suited for monitoring the progress of students receiving academic interventions because the measures are brief (1 to 5 minutes), can be administered frequently, and are based on students' own instructional materials or their generic equivalents. A voluminous body of evidence demonstrates that CBM procedures are reliable and valid methods of identifying students at risk for academic failure, monitoring progress, and evaluating the effectiveness of school-based interventions (see Deno, 2003, for a review).

Interventions to Improve Academic Productivity

This section includes five interventions targeting academic productivity in the classroom. One intervention—*ClassWide Peer Tutoring* (CWPT)—uses a peer tutoring format to increase academic engagement rates and to consolidate skills. Developed by Greenwood and his colleagues at the University of Kansas to improve the achievement of low-income urban students at risk for academic failure (Delquadri, Greenwood, Whorton, Carta, & Hall, 1986; Greenwood, 1991; Greenwood, Terry, Utley, Montagna, & Walker, 1993), CWPT includes several validated components from the instructional effectiveness literature, including frequent opportunities to respond, immediate error correction, frequent assessment, and public posting of performance. Unlike many other peer tutoring interventions, CWPT includes no contingencies, relying instead on a game-like atmosphere to motivate productivity. CWPT has been successful in improving student engagement, attitudes toward learning, and academic achievement in a wide variety of subjects, including reading, language arts, spelling, vocabulary, mathematics computation, and physical education, and across regular education, inclusive, and special education settings (see Greenwood et al., 2002, for a review). Moreover, longitudinal studies indicate that CWPT can help prevent school failure as measured by special education placement, school drop-out rates, and achievement on standardized tests (Greenwood & Delquadri, 1995; Greenwood et al., 1993). A growing body of research also supports the effectiveness of CWPT in enhancing outcomes for English language learners (Greenwood, Arreaga-Mayer, Utley, Gavin, & Terry, 2001; Mortweet et al., 1999). CWPT has been cited as a promising practice by the Promising Practice Network (*http://www.promisingpractices.net/research.asp*).

CROSS-REFERENCE: Several other interventions in this chapter use whole-class peer tutoring formats to enhance academic performance, including *Paired Reading*; *Partner Reading*; *Peer Tutoring in Vocabulary*; *Reciprocal Peer Tutoring in Math*; *Spelling Wizards: Accommodating Diverse Learners with Partner Spelling*; and *Admirals and Generals: Improving Content Area Performance with Strategy Instruction and Peer Tutoring*.

Using Response Cards to Increase Academic Engagement and Achievement targets academic engagement and productivity during whole-class instruction by giving every student an opportunity to respond to teacher questions. Although achievement is significantly associated with students' opportunities to respond to academic material (Randolph, 2007; Sutherland & Wehby, 2001), observational studies have found that typical classroom response rates are considerably lower than those recommended in the instructional effectiveness literature for both initial and practice/review lessons (Gunter, Reffel, Barnett, Lee, & Patrick, 2004). In the most common form of student participation during whole-class instruction, the teacher calls on one student at a time to answer questions or contribute to the discussion, an approach that provides active responding only for the student who is called on and results in less frequent participation by low-performing students, who rarely raise their hands (Heward et al., 1996). In *response card instruction,* all students respond to teacher questions by writing on cards and holding them up or by displaying preprinted cards indicating their answers. Response card instruction increases participation rates, achievement, and on-task behavior for students with and without disabilities across a variety of subject areas, including mathematics (Armendariz & Umbreit, 1999; Christie & Schuster, 2003), science (Gardner et al., 1994), and social studies (Narayan, Heward, Gardner, Courson, & Omness, 1990). Response cards have also been used successfully with diverse learners, including preschoolers with attention problems (Godfrey, Grishman-Brown, Schuster, & Hemmeter, 2003), elementary grade English language learners (Christie & Schuster, 2003), and high school students with disabilities in inclusive classrooms (Cavanaugh, Heward, & Donelson, 1996).

Two strategies in this section use *self-monitoring* as a primary intervention component to enhance academic productivity and performance. In contrast to peer-mediated academic interventions, in which students evaluate each other's responses and provide corrective feedback, self-monitoring strategies teach students to evaluate their own performance relative to a set of criteria. Self-monitoring includes at least two components: (1) self-observation and/or instruction and (2) self-recording. Two additional components—self-evaluation and self-reinforcement—are also often included (Shapiro, Durnan, Post, & Levinson, 2002). When self-monitoring procedures are used to enhance academic productivity, students record whether they have completed specific academic tasks or routines, with contingent reinforcement included in some applications. Successful outcomes have been obtained for self-monitoring interventions targeting academic productivity, performance, and on-task behavior for students in general education and students with learning disabilities and attentional and behavior disorders in inclusive and resource room settings (see Mooney, Ryan, Uhing, Reid, & Epstein, 2005, and Shapiro et al., 2002, for reviews). The vast majority of self-monitoring intervention studies have focused on only one or two students rather than entire classroom groups, however, and many strategies have relied on electronic audio cuing systems that are impractical in regular education settings. In contrast, *Self-Monitoring of Academic Productivity* teaches students to monitor their productivity and on-task behavior using a simple printed form and can be easily implemented on a whole-class, small-group, or individual basis.

Cover, Copy, and Compare: Enhancing Academic Performance with Self-Management (CCC) is a self-management intervention that can be used to enhance accuracy and fluency in a variety of subjects. In the CCC procedure, students look at an academic stimulus (such as a multiplication problem, vocabulary word, or spelling word), cover it, copy it, and evaluate their written response by comparing it to the original stimulus. CCC combines several empirically based intervention components, including self-instruction, increased opportunities to respond to academic material, and immediate corrective feedback (Skinner, McLaughlin, & Logan, 1997). Studies with CCC instruction have documented improvement in academic performance for students with and without disabilities in regular and special education settings and across a wide variety of academic subjects, including mathematics (Lee & Tingstrom, 1994; Stading, Williams, & McLaughlin, 1996), word recognition (Conley, Derby, Roberts-Gwinn, Weber, & McLaughlin, 2004), spelling (Hubbert, Weber, & McLaughlin, 2000), geography (Skinner, Belfiore, & Pierce, 1992), and science (Smith, Dittmer, & Skinner, 2002).

CROSS-REFERENCE: Many of the strategies in this book include a self-management or self-monitoring component as part of an intervention package. *Checking Stations* in Chapter 3 is a proactive strategy that teaches students to correct their own seatwork. For a variation on *Cover, Copy, and Compare* targeting written language skills, see *Add a Word for Successful Spelling* later in this chapter. Chapter 5 includes two self-management interventions designed to improve behavior and social competence: *Three Steps to Self-Managed Behavior* and *Self-Management to Decrease Negative Verbalizations*.

Many of the performance-based strategies in this text rely on *interdependent group contingencies* in which all or none of the students receive a reward depending on whether or not the class meets a group-oriented criterion. Although interdependent group contingencies can be highly effective in encouraging academic productivity and appropriate behavior (Stage & Quiroz, 1997), they are associated with some potential pitfalls. Some students may not be motivated by the reward, and others may stop putting forth effort or become disruptive if they believe that they have exceeded the criterion for reinforcement and lost the opportunity to receive the reward (Skinner, Cashwell, & Dunn, 1996). The *Rewards Box: Enhancing Academic Productivity with Randomized Group Contingencies* solves these problems by randomizing not only the rewards for academic productivity but also the criteria for reinforcement delivery. Classwide interventions using randomly selected group-oriented criteria have been successful in improving academic performance for students in regular education (Sharp & Skinner, 2004) and students with emotional and behavioral disorders (Popkin & Skinner, 2003).

CROSS-REFERENCE: For a strategy using randomized group contingencies to target reading comprehension, see *Motivating Reading Performance with Paired Reading and Randomized Group Contingencies* later in this chapter. Other interventions that incorporate randomized group contingencies include the *Timely Transitions Game: Reducing Room-to-Room Transition Time* in Chapter 3 and *Reducing Disruptive Behavior with Randomized Group Contingencies* in Chapter 5.

CLASSWIDE PEER TUTORING

Overview

ClassWide Peer Tutoring (CWPT) is a low-cost, efficient instructional intervention that enhances student achievement by increasing opportunities for active responding and immediate feedback. Unlike traditional peer tutoring, which is designed to remediate the deficiencies of individual pupils by pairing them with higher achieving students, CWPT was developed specifically to provide additional academic practice for every student in a classroom. Moreover, because peer tutors are provided with the correct answers for tutoring tasks, the strategy permits immediate error correction. In CWPT, students practice basic academic skills four times a week, with each student serving as tutor and tutee during a 30-minute tutoring period. On Fridays, students are tested on the material presented during the week and are pretested on the material for the upcoming week. CWPT includes both competitive and collaborative structures, with tutoring pairs organized into teams that earn points for accurate performance and appropriate tutoring behavior. CWPT has been successful in improving academic achievement, productivity, and attitudes toward learning in a wide variety of subjects and in regular, inclusive, and special education settings. Moreover, longitudinal studies indicate that students participating in CWPT show higher levels of academic engagement and achievement and are less likely to need special education services and to drop out of school, compared with students not receiving CWPT. In addition to general CWPT procedures, specific procedures for implementing CWPT in oral reading, word identification, and spelling are presented, including two adaptations for English language learners.

Purpose

To improve academic productivity and achievement by increasing opportunities for students to respond and receive immediate feedback without increasing the amount of instructional time.

Materials for CWPT in Any Subject

1. Box containing red and blue slips of construction paper, with an equal number of each color and summing to the number of students in the class.
2. Curricular materials appropriate for basic skills practice, one set per student pair.
3. Point sheets, consisting of sheets of paper or index cards with a list of consecutive numbers, one per student.
4. Kitchen timer with bell, stopwatch with audible signal, or watch.
5. "Team Points Chart," consisting of a posterboard chart or section of the chalkboard listing team names, with columns for posting team point totals and daily and weekly winning teams.
6. Adhesive stars or stickers.

Additional Materials for CWPT in Oral Reading

1. Copies of reading passages at the instructional level of the less proficient student in the tutoring pair, students' regular reading materials, or supplementary reading materials, such as *Weekly Reader*, one set of materials per student pair.

Additional Materials for CWPT in Vocabulary

1. Vocabulary flashcards (bilingual cards for the English language learner adaptation).
2. "Smiley faces" and question marks, about 5 inches in height, made of colored construction paper (English language learner adaptation).
3. Overhead projector and transparencies with lists of vocabulary words or colored chalk (English language learner adaptation).

Additional Materials for CWPT in Spelling

1. List of spelling words or regular spelling materials, one per student pair.
2. Notebooks or folders with sheets of ruled paper, one per student (see Variation 2).
3. Overhead projector and transparencies with lists of spelling words or colored chalk (English language learner adaptation).

Additional Materials for CWPT in Mathematics

1. Math flashcards or worksheets with math problems.

Additional Materials for CWPT in Social Studies, Science, Language Arts, or Other Subject Areas

1. Workbook pages or textbook-based reproducible skill sheets, one uncompleted page and one correctly completed page per student pair.

Observation (Select One or More)

Option 1

1. Calculate percent-correct scores on daily classwork, quizzes, or end-of-unit tests for the entire class or a group of target students in the selected subject for 5 to 10 days or for the current grading period.

Option 2

1. Using a *Group Interval Recording Form* with a 15-second interval, begin at the left side of the room and glance at each student in turn. Record a plus (+) if the student is on-task for the duration of the interval and a minus (–) if the student is off-task at any time during the interval. When you have rated each student, begin again at the left side of the room.
   a. *On-task behavior* is defined as looking at the teacher or an appropriately participating peer, answering teacher-delivered questions, working on lesson materials, and any other task-related behavior.
   b. *Off-task behavior* is defined as being out of seat, talking without permission, playing with nonlesson materials, and any other behavior interfering with task completion for oneself or others.
2. Conduct these observations for 30 to 45 minutes during the selected instructional period for 4 to 7 days.

Option 3

1. Administer *Curriculum-Based Measurement Probes* in the selected subject to a group of target students or to the entire class.

Intervention Steps

Introduction and Training

1. Explain to the students that they will be learning an enjoyable new way of working together to get more out of their lessons.
2. Demonstrate the tutoring procedures as described below, with yourself as tutor and a student as tutee. Then select two more students and guide them through the procedures, while the other students observe, and provide praise and corrective feedback as needed. Conduct two more brief demonstrations with other student pairs and then guide students through a class-

wide tutoring session. As part of the training, teach students to talk only during tutoring sessions, speak only to their tutoring partners, and use "inside" voices.

3. On Fridays, have students draw names from the box for assignment to one of two teams for the coming week. Within each team, form random pairs in subjects in which tutors can use a master sheet with the correct answers for checking tutees' responses, such as spelling, vocabulary, mathematics, and the content areas. For tutoring in oral reading, pair students with similar skill levels. For CWPT with English language learners, pair low-achieving with average-achieving students and average-achieving with high-achieving students, based on level of English proficiency and past progress in reading. Pair students new to the United States with bilingual students, if possible. Then assign each pair of students to one of two teams. Change tutoring pairs and team assignments each week.

General Implementation Procedures

1. The entire CWPT procedure requires 30 minutes, during which each student tutors for 10 minutes and receives tutoring for 10 minutes. An additional 5 to 10 minutes is needed to sum and post individual and team points. For students in grades one and two, shorten tutoring times from 10 minutes to 5 minutes per student.

2. Begin the session by asking students to move to their tutoring stations (paired desks or some other arrangement). Designate one partner in each pair as the first tutor and distribute point sheets and CWPT tutoring materials.

3. Set the timer for 10 minutes. The tutor presents the items one at a time (e.g., math flashcards, vocabulary or spelling words, social studies questions), and the tutee responds orally for oral reading or vocabulary and in writing for other subjects.

4. If the answer is correct, the tutor awards 2 points on the tutee's point sheet. If the answer is incorrect, the tutor provides the correct response, asks the tutee to write or say the correct answer three times, and then awards 1 point for the correction. Tutors present the reading passage, word or spelling list, flashcards, or set of items as many times as possible during the 10 minutes.

5. After 10 minutes, students switch roles and repeat the procedures for another 10 minutes.

6. During CWPT time, monitor tutoring by moving around the classroom, answering questions, giving corrective feedback, and awarding bonus points (1 point per pair per session) for correct tutoring procedures and cooperative behavior.

7. When the timer rings at the end of the next 10 minutes, have each pair of students report the total points earned (or their individual points; see below). Sum the points for each team and record the total score for each team on the Team Points Chart.

8. Lead the class in applauding the winning team for the day and place a star or sticker next to the team name. Also lead a round of applause for the losing team for its efforts.

9. On Friday, administer a test on the materials students have practiced. Have team pairs exchange papers, correct each other's answers, and award 5 to 10 points for each correct response. Enter these scores on the Team Points Chart and determine a weekly team winner. If desired, also administer a pretest of the material to be covered in the coming week. Have students exchange papers and correct them. Use these scores to help determine student pairs for the coming week.

10. Also on Friday, lead the class in applauding the winning team of the week. If desired, award a privilege to winning team members, such as lining up first for lunch. The losing team is also applauded for good effort and sportsmanship.

CWPT IN ORAL READING

1. Give each student in the pair a copy of the same reading selection and two point sheets.

2. The tutee reads aloud for 10 minutes while the tutor monitors and corrects errors. Tutors present the reading passage as many times as possible during the 10-minute period.

3. Tutors award 2 points for every sentence read correctly and 1 point for practicing the correct response three times after an error.
4. To add a comprehension component, have the tutor ask the tutee who, what, why, where, and when questions for 5 minutes after the 10-minute reading.
5. After 10 minutes (or 15 minutes with the comprehension component), students reverse roles and repeat the procedures.
6. For students in grades three and up, increase each reading session by 5 to 10 minutes for a total CWPT session of 40 to 45 minutes.

CWPT IN WORD IDENTIFICATION

1. Give each student pair a set of reading flashcards and two point sheets. The tutor shows the first flashcard to the tutee. If the tutee pronounces the word correctly, the tutor places the flashcard back in the pack and awards 2 points.
2. If the tutee does not pronounce the word correctly, the tutor supplies the correct word. The tutee then pronounces the word once and receives 1 point. If neither student in the pair knows the word, the students raise their hands to request teacher assistance.
3. Following the tutee's correct response, the tutor places the flashcard to the side for additional practice during the session.
4. After 10 minutes, students reverse roles and repeat the procedures.

CWPT IN WORD IDENTIFICATION: ADAPTATION FOR ENGLISH LANGUAGE LEARNERS (SPANISH EXAMPLE)

1. Prior to the CWPT session, introduce the new set of words in a whole-class format, using bilingual flashcards, as described below.
   a. First pronounce each word in Spanish and have students repeat the word in Spanish. Then pronounce each word in English and have students repeat the word in English.
   b. Verbally spell each word in English and have students verbally spell the words in English.
2. Pair students as described above for English language learners and then follow the CWPT word identification procedures.

CWPT IN SPELLING

1. Give each student pair the weekly spelling list for the entire class or their spelling group and two lined sheets of paper.
2. The tutor presents the first spelling word. The tutee pronounces the word and spells it aloud while writing it on the sheet of paper.
3. If the word is correct, the tutor says, "Correct, give yourself 2 points!" and the tutee marks a "2" beside the word on the practice sheet.
4. If the word is incorrect, the tutor points to, pronounces, and spells the missed word. The tutee must write the missed word correctly three times before receiving the next word.
5. If the tutee writes it correctly three times, the tutor awards 1 point. If any of the three practice words were spelled incorrectly, the tutee receives 0 points.
6. After 10 minutes, students switch roles.

CWPT IN SPELLING: ADAPTATION FOR ENGLISH LANGUAGE LEARNERS (SPANISH EXAMPLE)

1. Prior to the CWPT session, present the new spelling words on the chalkboard or using an overhead projector, with each word spelled in Spanish and English.
2. English words should be divided into syllables of different colors, with prefixes identified by the color red and suffixes by the color blue.

3. Pair students as described above for English language learners and then follow the CWPT spelling procedures.

Evaluation (Select One or More)

Option 1

1. Compare percent-correct scores on classwork, quizzes, or end-of-unit tests in the selected subject for the entire class or the target students before and after implementation.

Option 2

1. Compare classwide rates of on-task and off-task behavior during the selected instructional period before and after implementation.

Option 3

1. Compare scores on *Curriculum-Based Measurement Probes* in the target subject for the target students or the entire class before and after implementation.

Notes

1. Training takes two 30- to 45-minute sessions. During the first session, explain the partner and team formats, the process of awarding points, and tutoring procedures. During the second training session, review transitioning to and from CWPT sessions and provide additional practice in the tutoring procedures.
2. Creating a permanent classroom arrangement of paired desks greatly facilitates implementation and reduces downtime while students reposition their desks.
3. Field testing indicates that beginning with a highly structured subject, such as spelling or mathematics computation, facilitates implementation. When students have mastered the procedures, introduce CWPT in another area, such as word identification or oral reading.
4. Teachers considering CWPT sometimes express concern that the intervention will lead to increased noise levels and will diminish their control over student behavior. An orderly environment can be maintained by continually monitoring during CWPT (vs. grading papers or performing other administrative tasks), awarding bonus points for following the rules, and administering brief time-outs from the opportunity to earn points by having students put their pencils down for 15 to 30 seconds if classroom noise becomes excessive.
5. Although the standard version of CWPT does not include any contingencies other than teacher praise and public recognition, field testing indicates that awarding a small privilege to members of the daily and weekly winning team, such as lining up first for lunch, specials, or dismissal, enhances motivation.

Sources

Burks, M. (2004). Effects of ClassWide Peer Tutoring on the number of words spelled correctly by students with LD. *Intervention in School and Clinic, 39,* 301–304. Copyright 2004 by PRO-ED, Inc. Adapted by permission.

Greenwood, C. R., Arreaga-Mayer, C., Utley, C. A., Gavin, K. M., & Terry, B. J. (2001). Class-Wide Peer Tutoring Learning Management System: Applications with elementary-level English language learners. *Remedial and Special Education, 22,* 34–47. Copyright 2001 by PRO-ED, Inc. Adapted by permission.

Additional Resources

Greenwood, C. R., Delquadri, J., & Hall, R. V. (1997). *Together we can: ClassWide Peer Tutoring for basic academic skills.* Longmont, CO: Sopris West.

This 80-page guide to ClassWide Peer Tutoring includes reproducible forms and four dry-erase posters.

http://www.jgcp.ku.edu

The Juniper Gardens website provides information about CWPT, including the ClassWide Peer Tutoring Learning Management System (CWPT-LMS), a computerized teacher support program for managing student progress in CWPT instruction and program implementation. Included are a formative evaluation system, a CWPT advisor and teacher mentor, and the capability for creating data and performance graphics.

COVER, COPY, AND COMPARE:
INCREASING ACADEMIC PERFORMANCE WITH SELF-MANAGEMENT

Overview

The Cover, Copy, and Compare (CCC) strategy is a self-managed intervention that can be used to enhance accuracy and fluency in a variety of academic skill domains. Students look at an academic stimulus (such as a multiplication problem for CCC Mathematics or a spelling word for CCC Spelling), cover it, copy it, and evaluate their response by comparing it to the original model. If an error is made, the student engages in a brief error correction procedure before proceeding to the next item. CCC combines several empirically based intervention components, including self-instruction, increased opportunities to respond to academic material, and immediate corrective feedback. CCC has been successful in improving academic engagement and achievement for students with and without disabilities in elementary, middle school, and high school classrooms across a wide variety of subjects, including mathematics, science, geography, spelling, and word recognition. High in usability, it requires little student training or teacher time, other than worksheet preparation. CCC can be implemented as a whole-class activity or as part of an independent seatwork period while the teacher works with individual students or small groups. Procedures for a generic CCC version and for CCC in four academic subjects are presented. Two variations designed to enhance motivation during CCC sessions by means of group contingencies and public posting are also included.

Purpose

To improve accuracy and fluency in basic academic skills by teaching students a self-management procedure that provides increased opportunities to respond to academic material.

Materials for CCC in Any Subject

1. Worksheets with 10 to 15 problems or items in the target subject; problems should be listed on the left side of the paper with space at the right for copying and correction, one to three worksheets per student.
2. 3″ × 5″ index cards, one per student (optional, see Note 2).
3. Overhead projector and transparency with sample worksheet (optional).
4. Stopwatch, timer, or watch with second hand.
5. Folders containing sheets of lined paper or graph paper, one per student.
6. Posterboard chart for displaying the class average number of correctly completed problems during timed tests (optional, see Variation 2).

Additional Materials for CCC Mathematics

1. Math worksheets, with computation problems and the answers listed on the left side of the sheet and the same problems on the right, unsolved, one to three worksheets per student.

Additional Materials for CCC Spelling

1. Spelling worksheets, with 10 to 15 spelling words (5 to 10 words for early primary grade students) listed on the left side of the sheet and blank lines on the right for writing each word, including space for corrections, one to three worksheets per student. For classrooms using differentiated spelling instruction, prepare one set of worksheets per spelling group.

Additional Materials for CCC Vocabulary

1. Vocabulary worksheet, with 10 to 15 vocabulary words and their definitions listed on the left side of the sheet and blank lines on the right for writing each word and a definition for that word, one per student. For classrooms using differentiated reading instruction, prepare one set of worksheets per reading group.

Additional Materials for CCC Word Identification

1. Word list worksheet, divided into three vertical sections, with a list of 10 to 15 words (5 to 10 words for early primary grade students) in the left-hand section, the words written again in dashed lines in the middle section, and blank lines for writing each word in the right-hand section, one per student. For classrooms using differentiated reading instruction, prepare one set of worksheets per reading group.

Observation (Select One or Both)

1. Calculate percent-correct scores on daily classwork, quizzes, or tests in a selected subject for 5 to 10 days for the entire class or a target group of students.
2. Administer *Curriculum-Based Measurement Probes* in the selected subject to the entire class or a target group of students.

Intervention Steps

Introduction and Training

1. Tell the students that they will be learning a new method of improving their performance in the selected subject called Cover, Copy, and Compare, or CCC.
2. Give each student a copy of a CCC worksheet in the target subject. Demonstrate the use of the CCC procedure as described below, using your own copy of the worksheet or a transparency displayed on an overhead projector.
3. After the demonstration, conduct a classwide practice in which students complete one or more worksheets or item sets. Remind students that they will not benefit from the CCC strategy if they simply copy the correct item from the model rather than attempting to solve or study it first. Provide corrective feedback as needed and praise the students for managing their own learning.

CCC MATHEMATICS

1. Silently read the first problem and the answer on the left side of the paper.
2. Cover the problem and answer with an index card or your nonwriting hand.

3. Write the problem and answer from memory in the space on the right side of the paper.
4. Uncover the problem and answer on the left side to check your response.
5. Evaluate your response. If the problem is written incorrectly and/or the answer is incorrect, repeat the procedure with that item before proceeding to the next item.

CCC SPELLING

1. Silently read the first word on the list on the left side of the paper.
2. Cover the word with an index card or your nonwriting hand and write it again from memory on the blank line on the right side of the paper.
3. Uncover the word on the left and compare it to your spelling of the word.
4. Evaluate your response. If your spelling is incorrect, repeat the procedure with that word before proceeding to the next word.

CCC VOCABULARY

1. Silently read the first word on the list and its definition on the left side of the paper.
2. Cover the word with an index card or your nonwriting hand and write both the word and its definition on the blank line on the right side of the paper.
3. Uncover the word on the left and compare your definition with the model.
4. Evaluate your response. If the definition is inaccurate or incomplete, repeat the procedure with that word before proceeding to the next word.

CCC WORD IDENTIFICATION

1. Silently read the first word on the list on the left side of the paper.
2. Cover the word with an index card or your nonwriting hand and trace the dashed lines for that word in the second section of the paper while quietly saying the letter names aloud.
3. Write the word again on the blank line in the third section of paper while quietly saying the letter names aloud.
4. Pronounce the word quietly.
5. Repeat the procedure for the next word on the paper.

Implementation

1. Implement the CCC procedure several times a week in the target subject. Because CCC can become tedious if it is implemented too often and for too long a period, use it primarily as a review at the end of a lesson or as one of several activities during independent seatwork.
2. For instructional periods during which all students are simultaneously participating in CCC, set a fixed amount of time for the CCC session (5 to 15 minutes), signal students to begin, and have them complete as many trials as possible during that time.
3. When students reach mastery level (90% or above accuracy) on one set of problems or items, provide them with another set. For CCC Spelling, Vocabulary, and Word Identification, include two or three words from prior lists on the new list to promote retention.
4. Once a week, administer a worksheet based on the material that has been practiced during the CCC period as a timed 3-minute assessment. For CCC Spelling, dictate spelling words for 3 minutes. Have students exchange papers, score them under your direction, and graph the number of items completed correctly in 3 minutes or spelled correctly on the spelling assessment in their subject area folders.

Evaluation (Select One or Both)

1. Compare percent-correct scores on daily classwork, quizzes, or tests in the selected subject for the entire class or the target group of students before and after implementation.
2. Compare scores on *Curriculum-Based Measurement Probes* in the selected subject for the entire class or the target students before and after implementation.

Variations

Variation 1: CCC with Classwide Incentives for Behavior

1. During CCC sessions, record bonus points on the chalkboard for appropriate CCC behaviors and deduct points if you observe students copying the answers without going through the entire procedure. When the class has accumulated a specified number of points, deliver an activity-based reward, such as extra recess, music time, or an in-class game.

Variation 2: CCC with Classwide Incentives for Performance

1. Record the total number of problems completed correctly on the weekly timed CCC assessments on the chalkboard or chart. When the number reaches a specified goal (e.g., 300 correctly completed math problems), celebrate with a classwide reward, such as a pizza, popcorn, or ice cream party.

Notes

1. As students become proficient in using the CCC procedure in one subject, add CCC in another subject in which basic skills practice is needed.
2. Using index cards as covers may slow some students down and make the procedure more cumbersome (Skinner et al., 1992). Alternately, have students fold their worksheets in half lengthwise, so that the answers appear on one side and the blank lines or problems without solutions appear on the other side. For each item, have students look at the model and then fold the sheet over to the right side, covering the model with the correct answer, before responding.
3. Preparing worksheets with a larger number of problems or items (20 to 30) eliminates the need for several sets of sheets per session.

Sources

Conley, C. M., Derby, K. M., Roberts-Gwinn, M., Weber, K. P., & McLaughlin, T. F. (2004). An analysis of initial acquisition and maintenance of sight words following picture matching and copy, cover, and compare teaching methods. *Journal of Applied Behavior Analysis, 37,* 339–350. Copyright 2004 by the Society for the Experimental Analysis of Behavior. Adapted by permission.

Skinner, C. H., McLaughlin, T. F., & Logan, P. (1997). Cover, Copy, and Compare: A self-managed academic intervention effective across skills, students, and settings. *Journal of Behavioral Education, 7,* 295–306. Copyright 1997 by Springer Science and Business Media. Adapted by permission.

Additional Resources

http://www.interventioncentral.org/tools.php

This link from Jim Wright's Intervention Central website is to a math worksheet generator, which creates worksheets for the four basic math operations in a CCC format.

SELF-MONITORING OF ACADEMIC PRODUCTIVITY

Overview

Teachers often complain that they must waste valuable instructional time reminding students to begin and complete classroom tasks in a timely manner. In this simple, cost-effective strategy, students learn to monitor and rate themselves on a set of behaviors that enhance the likelihood of academic success, including attending to directions, beginning assignments promptly, and asking appropriately for help when needed. Self-monitoring interventions are especially appropriate for targeting academic productivity because they shift the responsibility for managing academic assignments and task-related behaviors from teachers to students. When used on a classwide basis, they not only help students become more independent learners, they also give teachers more time for instruction. The intervention can be used to promote on-task behavior and academic productivity in any instructional format, including whole-class instruction, small-group instruction, and independent seatwork. In the original study, implemented in language arts, reading, and computer classes with four at-risk middle school students, self-monitoring produced immediate increases in on-task behavior and improvement in academic performance for all four target students across all three classroom settings. Three variations are presented: one for use with an individual student or small group, one for multisubject implementation, and one with an interdependent group contingency to encourage productivity and accurate self-evaluation.

Purpose

To increase academic productivity by teaching students to monitor their own behaviors while performing daily classwork assignments.

Materials

1. Self-monitoring forms, one per student (see Figure 4.1 on p. 156).
2. Posterboard chart and gold adhesive stars (optional, see Variation 3).

Observation (Select One or More)

Option 1

1. Select an instructional period during which students are especially off-task and unproductive. Using a *Classwide Scanning Form* with a 5-minute interval, scan the room at the end of each interval, starting with the front of the room and ending with the back, and tally the number of students in each of the following behavior categories:
   a. *On-task behavior,* defined as working on the assigned task, asking or answering teacher-delivered questions, following teacher directions, and performing other behaviors relevant to the lesson.
   b. *Off-task behavior,* defined as sitting without having appropriate materials at hand, gazing around the room or at classmates, or any other nonengaged behavior.
   c. *Disruptive behavior,* defined as making noises, calling out, getting out of seat, arguing with peers, or any other behavior that interferes with ongoing instruction.
2. Conduct these observations for 30 to 45 minutes a day for 4 to 7 days.

Option 2

1. Calculate percent-correct scores on daily classwork assignments in a selected subject for a group of target students or the entire class for 5 to 10 days or the previous grading period. If desired, calculate the class average percent-correct score for daily classwork assignments by summing percent-correct scores for each student and dividing by the number of students in the class.

Option 3

1. Calculate the number of daily classwork assignments completed with 80% accuracy or above in the selected subject for a group of target students or the entire class for 5 to 10 days.

Intervention Steps

Introduction and Training

1. Explain to the class that they will be learning how to improve their grades in the selected subject by monitoring their own behavior during classwork time.
2. Lead a discussion about behaviors that facilitate successful completion of daily assignments (e.g., listening to directions, beginning promptly, and completing the entire assignment) and those that interfere with success (e.g., failing to pay attention to directions, not asking for help when needed, and not working hard until the task is completed).
3. Give each student a copy of the self-monitoring forms and review the behaviors that students will be observing and evaluating. Demonstrate examples of productive and unproductive behavior during classwork time and have students use their self-monitoring forms to rate your behavior. Circulate to review student responses, and provide assistance and feedback as needed.
4. Tell students that you will give them a few minutes each day at the end of the period to ask themselves if they have performed the target behaviors and to complete the self-monitoring forms. After they have completed the forms, you will walk around the room to review everyone's response.

Implementation

1. Distribute the self-monitoring forms at the beginning of the period.
2. Five minutes before the end of the period, instruct students to complete the forms. After students have had time to rate their behaviors, circulate and scan each form as you move around the room. If you observe that a student has been inaccurate in his or her self-evaluations, provide brief private feedback. If many students are inaccurate, conduct an additional review of the procedures.

Evaluation (Select One or More)

Option 1

1. Compare the percentages of students with on-task, off-task, and disruptive behavior during the selected period before and after implementation.

Option 2

1. Compare percent-correct scores on daily classwork assignments in the selected subject for a group of target students or the entire class before and after implementation. If desired, compare the class average percent-correct score for daily classwork assignments in the selected subject before and after implementation.

Option 3

1. Compare the number of daily assignments completed with 80% accuracy or above in the selected subject for the entire class or the target group before and after implementation.

Variations

Variation 1: Self-Monitoring with One Student or a Small Group of Target Students

1. To implement with one or a small group of target students, provide training on an individual basis and tailor the items on the form to the specific problem behaviors. Review the form privately with the students at the end of the period. If desired, have students take their forms home to be signed by parents and returned the following day.

Variation 2: Self-Monitoring in Multiple Subjects

1. For implementation in more than one subject, have students use one form per subject and keep the forms in their subject area folder or notebook. Conduct periodic spot checks of self-monitoring accuracy and provide praise and corrective feedback as needed.

Variation 3: Self-Monitoring with a Group Contingency

1. Each day that at least 80% of the students have 80% success or more on their self-monitoring sheets (or some other criterion) and you agree with those ratings, select a student to put a gold star on the chart. If the class accumulates four stars during the week, provide a group activity reward on Friday, such as extra recess, game time, or music time. Gradually raise the criterion as student productivity increases.

Source

Wood, S. J., Murdock, J. Y., Cronin, M. E., Dawson, N. M., & Kirby, P. C. (1998). Effects of self-monitoring on on-task behaviors of at-risk middle school students. *Journal of Behavioral Education, 8,* 263–279. Copyright 1998 by Springer Science and Business Media. Adapted by permission.

Checklist for Success

Name: _____ Date: _____ Subject: _____

	Yes	No
1. I was prepared for class.	____ Yes	____ No
2. I began the assignment promptly.	____ Yes	____ No
3. I worked without disturbing others.	____ Yes	____ No
4. I followed teacher directions.	____ Yes	____ No
5. I participated in the class.	____ Yes	____ No
6. I paid attention to the teacher and my work.	____ Yes	____ No
7. I asked for help appropriately when I needed it.	____ Yes	____ No
8. I completed the class assignment.	____ Yes	____ No
9. I checked over my paper before handing it in.	____ Yes	____ No
10. I turned in my assignment.	____ Yes	____ No

Total number of yeses = _____

Total number of nos = _____

Percent success (number of yeses divided by 10) = _____

FIGURE 4.1. Self-Monitoring Sheet. From Wood, Murdock, Cronin, Dawson, and Kirby (1998, pp. 266–268). Copyright 1998 by Springer Science and Business Media. Adapted by permission.

USING RESPONSE CARDS
TO INCREASE ACADEMIC ENGAGEMENT AND ACHIEVEMENT

Overview

Students learn and remember more when they actively respond during instruction. All too often, however, lesson formats fail to provide for sufficient participation, and students become passive observers of instruction. For low-performing students, this passivity compounds their problems because they lose opportunities to receive teacher feedback and improve their knowledge and skills. In this intervention, students write short answers on laminated boards in response to teacher questions during whole-class instruction. Response card lesson formats not only increase students' opportunities to respond but also enhance instructional effectiveness by permitting teachers to conduct ongoing assessments of student performance, provide immediate feedback, and modify instruction until all students demonstrate understanding. Response card instruction has been shown to enhance participation rates, on-task behavior, and academic achievement across a wide range of grade levels and subjects for students in general education, as well as for students with disabilities and English language learners. Moreover, students enjoy the novelty of the strategy and prefer using response cards to raising their hands. First developed for use in social studies and science classes, response card instruction can be implemented in any subject and is especially effective as a review strategy during the last 5 or 10 minutes of an instructional period. A variation with a preprinted card format appropriate for younger students is also presented.

Purpose

To improve participation and learning by providing frequent opportunities for active student responding and immediate teacher feedback.

Materials

1. Stopwatch or watch with second hand.
2. Weekly quiz, one quiz per student.
3. White laminated tileboards (9″ × 12″) or manila folders, cut in half and placed inside plastic sheet protectors, one per student.
4. Dry erase black markers, one per student.
5. Felt squares (about 4″ square), paper towels, or dry erasers, one per student.
6. 3″ × 5″ index cards with preprinted responses on either side (Yes/No or True/False), one per student; printing should be large enough to be easily read from the front of the room; alternately, use color-coded cards, with contrasting colors on either side of a single card (e.g., red for Yes, blue for No) or two differently colored cards (optional, see Variation).

Observation (Select One or More)

1. Calculate the class average on weekly quizzes and/or chapter tests for a selected subject for the previous month by summing individual student scores and dividing by the total number of students.
2. Using a sheet of paper with a list of student names or a copy of a seating chart attached to a clipboard, record the number of times one or more target students respond to a question by hand raising during a selected instructional period for 4 to 7 days.
3. Calculate the percentage of students with grades of D or F in a selected subject for the current grading period or for the school year thus far.

Intervention Steps

Introduction and Training

1. Explain to the students that they will be learning a new and more interesting way to participate in class. Distribute the tileboard cards, markers, and erasers and conduct a 10- to 15-minute training session using the procedures described below.
2. Tell students to answer your questions by printing their answers in one or two words on their response cards. Pose a question and say "Write your answer" to cue the students to begin writing. After 5 seconds, say "Cards up." Remind students to hold their cards above their heads so that you can see all responses.
3. Quickly scan all student responses and provide feedback as described below.
4. Say "Cards down" to signal students to lower their cards, erase the previous response, and prepare for the next response.

Implementation

1. During the lesson, present information for the first 15 or 20 minutes. After you present each new fact or concept, ask a question about it and have students respond by writing one- or two-word answers on their cards or folders and holding them up.
2. After visually scanning all of the response cards, provide praise for correct answers or corrective feedback for incorrect answers, as follows:
   a. If everyone has written the right answer, give the feedback to the whole class:

      "Good, class, I see that everyone wrote *gas*. Water vapor is a *gas*."

   b. If some students show incorrect answers, acknowledge that some have answered correctly and also provide the correct answer:

      "I see that many of you have *gas* as the answer. That is correct, water vapor is a *gas*."

   c. If no students have the correct answer, indicate this and provide the correct answer:

      "I do not see any correct answers. The correct answer is *gas*. Water vapor in the atmosphere is a *gas*."

3. Later in the lesson, ask a series of review questions related to the newly presented facts and concepts. Be sure to repeat any questions that were missed by a majority of students earlier in the lesson to ensure that students have understood their errors.
4. Praise students for using the response cards promptly and provide corrective feedback as needed.

Evaluation (Select One or More)

1. Compare the class average grade on weekly quizzes and/or chapter tests in the selected subject before and after implementation.
2. Compare response rates for hand raising versus response card use for the target students during the selected instructional period before and after implementation.
3. Compare the percentage of students with grades of D or F in the selected subject before and after implementation.

Variation: Preprinted Response Card Format

1. Distribute preprinted cards at the beginning of each lesson. Teach students to respond to questions by displaying the side of the card with the answer toward you. Pose a question and say "Cards up." After you scan the cards, say "Cards down."
2. Provide praise for correct answers and error feedback for incorrect answers. Conduct addi-

tional demonstrations and practice sessions if students are inadvertently displaying the wrong side of the card. For young students, use two differently colored cards.

Notes

1. For self-contained classes, have students keep response card materials at their desks. For departmentalized classes, collect response card materials at the end of each period and distribute them prior to instruction.
2. To prevent doodling, tell students that you will give them 2 minutes (or some other amount of time) at the end of the period to draw on their cards, provided that they write only answers to teacher questions on their cards during instruction.
3. Although preprinted response cards are easier for teachers to see than write-on response cards, they are more time-consuming to prepare and limit responses to predetermined recognition-type responses. Write-on cards slow student responses and instructional pacing because more time is needed for writing and erasing answers and for teacher inspection, but they permit a much wider range of responses.

Sources

Christie, C. A., & Schuster, J. W. (2003). The effects of using response cards on student participation, academic achievement, and on-task behavior during whole-class, math instruction. *Journal of Behavioral Education, 12,* 147–165. Copyright 2003 by Springer Science and Business Media. Adapted by permission.

Gardner, R. III, Heward, W. L., & Grossi, T. A. (1994). Effects of response cards on student participation and academic achievement: A systematic replication with inner-city students during whole-class science instruction. *Journal of Applied Behavior Analysis, 27,* 63–71. Copyright 1994 by the Society for the Experimental Analysis of Behavior. Adapted by permission.

THE REWARDS BOX: ENHANCING ACADEMIC PERFORMANCE WITH RANDOMIZED GROUP CONTINGENCIES

Overview

Interdependent group contingencies—reward systems based on the performance of all the students in the classroom—are efficient for teachers and encourage cooperation because every student has an opportunity to earn reinforcement. At the same time, however, group contingencies are limited by the fact that the rewards may be reinforcing for some students but neutral or even aversive for others. Moreover, if students perceive that they cannot meet the criterion for the reward after an initially poor performance, they have little incentive to engage in appropriate behavior for the rest of the intervention period. This intervention solves these problems by randomizing both the rewards and the performance criteria to target academic productivity and performance in a particular subject area. The teacher randomly selects a group criterion (class-wide average percent-correct score on daily assignments of 75%, 80%, 85%, etc.) and provides a group-oriented reward if the weekly class average meets that goal. First implemented in a self-contained classroom with five middle school students with emotional disorders, the intervention produced large, educationally meaningful gains in spelling, mathematics, and English for all participants. In the original study, the three academic subjects were targeted in succession. This adaptation targets a single academic subject, with the multiple-subject implementation included as a variation. Reward delivery has also been reduced from a daily to a weekly basis for usability purposes, with a daily reward system presented as a variation. Another highly usable variation that requires teachers to evaluate only a single student's performance is included, as are variations targeting homework and quiz or test performance.

Purpose

To improve achievement in one or more academic subjects with a randomized interdependent group contingency system.

Materials

1. *Reinforcement Menu,* optional.
2. Three shoe boxes, labeled "Rewards," "Goals," and "Suggestions," respectively.
3. 30 3″ × 5″ index cards, listing the criteria for student performance (e.g., one index card with "50%," three with "60%," three with "70%," four with "80%," four with "85%," five with "90%," five with "95%," and five with "100%"); 20–30 blank index cards.
4. Red pens, one per student (optional, see Note).
5. Shoe box containing slips of paper with the name of each student in the class, labeled "Student Names" (optional, see Variation 5).
6. Rewards, such as wrapped candy, school supplies, and stickers (optional).

Observation (Select One or Both)

1. Calculate percent-correct scores for each student on daily assignments in a selected academic subject for the past several weeks. Then calculate a class average percent-correct score by summing individual student scores and dividing by the total number of students.
2. Calculate the class average percent-correct score on weekly quizzes and/or chapter tests in the selected academic subject for the previous month by summing individual student scores and dividing by the total number of students.

Intervention Steps

Introduction and Training

1. Explain to the class that they will have a chance to earn rewards if they meet certain goals on their in-class assignments for Monday through Thursday in the selected subject. If the class meets the specified goal, you will randomly select a reward from a set of rewards on Fridays, and everyone will receive it.
2. Administer a *Reinforcement Menu* or conduct a discussion in which you give examples of group rewards (e.g., 15 minutes of computer time, 10 minutes of music, homework passes, 20 minutes of free time) and invite students to suggest other rewards. Write acceptable rewards on the chalkboard during the discussion.
3. Using this list, write each reward on an index card and put the cards in the Rewards Box. Place the Suggestions Box and the blank index cards on a table accessible to all students and tell them that they may put suggestions for other group rewards in the box. Explain that you will add their suggestions to the rewards if you believe that they are appropriate.
4. Next, display the Goals Box and explain that you will also randomly select a goal for group academic performance. Demonstrate by randomly selecting a card and reading the criterion (e.g., class average of 90% in the selected subject). Explain that if the class had met or exceeded this goal for their weekly average score, you would have randomly selected a card from the Rewards Box and given all students the reward or permitted all students to participate in the activity.
5. Tell the students that if they do not meet the selected goal, you will not draw a reward from the Rewards Box on Friday, but they will have an opportunity to earn a reward the following week.
6. Tell students the number of cards with each criterion in the Goals Box and answer any questions about the procedures. Place the Goals Box and the Rewards Box on your desk.

Implementation

1. Each Friday, randomly select a card from the Goals Box. Check your grade book to determine the class's average percent-correct score for the target subject, announce the criterion, and announce whether the class has met it.
2. If the class has met the criterion, randomly select a card from the Rewards Box and announce which reward has been drawn and when it will be delivered.
3. Return the goal and reward cards to their respective boxes so that they can be selected again at the next drawing.

Evaluation (Select One or Both)

1. Compare class average percent-correct scores in the selected academic subject before and after implementation.
2. Compare class average percent-correct scores on weekly quizzes and/or chapter tests in the selected academic subject before and after implementation.

Variations

Variation 1: The Daily Rewards Box

1. To provide rewards on a daily basis, calculate percent-correct scores on the daily assignment in the targeted subject area for each student in the class. Calculate the class average percent-correct score by summing individual scores and dividing by the number of students in class that day. Use this score to determine whether the class has met the performance criterion drawn from the Goals Box.
2. At the end of the day, randomly select a card from the Goals Box, check your grade book, announce the criterion, and announce if the class has met the criterion. If so, randomly select a card from the Rewards Box.
3. If possible, provide the reward at the end of the day. If not, deliver the reward as soon as possible the following day. Note that this version requires evaluating each student's performance before the end of the day; however, depending on the criterion drawn, the class average can be estimated. For example, if the goal selected is 80% and all students score above 90%, there is no need to calculate the exact average.

Variation 2: The Rewards Box for Multiple Subject Areas

1. After 2 weeks of implementation in one subject, tell students that you are adding goals for another subject to the Goals Box. Explain that the class will need to work hard in both subjects in order to increase their chances of earning a reward.
2. Add 30 more index cards with subject-specific goals to the Goals Box, for a total of 60 cards. To distinguish the two sets of goals, write the name of the subject as well as the goal on each card (e.g., Mathematics—70%; Spelling—85%).
3. Note that you must now evaluate and record each student's performance in two subjects by the end of the week so that you can calculate or estimate the class average score on both sets of assignments.
4. If desired, add a third subject after 2 weeks of two-subject implementation, using the same procedures. This version requires 90 cards in the Goals Box.

Variation 3: The Rewards Box for Homework Performance

1. Explain to the class that they will have a chance to earn rewards if they achieve a certain average score on their daily homework in the selected subject (e.g., a class average of 85% for

complete, accurate homework). Grade homework each night so that students can potentially receive a reward the following day.

2. After several weeks, require the class to achieve a specified weekly rather than daily homework average in order to receive the reward.

Variation 4: The Rewards Box for Quiz or Test Performance

1. Tell the students that they will have a chance to earn rewards if they achieve a certain average score on their quizzes or tests in the selected subject (e.g., a class average of 85% or better on the next four weekly quizzes). This variation enhances maintenance and generalization of academic gains because it requires students to achieve the same level of performance over a longer period of time to receive the reinforcement. Because students are not eligible for rewards for several weeks or longer, depending on the quiz or test schedule, however, do not implement this variation until students have responded positively to the daily assignment version.

Variation 5: The Rewards Box with Single-Student Performance Evaluation

1. After the classwide intervention has been implemented for several weeks, announce that you will now be randomly selecting one student and determining if that student's weekly average on daily assignments meets the randomly selected criterion.

2. Each Friday, randomly select a slip of paper from the Student Names Box and a card from the Goals Box. Check your grade book to determine the student's average daily assignment score, announce the criterion you have drawn, and announce whether the student has met this criterion. Be sure not to identify the student by name and to return the paper to the Student Names Box immediately.

3. If the student has met the criterion, randomly select a card from the Rewards Box and announce which reward has been drawn and when it will be delivered.

4. Note that this variation is easier to implement than the original version and the other variations because you must evaluate only one student's performance.

Note

1. For maximum usability, select subjects that have easy-to-grade daily assignments, such as spelling and mathematics. To speed up grading, have students exchange papers and use red pens to grade each other's papers while you go over the answers. Monitor students carefully during the grading process and if you detect cheating, do not deliver any rewards that day.

Source

Popkin, J., & Skinner, C. H. (2003). Enhancing academic performance in a classroom serving students with serious emotional disturbance: Interdependent group contingencies with randomly selected components. *School Psychology Review, 32,* 282–295. Copyright 2003 by the National Association of School Psychologists. Adapted by permission.

Interventions to Improve
Homework Completion and Accuracy

Although the benefits of homework have long been debated, the amount of homework students receive has substantially increased in recent years as the result of efforts to raise academic standards and improve achievement (Bryan, Burstein, & Bryan, 2001; National Center for Education Statistics, 2007a). Although studies have failed to document a significant positive relationship between the amount of homework completed and achievement for elementary school students, homework completion is strongly associated with achievement for secondary school students (Cooper, Lindsay, Nye, & Greathouse, 1998; Cooper & Valentine, 2001). Moreover, certain aspects of homework appear to be critical in the relationship between homework performance and achievement. In a large-scale study using data from the National Education Longitudinal Study gathered for the National Center for Education Statistics, homework completed outside of school had strong positive effects on learning, as measured by 12th-grade GPAs and achievement tests, whereas homework completed at school had no effect on performance (Keith, Diamond-Hallam, & Fine, 2004). Because homework assignments account for about 20% of students' total academic engaged time (Cooper & Nye, 1994), students who spend less time on homework or spend their homework time ineffectively are likely to make less academic progress than their peers (Cooper et al., 1998). Even for younger students, homework can have beneficial effects by promoting independent work habits, facilitating parent–child communication about school, and encouraging parental involvement in school (Cooper & Valentine, 2001; Miller & Kelley, 1994).

Despite the documented benefits of homework, many students lack the academic skills and/or self-discipline needed to complete their homework (Rathvon, 1996). Students with reading and writing problems and students with learning disabilities are especially vulnerable to homework completion problems and poor study habits, such as starting homework without making a list of their assignments or planning their study time (Bryan et al., 2001; Gajria & Salend, 1995; Margolis & McCabe, 1997). Homework problems typically increase from the elementary to the secondary level as teachers cover more content and assign longer, more complex homework tasks. Lack of homework completion may contribute to the widening of the achievement gap between students with disabilities and their nondisabled peers as students move through the middle and high school years (Hughes, Rudl, Schumaker, & Deshler, 2002).

Not withstanding the increasing use of homework as an instructional practice and the persistent concerns of teachers, parents, and students relative to homework completion (Bursuck et al., 1999; Epstein, Munk, Bursuck, Polloway, & Jayanthi, 1999; Harniss, Epstein, Bursuck, Nelson, & Jayanthi, 2001), there are surprisingly few experimentally based homework interventions in the literature. In addition, most of the published interventions have been implemented by researchers rather than teachers, involve small numbers of students, and/or require extensive training and additional curricular materials that make them impractical for classroom teachers (e.g., Eilam, 2001; Rhoades & Kratochwill, 1998). Because homework is assigned at school but completed at home, interventions that increase collaboration between teachers and parents have the potential to enhance homework quality and completion rates. Unfortunately, homework interventions involving parents often require substantial investments of time to implement and monitor, and obtaining adequate levels of parent participation can be difficult, even with extensive consultant support (e.g., Callahan et al., 1998).

HOMEWORK INTERVENTIONS

The three interventions in this section incorporate components drawn from one or more of three categories of homework enhancement strategies: (1) self-management interventions, (2) contingency-based strategies, and (3) direct instruction programs. Because students must do their homework away from direct teacher supervision, self-management strategies are ideally suited for targeting homework completion. *Team Up for Homework Success* combines self-management with group-oriented contingencies to prompt, monitor, and reinforce homework completion. This intervention addresses not only the skills needed for independent assignment completion through a collaborative learning format, but also the motivational aspects of homework completion by combining a peer-mediated form of self-management with a classroom lottery.

Instruction in organizational skills alone is insufficient to improve homework submission rates because students must also be motivated to complete their assignments (Hughes et al., 2002). *Promoting Homework Completion and Accuracy with Mystery Motivators* targets motivation directly by using unpredictable rewards and peer influence to improve homework productivity and performance. A *mystery motivator* is a description or symbol of a reward that is placed in an envelope with a question mark and displayed prominently in the classroom (Rhode et al., 1993). To gain access to the unknown reinforcer, students must meet specific academic or behavioral standards. Concealing the reinforcer while simultaneously signaling that it is potentially available increases the anticipation of the reward and motivates behavior directed toward the intervention target (Mottram, Bray, Kehle, Broudy, & Jenson, 2002). Interventions with mystery motivator components have been demonstrated to be effective in improving homework completion for elementary school students (Madaus, Kehle, Madaus, & Bray, 2003; Moore, Waguespack, Wickstrom, Witt, & Gaydos, 1994), as well as enhancing classroom behavior (Murphy, Theodore, Aloiso, Alric-Edwards, & Hughes, 2007; Musser et al., 2001).

Although numerous studies have focused on what teachers and/or parents can do to improve students' homework performance, such as providing contingencies for homework completion (e.g., Miller & Kelley, 1994) or increasing parental supervision (e.g., Rhoades & Kratchowill, 1998), very little research has focused on teaching students the complex sequence of skills necessary for adequate homework completion without additional supervision by teachers or parents. *Project Best: Seven Steps to Homework Completion* is a direct instruction intervention in which students learn to record and complete their homework assignments. The strategy provides instruction not only in planning and managing study time, but also in a set of metacognitive behaviors associated with successful homework completion, including self-monitoring, self-instruction, and self-evaluation.

CROSS-REFERENCE: *The Rewards Box: Enhancing Academic Performance with Randomized Group Contingencies* presented in the Academic Productivity section of this chapter includes a variation targeting homework completion. For two home-based interventions that teach parents how to tutor their children in reading, see *Paired Reading* and *Parents as Reading Tutors* later in this chapter. For a strategy that uses mystery motivators to enhance classroom behavior, see *A Multicomponent Intervention to Reduce Disruptive Behavior* in Chapter 5.

TEAM UP FOR HOMEWORK SUCCESS

Overview

Helping students assume responsibility for their own homework assignments can be challenging for teachers and students alike. This intervention package combines self-management strategies with interdependent group contingencies, public posting, and collaborative learning to help students monitor their own homework completion and accuracy. Teams of four students meet in structured sessions to monitor assignments, review effective homework strategies, and complete team scorecards. Three of the team roles incorporate research-based self-management strategies, including self-monitoring, self-instruction, and self-evaluation, while a fourth team member serves as a replacement if needed. Students of teams meeting a weekly criterion for homework accuracy have access to a classroom raffle. In the original study with 16 low-performing sixth graders, participants demonstrated substantial increases in homework completion rates in mathematics and scores on standardized math tests and curriculum-based measures. In addition, parents reported significantly fewer problems related to homework completion. Variations with whole-team rewards and randomized homework accuracy goals are also presented.

Purpose

To improve daily homework completion and accuracy with peer-mediated self-management procedures and a classwide raffle.

Materials

1. Daily homework assignment in the selected academic subject.
2. Answer sheets corresponding to homework assignments, one per team.
3. "Team Scorecards," consisting of 3″ × 5″ index cards listing team members' names down the left-hand side, with columns headed "Daily Score" and "Yes/No" (for goal completion rating), one per team per week.
4. Posterboard chart listing the duties for each team role.
5. "League Scorecard," consisting of a posterboard chart with team names and five columns, labeled with the days of the school week, for posting "win" stickers.
6. Stickers or stars.
7. Shoe box labeled "Raffle Tickets" and containing slips of paper with student or team names.
8. Opaque jar labeled "Homework Goals" and containing 16 slips of paper listing a variety of accuracy criteria, such as 4 "80%" slips, 4 "85%" slips, 4 "90%" slips, and 4 "95%" slips (optional, see Variation 2).
9. Raffle prizes, consisting of fast food cards, video game tokens, school supplies, wrapped candy, etc.

Observation (Select One or Both)

Option 1

1. Calculate homework completion rates in a selected subject for each student or a target group of students for 1 to 3 weeks by counting the number of days that homework is returned and expressing this number as a percentage. For example, if a student returns homework assignments on 9 out of 15 days, that student's homework completion rate is 60%.
2. If desired, calculate the percentage of students in the entire class whose homework completion rate is below 80% in the selected subject by summing the number of students with completion rates below 80% and dividing by the number of students in the class.

Option 2

1. Calculate homework accuracy rates in a selected subject for each student or a group of target students for 5 to 10 days by counting the number of correct problems completed, dividing by the number of problems assigned, and multiplying that number by 100%. For example, if a student answers 12 of 20 problems correctly, that student's homework accuracy rate is 60%.
2. If desired, calculate the percentage of students in the entire class whose homework accuracy rate is below 80% in the selected subject by summing the number of students with accuracy rates below 80% and dividing by the number of students in the class.

Intervention Steps

Introduction and Training

1. Explain to students that they will be playing a game to help them get more out of their homework assignments in the selected subject. Tell them that the game has teams like baseball (football, hockey, etc.), with each player on the team playing a special role in the group effort.
2. Explain that teams consist of four members: (a) "coach," (b) "scorekeeper," (c) "manager," and (d) "pinch hitter." Explain that the pinch hitter's role is to attend team meetings and take the role of other team members when they are absent. Assign students to teams and to roles within each team.
3. Review the steps in the team process and the team members' roles, as described below. Then conduct a demonstration of a team meeting, using four students to model the roles.

STEP 1: THE COACH

    a. Prompts and directs team functions.
    b. Assembles the team, reminds members of the weekly accuracy goal, and reviews homework completion strategies as needed.

STEP 2: THE SCOREKEEPER

    a. Counts the number of assignments turned in by team members and grades them according to the answer sheet supplied by the teacher.
    b. Determines each member's homework accuracy score and records it on each member's paper.
    c. Fills in each member's homework accuracy score on the team scorecard and checks "Yes" or No" to indicate whether or not all members obtained the weekly accuracy goal.

STEP 3: THE MANAGER

    a. Reviews the team scorecard and declares a "win" or "loss" depending on whether team performance met or exceeded the weekly accuracy goal.
    b. Posts a "win" sticker on the league scorecard if the team met or exceeded the goal.

STEP 4: THE COACH

    a. Reminds team members of the goal for the next day's homework and encourages team members to reach it.

Implementation

1. Have each team select a team name and discuss strategies for increasing homework accuracy and completion. Each student performs the assigned role for 3 days, after which roles are reassigned so that eventually each student has an opportunity to perform all team functions. Change teams every 4 weeks.
2. Each week, set an accuracy goal (e.g., 85% accuracy) on homework assignments to determine eligibility to participate in the raffle, and post the goal on the chalkboard. Team averages for the week must equal or exceed the goal for students to be eligible for the raffle.
3. Conduct team meetings daily (or each day that a homework assignment is due) at the beginning of the instructional period. Meetings should last 10 to 15 minutes, after which students hand in their corrected homework to you for review and managers return team scorecards until the next session.
4. Check homework papers for accuracy. If students have calculated homework scores incorrectly, rescore the papers and remind scorekeepers to check accurately.
5. On Fridays, have each manager check the weekly average for his or her team to determine whether the team has met the goal. Distribute raffle tickets to managers of teams that have met the weekly goal for distribution to team members.
6. Have members of winning teams write their names on slips of paper and place their raffle tickets in the Raffle Ticket Box. Draw three or four tickets (or a number corresponding to about 10 to 15% of the number of students in the class), and deliver rewards to the students whose names are drawn.
7. As homework performance improves, gradually raise the accuracy criterion or require that all students on a team meet the criterion in order for team members to be eligible for the raffle.

Evaluation (Select One or Both)

Option 1

1. Compare homework completion rates in the selected subject for each student or for the target group of students before and after implementation. If desired, also compare the percentage of students in the entire class whose homework completion rate is below 80% before and after implementation.

Option 2

1. Compare homework accuracy rates in the selected subject for each student or the group of target students before and after implementation. If desired, also compare the percentage of students in the entire class whose homework accuracy rate is below 80% before and after implementation.

Variations

Variation 1: Homework Teams with Whole-Team Rewards

1. Set a daily rather than a weekly criterion for homework accuracy. Have the manager of each team meeting the criterion place a raffle ticket with the team's name on it in the box. On Friday, draw a single ticket and deliver rewards to each member of the team whose name is drawn.

Variation 2: Homework Teams with Randomized Goals

1. Display the Homework Goals Jar and review the contents as described in the Materials section. Explain that you will draw a slip of paper from the jar each day during the team session to determine the goal for the day. Students of teams with averages that meet or exceed the selected goal may place a raffle ticket in the box. Conduct the raffle on Friday as described above and deliver rewards to students whose names are drawn.
2. Alternately, implement whole-team rewards as indicated in Variation 1 and deliver rewards to each member of the team whose name is drawn.

Notes

1. This intervention works best in a subject with homework assignments that can be easily scored using an answer key, such as mathematics, or with assignments that are dichotomously scored (i.e., true/false, multiple choice).
2. In the original study, there were only negligible differences in homework accuracy rates between treatment and control groups despite significant gains in homework completion rates and on other criterion measures for target students. As with any academic intervention, carefully assessing students for the presence of academic skills deficits versus performance deficits is critical to success.

Source

Olympia, D. E., Sheridan, S. M., Jenson, W. R., & Andrews, D. (1994). Using student-managed interventions to increase homework completion and accuracy. *Journal of Applied Behavior Analysis, 27,* 85–99. Copyright 1994 by the Society for the Experimental Analysis of Behavior. Adapted by permission.

PROJECT BEST:
SEVEN STEPS TO SUCCESSFUL HOMEWORK COMPLETION

Overview

Homework can provide students with additional opportunities to learn new content and practice new skills, but only if they complete their assignments with care and accuracy. Unfortunately, many students, especially those with disabilities, have difficulties mastering the complex sequence of behaviors required for homework completion, including recording assignments quickly and correctly, developing a plan for completing assignments, and following assignments through to completion. This intervention teaches students a seven-step strategy for managing homework assignments, as well as a set of metacognitive behaviors supporting effective homework practices, such as self-monitoring, self-instruction, and self-evaluation. The first letters of the major steps and the substeps of the strategy form the words *Project* and *Best*, respectively, which serve as mnemonic devices to guide students during the self-instruction process. As students work through the steps, they complete three forms: (1) a monthly calendar for long-range planning, (2) a weekly study schedule, and (3) an assignment sheet specifically designed for students with writing problems. First implemented with nine middle school students with learning disabilities enrolled in general education classes, the intervention had positive effects on homework completion rates, teacher ratings of the quality of completed homework assignments, and quarterly grades for eight of the nine target students. Moreover, the students maintained improvements in homework performance after strategy instruction was discontinued.

Purpose

To improve homework accuracy and completion rates using a seven-step self-management strategy.

Materials

1. Posterboard chart, labeled "Seven Steps to Successful Homework Completion" and displaying the PROJECT steps and the BEST substeps, as described below.
2. Homework assignment sheets, one per student per week (see Figure 4.2 on p. 172).
3. Weekly study schedule, consisting of an 8½″ × 11″ sheet of paper with eight columns, the first listing times in 30-minute increments and another seven columns for the days of the week, one per student per week.
4. Monthly planners, consisting of purchased homework planners or sheets of paper with dated blocks for each day of the month, one per student per month.
5. Manila folders, one per student.
6. Overhead projector and transparencies of samples of the homework assignment sheet, study schedule, and planner pages (optional).

Observation (Select One or More)

1. Calculate the percentage of completed homework assignments for a target group of students or the entire class in one or more subjects for 5 to 10 days or several weeks.
2. Calculate the percentage of homework assignments completed with 80% or above accuracy for a target group of students or the entire class in one or more subjects for 5 to 10 days or several weeks.
3. Using report card grades, calculate quarterly grade point averages for a group of target students by associating each letter grade with a number (i.e., A = 4, B = 3, C = 2, D = 1, F = 0), summing the numbers, and dividing by the total number of academic subjects.

Intervention Steps

Introduction and Training

1. Tell students that they are going to learn an effective strategy that will help them complete their homework and make better grades in school.
2. Display the folders, the chart with the PROJECT and BEST strategy steps, and examples of the monthly planner, weekly study schedule, and assignment sheet. Review the assignment completion steps as presented below, including where, when, why, and how the strategy can be used. Have students take notes about the strategy steps during the training.

STEP 1: PREPARE YOUR FORMS.

 a. *Prepare the monthly planners.* Fill in numbers corresponding to the days of the current and subsequent month on two monthly planning sheets. Note special events, such as holidays, athletic games, etc., so that you can plan study time on those days and on surrounding days.

 b. *Prepare the weekly study schedule.* Write in the date for each day of the week and block out time periods during each day when homework cannot be done (e.g., eating, sleeping, attending soccer practice, practicing the piano).

STEP 2: RECORD AND ASK.

 a. *Record assignments.* As soon as a teacher gives an assignment, record it on the assignment sheet, using abbreviations such as "SS" for social studies or "E" for English and circling words printed on the sheet instead of writing them. For example, if the assignment is to read Chapter 3 and answer questions 1 through 10, circle the word *read* and *answer* and then write the rest of the assignment on the lines provided (see Figure 4.2). Also note the due date. If the assignment is due on a different week than the current one, record the assignment and due date on the monthly planner. Remember to check the monthly planner each night to monitor upcoming due dates.

 b. *Ask questions.* Think about the instructions the teacher has given and ask about anything that is unclear immediately, after school, or at another appropriate time. Record any additional information learned on the assignment sheet.

STEP 3: ORGANIZE. (THIS STEP OCCURS AT THE END OF THE DAY AFTER ALL ASSIGNMENTS HAVE BEEN RECORDED.)

 a. *Break the assignment down into parts.* Break each task into parts and list each part on a piece of scrap paper. For example, for a book report, list the following parts: (1) selecting a book, (2) reading the book, (3) making notes, (4) completing a first draft, and (5) executing a final draft. Count each part and record that number next to "# of parts" on the assignment sheet.

 b. *Estimate the number of study sessions.* Estimate the number of study sessions, defined as a 30-minute block of time, required to complete the assignment and write this number on the assignment sheet next to "# of study sessions."

 c. *Schedule the sessions.* Write the abbreviation of the assignment (e.g., BK RPT for "book report") in a box on the weekly study schedule corresponding to the days and times you will work on the assignment. Remember to schedule study sessions far enough in advance that you can complete the assignment on time.

 d. *Take materials home.* Put all materials needed to complete each assignment that evening or weekend in your backpack and carry them home.

STEP 4: JUMP TO IT.

 a. Get out the materials you need, tell yourself you're going to do a good job, and check the requirements for each assignment.

STEP 5: ENGAGE IN THE WORK.

    a. Engage in the activities required to complete the assignment. If you have any problems doing the homework, seek assistance from your parents or a study partner from class (if permitted by your teacher).

STEP 6: CHECK YOUR WORK.

    a. Evaluate the quality of your work, based on your assessment of its neatness, completeness, and the effort you have put into it. Make any necessary corrections and circle a "quality grade" on the assignment sheet. Place the assignment in your homework folder.

STEP 7: TURN IN YOUR WORK.

    a. Put the assignment folder in a designated location so that you can find it easily.
    b. The next day, take the folder to school, check the monthly planner and assignment sheet to ensure that all due homework is turned in, and hand in the assignments.
    c. When the assignment has been turned in, record the date on the assignment sheet next to "Done" and give yourself a pat on the back for sticking to the plan and completing the work.

3. Model the use of all the steps of the strategy, using transparencies of the forms, if desired. Speak your thoughts aloud while showing the students how to perform each step and substep of the strategy.

> *Example*: "Now I need to schedule my study sessions for the homework assignments I got today. I'll start with the ones that are due tomorrow so I have time to get them done tonight." (Check the assignment sheet and monthly planner).
>
> "I have a math assignment and a Spanish assignment. I think math will take one session and Spanish will probably take two sessions. So I need three sessions for this evening." (Get out weekly study schedule.)
>
> "When I look at my weekly study schedule, I see that I have time open between 5:00 P.M. and 6:30 P.M. So I'll write 'math' in the first box and 'Spanish' in the next two boxes in that time slot." (Write the subject names in the appropriate boxes.)
>
> "Then I'll have dinner and still have time for guitar practice."

4. Ask questions about each step and substep until students have memorized the strategy and can answer questions about the steps and substeps fluently.
5. Distribute the manila folders with copies of the three forms, including a homework planner or two monthly planning sheets, and have students practice using the first three steps of the strategy with simulated assignments. Move around the room to provide assistance and corrective feedback as needed.

Implementation

1. Give each student an assignment sheet each Friday for the coming week. Distribute two monthly planning sheets every other month if students are not using their own planners.
2. Instruct students to take the assignment sheet to each class and write the next day's assignments on the sheet.
3. Conduct periodic classwide reviews of the strategy as needed.

ASSIGNMENT SHEET

Subject	(Read) Book	Partner John
Eng.	Answer	Phone 583-8888
	(Write) Report – 2 pgs.	
	Other	

A
B
C
D
F

# of parts	5	# of study sessions	10
Due	4/18	Done	4/17

FIGURE 4.2. Assignment sheet for *Project Best: Seven Steps to Homework Completion.* From Hughes, Ruhl, Schumaker, and Deshler (2002, p. 7). Copyright 2002 by Blackwell Publishing. Reprinted by permission.

Evaluation (Select One or More)

1. Compare the percentage of completed homework assignments for the target group of students or the entire class in the selected subject(s) before and after implementation.
2. Compare the percentage of homework assignments completed with 80% or above accuracy for the target group of students or the entire class in the selected subject(s) before and after implementation.
3. Compare quarterly grade point averages for the target students before and after implementation.

Note

1. In the original study, strategy instruction was conducted in a resource room setting four times a week for about 30 minutes per session. For classwide implementation, training takes about three 30-minute sessions, with reviews after holidays and vacations.

Source

Hughes, C. A., Ruhl, K. L., Schumaker, J. B., & Deshler, D. D. (2002). Effects of instruction in an assignment completion strategy on the homework performance of students with learning disabilities in general education class. *Learning Disabilities Research and Practice, 17,* 1–18. Copyright 2002 by Blackwell Publishing. Adapted by permission.

PROMOTING HOMEWORK COMPLETION
AND ACCURACY WITH MYSTERY MOTIVATORS

Overview

Although proficient homework completion is associated with academic success for students of every ability level, many students lack the motivation to complete their homework assignments. This strategy targets performance deficits in homework with a game-like intervention permitting access to an unknown reinforcer for students achieving a specific homework criterion. This "mystery motivator" is an unpredictable reward represented by a manila envelope with a question mark written on it, which is prominently displayed on the teacher's desk. Inside the envelope is a card indicating what the class will win if students attain the homework goal. The mystery motivator intervention has been demonstrated to have powerful effects on homework completion and accuracy for elementary school students and is highly rated by both students and teachers. In the original studies, target students received individual mystery motivator charts and earned rewards for their individual performance. Here the strategy is adapted for classwide application, with a single mystery motivator chart and an interdependent group contingency to capitalize on peer support for homework productivity. A variation with publicly posted reinforcers is also presented.

Purpose

To improve homework accuracy and completion with group contingencies that involve unknown rewards.

Materials

1. "Mystery Motivator Chart," consisting of a posterboard chart divided into boxes labeled with the five days of the school week. For younger students, use a novel format, such as a rocket ship divided into five parts to represent the days of the week.
2. Squares of construction paper and Scotch tape or a set of "invisible ink" and developer ink pens.
3. Manila envelope with a large question mark drawn on it with a black marker.
4. 3″ × 5″ index cards listing group activity rewards, such as extra recess, indoor games, and music time, or describing access to small tangible rewards, such as "candy for everyone" to indicate that each student may select a piece of wrapped candy from a jar.
5. Small tangible rewards, such as wrapped candy, stickers, colorful erasers, etc.
6. *Reinforcement Menus,* one per student (optional, see Variation).

Observation (Select One or More)

1. Calculate homework completion rates in one or more subjects for each student or a target group of students for 5 to 10 days or the previous marking period. *Homework completion rates* are defined as the number of completed assignments divided by the number of assignments given.
2. Calculate homework accuracy rates in one or more subjects for each student or a target group of students for 5 to 10 days or the previous marking period. *Homework accuracy rates* are defined as the number of correct items divided by the total number of items.
3. Calculate the percentage of students completing all homework assignments with at least 80% accuracy in one or more subjects for 5 to 10 days or the previous marking period.
4. Calculate grades in one or more subjects, such as those in which achievement is poorest, for the entire class or a target group of students for the marking period to date.

Intervention Steps

Preparation

1. Write the letter "M" (for mystery motivator) in the boxes on the Mystery Motivator Chart corresponding to the number of days that the reward is available (see Implementation Step 1 below). Then tape a square over each box so that the squares conceal which days are labeled with an "M" and which are blank.
2. Alternately, use the invisible ink marker to write an "M" in the squares corresponding to the days on which the reward is available.

Introduction and Training

1. Explain to the students that they will have an opportunity to earn rewards for good homework performance in the selected subject(s).
2. Display the manila envelope with the question mark on it. Explain that every day that all students turn in all assigned homework in the selected subject(s) with at least 80% accuracy (or some other criterion), you will choose someone to remove the tape and lift the tab on the Mystery Motivator Chart for that day or to color over the square with a developer pen. If an "M" appears beneath the tab or is revealed when the developer pen is applied, the class will earn the reward in the envelope.

Implementation

1. Begin by making the reward available (signaled by the "M") for at least 3 of 5 days each week. Be sure to make the "M's" random, so that students cannot predict on which days the reward will be available (e.g., not every other day).
2. Each day, check each student's homework in the target subject(s) to see if it is complete and to record a percent-accuracy score. As soon as you are able to determine whether the class has met the goal (which will probably be the following day after you have checked papers), announce the results. If the class has met the criterion, select a student to lift up the tab or apply the developer pen to color the square marking the day on which the goal was met. If an "M" appears on the square, open the envelope and announce the reward. Provide the reward immediately or as soon as possible (e.g., extra recess at the regular recess time).
3. If no "M" appears, lead the class in applauding their excellent homework performance and remind them that they will have another chance to earn a mystery motivator tomorrow.
4. If the class did not meet the criterion, encourage the students to try harder the next day.
5. After the class has met the original criterion for at least 3 of 5 days for several weeks, reduce the number of days per week on which the mystery motivator is available and/or raise the criterion (e.g., 85% accuracy).

Evaluation (Select One or More)

1. Compare homework completion rates in the selected subject(s) for each student or the target group of students before and after implementation.
2. Compare homework accuracy rates in the selected subject(s) for each student or the target students before and after implementation.
3. Compare the percentage of students completing all homework assignments with at least 80% accuracy in the selected subject(s) before and after implementation.
4. Compare grades in the selected subject(s) for the entire class or the target students before and after implementation.

Variation: Mystery Motivators with Publicly Posted Reward Menu

1. Distribute *Reinforcement Menus* and have students mark their preferences. Also invite students to add any favorite classroom activities not on the list. Based on student responses and classroom resources, develop a classwide reward menu and post it in the classroom when the mystery motivator intervention is in effect. When the "M" appears on the chart, permit students to vote on a reward from the menu and deliver it as soon as possible.
2. Alternately, number the rewards on the posted menu. Each day, place a slip of paper with a number on it corresponding to a reward in the envelope. If the "M" appears on the chart, deliver the reward matching that number.

Notes

1. To reduce the temptation for students to look under the tab on the chart, inform the class that if anyone turns up a tab without permission, the class will forfeit its chance to earn a reward that day.
2. Invisible and developer makers such as Crayola Changeables® are available at office and school supply stores and at *http://www.crayola.com*.

Sources

Madaus, M. M. R., Kehle, T. J., Madaus, J., & Bray, M. A. (2003). Mystery motivator as an intervention to promote homework completion and accuracy. *School Psychology International, 24,* 369–377. Copyright 2003 by Sage Publications. Adapted by permission.

Moore, L. A., Waguespack, A. M., Wickstrom, K. F., Witt, J. C., & Gaydos, G. R. (1994). Mystery motivator: An effective and time-efficient intervention. *School Psychology Review, 23,* 106–118. Copyright 1994 by the National Association of School Psychologists. Adapted by permission.

Interventions to Improve Reading Performance

Reading problems are the most frequent cause of referrals to school psychologists and intervention assistance programs (Bahr et al., 2006; Bramlett et al., 2002). Among students identified with learning disabilities, 80% have serious reading problems (Snow, Burns, & Griffin, 1998). Lack of reading proficiency in the general student population has also been documented on the National Assessment of Educational Progress (NAEP). On the 2005 NAEP reading assessment, more than a quarter of students at grades 4, 8, and 12 scored at a Below Basic level, indicating that they are unable to read and understand a simple paragraph from a grade-level text. Moreover, despite efforts to close the achievement gap among racial/ethnic groups, significant differences persist. At grade 4, 42% of Asian/Pacific Islander students and 41% of Caucasian students scored at or above the Proficient level, compared with only 18% of American Indian/Alaska Native students, 16% of Hispanic students, and 13% of African American students (National Center for Education Statistics, 2005). As more at-risk students, including children living in poverty and non-native English speakers, enter the school population, teachers must contend with increasing numbers of poor readers and a broadening range of reading skills within a single classroom. The problem is especially acute at the middle school and high school levels, where instruction is primarily text-based and students are expected to be able to use reading to learn (Bryant et al., 2000; Mastropieri, Scruggs, & Magnusen, 1999). Under these circumstances, it is not surprising that teachers report accommodating struggling readers as their greatest instructional challenge (Baumann, Hoffman, Duffy-Hester, & Ro, 2000).

The past two decades have witnessed tremendous advances in the understanding of the nature of reading acquisition and the development of effective approaches to help children learn to read (e.g., Catts & Kamhi, 1999; Simmons & Kame'enui, 1998). Researchers have reached a consensus that deficits in *phonological processing*—the use of phonological (sound-based) information to process oral and written language—are the primary cause of most reading disabilities and are characteristic of both "garden-variety" poor readers (readers not displaying ability–achievement discrepancies) and poor readers with such discrepancies (i.e., dyslexics; Torgesen & Burgess, 1998; Torgesen, Wagner, Rashotte, Alexander, & Conway, 1997). Research also documents that failure to acquire these foundational skills has profound and long-lasting consequences for subsequent reading development and academic success. As students progress through school, good readers read more and acquire larger vocabularies, which enhances their language skills, fund of general knowledge, and overall cognitive development, which in turn facilitates the development of higher order thinking and problem-solving skills in other academic areas (Baker et al., 1998; Cunningham & Stanovich, 1997). In contrast, poor readers read less and develop less adequate language skills, vocabularies, and background knowledge, limiting their ability to comprehend textual material and benefit from instruction. Stanovich (1986) has termed this phenomenon the "Matthew effect" from the passage in the Gospel according to St. Matthew: "For unto every one that hath shall be given, and he shall have abundance: but from him that hath not shall be taken away even that which he hath" (XXV: 29). Longitudinal studies have demonstrated that 75% of students identified with reading disabilities in third grade continue to display significant reading problems in ninth grade (Lyon, 1996). In addition, reading failure is associated with a heightened risk for a host of negative developmental outcomes, including dropping out of school, teen pregnancy, substance abuse, unemployment, and antisocial behavior (McGill-Franzen & Allington, 1991; Stanovich, 1993–1994).

Despite the growing database of empirically validated reading interventions, the often lamented gap between research and practice persists in reading instruction. Although schools have increased the amount of time allocated to reading instruction in response to federal legislation and state initiatives, instructional time is not always used optimally and typical practices fail to reflect scientifically based methods (Hirsch, 2003; Levy & Vaughn, 2002). For example, although alternative instructional formats such as small-group instruction and student pairing have been demonstrated to improve reading outcomes for students with and without disabilities (e.g., Elbaum et al., 1999; Fuchs et al., 1997; Vaughn, Gersten, & Chard, 2000), observational studies reveal that teachers seldom implement these instructional formats, even when they report that they do so (Moody, Vaughn, Hughes, & Fischer, 2000; Schumm et al., 2000; Vaughn, Moody, & Schumm, 1998). Moreover, many teachers lack an adequate knowledge base for teaching reading (Cunningham, Perry, Stanovich, & Stanovich, 2004; McCutchen et al., 2002; Spear-Swerling & Bruckner, 2003, 2004). Given the persistence of reading problems and their debilitating effects on academic and social development, working with teachers to implement interventions that help entire classes of students become proficient readers should be a priority for consultants at every level of schooling.

EVALUATING THE EFFECTIVENESS OF READING INTERVENTIONS

Methods for assessing the effectiveness of the reading interventions in this section include analyses of data that are naturally collected in classrooms, such as report card grades and percent-correct scores on quizzes and tests, as well as skill-specific measures, such as scores on *pseudoword* (nonsense word) lists and real word lists. Also presented below are guidelines for conducting curriculum-based measurement in reading, an assessment procedure that can be used to evaluate the effectiveness of any of the reading interventions in this chapter.

Curriculum-Based Measurement in Reading

Curriculum-based measurement (CBM) in reading consists of a set of brief, standardized procedures assessing reading fluency using a student's own curricular materials or generic grade-level materials. There are two types of CBMs in reading: (1) *oral reading fluency* and (2) *maze fluency*. In oral reading fluency (hereafter referred to as R-CBM), the student reads aloud for 1 minute in a passage selected to be at an end-of-year competency level (termed an *oral reading probe*), and the score is the number of words read correctly. In maze fluency, the student reads silently for a specified time (2.5–3 minutes) in a passage in which every seventh word has been deleted and replaced with three choices, and the score is the number of correct replacements. Maze fluency measures are more efficient because they can be administered to groups of students or delivered by computer (e.g., Shin, Deno, & Espin, 2000), but there is some evidence that maze fluency performance is less sensitive to reading growth and a poorer predictor of reading proficiency than R-CBM (Ardoin et al., 2004; Jenkins & Jewell, 1993). Although oral reading probes were originally taken from materials in students' own curricula, most practitioners now conduct R-CBM using generic probes, such as the passages in the *Dynamic Indicators of Basic Early Literacy Skills* (DIBELS; Good & Kaminski, 2002). Research has demonstrated that R-CBM is a valid performance indicator even when the reading probes are not drawn from the student's own curriculum (Fuchs & Deno, 1994) and that generic passages have less measurement error than passages randomly selected from graded readers (Hintze & Christ, 2004). Moreover, literature-based and trade-book probes are likely to underestimate performance levels compared with passages constructed from traditional basal reading materials or generic passages and are less sensitive to individual differences (Bradley-Klug, Shapiro, Lutz, & DuPaul, 1998; Hintze, Shapiro, & Lutz, 1994). For these reasons, and because today's classroom reading materials vary widely in difficulty level, R-CBMs for students instructed in literature-based or trade-book materials should be conducted using probes from a comparable basal series or from generic passages controlled for readability (Rathvon, 2004b). Numerous studies have demonstrated that R-CBM is a reliable, valid method of monitoring the progress of both proficient and poor readers (Fuchs, Fuchs, Hosp, & Jenkins, 2001; Hintze, Callahan, Matthews, Williams, & Tobin, 2001), predicting reading outcomes and performance on high-stakes assessments (Good, Simmons, & Kame'enui, 2001; McGlinchey & Hixson, 2004), and evaluating the effectiveness of reading interventions (Eckert, Ardoin, Daisey, & Scarola, 2000; Stoner, Scarpati, Phaneuf, & Hintze, 2002). R-CBM has also been successfully used to assess the progress of English language learners in early identification and intervention programs (Gunn, Biglan, Smolkowski, & Ary, 2000; Haager & Windmueller, 2001) and to predict performance on high-stakes tests (Wiley & Deno, 2005).

ASSESSING EARLY READING SKILLS WITH CURRICULUM-BASED MEASUREMENT

Because beginning readers have limited ability to access text, R-CBM is not sensitive to individual differences in oral reading skills until the second semester of first grade or even later for less proficient readers (Hartman & Fuller, 1997; Kaminski & Good, 1996). To bridge this gap, Good and Kaminski (2002) have developed the *Dynamic Indicators of Basic Early Literacy Skills* (DIBELS), a downward extension of R-CBM for preliterate children consisting of four fluency-based measures of phonemic awareness and alphabet knowledge. A growing body of evidence documents that the DIBELS prereading measures are reliable and valid predictors of future reading performance and can be used to identify children at risk for reading failure and to assess response to reading interventions (see Rathvon, 2004b, for a review). Several other CBM-type measures for children who cannot read fluently in text are also available, although there are less data on their reliability and validity (Fuchs, Fuchs, & Compton, 2004; Speece, Mills, Ritchey, & Hillman, 2003; Speece & Ritchey, 2005). The DIBELS measures and two additional CBM-type early reading measures are described below:

Initial sound fluency. The examiner asks the child to identify the one of four pictures that begins with a target sound. The child is also asked to produce the beginning sound of an orally presented word matching one of the pictures. The score is the number of initial sounds correct per minute for a set of four picture probes, obtained by multiplying the number of correct responses by 60 and dividing that product by the number of seconds needed to complete the task.

Letter naming fluency. The child names upper- and lowercase letters displayed in random order. The score is the number of letters correctly named in 1 minute.

Phoneme segmentation fluency. The child segments three- and four-phoneme words spoken by the examiner into individual phonemes. Credit is given for each correct sound segment, and the score is the number of correct sound segments per minute.

Nonsense word fluency. The child pronounces two- and three-phoneme pseudowords presented on a page. The child may pronounce the individual sounds or read the whole word. The score is the number of correct letter sounds per minute.

Letter sound fluency. The child identifies the sounds for lowercase letters displayed in random order. The score is the number of letter sounds correctly identified in 1 minute.

Word identification fluency. The child reads as many words as possible from a graded word list with 50 words. The score is the number of words correctly read in 1 minute.

The first four measures described above are available from the DIBELS website (*http://dibels.uoregon.edu*). AIMSweb (*http://www.aimsweb.com*) offers a slightly different set of four early literacy assessments, consisting of letter name, letter sound, phoneme segmentation, and nonsense word fluency measures, as well as a set of five early literacy assessments for Spanish speakers (letter name, letter sound, syllable segmentation, syllable reading fluency, and syllable and word reading fluency). Letter sound fluency and word identification fluency (WIF) materials are also available at Edcheckup (*http://www.edcheckup.com*) and Project AIM (Alternative Identification Models; *http://www.glue.umn.edu/%7Edlspeece/cbmreading/index.html*. WIF materials in English and Spanish are available at Intervention Central (*http://www.interventioncentral.org*).

CURRICULUM-BASED MEASUREMENT IN ORAL READING

Overview

Curriculum-based measurement in reading (R-CBM) consists of a set of standardized, fluency-based procedures in which students read aloud for 1 minute from a passage, termed an *oral reading probe*. Because R-CBM can have many alternate forms, oral reading fluency can be measured much more frequently than with norm-referenced tests and the results can be displayed graphically to monitor progress. There are two basic uses of R-CBM. R-CBM screening (also called *benchmarking*) is designed to identify students at risk for reading failure, with measures typically administered in fall, winter, and spring. R-CBM progress monitoring assesses students' progress toward end-of-year competency using goal-level material. R-CBM progress monitoring can also be conducted to assess response to reading interventions using year-end material or material at the student's individual goal level. Moreover, when R-CBM is conducted frequently and the results graphed and shared with students, it can have positive effects on reading achievement. Although oral reading probes were first constructed using materials from students' own curricula, generic reading probes, which are available from a variety of sources, are now more commonly used.

Purposes

1. To screen students for risk for reading problems and in need of supplementary instruction.
2. To monitor students' progress in reading and response to reading interventions.
3. To provide information for instructional planning and program improvement.
4. To evaluate the effectiveness of reading interventions and instructional programs.

Materials

1. For screening/benchmarking, select three reading passages, either from the student's current materials or, preferably, from a generic set of passages set at end-of-year competency levels. If materials are taken from the student's own text, select a passage from the beginning, middle, and end of the book, and administer them in that order. For progress monitoring, select one passage. Two copies of each passage are required: one for the student to read and the other for the examiner to score the student's oral reading.
2. Preprimer and primer level passages should be brief (less than 50 words). Passages should be approximately 150 words for grades 1–3 and approximately 250 words for grades 4–8. Passages should be prose text rather than poetry or plays, should not contain too much dialogue, should have no more than a single illustration, and need not be limited to the beginning of stories.
3. To assess comprehension, prepare five to eight comprehension questions for each passage. Questions should include both literal ("Who?," "What?," "When?," "Where?") and inferential questions ("How?," "Why?").
4. Stopwatch or timer.
5. Equal-interval graph paper or graphing program (optional).

Assessment Steps

Administration (Reading Fluency Only)

1. Give the student the copy of the first reading passage and give the following directions:

> "When I say, 'Begin,' begin reading aloud at the top of this page. Read across the page. Try to read each word. If you come to a word you don't know, I'll tell it to you. You will have 1 minute. Be sure to do your best reading. Are there any questions? Begin."

2. Place a slash over words read incorrectly, as indicated below. At the end of one minute, say, "Stop!" and place a vertical line on your copy of the passage after the last word read.
3. For screening/benchmarking, administer two more passages. For progress monitoring, only one passage is usually administered.

Administration (Reading Fluency and Comprehension)

1. Randomly select one of the three passages for the comprehension screening. Administer two probes as described above but give these directions for the third:

   "When I say, 'Begin,' begin reading aloud at the top of this page. Read across the page. Try to read each word. If you come to a word you don't know, I'll tell it to you. I will be asking you a few questions afterwards. Be sure to do your best reading. Are there any questions? Begin."

2. Allow the student to finish reading the entire passage, but mark where he or she is at the end of each minute.

3. Permit the student to look at the passage while you are asking the comprehension questions.

Scoring Reading Fluency

1. Mark errors as follows:
   a. *Mispronunciations*. If the student mispronounces a word, provide the correct word and count it as an error. If the student makes the same error several times, count it as an error each time unless it is a proper noun. If the error involves a proper noun, count it as an error the first time but not subsequently.
   b. *Omissions*. If the student leaves out an entire word, count it as an error but do not supply the word.
   c. *Substitutions*: If the student says the wrong word, provide the correct word and count it as an error.
   d. *Insertions*: If the student adds a word or words, count it as an error.
   e. *Hesitations*. If the student pauses for 3 seconds, supply the word and count it as an error.
   f. Repetitions, self-corrections, dialectical substitutions (e.g., *ax* for *ask*), and dialectical suffix deletions (e.g., *walk* for *walked*) are not counted as errors.
   g. If the student skips a line or loses his or her place, stop timing and redirect the student to the appropriate place in the text, but do not count it as an error. Then resume timing.

2. To determine words read correctly per minute (WCPM), count the number of words the student read correctly in 1 minute. If the student reads for more than 1 minute, as when comprehension questions are administered, multiply the total number of words read correctly by 60 and then divide that product by the number of seconds needed to read the passage, as follows:

$$\frac{\text{Number of words read correctly} \times 60}{\text{Total reading time in seconds}} = \text{Words read correctly per minute}$$

Scoring Comprehension

1. The comprehension score equals the percentage of questions answered correctly for that probe.

Interpretation

1. For screening/benchmarking, score each of the three probes as described above. The student's score on that book or set of probes is the *median* (middle) WCPM score on the three probes and the comprehension score (if used). The median score is used rather than the mean score to control for the effects of difficulty. For progress monitoring, score the probe as described above to determine WCPM.

2. Compare WCPM scores to national norms (see Table 4.1 for a recent set of national norms), local norms, or R-CBM benchmarks related to success on district or state assessments, if available.

3. If desired, graph WCPM scores for use in determining whether the student is making adequate progress toward end-of-year expectations or whether instructional modifications are needed.

Notes

1. Procedures for constructing oral reading probes from students' regular curriculum or alternative basal materials are presented in Rathvon (1999) and Shapiro (2004a).

2. Practitioners should note that the DIBELS passages and other generic passages are calibrated for the goal level of reading for each grade level, that is, they are set at a *year-end competency level.*

3. R-CBM can also be used in *survey-level assessment,* that is, to determine functional reading level (see Shapiro, 2004a). The available criteria consist of only two grade ranges (1–2 and 3–6), however, and the validation evidence is very outdated.

TABLE 4.1. Oral Reading Fluency Norms for Grades 1 through 8

Grade	Percentile	Fall WCPM	Winter WCPM	Spring WCPM
1	75		47	82
	50		23	53
	25		12	28
2	75	79	100	117
	50	51	72	89
	25	25	42	61
3	75	99	120	137
	50	71	92	107
	25	44	62	78
4	75	119	139	152
	50	94	112	123
	25	68	87	98
5	75	139	156	168
	50	110	127	139
	25	85	99	109
6	75	153	167	177
	50	127	140	150
	25	98	111	122
7	75	156	165	177
	50	128	136	150
	25	102	109	123
8	75	161	173	177
	50	133	146	151
	25	106	115	124

Note. WCPM, words correct per minute. Data were collected from fall of 2000 through spring of 2004, with between 3,496 and 20,128 students at each assessment window. There was no fall assessment for grade 1 students. Adapted from Hasbrouck and Tindal (2006, p. 639). Copyright 2006 by the International Reading Association. Adapted by permission.

4. R-CBM is most appropriate for students in grades 1–6. For younger students, CBM-type pre-reading measures are available from several sources, as noted above. To assess reading skills in older students, *Vocabulary Matching*—a metric described in the Content Area section of this chapter—is recommended.

5. Recent research indicates that administering only one oral reading probe may be sufficient for screening/benchmark purposes (Ardoin et al., 2004).

Sources

Hosp, M. K., Hosp, J. L., & Howell, K. W. (2007). *The ABCs of CBM: A practical guide to curriculum-based measurement*. New York: Guilford Press. Copyright 2007 by The Guilford Press. Adapted by permission.

Shapiro, E. S. (2004a). *Academic skills problems: Direct assessment and intervention* (3rd ed.). New York: Guilford Press. Copyright 2004 by The Guilford Press. Adapted by permission.

Additional Resources

Generic reading passages are available free of charge at the DIBELS home page (*http://dibels. uoregon.edu*), including a Spanish DIBELS version, and at Intervention Central (*http://www.interventioncentral.org*). A commercial version of the DIBELS measures is available from Sopris West (*http://www.sopriswest.com*). Other sets of generic reading passages are offered at Edcheckup (*http://www.edcheckup.com*) and AIMSweb (*http://www.aimsweb.com*). Web-based graphing and data management systems are available from the same sources.

OVERVIEW OF READING INTERVENTIONS

Three sets of skills are required for proficient reading: (1) *decoding*—the process leading to word recognition; (2) *fluency*—the ability to read quickly and accurately; and (3) *comprehension*—the ability to derive meaning from text. Although reading interventions can be categorized according to their primary subskill target, interventions focusing on one subskill have the potential to improve other skills because of the interrelated nature of the reading process (Rathvon, 2004b). This section includes 11 interventions targeting one or more of these three subskills.

Interventions to Improve Decoding and Word Recognition

Rapid and accurate *decoding*—using knowledge of letter–sound correspondences to identify written words—is the foundation of proficient reading. When decoding is slow or inaccurate, comprehension is impaired because so much cognitive energy must be allocated to the decoding process (Share, 1995; National Reading Panel, 2000). During the early stages of reading acquisition, children rely on letter-by-letter decoding, that is, pronouncing individual sounds in sequence and blending them together to form a word. By repeatedly associating a word's pronunciation with its visual representation, children gradually learn to process letter clusters and entire words as units, so that decoding becomes more rapid. Ultimately, repeated exposure leads to the ability to store words as whole spelling units that can be recognized accurately and automatically as "sight words" (Torgesen et al., 1997). In the final step of automatic word recognition, the word that has been translated into its phonological components is linked to its meaning in the mental lexicon (Chard, Simmons, & Kame'enui, 1998).

Word recognition skills are the major determinant of reading proficiency in the early elementary grades (Stanovich, 1991) and continue to exert an influence on reading ability throughout adulthood (Cunningham & Stanovich, 1997). Unfortunately, all too many students enter the middle and high school years with inadequate word recognition skills. Although these students are generally able to decode phonetically regular one-syllable words and can recognize a small number of high-frequency words, they lack strategies for decoding unfamiliar words, especially the content-oriented multisyllabic words they encounter in their textbooks (Archer, Gleason, & Vachon, 2003). The goal of word recognition instruction is to help students learn strategies for decoding novel words and to develop automaticity in word recognition, with the ultimate goal of facilitating comprehension.

Decoding Interventions

Three of the four interventions in this section target decoding skills by teaching students specific word analysis strategies. *Word Building* helps students decode multisyllabic words by focusing their attention on the effect of a single grapheme change on pronunciation and meaning in an instructional activity termed *progressive minimal contrasts*. In the progressive minimal contrast activity, students are guided through a series of transformations that changes one word into another by altering a single grapheme at the beginning, middle, or end of the word. Learning to focus on every letter in a word may help readers develop word representations in memory whose constituent letters and phonemes become increasingly specified in all word positions (Perfetti, 1992). Such an activity is especially helpful for students who have not progressed beyond the partial alphabetic decoding phase (Ehri, 1995). These so-called "partial decoders" are often able to decode the initial consonant or consonant cluster in a word but are unable to apply grapheme–phoneme decoding skills to each of the letter–sound units in a word.

Graphosyllabic Analysis: Decoding Multisyllable Words teaches students to conceptualize word identification as a problem-solving process, using a set of procedures for decoding multisyllabic words. This type of syllable training builds word identification skills by encouraging students to pay attention to all of the letters in words rather than only the first and final letters, a common practice among many poor readers. Syllable analysis has been recognized by researchers and practitioners as an important component of remedial reading instruction (Birsh, 1999; Gillingham & Stillman, 1997). *DISSECT: The Word Identification Strategy* also teaches students a set of procedures for rapidly decoding unfamiliar words in content area text. Students learn to break words into components and use context clues, along with additional resources, in a seven-step strategy that forms the mnemonic DISSECT. The DISSECT strategy is part of a multicomponent reading program with proven effectiveness in enhancing decoding and comprehension skills for average-achieving students, low-achieving students, and students with reading disabilities (Bryant et al., 2000).

The fourth intervention in this section, *Paired Reading*, is a parent-delivered intervention targeting fluency as well as word identification. Although parents play an important role in motivating struggling readers (Baker, 2003) and can learn to serve as reading tutors for their own children (Duvall, Delquadri, Elliott, & Hall, 1992; Taverne & Sheridan, 1993; Thurston & Dasta, 1990), many of the home-based reading interventions that have appeared in the literature require extensive parent training and supervision to ensure treatment fidelity and even then do not always increase children's reading skills (e.g., Law & Kratochwill, 1993). In contrast, *Paired Reading* requires a single parent training session and has documented effectiveness in improving reading performance for low-achieving elementary students (Fiala & Sheridan, 2003). Because of its simplicity, *Paired Reading* is also ideal for implementation in after-school tutoring programs delivered by paraprofessionals, volunteers, or community-based tutors.

BEST PRACTICES IN CORRECTING ORAL READING ERRORS

Numerous studies have demonstrated that feedback during oral reading improves students' reading accuracy on word lists and passages (e.g., Barbetta, Heron, & Heward, 1993; Singh, 1990; Espin & Deno, 1989). But what kind of feedback is most effective? When students read aloud, teachers use several methods to correct oral reading errors: (1) the *word supply procedure,* in which the teacher provides the correct word following a miscue; (2) the *phonetic emphasis procedure,* in which the teacher requires the student to use the letters to derive the word's pronunciation; and (3) the *sentence repeat procedure,* in which the teacher supplies the correct word following a miscue, after which the student repeats the word, completes the sentence, and rereads the entire sentence (Heubusch & Lloyd, 1998). Studies comparing oral reading error correction procedures have generally concluded that sentence repeat is the most effective procedure for increasing oral reading accuracy, probably because it provides an additional opportunity for the reader to pronounce the missed word and then practice it in the context of the sentence (Campbell, 1994; Singh, 1990). The sentence repeat procedure can be easily taught to parents, paraprofessionals, and community-based tutors and is incorporated in the *Paired Reading* intervention in this section and in the *Partner Reading* and *Parents as Reading Tutors* interventions in the fluency section.

WORD BUILDING

Overview

Teachers are all too familiar with so-called "partial decoders"—poor readers who can decode the initial grapheme of a novel word but have difficulty applying sound–symbol knowledge to other letter positions within words. This intervention assists students in fully decoding words by systematically directing their attention to each grapheme position within a word. Using letter cards, students form a chain of words that differ by a single grapheme at the beginning, middle, or end of the word in an activity called *progressive minimal contrasts*. Focusing attention on each individual letter–sound unit in a word plays a critical role in promoting the formation of more accurate and fully specified representations of printed words in memory. After each transformation, students decode the new word. To integrate decoding with text reading, students conclude each lesson by reading "silly sentences" that contain a high proportion of the new words. In the original study, implemented in an after-school tutoring program with 24 poor readers ages 7 to 10, participants showed significantly greater improvement in decoding for all grapheme positions as well as greater gains on standardized measures of decoding, reading comprehension, and phonological awareness, compared with a control group. In this adaptation, a peer-mediated format has been substituted for the one-to-one tutoring setting to facilitate classwide implementation. The one-to-one original version, which is also suitable for delivery in a small-group format, is presented as a variation.

Purpose

To build decoding skills with an activity that transforms one word into another by changing a grapheme at the beginning, middle, or end of the word.

Materials

For each intervention session or lesson
1. 5 to 16 letter cards, one set per student.
2. "Smiley faces" and question marks, about 5 inches in height, made of colored construction paper.

3. Overhead projector and transparencies (optional).
4. Plastic ziplock bags, one per student (optional, see Note 3).
5. 8 to 10 sentences consisting primarily of words formed in the lesson.
6. Flashcards for each word formed in the lesson or index cards, one set per student pair or instructional group (optional, see Variation).
7. Small whiteboard and whiteboard markers (optional, see Variation).

Observation (Select One or More)

Option 1

1. Construct a list of 20 one-syllable pseudowords by taking words from students' current reading material and recombining onset and rime units (e.g., *nan, vot, gip, glom*).
2. Administer the list to a group of target students or the entire class and calculate a percent-correct score for each student.

Option 2

1. Calculate average grades in reading for a group of target students or the entire class for the previous month or marking period.

Option 3

1. Using students' regular reading materials, administer *Curriculum-Based Oral Reading Probes* (R-CBM) with the comprehension option to a group of target students or the entire class.

Intervention Steps

Preparation

1. Divide the class into pairs, based on reading group or skill level. Change student pairs every 2 or 3 weeks, but match skill levels in each pair as much as possible.

   For each lesson:

PART 1: WORD BUILDING

1. Give each student a set of letter cards and conduct a brief review of those letter sounds.
2. Pronounce a word containing the letter–sound units for the lesson (e.g., *sat*) and ask students to use their cards to "build" the word. After students form the word, write the word on the chalkboard or transparency and have students modify their constructions as needed. Then have students chorally read the word.
3. Tell the students to insert, delete, or exchange a specific letter card to transform the current word into the next word in the lesson (e.g., *sat* to *sap*; see Figure 4.3 on p. 187). Sequences of letter changes should draw attention to each position within a word (e.g., initial consonant, second consonant within a consonant cluster, medial vowel, final consonant), and ensure that the same letters appearing in the initial position also appear in other positions. After each new word is formed, have students read it chorally.
4. Use the following error correction procedures:
   a. If students have difficulty pronouncing a word after forming it, avoid pronouncing the word for them. Instead, encourage an attempt based on the letter sounds. If students have trouble combining letter sounds, guide them through the process of progressively blending the sounds together.

b. If students mistake the word for a similarly spelled word, write out the target word and the error word on the chalkboard or transparency and help them analyze the differences between the two words in terms of letter–sound units.

PART 2: PEER TUTORING

1. After students have completed the Word Building sequence, have them move to their tutoring stations (pairs of adjacent desks). Give each student pair a set of flashcards and designate one student to begin as tutor.
2. The tutor shows the first flashcard to the tutee. If the tutee pronounces the word correctly, the tutor places the flashcard on the smiley face.
3. If the tutee cannot read the word, the tutor supplies it and places the flashcard on the question mark for additional practice. If neither of the students can read the word, they raise their hands to request teacher assistance.
4. After the tutee reads the missed word correctly, the tutor places the flashcard to the side for additional practice. After 5 minutes, students reverse roles and repeat the procedures.
5. During the tutoring session, circulate to provide assistance and corrective feedback. If most of the students can read at least 80% of the lesson words correctly, move on to the next lesson. If the accuracy criterion is not met, conduct more Word Building activities using the same set of words.

PART 3: SENTENCE READING

1. Using the chalkboard or a transparency, display a set of sentences containing a high proportion of words that students have just decoded and others that can be decoded based on the material taught to that point. Make the sentences silly and fun to read. *Examples*: "Did Tip sip and slip?" "Hot Spot does not sit on a pot."
2. Call on students to read the sentences aloud and provide help as needed using the procedures described above. For words containing phonics features that students have not yet mastered, encourage students' attempts to read the words but pronounce the words if necessary.
3. After students have successfully read the sentences, conduct a playful discussion about the meaning of the sentences.

Evaluation: Select One or More

Option 1

1. Compare percent-correct scores on the pseudoword list for the target students or the entire class before and after implementation.

Option 2

1. Compare scores on reading skill sheets, quizzes, or end-of-unit tests for the target students or the entire class before and after implementation.

Option 3

1. Compare R-CBM fluency and comprehension scores for the target students or the entire class before and after implementation.

Variation: Individualized or Differentiated Instructional Format

1. At the beginning of each unit, select a set of words from the unit lessons (e.g., vowel digraphs). If the target student(s) can read at least 90% of the words, skip that unit and proceed to the next unit pretest. Provide additional instruction based on the letter–sound correspondences in the skipped unit for students who did not reach the accuracy criterion.
2. At the end of each unit, administer a posttest of words drawn from the unit lessons. If the student(s) can read at least 90% of the lesson words, move to the next unit pretest. If the accuracy criterion is not met, provide additional activities based on the letter–sound units in the previous unit.

Notes

1. This intervention is appropriate for students who have completed grade 1 and have received instruction in the basic letter sounds.
2. In the original study, students participated in 77 lessons, grouped into 23 units containing 4 to 7 lessons each, as follows: (a) units 1–10, short vowels; (b) units 11–15, long vowel sounds controlled by silent *e*; (c) units 16–19, vowel digraphs (*ae, ee, oa, ow, oy*); and (d) units 20–23, changes in vowel pronunciation in different phonetic environments (e.g., *r*-controlled vowels).
3. To increase usability, have students create their own flashcards by writing the words to be studied on index cards. Have them store their cards in ziplock bags.

Source

McCandliss, B., Beck, I. L., Sandak, R., & Perfetti, C. (2003). Focusing attention on decoding for children with poor reading skills: Design and preliminary tests of the word building intervention. *Scientific Studies of Reading, 7,* 75–104. Copyright 2003 by Lawrence Erlbaum Associates, Inc. Adapted by permission.

FIGURE 4.3. Sample progression of word transformations for *Word Building.* The new grapheme card in each trial is shaded to illustrate how each successive transformation directs attention to different grapheme positions by holding constant the other letters from the previous word. From McCandliss, Beck, Sandak, and Perfetti (2003, p. 84). Copyright 2003 by Lawrence Erlbaum Associates, Inc. Reprinted by permission.

DISSECT: THE WORD IDENTIFICATION STRATEGY

Overview

As students progress through school, the ability to read, understand, and recall information from texts becomes increasingly important to academic success. Because middle school and secondary school texts are written at reading levels well above those of low-achieving students or students with reading disabilities, these students have great difficulty learning information presented in print form. The problem is especially acute in social studies and science classes, where assignments require students to decode and understand complex unfamiliar words in their textbooks and to cover large amounts of material independently. Even if these less skilled readers have learned basic sound–symbol relationships and have acquired a small sight vocabulary, their inability to apply structural analysis skills to identify new content-specific vocabulary can lead to academic failure. This intervention trains students in a general problem-solving strategy within which specific sub-strategies are used to identify difficult words rapidly. A mnemonic device (DISSECT) formed by the key words in each strategy step helps students remember the procedure. In the original study, conducted with 12 seventh-, eighth-, and ninth-grade students with learning disabilities, the DIS-SECT strategy was effective in improving reading accuracy for all of the target students in both ability-level and grade-level material and in improving comprehension for the majority of the students.

Purpose

To improve word identification skills in content area textbooks with a strategy for pronouncing and recognizing complex multisyllabic words.

Materials

1. Social studies or science textbooks or current classroom reading material in the content areas.
2. Posterboard chart listing common prefixes and suffixes.
3. Posterboard chart listing the DISSECT steps (see Implementation Step 3).
4. Posterboard chart listing the Rules of Twos or Threes (see Figure 4.4 on p. 190).
5. Sheet of paper listing common prefixes and suffixes (optional, one per student).
6. Sheet of paper listing the DISSECT steps and Rules of Twos or Threes (optional, one per student).
7. Classroom dictionaries, one per student.

Observation (Select One or More)

1. Have a group of target students read aloud a short passage (about 400 words) from the social studies or science textbook on an individual basis. Calculate a reading accuracy percentage score for each student by dividing the total number of words read correctly (total number of words in the passage minus the number of words missed) by the total number of words in the passage.
2. Calculate average grades on content area quizzes or tests for a group of target students or the entire class for the previous month or marking period. If desired, calculate a group or class-wide quiz or test average by dividing the sum of individual student scores by the total number of students in the group or class.
3. Using generic passages or passages from students' social studies or science textbooks, administer *Curriculum-Based Oral Reading Probes* (R-CBM) to a group of target students, using both the fluency and comprehension options.

Intervention Steps

Introduction and Training

1. Display the list of DISSECT steps, list of prefixes and suffixes, and chart with the Rules of Twos and Threes. If desired, give students individual copies of these materials to consult during classwork and/or homework assignments.
2. Conduct a general discussion of the importance of good reading skills to success in the targeted subject. If desired, have students calculate their averages on content area quizzes and tests for the current marking period or provide them with their averages.
3. Tell the students that they will be learning a seven-step strategy that will help them read and remember difficult words. Explain that the word *dissect*—"to separate into parts"—will help them remember the steps of the strategy.
4. Using the DISSECT chart and the chalkboard, describe and demonstrate the seven strategy steps to use when encountering a difficult word as follows:
   a. *D—Discover the Context.* Skip the difficult word, read to the end of the sentence, and use the meaning of the sentence to make your best guess as to a word that fits in the place of the unfamiliar word. If the guessed word does not match the difficult word, proceed to the next step.
   b. *I—Isolate the Prefix.* Using the list of prefixes, look at the beginning of the word to see if the first several letters form a prefix that you can pronounce. If so, box it off by drawing a line between the prefix and the rest of the word.
   c. *S—Separate the Suffix.* Using the list of suffixes, look at the end of the word to see if the last several letters form a suffix that you can pronounce. If so, box it off by drawing a line between the suffix and the rest of the word.
   d. *S—Say the Stem.* If you recognize the *stem* (the part of the word that remains after the prefix and the suffix have been boxed off), pronounce the prefix, stem, and suffix together. If you cannot recognize the stem, proceed to the next step.
   e. *E—Examine the Stem.* Using the Rules of Twos and Threes, dissect the stem into easy-to-pronounce word parts (see Figure 4.4).
   f. *C—Check with Someone.* If you still can't pronounce the word, ask someone (teacher, parent, or a better reader) in an appropriate way to help you. If someone is not available, go to the next step. (Model or have students model examples and nonexamples of appropriate ways to seek assistance.)
   g. *T—Try the Dictionary.* Look up the word in the dictionary, use the pronunciation guide to pronounce the word, and read the definition if you don't know the meaning of the word.
5. Discuss situations in which students can apply the strategy (e.g., homework assignments, leisure-time reading of newspapers and magazines) and the benefits students can expect if they learn and use the strategy, such as improved grades, more rewarding reading experiences, and greater knowledge of world and community events.
6. Include the following suggestions in your discussion: (a) the strategy is most effective on reading assignments that follow teachers' discussion of the content in class, (b) the first five steps of the strategy usually won't work on vocabulary words to which students have not been introduced, and (c) students should learn the strategy so thoroughly that they can complete the first five steps in no more than 10 seconds.
7. Write a multisyllabic word from a current reading assignment on the chalkboard and use it to demonstrate the entire strategy, using a think-aloud procedure so that students can observe all of the processes involved.
8. Write other multisyllabic words on the chalkboard and select students to demonstrate the strategy. Prompt students to think aloud as they go through the steps, and provide support and corrective feedback as needed.

Implementation

1. During social studies or science lessons, review the strategy when introducing new vocabulary. Select students to demonstrate the strategy on several words.
2. Provide time for students to apply the strategy during class assignments. If desired, divide the class into pairs and have the pairs work together to apply the strategy to a section of the text or reading materials while you circulate to provide assistance.

Evaluation (Select One or More)

1. Compare reading accuracy percentage scores for the group of target students before and after implementation.
2. Compare average grades on content area quizzes or tests for the group of target students or the entire class before and after implementation.
3. Compare R-CBM fluency and comprehension scores for the group of target students before and after implementation.

Note

1. For the purposes of this intervention, *prefix* and *suffix* are defined as any recognizable group of letters at the beginning or end of a word, respectively, that students can identify and pronounce correctly.

Source

Lenz, B. K., & Hughes, C. A. (1990). A word identification strategy for adolescents with learning disabilities. *Journal of Learning Disabilities, 23,* 149–158, 163. Copyright 1990 by PRO-ED, Inc. Adapted by permission.

Rules of Twos and Threes

Rule 1
- If a stem or any part of a stem begins with a **vowel,** separate the first **two** letters from the rest of the stem and pronounce them.
- If the stem or any part of the stem begins with a **consonant,** separate the first **three** letters from the rest of the stem and pronounce them.
- Once you have separated the first two or three letters from the stem, apply the same rules until you reach the end of the stem (example: al/ter/na/tor).
- Pronounce the stem by saying the dissected parts. If you can read the stem, add the prefix and suffix and reread the entire word. If you can't use Rule 1, use Rule 2.

Rule 2
- Isolate the first letter of the stem and try to apply Rule 1 again. Rule 2 is especially useful when the stem begins with two or three consonants.

Rule 3
- If two different vowels appear together in a word, pronounce both of the vowel sounds. If that doesn't sound right, pronounce one vowel sound at a time until it sounds right. Rule 3 can be applied in conjunction with either Rule 1 or Rule 2.

FIGURE 4.4. Rules of Twos and Threes. Adapted from Lentz and Hughes (1991). Copyright 1991 by PRO-ED, Inc. Adapted by permission.

GRAPHOSYLLABIC ANALYSIS:
FIVE STEPS TO DECODING COMPLEX WORDS

Overview

Syllabication—segmenting a multisyllabic word into its constituent syllables—is an important strategy for word reading, especially as students progress through school and encounter more complex vocabulary in their textbooks and reading materials. Unfortunately, all too many students fail to reach the full alphabetic phase of reading, in which readers are able to decode multisyllable words by forming complete connections between the spellings and pronunciations of syllabic units. In this intervention, students learn a strategy for analyzing words into their constituent parts as they practice reading a set of multisyllabic words over several trials. Only one syllabication rule is taught—the need to create a separate syllable for each vowel. In the original study, conducted with 60 students in sixth through ninth grade who were reading at a third- to fifth-grade level, the intervention group demonstrated greater improvement in spelling and reading unfamiliar real words and pseudowords than a no-treatment group and a group of struggling readers who practiced reading the same words as wholes, with the strongest effects for the poorest readers. In this adaptation, a response card format is used to facilitate classwide implementation, with the original one-to-one format included as a variation.

Purpose

To improve decoding skills by teaching students a five-step syllable segmentation strategy.

Materials

1. Word cards, consisting of four sets of 25 multisyllabic words written on 3″ × 5″ index cards, one set per student.
2. Sheets of paper listing the words in each set, one sheet each per student (optional, see Note 3).
3. Overhead projector and transparencies (optional).
4. 9″ × 12″ whiteboards, dry erase markers, and erasers, one each per student.
5. Index cards or a 9″ × 12″ whiteboard, dry erase markers, and erasers (optional, see Variation).

Observation (Select One or Both)

1. Administer a 20-item word list corresponding to the current grade placement or estimated reading level of a group of target students or the entire class. Continue to administer easier or more difficult word lists until you determine each student's instructional level, defined as the highest list on which a student can read 15 out of 20 words.
2. Using students' regular reading materials in a literature or content area class, administer *Curriculum-Based Oral Reading Probes* (R-CBM) with the comprehension option to a group of target students.

Intervention Steps

1. Tell students that you are going to teach them a strategy for reading complex and unfamiliar words by dividing words into syllables.
2. Using the chalkboard or an overhead transparency, demonstrate the five-step syllable analysis as follows:

Step 1: Read the word aloud.

    a. Display a sample multisyllabic word (e.g., *finish*) on the chalkboard or a transparency and pronounce it:

        "*Finish.*"

Step 2: Explain the word's meaning.

    a. Ask the students to give the word's meaning(s) and provide corrective feedback if needed:

        "That's right, *finish* means "to complete a task.""

Step 3: Orally divide the word into syllables.

    a. Pronounce each syllable aloud while raising one finger at a time to count the syllables:

        "There are two syllables in the word *finish*. I'll read it again—*fin-ish*."

    b. Explain the one-vowel, one-syllable rule:

        "Every syllable contains a vowel. Vowels are usually spelled with the letters *a, e, i, o, u, y,* or certain combinations of these letters, such as *ea, ee,* or *ai*. The word *finish* has one vowel in each syllable—/i/ in *fin* and /i/ in *ish*."

    c. Explain how to distinguish incorrect from correct segmentations:

        "Each letter can go in only one syllable. For example, I can't divide the word *finish* as *fin-nish*. I have to put the letter *n* in only one syllable—*fin-ish*."

    d. Explain that the sounds in the syllables must match sounds in the whole word:

        "The sounds in the syllables should be as close as possible to the sounds in the whole word. We don't say *fine-ish* because we don't hear *fine* and *ish* in *finish*. We don't say *fin-ush* because we don't hear *fin* and *ush* in *finish*. We say *fin-ish* because we hear *fin* and *ish* in *fin-ish*."

Step 4: Match the pronounced form of each syllable to its spelling.

    a. Pronounce each syllable aloud while you use your thumbs or a pointer to expose each syllable in turn while covering the other letters: "*Fin–ish.*"

Step 5: Blend the syllables to say the whole word.

    a. Moving your finger or pointer from left to right, slowly blend the syllables to pronounce the whole word.

        "Finally, I put the syllables together and read the whole word—*finish*."

    b. Present another slightly more complex example (e.g., *violinist*) and guide students through each step. Have students write the sample word on their whiteboards and practice pronouncing and exposing one syllable at a time while you circulate to provide help as needed. For Step 4, accept different ways of dividing words into syllables as long as each syllable contains only one vowel sound, the letters students expose match the sounds they pronounce, each letter is included in only one syllable, and the combination of letters forms a legal pronunciation (e.g., *fi-nish* but not *fini-sh*).

3. Divide the class into pairs of students with similar reading skills, give each pair the first set of words, and have them apply the five steps to read each word. Circulate to provide corrective feedback as needed.

4. Have the pairs repeat the steps three or four times for each set to help secure the words in memory.

Evaluation (Select One or Both)

1. Compare reading instructional levels for the target students or the entire class before and after implementation.
2. Compare R-CBM fluency and comprehension scores for the target students before and after implementation.

Variation: Individual or Small-Group Format

1. For delivery in an individual or small-group format, use index cards or a small whiteboard to demonstrate the strategy steps.

Notes

1. In the original study, target words were selected from *Basic Elementary Reading Vocabularies* (Harris & Jacobson, 1972).
2. Graded word lists from preprimer through high school are included in the *Qualitative Reading Inventory, Fourth Edition* (Leslie & Caldwell, 2006).
3. To increase usability, distribute sheets of paper listing the four word sets and have students copy the words on index cards. Have them store each word set in a separate ziplock bag.

Source

Bhattacharya, A., & Ehri, L. C. (2004). Graphosyllabic analysis helps adolescent struggling readers read and spell words. *Journal of Learning Disabilities, 37,* 331–348. Copyright 2004 by PRO-ED, Inc. Adapted by permission.

PAIRED READING

Overview

Consultants frequently receive requests from teachers and parents for home-based interventions that parents can use to improve their children's reading performance. Paired Reading is a simple, effective strategy that requires little training for parents and uses the student's regular classroom materials. During tutoring sessions, the parent and child begin reading aloud together and continue until the child makes an error. The parent supplies the correct word, the child repeats the word and rereads the sentence, and simultaneous ("duet") reading continues. When the child feels ready to read alone, he or she gives a prearranged signal, and the parent stops reading while the child continues. Paired Reading improves word identification, fluency, and comprehension for low-performing elementary grade readers, including students with ADHD, and is rated highly by parents and children alike. In this version, the individual training format has been modified to permit larger numbers of parents to participate in training at one time. Because of its simplicity, the strategy is also ideal for implementation in after-school or cross-grade tutoring programs. For best results, Paired Reading sessions should be conducted at least four times a week, whether at home or at school.

Purpose

To improve reading accuracy and rate with an easy-to-use paired reading procedure.

Materials

1. Copy of the story or materials currently being read in class or an older version of a basal reader corresponding to the child's instructional level, one per child.
2. Timer or watch with sound device.
3. School–home communication form indicating what story or materials should be read on Paired Reading days, one form per child per week.
4. Form for recording Paired Reading sessions (optional).

Observation (Select One or More)

1. Administer a 20-item word list corresponding to the current grade placement or estimated reading level of a group of target students or the entire class. Continue to administer easier or more difficult word lists until you determine each student's instructional level, defined as the highest list on which a student can read 15 out of 20 words.
2. Calculate percent-correct scores on reading skill exercises or end-of-unit tests for the previous month for a group of target students or the entire class.
3. Administer *Curriculum-Based Oral Reading Probes* (R-CBM) to a group of target students, using both the fluency and comprehension options.

Intervention Steps

Parent–Child Training

1. Parent training can be conducted in an individual, small-group, or large-group format (preferably not more than 20 parents in one session). If parents are delivering the intervention, include children in training sessions if possible. If children do not attend the training, have parents take turns role playing the child during practice sessions.
2. Have each child (or parent, if the student is not present at training) select a nonverbal signal for reading independently, such as a knock on the table, raised index finger, hand raise, etc.
3. Using a volunteer parent or colleague as the child, demonstrate the following Paired Reading procedures:
   a. Begin the session with a brief warm-up time during which you talk about the events of the day with the child.
   b. Set the timer for 10 minutes.
   c. Have the child choose a passage to read from among the materials sent by the teacher.
   d. Begin by reading simultaneously with the child (duet reading), adjusting your rate as needed.
   e. When the child makes an error, point to the place of error, provide the correct word, and have the child repeat it and then reread the entire sentence. Errors are defined as (1) substitutions, (2) omissions, (3) additions, and (4) hesitations lasting longer than a count of three.
   f. After the error correction procedure, begin duet reading again.
   g. When the child gives the signal to read alone, quietly praise the child (e.g., "Good, go ahead," "OK," "Right") and let the child begin reading alone. Give nonverbal approval (nod, smile, or thumbs-up) as the child reads independently.
   h. When the child makes another error, use the same correction procedure.
   i. Praise the child at least once more during the session for positive reading behaviors, such as sounding out a word and attempting a difficult word.
   j. End the session with a brief discussion about the material that has been read and praise for the child's efforts.

4. After training, distribute reading materials at the appropriate level for each pair and have the pairs practice while you circulate to provide feedback and encouragement.
5. Ask parents to conduct Paired Reading with their children for 10 minutes per session, 4 days a week.

Implementation

1. Each Monday, send home copies of the materials to be read and a form listing the selections for that week.
2. If desired, also provide parents with a form for recording Paired Reading sessions to be returned every Monday.

Evaluation (Select One or More)

1. Compare reading instructional levels for the target students before and after implementation.
2. Compare percent-correct scores on reading skill exercises or end-of-unit tests for the target students or the entire class before and after implementation.
3. Compare R-CBM fluency and comprehension scores for the target students before and after implementation.

Variation: Paired Reading as a Classroom Intervention

1. To implement Paired Reading as a classroom intervention, match higher performing students with lower performing students and provide reading material at the level of the less skilled reader in each pair.

Notes

1. Training sessions for parents or intervention agents take about 1 hour. If Paired Reading will be implemented using a cross-grade model, conduct the training in the classroom that houses the target students.
2. Graded word lists are available in many developmental reading inventories and on numerous literacy websites, such as *http://www.angelfire.com*.
3. If Paired Reading will be implemented as one component of an after-school tutoring program, train the tutors to conduct R-CBM on a weekly basis to monitor student progress. Graphing the results enhances motivation for both tutor and tutee.

Source

Fiala, C. L. & Sheridan, S. M. (2003). Parent involvement and reading: Using curriculum-based measurement to assess the effects of paired reading. *Psychology in the Schools, 40,* 613–626. Copyright 2003 by John Wiley & Sons, Inc. Adapted by permission.

Interventions to Improve Reading Fluency

Fluency—the ability to read quickly and accurately—is an essential feature of proficient reading (Allinder, Dunse, Brunken, & Obermiller-Krolikowski, 2001; Chard, Vaughn, & Tyler, 2002; Kame'enui & Simmons, 2001). Reading interventions that specifically target fluency are critical for several reasons. First, the relationship between fluency and overall reading ability, including comprehension, is well documented (Fuchs, Fuchs, Hosp, & Jenkins; 2001; Jenkins, Fuchs, Espin, van den Broek, & Deno, 2003; Meyer & Felton, 1999). If readers are to be able to focus on the meaning of what they are reading, they must be able to identify words quickly and automatically. A second reason for targeting fluency directly is that limited fluency leads to limited reading practice, which has deleterious consequences for reading development and learning in general (Moats, 2001). Because dysfluent readers read slowly, they are exposed to less text. They also experience reading as frustrating and avoid reading, while their more proficient peers can cover more text, building not only fluency but also vocabulary and content knowledge (Stanovich, 1986). Third, fluency directly affects work completion and academic achievement because students who read slowly and laboriously often fail to finish classroom and homework assignments that involve reading (Archer et al., 2003).

Fluency deficits also serve as early markers of reading problems, with pronounced differences in fluency between at-risk and typically developing children emerging as early as first grade (Deno, Fuchs, Marston, & Shin, 2001; Speece & Ritchey, 2005). As children progress through school, the importance of reading fluency increases, as the skill requirement shifts from *learning to read* to *reading to learn* (Chall, 1983). After third or fourth grade, fluency deficits become more apparent as textbooks and other classroom reading materials contain more multisyllabic, content-based words (Fuchs, Fuchs, & Kazdan, 1999). Especially likely to suffer from fluency deficits are students with disabilities, who typically read at about half the rate of students without disabilities in both narrative and expository text (Parmar, Deluca, & Janczak, 1994).

Despite the crucial role of fluency in the comprehension of textual material and the development of overall reading competency, reading for fluency received little attention from researchers or practitioners until quite recently. Within the past decade, however, syntheses of reading research have highlighted the importance of targeting fluency as a component of daily instruction (Chard et al., 1998; National Reading Panel, 2000; Snow et al., 1998). To build reading fluency, students need frequent opportunities to engage in oral reading and receive corrective feedback. Unfortunately, traditional classroom reading activities, such as round robin reading, provide insufficient practice for most students. Similarly, despite the widespread popularity of independent silent reading, there is little evidence that it is effective in building either fluency or comprehension (Chard et al., 2002; National Reading Panel, 2000). Typical instruction for students with learning disabilities also fails to incorporate research-based practices for enhancing fluency, with students spending large amounts of time doing seatwork, filling out worksheets, or waiting for instruction (Moody et al., 2000; Vaughn, Levy, Coleman, & Bos, 2002).

Reading Fluency Interventions

The three interventions in this section are designed to enhance students' ability to read rapidly and accurately in textual material. By increasing fluency, the strategies also have the potential to promote comprehension by permitting readers to allocate attention to meaning rather than to decoding. Two of the three strategies include repeated reading as an integral component. First studied by Samuels (1979), *repeated reading* combines guided oral reading practice with immediate error correction. One of the most widely investigated reading strategies, repeated reading has been successful in improving reading fluency for elementary students (Levy, Nicholls, & Kohen, 1993), middle school students (Homan, Klesius, & Hite, 1993), and high school students (Valleley & Shriver, 2003), as well as students with disabilities (Sindelar, Monda, & O'Shea, 1990; Weinstein & Cooke, 1992). Gains in comprehension have also been obtained in some studies (Homan et al., 1993; O'Shea, Sindelar, & O'Shea, 1985). Despite these positive outcomes, the traditional one-to-one format, in which an individual student reads the same passage aloud three or four times while the teacher listens and prompts, is impractical in general education settings. Moreover, it can be a tedious process for students and can have negative effects on attitudes toward reading, especially among struggling readers (Homan et al., 1993; Rasinski, 1990). In contrast, reading textual material with a peer partner is an efficient way of integrating oral reading practice into daily instruction. Peer-mediated oral reading formats capitalize on students' interest in interacting with their classmates and, unlike silent reading, can easily be monitored by the teacher because students are reading aloud (Archer et al., 2003).

In *Partner Reading,* repeated reading occurs in a peer collaboration context, with student dyads taking turns reading a passage aloud three times and evaluating their progress toward a specific goal. *Partner Reading* differs from *Class Wide Peer Tutoring* in that reading practice occurs in mixed-ability rather than random or matched-ability pairs. Because the higher performing student in each pair reads first, the strategy also incorporates *listening previewing,* another validated strategy for enhancing fluency. The procedure not only increases opportunities for all students to engage in active reading practice, but also accommodates diversity by providing less proficient readers with effective reading models. *Partner Reading* is part of a multicomponent reading intervention that has been successful in enhancing reading outcomes for a wide range of student populations, including students with learning disabilities (Bryant et al., 2000; Mathes, Fuchs, Fuchs, Henley, & Sanders, 1994; Vaughn et al., 2000). In *Parents as Reading Tutors* (PART), repeated reading is a core component in a parent–child tutoring routine. Although parents play a key role in motivating children's reading (Baker, 2003; Baker, Scher, & Machler, 1997), parents' efforts to tutor their own children do not always produce better reading outcomes (Law & Kratochwill, 1993; Miller & Kratochwill, 1996), and even when improvement is obtained at home, gains may not generalize to the classroom setting (Hook & DuPaul, 1999). In PART, parents learn a structured tutoring strategy that includes repeated reading, a simple error correction method, and 1-minute assessments. PART has been validated as an effective method of improving fluency and comprehension for both struggling and normally progressing readers (Delquadri et al., 1986; Duvall et al., 1992; Greenwood et al., 1989), as well as for students with ADHD (Hook & DuPaul, 1999).

The third intervention in this section uses a variation of listening previewing to build both fluency and comprehension. In the *listening previewing* procedure, a less proficient reader listens to a more proficient reader prior to independent reading. Listening previewing facilitates fluency because the previewer not only reads any words that may be unfamiliar to the listener but also models expressiveness and an appropriate fluency rate. Listening previewing has been successful in increasing reading fluency for elementary students (Rasinski, 1990; Tingstrom, Edwards, & Olmi, 1995), middle school students (Rose & Sherry, 1984), students with learning disabilities (Daly & Martens, 1994; Skinner et al., 1993; Skinner, Cooper, & Cole, 1997), and English language learners (O'Donnell, Weber, & McLaughlin, 2003; Rousseau & Tam, 1991; Rousseau, Tam, & Ramnarain, 1993). Moreover, listening previewing is superior to silent previewing (Rose & Sherry, 1984; Skinner, Cooper, et al., 1997; Skinner et al., 1993) and has been associated with comprehension gains in some investigations (Sindelar et al., 1990; Tingstrom et al., 1995). Like traditional forms of repeated reading, however, listening previewing can be time- and labor-intensive because it is typically delivered in a one-to-one setting. In contrast, *Listening Previewing with Discussion of Key Words* combines effectiveness with usability by means of classwide previewing, including a discussion of critical vocabulary words to be encountered by readers, followed by partner reading of the same selection. Because research demonstrates that adding performance-based (i.e., motivational) components to skill-based fluency interventions increases their effectiveness, especially for less proficient readers (Chafouleas, Martens, Dobson, Weinstein, & Gardner, 2004; Eckert, Ardoin, Daly, & Martens, 2002), a variation that trains the student pairs to monitor their own progress is also presented.

> **CROSS-REFERENCE:** Three other interventions in this chapter use paired learning formats to build reading fluency. *ClassWide Peer Tutoring in Reading* (Academic Productivity section) combines a structured paired tutoring routine with game-like procedures to provide opportunities for all students to practice oral reading. *Partner Reading with Retell,* the first component in the multifaceted *Peer-Assisted Learning Strategies in Reading* (Vocabulary and Comprehension section), includes peer-mediated repeated reading. *Admirals and Generals: Improving Content Area Performance with Strategy Instruction and Peer Tutoring* (Content Area section) primarily targets comprehension but includes repeated reading as one of several paired learning activities.

PARTNER READING

Overview

Although repeated reading of textual material has been demonstrated to increase fluency and comprehension, teachers and other intervention agents can listen to only one student read at a time. Partner Reading combines two strategies that have been demonstrated to enhance reading fluency—repeated reading and listening previewing—and delivers them in a peer-mediated format that permits all students in a classroom to participate simultaneously in active reading practice. During Partner Reading sessions, a higher performing student reads for 5 minutes, after which a lower performing student reads the same material for 5 minutes. Each 5-minute session is followed by a 1-minute fluency assessment based on the material that has just been read, beginning with the more proficient reader, so that the less proficient reader hears a fluent reading model twice during each Partner Reading session. Partner Reading includes competitive as well as cooperative features, with each student pair accumulating points to contribute to one of two teams. Partner Reading has been demonstrated to increase reading fluency significantly for elementary and middle school students with and without reading disabilities. Moreover, it is easy to implement and is ideal for classrooms with a wide range of reading abilities because not all student pairs must read from the same set of materials. A variation with a comprehension-enhancement component is also presented.

Purpose

To improve reading fluency by providing opportunities for structured oral reading practice within a paired learning framework.

Materials

1. Stopwatch or timer (optional).
2. Classroom clock with second hand or stop watches or watches with second hands, one per student pair.
3. Classroom reading materials, one set per student.
4. Notebooks or folders with sheets of graph paper, one per student.
5. Posterboard chart listing error correction procedures.
6. Score cards, consisting of index cards with a list of consecutive numbers, one per student pair per session.
7. Posterboard chart listing comprehension questions or index cards with comprehension questions, one per student pair (optional, see Variation).

Observation (Select One or Both)

1. Administer *Curriculum-Based Oral Reading Probes* (R-CBM), including the comprehension option, to a group of target students or the entire class and calculate each student's words-read-correctly-per-minute (WCPM) rate. If desired, calculate a class average WCPM rate by summing individual WCPM rates and dividing by the number of students in the class.
2. Calculate scores on reading skill sheets, quizzes, or end-of-unit tests for a group of target students or the entire class for the past several weeks.

Intervention Steps

Preparation

1. Rank order your students from strongest to weakest reader using scores on standardized tests, statewide reading tests, teacher judgment, or a combination.
2. Divide the list in half so that List A includes the stronger readers (who will serve as Partner 1) and List B includes the weaker readers (who will serve as Partner 2).
3. Pair the student at the top of List A with the student at the top of List B and so on until all of the students are matched. Make adjustments as needed to accommodate reading ability and compatibility. Assign each pair to one of two teams for use in awarding points.

Introduction and Training

1. Tell the class that they will be practicing reading in pairs to help everyone become better readers. Indicate student partner assignments and have students move to partner reading stations (i.e., paired desks). Also indicate teams for each pair.
2. Distribute reading materials to each pair and indicate what kind of timing device will be used for the sessions (i.e., classroom clock or student-held timers or watches). Display the chart with the error correction procedures where all students can see it.
3. Using a student as a partner, demonstrate a Partner Reading session, following the procedures presented below.
   a. When you give the signal, Partner 1 reads for 5 minutes (3 minutes for early primary grade students), modeling fluent reading, while Partner 2 follows along and times the reading. If Partner 1 comes to the end of the passage before the time is up, he or she returns to the beginning and starts again. Partner 2 then reads the same passage for the specified time, while Partner 1 follows along and keeps time.
   b. If the reader misreads a word, skips a word, or pauses for more than 4 seconds, the tutor points to the word and says, "Stop. You missed this word. Can you figure it out?" If the reader pronounces the correct word in 4 seconds, the tutor directs the reader to read the sentence again. If the reader cannot figure out the word in 4 seconds, the tutor says, "That word is ___. What word?" The reader repeats the word. The tutor says, "Good! Read the sentence again," and the reader rereads the sentence and continues. If the tutor cannot provide the word, the students raise their hands to ask for assistance.
   c. If a reader adds a word, the tutor says, "Stop. You added a word. Can you figure out what word you added?" If the reader cannot figure out what he or she added, the tutor says, "You added ___. Read the sentence again," and the reader rereads the sentence and continues.
   d. Students earn points as a pair. For each correctly read sentence, regardless of the number of trials that are necessary, the tutor awards a point by making a slash mark through the next number on the score card.
   e. After the tutoring session, students take turns conducting 1-minute timings and graphing their WCPM rates. While Partner 2 keeps time, Partner 1 reads the same passage for 1 minute and graphs his or her WCPM rate in the notebook or folder. The process is then

repeated for Partner 2. The error correction procedure is not used during the assessments. Students keep their score cards in their folders for the entire week.

4. Conduct a classwide practice session while you circulate to provide assistance and encouragement. For the first training session, have students practice Partner Reading without the error correction procedure. Introduce error correction in the second session and assessment and graphing procedures in a third session.

Implementation

1. At the end of the week, have each pair report their points so that you can determine total points for each team. The winning team is announced and applauded.
2. Create new pairs and team assignments every 4 weeks. For high school students, change partners more frequently.

Evaluation (Select One or Both)

1. Compare R-CBM fluency and comprehension scores for the target students or the entire class before and after implementation. If desired, compare the class average WCPM before and after implementation.
2. Compare scores on reading skill sheets, quizzes, or end-of-unit tests for the group of target students or the entire class before and after implementation.

Variation: Partner Reading with Comprehension Questions

1. To add a comprehension component, have student partners take turns asking each other five comprehension questions (Who?, What?, When?, Where?, and Why?) about the reading selection after the 1-minute timing.

Notes

1. Partner Reading can be used effectively with a wide variety of reading material, such as nonfiction student magazines, newspapers, basal texts, trade books, and leveled readers.
2. For maximum benefit, Partner Reading should be implemented three times a week for approximately 35 minutes per session.

Sources

Mathes, P. G., Fuchs, D., Fuchs, L. S., Henley, A. M., & Sanders, A. (1994). Increasing strategic reading practice with Peabody Classwide Peer Tutoring. *Learning Disabilities Research and Practice, 9,* 44–48. Copyright 1994 by Blackwell Publishing. Adapted by permission.

Vaughn, S., Chard, D. J., Bryant, D. P., Coleman, M., Tyler, B., Linan-Thompson, S., et al. (2000). Fluency and comprehension interventions for third-grade students. *Remedial and Special Education, 21,* 325–335. Copyright 2000 by PRO-ED, Inc. Adapted by permission.

PARENTS AS READING TUTORS

Overview

Parents often ask how they can help their children become more competent and confident readers. *Parents as Reading Tutors* (PART) is a simple but effective home-based intervention designed to increase the amount of time in which students actively engage in reading. Unlike many tutoring procedures that require students to struggle through a reading passage until they have completed it, PART provides the opportunity to read material to the point of mastery. Parents are trained in a two-step procedure: (1) 4 minutes of tutoring, using a simple error correction procedure and (2) 6 minutes of repeated reading of the tutored material. PART also includes an assessment component so that parent and child can monitor progress from session to session. In the original study with four elementary school children, three of whom had learning disabilities, mothers tutored their children daily during the summer, using materials that students would encounter at the beginning of the fall semester. All the target students displayed significant gains on standardized reading tests and immediate pronounced increases in reading rate that generalized to untutored passages at home as well as to more difficult material in school texts. In this adaptation, a comprehension check is added to each session. Because PART requires little training and relies on the student's regular classroom materials, it can be easily adapted for use by volunteers or community-based tutors in after-school supplementary instructional programs.

Purpose

To improve reading fluency with a simple tutoring procedure that can be delivered by parents.

Materials

1. Reading texts or copies of classroom reading materials, one set per parent–child pair.
2. Timer or watch with sound device, one per parent–child pair.
3. Notebook or folder with sheets of paper, one per parent–child pair.
4. Scratch paper, one sheet per tutoring session.
5. Home reading survey, consisting of a sheet of paper listing the following five questions: (a) How much do you enjoy reading? (b) How often do you read at home? (c) When do you read at home? (d) Do you read with your parents? and (e) If so, how often do you read with your parents? (optional, one per student; see Observation/Evaluation 3).
6. Home tutoring log, consisting of a sheet of paper listing days and times for parent tutoring, one per student per week (optional).
7. Small rewards, such as stickers, wrapped candy, and decorated erasers or pencils (optional).

Observation (Select One or More)

1. Administer *Curriculum-Based Oral Reading Probes* (R-CBM) to a group of target students, using both the fluency and comprehension options.
2. Calculate percent-correct scores on reading skill sheets, quizzes, or end-of-unit tests for a group of target students or the entire class for the previous grading period.
3. Administer the home reading survey to a group of target students or to the entire class.

Intervention Steps

Parent–Child Training

1. Parent training can be conducted in an individual, small-group, or large-group format (no more than 20 parents per session). Encourage parents to bring their children to the training session. If children are unable to attend the training, have parents take turns playing the roles of parent and child in the tutoring pairs.
2. Using a volunteer parent or a colleague as the child, train the parents in the procedures described below.
   a. Select a passage from the materials sent from school. Sit beside the child so that you can both see the passage, set the timer for 10 minutes, and ask the child to begin reading.
   b. When the child makes an error, stop the child, point to the location of the error in the text,

correctly pronounce the error word(s), ask the child to pronounce the error word(s) correctly, and then have the child reread the sentence. Errors are defined as (1) substitutions, (2) omissions, (3) additions, and (4) hesitations lasting longer than 4 seconds.

c. After the child has reread the entire sentence that previously involved one or more errors, praise him or her.

d. After tutoring for 4 minutes, mark the passage to indicate the farthest point of progress and have the child return to the beginning of the selection and continue reading between the beginning point and the end mark for the remaining 6 minutes. If desired, ask comprehension questions, such as Who?, What?, When?, Where?, and Why? for 3 or 4 additional minutes at the end of the session.

e. Set the timer for 1 minute and take a "parent check" by having the child read from the beginning point in the passage for 1 minute. Tally errors on a scratch sheet of paper while the child reads but do not correct any errors. At the end of 1 minute, count the total number of words between the beginning and ending points and subtract the number of errors from the total number of words to obtain a words-read-correctly-per-minute (WCPM) score. Help the child graph his or her WCPM score in the notebook or folder.

3. After the demonstration, distribute reading materials at the appropriate level for each participating student and have the parent–child or parent–parent pairs practice while you move among the room to provide encouragement and corrective feedback as needed.

Implementation

1. Each Monday, send home a set of tutoring materials with each target student for use during the week. Ask parents to use the procedure for 4 days a week, 10 minutes per session (plus 3 or 4 minutes for the comprehension option and 2 or 3 minutes for the timed assessment and graphing).

2. If desired, also send home a tutoring log and ask parents to return the completed log on the following Monday. To enhance motivation for both parents and children, provide small classroom-based rewards for students returning the completed logs, such as stickers, wrapped candy, and decorated erasers or pencils.

Evaluation (Select One or More)

1. Compare R-CBM fluency and comprehension scores for the target students before and after implementation.

2. Compare percent-correct scores on reading skill exercises, quizzes, or end-of-unit tests for the group of target students or the entire class before and after implementation.

3. Compare responses on the home reading survey for the group of target students before and after implementation.

Variation: Parent Tutoring with Classroom Generalization Check

1. To determine whether the student's reading gains are generalizing to unfamiliar material, conduct a weekly 1-minute assessment using material from a passage that is one or two pages ahead of the tutored material. Parents can conduct these assessments if the teacher provides the appropriate materials.

Note

1. In the original study, parents were taught to record reading rate (words read per minute) and reading errors on separate graphs. This adaptation uses the standard CBM metric of words

read correctly per minute (WCPM) to simplify data recording and facilitate comparisons with DIBELS benchmarks (available on the DIBELS website at *http://dibels.uoregon.edu*).

Source

Duvall, S. F., Delquadri, J. C., Elliott, M., & Hall, R. V. (1992). Parent-tutoring procedures: Experimental analysis and validation of generalization in oral reading across passages, settings, and time. *Journal of Behavioral Education, 2,* 281–303. Copyright 1992 by Springer Science and Business Media. Adapted by permission.

Additional Resources

Duvall, S. F., Delquadri, J. C., & Hall, R. V. (1996). *Parents as Reading Tutors.* Longmont, CO: Sopris West (*http://www.sopriswest.com*).

Designed for volunteers and paraprofessionals as well as parents, this handbook describes the PART procedures in detail and includes materials for graphing children's progress.

LISTENING PREVIEWING WITH KEY WORD DISCUSSION

Overview

In *Listening previewing,* also termed *passage previewing,* a more skilled reader reads a passage aloud while a less skilled reader follows along silently prior to independent reading of the same material. Listening previewing has been validated as an effective fluency-building strategy across a variety of student populations and settings from elementary through secondary levels. This version promotes vocabulary acquisition and comprehension in addition to fluency by including a discussion of key words prior to reading. In the original study, implemented with five English language learners in a class for students with speech and language impairments, listening previewing with key word discussion was more effective in increasing fluency and comprehension than listening previewing alone or silent previewing with key word discussion. This classwide adaptation uses choral responding and a peer-mediated format with a simple error correction procedure to enhance usability and increase students' opportunities for active oral reading practice during the reading instructional period. Two variations are presented: (1) a small-group format for classrooms using a differentiated reading instructional model and (2) a version with a self-monitoring component to enhance motivation. The strategy can be implemented with narrative or expository text in reading, literature, or content area classes.

Purpose

To enhance reading fluency and comprehension by discussing key vocabulary words and providing an opportunity for students to hear what they will read prior to independent reading.

Materials

1. Stopwatches or watches with second hands, one per student pair.
2. Classroom reading materials, one set per student.
3. Sets of five to eight comprehension questions for each passage, one set per student.
4. Notebooks or folders with sheets of paper, one per student (optional, see Variation 2).

Observation (Select One or Both)

1. Using students' regular reading materials, administer *Curriculum-Based Oral Reading Probes* (R-CBM) with the comprehension option to a group of target students or the entire class.
2. Calculate scores on reading skill sheets, quizzes, or end-of-unit tests for the entire class or a group of target students for 5 to 10 days or for the previous month.

Intervention Steps

Preparation

1. Using data collected during the observation period, create listening previewing pairs by matching higher performing readers with lower performing readers. Make adjustments as needed to accommodate reading proficiency and student compatibility.

Introduction and Training

1. Explain to the students that they will be working in pairs to practice their reading skills and learn new words. Using yourself as the more proficient reader and a student as the less proficient reader, demonstrate the paired listening previewing procedures as follows:
   a. The more proficient reader reads the first paragraph (the first sentence for younger and less skilled students) while the less proficient reader follows along. Then the less proficient reader reads the same paragraph or sentence.
   b. As one student reads, the other corrects four errors: (1) substitutions, (2) omissions, (3) additions, and (4) hesitations of more than 4 seconds. If neither student in the pair knows a word, the students raise their hands to ask for assistance.
2. Assign listening previewing partners and have students move to their partner stations (two desks placed together or some similar arrangement). To ensure that higher performing students read first, designate higher performing readers as the "red team" and lower performing students as the "blue team" or some other team names.
3. Conduct a classwide practice session while you move around the room providing encouragement and assistance as needed.

Implementation

1. At the beginning of the reading instructional period, write 10 to 12 key words from the reading selection on the chalkboard or add them to the word wall. *Key words* are defined as words that may be difficult for students to understand or pronounce, including vocabulary critical to understanding the assignment.
2. Read the first word to the students and have them repeat it chorally. Discuss the word's meaning by means of explanations, gestures, pictures, modeling, or other strategies, including the contexts in which it is used. Ask questions to determine if students understand the meaning of the word. Repeat this procedure for each of the key words.
3. Then read the selection aloud, while students follow along silently. To promote active attention, instruct students to follow along with a finger under each word as you read.
4. After you have finished reading the selection, have students move to their partner stations and take turns reading the same selection, one paragraph at a time, with the higher performing student in each pair reading first.
5. After the student pairs have read the selection, distribute a worksheet with five to eight comprehension questions based on the selection. If desired, have student pairs collaborate in preparing their answers.
6. Review the questions as a whole-class activity and have students correct their own or their

partner's papers. Collect the papers to check for scoring accuracy and provide corrective feedback as needed.

Evaluation (Select One or Both)

1. Compare R-CBM fluency and comprehension scores for the target students or the entire class before and after implementation.
2. Compare scores on reading skill sheets, quizzes, or end-of-unit tests for the target students or the entire class before and after implementation.

Variations

Variation 1: Listening Previewing in a Small-Group Format

1. Conduct the listening previewing and key word discussion during small-group reading instruction. If the group is small enough, have each student read aloud while you listen and provide corrective feedback after the preview. Alternately, have students work in pairs to conduct partner listening previews after the group preview and key word discussion while you move on to the next reading group.

Variation 2: Listening Previewing with Self-Monitoring

1. After each student in the pair has read, have partners conduct R-CBMs on a daily or weekly basis, as follows:
   a. The higher performing student returns to the beginning of the selection and reads for 1 minute while the lower performing student follows along, tallying errors on a sheet of paper and keeping time. The lower performing student counts the number of words read correctly per minute (WCPM), and the higher performing student graphs his or her results in a reading notebook or folder. The process is repeated for the lower performing student.
   b. To help students keep track of errors, teach them to make slash marks on a sheet of paper and to draw a line with a pencil in the passage to mark the last word read in 1 minute.

Notes

1. Including a self-monitoring component by having students graph their WCPM performance (Variation 2) helps to maintain interest and enhances the effectiveness of this intervention.
2. This intervention also lends itself to implementation in a cross-grade tutoring format or in an after-school tutoring program. Train tutors to conduct the R-CBMs and help their tutees graph their results.

Source

Rousseau, M. K., Tam, B. K., & Ramnarain, R. (1993). Increasing reading proficiency of language-minority students with speech and language impairments. *Education and Treatment of Children, 16,* 254–271. Copyright 1993 by West Virginia University Press. Adapted by permission.

Interventions to Improve Vocabulary

Vocabulary knowledge is essential for reading comprehension and for school success in general (Biemiller, 2003; National Reading Panel, 2000). Beginning around grade 3, deficits in vocabulary are a major contributor to comprehension problems, with the relationship between vocabulary and comprehension becoming stronger as reading material becomes more complex (Baker et al., 1998; Snow, 2002). Students face a formidable task in learning vocabulary. On average, students need to learn about 2,000 to 3,000 words per year, or about 6 to 8 new words per day (Beck & McKeown, 1991; D'Anna, Zechmeister, & Hall, 1991). Even before children enter school, however, they display dramatic differences in vocabulary size. Hart and Risley (1992, 1995) have estimated that the spoken vocabularies of 3-year-old children of families living in urban poverty are less than half the size of the vocabularies of their peers in middle-class families (500 vs. 1,100 unique words). Not only do children living in poverty enter school with much smaller vocabularies than their more advantaged classmates, they also acquire words at slower rates. Although, on average, children have acquired about 5,200 root words by the end of grade 2, the children in the lowest vocabulary quartile know 2,000 fewer root words than the children in the average quartile and 4,100 fewer root words than the children in the highest vocabulary quartile. These early vocabulary differences are likely to persist throughout elementary school, with profound implications for reading proficiency and overall academic success (Biemiller & Slonim, 2001). Vocabulary disparities among children from different socioeconomic backgrounds also play a role in the well-known decline in reading that has been termed "the fourth grade slump" (Chall, Jacobs, & Baldwin, 1990).

THE FOURTH GRADE SLUMP

In the critical transition from learning to read to reading to learn in the elementary grades, researchers and educators alike have often noted a decline in literacy development around grade 3 or 4, especially among students living in poverty. The term "fourth grade slump" was first coined by reading researcher Jeanne Chall and her colleagues (Chall et al., 1990) to describe the dropoff that occurs between third and fourth grade in the reading performance of students from low-income backgrounds. Their longitudinal research documented that although students from poor families performed as well as their more advantaged peers on standardized tests of language and literacy skills up to grade 3, the reading performance of poor children began a steady decline around grade 4 that became steeper with each higher grade level. The first and most pronounced skill to decline was knowledge of word meanings, especially less common and academically oriented words. Word recognition and spelling were next to decelerate, following by oral reading and reading comprehension.

Researchers have identified several factors that contribute to the fourth grade slump. First, because students can learn only about 8 to 10 words per week from direct vocabulary instruction (Beck & McKeown, 1991), most of the vocabulary growth after grade 3 must come from extensive reading. Children with weak decoding skills and limited reading fluency read less and avoid more difficult reading material and thus have fewer opportunities than more proficient readers to build vocabulary, domain knowledge, and comprehension skills (Cunningham & Stanovich, 1998; Stanovich, 1986). Children living in poverty may also read less because they are likely to have fewer reading experiences with adults and fewer role models for reading as an enjoyable activity compared with children from more advantaged backgrounds (Baker et al., 1997). Second, the shift from narrative to expository material has a negative impact on the reading development of many students, especially less skilled readers. In the early primary grades, the words that students encounter in their texts are generally high-frequency, familiar words. Beginning around grade 4, however, texts include an increasing number of less common words, including many abstract, literary, and technical words. Students who are unfamiliar with the organization and structure of expository texts, as well as those who have poor decoding skills and small vocabularies, will have difficulty understanding their textbooks and using reading to learn (Hirsch, 2003).

In contrast to the voluminous literature focusing on decoding instruction (i.e., instruction in learning to read), there has been much less research on effective instructional practices for helping children *understand* the words they are reading (i.e., building vocabulary knowledge) (Biemiller & Slonim, 2001; Coyne, Simmons, & Kame'enui, 2004). Although numerous studies have demonstrated that explicit vocabulary instruction can improve word knowledge and reading comprehension for students with and without learning disabilities (e.g., Baker et al., 1998; Bryant, Goodwin, Bryant, & Higgins, 2003; Harmon, Hedrick, & Fox, 2000), research-based practices are seldom integrated into classroom instruction. The traditional method of briefly introducing new words prior to having students read stories provides insufficient practice to master vocabulary, especially in the case of struggling readers and other diverse learners, such as English language learners (Sindelar & Stoddard, 1991). Similarly, although reading aloud is a frequent activity in the elementary grades, teacher-directed discussions before or after story reading that could be used to enhance vocabulary skills tend to be brief, typically less than 5 minutes (Hoffman, Rosner, & Battle, 1993). To close the vocabulary gap between lower and higher performing students, instruction must involve a more intentional, teacher-centered approach to vocabulary development (Biemiller & Slonim, 2001). At the middle and high school levels, where instruction is largely textbook-driven and texts include an increasing proportion of abstract, technical, and multisyllabic words, helping students to expand their word knowledge is essential if students are to master the content of the curriculum (Bryant, Ugel, Thompson, & Hamff, 1999; Hirsch, 2003). Vocabulary interventions are especially needed for students from linguistic minorities and students living in poverty, whose reading achievement levels remain consistently lower than those of Caucasian students and students from more affluent backgrounds (Carlos et al., 2004; National Center for Education Statistics, 2005).

Vocabulary Interventions

This section includes one intervention targeting reading vocabulary. *Peer Tutoring in Vocabulary* is a highly usable strategy that creates additional opportunities for all students to participate in supervised practice of new vocabulary without increasing the total amount of time set aside for vocabulary instruction. The strategy prevents the perpetuation of errors because student tutors provide immediate feedback on response accuracy. To enhance motivation and peer collaboration, rewards are delivered contingent on the combined performance of each tutoring pair. Interventions combining interdependent group contingencies with paired learning have been successful in improving academic skills across a variety of subjects and student populations (for a review, see Rohrbeck, Ginsburg-Block, Fantuzzo, & Miller, 2003).

CROSS-REFERENCE: The Academic Productivity section of this chapter includes two interventions that can be used to provide students with additional opportunities to practice vocabulary: *ClassWide Peer Tutoring in Vocabulary,* which embeds vocabulary practice within a peer tutoring context, and *Cover, Copy, and Compare—Vocabulary,* which teaches students to manage their own vocabulary practice. Chapter 6 includes two shared reading interventions targeting oral vocabulary development in preschoolers: *Building Vocabulary Skills with Interactive Book Reading* and *Enhancing Emergent Literacy Skills with Dialogic Reading.*

PEER TUTORING IN VOCABULARY

Overview

Maximizing the amount of active academic responding in the classroom has been demonstrated to be an effective method of increasing student achievement. In this peer tutoring strategy, pairs of students practice vocabulary words together, with rewards contingent upon the combined academic performance of both students. Because the intervention takes only about 20 minutes to complete after students have prepared their vocabulary flashcards for the week, it can be easily incorporated within the reading instructional period, using either a single list of vocabulary words for all students or different lists for small, skill-based instructional groups. Implemented in two seventh- and eighth-grade reading classes in the original study, it produced significant increases in vocabulary quiz scores compared with traditional vocabulary instruction. Four variations are presented, including one for reading classes that use a differentiated instructional format. This strategy is also ideal for implementation in social studies and science, with paired vocabulary practice serving as an introductory and/or review activity for a unit or chapter.

Purpose

To improve reading vocabulary by increasing opportunities for students to practice academic material in the context of an interdependent group contingency.

Materials

1. List of vocabulary words, one per student.
2. Vocabulary quizzes, consisting of one brief quiz per tutoring session and one more comprehensive quiz per week.
3. 3″ × 5″ index cards, 10 to 20 per student per week.
4. Dictionaries, one per student.
5. Posterboard chart or section of the chalkboard listing student names, with columns for posting stars or checks (see Variations 1 and 2).
6. Small and large gold stars (optional, see Variation 3).

Observation (Select One or Both)

1. Calculate percent-correct scores on weekly vocabulary quizzes for a target group of students or the entire class for several weeks or for the previous grading period. If desired, calculate the class average percent-correct score by summing individual scores and dividing by the number of students.
2. Administer *Curriculum-Based Vocabulary-Matching Probes* (VM-CBM) to the entire class. Calculate percent-correct scores for each student and, if desired, calculate the class average percent-correct score by summing individual scores and dividing by the number of students.

Intervention Steps

Introduction and Training

1. Explain to the students that they will be working in pairs to help them learn and remember more vocabulary words. Tell them that they will have an opportunity to earn homework passes that can be used for any daily assignment in the target subject (or some other reward).
2. Conduct a training session, using the procedures below. Allow about 30 minutes for the initial session, with 20 minutes for demonstration and modeling and 10 minutes for classwide practice. Be sure to model appropriate voice levels for students during practice sessions.

Implementation

1. On Monday, distribute the list of vocabulary words and assign tutoring partners. Pairs remain the same during the entire week. If students are grouped for reading instruction, pair members of the same group for tutoring (see Variation 4).
2. Begin by asking students to move to their tutoring stations (paired desks or a similar arrangement). Designate one student in each pair to serve as the first tutor. Distribute the new vocabulary list, index cards, and dictionaries.
3. Have students prepare individual sets of flashcards by looking up the vocabulary words in a dictionary and copying the word on one side of an index card and the definition on the other. Have tutoring partners check each other's definitions to ensure that they are accurate, complete, and legible while you circulate and provided assistance as needed.
4. On Tuesday, conduct a brief whole-class review of the definitions and provide corrective feedback as needed.
5. Have the tutoring pairs practice vocabulary definitions for 20 minutes, using the following procedures.
   a. For the first 10 minutes, the tutor shows the tutee a vocabulary card and asks the tutee to define it.
   b. If the definition is correct, the tutor praises the tutee, turns the card face down, and proceeds to the next card.
   c. If the tutee fails to define the word correctly, the tutor reads the definition from the back of the card and has the tutee repeat it. The tutor then inserts the missed card back into the stack of cards near the beginning and returns to it in a short period of time.
   d. After the tutor has gone through the stack of vocabulary cards, he or she starts over from the beginning and presents the words as many times as possible during the 10 minutes.
   e. After 10 minutes, call time and have students switch roles.
6. During tutoring, walk around the room, supervising and praising appropriate tutoring behavior and voice levels.
7. At the end of the tutoring session, administer a vocabulary quiz on the current words, as well as a few words drawn from earlier chapters or lessons.
8. Collect the papers for grading. Alternatively, have students exchange papers, correct each other's answers as you go over each item, and write the percentage of words correctly defined at the top of the paper.
9. Check over all test papers. Provide feedback to the class for scoring errors and adjust pair scores accordingly. (This may need to occur on the following day.)
10. When quizzes have been graded, put stars or checks on the chart to indicate which students have received scores of 90% or higher.
11. When both students in the tutoring pair receive three consecutive quiz scores of 90% or above, award a homework pass or the agreed-upon reward to each student.
12. Conduct one or two additional vocabulary tutoring sessions during the week, as needed, based on the first set of scores. Administer a more comprehensive vocabulary quiz on Friday.
13. After most student pairs have earned the reward once, administer vocabulary quizzes on a weekly rather than a daily basis.

Evaluation (Select One or Both)

1. Compare percent-correct scores on weekly vocabulary quizzes for the target group of students or the entire class and/or class average percent-correct scores before and after implementation.
2. Compare VM-CBM percent-correct scores for each student and/or class average VM-CBM percent-correct scores before and after implementation.

Variations

Variation 1: Self-Monitoring Variation

1. Have students record their vocabulary scores in their reading notebooks and request homework passes as they are earned.
2. Verify the reported scores in your grade book and award passes accordingly.

Variation 2: Public Posting Variation

1. Award checks or stars to student pairs that meet the 90% criterion but do not provide any tangible rewards.

Variation 3: Whole-Group Contingency Variation

1. Provide a classwide reward, such as extra recess, music time, or a pizza party, if all tutoring pairs achieve the 90% criterion on the weekly quiz.

Variation 4: Differentiated Instruction Variation

1. This variation is designed for reading classes using a small-group instructional format. Provide separate vocabulary lists and quizzes for each group and pair students according to their group placement.
2. Moving through each group in turn, administer a quiz to one group while the students in the other groups engage in peer tutoring.

Notes

1. For greatest benefit, tutoring sessions should be held at least three times a week.
2. To reduce preparation and grading time, use short-answer or item-matching formats on the daily quizzes, and have students check each other's papers under your guidance. If you detect cheating, do not permit students to check their partner's papers.

Source

Malone, R. A., & McLaughlin, T. F. (1997). The effects of reciprocal peer tutoring with a group contingency on quiz performance in vocabulary with seventh- and eighth-grade students. *Behavioral Interventions, 12,* 27–40. Copyright 1997 by John Wiley & Sons, Inc. Adapted by permission.

Interventions to Improve Reading Comprehension

Comprehension—the ability to derive meaning from text—is the most critical element in school learning (Cornoldi & Oakhill, 1996; Mastropieri & Scruggs, 1997). According to Gough's (1996) "simple view of reading," reading comprehension is the product of two component skills: (1) *decoding*—recognizing the words on the page—and (2) *comprehension*—understanding the words once they have been recognized. From this perspective, reading comprehension difficulties can arise from deficits in one or both of these component skills. Although considerable progress has been made toward the goal of promoting effective instruction in decoding, researchers have only recently recognized the need for a specific focus on comprehension (Snow, 2002; Williams, 2005). Improving comprehension is even more challenging than improving word recognition, however, because of the complex, multidimensional nature of comprehension and its relationship to domain knowledge and general cognitive ability (Baker, Gersten, & Grossen, 2002; Caccamise & Snyder, 2005). Moreover, despite the growing database of empirically validated comprehension-enhancing strategies for students with and without disabilities (for reviews, see Baker, Gersten, & Grossan, 2002, and Gersten et al., 2001), research-based practices have been slow to find their way into the classroom. Observational research reveals that teachers tend to assess comprehension rather than provide direct instruction in specific strategies for understanding text, whether in regular education classrooms (Pressley, Yokoi, Rankin, Wharton-McDonald, & Mistretta, 1997) or special education settings (Levy & Vaughn, 2002; Vaughn et al., 1998).

Students' comprehension difficulties are also related to their lack of exposure to *expository text* (informational or nonfiction text) compared with narrative text in the elementary grades. In a study of 20 first-grade classrooms (Duke, 2000), informational text made up less than 10% of classroom libraries and less than 3% of the materials displayed on classroom walls and other surfaces. Moreover, students spent on average only 3.6 minutes a day interacting with informational text during writing activities. Students in classrooms in low socioeconomic status (SES) settings had even fewer opportunities to interact with informational text. Over the course of four full-day observations, half of the low-SES classrooms spent no time interacting with informational texts. After the elementary grades, students are rarely grouped for instruction, and there is little emphasis on strategic reading comprehension (O'Connor et al., 2002; Pressley et al., 1997). In effect, comprehension is the *invisible curriculum* that all students are expected to master but in which few receive explicit instruction. At the secondary level, where reading achievement trends have been flat for more than a decade (National Center for Education Statistics, 2005), reading comprehension problems have reached crisis proportions, with many students unable to decode their texts or understand what they are reading, even if they can decode it (Caccamise & Snyder, 2005).

TEXT STRUCTURES AND READING COMPREHENSION

Text structure refers to the underlying pattern authors use to organize ideas and concepts in written text. *Narrative text structure* follows a consistent, generic pattern, often called *story grammar,* which includes such features as character, setting, problem or conflict, precipitating event, and plot with outcome and resolution. *Informational* or *expository text structure* comprises a variety of organizational patterns, such as sequence, description, compare–contrast, cause–effect, and problem–solution, all focusing on the logical organization of ideas and concepts (Williams, 2004, 2005). Knowledge of text structures, acquired through exposure, direct instruction, or both, helps readers to form *schemata,* or cognitive frameworks, for organizing information and constructing meaning from text. Although most students have been exposed repeatedly to narrative text structures through stories and children's literature, many have few encounters with informational text until grade 3 or 4, when they are expected to use reading as a vehicle for content area learning (Duke, 2000). Comprehending expository text is more challenging for readers compared with comprehending narrative text, not only because expository text includes a variety of structures, but also because it is more likely to include unfamiliar content and abstract, academically oriented vocabulary. The lack of exposure to informational text structures is especially problematic for students with learning disabilities, who have more difficulty with expository text than narrative text in terms of both fluency and comprehension (Parmar et al., 1994; Sáenz & Fuchs, 2002). Although research indicates that instruction focusing on text structure can enhance the comprehension skills of at-risk children as early as the second grade (Williams, 2004, 2005), teachers are often unprepared to provide explicit comprehension instruction, especially for expository material.

Reading Comprehension Interventions

Two of the interventions in this section use some form of strategy instruction to target reading comprehension. Because a major factor contributing to poor readers' difficulty comprehending text is their failure to use efficient cognitive (i.e., thinking) and metacognitive (i.e., regulating the learning process) strategies to understand textual material (Baker, Gersten, & Scanlon, 2002; Lebzelter & Nowacek, 1999), these interventions provide explicit instruction and guided practice in both sets of strategies, often with the support of *procedural facilitators* (see below). *Story Mapping* is based on the schema theory of reading comprehension, which proposes that adequate comprehension depends on the reader's ability to link previous knowledge structures (*schemata*) with textual material (Anderson, Spiro, & Anderson, 1978; Singer & Donlan, 1983). A *story map* is a pictorial technique that provides a framework for organizing important interrelated elements in narrative stories, such as setting, characters, problem, action, and outcome. First developed by Idol and her colleagues for use with students with learning disabilities (Idol, 1987b; Idol & Croll, 1987), story mapping has been demonstrated to improve reading comprehension for elementary students with and without disabilities (Babyak, Koorland, & Mathes, 2000; Boulineau, Fore, Hagan-Burke, & Burke, 2004; Johnson, Graham, & Harris, 1997; Taylor, Alber, & Walker, 2002), middle school students with disabilities (Boyle, 1996; Gardill & Jitendra, 1999; Vallecorsa & deBettencourt, 1997), and low-performing secondary level students (Dimino, Gersten, Carnine, & Blake, 1990; Gurney, Gersten, Dimino, & Carnine, 1990). The story mapping intervention included here combines the most effective components of several validated versions, including modeling, guided practice, and a collaborative learning format.

CROSS-REFERENCE: For a story mapping intervention designed to enhance comprehension of social studies and science textbooks, see *Improving Content Area Comprehension with a Critical Thinking Map* in the Content Area section of this chapter.

PROCEDURAL FACILITATORS:
TOOLS FOR ENHANCING READING COMPREHENSION AND WRITTEN EXPRESSION

A *procedural facilitator* is an instructional support designed to help students organize, structure, and sequence their cognitive processes during learning activities until they have learned to internalize those processes (Scardamalia & Bereiter, 1986). Often included in academic interventions, especially those targeting reading comprehension or writing, procedural facilitators include prompts, questions, study guides, outlines, or graphic organizers that guide students through the steps and processes used by proficient readers and writers. Procedural facilitators not only enhance performance by providing students with a plan of action for approaching an assignment, but also facilitate instruction by giving teachers and students a common language for discussing the strategies involved in task completion (Baker, Gersten, & Scanlon, 2002). Procedural facilitators in strategy-based interventions often incorporate mnemonic devices to help students remember the strategy steps (e.g., *DISSECT: The Word Identification Strategy; FAST DRAW: Strategy Instruction for Math Problem Solving; PLAN and WRITE: Self-Regulated Strategy Development for Essay Writing*). The interventions in this chapter include a wide variety of procedural facilitators for scaffolding student learning, including story maps, concept maps, summarization guides, writing guides, cue cards, and plans listing the steps in a strategy.

The second intervention in this section teaches comprehension strategies in the context of a paired learning format. Developed in the early 1990s by the Fuchs and their colleagues at Vanderbilt University (Mathes et al., 1994; Simmons, Fuchs, Fuchs, Mathes, & Hodge, 1995) as a variation of *ClassWide Peer Tutoring* (CWPT) that could accommodate students with learning disabilities, *Peer-Assisted Learning Strategies in Reading* (PALS-R) involves students in strategic reading behaviors that enhance textual understanding, such as retelling, summarization, and prediction. Like CWPT, PALS-R includes both cooperative (peer dyads) and competitive (teams) learning structures and can accommodate students with a range of reading levels. A growing body of evidence attests to the effectiveness of PALS-R in improving reading comprehension and fluency for low- and average-achieving students as well as students with learning disabilities and emotional/behavioral disorders (Falk & Wehby, 2001; Fuchs et al., 1997; Vaughn et al., 2000). PALS-R has been used effectively with students as young as kindergarten and first grade (Fuchs, Fuchs, Yazdian, & Powell, 2002; Fuchs & Fuchs, 2005), with middle and high school students in remedial and special education classes (Calhoon, 2005; Fuchs, Fuchs, et al., 2001; Fuchs et al., 1999), and with primary grade English language learners (Calhoon, Al Otaiba, Greenberg, King, & Avalos, 2006). PALS-R has also been cited as a promising practice by the Promising Practice Network (*http://www.promisingpractices.net/research.asp*).

The third intervention in this section, *Motivating Classwide Reading Performance with Paired Reading and Randomized Group Contingencies,* embeds partner reading within two interdependent group contingencies to enhance productivity during independent reading periods. For the least proficient readers, intervention packages combining skill-based and performance-based strategies (i.e., reinforcement contingencies) often yield the best outcomes (Chafouleas et al., 2004; Eckert et al., 2002). In contrast to the highly structured routines of other peer tutoring interventions in this text, such as *ClassWide Peer Tutoring* and *Peer-Assisted Learning Strategies in Reading,* the partner reading procedures in this strategy are more informal and focus on providing peer support for reading and understanding textual material. It is also one of two interventions in this chapter that include randomly selected group contingency components.

CROSS-REFERENCE: For other strategies using randomized group contingencies, see the *Timely Transitions Game: Reducing Room-to-Room Transition Time* in Chapter 3; the *Rewards Box: Enhancing Academic Performance with Randomized Group Contingencies* in the Academic Productivity section of this chapter; and *Reducing Disruptive Behaviors with Randomized Group Contingencies* in Chapter 5.

STORY MAPPING

Overview

Good readers use their knowledge of story structure to analyze, organize, and remember story content across a variety of reading contexts and materials. In contrast, poor readers have a limited understanding of text structure and how to apply it while reading to enhance comprehension. In story mapping, students learn to use a graphic framework that focuses their attention on key elements in narrative text, such as character, setting, and outcome, to help them organize and interpret information. Attending to the structural elements of the narrative during the story mapping process helps students to think about the content and relate it to prior knowledge, leading to better reading comprehension. The intervention is delivered in three phases that are designed to increase students' independent use of story mapping over time. Story map instruction has been associated with increased ability to identify narrative elements and improvement in literal and inferential comprehension for students with and without disabilities across a range of grade and skill levels. Three variations are presented: (1) a version with a self-questioning component, (2) a version with additional visual supports for primary grade students, and (3) a variation with a cooperative learning format.

Purpose

To improve reading comprehension by providing a visual framework and strategy for analyzing, organizing, and remembering story information.

Materials

1. Paper copies of the story map template appropriate for students' grade level (see Figures 4.5 and 4.6 on pp. 219 and 220, respectively), one copy per student per story.
2. Overhead projector and transparency of the story map template appropriate for students' grade level (optional).
3. Sheet of paper listing 10 story-specific comprehension questions or generic questions (see Figure 4.7 on p. 220), one list per story per student (optional, see Variation 1).
4. Chart with pictures illustrating each story element, such as a picture of a runner breaking the tape for outcome (optional, see Variation 2).
5. Reading notebooks or folders with sheets of paper, one per student (optional, see Variation 3).
6. Story retelling checklist, consisting of a list of the main events and details for two stories (optional, see Observation/Evaluation Option 2).

Additional Materials for Variation 3

1. Posterboard chart listing leader cues for story mapping steps or 3″ × 5″ index cards with cues, one card per group, as follows:
   a. *Tell*—tell the answer for your story part and give evidence to support your answer.
   b. *Ask*—ask other group members to share their answers and provide evidence to support their answers.
   c. *Discuss*—lead a discussion of your story part and try to reach a consensus. If the group can't agree, the leader has the final say.
   d. *Record*—write the group answer in that section of the story map.
   e. *Report*—be ready to report your group answers to the class.

Observation (Select One or More)

Option 1

1. Calculate scores on reading classwork, homework, or tests and quizzes for the entire class or a target group of students for the previous month.

Option 2

1. After the students in a target group have read a story independently, have each one tell you everything he or she can remember about the story from memory. Using a list of the story's main events and details, check off the information recalled as the student retells the story.
2. Calculate the percentage of key events and details recalled per story for each target student.

Option 3

1. Assign a story to the entire class, a selected reading group, or a group of target students. After reading, have the students complete a set of 10 generic questions (see Figure 4.7). Calculate percent-correct scores on the questions for each student.
2. If desired, calculate a classwide or group average percent-correct score by summing the individual scores and dividing by the number of students in the class or group.

Intervention Steps

Introduction and Training

1. Using reading material from narrative texts selected at the level of the weaker readers in the class, have students read a story silently during the reading instructional period or as a homework assignment. For classes that include very poor readers, create student pairs, consisting of a more proficient and a less proficient reader, and have the pairs read the story aloud together. For younger students, read the story aloud while they follow along.

PHASE 1: MODELING

1. Tell the students that they are going to learn the parts of a story and that this will help them understand and remember more about what they read.
2. Display the transparency with the story map template or draw the template on the chalkboard. Explain the meaning of each element, providing examples of story grammar elements from previously read stories.
3. Help students understand how the elements are interrelated. For example, tell students that identifying the theme requires studying the main character(s), the main problem, and the way in which the main characters solved or did not solve the problem.
4. Using a think-aloud procedure, identify the elements in the story students have just read, filling in the map as you move through the story.

PHASE 2: GUIDED PRACTICE

1. Distribute copies of the story map. Have students read another story and fill in their story maps independently.
2. Then call upon students to identify story map elements as described above. Respond positively to contributions and encourage students to state their opinions, but be clear about why some answers are correct, others are incorrect, and some answers are better than others. Redirect students to the text when necessary.
3. As consensus is reached, record responses on the story map template, and have students make any necessary corrections on their individual maps. Have students keep their maps as study aids.

PHASE 3: INDEPENDENT PRACTICE

1. Have students silently read stories and complete their story maps independently. Tell them that they can fill in the maps as they read a story, after they read it, or a combination.
2. Circulate to provide assistance and feedback as needed, but do not have students respond as a group to story map elements.

Implementation

1. Have students read silently and fill in the maps independently while reading or after reading.

2. Review student responses during a classwide discussion and have students make any necessary corrections on their individual maps.
3. Continue to identify classroom reading assignments on which students could apply the story mapping strategy and ways the strategy could be modified to fit different kinds of tasks.

Evaluation (Select One or More)

Option 1

1. Compare scores on reading classwork, homework, or tests and quizzes for the entire class or the target group of students before and after implementation.

Option 2

1. Have the target group of students read an unfamiliar story and retell it on an individual basis. Using the story retelling checklist, compare the percentage of elements recalled per story before and after implementation.

Option 3

1. Assign an unfamiliar story to the entire class, the selected reading group, or the group of target students. After reading, have the students complete the 10 generic comprehension questions and compare percent-correct scores before and after implementation.

Variation 1: Story Mapping with Self-Questioning

1. After students have completed their story maps, have them use the maps to answer 10 comprehension questions. If desired, have students work in pairs to complete their maps and answer the questions. Discuss the answers as a classwide activity and have students make corrections to their papers as needed.
2. After students are proficient in the use of the story maps, have them read silently and answer comprehension questions without the maps. If classwide comprehension scores fall below 80% accuracy for 2 consecutive days, reinstate the maps.

Variation 2: Story Mapping for Primary Grade Students

Introduction and Training

1. For the first training session, display the primary grade story map template (see Figure 4.6) on the overhead projector or chalkboard and tell students that a story map is like a road map. Just as a road map guides a traveler from one place to another, a story map leads the reader from the beginning of a story, through the middle of the story, and to the end of the story. Use locations familiar to the students to exemplify the road map analogy. Explain that by learning about and using story maps, students will be able to understand, remember, and enjoy stories more.
2. Display the chart with pictures illustrating the story elements. Using a story with a simple text structure, such as *The Three Billy Goats Gruff,* begin reading through the story and record the story map elements for *who* and *where* on the template. Call on students to identify the other four parts of the story as you continue reading.
3. In a second training session, review the story map parts and conduct a classwide practice in mapping, using another story. As you fill in the map, discuss the author's use of description, characterization, the relevance of the story to students' personal experiences, and other features.

4. Distribute copies of the story map template and have students work in pairs or small groups to complete a map for the story currently being read by the class or their reading group.
5. After students have completed the maps on their own, use the transparency or chalkboard to fill in the story map by calling on students for their responses. Have students correct their own maps as needed.

Implementation

1. Distribute copies of the story map during guided reading activities. Have students complete the maps individually as you proceed through the story.
2. After students are able to complete maps successfully in this format, have them complete the maps on their own during independent story reading for later review during whole-class or small-group instruction.

Variation 3: Cooperative Story Mapping

Introduction and Training

1. Explain to the class that they will be learning a new way of getting more out of what they read by working in teams to complete story maps.
2. Divide the class into teams of four students, including a range of skill levels in each group. Give each student a team assignment for the week, as described in Step 3 below. Guide students through the steps as follows.

STEP 1: READING THE STORY

1. All students in the class read the same story. Stories can be read during partner reading sessions, during the reading instructional period, or as homework. For weaker readers who cannot read the same story as the other students, assign a peer to read the story to the student or tape it and have the student listen while following along in the text.

STEP 2: SKIMMING THE STORY

1. After students have read the story, have them spend 2 minutes skimming the story silently to refamiliarize themselves with the details prior to completing the story maps.
2. Have students determine what they believe are the best answers for all the story elements and note on a sheet of paper where information supporting their answers is located in the story so that they can provide evidence for their answers during the map completion activity with their group.

STEP 3: COMPLETING THE STORY MAP

1. Have students move to their groups, give one copy of the story map to each group, and have the groups complete the maps under the direction of a leader. Each student is a leader for one story element and one major event, as follows: (a) main character and first major event, (b) setting and second major event, (c) problem and third major event, and (d) story outcome and fourth major event. For the first few sessions, assign weaker readers to the easier tasks of main character and setting.
2. The student assigned as leader for that element writes the group's answers for that element on the story map, according to the following five steps:
   a. Give your answer for a story part and provide evidence to support your answer.
   b. Ask other students in the group to share their answers and provide evidence in support.

  c. Lead a discussion of the story part.

  d. Reach a consensus and record the group's answer on the map.

  e. Be prepared to report the group's findings to the class.

STEP 4: DISCUSSING THE STORY

1. Lead a classwide discussion of the story elements, focusing on helping students to evaluate whether their answers are correct and reference portions of the text substantiating their answers.

2. For each story part, ask the leader for that element to report the group answer. Then restate it and ask if another group has a different response. Help students extend their understanding of the story beyond their own group by exploring whether some groups have different answers that may also be correct.

3. Have students make any necessary corrections to their maps and retain them as study aids.

Implementation

1. Have the groups work on their maps collaboratively while reading or after reading.

2. After map completion, conduct a classwide discussion as described above and have students correct their maps as needed.

3. Rotate leadership roles weekly so that students have an opportunity to guide group activities for each story element. Change groupings every few weeks or as needed based on student compatibility and ability levels.

Notes

1. Training for individual story mapping takes two to four sessions of about 45 minutes each. For Variation 3 (cooperative story mapping), two additional sessions are needed, one to explain cooperative learning and review cooperative learning rules (e.g., taking turns to respond, listening to what others are saying, disagreeing in a polite way) and another to demonstrate and practice mapping in the small-group format.

2. To help familiarize students with text structure, initially select texts in which all the story elements are easy to identify. Stories with more complex plot structures, such as abstract problems and unresolved conflicts, can be included as students become more competent in using the strategy.

3. Story maps can also be used to enhance the writing process. Have students create an original story map and write a story using it. Have students take turns reading their stories to each other. This can be conducted as an individual, paired, or small-group activity.

Sources

Baumann, J. F., & Bergeron, B. S. (1993). Story map instruction using children's literature: Effects on first graders' comprehension of central narrative elements. *Journal of Reading Behavior, 25*, 407–437. Copyright 1993 by the National Reading Conference. Adapted by permission.

Gurney, D., Gersten, R., Dimino, J., & Carnine, D. (1990). Story grammar: Effective literature instruction for high school students with learning disabilities. *Journal of Learning Disabilities, 23*, 335–342, 348. Copyright 1990 by PRO-ED, Inc. Adapted by permission.

Mathes, P. G., Fuchs, D., & Fuchs, L. S. (1997). Cooperative story mapping. *Remedial and Special Education, 18*, 20–27. Copyright 1997 by PRO-ED, Inc. Adapted by permission.

STORY MAP

Name of student: _____ Date: _____

Story title: _____

Main characters

Time and setting

Problem

Major events

1. _____

2. _____

3. _____

4. _____

Outcome or resolution

FIGURE 4.5. Story map for elementary and middle school students. Adapted from Mathes, Fuchs, and Fuchs (1997, p. 23). Copyright 1997 by PRO-ED, Inc. Adapted by permission.

WHAT'S IN A STORY?

WHO? The most important <u>people</u> or <u>animals</u> in the story

WHERE? The <u>places</u> the story happens

WHEN? The <u>times</u> the story happens

WHAT'S THE PROBLEM? The <u>problem</u> or <u>difficulty</u> the person or animal has

WHAT HAPPENED? The things that <u>happened</u> in the story and what was <u>done</u> to try to solve the problem

WHAT'S THE SOLUTION? How the problem was <u>solved</u>

FIGURE 4.6. Story map for primary grade students. Adapted from Baumann and Bergeron (1993, p. 415). Copyright 1993 by the National Reading Conference. Adapted by permission.

Story Questions

1. Who is the main character?
2. What is the main character like? Describe some of his or her personal characteristics, especially those that are important to what happened in the story.
3. Were there any other important characters in the story? Who? Describe some of their personal characteristics.
4. When did the story take place?
5. Where did the story take place?
6. What was the problem in the story?
7. How did the characters try to solve the problem?
8. Was there a twist or complication in the story? What was it?
9. Was the problem solved or not solved? Explain.
10. What is the theme or lesson of the story?

FIGURE 4.7. Generic comprehension questions for *Story Mapping*. Adapted from Gurney, Gersten, Dimino, and Carnine (1990, p. 338). Copyright 1990 by PRO-ED, Inc. Adapted by permission.

PEER-ASSISTED LEARNING STRATEGIES IN READING

Overview

Accommodating the diversity of reading skills in a single classroom and providing sufficient practice for struggling readers are among teachers' greatest challenges. *Peer-Assisted Learning Strategies in Reading* (PALS-R), a modification of *ClassWide Peer Tutoring,* is a set of strategy-based peer tutoring routines designed to address the needs of weaker readers while simultaneously expanding the comprehension skills of all students. In the fully implemented version of PALS-R, each tutoring session includes three activities: (1) Partner Reading with Retell, (2) Paragraph Shrinking, and (3) Prediction Relay. Partner Reading with Retell targets fluency with a combination of listening previewing and repeated reading and includes a brief retelling to enhance comprehension. Paragraph Shrinking and Prediction Relay are designed to promote comprehension by providing students with practice in summarizing, identifying the main idea, and formulating and verifying predictions. Each 35-minute session is divided into three 10-minute segments, with an additional 2 minutes for retelling and another 3 minutes for preparation, transitioning between activities, and putting materials away. To enhance motivation, student pairs are assigned to one of two teams and earn points for task completion and appropriate behavior. Compared with traditional reading instruction, PALS-R has been shown to be successful in accelerating the reading performance of struggling, average, and high-performing readers, as well as mainstreamed students with learning disabilities, with the largest effects for struggling readers.

Purpose

To improve reading comprehension and fluency by providing a sequence of structured activities within a paired learning framework.

Materials

1. Stopwatch or timer (optional).
2. Classroom clock with second hand or stopwatches or watches with second hands, one watch per student pair.
3. Classroom reading materials, one set per tutoring pair, with the materials at the level of the weaker reader.
4. Error prompt cards, consisting of 3" × 5" index cards with error correction procedures, one card per student pair.
5. Procedure prompt cards, consisting of 3" × 5" index cards listing PALS-R questions and procedures, one card per student pair (see Figure 4.8 on p. 225).
6. Posterboard chart listing the error correction procedures and PALS-R questions and procedures (optional).
7. Weekly score cards, consisting of 3" × 5" index cards with a list of consecutive numbers, one per student pair per week.

Observation (Select One or Both)

1. Calculate scores on reading classwork, homework, or tests and quizzes for the entire class or a target group of students for the previous month or marking period.
2. Have a group of target students or the entire class read a story and then respond to 10 generic comprehension questions (see Figure 4.7 for an example). Calculate percent-correct scores for each student. If desired, calculate the group or class average percent-correct score by summing individual scores and dividing by the total number of students in the group or class.

Intervention Steps

Preparation

1. Rank order the students from strongest to weakest reader using scores on standardized tests, statewide reading tests, classroom grades, teacher judgment, or a combination.
2. Divide the list in half so that List A includes the stronger readers (who will serve as Partner 1) and List B includes the weaker readers (who will serve as Partner 2).
3. Pair the student at the top of List A with the student at the top of List B and so on until all of the students are matched. Make adjustments as needed to accommodate reading ability and compatibility.
4. Assign each pair to one of two teams for use in awarding points.

Introduction and Training

1. Tell the class that they will be practicing reading in pairs and working as a team to help everyone become better readers. Select a student and demonstrate the first activity (Partner Reading with Retell), as described below.
2. Guide two other students through the procedures while the class observes and you provide encouragement and feedback. Use this format for introducing the other activities (see Note 1).

ACTIVITY 1: PARTNER READING WITH RETELL

1. Distribute the reading materials, prompt cards, and score cards to the student pairs. When you give the signal, Partner 1 reads for 5 minutes while Partner 2 follows along. If Partner 1 comes to the end of the passage before the time is up, he or she returns to the beginning and starts again. At the end of 5 minutes, Partner 2 reads the same passage.
2. Tutors correct four errors: (a) misread words, (b) omitted words, (c) added words, and (d) pauses of more than 4 seconds as follows:
   a. If the reader misreads a word, omits a word, or pauses for more than 4 seconds, the tutor says, "Stop. You missed that word. Can you figure it out?"
   b. If the reader cannot figure out the word, the tutor says, "That word is ___. What word?" The reader repeats the word. The tutor says, "Good! Read the sentence again," and the reader rereads the sentence and continues. If the tutor cannot provide the word, the students raise their hands for assistance.
   c. If the reader adds a word, the tutor says, "Stop. You added a word. Can you figure out what word you added?"
   d. If the reader cannot figure out what he or she added, the tutor says, "You added ___. Read the sentence again," and the reader rereads the sentence and continues.
3. After both students have read the same passage, Partner 2 retells in sequence what has been read for 2 minutes (1 minute for early primary grade students). If Partner 2 has trouble recalling information, Partner 1 prompts by asking, "What did you learn first?" and "What did you learn next?" If Partner 2 is unable to remember, Partner 1 provides the information. Both students may skim the text if needed, but they are not permitted to reread it.
4. Tutors record points for their partners by slashing consecutive numbers on the score cards. Students earn 1 point for each correctly read sentence. If an error correction is required, students earn 1 point after they have read the sentence correctly. The retell is worth 10 points.

ACTIVITY 2: PARAGRAPH SHRINKING

1. Paragraph Shrinking is designed to enhance comprehension through summarization and main idea identification. Partner 1 begins reading in the text where Partner Reading ended, but

unlike Partner Reading, new text is read by both students. Tutors continue to correct reading errors but no longer award points for sentence reading.

2. At the end of each paragraph, the tutor asks the reader: (a) "Who or what was the paragraph mainly about?" and (b) "Tell the most important thing about the who or what." The reader must summarize this information in 10 or fewer words.
3. If the tutor decides that the reader has made a paragraph summary error, he or she says, "That's not quite right. Skim the paragraph and try again." The reader skims the paragraph and tries again. If the reader still does not have the answer, the tutor provides it.
4. If the error involves using more than 10 words, the tutor says, "Shrink it."
5. After 5 minutes, students switch roles.
6. For each paragraph summary, students can earn up to 3 points: (a) 1 point for correctly identifying the subject of the paragraph, (b) 1 point for stating the main idea, and (c) 1 point for shrinking the summary statement to 10 words or less. Students are permitted multiple attempts to shrink their statements, and the subject of the answer (the who or what) counts as one word, regardless of how many words are used.

ACTIVITY 3: PREDICTION RELAY

1. The five-step Prediction Relay extends the Paragraph Shrinking activity to larger sections of text and requires students to make and confirm or disconfirm predictions.
2. The reader makes a prediction about what will be learned on the next half page of text.
3. The reader reads the half page aloud while the tutor follows along and uses the error correction procedure.
4. The reader confirms or disconfirms his or her prediction.
5. The reader summarizes the half page of text in 10 words or less.
6. The reader then makes a new prediction about the next half page. If the tutor judges that the prediction is not reasonable, he or she says, "I don't agree. Think of a better prediction."
7. Students can earn up to 6 points for each half-page summary: (a) 1 point for a reasonable prediction, (b) 1 point for reading each half page, (c) 1 point for accurately confirming or disconfirming the prediction, and (d) 1 point for each of the three paragraph summary components (the who or what, the most important thing about the who or what, and a summary of 10 or fewer words).
8. After 5 minutes, students switch roles.

Implementation

1. At the beginning of each PALS-R session, indicate student partner assignments and have students move to partner reading stations (i.e., paired desks). Also indicate teams for each pair.
2. Distribute reading materials, score cards, and prompt cards. Indicate the clock to be used for timing or make sure every student has a watch with a second hand for timing the sessions.
3. During PALS-R sessions, move around the room and award bonus points for cooperative behavior and accurate tutoring procedures. Collect prompt and score cards at the end of each session or have the Partner 1 students put them in their reading folders.
4. At the end of the week, have each pair report the last number slashed on the score card. Sum each team's points on the chalkboard and lead the class in applauding the winning team.
5. Create new pairs and team assignments every 4 weeks. For high school students, change partners more frequently.

Evaluation (Select One or Both)

1. Compare scores on reading classwork, homework, or tests and quizzes for the entire class or a target group before and after implementation.

2. Compare percent-correct scores on comprehension questions based on another story for the target students or the entire class on an individual and/or group basis before and after implementation.

Variation: Partner Reading with Retell Only

1. Implement Partner Reading with Retell as the sole tutoring activity. This variation reduces the time needed for the intervention as well as training time.

Notes

1. Teach students one activity at a time in a series of training sessions. For the first 45-minute training session, teach students how to set up materials, use the score cards, report points, and be a helpful tutoring partner. Train students in Partner Reading with Retell the first week. Add Paragraph Shrinking the second week, and have students practice Partner Reading with Retell for 15 minutes and Paragraph Summary for 20 minutes for another 4 weeks. In the fifth week, introduce Prediction Relay and reduce Paragraph Summary to 10 minutes to accommodate the new activity.
2. Because there are no answer keys for PALS-R activities, students must evaluate the correctness of their partners' responses in Paragraph Shrinking and Prediction Relay. Teach students to request your assistance if needed during these activities.
3. Use a set of detailed pictures to teach the comprehension strategies in Paragraph Shrinking and Prediction Relay. Display a picture and help students identify possible subjects (whos and whats) and the most important thing about the subjects from the details. Model the main idea statement for the picture by stating the subject, holding up one finger (to indicate one word), and stating the main idea about the subject in nine words or less. Once students can successfully identify the main idea for several pictures, repeat the process with text. Similarly, use pictures and simple text to model the process of formulating reasonable and unreasonable predictions.
4. To keep PALS-R interesting to students, vary the nature of reading materials and pairings. For example, occasionally have partners read from material at the more competent reader's level or arrange pairings so that proficient readers can read together (Fuchs, Fuchs, & Burish, 2000).

Sources

Fuchs, D., Fuchs, L. S., Mathes, P. G., & Simmons, D. G. (1997). Peer-assisted learning strategies: Making classrooms more responsive to diversity. *American Educational Research Journal, 34*, 174–206. Copyright 1997 by Sage Publications. Adapted by permission.

Mathes, P. G., Fuchs, D., Fuchs, L. S., Henley, A. M., & Sanders, A. (1994). Increasing strategic reading practice with Peabody Classwide Peer Tutoring. *Learning Disabilities Research and Practice, 9*, 44–48. Copyright 1994 by Blackwell Publishing. Adapted by permission.

Additional Resources

1. Commercially published PALS-R materials for students in prekindergarten, kindergarten, and grade 1 are available from Sopris West (*http://www.sopriswest.com*).
2. PALS-R materials for kindergarten, grade 1, grades 2 through 6, and high school, including manuals and training videos, are available for purchase at the PALS website (*http://www. kc.vanderbilt.edu/kennedy/pals*), which also provides links to ongoing PALS research.

```
┌─────────────────────────────────────────────────────────────────────────┐
│                              Prompt Card                                  │
│                                                                           │
│  Partner Retell                                                           │
│   1.  What did you learn first?                                           │
│   2.  What did you learn next?                                            │
│  *********************************************************************     │
│  Paragraph Shrinking                                                      │
│   1.  Who or what was the paragraph mainly about?                         │
│   2.  Tell the most important thing about the who or what.                │
│   3.  State the main idea in 10 words or less.                            │
│                                                                           │
│  *********************************************************************     │
│  Prediction Relay                                                         │
│   1.  Predict_____ What do you predict will happen next?               │
│   2.  Read _____ Read half a page.                                    │
│   3.  Check _____ Did your prediction come true?                        │
│   4.  Summarize      _____ Who or what was the paragraph mainly about?│
│                      _____ Tell the most important thing about the    │
│                                who or what.                               │
│                      _____ State the main idea in 10 words or less.   │
└─────────────────────────────────────────────────────────────────────────┘
```

FIGURE 4.8. Prompt card for *Peer-Assisted Learning Strategies in Reading*. Adapted from Mathes, Fuchs, Fuchs, Henley, and Sanders (1994, p. 46). Copyright 1994 by Blackwell Publishing. Adapted by permission.

MOTIVATING READING PERFORMANCE
WITH PAIRED READING AND RANDOMIZED GROUP CONTINGENCIES

Overview

Teachers often report that they have difficulty designing strategies that will motivate poor readers to put forth effort on their reading assignments. Although rewards can encourage productivity, it can be difficult to set a classwide criterion for performance. A low criterion may be too easy for proficient readers, whereas a high criterion may be so difficult for the poorest readers that they rarely if ever receive the reward. With interdependent group contingencies, however, all students have access to reinforcement when the class as a whole meets the criterion. This intervention uses group contingencies in a peer-mediated framework to encourage students to participate actively in classroom reading tasks. Unlike the highly structured tutoring routines typical of other forms of partner reading, the paired reading procedure in this intervention focuses on peer support rather than on error correction or strategy-based activities. To enhance motivation, paired reading occurs in the context of two interdependent group contingencies: one with a fixed criterion targeting individual performance and the other with a randomly selected criterion targeting group performance. Originally implemented in a second-grade classroom in which students read chapter books and then took computer-administered comprehension quizzes, the strategy resulted in immediate and sustained increases in quiz scores. In this adaptation, teacher-prepared quizzes are substituted for the computer-delivered tests. The intervention can be applied in classrooms using a whole-class or differentiated instructional model, as well as in any subject involving in-class reading of textual material, such as language arts, literature, social studies, or science. A variation with a self-monitoring component is also presented.

Purpose

To enhance motivation and productivity during independent reading periods with a partner reading procedure.

Materials

1. Two copies of the same chapter book or set of reading materials per student pair.
2. Brief comprehension quizzes based on each book or set of materials or a 10-question generic comprehension quiz, one per student per session (see Figure 4.7 for an example).
3. Opaque jar containing as many slips of paper as the number of students in the class and numbered from about 5 to 18, depending on class size; the lowest and highest numbers should correspond to about 25% and 75% of the total number of students.
4. Notebooks or folders containing sheets of paper, one per student (optional, see Variation).

Observation (Select One or More)

Option 1

1. Calculate percent-correct scores on classwork, quizzes, or tests in reading or the target subject for the entire class or a target group of students for 5 to 10 days or for the previous grading period.

Option 2

1. Calculate the percentage of students with grades of D or F in reading or the target subject for the current grading period or for the school year thus far.

Option 3

1. With your eye, divide the class into four quadrants of approximately equal numbers of students. Using a *Group Time Sampling Form* with a 5-minute interval, glance at the first of four quadrants and record a plus (+) if all of the students in the quadrant are on-task at the moment of observation or a minus (–) if any of the students in the quadrant are off-task, as defined below. During the next interval, observe the next group, and so on until you have observed all four groups. Then begin again with the first quadrant.
   a. *On-task behavior* is defined as reading assigned materials, working on assignments, answering teacher-delivered questions, looking at the teacher, and other lesson-related behaviors.
   b. *Off-task behavior* is defined as failing to attend to the assigned task or to the teacher, playing with materials, fidgeting, talking out of turn, or any other nonlesson behavior.
2. Conduct these observations for 30 to 45 minutes during the selected instructional period for 4 to 7 days.

Intervention Steps

Preparation

1. Create student pairs based on reading levels or reading group assignment. Pair very poor readers with higher level readers who can provide assistance with decoding and comprehension.
2. For each pair, select a book at the reading level of the weaker reader in the pair or provide access to several appropriate selections. If possible, select books for which there are two copies available. If only one copy of the selected book is available, students share the book.

Introduction and Training

1. Explain to the class that they will be playing a tutoring game to help everyone become a better reader and to make reading more fun.
2. Tell students that the class will earn an ice cream party (popcorn party, pizza party, etc.) if each student passes at least one reading quiz (or some other criterion) during the next marking period. If even one student fails to reach this goal, however, no party will be provided.
3. Display the jar with the slips of paper and tell students that you will draw a slip of paper each Friday. If the number of reading quizzes passed by students that week equals or exceeds the number drawn, the whole class will receive an activity reward (30 minutes of extra recess, music time, in-class game time, etc.) on Friday afternoon. For departmentalized classes, tell students that you will deliver the reward during the last part of the instructional period.
4. Using a student as a partner, demonstrate the procedures described below.
   a. Students take turns reading a page at a time in the material (a paragraph at a time for younger readers). While one student reads, the other follows along and helps the other read difficult words.
   b. If both students are unable to read a word, they raise their hands to ask for assistance.
   c. After the pair has finished reading the book or selection, they take a brief quiz on the material.
5. Discuss ways partners can help each other, such as providing an unfamiliar word, encouraging the reader to sound out the word or use context clues, and supporting each other's efforts to read and understand the material.
6. Assign students to pairs, have partners move their desks together or find a suitable place in the classroom, and conduct a classwide practice while you circulate to provide encouragement and assistance as needed.

Implementation

1. At the beginning of each tutoring session, indicate student pairings, have students move to their partner reading area, and distribute reading materials.
2. When students have finished reading, distribute the quizzes and have students complete them individually or as a pair. Grade the quizzes as soon as possible and return them to students.
3. On Friday, announce the number of quizzes passed by students that week. Draw a slip of paper from the box or jar and announce the number. If the number of reading quizzes passed by students that week equals or exceeds the number drawn, deliver the activity reward.
4. As the intervention proceeds, remind individual students in private on Monday of the third week and each week thereafter if they still have not passed a quiz. At the end of the grading period, deliver the party reward if every student has passed at least one quiz (or met the criterion).
5. As students become more successful, alter the criterion pool by removing slips with lower numbers (e.g., 5 to 8 quizzes passed each week) and adding slips with higher numbers (e.g., 15 to 25 quizzes passed per week).

Variation: Paired Reading with Self-Monitoring

1. Have students monitor their own progress by recording their quiz grades in their reading or subject area folders. If desired, teach them to record their grades on a line or bar graph for greater visual impact.

Notes

1. In the original study, students read chapter books for 30 minutes during sustained silent reading time and then took multiple-choice quizzes assessing comprehension for those books using the Accelerated Reading software (Renaissance Learning, 2002).
2. In the original study, the teacher wrote the number 6 (the number of quizzes students actually passed) on all of the slips of paper for the initial drawing to ensure that students earned the activity reward during the first week of implementation.
3. If student pairs will be reading different materials, using a generic comprehension quiz is highly recommended to reduce preparation time (see Figure 4.7 for an example).

Source

Sharp, S. R., & Skinner, C. H. (2004). Using interdependent group contingencies with randomly selected criteria and paired reading to enhance class-wide reading performance. *Journal of Applied School Psychology, 20,* 29–45. Copyright 2004 by The Haworth Press. Adapted by permission.

Interventions to Improve Mathematics Performance

With the growing emphasis on technology in the marketplace, proficiency in mathematics is a critical skill for individual success and national growth (National Research Council, 2001). Despite the importance of math competency in today's society, the most recent National Assessment of Educational Progress (NAEP) in mathematics (National Center for Education Statistics, 2006a, 2007a, 2007c) reveals serious deficiencies in math achievement among the general student population. Although average mathematics scores at grades 4 and 8 were higher in 2005 than in all previous assessment years, only about a third of students at either grade level scored at the Proficient level (36% and 30%, respectively), and nearly one-third (31%) of grade 8 students failed to reach even the Basic level. At grade 12, where the use of a new framework prevents comparisons with previous NAEP data, more than a third (39%) of the students scored below Basic. At grade 4, the score gap between Caucasian and African American students was smaller in 2005 than any previous assessment year, but the gap between Caucasian and Hispanic students was not significantly different compared with previous years. Similarly, at grade 8, the gaps between the performance of Caucasian students and that of African American and Hispanic students were not significantly different in 2005 than in any of the previous assessment years. Cross-national studies of mathematics achievement, such as the Trends in International Mathematics and Science Study (TIMSS), an educational survey of students in 40 countries, have also documented significant performance disparities between American students and students in other industrialized nations. Although U.S. grade 8 students showed significant improvement in average math performance from 1995 to 2003 and an increase in their relative standing compared with their grade peers in other participating countries, U.S. grade 4 students showed no measurable growth over the same period, and their average performance was lower in 2003 than in 1995 relative to students in the 14 other countries participating in both studies (National Center for Education Statistics, 2004a).

Diverse learners, such as students with learning disabilities and students from families living in poverty, are especially at risk for poor math performance. Students with learning disabilities experience difficulty with virtually all aspects of mathematics, including counting and basic operations (Cawley, Parmar, Yan, & Miller, 1998; Geary, Hamson, & Hoard, 2000) and higher level applications, such as problem-solving skills and strategy use (Jitendra, Hoff, & Beck, 1999; Jitendra, DiPipi, & Perron-Jones, 2002; Torbeyns, Verschaffel, & Ghesquière, 2004). Students from high-poverty backgrounds also display lower levels of math achievement compared with their more advantaged peers, with performance disparities apparent as early as preschool (Fuchs et al., 2002; National Center for Education Statistics, 2006a). For many students, poor mathematics achievement may be more related to so-called "curriculum and instructional disabilities" arising from the shortcomings of current textbooks and instructional practices rather than to learning disabilities internal to students (Schmidt, McKnight, & Raizen, 1997; Valverde & Schmidt, 1997–1998). Despite efforts to improve mathematics instruction by professional groups such as the National Council of Teachers of Mathematics (NCTM; 2000, 2006), math texts, which provide the primary method of presenting new information, often fail to adhere to important instructional design principles, such as providing clear learning objectives and structuring adequate opportunities for review and practice (Jitendra et al., 2005; Jitendra, Salmento, & Haydt, 1999). Moreover, compared with textbooks of other countries, U.S. math textbooks emphasize breadth at the expense of depth, covering more topics but in a superficial, unfocused manner. As a result, school mathematics in the United States has been characterized as "a mile wide and an inch deep" (Schmidt et al., 1997, p. 62). Compounding the problem is the lack of consensus regarding the topics that should be covered at specific grade levels or the amount of time that should be allocated to different skill areas (Reys, Dingman, Sutter, & Teuscher, 2005).

Moreover, unlike reading instruction, which is typically conducted in groups on the basis of students' skill levels in the elementary grades, math instruction tends to be provided in a whole-class format, regardless of differences in terms of students' mastery of basic operations or depth of conceptual understanding (Fleischner & Manheimer, 1997). At the elementary and middle school level, students are often taught by teachers who are poorly prepared to help students build math proficiency (National Research Council, 2001; U.S. Department of Education, 2003). Math instruction for students in special education settings is especially inadequate, with excessive use of seatwork, limited access to standards-based content, and infrequent small-group learning activities (Jackson & Neel, 2006).

TYPES OF MATHEMATICS PROBLEMS

Although students with mathematics difficulties constitute a very heterogeneous group, they generally exhibit deficits in one or more of three areas: (1) computational skills, including the basic operations of addition, subtraction, multiplication, and division; (2) computational fluency, that is, speed and automaticity with math facts; and (3) mathematics applications and reasoning, including areas such as money, measurement, time, and word problems (Shapiro, 2004a). Just as students with limited decoding skills and lack of automaticity in word recognition have difficulty comprehending what they read, so students with deficits in math computation and fluency have trouble performing math tasks that involve skill application, reasoning, and problem solving. In addition, because of the sequential nature of the mathematics curriculum, deficits in basic math skills limit further mathematical development, so that low-performing students experience increasing difficulty as they move from grade to grade and encounter more complex math topics (Woodward, 2004).

Despite the prevalence of mathematics deficits in the general student population as well as among students with disabilities and other at-risk groups, researchers have devoted much less attention to math interventions compared with strategies targeting reading. In an analysis of 20 years of classroom-based research for students with disabilities, Swanson, Hoskyn, and Lee (1999) found that a mere 10% of intervention studies focused specifically on mathematics. Moreover, the success of math interventions varies with the target. Meta-analyses of mathematics interventions with low-achieving students and/or students with disabilities (Baker, Gersten, & Lee, 2002; Kroesbergen & Van Luit, 2003; Xin & Jitendra, 1999) have consistently reported the greatest efficacy for interventions targeting basic computational skills and the least efficacy for interventions focusing on higher order skills, such as conceptual and application skills.

MATHEMATICS INTERVENTIONS

The interventions in this section are designed to enhance mathematics skills acquisition, fluency, and problem solving using empirically validated practices such as increasing opportunities to respond, collaborative learning, and strategy-based instruction. Two interventions use peer tutoring formats to build computational skills and fluency. *Improving Math Fluency with a Multicomponent Intervention* embeds explicit timing and performance feedback within a peer tutoring routine to improve fluency with math facts. This intervention also incorporates *positive practice overcorrection,* a procedure requiring students to repeat a correct response several times after making an error to reinforce learning and ensure that the last response made is correct (Sulzer-Azaroff & Mayer, 1991). *Reciprocal Peer Tutoring in Math* (RPT-M) combines self-management procedures and group contingencies within a collaborative learning format. Developed by Fantuzzo and his associates at the University of Pennsylvania, RPT-M was specifically designed to enhance mathematics skills in low-achieving urban elementary school students. RPT-M is associated with significant positive effects not only for math computation skills, but also for social competencies, including classroom behavior, students' perceptions of their own academic skills, peer acceptance, and academic motivation (Fantuzzo, Davis, & Ginsburg, 1995; Fantuzzo et al., 1992; Fantuzzo & Polite, 1990; Ginsburg-Block & Fantuzzo, 1997). Because collaborating with parents of students participating in RPT-M has additive benefits in terms of both academic and social outcomes (Fantuzzo et al., 1995; Heller & Fantuzzo, 1993), a variation with a parent involvement component is also presented.

One intervention uses strategy instruction to improve math problem-solving skills. In strategy instruction in mathematics, students learn to follow a series of steps to facilitate conceptual understanding and problem solving. Although strategy instruction has been successful in enhancing math problem-solving skills for students with and without disabilities (Cassel & Reid, 1996; Maccini & Hughes, 1997; Montague, 1997; Tournaki, 2003), most published interventions have been delivered by researchers rather than by classroom teachers and require supplementary curricular materials, such as scripted lessons. In contrast, *FAST DRAW: Strategy Instruction for Math Problem Solving* combines efficacy with practicality. Students learn an eight-step problem-solving strategy embedded in a self-regulation procedure (Case, Harris, & Graham, 1992; Harris & Graham, 1999) that helps them build the prerequisite skills needed for strategy use. In this adaptation, strategy instruction occurs in a collaborative learning context to enhance usability and motivation and provide all students with additional practice opportunities.

CROSS-REFERENCE: For other interventions targeting mathematics performance, see *Class Wide Peer Tutoring in Mathematics* and *Cover Copy Compare in Mathematics* in the Academic Productivity section of this chapter.

Evaluating the Effectiveness of Mathematics Interventions

Measures for assessing the effectiveness of the strategies in this section range from typical classroom math assessments, such as percent-correct scores on quizzes and tests, to group-oriented measures, such as classwide percent-correct rates on daily assignments. For interventions that target academic engagement as well as skill development, classwide measures of on-task behavior rates are also included. In addition to the evaluation procedures provided for each intervention, procedures for curriculum-based measurement in mathematics (M-CBM) are provided below.

Curriculum-Based Measurement in Mathematics

Curriculum-based measurement in mathematics (M-CBM) consists of a set of brief, fluency-based standardized procedures that can be used to measure mathematics competence and progress toward grade-level standards. There are two basic types of M-CBM problem sets, termed *math probes,* (1) computation probes and (2) concepts and application probes, each of which can consist of single-skill probes sampling only one type of problem (e.g., addition, subtraction, money problems) or multiple-skill probes sampling several different types of computation or concept problems. Like R-CBM, M-CBM can be used in screening/benchmarking programs and in monitoring student progress toward intervention goals or end-of-year objectives. Math probes can be constructed to align with the student's own curriculum or a general mathematics scope and sequence (see Shapiro, 2004a), but the process is very time-consuming and offers little control over variability in difficulty or content. Generic math probes, which are available from a variety of sources, are therefore recommended.

When used for screening/benchmarking or progress monitoring purposes, each M-CBM probe has the same number of items sampling the problems covered in the entire year's curriculum. For computation probes, the student is presented with 25 items sampling the problems covered in the annual curriculum and given 2 minutes to answer as many items as possible. Answers are scored in terms of correct digits written in 2 minutes. For concepts and applications probes, the student is presented with 18 to 25 items covering topics such as number concepts, money, measurement, graphs and charts, and problem solving. The student has 5 to 10 minutes, depending on grade level, and the score is the number of correct answers. As with R-CBM, results can be graphed and analyzed to determine whether student progress is sufficient to meet intervention goals and/or end-of-year expectations and whether the instructional program should be modified. Teachers' implementation of M-CBM has been associated with accelerated growth in mathematics for elementary school students (Allinder & Oats, 1997; Fuchs, Fuchs, Karns, Hamlett, & Katzaroff, 1999; VanDerHeyden & Burns, 2005). M-CBM is also a moderate to strong predictor of performance on criterion measures, such as norm-referenced and end-of-year achievement tests, although the correlations are lower than those for R-CBM (Shapiro, Keller, Lutz, Santoro, & Hintze, 2006). Moreover, low interscorer agreement for digits correct has been reported, even for trained scorers (Thurber, Shinn, & Smolkowski, 2002), and many teachers are unfamiliar with that scoring procedure. For that reason, problems-correct is included as an optional scoring metric for computation probes in the discussion below.

ASSESSING EARLY MATH SKILLS
WITH CURRICULUM-BASED MEASUREMENT IN MATHEMATICS

Although CBM-type measures assessing the emergent literacy skills of prereaders were developed over a decade ago, no comparable measures of foundational math skills for identifying young students at risk for early math failure or monitoring progress in early math skills were available until quite recently. Clarke and Shinn (2004) have developed a set of four early math measures that index young children's informal number sense development, including the ability to understand the meaning of numbers and discriminate relationships among numbers. Preliminary evidence of reliability, concurrent and predictive validity, and sensitivity to growth over time has been documented in a small sample of grade 1 students (Clarke & Shinn, 2004). Preliminary evidence of concurrent and predictive validity is also available for kindergarten students (Chard et al., 2005). The four measures are available as the *Test of Early Numeracy* at AIMSweb (*http://aimsweb.com*), along with user norms and rate of improvement statistics for fall, winter, and spring for kindergarten and grade 1. Variations of three of the measures (excluding Oral Counting) and an additional measure are available for free download at the Research Institute of Progress Monitoring website (*http://www.progressmonitoring.org*. The five measures are described below:

Oral Counting. The student counts orally, beginning with 1. The score is the number of numbers correctly counted in 1 minute.

Number Identification. The student identifies numerals between 0 and 20 randomly presented on a sheet of paper. The score is the number of numerals correctly identified in 1 minute.

Quantity Discrimination. The student identifies the larger of two numbers presented in a grid of boxes on a sheet of paper. Each box contains two randomly sampled numbers from 0 to 20. The score is the number of correctly identified larger numbers in 1 minute.

Missing Number. The student is presented with a series of boxes containing a string of three numbers between 0 and 20 in a pattern (e.g., counting by 2's) displayed on a sheet of paper. The first, middle, or last number of the string is missing, and the student is asked to state the number that is missing. The score is the number of missing numbers correctly identified in 1 minute.

Quantity Array. The student identifies the number of dots in a series of boxes presented on a sheet of paper. The score is the number of correctly counted dots per box in 1 minute.

CURRICULUM-BASED MEASUREMENT IN MATHEMATICS

Overview

Curriculum-based measurement in mathematics (M-CBM) consists of a set of fluency-based standardized procedures that are used to index students' performance in math and monitor progress over time. In M-CBM screening/benchmarking and progress monitoring programs, each probe is designed to sample all of the curriculum objectives for that grade, and the results are used to identify students at risk for math failure or to evaluate students' progress toward intervention goals or end-of-grade expectations. M-CBM probes can be designed to index competency in two basic areas: (1) computation and (2) concepts/applications. Because M-CBM math probes yield information on fluency as well as accuracy, they are especially helpful for identifying students who have learned basic computational skills but cannot perform them fast enough to keep up with the pace of classroom instruction or achieve at grade-level expectations. Math probes can be administered to individuals or groups of students. Although the digits-correct scoring method is more sensitive to individual growth, many teachers and consultants are unfamiliar with this procedure, and it is much more time-consuming. A problems-correct metric is therefore included as a scoring option. Because many of the items on concepts/applications probes have multiple-part answers, they must be scored on a blanks-correct basis.

Purpose

1. To identify students at risk for math problems and in need of additional instruction in math.
2. To monitor students' progress in mathematics and response to math interventions.
3. To provide information for designing math interventions and improving instructional programs.
4. To evaluate the effectiveness of reading interventions and instructional programs.

Materials

1. Stopwatch or timer.
2. Pencils with erasers, two per student.
3. Equal-interval graph paper or graphing program (optional).

Computation Probes

1. For each student, two or three sheets of math problems, 25 problems per probe.

Concepts and Application Probes

1. For each student, two or three sheets of math problems, 18 to 25 problems per probe.

Assessment Steps

Administration

1. Distribute the worksheets, give each student two pencils with erasers, and give the following instructions:

DIRECTIONS FOR SINGLE-SKILL PROBES:

"The sheets on your desk have math facts/math problems on them. All the problems are [addition or subtraction or multiplication or division] facts/[measurement, money, graphing, etc.] problems. When I say, 'Begin,' turn the sheets over and begin answering the problems. Start with the first problem on the left on the top row [point]. Work across and then go to the next row. If you can't answer the problem, make an x on it and go on to the next one. If you finish one sheet, go on to the next. Are there any questions? Begin!"

DIRECTIONS FOR MULTIPLE-SKILL AND CONCEPT/APPLICATIONS PROBES:

"The sheets on your desk are math facts/math problems. There are several types of problems on the sheets. Look at each problem carefully before you answer it. Some problems may have more than one blank. Try to fill in as many blanks as you can because you will get credit for each blank you answer. When I say, 'Begin,' turn the sheets over and begin answering the problems. Start with the first problem on the left on the top row [point]. Work across and then go to the next row. If you can't answer the problem, make an x on it and go on to the next one. If you finish one sheet, go on to the next. Are there any questions? Begin!"

2. At the end of 2 minutes, say, "Stop! Put your pencils down."
3. For screening/benchmarking, administer three M-CBMs probes and use the median score of the three probes for interpretive purposes. For progress monitoring, administer a single probe.

4. If desired, graph digits-correct scores for use in determining whether the student is making adequate progress toward intervention goals or end-of-year expectations or whether instructional modifications are needed.

Scoring and Interpretation

OPTION 1: DIGITS-CORRECT SCORING METHOD (COMPUTATION PROBLEMS)

1. Count the separate correct digits in an answer. For all problems except division, only digits below the answer line are counted. When scoring multiplication problems, however, score digits as correct if the addition operations are performed correctly, even if the answer is incorrect. That is, do not penalize students twice for a single error.
2. When scoring division problems, count digits as incorrect if the incorrect operation is performed or if incorrect place values are used.
3. If the student completes the worksheets before the time is up, divide the number of correctly written digits in the answer by the total number of seconds and multiply by 120 to obtain an estimate of the digits-correct score, as in

$$\frac{\text{Total number of correct digits}}{\text{Number of seconds to finish}} \times 120$$

4. Count omitted problems as errors.
5. Count reversed digits as correct, with the exception of 6's and 9's.
6. Compare digits-correct scores to local norms, web-based norms, or end-of-year goals.

OPTION 2: PROBLEMS-CORRECT SCORING METHOD (CONCEPTS/APPLICATIONS PROBLEMS AND/OR COMPUTATION PROBLEMS)

1. Give credit for each correct answer. For multiple-answer problems, award one point for each correct blank. Score omitted problems as errors. The score is the number of correct problems/blanks within the time limit. If desired, divide the number of correct problems/blanks by the total number of problems/blanks to obtain a percent-correct score.
2. Compare problems-correct or percent-correct scores to local norms, web-based norms, or end-of-year goals.
3. If desired, graph digits-correct, problems-correct, or percent-correct scores for use in determining whether the student is making adequate progress toward end-of-year expectations or whether instructional modifications are needed.

Notes

1. M-CBM can also be used in *survey-level assessment,* that is, to determine students' math instructional level (see Shapiro, 2004a, and Hosp et al., 2007), but the most widely cited placement standards date to the 1970s and consist of only two broad grade levels (grades 1–2 and 3–6). More recent data are available from Burns, VanDerHeyden, and Jiban (2006) but again, criteria are available for only two grade ranges (grades 2–3 and 4–5).
2. Very little normative data are currently available for interpreting the results of concepts/applications probes. For practitioners interested in developing local norms, see the procedures described in Stewart and Kaminski (2002).
3. Benchmark (end-of-year) goals and norms for weekly M-CBM growth rates for students in grades 1–6 in computation and grades 2–6 in concepts and applications are available in Fuchs and Fuchs (2005, p. 64) and on the AIMSweb site (*http://www.AIMSweb.com*).
4. M-CBM is most appropriate for students in grades 1–6. For younger students, CBM-type early numeracy measures are available from several web-based sources.

Sources

Hosp, M. K., Hosp, J. L., & Howell, K. W. (2007). *The ABCs of CBM: A practical guide to curriculum-based measurement.* New York: Guilford Press. Copyright 2007 by The Guilford Press. Adapted by permission.

Shapiro, E. S. (2004a). *Academic skills problems: Direct assessment and intervention* (3rd ed.). New York: Guilford Press. Copyright 2004 by The Guilford Press. Adapted by permission.

Additional Resources

M-CBM sheets are available free of charge at Intervention Central (*http://www.interventioncentral.org*). The fee-based AIMSweb (*http://www.aimsweb.com*) offers M-CBM benchmarking and progress monitoring sets for grades 1–6. Web-based graphing and data management systems are available from the same sources. Several websites permit users to create customized M-CBM sheets, including *http://www.aplusmath.com* and *http://www.schoolhousetech.com*.

IMPROVING MATH FLUENCY WITH A MULTICOMPONENT INTERVENTION

Overview

Developing fluency with math facts is an important competency for students. Students with limited fluency in computational skills are at a severe disadvantage because they cannot keep up with the pace of classroom instruction, which can lead to failure in the mathematics curriculum. Moreover, students with adequate fluency are more successful in applying their skills to new math tasks and are able to stay academically engaged for longer periods of time. Although increasing opportunities for practice and providing immediate response evaluation and error correction can improve math fluency, it can be difficult for teachers to build in supplementary instructional time or provide individualized feedback. This intervention includes several validated components for building fluency, including explicit timing, positive practice overcorrection, and performance feedback, without increasing instructional time or teacher supervision by embedding them within a peer tutoring structure that requires less than 10 minutes per session. In the original study, implemented with four low-performing fourth graders, the strategy was successful in improving fluency in multiplication facts for all participants. In this version, tutoring and assessment materials are prepared on a whole-class rather than on an individualized basis for usability purposes, with public posting of class performance added to enhance motivation. Also presented is a variation with classwide timing for tutoring and assessments that is especially appropriate for younger students. The intervention can be implemented in any subject area to provide additional opportunities for students to practice basic skills and facts.

Purpose

To improve speed and accuracy with math facts with a peer tutoring procedure combining explicit timing, immediate response feedback, and overcorrection.

Materials

1. Stopwatches, one per student pair and one per teacher.
2. Math flashcards, consisting of 3" × 5" index cards with two or three same-factor problems (e.g., 4 × 4 = __) on one side and the problem with the answer on the other side (e.g., 4 × 4 = 16), one set per student pair.
3. Red and green felt or construction paper circles, approximately 4 inches in diameter, one of each color per student pair.

4. Assessment sheets, consisting of 8½″ × 11″ sheets of paper listing the same problems as those on the flashcards, presented in random order, one sheet per student.
5. Assessment answer keys, consisting of 8½″ × 11″ sheets of paper listing the same problems on the flashcards presented in random order, including the answers, one sheet per student (optional).
6. Red marking pens, one per student.
7. Scratch paper, one or two sheets per student.
8. Posterboard chart labeled "We're on the Fast Track!" and displaying a racetrack divided into segments for displaying the class average number of correctly completed problems per minute.
9. Math folders containing sheets of graph paper, one per student (optional).

Observation (Select One or More)

Option 1

1. Create three math tests with sets of computational problems related to the math facts currently being taught. For 3 consecutive days, distribute one of the tests and give students 1 minute to complete as many problems as possible. Calculate a percent-correct score to yield a problems-correct-per-minute score for each student on each test. At the end of the 3 days, obtain an average problems-correct-per-minute score for each student by dividing by three.
2. If desired, calculate a classwide problems-correct-per-minute score by summing individual student average problems-correct-per-minute scores and dividing by the number of students in the class.

Option 2

1. Calculate problems-correct-per-minute scores on math daily worksheets for a target group of students or the entire class for 5 to 10 days by dividing the number of problems worked correctly by the number of minutes students are given to work. For example, if students have 15 minutes available to work and a student completes 18 problems correctly, the problems-correct-per-minute rate for that student is 1.2.

Option 3

1. Administer *Curriculum-Based Mathematics Probes* (M-CBM) to the entire class or a selected group of students.

Intervention Steps

Introduction and Training

1. Explain to the class that they will be learning to work together in pairs to improve their math skills. Display the chart with the racetrack and explain that they will be able to see their progress as a class in solving math problems quickly and accurately.
2. Using a student as a tutee, demonstrate the tutoring procedures described below, including timing and error correction.
   a. Each tutoring pair receives a stack of flashcards, a red and a green circle, and two assessment sheets.
   b. At your signal, each tutor sets the stopwatch for 2 minutes and begins showing flashcards to the tutee while the tutee verbally responds.
   c. If the answer is correct, the tutor responds, "Correct," places the card on the green ("Go—Correct") circle, and presents the next flashcard in the stack.

d. If the answer is incorrect, the tutor responds, "Incorrect, the answer is ___," places the card on the red ("Stop—Incorrect") circle, and the tutee writes the problem and the correct answer three times on scratch paper. After the tutee has completed this correction process, the tutor presents the next flashcard and continues with the procedure until the 2 minutes have expired. If tutors run out of flashcards before the 2 minutes have elapsed, they go through the Stop cards again.

e. Students then exchange roles and participate in another 2-minute tutoring session.

f. When both tutoring sessions have been completed, the students set their stopwatch for 1 minute and work independently to complete as many problems as possible on their assessment sheets.

g. The students in each pair exchange papers and, using their red pens, score the assessments by referring to the answer sheets. Alternatively, wait until all tutoring pairs have completed their sessions and assessments and call out the answers while students check their partners' papers.

3. Select two more students and guide them through the procedures, while the other students observe and you provide encouragement and corrective feedback as needed.

4. Then conduct a classwide practice tutoring session, using sets of addition flashcards. Have students practice until every pair can perform each step accurately for both tutee and tutor roles with 10 flashcards.

Implementation

1. Divide the class into pairs and designate one student in each pair to serve as tutor first. Students remain as partners for a week at a time but change initial roles for each session.

2. At the beginning of the period, conduct a brief review session of the math computational skills being taught that week.

3. Have students work in tutoring pairs as described above.

4. Collect the assessment sheets to verify scoring accuracy and compute a class average problems-correct-per-minute score by summing individual student scores and dividing by the number of students in the class.

5. After the initial session, begin each session by distributing the previous session's assignment sheets (corrected for accuracy, if necessary) and providing a minute or two for the pairs to review their progress. Have students record their scores on a bar graph in their math folders, if desired.

6. Report the class average problems-correct-per-minute score, and select a student to fill in that number on the racetrack chart. Praise the students for their efforts and remind them to encourage each other during tutoring sessions. If desired, deliver a group activity reward, such as a math game time using board or web-based games (see Additional Resources below), when the score reaches a certain criterion.

Evaluation (Select One or More)

Option 1

1. Compare individual student and/or classwide average problems-correct-per-minute scores on math computational tests before and after implementation.

Option 2

1. Compare problems-correct-per-minute scores on math daily worksheets for the target group of students or the entire class before and after implementation.

Option 3

1. Compare M-CBM scores for the entire class or the target students before and after implementation.

Variation: Classwide Timing

1. Using a stopwatch, signal all students to begin the 2-minute tutoring session at the same time. At the end of 2 minutes, call time and allow a minute or two for tutors to count up the number of correctly answered flashcards and praise their tutees. Then have students switch roles and repeat the procedures while you keep time. After each student has served in both roles, conduct the 1-minute assessment as described above.

Note

1. Training requires two 30-minute sessions over a 2-day period.

Source

Rhymer, K. N., Dittmer, K. I., Skinner, C. H., & Jackson, B. (2000). Effectiveness of a multi-component treatment for improving mathematics fluency. *School Psychology Quarterly, 15*, 40–51. Copyright 2000 by The Guilford Press. Adapted by permission.

Additional Resources

1. Printable math flashcards and online math flashcards games are available on numerous web sites, including *http://www.coolmath4kids.com, http://www.funbrain.com/math*, and *http://www.aplusmath.com.*
2. Premade and customized math worksheets with computation problems and keys for grades 1–4 are available at *http://www.mathfactcafe.com* and for elementary through high school mathematics at *http://www.edhelper.com.*

RECIPROCAL PEER TUTORING IN MATH

Overview

Reciprocal peer tutoring in mathematics (RPT-M) is a collaborative learning intervention that targets math performance and productivity with self-management procedures and group contingencies within a structured peer tutoring format. Unlike the majority of self-management strategies, which focus on individual students, RPT-M is designed to help students manage their academic progress in a group context. In RPT-M, students are trained to serve as instructional partners for each other, select team goals for academic performance, and manage their own reward contingencies. Because the intervention takes only about 30 minutes—20 minutes for peer tutoring and 10 minutes for individual drills and checking—it can be easily incorporated into a typical math instructional period. Studies with RPT-M have reported significant gains in academic achievement, academic engagement, and prosocial interactions, as well as reductions in disruptive behavior, for participating students. RPT-M also enhances students' perceptions of their own scholastic competence and self-control and earns high satisfaction ratings from both teachers and students. In the original studies, implemented with academically at-risk elementary school students in urban schools, student teams selected their own rewards. Two variations are included: one with home-based incentives that has been validated with urban low-achieving students and another with classwide rather than team rewards.

Purpose

To improve mathematics performance and engagement during math instruction with peer tutoring, group rewards, and self-management procedures.

Materials

1. *Reinforcement Menus* with activity rewards, one per student pair.
2. Team score cards, consisting of 3" × 5" index cards, one per student pair per week.
3. Happy face stickers or happy face rubber stamps, one set of stickers or stamp per student pair.
4. Flashcards with mathematics problems printed on the front and the problems with the computational steps and answers printed on the back, one problem per card, one set of cards per student pair.
5. Worksheets, consisting of 8½" × 11" sheets of paper divided into four sections labeled: "Try 1," "Try 2," "Help," and "Try 3."
6. Instructional prompt cards, consisting of 3" × 5" index cards with specific instructions related to common mistakes in solving math problems, one prompt card per student pair.
7. Quizzes with 10 to 16 math problems, one per student.
8. Answer sheets for quizzes, one per student (optional).
9. Red pens, one per student (optional).
10. Posterboard chart or section of the chalkboard to record team wins (optional, see Variation 1).
11. Introductory parent letter (see Figure 4.9 on p. 242), one per student (optional, see Variation 2).
12. Recognition certificates (optional, see Variation 2).

Observation (Select One or More)

Option 1

1. Calculate percent-correct scores on daily math drill sheets or weekly math quizzes for a target group of students or the entire class for 5 to 10 days or several weeks.

Option 2

1. Administer *Curriculum-Based Mathematics Probes* (M-CBM) to a group of target students.

Option 3

1. With your eye, divide the class into four quadrants of approximately equal numbers of students. Using a *Group Time Sampling Form* with a 5-minute interval, glance at the first of four quadrants and record a plus (+) if all of the students in the quadrant are on-task at the moment of observation as defined below. If any of the students in the quadrant being observed are not on task, record a minus (–). During the next interval, observe the next group, and so on until you have observed all four groups. Then begin again with the first quadrant.
    a. *On-task behavior* is defined as looking at the teacher during instruction, working on the assignment, asking or answering lesson-oriented questions, and any other lesson-relevant behavior.
    b. *Off-task behavior* is defined as failing to attend to the teacher or the assignment, playing with materials, talking, being out of seat, or any other nonlesson behavior.
3. Conduct these observations for 30 to 45 minutes during the math instructional period for 4 to 7 days.

Intervention Steps

Introduction and Training

1. Tell the students that they will be learning to work in pairs to help each other do well in mathematics. Using two students, conduct a demonstration of the goal-setting process and tutoring procedures as described below.
2. Divide the class into pairs. Provide each pair with a *Reinforcement Menu* listing activity rewards, such as serving as a classroom helper or messenger, working on special projects in the classroom, using classroom computers, and working in centers, and have each pair select a reward for the week.
3. Conduct a brief meeting with each pair to help the students select their team goal for the week (the number of problems they believe they can answer correctly as a team). Teams select goals from a list of recommended choices, based on your estimates of realistic academic objectives for that team and the results of the previous week's math assessments.
4. After each pair has chosen a team goal, have each student record his or her expected individual contribution to the team (each student's individual goal), the sum of the individual goals (each pair's team goal), and their choice of a reward on the team score card.

Implementation

1. For the first 5 minutes of each session, conduct a review or skills drill with the math facts students are currently learning.
2. Begin the RPT-M session by giving a set of flashcards to each pair. Tell the students to choose who will act as "teacher" first. Flashcard sets can be identical across all pairs or individualized according to student needs, based on assessment results.
3. The teacher holds up a flashcard for the student and tells the student to work the problem on his or her worksheet in the section marked "Try 1" while the teacher observes.
4. If the student solves the problem correctly, the teacher praises the student, marks his or her worksheet with a happy face sticker or stamp in the "Try 1" section, and presents the next problem. If the solution is incorrect, the teacher gives the student instructional prompts read from the prompt card and tells the student to compute the problem again in the worksheet section marked "Try 2."
5. If the student does not solve the problem correctly on the second try, the teacher computes the problem in the "Help" section. As the teacher works the problem, he or she explains each step and answers the student's questions. Then the teacher tells the student to work the problem again in the "Try 3" section. If the teacher has trouble answering the student's questions, the pair raise their hands to request help from the classroom teacher.
6. After 10 minutes, signal the pairs to switch roles for a second 10-minute tutoring session.
7. During tutoring sessions, circulate around the room, praising appropriate behavior and identifying strategies teachers can use to help their students.
8. After the second tutoring session, give all the students a problem drill sheet and have them work on their own for a fixed period of time, such as 7 to 10 minutes.
9. Have students switch papers with their team partners. Go over the problems as a class while students check each other's papers, using red pens. Alternatively, provide students with answer sheets and have them score each other's papers.
10. Have student pairs first determine their team's total score by counting the number of problems each team member completed correctly and then compare their team score with their team goal to see if they have "won" (met their goal).
11. Give winning teams a sticker to put on their score card for that day. After five wins, schedule a time when the team can engage in the previously selected rewarding activity.

Evaluation (Select One or More)

Option 1

1. Compare percent-correct scores on daily math drill sheets or weekly math quizzes for the selected group of students or the entire class before and after implementation.

Option 2

1. Compare M-CBM scores for the target group of students before and after implementation.

Option 3

1. Compare the percentages of classwide on-task and off-task behavior before and after implementation.

Variations

Variation 1: RPT-M with Home-Based Rewards

1. Send a letter home providing information about RPT-M and inviting parents to consider several options for involvement (see Figure 4.9).
2. After a team achieves three wins, give the students a recognition certificate to take home to their parents.
3. If desired, have parents sign the certificates, indicate the type of reward they provided (if any), add any additional comments or questions, and return.

Variation 2: RPT-M with Classwide Rewards

1. Using the *Reinforcement Menu,* have the class vote to select one reward for the week.
2. In addition to having teams record their wins on team score cards, record daily team wins on a posterboard chart or a section of the chalkboard.
3. Set a criterion for weekly classwide rewards, such as 80% of the teams achieving their goals on 4 of 5 days. Deliver rewards, if earned, to the entire class on Friday. Gradually increase the criterion as students become more successful.

Notes

1. Training takes two sessions of approximately 45 minutes each.
2. The RPT-M procedure can be adapted to any subject that includes fact drills, such as spelling, vocabulary, history, and geography.
3. In the original study that included a home-based reward system (Heller & Fantuzzo, 1993), school meetings were held with parents to provide information about RPT-M, with follow-up telephone calls to monitor home reward delivery.

Sources

Fantuzzo, J. W., King, J. A., & Heller, L. R. (1992). Effects of reciprocal peer tutoring on mathematics and school adjustment: A component analysis. *Journal of Educational Psychology, 84,* 331–339. Copyright 1992 by the American Psychological Association. Adapted by permission.

School Letterhead

Date:

Dear parent/guardian:

I am delighted to inform you that our class will be participating in a reciprocal peer tutoring program designed to improve students' skills in mathematics (RPT-M). RPT-M is a collaborative learning strategy in which students work in pairs to set goals for improving their math skills, practice math problems, and provide each other with helpful feedback. Students who meet their goals three times in a row will earn a classroom reward and will receive a reward certificate to take home to let you know that they have achieved their goals. RPT-M will take place (number of times a week) at (time of day) for about 30 minutes per session.

A key component of RPT-M is parent involvement. Studies have shown that when parents participate in the program, children not only improve their math skills substantially but also develop more positive attitudes toward school. You can be involved in several ways:

1. By providing rewards and privileges to your child when he or she brings home a reward certificate.

2. By attending classroom sessions to observe your child participating in RPT-M.

3. By serving as a classroom helper during RPT-M sessions.

If you would like to participate by providing your child with home rewards, suggested rewards include special time or activities with parents, special snacks, or extra privileges, such as staying up later, having a slumber party on the weekend, or getting to pick first among chores for the children that week. Please indicate below how you would like to participate and have your child return the bottom half of this letter. Please feel free to call me if you have any questions about RPT-M or ways in which you can participate. Your participation is completely voluntary and very welcome! I look forward to working with you to help your child become the best mathematics student he or she can be!

Sincerely yours,

Name of teacher

===
Reciprocal Peer Tutoring in Mathematics (RPT-M) Program

____ I would like to participate by providing my child with home rewards.

____ I would like to participate by attending classroom sessions to observe my child participating in RPT-M.

____ I would like to participate by helping in the classroom during RPT-M sessions.

____ I do not wish to participate at this time.

Name of parent/guardian: _____

Name of student: _____

FIGURE 4.9. Introductory parent letter for *Reciprocal Peer Tutoring in Mathematics*. Adapted from Heller and Fantuzzo (1993). Copyright 1993 by the National Association of School Psychologists. Adapted by permission.

Fantuzzo, J. W., & Rohrbeck, C. A. (1992). Self-managed groups: Fitting self-management approaches into classroom systems. *School Psychology Review, 21*, 255–263. Copyright 1992 by the National Association of School Psychologists. Adapted by permission.

Heller, L. R., & Fantuzzo, J. W. (1993). Reciprocal peer tutoring and parent partnership: Does parent involvement make a difference? *School Psychology Review, 22*, 517–534. Copyright 1992 by the National Association of School Psychologists. Adapted by permission.

FAST DRAW: IMPROVING MATH WORD PROBLEM SOLVING WITH STRATEGY INSTRUCTION

Overview

Many students, especially those with learning disabilities, perform reasonably well on low-level math skills, such as calculation, but have difficulty with the higher level skills needed for problem solving and applications. To solve word problems successfully, students must not only be able to perform the necessary computations, but must also understand the questions that are being asked, identify the relevant information within the problem, and determine the specific operations needed to solve the problem. In this multicomponent intervention, students learn an eight-step strategy for solving math word problems, along with self-regulation procedures to assist them in completing the strategy successfully. The strategy is taught in a series of stages, and the mnemonic FAST DRAW is used to help students remember the eight strategy steps. In the original study with four elementary grade students, two with learning disabilities and two with mild mental retardation, math word problem-solving performance improved significantly for all participants, with gains maintained at 6- and 8-week follow-ups. Moreover, students' attitudes toward word problems became much more positive during the intervention period. Originally delivered in a one-to-one format, the strategy is adapted here for classwide application using a peer tutoring format.

Purpose

To increase students' ability to solve math word problems using self-regulated strategy instruction.

Materials

1. Math folders containing sheets of paper, one folder per student.
2. Math manipulatives.
3. Prompt cards, consisting of 3″ × 5″ inch index cards listing the strategy steps and FAST DRAW mnemonic, one per student (see Intervention Steps, Stage 3).
4. Self-monitoring strategy check-off sheet, one per student (see Intervention Steps, Stage 3).
5. Math word problem worksheets, one per student.
6. Colored marking pens and highlighters, one each per student.
7. Overhead projector and transparencies of math word problems and the strategy steps and mnemonic (optional).

Observation (Select One or Both)

Option 1

1. Administer to the entire class a 20-problem math test consisting of 10 problems involving addition and subtraction facts and problems with regrouping and 10 one-step word problems involving application of knowledge about basic facts and regrouping in addition or subtraction. *Example*: The fifth grade class has nine goldfish. The fourth grade class has seven goldfish. How many goldfish does the fifth grade need to give away to have as many as the fourth grade?

2. Calculate a word problem-solving percent-accuracy score for each student by dividing the number of problems worked correctly by the total number of problems. If desired, calculate a class average word problem-solving percent-accuracy score by summing scores for individual students and dividing by the number of students in the class.

Option 2

1. Calculate grades on math quizzes and tests for a group of target students or all of the students in the class for the past several weeks or the current marking period.

Intervention Steps

Stage 1: Introduction and Initial Group Conferencing

1. Explain to the students that they will be learning a strategy called "FAST DRAW" that will help them be more successful in solving math word problems. Tell them that they will have an opportunity to work in pairs while they are learning the strategy.
2. Lead a discussion of the reasons why it is important to know how to solve math word problems in terms of being a future consumer, worker, and citizen, and list the reasons on the chalkboard.
3. Distribute to students their individual results on the 20-item math test administered during the observation period or a list of their grades on math quizzes and tests for the past several weeks. Using the chalkboard or an overhead projector, demonstrate how to construct a bar graph of percent-correct scores. Then help students construct bar graphs in their math folders, using their performance on the pretest or on previous math assessments as initial data. Explain that they can use the bar graphs to monitor their own progress in solving word problems.

Stage 2: Preskill Development

1. Use manipulatives and simple computation problems to demonstrate the following relationships found in addition and subtraction problems:
   a. The relationship of addition and subtraction to the action implied in a word problem (i.e., for addition, objects are put together; for subtraction, they are separated or removed).
   b. The relationship of addition and subtraction to the size of an answer (i.e., for addition, the largest number in the problem will get larger; for subtraction, it will get smaller).
2. Conduct a classwide practice with each concept that will be taught until students reach an 80% mastery criterion (four out of five problems correct) for each concept.

Stage 3: Discussion of the FAST DRAW Strategy and Self-Regulation Procedures

1. Give each student a prompt card listing the eight strategy steps and the FAST DRAW mnemonic for remembering the steps, as follows:
   F: Find and highlight the question, and then write the label (e.g., addition—change).
   A: Ask what the parts of the problem are and then circle the numbers needed to solve it.
   S: Set up the problem by writing and labeling the numbers.
   T: Tie down the sign by rereading the problem (i.e., decide whether addition or subtraction should be used).
   D: Discover the sign by rechecking the operation.
   R: Read the number problem.
   A: Answer the number problem.
   W: Write the answer and check to see if it makes sense.

2. Discuss how and why each step is used in solving word problems, using examples displayed on the chalkboard or overhead projector.
3. Discuss the importance of using self-statements while applying each step, such as:
    a. (A) "To find the question, look for the sentence ending with a question mark."
    b. (S) "When setting up the problem, remember to write the larger number on top."
    c. (T) "To tie down the sign, ask if I am putting together so the answer will be larger than the other numbers (if yes, use addition), or if I am taking apart so the answer will be smaller than the largest number (if yes, use subtraction)."
4. Show students how these self-statements can be used to create a self-monitoring check-off sheet for use during word problem solving. Guide students in generating their own self-statements for using the strategy and have them record them on check-off sheets in their math folders.

Stage 4: Modeling

1. Model the use of the strategy using the following six self-instructions:
    a. *Problem definition:* "What is it I have to do?"
    b. *Planning:* "How can I solve the problem?"
    c. *Strategy use:* "FAST DRAW will help me remember all the things I need to do to solve a word problem successfully."
    d. *Self-monitoring:* "I can check off the steps of the strategy as I complete them so I can remember what I've done."
    e. *Self-evaluation:* "How am I doing? Does what I'm doing make sense? Did I complete all the steps?"
    f. *Self-reinforcement:* "Great, I'm half-way through the strategy!" or "Oops, I made a mistake, but that's OK because I can fix it. Yay, I did it!"
    g. Have students record examples of statements for each of the six categories on their self-monitoring strategy check-off sheets. Stress that self-instructional statements do not have to be verbalized aloud; once they are learned, they can be whispered or said to oneself.

Stage 5: Mastery of the Strategy Steps

1. Divide the class into pairs and have students work together to rehearse the strategy until they have memorized all eight steps, including the FAST DRAW mnemonic, and several positive self-statements about solving math word problems.

Stage 6: Collaborative Practice with Self-Instructions

1. Distribute a worksheet with a set of 7 to 10 problems of the first problem type to be taught (i.e., addition–change problems; see Table 4.2).
2. As students work in pairs, move around the room and provide assistance in the correct use of the strategy steps and self-instructions by asking questions and referring to the prompt cards and check-off sheets. Encourage students to verbalize their self-statements softly to each other and then silently to themselves.
3. After all of the pairs have completed the worksheet, have the students exchange papers and go over the answers as a class. Have students graph the number of items they answered correctly on the bar graphs in their math folders.
4. Continue collaborative practice sessions until students meet a criterion of five out of six problems correct for that problem type.

Stage 7: Independent Performance

1. During the math instructional period, remind students to use the strategy and self-instructions for addition–change problems, but do not provide assistance for that problem type. If students experience difficulty, return to the collaborative practice stage until they demonstrate mastery again.

2. Return to the collaborative practice stage for the next problem type (subtraction–change problems). Continue introducing word problem types sequentially, alternating collaborative practice and independent performance stages until students are performing at the criterion level on change and equalize problem types in both addition and subtraction. Then follow the same procedure for combine and compare problem types.

Evaluation (Select One or Both)

Option 1

1. Compare individual student and/or class average percent-accuracy scores on word problem-solving tests before and after implementation.

Option 2

1. Compare grades on math quizzes and tests for the target group or the entire class before and after implementation.

Note

1. The problem types taught in the intervention are based on the Riley, Greeno, and Heller classification of word problems (Pellegrino & Goldman, 1987), which consists of four basic problem types (change, equalize, combine, and compare) and 16 problem subtypes. In the original investigation, four of the most difficult subtypes were omitted from instruction and assessment probes.

TABLE 4.2. Examples of Word Problem Types Used in Math Strategy Instruction

Problem type		Example
Addition	Change (result unknown)	Peter had 7 comic books. Then Miguel gave him 5 more comic books. How many comic books does Peter have now?
	Combine (total set unknown)	Twanda has 7 comic books. Sarah has 5 comic books. How many comic books do they have altogether?
	Compare (quantity unknown)	Raymond has 9 comic books. James has 7 more comic books than Raymond. How many comic books does James have?
Subtraction	Change (result unknown)	Tabitha had 12 comic books. Then she gave 4 comic books to Patricia. How many comic books does Tabitha have now?
	Equalize (must get)	Injila has 7 comic books. Dennis has 10 comic books. How many comic books must Injila get to have as many as Dennis?
	Compare (difference unknown— more than)	Jack has 11 comic books. LaShawn has 3 comic books. How many more comic books does LaShawn have than Jack?

Note. Examples of word problem types for *Fast Draw: Math Word Problem Solving with Strategy Instruction.* Adapted from Cassel and Reid (1996, p. 157). Copyright 1996 by Springer. Adapted by permission.

Interventions to Improve Writing Performance

Writing is a crucial skill for school success because it is a fundamental way of communicating ideas and demonstrating knowledge in the content areas. Although there is much less research on writing instruction compared with reading instruction, recent reports by the National Commission on Writing (2003, 2004, 2005) have underscored the importance of writing proficiency to academic success and participation in today's global economy. Unfortunately, most students are not graduating from high school with adequate writing skills. According to the most recent National Assessment of Educational Progress (NAEP) in writing (National Center for Education Statistics, 2003), less than a third of students at each of the three grades assessed scored at or above the Proficient level. Although modest gains were noted for fourth and eighth graders compared with the 1998 assessment, the average score for 12th graders declined, with more than a quarter (26%) scoring at the Below Basic level. Writing problems are also characteristic of most students with learning disabilities, who have deficits in basic writing skills, such as handwriting, spelling, capitalization, and sentence formation (Graham, Harris, MacArthur, & Schwartz, 1991); have difficulty sustaining effort during writing (Graham, 1990); and produce compositions that are typically brief, poorly organized, and impoverished in both content and development (De La Paz, 1997; Graham & Harris, 2002; Graham, Harris, & Larsen, 2001).

The pervasiveness of writing problems in the general student population as well as among students with learning disabilities suggests that poor writing achievement is related less to internal student disabilities than to inadequate writing instruction. Although there is a growing body of research on effective writing strategies (see Graham & Harris, 2006a, and Graham & Perin, 2007, for reviews), the myth that writing develops naturally and that good writing cannot be taught has had a negative impact on typical classroom instruction. Despite a greater emphasis in recent years on providing classroom writing experiences for students, informal approaches are still prevalent. Unfortunately, simply increasing the amount of writing students engage in each day is insufficient to improve writing performance, especially for less skilled writers (Graham & Harris, 1997). Similarly, teachers often fail to provide students with high-quality writing assignments and tend to deliver feedback that focuses primarily on improving the surface features of writing rather than on enhancing organization or content (Matsumura, Patthey-Chavez, Valdés, & Garnier, 2002). Research also demonstrates that teachers have difficulty differentiating writing instruction to meet individual student needs. A recent national survey of primary grade teachers (Graham, Harris, Fink-Chorzempa, & MacArthur, 2003) found that nearly half of the teachers made few or no adaptations for struggling writers, and approximately one-sixth of classroom adaptations limited student participation or decision making in some way rather than providing additional learning opportunities. Writing instruction for students with learning disabilities is especially likely to be inadequate. Instruction focuses largely on lower level writing skills, such as spelling and handwriting, with students spending most of their time completing worksheets and copying single words rather than practicing compositional aspects, such as planning, text production, and editing (Graham & Harris, 1997; Palinscar & Klenk, 1992).

Although there is still much less research on effective writing practices compared with reading practices, recent federal initiatives, such as the National Commission on Writing for America's Families, Schools, and Colleges, established in 2002 by the College Board (*http://www.writingcommission.org*), and the growing use of statewide writing assessments have generated interest in interventions that can enhance the writing skills of all students as well as students with disabilities. This section includes interventions targeting two aspects of writing: (1) spelling and (2) written expression. Helping students to attain an adequate level of competence in basic writing mechanics so that mechanical difficulties do not interfere with higher order writing processes is an essential goal of writing instruction (Graham, Harris, & MacArthur, 1993). Students also need carefully designed composition instruction focusing on the important ideas of writing, such as the writing process, text structures, and writing for an audience (Stein, Dixon, & Isaacson, 1994).

INTERVENTIONS TO IMPROVE SPELLING PERFORMANCE

Spelling is a critical component of written communication. Without adequate spelling skills, students have difficulty communicating in written form and demonstrating what they have learned. Spelling problems are not only common among students with learning disabilities (Darch, Kim, Johnson, & James, 2000; Fulk & Stormont-Spurgin, 1995; Gordon, Vaughn, & Schumm, 1993), but are widespread in the general student population. In a year-long study of six elementary classrooms (Morris, Blanton, Blanton, & Perney, 1995), only two-thirds of the students observed could spell 86% of a curriculum-based list correctly, and the lowest third could spell only 46% of that list correctly. Moreover, students taught using spelling textbooks varied greatly in their mastery of grade-level spelling patterns. Spelling problems exert detrimental effects on writing in several ways. First, having to focus on spelling interferes with higher order writing processes, such as planning, generating text, and revising (Graham et al., 1993; Graham, 1999). Spelling skills account for a sizable proportion of the variance in compositional fluency (66%) and quality (42%) throughout the elementary grades (Graham, Berninger, Abbott, Abbott, & Whitaker, 1997). Second, misspelled words not only interfere with the message the writer is trying to convey, but may also influence perceptions of the student's competency as a writer (Graham, Harris, & Fink-Chorzempa, 2002). Third, spelling problems may lead students to avoid writing and ultimately to develop the belief that they cannot write, limiting not only their literacy development but also their performance in a wide variety of subject areas (Graham, 1999).

Despite frequent calls to incorporate evidence-based practices into spelling instruction (Fresch, 2003; Graham & Harris, 2006b; Moats, 1995), many teachers appear to lack the knowledge and resources needed to teach spelling effectively. Teachers persist in using traditional but unvalidated activities, such as assigning weekly spelling lists, administering weekly tests, and having students write words multiple times or use them in sentences (Fresch, 2003; Johnston, 2001). Unfortunately, these practices provide insufficient opportunities to improve spelling, especially for poor spellers and students with disabilities. Moreover, some students may be able to score satisfactorily on weekly tests by memorizing the words on the list, only to misspell the same words later because they have not learned the underlying spelling patterns (Templeton & Morris, 1999). Similarly, although current spelling textbooks provide lists of grade-appropriate words, they often fail to emphasize empirically validated strategies for learning the words, such as instruction based on functional spelling units (Berninger et al., 1998; Morris et al., 1995). Spelling instruction has also been complicated by the fact that many districts have replaced textbook-based instruction with instruction that is integrated within language arts and content area subjects. With this approach, words for spelling tests are drawn from a number of nonstandardized sources. Unfortunately, this method not only fails to accommodate the wide range of spelling abilities and spelling problems within most classrooms, but also introduces variability in terms of what students are taught at each grade level. At the middle school and high school levels, teachers rarely provide direct instruction in effective spelling strategies, perhaps because they believe that spelling is less important in the curriculum or that students have already acquired—or should have already acquired—spelling techniques in the elementary grades (Fulk & Stormont-Spurgin, 1995). Fortunately, researchers have focused more attention on spelling interventions in recent years (see Wanzek et al., 2006, for a review), based on evidence that targeted spelling instruction can not only improve writing fluency and expressive writing skills (Baker, Gersten, & Graham, 2003), but also facilitate the acquisition of foundational literacy skills, such as word recognition and sentence writing for at-risk students (Graham & Harris, 2006a, 2006b; Graham et al., 2002).

WHAT SPELLING WORDS SHOULD BE TAUGHT?

When spelling instruction is integrated into the curriculum rather than based on a separate textbook or set of materials, teachers often wonder how to select words to teach their students. One approach to spelling instruction in these circumstances is to teach the words that students at each grade level are most likely to use in their writing. This method has the advantage of reducing the number of preassigned words so that although all students study the most common grade-specific words, teachers can also help students select their own spelling words from the vocabularies in reading, language arts, and content area classes. Including a subset of student-chosen words not only links spelling instruction to classroom reading and writing activities, but also permits students to study words that are of personal interest. Graham and his colleagues have developed two high-frequency graded spelling word lists for use in selecting words to teach—(1) the *Basic Spelling Vocabulary List,* consisting of 850 high-frequency words for students in grades 1 through 5 (Graham, Harris, & Loynachan, 1993), and (2) the *Spelling for Writing List,* consisting of the 335 words most commonly used in writing by students in grades 1 through 3 (Graham, Harris, & Loynachan, 1994).

Evaluating the Effectiveness of Spelling Interventions

Methods for evaluating the effectiveness of the spelling interventions presented in this section include typical classroom measures, such as individual student scores on weekly spelling tests, as well as classwide metrics, such as the percentage of students meeting a specified accuracy criterion on spelling tests. Two other types of measures are especially useful for assessing students' response to spelling interventions: (1) developmental spelling inventories and (2) curriculum-based measurement in spelling (S-CBM). *Developmental spelling inventories* consist of word lists that reflect a hierarchical progression of spelling features and are scored not only for whole-word correctness but also for the presence or absence of spelling features representing a specific developmental stage (Rathvon, 2004b). Compared with traditional spelling achievement tests, developmental spelling inventories are much more sensitive to differences among students and to small changes in spelling performance (Moats, 1995). Moreover, the results provide a blueprint for differentiated spelling instruction. Developmental spelling inventories, including scoring feature guides, for students in kindergarten through high school are available in *Words Their Way: Word Study for Phonics, Vocabulary, and Spelling Instruction* (Bear, Invernizzi, Templeton, & Johnston, 2004). Procedures for administering and scoring S-CBM are presented below.

Curriculum-Based Measurement in Spelling

Curriculum-based measurement in spelling (S-CBM) is a set of brief, fluency-based standardized procedures used to index spelling performance and progress toward grade-level expectations in spelling. As with R-CBM and M-CBM, S-CBM can be used for universal screening/benchmarking programs, in which sets of three spelling probes are administered to all students three or four times a year, and for more frequent monitoring of student progress toward intervention goals or end-of-year objectives for at-risk students. Each spelling probe consists of 12 to 17 words randomly sampled from the pool of words students are expected to master during the year and dictated for 2 minutes. If students are taught from a grade-based spelling textbook, spelling probes can be constructed using the classroom curricular materials. As noted above, however, most school districts have replaced textbook-based spelling instruction with instruction integrated within language arts and content area subjects, so that words for spelling instruction and assessments are drawn from a variety of sources. When this is the case, graded word lists controlled for difficulty should be used.

Two options are included for scoring S-CBMs: (1) correct letter sequences (CLS), defined as an adjacent pair of correctly spelled letters, and (2) number of words spelled correctly. Although the CLS method is more sensitive to differences among students and small changes in student performance, it is also more complex and time-consuming. Moreover, because improving skills in spelling whole words is the ultimate goal, the number of words spelled correctly should be monitored at periodic intervals (Fuchs, Fuchs, Hamlett, Walz, & Germann, 1993). Studies have documented that both metrics are highly correlated with standardized measures of spelling and that spelling CBMs can reliably distinguish among students with disabilities, students receiving Title I services, and regular education students, regardless of which of the two scoring methods is used (Shinn & Marston, 1985; Shinn, Ysseldyke, Deno, & Tindal, 1986). Moreover, higher spelling achievement is associated with teacher use of skills analysis based on S-CBM performance (Fuchs, Fuchs, Hamlett, & Allinder, 1991).

CURRICULUM-BASED MEASUREMENT IN SPELLING

Overview

In spelling, all students in a classroom are usually placed in the same level of the curriculum regardless of their skill development. For that reason, the results of curriculum-based measurements in spelling (S-CBM) are not generally used to make decisions about moving students to a different level of the curriculum. Instead, spelling probes are conducted to identify students who would benefit from supplementary targeted instruction and to indicate the degree to which students are acquiring spelling skills relative to their classmates and end-of-year expectations. In S-CBM screening/benchmarking, measures are administered in fall, winter, and spring to index spelling achievement and identify at-risk students. S-CBM progress monitoring is conducted at more frequent intervals to measure students' response to spelling interventions and/or progress toward end-of-year standards. S-CBM results can also be analyzed to provide information for instructional planning based on the types of errors frequently made by students. Research has demonstrated that S-CBM is a reliable and valid predictor of performance on norm- and criterion-referenced spelling measures and that it can differentiate between students with and without disabilities. Two scoring options are presented: (1) the number of correct letter sequences (pairs of adjacent letters) spelled correctly and (2) the number of words spelled correctly. S-CBMs may be administered to students individually or in groups. S-CBM performance can be evaluated by means of local norms, intrastudent comparisons, and, for correct letter sequences, web-based user norms.

Purpose

1. To identify students in need of supplementary instruction in spelling.
2. To monitor students' progress toward intervention or end-of-year spelling goals.
3. To evaluate the effectiveness of spelling interventions and instructional practices.
4. To provide information for instructional planning and program improvement.

Materials

1. Spelling lists of words randomly sampled from the spelling textbook or, preferably, grade-level curriculum-independent lists; for students in grades 1 and 2, use 12-word lists; for students in grades 3 and up, use 17-word lists.
2. Pencils with erasers, two per student.
3. Sheets of lined paper, two per student, or spelling notebooks, one per student.
4. Stopwatch or timer.
5. Equal-interval graph paper or graphing program (optional).

Assessment Steps

Administration

1. Distribute the writing materials and give the following directions:

   "I am going to read some words to you. I want you to write the words on the sheet in front of you. Write the first word on the first line, the second word on the second line, and so on. I'll give you 7 seconds (10 seconds for students in grades 1 and 2) to spell each word. When I say the next word, try to write it, even if you haven't finished the last one. Are there any questions? Begin!"

2. Dictate each word in order at the appropriate interval, repeating each word twice. If a word is a homonym, use it in a short sentence.
3. At the end of 2 minutes, say, "Stop! Put your pencils down." If students have nearly completed a word and the time has expired, permit them to finish writing that final word.
4. For screening/benchmarking, administer two more lists. For progress monitoring, administer one list.

Scoring and Interpretation

OPTION 1: CORRECT LETTER SEQUENCES (CLS)

1. For scoring purposes, each word has an extra character placed before and after it and one more letter sequence than the number of letters in the word. For example, the six-letter word BUTTER has seven possible letter sequences (_B, BU, UT, TT, TE, ER, and R_).
2. Count the number of correct letter sequences. *Examples*:
   BUTTER has seven letter sequences correct.
   BUTTAR has five letter sequences correct.
   BUTER has five letter sequences correct.
   BATTAR has three letter sequences correct.

3. For screening/benchmarking, score each of the three probes as described above and use the median score for interpretative purposes. For progress monitoring, score the probe as described above.
4. Compare the CLS rate to intrastudent norms, local norms, or web-based norms.

OPTION 2: WORDS SPELLED CORRECTLY (WSC)

1. Count the number of words spelled correctly to obtain a words-spelled-correctly rate (WSC).
2. For screening/benchmarking, score each of the three probes as described above and use the median score for interpretative purposes. For progress monitoring, score the probe as described above.
3. Compare the WCS rate to intrastudent norms, local norms, or web-based norms.

Notes

1. Lists can be generated by writing grade-level words on index cards or entering them in a word processing program and then randomly selecting sets. If CLS will be used as the metric, each list should include the same number of three-, four-, five-, etc., -letter words.
2. To evaluate S-CBM performance using a whole-word metric, local norms at the classroom, school, or district level can be developed, using guidelines described in Stewart and Hadebank (2002).
3. Having students respond to S-CBMs in their spelling notebooks permits both teachers and students to assess progress over time.

Sources

Hosp, M. K., Hosp, J. L., & Howell, K. W. (2007). *The ABCs of CBM: A practical guide to curriculum-based measurement*. New York: Guilford Press. Copyright 2007 by The Guilford Press. Adapted by permission.
Shapiro, E. S. (2004a). *Academic skills problems: Direct assessment and intervention* (3rd ed.). New York: Guilford Press. Copyright 2004 by The Guilford Press. Adapted by permission.

Additional Resources

AIMSweb (*http://www.aimsweb.com*) offers sets of 3 benchmarking lists and 30 progress monitoring lists for each of grades 1 through 8 based on seven commonly used spelling series and reading word lists. Also available are fall, winter, and spring norms for correct letter sequences for students in grades 1 through 8.

Spelling Interventions

This section includes three interventions that target spelling. *Three Steps to Better Spelling with Word Boxes* helps students make connections between sound and print by directly manipulating the phonological and orthographic features of words. *Word boxes,* Clay's (1993) extension of Elkonin's (1973) sound boxes, provide a concrete method of demonstrating that words are composed of a sequence of sound segments. Word boxes have been used to enhance early literacy skills in phonemic awareness training programs (Ball & Blachman, 1991; Byrne & Fielding-Barnsley, 1991) and to improve writing skills in Reading Recovery lessons (Clay, 1993). In word box spelling activities, students write letters in the boxes of a drawn rectangle as they pronounce each sound in sequence. Word box instruction has been validated as a strategy for enhancing word identification and spelling skills for early primary grade students in regular education classes (Joseph, 2000a, 2000b), early primary grade students with learning disabilities (Joseph, 1998–1999), and elementary grade students with mild mental retardation (Joseph, 2002) and is superior to traditional phonics instruction in increasing spelling and word identification skills (Joseph, 2000a, 2000b).

Two strategies provide structured practice and immediate performance feedback within a collaborative learning structure. *Spelling Wizardry* creates a partner learning format that can accommodate students with disabilities while simultaneously promoting high levels of productivity for all students. Unlike typical peer tutoring routines, which involve dyads of students, this intervention uses triads to provide additional support to very poor spellers and students with disabilities and is ideal for implementation in inclusive classrooms. The *Add-A-Word for Spelling Success* intervention consists of a directed study technique with a self-managed error correction procedure. Rather than studying a fixed weekly list common to all students, each student uses a four-step practice strategy to learn an individualized "flow list" that is modified each day, based on performance on a daily assessment. In this adaptation, the original individual format has been changed to a peer tutoring format to enhance usability and increase academic responding for all students in the classroom. Studies of the Add-A-Word strategy have documented its effectiveness in improving spelling outcomes across diverse student populations, including low-achieving primary grade students (McAuley & McLaughlin, 1992), elementary school students in regular education (Schermerhorn & McLaughlin, 1997) and special education settings (Pratt-Struthers, Struthers, & Williams, 1983, 1989; Struthers, Bartalamay, Bell, & McLaughlin, 1994), and middle school students with disabilities (McLaughlin, Reiter, Mabee, & Byram, 1991). It is also superior to traditional textbook-based spelling instruction (Schermerhorn & McLaughlin, 1997). Moreover, unlike many other spelling interventions, improvements in spelling performance for Add-A-Word participants generalize to written composition tasks (Pratt-Struthers et al., 1983; Pratt-Struthers, Bartalamay, Williams, & McLaughlin, 1989).

CROSS-REFERENCE: Two interventions in the Academic Productivity section of this chapter also target spelling. The practice and error correction procedures in *Cover Copy Compare–Spelling* are similar to the *Add-A-Word* strategy, but a single spelling list is used for the entire class. *ClassWide Peer Tutoring in Spelling* also uses a partner learning format to provide students with additional practice opportunities and immediate feedback for errors but embeds peer practice within a team-based format.

THREE STEPS TO BETTER SPELLING WITH WORD BOXES

Overview

Word boxes—drawn rectangles divided into sections corresponding to the number of phonemes in words—provide a visual structure for analyzing the sounds of spoken words. When used to target spelling, word box activities help students make connections among the sounds in a word, the letters matching the sounds, and the orthographic pattern of the word. This strategy presents a three-part word box activity consisting of sound segmentation, letter-to-sound matching, and spelling. As the teacher articulates each sound in a word, students first move counters into the boxes, then move letters into the boxes, and finally write letters in the boxes. Typically implemented in one-to-one or small-group settings, word box instruction has also been validated in a whole-class format. Compared with students receiving traditional phonics instruction, students receiving word box instruction display better word identification and spelling skills on taught words as well as on nontaught words. Two variations are presented: (1) a peer-mediated version that increases students' opportunities to respond in a whole-class format and (2) a version suitable for classrooms using a differentiated spelling instructional model.

Purpose

To help students attend to the phonological and orthographic features of words using a visual spelling framework and a guided interactive procedure.

Materials

1. 9″ × 12″ dry erase boards, each with a drawn rectangle divided into boxes according to the number of sounds in the target words (e.g., three boxes for consonant–vowel–consonant words), one per student.
2. Dry erase markers, one per student.
3. Dry erasers or felt squares, one per student.
4. Two to four colored chips (the number corresponding to the number of phonemes in the target words), one set per student.
5. Two to four plastic or tile letters (the number corresponding to the number of letters in the taught words), one set per student.
6. Plastic ziplock bags, each containing a set of the five items listed above, one bag per student.
7. Pictures for target words (optional, see Note 2).
8. List of spelling words for the week, one copy per student pair (optional, see Variation).

Observation (Select One or More)

Option 1

1. Create a spelling test of 20 words based on the phonograms (consonant–vowel–consonant patterns) that have been introduced.
2. Administer the test and calculate percent-correct scores for each student in the class or a target group of students.

Option 2

1. Calculate percent-correct scores on weekly spelling tests for the entire class or a group of target students for several weeks or the previous month.

Option 3

1. Calculate the percentage of students in the entire class with grades of B or better in spelling for the previous grading period.

Intervention Steps

Introduction and Training

1. Tell the class that they are going to play a game called Word Boxes to help everyone become better spellers. Distribute the boards, markers, erasers, and ziplock bags with chips (counters) and letters.
2. Using the procedures presented below, model the word box activity step by step on the chalkboard. Then, using the same target word, have all of the students complete the word box activ-

ity independently and circulate to provide corrective feedback as needed. Provide additional practice with other words until students are familiar with the procedures.

STEP 1: SEGMENTING SOUNDS

1. Ask the students to take out their counters and place them beneath each section of the divided box.
2. As you slowly articulate a word (e.g., "mmmm-aaaa-nnnn" for *man*), have them place the counters sequentially in the respective sections of the box. Move around the room to check students' responses and provide encouragement and feedback as needed.
3. For additional practice, have the students replace the counters beneath each section of the box and then chorally say the word slowly as they simultaneously move the counters one at a time into each section of the box.

STEP 2: LETTER-TO-SOUND MATCHING

1. Have students remove the counters and take out the letters.
2. Have students chorally articulate the word slowly as they place the letters in the appropriate sections of the box.

STEP 3: SPELLING

1. Have students put away the letters, take out their markers, and write the letters of the word in the respective divided sections of the boxes as they slowly pronounce each sound in the word.
2. Have students hold up their boards for you to inspect or move around the room and give corrective feedback as needed.
3. After you have checked students' responses, have them wipe the letters off their boards. At this point, they may need to redraw the divided rectangles on their boards.
4. Repeat all three steps for each of the target words in the lesson.

IMPLEMENTATION

1. Conduct word box activities for 15 to 20 minutes per session, presenting between 6 and 10 words per session, depending on students' literacy development. A new word family can be presented about once a week. Be sure to review previously taught words in subsequent sessions.
2. As students become more proficient in the word box procedure, they can work in pairs or small groups as described in the variations.

Evaluation (Select One or More)

Option 1

1. Compare percent-correct scores on the phonogram spelling test for the entire class or the target students before and after implementation.

Option 2

1. Compare percent-correct scores on weekly spelling tests for the entire class or the target students before and after implementation.

Option 3

1. Compare the percentage of students in the entire class with grades of B or better in spelling before and after implementation.

Variations

Variation 1: Peer Tutoring Format

1. Review the target words by writing them on the chalkboard and having students chorally pronounce each word. Divide the class into pairs of students. Give each pair a copy of the spelling list and a set of word box materials (omitting the counters). Have students take turns administering the list of spelling words to their partners and performing the word box activity. Have students check off each correctly spelled word on the list. If time permits, have students readminister any misspelled words to each other.

Variation 2: Differentiated Instructional Format

1. After initial classwide training, give students a copy of the list for their spelling group. Review the words for the first group by writing them on a dry erase board and having students chorally pronounce the words. Then pair students as described in Variation 1 above and have them practice while you move on to the next group.

Note

1. For younger children or English language learners, display pictures of the target words and have students chorally name and discuss their meaning prior to the word box activity.

Source

Joseph, L. M. (2000b). Using word boxes as a large group phonics approach in a first grade classroom. *Reading Horizons, 41,* 117–127. Copyright 2000 by Western Michigan University. Adapted by permission.

Additional Resources

Daly, E. J., Chafouleas, S., & Skinner, C. H. (2005). *Interventions for reading problems: Designing and evaluating effective strategies.* New York: Guilford Press.

This text presents a framework for selecting, implementing, and monitoring evidence-based strategies targeting phonological awareness, fluency, and comprehension. Included among the reproducible forms are examples of word boxes for two-, three-, and four-phoneme words.

SPELLING WIZARDS: ACCOMMODATING DIVERSE LEARNERS WITH PARTNER SPELLING

Overview

As more children with special needs enter the regular classroom, teachers are encountering a wider range of spelling abilities among their students. In this game-like intervention, students work in mixed-ability triads to provide each other with active spelling practice and immediate corrective feedback in a 20-minute three-step tutoring routine. The structure of the partner spelling strategy permits teachers to incorporate a variety of accommodations and adaptations to meet individual learning needs, including individualizing spelling lists based on students' IEP objectives and previous spelling performance. In the original study, implemented in one fourth- and two fifth-grade general education classrooms, each of which included a student with severe disabilities, the strategy resulted in substantial gains in spelling accuracy for all three students with special needs without negatively affecting the performance of three normally achieving comparison peers. Partner spelling also increased rates of academic responding and reduced rates of competing behavior for five of the six target students, compared with traditional spelling instruction. Participating teachers rated the strategy highly and reported that it helped their low-performing students became more confident spellers. A variation for classrooms using a differentiated spelling instructional model is also presented.

Purpose

To improve spelling performance with a collaborative learning format designed to accommodate students with a wide range of spelling skills.

Materials

1. List of 20 spelling words drawn from the regular spelling curriculum or grade-level word lists, one per student triad.
2. List of 5 to 20 spelling words for students with identified disabilities or very poor spelling skills; words for students with disabilities should be selected jointly by the general education teacher and the special education teacher to be consistent with students' IEP goals and objectives.
3. Sheets of lined paper, one per student.

Observation (Select One or Both)

Option 1

1. Calculate percent-correct scores on weekly spelling tests for the entire class or a group of target students for several weeks or the previous month.

Option 2

1. Using a *Classwide Scanning Form* with a 3-, 5-, or 10-minute interval, scan the room, starting with the front and ending with the back, and tally the number of students exhibiting academic responding and competing behaviors as defined below.
   a. *Academic responding* is defined as working on the task at hand, looking at the teacher during presentations, engaging in verbal behaviors related to the academic task, and any other behavior relevant to the lesson.
   b. *Competing behavior* is defined as playing with nonlesson materials, failing to look at the teacher during presentations, talking about subjects unrelated to the task, failing to comply with teacher directions, and any other behavior not relevant to the lesson.
2. Conduct these observations during the spelling period for 30 to 45 minutes for 4 to 7 days.

Intervention Steps

1. Divide the class into triads consisting of students with a range of spelling performance levels. If the class includes students with disabilities or very poor spelling skills, include no more than one student with a disability or one very low-performing student in each triad.

2. Tell the students that they will be working in teams of three so everyone can have more fun and get the most out of the spelling lesson. Explain that students will take turns serving in one of three roles: (a) the "word wizard," who writes and orally spells words; (b) the "word conjurer," who presents the words and gives feedback; and (c) the "word keeper," who checks the word wizard's spelling.

3. Select three students to demonstrate the strategy while the rest of the class observes. Guide the students through the steps described below, emphasizing the roles played by each member of the team.

   a. The word conjurer randomly selects a word from the appropriate spelling list (the general word list for students without disabilities or an individualized list for a poor speller or student with disabilities), and says, "Spell ___" to the word wizard. If the word conjurer cannot read the word to be spelled, the word keeper supplies the word or raises his or her hand to ask for assistance.

   b. The word wizard has 5 seconds to write the word and spell it aloud.

   c. The word conjurer and the word keeper jointly check the spelling accuracy of the response. The word conjurer then provides feedback to the word wizard by saying, "I agree" or "I disagree." If the word wizard did not spell the word correctly, the word keeper shows him or her the word on the list, and the steps are repeated until the word wizard spells the word correctly.

   d. After the word wizard has had an opportunity to spell all of the words on his or her list, the roles are rotated until each student has had an opportunity to serve as word wizard. Students should receive at least one trial on each word on their list during partner spelling sessions.

4. Conduct one more demonstration, using another student triad. Then have the entire class practice the procedures while you circulate, giving praise for appropriate tutoring and corrective feedback as needed. Also point out examples of cooperative and helpful tutoring behaviors as you move around the room.

5. Conduct partner spelling for 20 minutes twice a week during the regularly scheduled spelling instructional period, or more frequently, if desired.

Evaluation (Select One or Both)

Option 1

1. Compare percent-correct scores on weekly spelling tests for the entire class or a group of target students before and after implementation.

Option 2

1. Compare classwide rates of academic responding and competing behavior during the spelling instructional period before and after implementation.

Variation: Differentiated Instructional Format

1. Form student triads based on spelling groups and provide each triad with a list appropriate for that group.

Note

1. Because triads that include very low-performing students or students with disabilities may proceed through the tutoring routine at a slower pace than the rest of the groups, even with individualized lists, have enrichment spelling activities available for early finishers.

Source

McDonnell, J., Thorson, N., Allen, C., & Mathot-Buckner, C. (2000). The effects of partner learning during spelling for students with severe disabilities and their peers. *Journal of Behavioral Education, 10,* 107–121. Copyright 2000 by Springer Science and Business Media. Adapted by permission.

ADD-A-WORD FOR SPELLING SUCCESS

Overview

In many classrooms, the typical spelling program consists of assigning the same list of words to the entire class on Monday, having students complete various spelling activities during the week, and administering a test on Friday. Unfortunately, such a program is ineffective for many students, especially students with disabilities, because it fails to provide sufficient practice or accommodate individual rates of progress. In this intervention, students learn a five-step self-managed procedure for daily spelling practice, using words from individual "flow lists" that are adjusted based on performance on daily tests. Words must be spelled correctly for two consecutive days before they are dropped from the list and a new word added. Correctly spelled words are retested at two later dates to assess retention and mastery, after which they are dropped from the student's list. The Add-A-Word procedure has resulted in improved spelling achievement for poor spellers, normally progressing students, and students with disabilities in elementary and middle school settings, with improvements generalizing to creative writing assignments. In this adaptation, spelling practice and assessments occur in a partner learning format to reduce teacher preparation and testing time and permit students to receive feedback more promptly. A variation with a public posting component to enhance motivation is also presented.

Purpose

To improve spelling performance with individualized spelling lists, daily practice sessions with a structured error correction procedure, and daily progress monitoring.

Materials

1. List of spelling words drawn from the regular spelling curriculum, grade-level word lists, and/ or errors in the student's creative writing or other written productions, one per student with the student's name and date on it. Use lists of 5 to 10 words for primary grade students and 10 to 18 words for elementary to middle school students; you will need to prepare new lists each day, based on students' performance on the previous day.
2. Individual master spelling lists, consisting of words consistently spelled correctly, one per student.
3. Spelling notebooks or folders, containing an index card and sheets of lined paper, one per student.
4. Spelling practice sheet, one per student (see Figure 4.10 on p. 261).
5. Overhead projector and transparency (optional).
6. Posterboard chart with a list of student names or student pairs on the left-hand side and columns for the days of the week on the right-hand side (optional, see Variation 2).
7. Gold stars (optional, see Variation 2).

Observation (Select One or More)

1. Calculate percent-correct scores on weekly spelling tests for the entire class or a group of target students for several weeks or for the previous month.
2. Calculate the percentage of students in the entire class who score 90% or better on weekly spelling tests for several weeks or the previous month.
3. Administer *Curriculum-Based Spelling Probes* (S-CBM) to a target group of students.

Intervention Steps

Introduction and Training

1. Using information obtained during the observation period, create student pairs by matching students with similar spelling skills. Rotate spelling pairs every 3 or 4 weeks.
2. Tell the students that they will be working in pairs to become better spellers, using a method called "Add-A-Word." Explain that they will be practicing and taking daily tests on their own individual spelling lists. The results of the daily tests will be used to create a master list consisting of words they have learned to spell. Once a word has been spelled correctly on 2 consecutive days, it will be dropped from the daily practice list and placed on the master list, and a new word will be added to the daily list. After 5 days, any words that have been removed from the list will be placed on the list again as a review word and retested. If spelled correctly, the word or words will be placed on the list again in 1 month. If a word is misspelled at any time, it will be returned to the list.
3. Using the chalkboard or the overhead projector, demonstrate the steps in the procedure as described below.
   a. *Step 1: Study.* The student softly pronounces the first word on his or her list and looks closely at its spelling features.
   b. *Step 2: Copy.* The student copies the word from the list onto the spelling practice sheet and checks the original list to see that the word has been correctly copied.
   c. *Step 3: Cover.* The student covers the word with an index card and writes the word from memory next to the covered word.
   d. *Step 4: Compare.* The student uncovers the word and compares his or her second spelling of the word with the spelling on the list to determine correctness. If the word is spelled correctly, the student goes on to the next word. If the word is misspelled, the student erases the word and repeats the copy, cover, and compare procedure with that word until the word is written correctly.
4. Assign pairs and have the students move to partner spelling stations (paired desks or some other arrangement). Distribute the spelling folders and spelling lists and conduct a classwide practice session while you circulate to provide encouragement and assistance, as needed.
5. When both students in the pair have written each word on their list correctly from memory twice, have them exchange lists and use their partner's list to administer spelling tests to each other in their spelling notebooks.
6. Using the original lists, have the partners correct each other's tests, while you circulate to provide assistance as needed.

Implementation

1. At the end of each spelling period, collect the notebooks and spelling lists and review the tests for accuracy. Use the results to prepare a new list for each student for the following day based on his or her performance. Also update students' master lists as needed.
2. For best results, implement the Add-A-Word strategy three or four times a week.

Evaluation (Select One or More)

1. Compare percent-correct scores on weekly spelling tests for the entire class or the group of target students before and after implementation.
2. Compare the percentage of students in the entire class who score 90% or better on weekly spelling tests before and after implementation.
3. Compare S-CBM scores for the target group of students before and after implementation.

Variation: Add-A-Word with Public Posting

1. For public posting based on individual performance, list student names in alphabetical order on the chart. Each day that a student achieves 80% correct or better (or some other criterion) on his or her list, give that student a gold star to place on the chart beside his or her name. Alternately, have students post color-coded stars to indicate improvement (red star) and perfect performance (blue star) rather than a specific accuracy criterion.
2. For public posting based on team performance, list the names of students by assigned pairs on the chart. Permit a team to post a gold star if both partners meet the accuracy criterion or a red or blue star if both partners achieve an improved or perfect performance, respectively. If one partner earns a red star and the other earns a blue star on the same day, the pair may choose which star they prefer to post.

Notes

1. Allow two sessions of about 30 to 45 minutes for training, the first for demonstrating the individual practice procedures and the second for reviewing the procedures and demonstrating test administration, scoring, and recording procedures in the paired format.
2. Using a word processing program to generate daily spelling lists and maintain master lists greatly enhances the usability of this intervention.

Name of student: _____ Date: _____				Spelling Practice Sheet	
Words to practice	Check spelling	Copy word	Cover and compare	Spelling correct?	Correct if needed
	+ —			+ —	
	+ —			+ —	
	+ —			+ —	
	+ —			+ —	
	+ —			+ —	
	+ —			+ —	
	+ —			+ —	
	+ —			+ —	
	+ —			+ —	
	+ —			+ —	

FIGURE 4.10. Add-A-Word spelling practice sheet. Adapted from Schermerhorn and McLaughlin (1997, p. 29). Copyright 1997 by The Haworth Press. Adapted by permission.

Sources

Schermerhorn, P. K., & McLaughlin, T. F. (1997). Effects of the Add-A-Word Spelling Program on test accuracy, grades, and retention of spelling words with fifth and sixth grade regular education students. *Child and Family Behavior Therapy, 19,* 23–35. The Haworth Press. Adapted by permission.

Struthers, J. P., Bartalamay, H., Bell, S., & McLaughlin, T. F. (1994). An analysis of the Add-A-Word Spelling Program and public posting across three categories of children with special needs. *Reading Improvement, 31,* 28–36. Copyright 1994 by Project Innovation, Inc. Adapted by permission.

INTERVENTIONS TO IMPROVE WRITTEN EXPRESSION

Helping students to improve their writing performance is a complex and challenging task because of the multiple skills required for proficient writing, including strategies for regulating the writing process, text-production skills, and knowledge of writing types (De La Paz & Graham, 2002; Graham & Harris, 2002). In the past two decades, research on the cognitive processes underlying writing has led to a shift in writing instruction from an emphasis on *product* (e.g., grammar, mechanics, and content) to the *processes* used to generate written productions (e.g., internal dialoguing, developing a sense of audience, and incorporating feedback from others). As a result, writing interventions increasingly target skills related to process-oriented aspects of writing, including planning, content generation, and revising (Gersten & Baker, 2001). One of the most promising approaches to improving writing skills is *Self-Regulated Strategy Development* (SRSD), an instructional model that combines explicit teaching of compositional strategies with instruction in a set of self-regulatory procedures, including goal setting, self-instruction, and self-monitoring. Developed by Graham and Harris and their colleagues at the University of Maryland for low-performing students, it also incorporates components targeting the limited persistence and low levels of productivity characteristic of struggling writers (Graham & Harris, 2003; Graham, Harris, & Troia, 2000). More than 25 years of research have demonstrated that SRSD improves the quantity and quality of narrative and expository writing for students with writing disabilities, students with emotional and behavioral problems, and normally developing writers in a variety of settings, including one-to-one after-school tutoring (Troia, Graham, & Harris, 1999), small-group resource room programs (Graham & Harris, 1989), and whole-group instruction in regular and inclusive classrooms (Danoff, Harris, & Graham, 1993; De La Paz, 1999; Mason, Harris & Graham, 2002; Sexton, Harris, & Graham, 1998). In addition to enhancing writing performance, SRSD is also associated with higher levels of self-efficacy and more positive attitudes toward writing for students (Harris & Graham, 1999; Sexton et al., 1998).

Writing Interventions

This section includes four SRSD-based interventions that focus on different types of writing, including narrative writing, general expository writing, and essay writing, or specific aspects of the writing process, such as planning and revising. In *Strategy Instruction in Story Writing,* students are trained to use a self-questioning text evaluation strategy that targets motivation to write as well as story writing performance. Strategy instruction components in this intervention include the development of metacognitive knowledge, teacher–student and student–student dialogues, and direct instruction in text structures and the writing process. Although expository writing is an important competency for students, beginning in the upper elementary grades, surprisingly few studies have evaluated the effectiveness of interventions focusing on expository writing skills and even fewer for students in general education. *Writing Power: Cognitive Strategy Instruction in Expository Writing* incorporates several features characteristic of effective strategy instruction: (1) writing-related dialogue, including teacher "think-alouds" and student–student dialogues; (2) scaffolded instruction during lessons and writing sessions; and (3) an emphasis on writing as a collaborative rather than a solitary activity. Procedural facilitators in the form of written prompts are also provided to help make the strategies, self-talk, and text structures involved in the writing process visible to students.

Poor writers, especially students with learning disabilities, typically plan minimally or not at all during the composition process (De La Paz, 1999; De La Paz, Owen, Harris, & Graham, 2000). In *PLAN and WRITE: Self-Regulated Strategy Development for Essay Writing*, students learn a strategy for planning and writing expository essays that is embedded in a set of self-regulatory procedures. Two mnemonics are incorporated to remind students of the planning steps that occur before and during the writing process. The PLAN and WRITE strategy has been validated as an effective intervention for middle school students in regular classrooms (De La Paz & Graham, 1997, 2002) and middle school students with and without disabilities in inclusive classrooms (De La Paz, 1999).

The fourth intervention in this section focuses on teaching revision strategies. For most skilled writers, revising plays a critical role in the composing process. In contrast, less skilled writers often fail to revise their compositions, and when they do, their revisions generally fail to improve the quality of their work (Beal, Garrod, & Bonitatibus, 1990; De La Paz, Swanson, & Graham, 1998). In *Peer Editing for Effective Revision*, pairs of students work together to learn and practice a four-question editing strategy. In keeping with the increasing use of computers in the writing process in the classroom, this intervention uses word processing programs to facilitate text revisions. A paper-and-pencil variation is included for teachers who have limited access to computers or who prefer not to use them as part of writing instruction.

Evaluating the Effectiveness of Writing Interventions

Evaluating the effectiveness of interventions targeting written expression presents numerous challenges because of the complexity of the writing process and the lack of a generally agreed upon theory of writing development (Rathvon, 2004b). In fact, deciding how to rate students' written productions is perhaps the greatest problem in evaluating writing curricula and instructional practices. In addition, evaluating the impact of writing interventions on student writing assignments can be extremely time-consuming, especially on a classwide basis. The evaluation strategies in this section have been designed to be as brief and practical as possible and still provide meaningful information about students' response to interventions and progress toward end-of-year standards. Measures include simple holistic scales of writing quality, proportion of mechanical errors, number and quality of revisions, and scales assessing the inclusion of story grammar elements. In addition to the evaluation procedures provided for each intervention, procedures for curriculum-based measurement in writing (W-CBM) are also provided.

Curriculum-Based Measurement in Writing

Curriculum-based measurement in writing (W-CBM) consists of a standardized set of procedures requiring students to write for 3 minutes in response to an instructional-level story starter or essay prompt. Because the utility of W-CBM scoring methods varies by grade level, separate versions are presented for early primary grade students, elementary students, and secondary level students. For students in the elementary grades, the number of words written, number of words spelled correctly, and number of correct word sequences produced during writing probes are strongly correlated with standardized measures of written expression and teacher ratings of writing skill (Gansle, Noell, VanDerHeyden, Naquin, & Slider, 2002; Marston, 1989; Parker, Tindal, & Hasbrouck, 1991) and can differentiate between students with learning disabilities and typically achieving students (Watkinson & Lee, 1992). At the secondary level, however, where the writing process is more complex, words written and words spelled correctly are not sensitive to individual differences and are only weakly or moderately correlated with criterion measures. Instead, more complex metrics, such as the number of correct word sequences or the number of correct word sequences minus incorrect word sequences, are better predictors of writing proficiency (Espin, Scierka, Skare, & Halverson, 1999; Espin & Tindal, 1998; Espin et al., 2000; Jewell & Malecki, 2005; Malecki & Jewell, 2003). Similarly, for students in the early primary grades, who are just beginning to develop written production skills, the standard W-CBM procedure is of limited utility in monitoring writing progress or evaluating the effectiveness of writing interventions because of *floor effects* (i.e., many students obtain very low scores). At this stage of writing development, W-CBM probes consisting of dictated words or sentences are highly correlated with teacher ratings of writing ability and other global judgments of writing performance (Lembke, Deno, & Hall, 2003).

CURRICULUM-BASED MEASUREMENT IN WRITING

Overview

In curriculum-based measurement in writing (W-CBM), students are provided with story starters or writing prompts and asked to write for 3 minutes. The number of words written, the number of words spelled correctly, and the number of correct word sequences during these writing probes are strongly correlated with standardized measures of written expression, teacher ratings of students' writing skills, and other measures of general writing proficiency. Moreover, W-CBM can reliably differentiate between students with learning disabilities and their normally achieving peers, as well as among students enrolled in basic, regular, and enriched levels of English class, and is sensitive to changes in writing performance over time. Because the predictive power of W-CBM tasks and metrics varies across grade levels, three versions of W-CBM are presented: (1) one for early primary grade students that substitutes word or sentence dictation tasks for story starters; (2) one for elementary school students; and (3) one for middle and high school students. Each version includes several validated scoring options, ranging from simple to more complex. Writing probes may be administered to students individually, in small groups, or in whole-class settings. Student performance can be evaluated by means of local norms, intrastudent comparisons, and, for certain metrics, web-based norms.

Purpose

1. To identify students in need of additional instruction and intervention in writing.
2. To provide information for planning writing instruction.
3. To monitor student progress in general writing proficiency.
4. To evaluate the effectiveness of writing interventions and instructional programs.

Materials

1. Pencils with erasers, two per student (early primary grade students); pencils with erasers or pens, two per student (elementary and secondary students).

2. Stopwatch or timer.
3. Equal-interval graph paper or graphing program (optional).

Additional Materials for Early Primary Grade Students

1. Sheets of lined paper, one per student.
2. Lists of high-frequency words, 30 words per list (word dictation task), and/or lists of 12 sentences, each consisting of 5 to 7 words (sentence dictation task).

Additional Materials for Elementary and Secondary Students

1. Sheets of lined paper with a writing prompt printed at the top, one per student, with additional sheets of lined paper.
2. Story starters or topic sentences, such as:
   a. When Marcus woke up that morning, he knew that his life was about to change.
   b. It was a dark and stormy night.
   c. I will never forget the first time I met my best friend.
   d. Describe the clothing that students in your school wear.
   e. Explain why local school boards should include a student representative.

Assessment Steps: Early Primary Grade Students (Grades 1–2)

Administration

1. Give each student a sheet of lined paper and two pencils. Word diction is recommended for first-semester first graders and lower performing students. Either word or sentence dictation may be used for second-semester first graders, second graders, and higher performing early primary grade students. Give the following directions:

   > "I want you to write some words (sentences). I am going to read each word (sentence) twice and then I want you to write it. If you don't know how to spell a word, do your best to write it anyway. Are there any questions?"

2. Dictate each word (sentence) twice and then pause for students to write. After students have finished the current word (sentence) or have paused for 5 (10) seconds, move on to the next word (sentence).
3. Continue dictating words or sentences for 3 minutes. After 3 minutes, say, "Stop and put your pencil down."

Scoring and Interpretation

OPTION 1: WORDS WRITTEN (WW)

1. Count the number of written words. A *word* is defined as a sequence of letters that can be recognized, even if it is misspelled. Do not count numerals as words.
2. Compare the WW score to local norms or students' previous scores.

OPTION 2: WORDS SPELLED CORRECTLY (WSC)

1. Count the number of words spelled correctly. A *correctly spelled word* is defined as a recognizable, correctly spelled word. Do not award credit to words containing reversals.
2. Compare the WSC score to local norms or students' previous scores.

OPTION 3: CORRECT LETTER SEQUENCES (CLS; WORD DICTATION TASK ONLY)

1. Count the number of correct letter sequences. A *correct letter sequence* is defined as two adjacent letters that are correctly placed in a word.
2. Compare the CLS score to local norms or students' previous scores.

OPTION 4: CORRECT WORD SEQUENCES (CWS; SENTENCE DICTATION TASK ONLY)

1. Count the number of correct word sequences. A *correct word sequence* is defined as two adjacent correctly spelled words that are semantically and syntactically acceptable within the context of the sentence. Beginning and ending punctuation are counted in the sequences. Give credit for capitalization on the first word of a sentence and appropriate punctuation at the end of a sentence, and do not award credit if appropriate capitalization and end punctuation are omitted.
2. Compare the CWS score to local norms or students' previous scores.

OPTION 5: CORRECT MINUS INCORRECT WORD SEQUENCES (C-IWS; SENTENCE DICTATION TASK ONLY)

1. Count the number of correct word sequences as described above. Then count the number of incorrect word sequences. An *incorrect word sequence* is defined as two adjacent words, one or both of which is syntactically incorrect, grammatically incorrect, incorrectly spelled, and/or incorrectly capitalized if it occurs at the beginning of a sentence, and/or incorrectly punctuated if it occurs at the end of the sentence.
2. Calculate the number of correct minus incorrect word sequences by subtracting the number of incorrect word sequences from the number of correct word sequences (see Figure 4.11 on p. 268).
3. Compare the C-IWS score to local norms, students' previous scores, or web-based norms.

Assessment Steps: Elementary Grade Students (Grades 1–6)

Administration

1. Give each student a sheet of lined paper with a story starter printed across the top, an extra sheet of lined paper, and two pencils or pens. Give the following directions:

   > "I want you to write a story. I am going to read a sentence to you first, and then I want you to write a short story about what happens. You will have 1 minute to think about the story you will write and then have 3 minutes to write it. Do your best work. If you don't know how to spell a word, you should guess. Use the sentence I read as your first sentence but don't write that sentence again. Are there any questions? For the next minute, think about … [read story starter]."

2. After 1 minute, say, "Begin writing."
3. After 3 minutes, say, "Stop and put your pencil/pen down."

Scoring and Interpretation

OPTION 1: WORDS WRITTEN (WW)

1. Count the number of written words. A *written word* is defined as a word that can be recognized, even if it is misspelled. If the student writes a title, include the title in the scoring. Do not count dates or numerals (e.g., *2007, 3*) as words.
2. If a student stops writing before the 3 minutes are up, divide the number of correctly written words by the number of seconds spent writing and multiply by 180 to obtain the words-written-correctly rate per 3 minutes.

3. If the student writes the story starter as part of the story, include the words in the starter as part of the total word count.
4. Compare the WW score to local norms, students' previous scores, or web-based norms.

OPTION 2: WORDS SPELLED CORRECTLY (WSC; SEE ABOVE)

OPTION 3: CORRECT LETTER SEQUENCES (CLS; SEE ABOVE)

OPTION 4: CORRECT WORD SEQUENCES (CWS)

1. Score as above. Compare the CWS score to local norms, students' previous scores, or web-based norms.

OPTION 5: QUALITY EVALUATION OF WRITING MECHANICS

1. Based on writing mechanics such as capitalization, spelling, punctuation, sentence construction, and paragraph construction, as well as the overall appearance of the written product, assign a quality rating from 1 to 5 (1 = poor; 2 = fair; 3 = average; 4 = good; 5 = very good).

Assessment Steps: Middle and High School Students (Grades 6 or 7–12)

Administration

1. Give each student a sheet of lined paper with a story starter (topic sentence) printed across the top, an extra sheet of lined paper, and two pencils or pens. Give the following directions:

> "I want you to write a short story (essay). I am going to read a sentence to you first, and then I want you to write a short story about what happens (a short essay about that topic). You will have 1 minute to think about the story (essay) you will write and then have 3 minutes to write it. Do your best work. If you don't know how to spell a word, you should guess. Use the sentence I read as your first sentence but don't write that sentence again. Are there any questions? For the next minute, think about … [read writing prompt]."

2. After 1 minute, say, "Begin writing."
3. After 3 minutes, say, "Stop and put your pencil/pen down."

Scoring and Interpretation

OPTION 1: CORRECT WORD SEQUENCES (CWS; SEE ABOVE)

OPTION 2: CORRECT MINUS INCORRECT WORD SEQUENCES (C-IWS; SEE ABOVE)

OPTION 3: SENTENCES WRITTEN (SW)

1. Count the number of sentences written. A *sentence* is defined as any string of words separated from another group of words by a period, question mark, or exclamation point. Sentences do not have to be complete or grammatically correct to receive credit.
2. Compare the SW score to local norms or students' previous scores.

Notes

1. Guidelines for developing local writing norms are provided below.
2. High-frequency words for word dictation and sentence dictation tasks can be found in Harris and Jacobson (1972) or on one of the many Dolch word list websites (e.g., *http://reading.indiana.edu/ieo/bibs/dolchwordlist.html*). Examples of narrative story starters can be found in Shapiro (2004a) and Hosp et al. (2007).

[+ The + boy + went + to + the] – stor – [but + he] – forgott – [his + money +.] – he – gone – home [+ to + get + it +.]

FIGURE 4.11. Example of a correct-minus-incorrect-word-sequence (C–IWS) scoring for a sentence from a written expression probe. Plus signs indicate correct word sequences (CWS), whereas minus signs indicate incorrect word sequences (I–CWS). Errors are underlined, and strings of correct word sequences are set off by brackets. In this sentence, there are 12 CWS and 7 I–CWS, for a C–IWS score of 5. Adapted from Espin et al. (2000, p. 144). Copyright 2000 by PRO-ED, Inc. Adapted by permission.

Sources

Espin, C. A., Scierka, B. J., Skare, S., & Halverson, N. (1999). Criterion-related validity of curriculum-based measures in writing for secondary school students. *Reading and Writing Quarterly, 14,* 5–27. Copyright 1999 by Taylor & Francis Group, LLC., *http://www.taylorandfrancis.com.* Adapted by permission.

Espin, C., Shin, J., Deno, S. L., Skare, S., Robinson, S., & Benner, B. (2000). Identifying indicators of written expression proficiency for middle school students. *Journal of Special Education, 34,* 140–153. Copyright 2000 by PRO-ED, Inc. Adapted by permission.

Lembke, E., Deno, S. L., & Hall, K. (2003). Identifying an indicator of growth in early writing proficiency for elementary school students. *Assessment for Effective Intervention, 28,* 23–36. Copyright 2003 by PRO-ED, Inc. Adapted by permission.

Shapiro, E. S. (2004a). *Academic skills problems: Direct assessment and intervention* (3rd ed.). New York: Guilford Press. Copyright 2004 by The Guilford Press. Adapted by permission.

Weissenburger, J. W., & Espin, C. (2005). Curriculum-based measures of writing across grade levels. *Journal of School Psychology, 43,* 153–169. Copyright 2005 by Elsevier. Adapted by permission.

Additional Resources

Intervention Central (*http://www.interventioncentral.org*) offers W-CBM administration and scoring sheets for total words, correctly spelled words, and correct word sequences. AIMSweb (*http://www.aimsweb.com*) provides fall, winter, and spring norms for correct word sequences and total words written for students in grades 1 through 8, as well as web-based data management and graphing.

DEVELOPING LOCAL NORMS FOR CURRICULUM-BASED MEASUREMENT IN WRITING

Although web-based user norms are now available for W-CBM at AIMSweb (*http://www. AIMSweb.com*), developing local norms is recommended because of wide variations in writing instruction across districts and states. Moreover, normative data are available for only two scoring options: words written and correct word sequences. Procedures for creating local norms at the classroom, building, and district level are described below, based on Stewart and Kaminski's (2002) sampling plan suggestions.

Classroom/Grade Norms

1. Three methods can be used to sample students for classroom or grade norms: (1) testing a randomly selected subset of 7 to 10 students chosen from among the students in the classroom who are *not* experiencing difficulty in written expression, (2) testing a randomly selected subset of 7 to 10 students from the entire class, or (3) testing all the students in

the classroom. For schools with more than one classroom per grade, use one of these three methods to select students and include a minimum of 7 to 10 students from each classroom.

2. Administer a grade-appropriate W-CBM (i.e., word list, sentence list, story starter, or topic sentence) to the sample of students.
3. Score the results, using one or more grade-appropriate metrics.
4. Calculate the median (middle) score for each metric and use it to evaluate the writing performance of individual students in that classroom or grade.

Building- and/or District-Level Norms

1. Randomly select 15 to 20% of students at each grade level (at least 20 students per grade). A sample of 100 students per grade is necessary to obtain reliable percentile ranks.
2. Administer a grade-appropriate W-CBM (i.e., word list, sentence list, story starter, or topic sentence) as described above.
3. Score the results, using one or more grade-appropriate metrics.
4. Calculate the median score for each metric and use it to evaluate the writing performance of individual students in the building.
5. For district-level norms, combine building-level norms, aggregating across years if needed to obtain samples of 100 students per grade.

STRATEGY INSTRUCTION IN STORY WRITING

Overview

Self-regulated strategy development (SRSD) is an instructional approach that teaches students a multistep strategy for planning, writing, and revising in the context of a set of self-regulation procedures, including goal setting, self-instruction, and self-reinforcement. In this classwide version, students learn a five-step strategy for composing stories, as well as strategies for regulating the writing process in a series of minilessons. Paired and small-group activities are included at several steps to provide opportunities for feedback and collaborative practice without direct teacher supervision. Students also learn a mnemonic to help them remember the story grammar elements taught in the strategy lessons. In the original study, implemented in two fifth-grade classrooms and one fourth-grade classroom, each of which included a student with learning disabilities, the story writing strategy resulted in longer, more complete, and higher quality stories for the students with learning disabilities and their normally achieving peers. Moreover, the improvements in story structure and quality were maintained and generalized to other story writing tasks for the majority of students. A variation that extends partner learning opportunities to additional stages of the training is also included.

Purpose

To improve narrative writing performance with a self-regulated story grammar strategy.

Materials

1. Posterboard chart listing the five strategy steps and the mnemonic for remembering the seven story parts (see Intervention Steps, Stage 3).
2. Strategy cue cards, consisting of index cards listing the five steps and mnemonic, one each per student.
3. Previously written stories or typed sets of sample stories, two or three per student.

4. Overhead projector, blank transparencies, and transparencies of sample stories and the five steps and mnemonic (optional).
5. Writing portfolios or notebooks containing sheets of lined paper and, if desired, graph paper, one per student.
6. Story starters (e.g., "When Martina walked into her homeroom Friday morning, she noticed right away that something had changed.").

Observation (Select One or Both)

Option 1

1. Select a picture that would be interesting to your students and easy to write about, and display it so that the entire class can see it. Give the following instructions:

   "Look at this picture and write a story to go with it in your writing notebook. Do your best."

2. Score the stories for each of the following seven elements: (a) main character[s], (b) location, (c) time, (d) characters' goal(s), (e) action to achieve the goals, (f) resolution, and (g) characters' reaction, as follows: 0 points = element is not present; 1 point = element is present; 2 points = element is highly developed.
3. Award 1 additional point for each of the following characteristics: (a) the story contains two or more goals, (b) the story contains more than one well-defined episode, and (c) story events happen in a logical manner (total of 17 possible points per story).

Option 2

1. Evaluate two or three previously written stories for a group of target students or the entire class according to the following 4-point rating scale: 1 = poor, 2 = fair, 3 = good, 4 = excellent. Consider organization, sentence structure, grammar, vocabulary, spelling, and imaginative content in evaluating overall story quality.

Intervention Steps

Stage 1: Initial Conference

1. Tell the students that they will be learning a strategy to help them write better stories and to have more fun doing it.
2. Lead a discussion of story writing that includes the following: (a) the seven common parts of a story (see Intervention Steps, Stage 3); (b) the goal for learning the composition strategy, that is, to write stories that are more fun to write and more fun for others to read; and (c) the role of story parts in improving story quality.

Stage 2: Preskill Development

1. Discuss the parts commonly included in the two major components of a story: (a) *setting*, including main character[s], time, and place; and (b) *episode*, including the characters' goals, actions to achieve goals, resolution, and the characters' reactions.
2. Guide students in identifying examples of the seven story elements in literature the class is currently reading and discuss the different ways that writers develop and expand story parts.
3. Using sample story starters or writing prompts, have the class practice generating ideas for story parts.
4. Have students select two or three previously written stories from their portfolios or provide

handouts of two or three sample stories, and have them determine which story parts are present in each story.

5. Using an overhead projector or the chalkboard, demonstrate how to create a bar graph recording the number of parts in a story. Explain that students can use graphing to monitor their own use of story parts and their progress in learning the composition strategy.

Stage 3: Discussion of the Composition Strategy

1. Display the chart and distribute the cue cards listing the five strategy steps and the story part reminder (mnemonic), as follows:

THE COMPOSITION STRATEGY

Step 1: Think of a story you would like to share with others.
Step 2: Let your mind be free.
Step 3: Write down the story part reminder: W(ho)–W(hen)–W(here); What =2; How = 2.
Step 4: Write down ideas for each part.
Step 5: Write your story, using good story parts and making sure your story makes sense.

THE STORY PART REMINDER

Who is the main character? Who else is in the story?
When does the story take place?
Where does the story take place?
What does the main character do or want to do? What do other characters do or want to do?
What happens when the main character does it or tries to do it? What happens with other characters?
How does the story end?
How does the main character feel? How do other characters feel?

2. Discuss the rationale for each of the five steps of the composition strategy.
3. Explain the procedures for learning the strategy, stressing students' roles as collaborators and the importance of effort in mastering the strategy.
4. Provide models of self-statements that can help students generate good ideas and story parts when writing. Invite students to volunteer self-statements they find useful (e.g., "Slow down, I can take my time," "I can do it," etc.). Then have students generate three creativity self-statements and record them in their writing portfolios.

STAGE 4: MODELING

1. Share a story idea with the class and model how to use the strategy to develop the idea further while "thinking aloud."
2. Call on students for assistance as you plan and make notes for each story part on the chalkboard and write a first draft of the story.
3. While composing the story, model five types of self-statements: (a) problem definition ("What do I need to do?"), (b) planning ("First, I need to think of a story to share"), (c) self-evaluation ("Does this part make sense?"), (d) self-reinforcement ("People are going to like this part!"), and (e) coping ("I can write good stories!").
4. When the story is completed, lead a discussion of the importance of what we say to ourselves during the creative process, and identify the types of self-statements you have used. Have students review their previously recorded self-statements and revise them as desired.

STAGE 5: MEMORIZATION OF THE STRATEGY AND MNEMONIC

1. Divide the class into pairs and have students work together to memorize the five-step strategy, the mnemonic, and several positive self-statements about writing.
2. Have the pairs review the story parts in one or more of their own previously written stories or sample stories and graph the number of parts in their writing portfolios. Circulate to provide encouragement and assistance, as needed.

STAGE 6: COLLABORATIVE PRACTICE

1. Have students work in pairs to plan stories collaboratively. Remind students that the goal is to include all seven of the story parts in each story. For students who typically use all or nearly all of the story parts, discuss how they can improve their parts with more detail, elaboration, and action.
2. Circulate to make sure students are using the strategy steps and mnemonic appropriately. Encourage students to use their self-statements covertly, if they are not already doing so.
3. When students complete a story, have them work with their partners to identify the story parts, compare their counts of the parts, fill in their graphs, and compare the numbers to the goal of seven parts per story.
4. Lead a class discussion of the ways students can maintain the strategy and generalize it to other experiences and tasks (e.g., when reading stories in English class or when writing outlines).

STAGE 7: INDEPENDENT PERFORMANCE

1. Allow students to continue to refer to their strategy cue cards and self-statements if they wish to do so, but encourage them to try writing without them.
2. Encourage students to continue using the graphing process for two more stories and then tell them that future graphing is up to them.

Evaluation (Select One or Both)

Option 1

1. Compare story element scores on two or three stories written by the entire class before and after implementation.

Option 2

1. Compare quality ratings for two or three stories for the target group or the entire class before and after implementation.

Variation: Partner Learning Format

1. Divide the class into dyads by pairing a higher performing student with a lower performing student. Have students work in pairs beginning in Stage 2 to determine the number of parts in their previously written stories or the sample stories. This variation is especially useful for classrooms containing students with disabilities or very diverse writing skills.

Notes

1. Between one and three collaborative writing experiences (see Stage 6) are typically needed before students are ready to use the strategy independently.
2. Because self-regulated strategy development (SRSD) in writing targets only selected aspects

of the writing process, it should be integrated into existing programs or combined with other approaches to provide a comprehensive writing program. For example, SRSD can be implemented during writer's workshop in a program that uses a process approach to writing.

Source

Danoff, B., Harris, K. R., & Graham, S. (1993). Incorporating strategy instruction within the writing process in the regular classroom: Effects on the writing of students with and without learning disabilities. *Journal of Reading Behavior, 25,* 295–322. Copyright 1993 by Lawrence Erlbaum Associates, Inc. Adapted by permission.

WRITING POWER:
COGNITIVE STRATEGY INSTRUCTION IN EXPOSITORY WRITING

Overview

Effective expository writing requires metacognitive knowledge of the processes of planning, drafting, and revising, as well as the ability to use text structure to organize and improve compositions. Unfortunately, many students, especially those with learning disabilities, have a limited understanding of the processes involved in writing expository material and have difficulty using text structures to produce well-organized compositions. This multicomponent intervention teaches expository writing strategies and text structure processes in a four-stage instructional sequence: (1) text analysis, (2) modeling of the writing process, (3) guided practice, and (4) independent strategy use. A series of "think sheets" linked to different aspects of the writing process prompt students to engage in self-questions or self-instructional statements that promote the development of the inner language critical to planning and composing. The acronym POWER is used to help students remember the five subprocesses in the writing process (plan, organize, write, edit/editor, and review). In the original study, conducted with 183 fourth and fifth graders from 12 schools in high-poverty neighborhoods, students with and without learning disabilities demonstrated significant gains in writing ability for two text structures taught during the intervention and a text structure on which they were not instructed.

Purpose

To improve students' expository writing skills with multistage strategy instruction, written prompts, self-editing, and peer collaboration.

Materials

1. Overhead projector and transparencies of four passages taken from student writing examples from the previous year or mock examples illustrating one or more types of expository text structures (explanation, compare/contrast, problem/solution, expert, etc.) and varying in quality from poor to good.
2. Transparencies and print copies of six "think sheets," one copy of each think sheet per student, as follows:
   a. *Plan* think sheet (see Figure 4.12 on p. 276 for a completed example).
   b. *Organize* think sheet, consisting of a text structure map or set of questions related to the target text structure; for example, an explanation think sheet would list questions such as "What is being explained?", "What materials/things do I need?", "What is the setting?", and "What are the steps?"
   c. *Write* think sheet, consisting of lined sheets of paper for translating ideas from the Plan and Organize think sheets into a first draft.

     d. *Edit* think sheet listing questions such as "What do I like best?", "Why?", "What parts are not clear?", "Why not?", "What do I need to add?", and "What questions do I have for my editor?"

     e. *Editor* think sheet, with a list of instructions parallel to the questions on the Edit think sheet, such as: (a) Read your classmate's paper. (b) Star the parts you liked best. (c) Place question marks by places that are not clear. (d) List your suggestions about what needs to be added.

     f. *Revise* think sheet, consisting of a sheet of lined paper for listing the suggestions made by the author and reader during the editing step.

3. Posterboard chart displaying the acronym POWER (Plan, Organize, Write, Edit/Editor, Review) for the strategy steps.

Observation (Select One or More)

Option 1

1. Have a group of target students or the entire class write a composition comparing and contrasting two people, places, or things (comparison/contrast text structure). Emphasize that they should write their papers for someone who does not know anything about their subject.

2. Score the papers for each of five traits: (a) identification of the two things being compared and contrasted; (b) description of how the two things are alike; (c) explanation of how the two things are different; (d) use of key words (e.g., *alike, different, but*); and (e) adherence to comparison/contrast text structure (i.e., introduction sentence, similarities/differences, conclusion).

3. For each trait, award a score of "0" if the trait is not present, "1" if the trait is present, and "2" if the trait is highly developed (maximum score = 10 points).

Option 2

1. Have a group of target students or the entire class write a paper explaining how to do something (explanation text structure). Emphasize that they should write their papers for someone who does not know anything about their subject.

2. Score the papers for each of four traits: (a) introduction to the topic being explained; (b) inclusion of a comprehensive sequence of steps; (c) inclusion of key or signal words (e.g., *first, second, third, finally*); and (d) adherence to explanation text structure (i.e., introduction, logical sequence of steps, and closure).

3. For each trait, award a score of "0" if the trait is not present, "1" if the trait is present, and "2" if the trait is highly developed (maximum score = 8 points).

Option 3

1. Have the entire class write a comparison/contrast or explanation paper, as described above.

2. Score the papers according to the following 5-point holistic scale to indicate the overall appeal of the paper and the extent to which the student accomplished the purpose of writing a comparison/contrast or explanation paper: 1 = unacceptable quality, 2 = poor quality, 3 = fair quality, 4 = average quality, 5 = high quality.

Intervention Steps

Stage 1: Text Analysis

1. Explain to the students that they will be learning a set of strategies for planning and writing that can help them write better compositions. Explain that they will have the opportunity to practice the strategies in pairs so that they can give and receive feedback from their classmates on their compositions.

2. Display the chart and tell the students that they can remember the strategies by using the acronym "POWER," which stands for the five subprocesses in the writing process: *plan, organize, write, edit/editor,* and *revise.* Encourage the students to memorize the subprocesses, using the acronym.

3. Display a transparency of a student writing example or mock example of the first target text structure on the overhead projector while you lead a think-aloud discussion of the features of the text structure and the quality of the writing sample.

4. For example, for an explanation text structure, discuss the text aids to comprehension (e.g., key words such as "first" and "second" that indicate the location of steps) and the kinds of questions the text was intended to answer (e.g., did the writer address, "What is being explained?", "Who or what materials are involved?", "Where does it take place?", and "What are the steps?").

5. Also think aloud about your own problems in understanding the example and invite students to discuss the type of additional information that would answer readers' questions.

6. Using additional examples of varying quality, invite students to participate in the text analysis process themselves by identifying signal words, asking text structure questions, and posing readers' questions.

Stage 2: Modeling the Writing Process

1. Using the overhead projector and transparency, introduce the *plan* think sheet. Explain to students that it will help them remember ideas from their own knowledge and experiences, consider strategies related to identifying their audience and purpose for writing, and develop a plan for grouping their ideas into categories. Stress that all of the think sheets are simply note-taking tools to help them record their ideas for later reference.

Stage 3: Guided and Collaborative Practice

1. Invite students to participate in a dialogue about the writing process as you use the *plan* think sheet to construct a class paper on a topic related to the target text structure (comparison/contrast, explanation, or expert).

2. As instruction proceeds, have students assume increasing responsibility for self-questions and planning strategies, while you act as scribe to record students' ideas on the *plan* think sheet and guide students' strategy use and assumption of the writing dialogue.

3. Introduce the other think sheets in a similar way by modeling and thinking aloud while performing the writing process. For example, demonstrate how the *organize* think sheet can help students organize their ideas into text structure categories and use the target text structure as a map to plan their compositions.

Stage 4: Collaborative and Independent Practice

1. Have students develop plans for individual papers involving the same text structure as the modeled paper.

2. After students have planned their individual papers, divide the class into pairs and have partners share their plans, including their *plan* think sheets, to elicit feedback, questions, and advice from each other.

3. Display examples of strategy use and problems encountered by students on overhead transparencies to guide the writing discussion.

4. Continue to provide modeling and feedback on the strategies as students develop more independence in writing. If desired, have students prepare independently a paper for publication in a class book.

5. Repeat these stages for each of the targeted text structures.

Elaine's *Plan* think sheet

Author's name Mrs. G.   Date _____

TOPIC: Making Peanut Butter Fudge

WHO: Who am I writing for?
Parents, brothers, sisters, + friends of my students

WHY: Why am I writing this?
So my students can make peanut butter fudge at home, + so we can remember how we made it in school

WHAT: What do I already know about my topic? (Brainstorm)
we made it after lunch

1. peanut butter   Matthew got the first piece
2. chocolate   need an "8" pan (a reversal)
3. measuring cups   tastes great!!!   taking turns stirring
4. Cosette got to lick the spoon clean   salt sugar
   wooden spoons glass bowls need patience stirring
                it was a surprise

HOW: How do I group my ideas?

Materials I'll need	Steps
Chocolate - 2 ounces hot plate, bowls, wooden spoons, aprons, buttered pans peanut butter 2 cups sugar measuring cups	melt chocolate + peanut butter took turns stirring add things put in refrigerator

Things that happened when we made it	Beginning + ending ideas
Cosette licked the spoon We put on aprons + took turns we ate fudge at recess ? →	? tastes great!! ? Matthew took the first bite we wanted to make it again

FIGURE 4.12. *Plan* think sheet. From Raphael and Englert (1990, p. 392). Copyright 1990 by the International Reading Association. Reprinted by permission.

Evaluation (Select One or More)

Option 1

1. Compare trait scores on one or more comparison/contrast papers for the target students or the entire class before and after implementation.

Option 2

1. Compare trait scores on one or more explanation papers for the target students or the entire class before and after implementation.

Option 3

1. Compare quality ratings for one or more comparison/contrast or explanation papers for the target students before and after implementation.

Notes

1. Allow one training session per think sheet. Teachers should individualize think sheets according to their own preferences, the types of texts students are writing, and the individual needs of students.
2. To avoid embarrassing students by displaying their low-quality written productions, select examples saved from the previous year, create sample papers, or retype student papers on a word processor and edit them until the authors cannot be recognized.

Sources

Englert, C. S., Raphael, T. E., Anderson, L. M., Anthony, H. M., & Stevens, D. D. (1991). Making writing strategies and self-talk visible: Writing instruction in regular and special education classrooms. *American Educational Research Journal, 28,* 337–372. Copyright 1991 by Sage Publications. Adapted by permission.

Raphael, T. E., & Englert, C. S. (1990). Writing and reading: Partners in constructing meaning. *Reading Teacher, 43,* 388–400. Copyright 1990 by the International Reading Association. Adapted by permission.

PLAN AND WRITE: SELF-REGULATED STRATEGY DEVELOPMENT FOR ESSAY WRITING

Overview

Writing essays is a frequent requirement in the middle and high school curriculum and, increasingly, on high-stakes assessments. In this intervention, students learn to plan and write expository essays using the Self-Regulated Strategy Development (SRSD) model of instruction. Six instructional stages provide a framework for strategy development and can be combined, reordered, repeated, or modified, depending on teacher preference and student needs. In the original investigations, implemented with seventh and eighth graders in six regular education and three inclusive classrooms, the strategy had positive effects on essay length, quality, and completeness for all of the target students, including low-achieving, average, and high-achieving writers, as well as students with learning disabilities. Moreover, the positive changes in writing performance and writing behaviors, such as planning, were maintained over a 1-month follow-up. Teachers and students alike were enthusiastic about the effects of the intervention, and the seventh-grade participants in one study reported that they applied the strategy on their high-stakes competency examination. A variation for enhancing vocabulary and spelling is also presented.

Purpose

To teach students a strategy for planning, writing, and revising expository essays, as well as a set of strategies for regulating their own writing behavior.

Materials

1. Posterboard chart listing the planning and writing strategy steps (see Figure 4.13 on p. 281).
2. Cue cards, consisting of index cards listing the strategy steps, one per student (see Figure 4.14 on p. 282).
3. Overhead projector with transparencies and print copies of several student essay examples from the previous year or mock examples, one copy of each example per student.
4. Brainstorming sheet, consisting of a sheet of paper for identifying possible responses to a writing prompt and outlining main and supporting ideas, one per student.
5. Essay sheet, consisting of a sheet of paper with a space at the top for writing the thesis statement and preprinted subheadings, such as "introductory paragraph"; "body paragraphs one, two, and three"; and "conclusion," one per student.
6. Highlighters, one per student.
7. Copies of essay prompts, one per student; prompts should elicit expository text, such as:
   a. Choose a country you would like to visit. Write an essay explaining why you would like to visit this country.
   b. Think about how students can improve their grades. Write an essay explaining why getting good grades is important and what students can do to improve their grades.
   c. Think about rules you believe are unfair. Write an essay stating the rules you think should be changed and explaining why you think so.
8. Copies of the classroom rubric or standards for grading essays or the state assessment scoring rubric (optional, see Intervention Steps, Stage 3).
9. Quiz with questions about strategy use in essay writing (optional, see Intervention Steps, Stage 6).
10. Posterboard chart or section of the chalkboard listing "Million Dollar Words" (optional, see Variation).

Observation (Select One or Both)

Option 1

1. Distribute copies of an essay prompt to the entire class. Have students write an essay based on the prompt within a 35-minute time limit, a period equivalent to the requirements of your state's writing assessment, or another appropriate time frame. Note that the essays obtained in this or the next option can be used as baseline essays in the individual student conferences conducted in Stage 3 of the Intervention Steps.
2. For each essay, count the number of functional essay elements as follows: (a) *premise,* defined as a statement specifying the writer's position on the topic; (b) *reasons,* defined as explanations to support or refute a position; (c) *conclusion,* defined as a closing statement summing up an individual paragraph or the overall premise of the essay; and (d) *elaborations,* defined as a unit of text that expands on a premise, reason, or conclusion in terms of emphasis, examples, or other functional content.

Option 2

1. Administer an essay prompt to a group of target students or the entire class as described above.
2. Rate each essay on a holistic scale from 1 to 7 based on the quality of the ideas, development

and organization, coherence, mechanics, and the quality of vocabulary as follows: 1 = unacceptable, 2 = poor, 3 = fair, 4 = average, 5 = good, 6 = very good, 7 = outstanding.

Intervention Steps

Stage 1: Overview of Purpose

1. Tell students that they are going to learn a writing strategy for composing expository essays that will help them be more capable and confident writers.
2. Set the goal of learning, such as preparing for the writing proficiency essay on the state assessment, improving essay writing ability for use in content area classes, and so on.
3. Discuss how writers use planning strategies when they write and the benefits of using those strategies.
4. Using the chart, present the PLAN and WRITE strategy and the rationale for each step (see Figure 4.13).

Stage 2: Activating Background Knowledge

1. For the first session in this stage, display a sample essay on the overhead projector and have students read it collaboratively. Ask them to identify the introductory, body, and concluding paragraphs. Help them to determine whether the sample essay contains a good thesis statement and to identify transition words in each paragraph.
2. Have students search the essay for different sentence types in terms of form (simple, compound, and complex) and function (declarative, imperative, exclamatory, and question). Have students take notes during the discussion and incorporate their suggestions for revision on the transparency.
3. During a second session, conduct a similar review of the same essay with the primary focus on the writer's use of vocabulary. Help student identify "million dollar words," that is, words they consider to be exciting, interesting, and unique. Have them make suggestions for changes in vocabulary that would improve the essay.

Stage 3: Review of Students' Initial Writing Abilities

1. Explain the classroom rubrics or standards for grading essays or the scoring rubric used in the state assessment, if appropriate.
2. Distribute copies of an essay prompt, and have students practice Step 1 of the PLAN and WRITE strategy while you conduct brief individual conferences reviewing students' performance on their most recent baseline essay.
3. If desired, give students individual copies of the classroom or state assessment scoring rubric and identify one or two features in need of improvement. Encourage students to select one or two writing goals to address the identified weaknesses, such as keeping on topic, using mature vocabulary, having few or no errors in grammar, and making the essay lively and fun to read.

Stage 4: Modeling the Planning Strategy

1. Using the projector, display another essay prompt and model the use of the PLAN and WRITE strategy by thinking aloud through the planning and writing process. Include a variety of self-instructions to show students how to manage the process (e.g., "OK, I've decided to write my thesis statement first, so it goes at the beginning of my introductory paragraph").
2. Identify the essential components of the prompt and model the use of the brainstorming sheet to record and organize your ideas. Also demonstrate how to use the essay sheet to write the thesis statement and decide whether to place it as the first or last sentence in the introductory paragraph.

3. Distribute cue cards to students and demonstrate how to use them as reminders of what each paragraph should include.
4. Throughout the demonstration, emphasize how good writers use the processes and procedures several times during planning and composition. For example, during the last two steps of WRITE, revise sentence types and vocabulary as you model writing the paper.

Stage 5: Collaborative Practice

1. Display an essay prompt on the projector, and help students use the PLAN and WRITE strategy to plan and compose an essay on a classwide basis.
2. Divide students into dyads or triads. Distribute copies of another essay prompt, and have the students collaborate in planning and composing a second essay. Discuss and model expected behaviors for collaborative writing practice. Circulate to monitor behavior and provide assistance as needed. As you circulate, write brief positive comments on students' papers and note where revisions would be helpful.
3. After students have composed their essays, conduct a whole-class discussion about various essay components, such as the relationship between introductory and concluding paragraphs, different sentence types and forms, and examples of mature vocabulary in student essays.
4. Have students work again in dyads or triads to give each other feedback and suggestions for revision. Give students highlighters and a list of criteria to search for in their partners' papers (e.g., appropriate content, focus on the topic, use of transition words, use of mature vocabulary words). Allow time for students to revise their papers and circulate to answer questions, prompt, and provide assistance as needed.

Stage 6: Independent Practice

1. Explain to students that their goal is to be able to use the strategy without relying on the procedural supports (cue cards and brainstorming and essay sheets) to generate an essay within class or state assessment time limits and to demonstrate mastery of at least one of their self-selected goals.
2. Distribute an essay prompt and have students use the strategy to write an essay. Provide assistance as needed but gradually fade prompting and the use of the procedural supports as students become more proficient in using the strategy.
3. During independent practice sessions, conduct a second set of individual conferences to assess students' mastery of the strategy. Ask students to recall each strategy step, provide examples of transition words, provide a word and a synonym for that word, and state how they plan to write an introductory paragraph. Alternately, administer a quiz requiring students to respond to these questions in writing and lead a classwide discussion of the results afterward.
4. Have students select one of their essays for inclusion in a class writing portfolio.

Evaluation (Select One or Both)

Option 1

1. Compare the number of functional elements in two or three essays written by the entire class before and after implementation.

Option 2

1. Compare quality ratings for two or three essays for the target group or the entire class before and after implementation.

The Expository Planning Strategy: Nine Steps to Success

Planning strategy: PLAN	Instructions for each planning step
1. **P**ay attention to the prompt.	Read the prompt. Underline what you are being asked to write about once. Underline how you are to develop it twice.
2. **L**ist main ideas.	Brainstorm possible responses to the prompt and decide on one topic. Then brainstorm at least three main ideas for the development of your essay.
3. **A**dd supporting ideas.	Think of at least three details, examples, and elaborations to support each of your main ideas.
4. **N**umber your ideas.	Number your main ideas in the order you will use them.

Keep planning while composing your essay: WRITE

5. **W**ork from your plan to develop your thesis statement.	Look at your cue cards for basic and advanced ways to develop the introductory paragraph.
6. **R**emember your goals.	Write one or two goals on the top of your plan.
7. **I**nclude transition words for each paragraph.	Look at your cue cards for sample transition words and phrases for each paragraph.
8. **T**ry to use different kinds of sentences.	Remember to use simple, compound, complex, declarative, interrogative, and exclamatory sentences.
9. (Use) **e**xciting, interesting $1,000,000 words in your essay.	Use synonyms for words occurring more than once.

FIGURE 4.13. The PLAN and WRITE strategy for *PLAN and WRITE: Self-Regulated Strategy Development for Essay Writing*. Adapted from De La Paz, Owen, Harris, and Graham (2000, p. 102). Copyright 2000 by Blackwell Publishing. Adapted by permission.

Variation: PLAN and WRITE with Million-Dollar Word Search

1. As part of Stage 5, have students search each other's papers for "million-dollar words" and highlight the words they identify. Have students add their million-dollar words to a list posted at the front of the classroom or written on the chalkboard. As the words accumulate, group them in sets of 5 to 10 to create weekly vocabulary and spelling lists or use them as bonus words in the regular weekly spelling test.

Notes

1. In the original studies, teachers taught the strategy over periods ranging from 2 weeks (De La Paz et al., 2000) to 4 to 6 weeks (De La Paz, 1999). Several sessions are needed for each of Stages 2, 4, 5, and 6.
2. This strategy allows for paired or small-group collaborative learning during many aspects of the writing process. Change pairs or groupings each week so that students have an opportunity to work with peers with a variety of writing abilities.

Sources

De La Paz, S. (1999). Self-regulated strategy instruction in regular education settings: Improving outcomes for students with and without learning disabilities. *Learning Disabilities Research and Practice, 14,* 92–106. Copyright 1999 by Blackwell Publishing. Adapted by permission.

Introductory paragraph: Thesis statement first • Answer the prompt in your first sentence. • Write your first main idea in the second sentence. • Write your second main idea in the third sentence. • Write your third main idea in the last sentence <div align="center">(1)</div>	*Introductory paragraph:* Thesis statement last • Start with an "attention getter" and lead up to the thesis statement. • Answer the prompt in your last sentence. • Include your first, second, and third main idea in a series. <div align="center">(2)</div>
How to start with an "attention getter": • Use a series of questions. • Use a series of statements. • Use a brief or funny story. • Use an angry or surprising statement. • Start with the opposite opinion from what you believe. <div align="center">(3)</div>	*First body paragraph:* Use transition words to introduce ideas. • First (of all) … • (The/My) first (reason/example) is … • One (reason why/example is) … • To begin with … • In the first step … • To explain … <div align="center">(4)</div>
Second and third body paragraph: Use transition words to connect or add ideas, or give examples. • Second … Third … • My second (reason/example) is … • Furthermore … • Another (reason) to support this is … • What is more … • The next step … <div align="center">(5)</div>	*Concluding paragraph:* Use transition words to summarize ideas. • In conclusion/To conclude … • In summary/To sum up … • As one can see … /As a result … • In short/All in all … • It follows that … • For these reasons … <div align="center">(6)</div>

FIGURE 4.14. Cue cards for *PLAN and WRITE: Self-Regulated Strategy Development for Essay Writing.* Italicized cards are designed for students who wish to attempt more sophisticated introductory paragraphs. Adapted from De La Paz et al. (2000, p. 102). Copyright 2000 by Blackwell Publishing. Adapted by permission.

De La Paz, S., Owen, B., Harris, K. R., & Graham, S. (2000). Riding Elvis' motorcycle: Using self-regulated strategy development to PLAN and WRITE for a state writing exam. *Learning Disabilities Research and Practice, 15,* 101–109. Copyright 2000 by Blackwell Publishing. Adapted by permission.

Additional Resources

The Center on Accelerating Student Learning (CASL) website *http://www.kc.vanderbilt.edu/casl/ srsd.html* provides links to sample lesson plans for writing interventions based on the Self-Regulated Strategy Instruction Model, including strategies for story writing and early opinion essays.

PEER EDITING FOR EFFECTIVE REVISION

Overview

Learning to revise is an important component skill in the writing process. To revise successfully, students must reflect on what they have written, develop criteria for evaluating their work, and implement the revisions. Compared with more proficient writers, less skilled writers make fewer revisions, and the changes they do make are usually attempts to correct mechanical errors that have little impact on overall quality. In this intervention, students work in pairs to help each other revise written productions, using a nine-step strategy that incorporates word processing in the composing and revising stages. In the original study, implemented with six seventh graders with learning disabilities in a school computer laboratory, the peer editing intervention was successful not only in increasing the number and quality of revisions for all target students, but also increasing overall writing quality in terms of content, organization, and style. Moreover, gains made during instruction using word processors for composition and peer-supported revision generalized to independently prepared handwritten compositions. The strategy can be easily adapted for students of diverse writing abilities and for a variety of writing instructional goals. Two variations are presented: a paper-and-pencil version and a version for elementary grade students.

Purpose

To improve writing performance by integrating strategy instruction in the writing process, peer collaboration, and word processing.

Materials

1. Computers and software word processing programs.
2. Prompt sheets, consisting of printed copies of the nine steps in the peer editing strategy (see *Introduction and Training 5*), one per student.
3. Eight to 10 writing prompts on computer disks, memory sticks, or in a computer file; prompts should be designed to elicit personal narratives, such as: "Think about a time when you were surprised by something. What happened and why were you surprised? Write a story for your friends to read about the time when you were surprised."
4. Printed copies of sample personal narratives, one per student.
5. Overhead projector and transparency of a sample personal narrative (optional).
6. Writing portfolios or notebooks with lined paper, one per student (see Variation 1).
7. Paper copies of writing prompts, one per student (see Variation 1).

Observation (Select One or Both)

Option 1

1. Have a group of target students or the entire class write and revise between one and three stories according to the following procedures:
   a. In an initial session using computers, have students call up the class file with a writing prompt printed at the top. Tell them to take a minute to read the prompt and plan their composition. Explain that they will have a chance to make revisions later. Have students compose their stories at the computers, save them, and print hard copies.
   b. In a second session, give students printed copies of their stories and tell them to think about changes they can make to improve their stories and to make notes on the first draft with a pencil or pen. Then have them make revisions on the computer and print a final draft.
   c. Score student compositions using one or more of the following measures:
      1. Number of words, counting each word that is recognizable as a word.
      2. Proportion of mechanical errors, defined as the number of errors in spelling, capitalization, and punctuation, divided by the total number of words.
      3. Number of appropriate revisions, including changes in mechanics, organization, vocabulary, and other features that improve the quality of the composition.
      4. Overall quality on a scale from 1 to 7, as follows: 1 = unsatisfactory, 2 = poor, 3 = fair, 4 = average, 5 = good, 6 = very good, 7 = excellent.
      5. Quality change from first to second draft on a 5-point scale, as follows: −2 = second draft much worse than first, −1 = second draft worse than first, 0 = second draft same quality as first, +1 = second draft better than first, +2 = second draft much better than first.

Option 2

1. Have a group of target students or the entire class write and revise between one and three stories, using a paper-and-pencil format.
2. Rate the revised stories on a 3-point scale, as follows: –1 = worse than the first draft, 0 = no change, +1 = better than the first draft.

Intervention Steps

Introduction and Training

1. Tell students that they are going to work in pairs to learn a strategy for improving their written compositions. Explain that the class will be focusing on writing personal narratives and using computers to make the task easier and more fun.
2. If necessary, conduct a training session on the use of the computers and the word processing program that will be used for the intervention. Conduct the initial peer editing training session in the classroom rather than in a computer laboratory, however.
3. Discuss with students the characteristics of a personal narrative. *Example:* "A personal narrative is a true story about you that describes something that happened to you so clearly that readers feel as if they had been there."
4. Give each student copies of a sample personal narrative and the peer editing procedures. Lead a discussion of importance of revision in the overall writing process.
5. Explain each step of the peer editing strategy as described below. If desired, use an overhead projector with a transparency of the sample narrative to demonstrate the revision procedures. Explain that both students in a pair complete the first two steps in turn. Then each student works independently on the other student's paper as a peer editor, after which the partners take turns discussing the two papers.
   Step 1: Listen carefully and follow along as the author reads the first draft of his or her composition aloud.
   Step 2: Tell the author what you liked best.
   Step 3: Reread your peer editor's paper to yourself.
   Step 4: Ask yourself the four key revision questions about the composition:
      Parts? Does it have a good beginning, middle, and ending?
      Order? Does it follow a logical sequence?
      Details? Where could the writer add more details?
      Clarity? Is there any part that is hard to understand?
   Step 5: Make notes on your peer editor's draft based on the revision questions.
   Step 6: Discuss your suggestions with the author.
   Step 7: Work independently at the computer to revise your own paper.
   Step 8: Meet again with your partner to discuss the revisions you each have made and to check each other's papers for mechanical errors.
   Step 9: Work independently at the computer to make final revisions and print out your composition.
6. Guide a pair of students through a demonstration of the strategy in a paper-and-pencil format, using the same sample narrative. Be sure to discuss the importance of positive peer support during the demonstration.
7. Assign partners, distribute copies of a second sample personal narrative, and conduct a class-wide practice. Circulate to provide assistance and encourage appropriate peer editing behaviors as needed.
8. Using another sample narrative or students' own compositions from the observation period, conduct at least one more training session in the classroom with a paper-and-pencil format.

Implementation

1. Using a prepared prompt, have students compose a personal narrative on computers and then work in pairs to apply the peer editing strategy. Encourage students to refer to their prompt sheets and to memorize the four key words in the revision questions. Circulate to provide assistance and prompt positive peer editing behaviors as needed.
2. In a second session, have students make the final revisions to their drafts on computers and print out hard copies. Change pairs every few weeks to give students an opportunity to work with peer editors with a range of writing abilities.

Evaluation (Select One or Both)

Option 1

1. Have the group of target students or the entire class compose and revise two or three more personal narratives and compare their performance on one or more of the following measures before and after implementation: (a) number of words, (b) proportion of mechanical errors, (c) number of appropriate revisions, (d) overall quality of the final draft, and/or (e) quality change from first to second draft.

Option 2

1. Have the entire class or the target students compose and revise two or three more personal narratives and compare the quality of the revisions before and after implementation.

Variations

Variation 1: Paper-and-Pencil Variation

1. Teach the strategy using a paper-and-pencil format, with printed copies of writing prompts. After the peer editing pairs make notes about suggested changes on each other's first drafts, have students recopy their own stories, incorporating the revisions.

Variation 2: Elementary Grade Variation

1. Initially teach the strategy using a paper-and-pencil format as described in Variation 1. Include only two revision questions in Step 4 of the peer editing process: (a) *Clarity?* Is there anything that is not clear? (b) *Details?* Where could more information be added?
2. When most of the students are demonstrating improvement in their revisions, introduce the word processing composition and revision format.

Notes

1. In the original study, students made more revisions with handwriting than with word processing, both before and after implementation. The authors suggest that the greater number of revisions for handwritten narratives was due to incidental revisions made during recopying, whereas revisions made with the word processor were intentional.
2. Allow two sessions for writing and revising each composition.

Source

Stoddard, B., & MacArthur, C. A. (1993). A peer editor strategy: Guiding learning-disabled students in response and revision. *Research in the Teaching of English, 27,* 76–103. Copyright 1993 by the National Council of Teachers of English. Adapted by permission.

Interventions to Improve
Social Studies and Science Performance

Recent national assessments have documented alarming low levels of achievement in social studies and science among U.S. students. The 2007 National Assessment of Educational Progress (NAEP) in civics found that only 24% of fourth graders, 22% of eighth graders, and 27% of 12th graders scored at or above the Proficient level, indicating solid academic performance for the grade assessed, with no significant increase in the percentages of students at or above Proficient since 1998 (National Center for Education Statistics, 2007b). Performance on the 2007 NAEP U.S. history assessment was even more disappointing. Although the percentage of students performing at or above the Basic level increased from 1994 to 2006 at all three grade levels, less than one-fifth of students at the three grade levels scored at or above Proficient (18%, 17%, and 13%, respectively), and there was no significant change in the percentages performing at or above Proficient (National Center for Education Statistics, 2007d).

Students' performance in science has also long been viewed with concern. NAEP science assessments conducted from 1996 to 2005 reveal that although the percentage of students scoring at or above Basic increased from 63% to 68% in grade 4, the average score for grade 8 students remained unchanged. At grade 12, the average score declined over the same period, with nearly half (46%) of students failing to reach even the Basic level in 2005. Moreover, although African American students demonstrated some gains over the period, significant score gaps persist between Caucasian students and minority students. At all three grade levels, more than 80% of the students scoring at or above Proficient were Caucasian, compared with 6% or fewer for students in other racial/ethic groups (National Center for Education Statistics, 2006b). Similarly, on the 2003 Trends in International Mathematics and Science Study (TIMSS), the science performance of U.S. eighth graders improved between 1995 and 2003, but fourth graders made no measurable improvement over the same period, and their performance was lower in 2003 than in 1995 relative to the fourth graders in the 14 other nations participating in the studies (National Center for Education Statistics, 2004a).

READING SKILLS AND SUCCESS IN THE CONTENT AREAS

Successful performance in social studies and science is strongly associated with students' ability to read and obtain meaning from their textbooks. Unfortunately, many students, including students with disabilities and non-native English speakers, have reading deficits that prevent them from reading their textbooks with sufficient proficiency to acquire information from them and integrate that information with previously acquired knowledge (Bryant et al., 2000; De La Paz & MacArthur, 2000; Parmar et al., 1994). As these poor readers progress through school, the gap between their skill level and the reading level of their textbooks widens, reducing their ability to profit from instruction. By the time they reach high school, struggling readers and students with learning disabilities are typically reading on a fourth- or fifth-grade level, whereas the reading level of their content area textbooks may be even higher than the assigned grade level (Deshler et al., 2001). Already at risk for school failure, poor readers may become so frustrated that they become passive observers of instruction or resort to disruptive behavior in an effort to distract themselves and their classmates from their academic problems.

The problems that many students face in reading and obtaining meaning from their content area textbooks are compounded by the mismatch between their learning needs and typical instructional practices in content area classrooms. Although textbooks serve as the major instructional medium in science and social studies, teachers seldom provide explicit instruction in reading comprehension strategies (Scruggs & Mastropieri, 2003). Instead, observational studies of content area classrooms reveal that teachers typically focus on covering the curriculum and maintaining classroom control rather than on helping students comprehend textual material (Alvermann, O'Brien, & Dillon, 1990). Moreover, because of the pressures created by higher expectations for all students arising from No Child Left Behind and the heightened focus on outcome-based programming, many teachers have increased the pace of instruction, further widening the gap between the instructional demands of the classroom and students' skill levels.

Problems with Content Area Textbooks

In addition, content area texts are often poorly written and "inconsiderate" of their readers in terms of structure, coherence, and audience appropriateness (Armbruster & Anderson, 1988). Despite recent efforts, a serious discrepancy remains between research about learning from text and many of today's textbooks (Armbruster & Ostertag, 1993). Science and social studies texts tend to emphasize breath over depth, covering many more topics than is typical in texts in other nations (Schmidt et al., 1997; Valverde & Schmidt, 1997–1998). Similarly, textbooks fail to reflect current knowledge about effective instructional practices that would assist students in engaging in high-level text processing and exploring concepts deeply (Harmon et al., 2000). Instead, textbooks require students to acquire and apply skills and concepts without providing sufficient help for teachers in teaching those skills and concepts or students in learning them. History textbooks have been criticized for being dull, overly broad, and difficult to understand (Paxton, 1999), whereas science textbooks have been criticized for including too many topics and presenting excessive numbers of complex vocabulary words and concepts with insufficient opportunities for practice and application (Best, Rowe, Ozuru, & McNamara, 2005; Schmidt et al., 1997). Moreover, many of today's students possess minimal background knowledge in the content areas, making it difficult for them to generate the kinds of inferences about what they are reading that are necessary for textual comprehension (Best et al., 2005; Otero, León, & Graesser, 2002). Under these circumstances, it is not surprising that students themselves feel that they do not receive enough help from their teachers in understanding textbook material in their content area classes (Guthrie & Davis, 2003).

Interventions to Improve Performance in the Content Areas

As the pressure to improve student achievement in the content areas increases, the need for classroom-based strategies that enhance students' ability to understand and remember material in their textbooks is greater than ever. Although instructional models targeting the content areas have been developed to assist at-risk students in regular education settings (e.g., Deshler et al., 2001; Schumaker, Deshler, & McKnight, 2002), surprisingly few "stand-alone" interventions focusing on social studies or science have appeared in the literature, perhaps because content area achievement is affected by a wide range of interrelated skills and competencies, including cognitive ability, vocabulary, background knowledge, reading proficiency, and task persistence. Two of the five interventions in this section use *graphic organizers* to enhance reading comprehension of textual material. A graphic organizer is a type of procedural facilitator that provides a visual framework for organizing and understanding textual material. Visual models of text organization have been successful in improving reading comprehension and content area knowledge for students with and without disabilities in elementary and secondary school settings (see Kim, Vaughn, Wanzek, & Wei, 2004, for a review). *Improving Content Area Comprehension with a Critical Thinking Map* targets comprehension skills by providing a structured framework for understanding and remembering expository text. This text structure strategy can be used to promote comprehension in any subject in which students must read to gather information. *Concept Mapping to Improve Science Content Comprehension* facilitates comprehension skills by providing a visual framework in the form of a concept map for understanding, relating, and remembering informational material in science texts. This strategy, like the others in this section, can also be applied to other text-based academic subjects.

Three interventions use some form of strategy instruction as a primary intervention component. When applied to content area subjects, *strategy instruction* involves teaching procedures that students can use before, during, and after reading to understand text structures, self-monitor for understanding, and activate prior knowledge. Strategy instruction is especially beneficial for students who have difficulty with expository text, such as poor readers and students with learning disabilities (Parmar et al., 1994; Mason, 2004). *Improving Comprehension of Science Text with a Summarization Strategy* teaches students to apply a structured summarization procedure to textbook passages to improve learning and retention. Although research attests to the effectiveness of summarization training in improving comprehension of expository text for poor readers and students with disabilities (Gajria & Salvia, 1992; Jitendra, Hoppes, & Xin, 2000; Malone & Mastropieri, 1992), the vast majority of studies have been conducted using passages that were especially developed or modified by researchers to meet the task demands associated with summarization strategies. In contrast, the intervention included here was designed to be implemented with regular classroom textbook material.

In two of the three strategy-based interventions, strategy instruction is embedded within a peer tutoring framework to increase students' opportunities to be actively engaged with content area text and to encourage task persistence. *Admirals and Generals: Improving Content Area Performance with Strategy Instruction and Peer Tutoring* targets content area learning and reading comprehension with a combination of repeated oral reading and strategy questioning delivered in a paired learning format. Students take turns reading paragraphs from their textbooks, after which they work together to apply summarization strategies to what they have read. The intervention has been successful in improving performance on content area tests and increasing on-task behavior for middle school students with learning disabilities (Spencer, Scruggs, & Mastropieri, 2003) and high school students with emotional or behavior disorders (Mastropieri, Scruggs, Spencer, & Fontana, 2003). *Collaborative Strategic Reading* (CSR) also combines reading comprehension strategy instruction with a cooperative learning structure. Based on the principles of reciprocal teaching (Palincsar & Brown, 1984), CSR teaches students strategies for comprehending content area material, as well as a structured routine for implementing those strategies within mixed-ability cooperative groups. CSR is more effective than regular instruction in improving reading comprehension for expository text (Klingner, Vaughn, Hughes, & Arguelles, 1999) and has documented effectiveness in improving comprehension and content learning for students at the elementary and middle school level, including English language learners, students with disabilities, and average and high-achieving students (Klingner & Vaughn, 1996; Klingner, Vaughn, & Schumm, 1998; Vaughn et al., 2000).

CROSS-REFERENCE: The Academic Productivity section of this chapter includes three interventions that have been validated for implementation in content area subjects: *ClassWide Peer Tutoring, Cover, Copy, and Compare*, and *Using Response Cards to Increase Academic Engagement and Achievement*. For an intervention that uses a graphic organizer to enhance comprehension of narrative textual material, see *Story Mapping* in the Reading section of this chapter.

Evaluating the Effectiveness of Social Studies and Science Interventions

Methods for assessing the effectiveness of the strategies in this section include quiz and test grades, classwide percentages of students with low grades, classwide academic engagement rates, and comprehension-based measures, such as the number of important elements included in summaries and self-reports of strategy use. In addition to the evaluation procedures provided for each intervention, directions for constructing and administering *vocabulary-matching probes*, a form of curriculum-based measurement (CBM) in the content areas, are provided below.

Curriculum-Based Measurement in the Content Areas

Although CBM methods have been used since the 1980s to monitor student progress in reading, mathematics, spelling, and writing, researchers have only recently extended CBM technology to content area learning. A series of studies by Espin and her colleagues have demonstrated that a 5-minute vocabulary-matching measure, consisting of 20 terms and 22 definitions (including two distractors) drawn from students' own texts, is a reliable and valid indicator of performance and growth in content area learning for middle school and high school students (Busch & Espin, 2003; Espin, Busch, Shin, & Kruschwitz, 2001; Espin & Foegen, 1996; Espin, Shin, & Busch, 2005). Results of vocabulary-matching probes can be interpreted by means of intraclass comparisons (i.e., comparing an individual student's score to the class mean or median) and by creating expectancy tables that incorporate scores on end-of-year examinations or high-stakes assessments (Espin & Tindal, 1998).

CURRICULUM-BASED MEASUREMENT IN THE CONTENT AREAS: VOCABULARY MATCHING

Overview

For many middle and high school students, limited vocabulary knowledge, poor decoding skills, and impaired fluency interfere with their ability to read and understand their content area texts, putting them at risk for failure in those classes. *Vocabulary matching*, a 5-minute assessment tapping these three critical skills, uses curriculum-based procedures to monitor student progress in content area classes. A growing body of research demonstrates that vocabulary matching is a reliable and valid indicator of student performance on content area tasks, including standardized tests, grades, and tests of subject area knowledge, and is sensitive to individual differences in growth. Moreover, scores on vocabulary-matching probes reliably differentiate between students with and without learning disabilities. Data from vocabulary-matching probes can be used to identify students at risk for failure in content area classes early in the school year and to evaluate the appropriateness of content area classes for students with disabilities. After the initial benchmark assessment, vocabulary-matching probes can be administered on a weekly or biweekly basis to target students to monitor learning and determine the need for additional interventions. The probes can be administered on an individual, small-group, or whole-class basis.

Purpose

1. To provide information for making placement decisions for students with disabilities in general education content area classes.
2. To identify students who are at risk for failure in content area classes and in need of additional support.
3. To monitor student learning and growth in content areas subjects.
4. To evaluate the effectiveness of content area curricular programs and interventions.

Materials

1. Create a pool of vocabulary terms with their definitions from the content to be covered during the semester or school year. For performance-level (benchmark) testing, a pool of 100 to 150 terms is sufficient. For progress monitoring, a larger pool is needed, depending on the frequency of assessment. Select terms from the textbook glossary, teacher lectures and notes, or a combination. Develop a short definition (fewer than 15 words) for each term, using the textbook glossary, teacher notes or lectures, or a student dictionary.
2. For each probe, randomly select 20 terms with their definitions and two additional definitions not matching any of the 20 terms. List the terms alphabetically down the left side of the page and the definitions on the right side of the page with a blank next to each definition (see Table 4.3). For benchmark testing, create three probes. For progress monitoring, generate a weekly or biweekly probe.
3. Stopwatch or timer.
4. Pencils with erasers, one or two per student.
5. Equal-interval graph paper or graphing program (optional).

Assessment Steps

Administration

1. Give each student a vocabulary-matching probe and give the following directions:

> "Here is a list of terms and definitions from this course. When I say, 'Begin,' match as many definitions with their terms as you can by writing the number of the definition in the blank next to the correct term. You will have 5 minutes. You will see terms we have not covered yet, so don't worry if you don't know all of the words. Are there any questions? Ready? Begin."

2. At the end of 5 minutes, say, "Stop!" and collect the probes.
3. For benchmark testing, administer two more probes. For progress monitoring, administer only one probe.

Scoring

1. Award one point for each correct match. Sum the number of correct matches to obtain a percent-correct score.
2. For benchmark testing, use the median (middle) score on the three probes to control for the effects of difficulty across probes.
3. For greater reliability in progress monitoring, administer two probes weekly and record the mean score of each pair of adjacent probes.

Interpretation

1. For benchmark testing, rank student results from highest to lowest, and calculate a class mean and median. Students whose performance is very discrepant from that of their average peers are likely to need additional interventions to be successful in the content area class from which the vocabulary terms are drawn.
2. For progress monitoring, graph or have students graph their weekly or biweekly scores. Compare the results to end-of-semester or end-of-year goals you set collaboratively with the students. If progress monitoring data indicate that students are making limited progress, modify or intensify content area interventions.

Notes

1. To reduce preparation time, use a word processing program to create a master list of vocabulary terms and definitions and generate probes.
2. Local norms can be developed for use in predicting performance on end-of-year examinations or high-stakes assessments. Create an expectancy table by recording student scores on vocabulary probes along with their scores on final examinations or high-stakes assessments. The following year, use the data in the table to estimate the likelihood that students with specific vocabulary scores will have difficulty achieving success in the content area classes or passing high-stakes examinations (Espin & Tindal, 1998).

Sources

Espin, C. A., Busch, T. W., Shin, J., & Kruschwitz, R. (2001). Curriculum-based measurement in the content areas: Validity of vocabulary-matching as an indicator of performance in social studies. *Learning Disabilities Research and Practice, 16,* 142–151. Copyright 2001 by Blackwell Publishing. Adapted by permission.

Espin, C. A., Shin, J., & Busch, T. W. (2005). Curriculum-based measurement in the content areas: Vocabulary matching as an indicator of progress in social studies learning. *Journal of Learning Disabilities, 38,* 353–363. Copyright 2005 by PRO-ED, Inc. Adapted by permission.

TABLE 4.3. Sample Items from a Vocabulary-Matching Probe

<u>5</u>	Classical conditioning	1. A resource that is important for a country's industries or national securities
<u>2</u>	Empathy	2. Feeling as another person does; putting yourself in someone else's place
<u>4</u>	First World	3. According to Freud, a part of the personality concerned with right and wrong
<u>6</u>	Socialization	4. The wealthy, industrialized nations
<u>1</u>	Strategic resource	5. Pairing of a neutral stimulus with an unconditioned stimulus so they produce the same response
<u>3</u>	Superego	6. Process through which an individual learns the rules of society

Note. From Espin, Busch, Shin, and Kruschwitz (2001, p. 145). Copyright 2001 by Blackwell Publishing. Reprinted by permission.

IMPROVING CONTENT AREA COMPREHENSION
WITH A CRITICAL THINKING MAP

Overview

Students often make poor grades in content area subjects because they have difficulty comprehending their textbooks. Although they may have adequate word recognition skills, they have
trouble learning and remembering textual information because they lack strategies for thinking
critically about what they are reading and are unfamiliar with expository text structures. This
intervention uses a model–lead–test format to teach students a mapping strategy that provides
a framework for guiding their thinking processes as they read. In the original study, conducted
with six high school students, four in a remedial reading program and two in a special education
program for students with mild retardation, use of critical thinking maps was associated with
significant increases on standardized vocabulary and comprehension tests and comprehension of
lesson material, with improvement generalizing to similar content. In this adaptation, the one-to-
one instructional format has been modified for classwide implementation. Critical thinking maps
can be used in any subject that requires students to read expository text. Also included is a variation with a self-monitoring component to enhance motivation and task persistence.

Purpose

To improve comprehension of social studies textual material by teaching students to use a five-
component graphic organizer during reading.

Materials

1. Printed copies of critical thinking maps, one per student (see Figure 4.15 on p. 295).
2. Copies of generic comprehension questions, one per student (see Figure 4.16 on p. 296).
3. Overhead projector and a transparency of the map (optional).
4. Red pens for checking papers, one per student.
5. Social studies folders with paper for graphing scores on comprehension questions (see Variation).

Observation (Select One or More)

Option 1

1. Administer a five-question generic comprehension quiz (see Figure 4.16) to the entire class
   after students have read the social studies lesson for the day.
2. Score each question using the following 5-point rating scale: 0 = no response or completely
   wrong, 1 = poor response, 2 = partially correct but incomplete response, 3 = satisfactory
   response, 4 = excellent response (total possible points = 20).
3. Record comprehension scores for 4 to 7 days. If desired, calculate a class daily average score
   by summing individual scores and dividing by the number of students in the class.

Option 2

1. Calculate grades on weekly or end-of-unit social studies quizzes and tests for the entire class
   for several weeks.

Option 3

1. Have a group of target students respond orally or in writing to the following question: What do you do to help yourself understand and remember what you read?
2. Tally the number of acceptable strategies reported by each student. Acceptable strategies include paying attention to the text, reading slower, repeated reading, skimming for main ideas, using section headings and illustrations, self-questioning, and so on.
3. If desired, calculate a group average number of acceptable strategies by dividing the total number of strategies by the number of students in the group.

Intervention Steps

Stage 1: Modeling Phase

1. Using an overhead projector, display a transparency of the critical thinking map or reproduce it on the chalkboard. Explain to the students that they will be learning to use the map to get more out of reading their social studies textbooks.
2. Explain each of the map components as follows:
   a. *Important events*: important events, points, or steps that lead to the main intent or idea of the lesson, such as the positive and negative attributes of an issue or the causal and/or temporal points.
   b. *Main idea*: the most important message conveyed by the author, whether explicit or implicit, reflecting the author's attitudes toward the information presented in the text.
   c. *Other viewpoints/opinions*: the reader's own perspective and opinions about what has been read, including the background information and knowledge the reader has already acquired about the topic.
   d. *Reader's conclusions*: the reader's final conclusions about the passage and reasons to support them, based on information from all of the preceding map components.
   e. *Relevance to today*: the reader's comparisons between the historical lesson and present-day events and ideas about what today's individuals can learn from past events.
3. Note the number of pages in the lesson to be read. Then read the passage aloud, pausing as you encounter answers to map components in the text. Fill in the map components on the transparency or chalkboard as you identify answers to them in the lesson.
4. After you have read through the entire lesson, read the map components aloud or call on students to do so. Guide the class in checking what you have written for accuracy and completeness, and add more information as necessary.
5. Distribute copies of the five generic comprehension questions and have students silently read the questions and write down their responses without referring back to the text.
6. Review the answers to the questions and have students correct their responses using red pens.
7. Continue this modeling phase for two more lessons or until most students are achieving ratings of "3" (satisfactory) or higher on four of the five questions.

Stage 2: Lead Phase

1. Distribute copies of the map and instruct the students to read the lesson silently.
2. Demonstrating with the overhead projector or on the chalkboard, help students reexamine the lesson for answers to map components and complete their maps.
3. Have students take turns orally rereading the contents of the map components, checking for accuracy, and adding more information if necessary.

4. Collect the maps, distribute the comprehension questions, and have students complete them.
5. Have students correct their papers with red pens while you review answers to the questions and discuss any discrepancies between incorrect comprehension answers and correct map information. Have students rewrite any incorrect answers.

Stage 3: Test Phase

1. As students become successful in completing the map components, discontinue classwide demonstrations and provide individual help as needed.
2. When the majority of students are obtaining satisfactory ratings on all five of the comprehension questions with little or no assistance, discontinue use of the map.
3. If desired, discontinue the use of the comprehension questions. Instead, have students read the lesson silently and then write a paragraph pertaining to each of the map components during class time or as a homework assignment.

Evaluation (Select One or More)

Option 1

1. Compare individual and/or class daily average scores on the five generic comprehension questions before and after implementation.

Option 2

1. Compare grades on weekly or end-of-unit social studies quizzes and tests for the entire class before and after implementation.

Option 3

1. Compare the average number of comprehension strategies reported by the target group of students before and after implementation.

Variation: Critical Thinking Maps with a Self-Monitoring Component

1. Have students monitor their own progress by graphing their scores on the comprehension quizzes in their social studies folders.

Notes

1. This intervention lends itself readily to a collaborative learning format. After students work in pairs or small groups to complete their maps, have the pairs or groups help you as you complete a map on the chalkboard or a transparency. Provide time for students to correct their maps if necessary so that they can use them as study aids.
2. To save instructional time, have students read the lesson as homework and conduct a brief review prior to map completion (see Stage 2, Step 2).

Source

Idol, L. (1987a). A critical thinking map to improve content area comprehension of poor readers. *Remedial and Special Education, 8*(4), 28–40. Copyright 1987 by PRO-ED, Inc. Adapted by permission.

A Map for Critical Thinking

Name: _____ Chapter: _____ Section/Pages: _____

Date: _____ Topic: _____

Important events, points, or steps

```
┌─────────────────────────────────────────────────────────────────┐
│                                                                   │
│                                                                   │
│                                                                   │
│                                                                   │
│                                                                   │
└─────────────────────────────────────────────────────────────────┘
```

Main idea

```
┌─────────────────────────────────────────────────────────────────┐
│                                                                   │
│                                                                   │
│                                                                   │
│                                                                   │
└─────────────────────────────────────────────────────────────────┘
```

Other viewpoints/opinions about this topic

```
┌─────────────────────────────────────────────────────────────────┐
│                                                                   │
│                                                                   │
│                                                                   │
│                                                                   │
│                                                                   │
└─────────────────────────────────────────────────────────────────┘
```

Reader's conclusion

```
┌─────────────────────────────────────────────────────────────────┐
│                                                                   │
│                                                                   │
│                                                                   │
│                                                                   │
└─────────────────────────────────────────────────────────────────┘
```

Relevance to today

```
┌─────────────────────────────────────────────────────────────────┐
│                                                                   │
│                                                                   │
│                                                                   │
│                                                                   │
└─────────────────────────────────────────────────────────────────┘
```

FIGURE 4.15. Map for *Improving Content Area Comprehension with a Critical Thinking Map*. From Idol (1987a, p. 30). Copyright 1987 by PRO-ED, Inc. Adapted by permission.

Showing What You've Learned

Name: _____ Chapter: _____ Section/Pages: _____
Date: _____ Topic: _____

1. What is the main idea in this passage?

2. What were the important steps that led to the main idea?

3. What are some other points of view or missing information about this topic?

4. What is your own conclusion?

5. How is this passage relevant to a problem or issue in today's world?

FIGURE 4.16. Generic comprehension questions for *Improving Content Area Comprehension with a Critical Thinking Map*. Adapted from Idol (1987a, p. 32). Copyright 1987 by PRO-ED, Inc. Adapted by permission.

ADMIRALS AND GENERALS: IMPROVING CONTENT AREA PERFORMANCE WITH STRATEGY INSTRUCTION AND PEER TUTORING

Overview

For success in the content areas of social studies and science, students must be able to read the textbook, organize and remember content, retrieve important facts and concepts for tests, and express themselves in written form on classroom tasks and assessments. In this intervention, which combines comprehension strategy instruction with peer tutoring, students work in pairs to read textbook passages aloud, apply summarization strategies to the material, and tutor each other using the summary fact sheets they have prepared. During the oral reading portion, the higher performing student reads first to provide a more effective reading model before the lower performing student reads the same material. Originally implemented with middle and high school students with disabilities in history and social studies classes, the strategy was successful in improving student summarization skills and performance on tests and quizzes, as well as increasing on-task behavior, compared with traditional instruction or a guided-notes condition. Moreover, teachers and students alike rated the strategy highly. A variation that permits more rapid content coverage is also presented.

Purpose

To improve performance in social studies and history classes by teaching students a summarization strategy in the context of a peer tutoring format.

Materials

1. Overhead projector and blank transparencies (optional).
2. Social studies or history textbook, one per student.

3. Posterboard charts listing (a) the rules for peer tutoring, (b) procedures for identifying and correcting oral reading errors, and (c) questions included on the summarization sheets.
4. Cue cards, consisting of index cards listing the same information as the charts, one card per student.
5. Review sheets listing key points and vocabulary terms from the target chapter, one review sheet per student per week.
6. 10-item multiple-choice or short-answer quizzes covering the content on the review sheets, one quiz per student per week.
7. Manila folders containing sheets of lined paper (for summaries), review sheets, and cue cards, one folder per student.

Observation (Select One or More)

Option 1

1. Have the entire class or a group of target students silently read a paragraph from the social studies or history textbook. Then have the students write a 10- to 15-word sentence summarizing the paragraph they have just read.
2. Score summary sentences on a 5-point scale for completeness and accuracy as follows: 1 = very poor, 2 = fair, 3 = average, 4 = good, and 5 = excellent.
3. If desired, calculate a class average summarization score by summing individual scores and dividing by the number of students in the class.

Option 2

1. Calculate the class average percent-correct score on social studies or history tests for the previous grading period.

Option 3

1. Using a *Classwide Scanning Form* with a 3- or 5-minute interval, scan the room at the end of each interval, starting with the front of the room and ending with the back, and tally the number of students in each of the following behavior categories:
   a. *Active engagement,* defined as writing when requested, looking at the teacher, reading aloud from or following along in the textbook, responding to teacher-delivered questions, or any other behavior relevant to the lesson.
   b. *Passive off-task behavior,* defined as sitting quietly but not attending to the lesson.
   c. *Disruptive behavior,* defined as making noises, getting out of seat, calling out, or any other behavior that interferes with instruction or the on-task behavior of other students.
2. Conduct these observations for 30 to 45 minutes for 4 to 7 days during the social studies or history instructional period.

Intervention Steps

Introduction and Training

1. Using grades, standardized tests, and/or teacher judgment, divide the class into pairs, each consisting of one higher performing and one lower performing student.
2. Explain to the students that they will be working together in pairs to help them learn and remember the information in their textbooks. Tell them that one student in the pair (the higher performing reader) is the admiral and the other (lower performing reader) is the general. (Admirals always read first so that the lower performing student has a more fluent model prior to reading independently.)

3. Demonstrate the rules and procedures for partner reading as described below, using a student as the tutee. Then distribute the folders containing the cue cards and other materials, have students move to their tutoring stations (i.e., paired desks), and conduct a classwide practice while you circulate to provide assistance and support as needed.

Implementation

1. Begin with a brief whole-class review of the information covered the previous day. Then present key new concepts to activate students' prior knowledge and build background knowledge of the content to be covered.
2. Distribute the folders and have students work in pairs to apply the following procedures to each assigned paragraph in the textbook or curricular materials:
    a. The admirals (readers) read one paragraph while the generals (tutors) follow along and listen. If the reader misreads a word, omits a word, or pauses for more than 4 seconds, the tutor stops the reader, indicates which error has been made, and asks him or her to correct it. If the reader cannot correct the error, the tutor prompts, corrects the error, or asks for teacher assistance if the word is unfamiliar. The reader then rereads the sentence and continues.
    b. Then students reverse roles, with the generals reading the same paragraph a second time and the admirals correcting reading errors and prompting as described above.
    c. After reading each paragraph, students ask each other the following three questions in order: (1) "Who or what is the section about?" (2) "What is happening to the who or what?" and (3) "What is the summary sentence (in 10 to 15 words)?"
3. Students work with their partners to develop answers to the three questions but record their answers independently on their own summarization sheets.
4. After completing the summarization sheets, students use the review sheets to take turns asking each other questions from the chapter.
5. During tutoring sessions, circulate to answer questions and assist students in generating correct answers and summary sentences as needed. Tutoring sessions should last about 35 minutes. If a pair completes the assigned reading before the allotted time is up, have them quiz each other on additional material from the chapter.
6. When about 10 minutes remain in the period, conduct a whole-class review session. Using the chalkboard or overhead projector, call on students to supply their responses to the three questions. Discuss responses that differ and encourage students to modify their own answers to reflect information based on the classwide discussion.
7. As students become more proficient in the summarization strategy, have the pairs read three paragraphs at a time and then answer the questions for those three paragraphs.

Evaluation (Select One or More)

Option 1

1. Compare summarization scores for the entire class or the target students before and after implementation.

Option 2

1. Compare class average percent-correct scores on social studies or history tests before and after implementation.

Option 3

1. Compare classwide rates of active engagement, passive off-task behavior, and disruptive behavior before and after implementation.

Variation: Peer Tutoring without Listening Previewing

1. Rather than having the generals read the passages previously read by the admirals, have students read successive paragraphs during tutoring sessions. This variation permits greater content coverage and may be more acceptable to students. In the original studies, some of the students complained about having to read material previously read by their partners. Monitor students' progress carefully, however, and reinstitute the repeated reading if the class shows signs of struggling.

Notes

1. Training takes three to four sessions. Introduce the rules and procedures for partner reading and error correction in the first one or two sessions. In subsequent sessions, introduce the summarization strategies and the review sheet activity.
2. To assist students in decoding and understanding unfamiliar terms and proper names during oral reading, review key vocabulary terms, including people and places in the text, as part of the whole-class discussion prior to each peer tutoring session.
3. Teachers in the original investigations commented that careful partner pairing was critical to keeping students on task and maintaining a positive learning environment.

Sources

Mastropieri, M. A., Scruggs, T. E., Spencer, V., & Fontana, J. (2003). Promoting success in high school world history: Peer tutoring versus guided notes. *Learning Disabilities Research and Practice, 18,* 52–65. Copyright 2003 by Blackwell Publishing. Adapted by permission.

Spencer, V. G., Scruggs, T. E., & Mastropieri, M. A. (2003). Content area learning in middle school social studies classrooms and students with emotional or behavioral disorders: A comparison of strategies. *Behavioral Disorders, 28,* 77–93. Copyright 2003 by the Council for Children with Behavioral Disorders. Adapted by permission.

CONCEPT MAPPING
TO IMPROVE SCIENCE CONTENT COMPREHENSION

Overview

Concept maps, also called *cognitive maps* or *graphic organizers,* use lines, arrows, figures, and diagrams to show how key ideas in textual material are organized and related. Concept mapping facilitates both teaching and learning in the content areas by translating textbook information into a visual display that serves as a blueprint for organizing a reading assignment or a written report based on that reading. Moreover, in contrast to a traditional lecture format, in which students listen passively to teacher-delivered instruction, concept mapping increases academic engagement by requiring students to analyze and organize relevant textual information. In this intervention, students learn to use concept maps displaying the connections between major and minor concepts in science lessons. In the original study, conducted with 124 low-achieving, predominantly Hispanic, inner-city seventh graders, concept mapping instruction improved comprehension scores on an end-of-unit test by approximately six standard deviations over traditional read-and-discuss science instruction. The strategy can be used to enhance comprehension in any subject in which students must understand and remember textual material. A variation with text reading at home that permits more rapid coverage of the curriculum is also included.

Purpose

To help students understand, categorize, and remember science content by using concept maps during whole-class instruction.

Materials

1. Science curricular materials, including a teacher's guide and student textbooks or materials, one textbook or set of materials per student.
2. Transparency or paper copy of a sample concept map for a previously taught chapter or unit of study.
3. Two concept maps for each unit of study to be targeted (one completed map as a key and one blank map per student; see Figure 4.17 for an example).
4. Overhead projector and transparencies with completed and blank concept maps (optional).

Observation (Select One or More)

1. Calculate the class average percent-correct score on science quizzes and tests for several weeks or for the previous grading period.
2. Calculate the number of students with grades of D or F in science for the current marking period or the school year thus far.
3. Administer *Curriculum-Based Vocabulary-Matching Probes* to the entire class or a group of target students.

Intervention Steps

1. Explain to the students that they will be learning a new way of analyzing and organizing information in their science textbooks so that they can understand and remember the material better and do better on tests and quizzes.
2. Introduce the unit of study by asking questions to assess students' prior knowledge of the content. Also ask students what they would like to learn about the topic and help them to make predictions about the topic.
3. Give a global overview of the unit and introduce the main unit objectives. *Example:* For a unit on the circulatory system, the main objectives are: (a) understanding the three main parts of the circulatory system, (b) identifying the subcategories of the circulatory system, and (c) describing the subcategory characteristics and functions.
4. Display the concept map based on familiar material on a transparency or reproduce it on the chalkboard. Explain how the map depicts the main concept and graphically illustrates how the subordinate ideas and details in the material are related to the main concept. Explain that you will be helping them construct concept maps for the new material to be covered.
5. At the beginning of the unit, display the blank map. During each lesson, continue constructing the map as you read through the unit with the students section by section. As you fill in the map, call on students to help you locate the information to be included.
6. After each section has been read, conduct a discussion of the key ideas, and have students fill in the relevant parts of their own concept maps.
7. Continue discussing the material in the unit and helping students to map each major component and specific details under each of the subheadings. Repeat this process until you have completed the entire unit and students have completed their concept maps.
8. Have students take the concept maps home as study guides for the unit test.

9. As students become more proficient in constructing the maps, have them work in pairs to map an assignment independently, using a concept map template previously introduced in class. Then have the student pairs construct concept maps on their own for a section in a unit. Review the maps as a whole-class activity, and have students modify their maps as needed.

Evaluation (Select One or More)

Option 1

1. Compare the class average percent-accuracy scores on science quizzes or chapter tests before and after implementation.

Option 2

1. Compare the number of students with grades of D or F in science before and after implementation.

Option 3

1. Compare scores on *Curriculum-Based Vocabulary-Matching Probes* for the entire class or the target students before and after implementation.

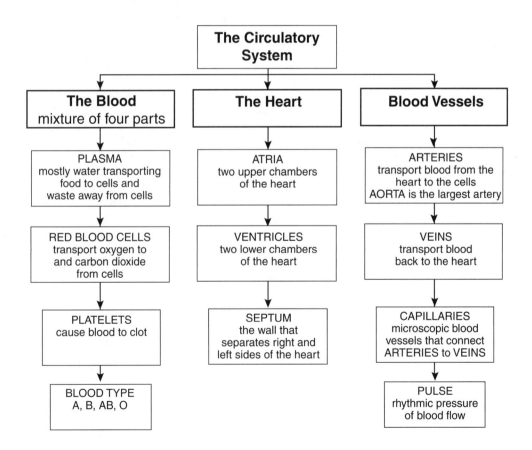

FIGURE 4.17. Example of a concept map for the circulatory system. From Guastello, Beasley, and Sinatra (2000, p. 361). Copyright 2000 by PRO-ED, Inc. Reprinted by permission.

Variation: Concept Mapping with Home Prereading

1. Have students read sections of the target unit as homework the night before you conduct concept mapping instruction with that content. This variation permits more rapid coverage of the curriculum, but it is not recommended for classes with large numbers of very poor readers.

Source

Guastello, E. F., Beasley, T. M., & Sinatra, R. C. (2000). Concept mapping effects on science content comprehension of low-achieving inner-city seventh graders. *Remedial and Special Education, 21,* 356–365. Copyright 2000 by PRO-ED, Inc. Adapted by permission.

Additional Resources

Concept map templates and concept map-generation programs are available for free download on numerous websites, including the University of Oregon's Computer-Based Study Strategies (*http://cbss.uoregon.edu/clearing/index.html*), Houghton Mifflin's Education Place (*http://www. eduplace.com/graphicorganizer/index.html*), Teach-nology (*http://www.teach-nology.com*), and the International Reading Association's Read Write Think site (*http://www.readwritethink.org*).

IMPROVING COMPREHENSION OF SCIENCE TEXT WITH A SUMMARIZATION STRATEGY

Overview

Many students have trouble in content area courses because they lack effective reading strategies, such as identifying main ideas, summarizing information, and monitoring their own learning. Summarization is an especially important strategy for students with poor comprehension skills because it helps them to organize and retain important textual information for use in reading and writing assignments. In this intervention, a three-part instructional sequence—review, modeling, and guided practice—is used to teach a summarization strategy for comprehending science text. A peer review component is included to provide performance feedback and reinforce learning. In the original study, implemented in a summer remedial program with five elementary school students with learning disabilities, the intervention produced substantial increases in science text comprehension and completeness of written summaries for all the participants, with the results maintained at a 4-week follow-up. Moreover, the students reported that the strategy helped them understand their science texts, and a group of general education elementary school teachers judged the strategy to be effective and easy to implement. In this adaptation, a second peer-mediated practice component has been added to increase usability and motivation. The intervention can be implemented in any content area subject to enhance textual comprehension.

Purpose

To improve the comprehension of science text using a nine-step summarization strategy with a peer collaboration component.

Materials

1. Overhead projector and transparencies of a text passage and the summary writing guide, optional (see Figure 4.18 on p. 305).
2. Paper copies of the summary writing guide, one per student.
3. Short comprehension quizzes, one per training passage (optional).

Observation (Select One or More)

Option 1

1. Select a passage in the science textbook that students have not read. Develop a list of the most important information items in the passage.
2. Have a group of target students or the entire class read the passage and write a half-page summary of the content.
3. Calculate the percentage of important information items included in each summary by summing the number of important items included, dividing by the total number of important items, and multiplying by 100.

Option 2

1. Calculate the class average percent-correct score on science quizzes and tests for several weeks or for the previous grading period.

Option 3

1. Calculate the percentage of students with grades of D or F in science for the current grading period or the school year thus far.

Intervention Steps

Introduction and Training

1. Tell students that they will be learning a summarization strategy to help them understand and remember the information in their science texts.
2. Describe a summary as follows: (a) a summary should contain only important information from what you have read, (b) it should not include personal and unnecessary information, (c) it should combine information when possible, and (d) it should be written in your own words.
3. Describe the cues that help identify the main ideas in a textbook passage, including (a) large type size; (b) italicized and underlined words; (c) words and phrases such as *important, relevant,* and *the purpose is*; (d) pictures and tables; (e) introductory and summary sentences; and (f) repeated words and sentences.
4. Display the transparency of the summary writing guide on the projector or create it on the chalkboard. Review each step in the strategy, including a rationale for its inclusion (see Figure 4.18).
5. Have students follow along in their textbooks as you read through a selected passage and model how to use the summary writing guide. If desired, select a passage that students have read the night before as part of a homework assignment so that they are familiar with the content.
6. Work through the nine steps, using a think-aloud format and including self-instruction statements such as, "What is it I have to do? I need to ... " As you fill in the guide, call on students to help you identify cues to the main ideas that can help in writing the summary.
7. During a second training session, model completing the guide for another passage as described above, but have students fill in their guides as you fill in each step on the transparency or chalkboard. Then have students use their completed guides to write a summary of the passage.
8. When students have completed their summaries, have them work in pairs to share their summaries and give each other feedback. Allow time for students to revise their summaries, based on their partner's feedback.

9. Have several students read their summaries aloud, and provide praise and corrective feedback as needed. Conduct a brief discussion reviewing elements of the most effective summaries, and allow time for students to revise their summaries based on the discussion.

10. If desired, administer a short comprehension test based on the target passage, and have students exchange and score each other's papers while you go over the answers. Remind students that using the summarization strategy can help them improve their performance on tests and quizzes.

11. Conduct several more practice sessions until students are proficient in the strategy, as demonstrated by the ability to state the nine steps in order and use the guides to complete summaries of assigned passages with at least 90% accuracy and completeness.

Implementation

1. Continue to have students use the guides to write summaries of passages read in class or as homework assignments. For passages read in class, have students work in pairs to provide each other with feedback on the completeness and accuracy of their summaries.

2. Begin by having students write summaries of a few paragraphs at a time and gradually increase the length of the passages and summaries as students become proficient in the use of the strategy.

3. Gradually fade the use of the guides and summaries as an in-class activity, but encourage students to continue to apply the strategy while reading their textbooks at home and to retain their guides and summaries as study aids for tests.

Evaluation (Select One or More)

Option 1

1. Compare the percentage of important information items included in passage summaries for the target students or the entire class before and after implementation.

Option 2

1. Compare the class average percent-correct score on science quizzes and tests before and after implementation.

Option 3

1. Calculate the percentage of students with grades of D or F in science before and after implementation.

Note

1. In the original study, the teacher used two overhead projectors simultaneously during training, one to display the training passage and one to display the summary writing guide.

Source

Nelson, J. R., Smith, D. J., & Dodd, J. M. (1992). The effects of teaching a summary skills strategy to students identified as learning disabled on their comprehension of science text. *Education and Treatment of Children, 15*, 228–243. Copyright 1992 by West Virginia University Press. Adapted by permission.

Summary Writing Guide

Part 1: Identify and Organize the Main Idea and Important Information

Step 1: Think to yourself—"What was the main idea?" Write down the main idea.

_____

Step 2: Think to yourself—"What important things did the writer say about the main idea?"
Write down the important things that the writer said.

      1. _____

      2. _____

      3. _____

      4. _____

Step 3: Go back and check to make sure you understood what the main idea was and the important things the writer said about this.

Step 4: Think to yourself—"What is the main idea or topic that I am going to write about?"
      Write a topic sentence for your summary. _____

Step 5: Think to yourself—"How should I group my ideas?" Put a "1" next to the idea you want to be first, put a "2" next to the idea you want to be second, and so on.

Step 6: Think to yourself—"Is there any important information that I left out? Or is there any unimportant information than I can take out?" Revise your summary if necessary.

Step 7: Write a summary about what you have read.

Part 2: Clarify and Revise the Summary

Step 8: Read your summary and think to yourself—"Is there anything that is not clear?"
      Rewrite your summary if necessary.

Step 9: Ask a classmate to read your summary and tell you if there is anything that is not clear.
      Rewrite your summary if necessary.

FIGURE 4.18. Summary Writing Guide for *Improving Comprehension of Science Text with a Summary Skills Strategy*. Adapted from Nelson, Smith, and Dodd (1992, p. 233). Copyright 1992 by West Virginia University Press. Adapted by permission.

COLLABORATIVE STRATEGIC READING

Overview

Many students perform poorly in content area subjects because they lack the metacognitive skills necessary to monitor their reading comprehension, as well as strategies to improve their understanding when they have difficulty. Collaborative strategic reading (CSR) combines reading comprehension strategy instruction with cooperative learning to enhance students' understanding of expository textual material. Students learn four strategies through direct instruction and teacher modeling: (1) *Preview* (previewing and predicting), (2) *Click and Clunk* (monitoring for understanding and vocabulary knowledge), (3) *Get the Gist* (identifying the main idea), and (4) *Wrap-Up* (self-questioning for understanding). After students have become proficient in applying the strategies during teacher-directed activities, they work in groups to implement the strategies collaboratively, with each student performing a designated role. Originally developed to enhance comprehension and content knowledge acquisition for students with learning disabilities and low-achieving students, CSR has also yielded positive outcomes for English language learners and average- and high-achieving students across a range of grade levels, including elementary, middle, and high school. CSR can be used to enhance comprehension and domain knowledge in any content area subject or with narrative textual material.

Purpose

To improve reading comprehension, increase conceptual learning, and promote active student involvement in content area classes by teaching comprehension strategies within a collaborative peer context.

Materials

1. "Cue cards," consisting of index cards listing the responsibilities for each group member, one set of cards per group.
2. "Learning logs," consisting of preprinted sheets of paper, one per student (see Figure 4.19).
3. Three-hole binders or folders with sheets of lined paper and pockets for learning logs, one per student.
4. Posterboard charts or overhead projector with transparencies of the learning log form and CSR plan (see Figures 4.19 and 4.20 on p. 310).
5. Curricular materials, such as content area textbooks and student newspapers or magazines.
6. Timers or watches with second hands, one per group (optional).

Observation (Select One or More)

Option 1

1. Calculate scores on homework, quizzes, or unit tests in the selected content area subject for the entire class or a target group of students for the grading period to date.

Option 2

1. Administer *Curriculum-Based Vocabulary-Matching Probes* to the entire class or a group of target students.

Option 3

1. Using a *Classwide Scanning Form* with a 3- or 5-minute interval, scan the room at the end of each interval, starting with the front of the room and ending with the back, and tally the number of students in each of the following behavior categories:
   a. *On-task behavior,* defined as asking or answering lesson-oriented questions, writing when requested, looking at the teacher during presentations, and any other behavior relevant to the lesson.
   b. *Off-task behavior,* defined as sitting without appropriate materials, looking at nonlesson materials, or failing to work after assignments have been made.
   c. *Disruptive behavior,* defined as any behavior interfering with instruction or the on-task behavior of other students, such as talking without permission, getting out of seat, or making noises.
2. Conduct these observations for 30 to 45 minutes for 4 to 7 days during the selected content area class.

Intervention Steps

Introduction and Training

1. Explain to students that they will be learning a set of strategies to help them understand and remember what they read. These are strategies that good readers use automatically when they read, but everyone can learn them. After students learn the strategies, they will be working in groups to apply them.
2. Display the Plan for Strategic Reading Chart (see Figure 4.20). Explain that the *Preview* and *Wrap Up* strategies are used only once per reading selection (*Preview* before reading the entire passage for that session [typically 12 to 14 paragraphs] and *Wrap Up* after reading the entire passage), whereas the *Click and Clunk* and *Get the Gist* strategies are used after each paragraph or two.
3. Using a selection from a student magazine or newspaper, model the strategies described below, using a think-aloud procedure. Verbalize your thoughts to make explicit why, how, and when you apply each of the strategies while reading. As you model the strategies, display the learning log form on a chart or overhead projector (see Figure 4.19). Explain that learning logs can be used for recording ideas while applying each strategy or for writing down "clunks" (unfamiliar words and concepts) and "gists" (main ideas).

STEP 1: PREVIEW

1. *Preview* is designed to generate interest and questions about the material, stimulate background knowledge and associations, and assist in predictions. When students have little background information about a topic, conduct this step as a whole-class activity prior to small-group work.
2. Using the selected passage, model the Preview steps as follows: (a) read the title; (b) examine the visual clues, such as pictures, tables, charts, and graphs; (c) read the headings and predict what they mean; (d) look for key words, as indicated by highlighting, underlining, and italics; (e) read the first and last paragraphs of the selection; and (f) predict what you think you will learn from the selection.
3. Using another selection, conduct a whole-class practice of the Preview step and provide feedback and assistance as needed.

STEP 2: CLICK AND CLUNK

1. Tell students that this step will help them think about what they do and don't understand about what they are reading. A "click" occurs when readers identify something they know—it clicks because it makes sense. A "clunk" is a word or concept that readers don't understand—it's like a running into a brick wall.
2. Display the learning log form and explain that learning logs can be used to record ideas while applying each strategy or to write down clunks.
3. Tell students that readers can "de-clunk" words by using "fix-up strategies," such as consulting a dictionary, rereading, or asking a classmate or the teacher. Refer to the fix-up strategies on the Plan for Strategic Reading chart, and tell students that these strategies can help them de-clunk difficult words and ideas.
4. Using the same selection as in Step 1, model the Click and Clunk process. Then have students read another short selection and practice clicking and clunking. Provide photocopies of the selection, so that students can mark their clicks and clunks in the margins of the text.

STEP 3: GET THE GIST

1. Explain that "getting the gist" means identifying the main idea or most critical information in a section of text (one or two paragraphs) and rephrasing it in one's own words.

2. Have students read two paragraphs in their text, think of a gist (a sentence of no more than 12 words summarizing the main idea), and write it on a sheet of paper. Call on students to share their gists and ask them to provide evidence to support them. Then have the students vote as a class on which gist is the best and why.

STEP 4: WRAP UP

1. Tell students that *Wrap Up* is an opportunity to review what they have read by asking themselves questions about the passage and thinking about the most important ideas.
2. Model a series of literal and inferential questions about the passage, such as: (a) "How would you ... ?", (b) "How were ___ and ___ the same or different?", and (c) "How would you interpret ... ?"
3. After modeling questions for the selection, help students generate their own questions.

Implementation

1. After conducting whole-class training and practice sessions for each step, divide the class into groups of four or five. Be sure that each group includes students with a variety of reading levels and at least one student with leadership skills.
2. Assign the following roles in each group and explain the tasks for each role as follows:
   a. *Leader*: Focuses the group on the four strategies by saying what to read next and what strategy to apply next. The leader also asks the teacher for assistance, if necessary.
   b. *Clunk expert*: Reminds the group of fix-up strategies for figuring out difficult words or concepts.
   c. *Gist expert*: Helps the group remember the steps in figuring out the main idea and makes sure that the main idea includes the key ideas without unnecessary details.
   d. *Announcer*: Calls on group members to read or share ideas and represents the group during whole-class group reporting.
   e. *Encourager* (if there is a fifth student in a group): Encourages all group members to participate, gives feedback to members, evaluates how well the group has worked together, and provides suggestions for improvement.
3. Initially, the clunk expert records the clunks and the gist expert records the gists. As students become more skillful in performing their roles, introduce the learning logs so that each student can record his or her own clunks and gists.
4. Give each group a set of cue cards. Explain that the cue cards are reminders of the steps each student in the group should follow. Rotate roles each week so that each student has an opportunity to practice all the functions.
5. Assign a selection from the textbook, and have the groups practice applying the four strategies. Initially, have the leader select group members to read the text aloud, two paragraphs at a time. Also specify time limits for each of the steps, depending on the length of the instructional period, and call time for each step. If desired, have group members share their gists orally to save time as they work through the material. As the groups work, circulate to clarify difficult words, model strategy use, and provide positive feedback or redirection as needed.
6. After the group sessions, conduct a whole-class debriefing, during which you invite the groups to share their gists, clunks, and effective fix-up strategies.
7. Have the students work in CSR groups several times a week with expository text until they can use the strategies effectively (about 2 to 3 weeks for elementary school students or 1 week for middle and high school students). After students have reached proficiency, substitute CSR two or three times a week for whole-class textbook reading sessions.
8. Discontinue the cue cards as students become more proficient in using the strategies and carrying out their roles. Gradually discontinue whole-class timing, or have the groups serve as their own timekeepers.

Evaluation (Select One or More)

Option 1

1. Compare scores on content area homework assignments, quizzes, or unit tests for the entire class or the target group of students before and after implementation.

Option 2

1. Compare scores on *Curriculum-Based Vocabulary-Matching Probes* for the entire class or the target students before and after implementation.

Option 3

1. Compare rates of on-task, off-task, and disruptive behavior during the selected content area class before and after implementation.

Variation: Group-Prepared Learning Logs

1. Have students prepare learning logs as a collaborative rather than an individual activity. Assign one student per group to serve as recorder, and have the groups refer to their logs during whole-class discussions.

Notes

1. Training takes about 4 days. For the first day of training, model the entire CSR plan to help students get the big picture. On subsequent days, provide instruction in how to implement each of the CSR strategies. Starting with the fourth day, teach students how to work in groups to implement the strategies on a collaborative basis.
2. When beginning CSR, use short selections from high-interest nonfiction publications, such as student news magazines or community-based newspapers, rather than from a textbook.

Sources

Klingner, J. K., Vaughn, S., & Schumm, J. S. (1998). Collaborative strategic reading during social studies in heterogeneous fourth-grade classrooms. *Elementary School Journal, 99,* 3–22. Copyright 1998 by the University of Chicago. Adapted by permission.

Vaughn, S., & Klingner, J. K. (1999). Teaching reading comprehension through collaborative strategic reading. *Intervention in School and Clinic, 34,* 284–292. Copyright 1999 by PRO-ED, Inc. Adapted by permission.

Additional Resources

Resources for implementing Collaborative Strategic Reading, including overheads for use in professional development, are available at the Vaughn Gross Center for Reading and Language Arts, University of Texas at Austin, website (*http://www.texasreading.org/utcrla/*). A variety of CSR forms are also available at the International Reading Association's Read Write Think website (*http://www.readwritethink.org/lessons/lesson_view.asp?id=95*). A commercially published version of CSR is available from Sopris West (*http://www.sopriswest.com*).

Today's topic: _____ Date:_____

Before Reading: PREVIEW	During Reading: CLUNKS	After Reading: WRAP UP
What I already know about the topic		My questions about the important ideas in the passage
What I predict I will learn		What I learned

FIGURE 4.19. Example of a *Collaborative Strategic Reading* learning log. Adapted from Vaughn and Klingner (1999, p. 291). Copyright 1999 by PRO-ED, Inc. Adapted by permission.

A Plan for Strategic Reading

Before Reading
Step 1: Preview
1. *Brainstorm:* What do we already know about the topic?
2. *Predict:* What do we think we will learn about the topic when we read the passage?
Read the first paragraph or section.

During Reading
Step 2: Click and Clunk
1. Were there any parts that were hard to understand (clunks)?
2. How can we fix the clunks? Use **fix-up strategies**.
   a. Reread the sentence with the clunk and the sentences before and after the clunk looking for clues.
   b. Reread the sentence without the clunk. Think about what would make sense.
   c. Look for a prefix or suffix in the clunk that might help.
   d. Break the clunk apart and look for smaller words you already know.

Step 3: Get the Gist
1. What is the most important who or what?
2. What is the most important idea about the who or what?
Read: Do Steps 2 and 3 again with all the paragraphs or sections in the passage.

After Reading
Step 4: Wrap Up
1. *Ask questions:* What questions would show we understand the most important information?
2. *Review:* What did we learn?

FIGURE 4.20. Plan for *Collaborative Strategic Reading*. Adapted from Klingner, Vaughn, and Schumm (1998, pp. 19–20). Copyright 1998 by the University of Chicago. Adapted by permission.

PRINT RESOURCES

Rathvon, N. (2004b). *Early reading assessment: A practitioner's handbook*. New York: Guilford Press.

This text provides a comprehensive overview of the field of early reading assessment, including a discussion of the essential components of reading acquisition and critical reviews of 42 measures selected for optimal technical adequacy and usability.

Shapiro, E. S. (2004a). *Academic skills problems: Direct assessment and intervention* (3rd ed.). New York: Guilford Press.
Shapiro, E. S. (2004b). *Academic skills problems workbook* (rev. ed.). New York: Guilford Press.

The author presents a four-step model of direct academic assessment and intervention: (1) assessing the academic environment, (2) assessing instructional placement, (3) designing and implementing instructional modifications, and (4) monitoring progress. Detailed case examples for applying the model and the assessment and intervention strategies are provided. The companion workbook includes the complete manual for the Behavioral Observation of Students in Schools (BOSS), and a wealth of reproducible forms and practice exercises.

WEBSITES

National Center for Culturally Responsive Educational Systems (NCCRESt)
http://www.nccrest.org

Funded by the U.S. Department of Education' Office of Special Education Programs (OSEP), NCCRESt provides technical assistance and professional development to close the achievement gap between students from culturally and linguistically diverse backgrounds and their peers and reduce inappropriate referrals to special education. Available evidence-based publications include practitioner briefs, technical reports, and "exemplars" summarizing models and activities of culturally responsive schools.

National Center on Student Progress Monitoring
http://www.studentprogress.org

Funded by OSEP, the National Center on Student Progress Monitoring provides information and technical assistance to states and districts to implement progress monitoring in different content areas for grades K–5.

Special Connections
http://www.specialconnections.ku.edu

Funded by OSEP and coordinated by the University of Kansas, Special Connections provides resources to support students with special needs in accessing the general education curriculum. Best practices, teacher tools, case studies, and resources are provided for four main areas of focus: Instruction, Assessment, Behavior Plans, and Collaboration.

APPENDIX 4.1. Summary Characteristics of Academic Interventions

Intervention	Description	Comments
Interventions to Enhance Academic Productivity		
ClassWide Peer Tutoring	In this team-based strategy, pairs of students practice oral reading, math facts, or basic academic skills.	CWPT can be implemented in any subject area to provide additional opportunities to practice basic skills.
Cover, Copy, Compare: Increasing Academic Performance with Self-Management	Students respond in writing to questions or problems, compare their answers with a model, and correct their own errors.	CCC is ideal for use during the practice portion of a lesson. Including some form of incentive is recommended to maintain interest and motivation.
Self-Monitoring of Academic Productivity	Students monitor their own academic productivity and academically related behavior using a simple printed form.	Because self-monitoring occurs on an individual basis, this strategy can be unobtrusively implemented with individuals or small groups of target students.
Using Response Cards to Increase Academic Engagement and Achievement	Students respond to teacher questions using preprinted or write-on cards.	Brief (5- to 10-minute) response card periods can be included to check for student understanding after whole-class presentations. Preprinted cards are more efficient than write-on cards but limit the types of teacher questions that can be asked.
The Rewards Box: Enhancing Academic Performance with Randomized Group Contingencies	Students work to earn group rewards under contingency systems that randomize the criteria for reinforcement.	Teachers and students alike enjoy the unpredictable aspects of this intervention, which lends itself to numerous variations.
Interventions to Enhance Homework Performance		
Team Up for Homework Success	Students work in groups of four to set goals for home-work performance, monitor their own progress, and earn access to a classwide raffle.	Randomizing the criterion for the daily homework goal enhances student motivation and task persistence.
Project Best: Seven Steps to Homework Completion	Students learn a seven-step strategy for managing homework assignments, as well as a set of metacognitive behaviors supporting effective homework practices.	Conduct "refresher" sessions after holiday breaks to help students sustain positive homework practices. The effectiveness of this strategy is enhanced when parents participate in the training along with the student.
Promoting Homework Completion and Accuracy with Mystery Motivators	This game-like intervention permits access to an unknown reinforcer if the class achieves a group-oriented homework criterion.	During the first week or two of implementation, set the criterion low enough so that students are successful in obtaining the reward, and then gradually raise the criterion or reduce the number of days per week on which the reinforcer is available.
Reading Interventions: Interventions to Enhance Decoding and Word Identification		
Word Building	Students are guided through a series of three-step lessons in which they form new words by changing a single grapheme in a target word.	This intervention also works well in a differentiated instructional model. Teachers can lead one group through the activity while the other groups engage in the peer tutoring practice component. Trained parents can also deliver this intervention.
DISSECT: The Word Identification Strategy	Students learn a seven-step strategy for pronouncing and recognizing multisyllabic words.	To enhance learning and motivation for use, provide opportunities for students to work in pairs to apply the strategy to classwork assignments.

(continued)

312

Intervention	Description	Comments
Graphosyllabic Analysis: Five Steps to Decoding Complex Words	Students learn a strategy for segmenting a word into syllables and then practice the strategy in pairs.	This strategy is ideal for introducing key vocabulary words prior to lessons in content area subjects.
Paired Reading	This parent-delivered intervention combines simultaneous and independent reading with a simple error correction procedure.	For classroom implementation, pair higher performing students with lower performing students and circulate to provide assistance as needed.

Interventions to Enhance Reading Fluency

Partner Reading	Pairs of students take turns reading the same passage and earn points for their team for positive reading behaviors.	Partner Reading can be easily implemented in inclusive classrooms and classrooms using a differentiated instructional format because student pairs do not have to read the same material.
Parents as Reading Tutors	Parents learn a structured tutoring routine that includes repeated reading and progress monitoring to use with their children at home.	Although originally designed for parent delivery, this strategy is also suitable for cross-grade or after-school tutoring programs.
Listening Previewing with Key Word Discussion	After a discussion of key content words, pairs of students engage in repeated reading, with the more proficient reader reading first.	The previewing and repeated reading features are especially helpful for English language learners. Having student pairs monitor their own progress in reading fluency increases engagement and task persistence. This intervention is suitable for parent delivery.

Interventions to Enhance Vocabulary and Reading Comprehension

Peer Tutoring in Vocabulary	Pairs of students practice new vocabulary words and earn rewards based on the performance of both students.	Use this strategy to teach key vocabulary at the beginning of a new unit and as a review format before tests.
Story Mapping	Students learn to use a visual framework to organize and remember story information.	Adding a self-questioning component, in which students respond to 10 comprehension questions following story mapping, enhances the effectiveness of this intervention.
Peer-Assisted Learning Strategies in Reading	Students learn a three-part peer tutoring routine that includes paired reading with retelling, main idea identification, and prediction.	Full implementation of this multistep strategy works best in extended reading/language arts periods (blocks). Alternately, implement only one or two of the three activities several times a week.
Motivating Reading Performance with Paired Reading and Randomized Group Contingencies	After paired reading, students take brief quizzes on what they have read, with a classwide reward if students meet a randomly selected criterion.	Originally designed for classes using computer-delivered comprehension quizzes, this strategy can be implemented in any subject involving in-class reading of textual material.

(continued)

Intervention	Description	Comments
Interventions to Enhance Mathematics Performance		
Improving Math Fluency with a Multicomponent Intervention	After student pairs practice math facts and take 1-minute assessments, classwide math progress is recorded on a racetrack chart.	This intervention can be used to provide basic skills practice in any subject area. For early primary grade children, the 1-minute assessment can be omitted to enhance usability.
Reciprocal Peer Tutoring in Math	Tutoring pairs select their own math goals and work toward group-oriented rewards.	Parent involvement enhances the effectiveness of this strategy in terms of students' math achievement and their attitudes toward mathematics.
FAST DRAW: Improving Math Word Problem Solving with Strategy Instruction	Students learn an eight-step strategy for solving common word problems and practice it in pairs.	The paired practice portion of this intervention permits teachers to provide additional assistance and support to low-performing students.
Interventions to Enhance Spelling Performance		
Three Steps to Better Spelling with Word Boxes	Students make connections between sound and print by writing letters as they pronounce sounds in sequence.	Word box instruction can also be used to enhance phonemic awareness by using tokens rather than letter tiles. This intervention is suitable for parent delivery.
Spelling Wizards: Accommodating Diverse Learners with Partner Spelling	Students work in tutoring triads to increase opportunities for spelling practice and performance feedback.	Ideal for inclusive classrooms and classrooms serving students with a broad range of spelling skills, this strategy provides more support for low-performing students than traditional paired tutoring formats.
Add-A-Word for Spelling Success	Pairs of students practice spelling words using a four-step self-managed procedure.	This strategy differs from the standard Cover Copy Compare procedure in that students' spelling lists are adjusted based on daily assessments.
Interventions to Enhance Written Expression Performance		
Strategy Instruction in Story Writing	Students learn a self-questioning strategy for composing stories and regulating the writing process in a series of minilessons.	Paired practice is included at several stages to provide additional feedback and enhance motivation.
Writing Power: Cognitive Strategy Instruction in Expository Writing	Students learn five writing subprocesses with the support of "think sheets" linked to each process.	"Think sheets" can be individualized depending on the target writing text structure, students' level of writing skills, and teacher preference.
PLAN and WRITE: Self-Regulated Strategy Development for Essay Writing	Students learn a six-stage strategy for planning, composing, and revising expository essays.	This intervention lends itself to paired or small-group collaborative practice during several stages of the writing process.
Peer Editing for Effective Revision	Students work in pairs to learn and practice a revision strategy that incorporates word processing in the composing and revision stages.	Originally designed for use with a word processing program, this strategy can also be implemented as a paper-and-pencil intervention.

(continued)

Intervention	Description	Comments
Interventions to Enhance Social Studies and Science Performance		
Improving Content Area Comprehension with a Critical Thinking Map	Students learn to use a visual framework to organize and remember information in their content area textbooks.	This intervention can be implemented in any subject in which students must read textual material in order to learn content.
Concept Mapping to Improve Science Content Comprehension	Students use a visual framework to organize and analyze connections between major and minor concepts in science lessons.	For more rapid content coverage, have students read the target unit for homework prior to completing the concept map in the classroom.
Admirals and Generals: Improving Content Area Performance with Strategy Instruction and Peer Tutoring	Student pairs read textbook passages in turn, summarize the material, and then quiz each other using fact sheets they have prepared.	For more rapid content coverage, have students read successive passages rather than having the second student reread the passage previously read by the first student in the pair.
Improving Comprehension of Science Text with a Summarization Strategy	Students learn to use a nine-step strategy to summarize information in their science textbooks.	The summarization strategy and writing guide can be implemented to enhance comprehension in any textbook-based subject.
Collaborative Strategic Reading	Students learn four strategies for comprehending text and practice them as a four-step process in small groups.	To help students stay on task and work productively, assign time limits to each of the four steps and circulate to provide assistance as needed.

CHAPTER 5

Interventions to Improve Behavior and Enhance Social Competence

Dealing with students with problem behavior has been consistently identified as one of the greatest challenges facing today's educators (Martens, Witt, Daly, & Vollmer, 1999; Rose & Gallup, 2006). Behaviors such as calling out, arguing, and failing to comply with teachers' directions not only disrupt instruction, but create a tension-filled classroom environment for teachers and students alike. Managing student behavior can be especially difficult for beginning teachers, who have less experience establishing classroom behavior norms and dealing with unproductive, oppositional, and aggressive students. Although the consistent use of proactive classroom management strategies helps to minimize opportunities for inappropriate behavior, teachers also need a repertoire of practical techniques for responding effectively to problem behaviors when they arise. Strategies that enhance on-task behavior and reduce disruptive behavior are especially critical for promoting the academic and social competence of students at risk for school failure, such as children living in poverty, who are already at risk for lower academic engagement rates and higher levels of aggression (Greenwood, 1991; Kellam, Ling, Merisca, Brown, & Ialongo, 1998).

The interventions in this chapter are organized into two categories, based on setting: (1) strategies for improving behavior and enhancing social competence in the classroom and (2) strategies for improving behavior in nonclassroom situations, such as lunchrooms, gymnasiums, playgrounds, and hallways. Regardless of setting, all of the strategies consist of intervention "packages" containing both proactive components, such as public posting of classroom rules and guided practice in desired behaviors, and reactive components, such as group contingencies and response cost. In keeping with the ecological perspective in this book, emphasis is placed on group-oriented strategies that utilize peer influence to encourage and maintain appropriate behavior. Peer-mediated components can enhance intervention effectiveness for students with problem behavior, who are often more responsive to peer influence than to inducements offered by their teachers for behavior improvement (Utley, Mortweet, & Greenwood, 1997). Similarly, several of the interventions rely on team-based formats in which intraclass teams compete to earn rewards or privileges contingent upon complying with classroom rules or displaying specific prosocial behaviors. Team-based and classwide contingencies are especially helpful for students with poor social skills and/or problem behaviors, who receive lower rates of reinforcement from teachers and peers under typical classroom reward systems (Forehand & Wierson, 1993; Hoff & Robinson, 2002).

Evaluating the Effectiveness of Behavioral Interventions

Researchers have developed a wide variety of instruments for measuring student behavior and social competence, ranging from complex systems assessing dozens of teacher- and student-related variables (e.g., Greenwood, Carta, Kamps, Terry, & Delquadri, 1994; Greenwood et al., 1997) to a single-item measure asking teachers to rate overall class disruption on a scale from 1 to 5: "How disruptive was your class today?" (Bahl, McNeil, Cleavenger, Blanc, & Bennett, 2000, p. 65). Many of the evaluation measures for the interventions in this chapter rely on direct observational recording of target behaviors, such as on- and off-task behavior rates, frequency of positive and negative verbalizations, and frequency of rule infractions. Other assessments involve monitoring teacher responses to student problem behaviors, such as number of reprimands, and student responses to teacher behaviors, such as rates of compliance with teacher directives. Because disruptive behavior interferes with the academic engagement of misbehaving students and often that of their classmates as well, measures of academic productivity are included for some interventions. As in the other strategies in this text, the emphasis is on classwide evaluation procedures, although measures suitable for monitoring the behavior of individuals or a group of target students are provided for most interventions. Evaluation options for several interventions designed for schoolwide implementation include office disciplinary referrals (ODRs), an index frequently used to document problem behavior patterns and response to schoolwide behavior support strategies (e.g., McCurdy, Manella, & Eldridge, 2003; Sugai, Sprague, Horner, & Walker, 2000). In addition, information about functional behavioral assessment (FBA), a critical tool in designing effective behavioral interventions, is provided below.

FUNCTIONAL BEHAVIORAL ASSESSMENT: A NEW APPROACH TO ADDRESSING STUDENT PROBLEM BEHAVIORS

Functional behavioral assessment (FBA) consists of a set of procedures for gathering information to develop hypotheses about the purpose or function of a student's problem behavior in order to develop effective interventions (Reid & Nelson, 2002; Tilly, Knoster, & Ikeda, 2000). FBA includes a wide variety of assessment methods, including observations, interviews, questionnaires, record reviews, and permanent product recording (e.g., samples of academic work). When an FBA involves the experimental manipulation of environmental variables to test the validity of the hypotheses related to the problem behavior, it is termed a *functional analysis* (Sterling-Turner, Robinson, & Wilczynski, 2001). For example, if the data suggest that peer attention is maintaining the inappropriate behavior, that hypothesis can be tested by permitting the student to work with a peer helper contingent on appropriate behavior.

FBA methods are considered best practices for identifying and designing interventions (Gartin & Murdick, 2001; McNamara, 2002) and are an integral part of Tier 2 problem-solving process in response-to-intervention (RTI) approaches. Moreover, FBA methods are recommended or mandated under IDEA 2004 in certain circumstances. Specifically, the IEP team must "consider the use of positive behavioral interventions and supports, and other strategies" to address the behavior of concern in developing an IEP for a student with disabilities whose behavior impedes his or her own learning or the learning of others (34 C.F.R. § 300.324[a][2] [i]). If the current IEP does not address the behavior that is impeding learning, the IEP team must revise the IEP to ensure that appropriate positive behavioral interventions and supports are provided (34 C.F.R. § 300.324[a][2][i]). The requirement for an FBA and a behavior intervention plan (BIP) is also triggered when a student with a disability is removed for more than 10 consecutive school days due to a violation of the code of student conduct. If the manifest determination team (consisting of a subset of the IEP team, including the parent, the district representative, and other "relevant members") determines that the student's behavior was a manifestation of the disability, the local education agency (LEA) must conduct an FBA and implement a BIP based on the FBA. If a BIP was already in place, it must be reviewed and modified to address the problem behavior, and except in cases involving weapons, drugs, or infliction of serious body injury, the student must be returned to the original placement, unless the LEA and parent agree to a change of placement as part of the modified BIP (34 C.F.R. § 300.530[e][f][g]). If the behavior is not judged to be a manifestation of the student's disability, the student may still "receive, as appropriate, a functional behavioral assessment, and behavioral intervention services and modifications" to prevent the problem behavior from reoccurring (34 C.F.R. § 300.530[d][ii]). Although IDEA does not include a definition of FBA or provide guidance in selecting measures or identifying key components, states are beginning to develop definitions and guidance to assist educators in this process (von Ravensberg & Tobin, 2006; Weber, Killu, Derby, & Barretto, 2005).

In evaluating students' response to behavioral interventions, practitioners may also wish to consider the *Social Skills Rating System* (SSRS; Gresham & Elliott, 1990), a user-friendly norm-referenced multirater battery with teacher, parent, and student self-report scales. Norms are stratified into three levels: preschool (ages 3–5; no self-report scale), elementary (ages 5–12), and secondary (ages 13–18). The SSRS assesses three domains: Social Skills, Problem Behaviors, and Academic Competence. The Social Skills Scale includes five subscales (Cooperation, Assertion, Responsibility, Empathy, and Self-Control), with ratings based on frequency and importance. The Problem Behaviors Scale, which is included only in the teacher and parent forms, measures three areas (Externalizing Problems, Internalizing Problems, and Hyperactivity). The Academic Competence Scale is a 5-point scale consisting of items assessing reading and math performance, motivation, parental support, and cognitive functioning. A computer-assisted scoring program that provides behavioral objectives and suggestions for planning interventions is also available. Although the norms are in need of updating, the SSRS has been widely used to predict academic and social outcomes for children (e.g., Agostin & Bain, 1997; Eisenhower, Baker, & Blacher, 2007; Maleki & Elliott, 2002) and evaluate the effectiveness of classroom and schoolwide social skills interventions (e.g., Hennessey, 2007; Lane & Menzies, 2003; Rimm-Kaufman & Chiu, 2007).

Interventions to Improve Behavior and Enhance Social Competence in the Classroom

Designing effective interventions to help students manage negative emotions and cooperate with adults and peers is critical not only in creating an orderly learning environment, but also in promoting the long-term functioning of aggressive and noncompliant children. Students who display aggressive and oppositional/defiant behaviors are at risk for a host of negative developmental outcomes, including school failure, peer rejection, substance abuse, delinquency, and antisocial behavior (Coie, Lochman, Terry, & Hyman, 1992; Hinshaw, 1992a, 1992b; Trembley et al., 1992; Walker, Stieber, Ramsey, & O'Neill, 1991). Although the link between childhood physical aggression and delinquency appears to be much stronger for boys than for girls (Broidy et al., 2003), behavior problems in the early school years are strong predictors of antisocial behavior and psychopathology in adolescence (Egeland, Pianta, & Ogawa, 1996; Lacourse et al., 2002). Given that antisocial behavior patterns become increasingly stable over time (Bennett et al., 1999; Egeland et al., 1996), early intervention is critical to students' future academic and social outcomes.

PATHWAYS TO ANTISOCIAL BEHAVIOR

The importance of early intervention is underscored by research demonstrating the rapidity with which a vicious cycle of ineffective behavior, teacher and peer rejection, and school and social failure can be set in motion. Many aggressive and defiant children have acquired their inappropriate behavioral patterns in homes where parents have failed to teach developmentally appropriate ways of managing negative emotions and have inadvertently reinforced coercive interactional patterns (Patterson, Reid, & Dishion, 1992). When these children enter school, they are likely to continue to engage in similar coercive interactions with their teachers and classmates (Eddy, Reid, & Curry, 2002; Wehby et al., 1998). Because their inappropriate behavior interferes with their ability to succeed academically and to form positive relationships with adults and peers, they fail to earn typical school rewards, such as good grades, positive peer attention, and teacher praise. Deprived of these rewards and increasingly isolated from positive social models, they gravitate to groups of rejected youngsters like themselves who do not require them to display the appropriate behaviors they have failed to acquire (Dishion et al., 1991; Dishion, Nelson, Winter, & Bullock, 2004). Patterson and his colleagues (Patterson et al., 1992) have termed this phenomenon "limited shopping," reflecting the fact that the development of antisocial behaviors increasingly restricts the number and quality of the social settings available to these youngsters. Over time, the limited shopping situation becomes more pronounced, so that children participate in fewer positive social experiences and spend more time associating with deviant peers who provide modeling and encouragement for antisocial behaviors. As the vicious cycle progresses, children's membership in these antisocial peer groups contributes to an escalation of aggressive and defiant behaviors and to the formation of an antisocial identity in which conforming to deviant peer norms overrides the desire to conform to classroom and school norms (Forehand & Wierson, 1993; Loeber & Stouthamer-Loeber, 1998).

Under these circumstances, the power of school personnel to influence student behavior in positive directions is severely compromised. When consultants and teachers attempt to intervene on behalf of these students, the rewards they can offer for appropriate behavior are far less powerful than those provided by the deviant peer group for antisocial actions, such as disrupting class, defying authority figures, or bullying other students (Dishion et al., 1991; Forehand & Wierson, 1993). By the time they enter middle school, these students may have become so attached to the antisocial peer group that they have difficulty altering their image with teachers and peers even if they learn more appropriate ways of behaving (Webster-Stratton, 1993). To counter this problem, many of the interventions in this section capitalize on peer-mediated strategies to mobilize peer support for prosocial behaviors and group-oriented contingencies to encourage peer collaboration in obtaining socially sanctioned rewards.

SOCIAL COMPETENCE AND ACADEMIC ACHIEVEMENT

In contrast to the negative effects of aggressive and disruptive behavior on children's developmental trajectories, social competence, measured as early as kindergarten or first grade, is a strong predictor of academic success (Agostin & Bain, 1997; Alexander, Entwisle, & Dauber, 1993; McClelland et al., 2000). Teachers and researchers alike have consistently identified two key social competencies as essential for school success: (1) self-control and (2) cooperation (Gumpel, 2007; Gumpel & David, 2000; Lane et al., 2002; Pelco & Reed-Victor, 2007). The importance of early interventions to reduce inappropriate behavior and enhance social competence is underscored by an accumulating body of evidence attesting to the powerful negative impact of behavior problems on children's responsiveness to early literacy interventions (see Al Otaiba & Fuchs, 2002, and Nelson, Benner, & Gonzalez, 2003, for reviews). In some treatment studies, attentional or behavior problems prevented children from benefiting even when interventions were delivered in one-to-one tutoring settings (Torgesen et al., 1999; Vadasy, Jenkins, Antil, Wayne, & O'Connor, 1997).

In designing classroom interventions for students with problem behavior, consultants should also carefully assess the need for adjunctive academic interventions (Scott, Nelson, & Liaupsin, 2001). Although it is not clear whether poor school achievement precedes or follows disruptive behavior problems, students with a combination of learning and behavior problems are especially at risk for developing antisocial behavior patterns and thus require a comprehensive set of interventions targeting both sets of problems (Hinshaw, 1992a, 1992b; Tremblay et al., 1992). Observational studies indicate that classroom behavior problems often arise from students' attempts to avoid or escape from academic tasks and that teachers reduce instructional demands to order to avoid confrontations with chronically misbehaving students, thereby reducing opportunities to learn for the very students who are at greatest risk for school failure (Carr, Taylor, & Robinson, 1991; Lalli et al., 1999; Wehby, Tally, & Falk, 2004). Moreover, evidence is accumulating that students with academic deficits are at risk not only for future problem behavior but also for nonresponse to schoolwide behavioral supports (McIntosh et al., 2006).

Types of Social Competence Problems

Social competence problems arise from two basic types of deficits: (1) *acquisition deficits*—deficits resulting from failure to develop the appropriate skills; and (2) *performance deficits*—deficits resulting from inappropriate or insufficient use of skills already in the individual repertoire (Gumpel, 2007; Gumpel & Golan, 2000). If students lack the appropriate social skills, interventions should provide direct instruction and guided practice in prosocial competencies. If the desired skills are in students' repertoires but are not being used, interventions should focus on activation strategies (i.e., performance-based interventions) that motivate students to use the skills they possess. Diverse learners, including children living in poverty and children with disabilities, are especially in need of interventions to enhance social competence (Gresham & MacMillan, 1997). Children living in high-poverty urban environments display higher rates of aggression in the classroom (Greenwood, 1991; Kellam et al., 1998) and are more likely to be exposed to violent models of behavior, with fewer opportunities to learn or receive reinforcement for engaging in socially effective behaviors than are children from more advantaged backgrounds (Barnett et al., 1999). In addition, although there is limited evidence supporting the notion that social skills deficits constitute a specific learning disability, children with learning disabilities, behavior disorders, and mental retardation tend to have poorer social skills and to suffer peer rejection more frequently, compared with their nondisabled classmates (Gresham, 1992; Merrell, Johnson, Merz, & Ring, 1992). Interventions that assist at-risk children in acquiring and practicing effective social behaviors can not only prevent inappropriate special education placements but also enhance the likelihood that students with identified disabilities can be successfully included in regular classroom settings.

The Importance of Classroom-Based Strategies for Problem Behavior

The critical role of the classroom environment in preventing and ameliorating patterns of ineffective behavior cannot be overestimated (Hughes, 2002; Nucci, 2006). Reviews of the efficacy of social skills training interventions have generally reported only modest improvement in social functioning, either for students in general education (Forness, Kavale, Blum, & Lloyd, 1997) or at-risk groups, such as students with emotional and behavioral disorders (Mathur & Rutherford, 1996; Quinn et al., 1999) or young children with disabilities (Vaughn et al., 2003). Disruptive and aggressive behaviors are especially resistant to treatment delivered through formal social skills training programs (Mathur et al., 1998; Quinn et al., 1999). Moreover, even when social skills programs result in positive outcomes, there is limited evidence that gains generalize to other settings or produce meaningful improvements in students' overall social competence (Gresham, 1997, 1998). In fact, in some cases, social skills training programs have had unintended negative effects (Ang & Hughes, 2001; Quinn et al., 1999)!

In contrast, interventions delivered in the regular classroom have the greatest potential to enhance prosocial competencies by altering the classroom social system to support all students, including rejected and isolated students, students with disabilities, and low-performing students, all of whom are at risk for social difficulties (Bullis et al., 2001; Nowicki, 2003). Rather than removing aggressive and noncompliant students from the classroom for individual or small-group training, as many programs have done, interventions should be integrated into the regular curriculum, not only to teach prosocial behaviors in the setting in which they will be used, but also to prevent socially competent students from rejecting their socially inept classmates and driving them further into deviant peer groups (Webster-Stratton, 1993). Given the negative impact of early problem behavior on children's health, academic, and psychosocial outcomes (Egeland et al., 1996; Loeber & Stouthamer-Loeber, 1998) and the increasing prevalence of conduct disorders in children (American Psychiatric Association, 2000), implementing school-based strategies to reduce disruptive behavior and increase social competence should be a top priority for consultants and other educators.

INTERVENTIONS TO IMPROVE BEHAVIOR AND ENHANCE SOCIAL COMPETENCE IN THE CLASSROOM

The interventions in this section rely on a variety of techniques, including group contingencies, response cost, self-monitoring, and social recognition, to help students focus on instruction, manage frustration, and acquire and practice key prosocial behaviors. They are designed not only to reduce inappropriate behavior but also to create a classroom climate that motivates students to put forth effort on their academic tasks and cooperate with their teachers and classmates. The first two interventions rely on *group contingencies* in the context of team competitions that enlist peer influence processes to support appropriate behavior. Among the most popular behavioral interventions in the field testing, they can have rapid, dramatic positive effects on classroom behavior. In the *Good Behavior Game* (GBG), teams compete to earn rewards or privileges delivered for low levels of rule infractions. First studied in the late 1960s (Barrish, Saunders, & Wolf, 1969), the GBG has proven to be effective in reducing inappropriate and aggressive behavior in preschool settings (Swiezy, Matson, & Box, 1992), elementary and middle school classrooms (Dolan et al., 1993), and special education classrooms (Salend, Reynolds, & Coyle, 1989), as well as in nonclassroom settings, such as media centers (Fishbein & Wasik, 1981) and gymnasiums (Patrick, Ward, & Crouch, 1997). Longitudinal studies have demonstrated that GBG participation in first and second grade significantly reduces disruptive and aggressive behavior for at-risk students not only in the early primary grades but also at entry to middle school 6 years later (Kellam et al., 1998; Kellam, Rebok, Ialongo, & Mayer, 1994). The GBG has been designated as a "best practice" for preventing substance abuse or violent behavior by several federal agencies (see Embry, 2002, for a review). The *Good Behavior Game Plus Merit,* a variation in which teams earn bonus points to offset demerits by displaying specific positive academic or social behaviors, is presented as a separate intervention.

CROSS-REFERENCE: For a variation of the *Good Behavior Game* (GBG) designed for implementation in a nonclassroom setting, see *Promoting Sportsmanship in Physical Education Classes with the Good Behavior Game Plus Merit* later in this chapter. *Red Light/Green Light*, a GBG variation for preschoolers, is presented in Chapter 6.

GROUP CONTINGENCIES: KEY COMPONENT OF PERFORMANCE-BASED INTERVENTIONS

Group contingencies specify the relationship between the behavior of a group and the delivery of a consequence to the individuals in that group. There are three basic types of group-oriented contingencies: (1) independent, (2) interdependent, and (3) dependent (Skinner, Skinner, & Sterling-Turner, 2002). In *independent group contingencies,* the target behavior, criteria for earning reinforcement, and reinforcement are the same for all group members, but access to the reinforcer depends on the behavior of each individual. For example, any student who scores 90% or higher on a mathematics test earns a homework pass for that day. In contrast, *interdependent group contingencies* permit access to reinforcement based on some aspect of the behavior or performance of the group as a whole, so that all or none of the students in the group receive the reward. For example, if a class incurs fewer than five rule infractions during the intervention period, the entire class earns 15 minutes of extra recess. Many of the interventions in this text include interdependent group contingencies to encourage academic productivity and/or prosocial behavior (e.g., *The Rewards Box: Enhancing Academic Performance with Randomized Group Contingencies*; *Good Behavior Game*). *Dependent group contingencies* allow an entire group to have access to reinforcement contingent on the behavior of only one or a few target students. As with interdependent group contingencies, all or none of the group members receive the reward if the criterion is met, but delivery is based on the behavior of the target student(s) rather than on the group as a whole. For example, if the target student refrains from emitting negative verbalizations during the intervention period, all of the students in the class earn 10 minutes of free time. Several interventions in this chapter make use of dependent group contingencies to streamline or randomize reward delivery (e.g., *Three-Steps to Self-Managed Behavior*; *Reducing Disruptive Behavior with Randomized Group Contingencies*).

Research demonstrates that group contingencies can be highly effective in improving academic performance and behavior across student populations and settings. In a meta-analysis of 99 studies of interventions targeting disruptive classroom behavior, group contingencies had the largest effect size compared with other types of strategies (Stage & Quiroz, 1997). Group contingencies are also practical for teachers, especially if a teacher has more than one student in need of individual behavior programming (Skinner, Cashwell, & Dunn, 1996). Despite the efficacy and usability of group-oriented contingencies, several problems may arise during implementation. First, in any group contingency system, students may not behave appropriately if they do not value the reward. Second, in the case of interdependent and independent group contingencies, the academic or behavior criterion for earning the reward may be too high for some students, so that students with low rates of productivity or prosocial behaviors seldom or never receive the reward. Third, students may abandon the effort to behave appropriately if they perceive that they have exceeded the criterion for reinforcement delivery and can no longer earn the reward (Skinner, Williams, & Neddenriep, 2004). For example, if the criterion for reward is set at no more than six rule infractions and a seventh rule infraction occurs, disruptive behavior may escalate when students perceive that they have lost the opportunity to obtain a reward.

Randomized Group Contingency Components

One solution to the problems associated with group contingencies is to randomize one or more of the contingency components—that is, the rewards, target behaviors, and/or criteria for earning reinforcement. Randomizing the rewards increases the likelihood that students will continue to put forth effort because the specific reinforcer cannot be determined. Similarly, if students do not know which of several possible target behaviors will be selected for reinforcement, students are likely to attempt to modify each behavior in a positive direction. When the criteria for reinforcement are randomized, students cannot determine which aspect of behavior will be selected for evaluation or what level of performance will be required, reducing the likelihood that students will misbehave or stop putting forth effort in the belief that they have lost the opportunity for reinforcement. A growing body of evidence documents the effectiveness of interventions with randomized group contingencies in reducing disruptive behavior (Kelshaw-Levering et al., 2000; Theodore, Bray, & Kehle, 2004; Theodore et al., 2001) and enhancing academic performance (Popkin & Skinner, 2003; Sharp & Skinner, 2004).

Two of the strategies in this section incorporate randomized group contingencies to target inappropriate classroom behavior. *Reducing Disruptive Behavior with Randomized Group Contingencies* is an innovative intervention package that embeds randomly selected components within an interdependent group contingency. As noted above, randomizing contingency components solves many of the problems associated with group contingencies because students cannot predict which rewards are available, which behaviors will be reinforced, or the criteria for earning reinforcement. Variations of this strategy randomizing as few as one and as many as four contingency components are presented. *A Multicomponent Intervention to Reduce Disruptive Behavior* increases the effectiveness of group contingency systems by capitalizing on the power of unpredictable reinforcers in a reward structure known as the "mystery motivator" (Rhode et al., 1992). A *mystery motivator* consists of a description or symbol of a reward that is placed in an envelope with a question mark and displayed where the target student(s) can see it. Concealing the reinforcer while simultaneously signaling that it is potentially available increases the anticipation of the reward and helps maintain motivation to perform the desired behaviors or refrain from the undesired behaviors (Mottram et al., 2002). Interventions incorporating mystery motivators have been successful in reducing disruptive behavior for preschoolers in Head Start settings (Murphy et al., 2007) and elementary students in regular and special education settings (De Martini-Scully et al., 2000; Kehle, Madaus, Baratta, & Bray, 1998; Madaus et al., 2003; Moore et al., 1994; Mottram et al., 2002; Musser et al., 2001).

CROSS-REFERENCE: Chapter 4 includes two interventions that combine mystery motivators with interdependent group contingencies: *Promoting Homework Completion and Accuracy with Mystery Motivators* in the Academic Productivity section and *Motivating Reading Performance with Paired Reading and Randomized Group Contingencies* in the Reading section.

One intervention includes response cost as a primary intervention component. *Response cost* involves removing a predetermined amount of positive reinforcement following the occurrence of an undesired behavior. In the *Response Cost Raffle,* response cost is implemented in the context of a classwide lottery system. First studied by Witt and Elliott (1982), the *Response Cost Raffle* can have immediate, dramatic effects on student behavior and earns high acceptability ratings from both students and teachers. Response cost has been validated as an effective component in intervention packages targeting academic performance (Reynolds & Kelley, 1997) and social behavior (Conyers et al., 2004; Musser et al., 2001). Two other interventions in this chapter—the *Good Behavior Game* and the *Good Behavior Game Plus Merit*—include response cost variations that have been validated in field testing.

Two interventions use self-management as a key intervention component. *Self-management* strategies typically involve at least three components: (1) *self-monitoring*—observing some aspect of one's own behavior, (2) *self-evaluation*—comparing the observed behavior to a specified criterion level of performance, and (3) *self-correction*—modifying the target behavior in the desired direction (Gumpel & Golan, 2000). Reinforcement contingent on accurate self-monitoring and/or behavior improvement is also often included, either self-administered or delivered by an external intervention agent. Self-management procedures are especially appropriate for interventions targeting inappropriate behavior because the self-monitoring process not only increases students' sense of control over their own actions but also increases the likelihood that they will generalize their newly learned competencies to other situations. Although self-management interventions have been successful in increasing on-task behavior and reducing inappropriate behavior for students across a wide range of grade levels (see Shapiro et al., 2002, for a review), many treatment investigations have relied on individual audio cuing devices (e.g., Todd, Horner, & Sugai, 1999) that are impractical in regular education settings, especially on a classwide basis. In *Three Steps to Self-Management,* students use the classroom clock as the cue for self-observation and record their own productivity and behavior on an easy-to-use form. Moreover, in contrast to the labor-intensive teacher–student matching typical of self-monitoring interventions (e.g., Hoff & DuPaul, 1998; Kern, Dunlap, Childs, & Clarke, 1994), this intervention uses a streamlined teacher–student matching procedure that interferes minimally with ongoing instruction.

Unwanted verbalizations, such as humming, talking out, or making noises, or negative student–student comments, such as name calling and teasing, can interfere with instruction and create a hostile learning environment for both students and teachers (Courson-Krause, Marchand-Martella, Martella, & Schmitt, 1997; Martella, Leonard, Marchand-Martella, & Agran, 1993). *Decreasing Inappropriate Verbalizations with a Peer-Monitored Self-Management Program* is a multicomponent intervention that targets negative verbalizations with a combination of self-management and peer monitoring, embedded within a group contingency. In this strategy, the problem of time-consuming teacher–student matching is solved by training students to check each other's self-monitoring accuracy.

Helping socially rejected students and students with poor peer relationships is an important goal of classroom interventions. Socially isolated and rejected students can become trapped in a negative coercive process, in which they escalate their inappropriate or provocative behavior in an effort to obtain peer attention, followed by teacher and peer negative attention (Bowers, McGinnis, Ervin, & Friman, 1999; Patterson et al., 1992). In contrast to social skills training programs that provide direct instruction in the desired social competencies, *Positive Peer Reporting* (PPR) targets the classroom social system by reinforcing students for observing and acknowledging the appropriate behavior of their isolated and rejected peers (Ervin, Johnston, & Friman, 1998). A large body of research demonstrates that PPR enhances social involvement and peer acceptance and reduces problem behavior for socially withdrawn and rejected students and students with poor social skills (Bowers, Woods, Carlyon, & Friman, 2000; Ervin, Miller, & Friman, 1996; Jones, Young, & Friman, 2000; Moroz & Jones, 2002). Although most of the PPR studies have been conducted in residential treatment settings, PPR has also been applied successfully in regular education classrooms (Ervin et al., 1998; Moroz & Jones, 2002).

CROSS-REFERENCE: A proactive variation of positive peer reporting—*Tootling: Enhancing Peer Relationships with Public Posting and Group Contingencies*—is presented in Chapter 3.

THE GOOD BEHAVIOR GAME

Overview

The *Good Behavior Game* (GBG) is a simple but effective intervention that uses team competitiveness and group incentives to reduce disruptive behavior in the classroom. Student teams compete for rewards or privileges, which are awarded to teams not exceeding a specific number of rule violations. If all of the teams meet the behavior standards, all earn the reward. Critical components in the game's effectiveness include positive peer pressure, specific performance criteria for winning, immediate behavior feedback, and group-based reinforcement. The GBG has been proven to be effective in reducing disruptive and aggressive behavior in elementary and middle school classrooms with regular education, at-risk, and special needs student populations. Moreover, longitudinal research demonstrates that enrollment in GBG classrooms in first and second grade significantly reduces aggressive and disruptive behavior among at-risk students at the end of first and second grade and at entry to middle school. Three variations are presented: (1) a response cost version, in which points are deducted for rule infractions, (2) a version with unpredictable rewards, and (3) a version with positive behavior incentives for teams that have exceeded the day's limit for rule infractions. The *Good Behavior Game Plus Merit,* a variation in which bonus points are awarded for positive academic or social behavior to offset demerits, is presented as a separate intervention.

Purpose

To increase on-task behavior and reduce inappropriate and disruptive behavior with team-based contingencies.

Materials

1. Posterboard chart displaying the classroom rules, such as:
   a. Talk only when you have the teacher's permission.
   b. Stay in your seat unless you have permission to get up.
   c. Be polite and kind to others.
   d. Follow the teacher's instructions the first time they are given.
2. Posterboard chart or section of the chalkboard divided into two parts labeled "Team 1," "Team 2," etc. (or labeled with team names), and listing team members' names, if desired, with a column for each day of the week.
3. Victory tags, consisting of "winner" stickers or circles of colored construction paper with "winner" stickers affixed to them and threaded with yarn, to be worn around the neck (optional, for early primary grade students).
4. Manila envelope with a question mark on it, containing a slip of paper describing a tangible reward (e.g., "Draw from the candy jar," "Homework pass") or an activity-based reward (e.g., "10 minutes of music time," "5 minutes of extra recess," "Line up first for lunch") (optional, see Variation 2).
5. Small rewards, such as stickers, wrapped candy, and decorated pencils and erasers (optional).

Observation (Select One or More)

Option 1

1. Using a *Classwide Scanning Form* with a 3- or 5-minute interval, scan the room at the end of each interval, starting with the front of the room and ending with the back, and tally the number of students in each of the following behavior categories:
   a. *On-task behavior,* defined as asking or answering lesson-oriented questions, writing when

requested, looking at the teacher during presentations, and any other behavior relevant to the lesson.

   b. *Off-task behavior,* defined as sitting without having appropriate materials at hand, looking at nonlesson materials, and looking around the room after assignments have been made.

   c. *Disruptive behavior,* defined as any behavior disrupting instruction or the on-task behavior of other students, such as inappropriate verbal or motor behavior, failing to follow directions, and aggression.

2. Conduct these observations during a selected instructional period for 30 to 45 minutes for 4 to 7 days.

Option 2

1. Using a *Group Event Recording Form,* record the frequencies of three or four disruptive behaviors, such as getting out of seat, name calling, talking out, and failing to follow directions, during a selected instructional period for a target group of students or the entire class for 4 to 7 days.

2. Use these baseline data to set a demerit criterion at a value that is approximately half of the average number of disruptive behaviors. For example, if students display an average of 30 disruptive behaviors during the selected period, set the initial criterion at 15.

Option 3

1. Using a sheet of paper attached to a clipboard, record the number of classroom rule infractions during a selected instructional period for the entire class for 4 to 7 days.

2. Use these baseline data to set the demerit criterion at a value that is approximately half of the average number of rule infractions. For example, if students display an average of 20 rule infractions during the selected period, set the initial criterion at 10.

Intervention Steps

Introduction and Training

1. Select a time for implementation, such as the morning work period or an instructional period when students are especially unproductive and disruptive. Tell the students that they will be playing a game to help everyone get more out of the period during which the game will be played. Explain the times when the game will be played and post the times on the chalkboard.

2. Divide the class into two or three teams. Be sure that teams contain approximately equal numbers of male and female students and that students with problem behavior are divided equally among teams. To facilitate monitoring behavior and delivering rewards, use rows or desk groupings to assign teams or change seating arrangements to reflect team membership. Allowing teams to select names fosters team spirit and makes it easier to encourage or reprimand teams.

3. Write the team names or numbers and names of team members if desired on the chalkboard, as described above, with a column for each day of the week.

4. Explain the game's procedures as described below, including the criterion for the maximum number of demerits permitted to earn the reward. Also describe the rewards for the winning team(s), such as wearing victory tags for the rest of the day, lining up first for lunch, getting to pack up first at the end of the day, or small tangible rewards. If all the teams win, possible rewards include a video or DVD, 15 minutes of free time, or a special art activity at the end of the day.

5. Review the classroom rules and demonstrate the process of giving demerits for rule infractions

as described below. Be sure to model how students should respond to receiving a demerit and explain that arguing or other inappropriate reactions will result in an additional demerit.

Implementation

1. At the beginning of the intervention period, conduct a brief review of the classroom rules and the GBG criterion (e.g., no more than 10 demerits for the period).
2. During the intervention period, record a demerit beside the team name each time a student on that team breaks a rule. As you record the demerit, state the reason. *Example*: Say, "Anthony, that's an 'out of seat,' " while putting a check mark under the appropriate team's name. If you have listed individual team members' names on the chart or chalkboard, put the check mark next to the name of the student who committed the infraction.
3. Tally demerits at the end of the intervention period and determine which, if any, teams have met the criterion. If none of the teams exceeds the predetermined limit, all teams are winners and receive the reward.
4. Begin by playing the GBG three times a week for 15 minutes or during the selected instructional period. Gradually increase the duration by approximately 10 minutes per intervention period every 3 weeks, up to a maximum of 3 hours or three or four instructional periods per day.
5. If necessary, adjust the criterion slightly to reflect the longer periods of implementation, but gradually lower the limit for demerits to no more than four or five infractions per day.
6. Initially, announce the game period and deliver the rewards immediately afterward or as soon as possible. As students become more familiar with the procedure, initiate the game period without prior notice at different times of the day and during different activities and routines, such as walking down the hall to the cafeteria. Delay rewards until the end of the school day.
7. After several weeks of implementation, fade the rewards to once a week. Record the number of daily demerits for each team and deliver the reward on Fridays to teams meeting the criterion on 4 out of 5 days.

Evaluation (Select One or More)

Option 1

1. Compare the percentages of students exhibiting on-task, off-task, and disruptive behavior during the selected instructional period before and after implementation.

Option 2

1. Compare the frequencies of disruptive behaviors for the target group of students or the entire class during the selected instructional period before and after implementation.

Option 3

1. Compare the number of rule infractions for the entire class during the selected instructional period before and after implementation.

Variations

Variation 1: The Good Behavior Game with Response Cost

1. Begin the intervention period by awarding each team a fixed number of credits, such as 10 credits. Set a minimum criterion for winning, such as five credits remaining at the end of the intervention period.

2. Remove one credit each time a member of a team breaks a rule.
3. Deliver the reward to teams that meet or exceed the criterion. If all teams meet or exceed the criterion, all teams are winners.

Variation 2: The Good Behavior Game with Mystery Motivators

1. Implement the standard GBG or the GBG as described above in Variation 1.
2. Display a manila envelope with a question mark written on the front of it and containing a slip of paper describing a reward on it on a desk or table where all students can see it. Explain that winning teams will receive the reward written on the hidden slip of paper.
3. At the end of the day, open the envelope and deliver the reward to teams that meet the criterion.

Variation 3: The Good Behavior Game with a "Better Behavior Booster"

1. This variation helps to prevent the number of rule infractions from increasing if students perceive that their team has exceeded the limit on a particular day and can no longer obtain the daily reward.
2. Provide a larger group reward, such as 15 minutes of free time, at the end of the week to teams with five or less "extra" rule infractions (i.e., demerits exceeding the daily criterion). Record the extra marks on bar graphs drawn on the chalkboard and labeled with team names so that teams can monitor their progress during the week. Deliver the reward at the end of the week to teams meeting this criterion.

Notes

1. Occasionally, chronically defiant and disruptive students will declare that they do not want to play the game and will deliberately violate the rules to incur penalty points for their team. If this occurs, explain to the class that it is not fair to penalize an entire team because a few students will not control their behavior. Create another team consisting of the problem student(s) and add a negative contingency, such as requiring losing teams to have a "silent lunch" or deducting 5 minutes of recess for each mark scored over the criterion. If the problem persists, conduct a *Debriefing* session to help identify factors contributing to the problem and support the student(s) in displaying acceptable replacement behaviors (see *Debriefing: Helping Students Solve Their Own Behavior Problems*).
2. Teachers sometimes express concern about monitoring only inappropriate behavior. In that case, the *Good Behavior Game Plus Merit,* which provides bonuses for appropriate behavior, can be substituted (see below).
3. Field testing suggests that the response cost variation (Variation 1) is more effective than the original procedure of recording demerits. Moreover, teachers have consistently preferred the response cost version to the original.

Sources

Barrish, H. H., Saunders, M., & Wolf, M. M. (1969). Good behavior game: Effects of individual contingencies for group consequences on disruptive behavior in a classroom. *Journal of Applied Behavior Analysis, 2,* 119–124. Copyright 1969 by the Society for the Experimental Analysis of Behavior. Adapted by permission.

Kellam, S. G., Ling, X., Merisca, R., Brown, C. H., & Ialongo, N. (1998). The effect of the level of aggression in the first grade classroom on the course and malleability of aggressive behavior into middle school. *Development and Psychopathology, 10,* 165–185. Copyright 1998 by Cambridge University Press. Adapted by permission.

THE GOOD BEHAVIOR GAME PLUS MERIT

Overview

This variation of the *Good Behavior Game* (GBG) combines group contingencies for reducing disruptive behavior with a bonus for positive academic behavior. As in the GBG, teams receive a reward if the number of demerits they accumulate for rule infractions remains below a fixed criterion. In contrast to the original, however, the *Good Behavior Game Plus Merit* permits students to compensate for inappropriate behavior by earning credits for improvement in academic performance. It is especially useful with students who become argumentative or unproductive when corrected because the opportunity to remove demerits and regain access to rewards is built into the procedure. In the original study, the strategy was successful not only in reducing disruptive behavior for two students with behavior disorders in a second-grade classroom but also in improving assignment completion and increasing active participation for both targeted and nontargeted students. Two variations are presented: (1) a response cost variation in which teams are awarded a fixed number of credits that are deducted for rule infractions and (2) a variation awarding merit points for exemplary behavior as well as for academic improvement.

Purpose

To increase on-task behavior and academic productivity and reduce disruptive behavior with positive team competitions.

Materials

1. Posterboard chart with a list of classroom rules, such as:
   a. Raise your hand and wait to be recognized when you want to talk.
   b. Keep from making too much noise.
   c. Stay in your seat unless you have permission to get up.
   d. Keep from tattling on other students.
   e. Follow teacher directions the first time they are given.
2. Posterboard chart listing the ways students can earn merit points, such as:
   a. Earn a score of 80% or better on your classwork.
   b. Participate actively in class discussions.
   c. Be especially polite and helpful to others (see Variation 2).
3. 3″ × 5″ index cards with the words "One Merit" written on each; the number of cards should equal the number of students in the class (optional).

Observation (Select One or More)

Option 1

1. Record percent-correct scores on classwork assignments for the entire class or a target group of students during a selected instructional period for 5 to 10 days or for several weeks.

Option 2

1. Using a sheet of paper attached to a clipboard, record the frequency of active classroom participation for the entire class or a target group of students during a selected instructional period for 4 to 7 days. *Active classroom participation* is defined as responding appropriately to a teacher-delivered question or contributing an appropriate statement or question to class discussion.

Option 3

1. Using a *Classwide Scanning Form* with a 3-, 5-, or 10-minute interval, scan the room, starting with the front and ending with the back, and tally the number of students exhibiting on-task, off-task, and disruptive behavior as defined below.
   a. *On-task behavior:* working on the task at hand, looking at the teacher during presentations, and any other behavior relevant to the lesson.
   b. *Off-task behavior:* sitting without having appropriate materials at hand, looking at noninstructional materials, and looking around the room after assignments have been made.
   c. *Disruptive behavior:* any behavior disrupting the on-task behavior of other students, such as inappropriate verbal or motor behaviors.
2. Conduct these observations during a selected instructional period for 30 to 45 minutes for 4 to 7 days.

Intervention Steps

Introduction and Training

1. Select an instructional period for implementation, such as the period when students are most disruptive, least productive, and/or participate least often in class discussions. Explain to the students that they will be playing a game during the period to help everyone get the most out of that subject.
2. Divide the class into two or three teams. Be sure to distribute students with problem behavior between teams. If desired, have the teams select their own names.
3. On a section of the chalkboard visible to all students, write "Team 1," "Team 2," etc. (or the names of the teams), with a column for each day of the week. If desired, list names of team members under each team name.
4. Set a criterion for winning the game, such as no more than five demerits during the intervention period. Also describe the rewards for the winning team(s), such as 10 minutes of free time, 10 minutes of computer time, homework passes, extra recess, lining up first to go home, etc. Both teams can win or lose.
5. Demonstrate the process of giving demerits as described below. Model how students should respond to receiving a demerit and explain that arguing or other inappropriate reactions will result in an additional demerit for the team.
6. Using the charts, review the classroom rules and the ways students can earn merit points.

Implementation

1. During the selected period, record a demerit beside the team name each time a student breaks a rule. State the reason for the demerit as you record it. *Example:* Say, "Sonya, you didn't follow directions" while putting a check mark under the appropriate team's name and a check mark next to the student's name, if listed.
2. During the intervention period, give merit cards to students who display the designated positive academic and/or social behaviors. Alternately, record merit points in the form of plus (+) marks on the chalkboard next to team names and, if desired, student names.
3. At the end of the period, have students hold up their merit cards for you to count or tally the number of pluses per team. Erase one demerit for every five merit points earned by a team. Collect the merit cards, if used.
4. At the end of the period or the end of the day, deliver rewards to teams not exceeding the criterion.
5. As student behavior improves, post the winning team(s) for an entire week and deliver a reward to teams meeting the criterion on 4 out of 5 days.

Evaluation (Select One or More)

Option 1

1. Compare percent-correct scores on classwork assignments for the entire class or the target students during the selected instructional period before and after implementation.

Option 2

1. Compare the frequency of active classroom participation for the entire class or the target students during the selected instructional period before and after implementation.

Option 3

1. Compare the percentages of students exhibiting on-task, off-task, and disruptive behavior during the selected instructional period before and after implementation.

Variations

Variation 1: Good Behavior Game Plus Merit with Response Cost

1. Begin the period with a certain number of credits per team, such as 10. Set a minimum criterion for winning, such as five credits. Remove one credit each time a member of a team breaks a rule. Restore one credit for every five merit points earned by members of that team.
2. Deliver rewards to teams with the designated number of credits remaining at the end of the intervention period. If both teams meet or exceed the criterion, both teams are winners.

Variation 2: Good Behavior Game Plus Merit for Behavior Improvement

1. Award merit points for prosocial behavior as well as for improved academic performance. For example, if you observe a student being especially helpful, cooperative, or kind, publicly identify the student and the prosocial behavior and award a merit point to that team.

Notes

1. This has been one of the most popular interventions in the field testing. Teachers find it very easy to use and often develop their own variations. Most teachers prefer to record merit points on the chalkboard rather than to distribute merit cards.
2. As with the *Good Behavior Game,* the response cost variation (Variation 1) appears to be more effective and more acceptable to teachers than the original.

Source

Darveaux, D. X. (1984). The good behavior game plus merit: Controlling disruptive behavior and improving student motivation. *School Psychology Review, 13,* 510–514. Copyright 1984 by the National Association of School Psychologists. Adapted by permission.

THREE STEPS TO SELF-MANAGED BEHAVIOR

Overview

Helping students learn to manage their own behavior is an important goal for teachers at any level. Self-management of behavior increases student independence and self-reliance and helps ensure that newly acquired competencies will transfer to other settings and situations. In this intervention, a three-component self-monitoring procedure is paired with a token economy to reduce inappropriate behavior and improve academic productivity. Implemented with two eighth graders with learning disabilities and behavior problems in two general education classes and a study hall class, the self-management package was successful in decreasing off-task and disruptive behavior and increasing academic performance and assignment completion rates in all targeted classes. Moreover, all of the participating teachers indicated that they would use the strategy again to reduce unwanted behaviors. In this classwide adaptation, data collection measures for the three self-monitoring components have been combined into a single form, and a team-based format with a dependent group contingency has been substituted for an individualized matching and reward system. Two variations are presented: one with a single overall behavior self-rating scale and another with a classwide group contingency.

Purpose

To reduce disruptive behavior and increase academic productivity with self-monitoring and interdependent group contingencies.

Materials

1. Self-monitoring form (see Figure 5.1 on p. 335), one form per student.
2. *Reinforcement Menu,* one per student.
3. Classroom clock, large enough to be visible to all students.
4. Overhead projector and transparency of the self-monitoring form (optional).
5. Posterboard chart with a list of classroom rules, such as:
    a. Stay in your seat unless you have permission to get up.
    b. Raise your hand and wait to be called on to speak.
    c. Use appropriate language.
    d. Follow the teacher's directions at all times.
    e. Do your best on all assignments.
6. Posterboard chart listing the rating criteria for the point system, as described below (see Intervention Step #5).
7. Section of the chalkboard divided into two parts labeled "Team 1" and "Team 2" (or labeled with team names), with a column for each day of the week.
8. Small tangible reinforcers, such as stickers, wrapped candy, decorated pencils and erasers, etc.
9. Red felt-tip pen or marker.

Observation (Select One or Both)

Option 1

1. Select an instructional period during which students are especially disruptive or unproductive. Using a *Group Interval Recording Form* with a 30-second interval and beginning at the left side of the room, glance at each student in turn at 30-second intervals. Record a plus (+) if the student is off-task at any time during the interval until one rating is made for each student. When you have rated all students, begin again at the left side of the room.
    a. *Off-task behavior* is defined as being out of seat, talking with classmates without permission, playing with nonlesson materials, and engaging in any other behavior interfering with task completion for oneself or others.
2. Conduct these observations for 30 to 45 minutes during the selected instructional period for 4 to 7 days.

Option 2

1. Using a sheet of paper attached to a clipboard, tally the number of classroom rule infractions during the selected instructional period for the entire class or a target group of students for 4 to 7 days.

Intervention Steps

Introduction and Training

1. Explain to the students that they will be learning a new way of managing their own behavior so that they can get more out of each lesson. Also explain that they will be able to earn points toward rewards for positive behavior as part of the self-management process.
2. Using the rules chart, review the classroom rules, including the rationale for each rule.
3. Using the *Reinforcement Menus*, help students develop a set of rewards, including group activity rewards.
4. Using *Say Show Check: Teaching Classroom Procedures,* sit at a student desk near the chalkboard and have the class observe while you demonstrate examples of on-task and off-task behavior. Have students indicate if your behavior is on-task or off-task by responding chorally or giving a thumbs-up for on-task behavior and a thumbs-down for off-task behavior. Praise students when they evaluate your behavior accurately. If they respond incorrectly to an example, demonstrate the behavior again and ask, "Is this on-task or off-task behavior?"
5. Using the ratings chart, review the following criteria for the overall behavior rating scale (see Figure 5.1):
   a. 5 = great: working on the assignment and following the rules throughout the period.
   b. 4 = good: working on the assignment and following the rules throughout the period, with one minor infraction, such as talking without permission.
   c. 3 = OK: working on the assignment and following the rules for more than half of the period, with one or two behavior reminders.
   d. 2 = needs improvement: working on the assignment and following the rules for less than half of the period, with more than two behavior reminders.
   e. 1 = poor: off-task for most of the period, failing to follow the rules, and more than two behavior reminders.
6. Divide the class into two teams, based on seating arrangements. If necessary, change the seating arrangement so that students with attention and/or behavior problems are approximately equally distributed between the teams.
7. Distribute copies of the self-monitoring form, and lead students through the three sections of the form, using the overhead projector and transparency, if desired, as follows:
   a. At the beginning of class, respond to the three questions in the Before Class section by circling "Yes" or "No."
   b. During the period, glance at the classroom clock every 5 minutes and ask yourself, "Am I working?" Circle "Yes" if you are on-task and "No" if you are off-task.
   c. At the end of the period, respond to the five questions in the After Class section by circling "Yes" or "No."
   d. Then rate your overall behavior by circling one of the numbers at the bottom of the form.
8. Tell students that during the last few minutes of the period, you will collect the self-monitoring forms by team, randomly select one form from each team, review the forms, give an overall behavior rating to that student, and award points as follows:
   a. 5 points = all of the components completed correctly.
   b. Additional 5 points = teacher rating of 4 or 5.
9. Explain that when a team receives a total of 10 points for 4 consecutive days, all of the members of that team will receive a reward.

10. Conduct a training session during which students practice using the self-monitoring forms and rating themselves. Provide feedback on the completeness of the forms and the accuracy of their self-ratings.

Implementation

1. At the beginning of the instructional period, distribute the self-monitoring forms and remind students to check the classroom clock at the appropriate interval.
2. Near the end of the period, instruct students to mark the After Class section and the overall rating scale.
3. Collect the forms by team and randomly draw one form from each team. Do not reveal the identity of the students whose forms have been drawn.
4. Review the forms, award points as appropriate, and announce to the class when a team has achieved the criterion. Have a team member write the points total on the chalkboard under the team number or name.
5. When a team earns a total of 10 points for 4 consecutive days, deliver a reward to all of the members of that team. If both teams earn 10 points for 4 consecutive days, deliver a classwide activity reward, such as a popcorn party, 15 minutes of music time, etc.
6. When most students are receiving teacher ratings of 3 or above, increase the length of the During Class self-monitoring interval to 15 minutes. When most students are receiving teacher ratings of 4 or 5, implement the overall behavior rating scale as the sole component (see Variation 1).

Evaluation (Select One or Both)

Option 1

1. Compare the percentage of off-task behavior for the entire class or the target group of students during the selected instructional period before and after implementation.

Option 2

1. Compare the frequency of rule infractions for the entire class or the target group of students during the selected instructional period before and after implementation.

Variations

Variation 1: Single Behavior Rating Scale Version

1. Implement the 5-point overall behavior rating scale as the sole component (see Note 2) and modify the self-monitoring form accordingly. Award points and deliver rewards as described above. Because only one match is required per student, this version can be easily implemented on an individualized basis with one student or a small group of students.

Variation 2: Classwide Version

1. Implement the intervention as described above but do not divide the class into teams. After the class period, have students turn in their forms. Randomly select a single form and rate it, without revealing the identity of the student. Award points as described above and record earned points on the chalkboard each day. Deliver a group activity reward or small tangible rewards to each student when the class has earned 10 points on 4 consecutive days.

Notes

1. If the intervention is implemented with an individual student or a small group of students, have students keep their self-monitoring forms inside their subject area folders to make the procedure less intrusive. At the end of the period, have them bring their forms to be matched or go to their desks to conduct the teacher–student matching. Rewards should be social in nature (lunch with the teacher, a day as classroom messenger, etc.) rather than tangible so that other students do not feel deprived of the opportunity to earn reinforcement.
2. In the original study, teachers and students alike selected the overall behavior rating scale as the most effective of the three components in the self-monitoring system.

Source

Dalton, T., Martella, R. C., & Marchand-Martella, N. E. (1999). The effects of a self-management program in reducing off-task behavior. *Journal of Behavioral Education, 9,* 157–176. Copyright 1999 by Springer Science and Business Media. Adapted by permission.

My Class Checklist

Name: _____ Subject: _____ Date: _____

Before Class:

1. Do I have my class materials and homework ready?	Yes	No
2. Did I listen to directions?	Yes	No
3. Did I get started on time?	Yes	No

During Class:
- Am I working? (Check the classroom clock every 5 minutes and circle **Yes** if on-task and **No** if off-task.)

Yes No	Yes No	Yes No	Yes No	Yes No	Yes No	Yes No	Yes No	Yes No	Yes No

After Class:

4. Did I self-monitor to stay on-task?	Yes	No
5. Did I follow all teacher directions?	Yes	No
6. Did I work on the assignment during the entire time I was given?	Yes	No
7. Do I have homework tonight?	Yes	No

My overall behavior in this class:	1	2	3	4	5
(my rating)	Poor	Needs Improvement	OK	Good	Great

My overall behavior in this class:	1	2	3	4	5
(teacher rating)	Poor	Needs Improvement	OK	Good	Great

Form complete = 5 points
Teacher rating of 4 or 5 = 5 points
Total points = _____

FIGURE 5.1. Self-monitoring form for *Three Steps to Self-Managed Behavior*. Adapted from Dalton, Martella, and Marchand-Martella (1999, p. 162). Copyright 1999 by Springer Science and Business Media. Adapted by permission.

REDUCING DISRUPTIVE BEHAVIOR
WITH RANDOMIZED GROUP CONTINGENCIES

Overview

Although group contingencies can be effective in increasing appropriate behavior and are easier to deliver than individual reinforcers, it can be difficult to identify rewards that are not only practical for teachers but also reinforcing for every student. If some students do not value the reinforcers, group contingency procedures may not alter their behavior in the desired direction. This intervention addresses this limitation by randomizing reinforcements so that students cannot determine which reward is available for displaying the desired behavior. Similarly, randomizing the targeted behaviors and the criteria for earning rewards can encourage students to maintain appropriate behavior throughout the intervention period because they are unsure of the behavior that will be selected or the exact criteria for reinforcement. In the original studies, interventions with randomized group contingency components produced immediate dramatic improvement in the behavior of elementary students in regular education classes and secondary students with emotional disorders in a self-contained special education classroom. Two variations are presented: one randomizing rewards and the criteria for receiving them and another randomizing two additional group contingency components.

Purpose

To reduce disruptive behavior and increase appropriate behavior with a randomized group contingency program.

Materials

1. "Rules chart," consisting of a posterboard chart listing the class rules, such as:
   a. Stay in your seat unless you have permission to be out of it.
   b. Raise your hand before speaking.
   c. Keep from talking to others unless given permission.
   d. Pay attention when the teacher is talking.
   e. Do what the teacher tells you to do at once.
2. One opaque glass or plastic jar with slips of paper (two jars for Variation 1 and four jars for Variation 2).
3. List of student names attached to a clipboard (for Variations 1 and 2; also label five columns corresponding to the target behaviors [i.e., infractions of each of the classroom rules]).
4. "Rewards chart," consisting of a posterboard chart listing a variety of activity and social rewards.

Materials Preparation

1. Label the first jar "Rewards." On 15 to 20 slips of paper, write a variety of activity and social rewards, such as intervals for extra recess (e.g., 5 minutes, 10 minutes), intervals of free time (e.g., 5 minutes, 10 minutes, 15 minutes), special snacks (e.g., peanut butter cups, lollipops), and "party points" (points ranging from 1 to 5, with a total of 45 needed for a class party). Place the slips of paper in the jar.

ADDITIONAL PREPARATION FOR VARIATION 1

1. Label the second jar "Behavior." Place in the jar 15 to 20 slips of paper listing either (a) a target behavior corresponding to the classroom rules (e.g., out of seat, call-out, talk-out, off-task, or noncompliance) and a number ranging from 0 to the criterion number (e.g., Off-task–3),

or (b) the word "All" and a number (e.g., All–5). The number represents the number of times the target behavior(s) can occur during a given interval. "All" indicates that you will evaluate all of the target behaviors, that is, the total number of marks across behaviors.

ADDITIONAL PREPARATION FOR VARIATION 3

1. Label the third and fourth jars as "Whole Class or Individual Student" and "Names." Place 10 to 15 slips of paper labeled "Whole Class" and "Individual Student" in the Whole Class or Individual Student jar. Put a slip of paper with the name of each individual student in the Names jar. Alternatively, to reduce preparation time and enhance motivation, have students write their names on the slips of papers and place them in the jar.

Observation (Select One or Both)

Option 1

1. Using a sheet of paper attached to a clipboard, tally the number of rule infractions for the entire class during a selected instructional period or a fixed interval, such as the first third of the day, for 4 to 7 days.
2. Calculate the average number of rule infractions per period or interval and use that number to set the initial criterion (see Intervention Step #5) at about half that number.

Option 2

1. Using a *Group Interval Recording Form* with a 10-second interval, code the behavior of each student in turn as on-task (+) or off-task/disruptive (–), beginning at the left side of the room. Record a minus (–) if the student is off-task or disruptive at any time during the interval, as defined below.
   a. *On-task behavior* is defined as attending to the teacher or the assignment, participating in class discussions, and any other lesson-related behavior.
   b. *Off-task/disruptive behavior* is defined as failing to follow teacher instructions; calling out; talking without permission; being out of seat without permission; looking at something other than the teacher, participating peers, or classwork; or any other behavior interfering with one's own learning or that of others.
2. Conduct these observations for 30 to 45 minutes during a selected instructional period for 4 to 7 days.

Intervention Steps

Introduction and Training

1. Using the Rules chart, review the classroom rules with the students and post the chart where it is visible to everyone. Explain to the students that they will be able to earn certain privileges or treats by following the rules.
2. Display the clipboard with the list of students' names and explain that you will put a check beside the name of any student who breaks a classroom rule.
3. Explain that you have divided the school day into three intervals during which students can earn rewards. Set the intervals to accommodate regular breaks in the day for ease of reinforcement delivery. For implementation within a single instructional period, explain that students can earn rewards at the end of the period.
4. Display the Rewards chart, the Rewards jar and slips of paper, and review the available reinforcers.
5. State the criterion for earning rewards.

Example: Say, "If our class has less than 15 checks [or some value approximately half of the baseline rate] for breaking the rules, I will choose someone to draw a reward from the jar."

Implementation

1. If a student breaks a rule, state the student's name and the infraction, and place a mark on the checklist next to the student's name.

    Example: "Heather, that's a talk-out."
2. Halfway through each of the three daily intervals (or halfway through the instructional period), remind students that they are working to try to earn a reward at the end of the interval or period. Deliver this reminder regardless of the frequency of target behaviors. Do not comment on the appropriateness or inappropriateness of student behavior at this time or the number of checks earned by individual students or the class as a whole.
3. At the end of the interval, consult the checklist to determine if students have met the criterion. If the class has met the criterion, praise the class and permit a randomly selected student to draw a slip of paper from the Rewards jar and hand it to you without reading what is written on it. Identify the reward and deliver it to the class as soon as possible.
4. As student behavior improves, gradually increase the length of the interval until you are drawing from the jar and delivering rewards once a day. Then conduct the drawing and reward delivery on a weekly basis. If you are implementing the intervention within a single period, gradually increase the number of consecutive days on which students must meet the criterion to receive a reward until you are delivering a reward for 4 consecutive days of successful behavior.

Evaluation (Select One or Both)

Option 1

1. Compare the average number of rule infractions committed during the selected instructional period or intervention interval before and after implementation.

Option 2

1. Compare classwide off-task/disruptive behavior rates during the selected instructional period or intervention interval before and after implementation.

Variations

Variation 1: Randomized Reinforcements and Randomized Criteria

1. Display the Rewards chart and jar and discuss the available rewards as described above.
2. Display the Behavior jar and the slips of paper and review their contents, as described above. Explain that students will not know the criterion for reinforcement or what the reward may be. Instead, the reward and criterion may change from period to period, depending on what is drawn from the jar.
3. During the intervention period, use the checklist to record rule infractions by student name and rule. Halfway through each of the three daily intervals (or halfway through the instructional period), remind students that they are working for a chance to earn a reward at the end of the interval.
4. At the end of the interval, draw a slip of paper from the Behavior jar. State the target behavior(s) and the number that has been drawn.

5. Consult the checklist to determine if the class has met the criterion. *Example 1:* If you draw a slip of paper with "Noncompliance–9" on it, there must be no more than 9 checks in the noncompliance column for that interval for the class to meet the criterion. *Example 2:* If you draw a slip of paper with "All–12" on it, there must be no more than 12 marks across all behaviors for that interval for the class to meet the criterion.

6. If the class has met the criterion corresponding to the slip of paper that has been drawn, randomly select a student to draw a slip of paper from the Rewards jar. Identify the reward and deliver it to the class as soon as possible.

Variation 2: Randomized Reinforcements, Criteria, Behaviors, and Target Students

1. Display the first two jars and the rewards as described above. Explain that students will not know the criterion for earning reinforcement or what the reward may be. Instead, the reward and criterion may change from period to period, depending on what is drawn from the jar.

2. Display the Whole Class or Individual Student jar and the Names jar. Review their contents as described in the Materials section above. Explain that students will not know whether the behavior of the entire class or an individual student will be evaluated according to the criterion that is drawn.

3. Use the checklist to record rule infractions by student name and rule and provide the prompt halfway through each of the intervals as described above for Variation 1.

4. At the end of the interval, draw a slip of paper from each of the four jars in the following order:
   a. First, draw a slip of paper from the Behavior jar. State the target behavior(s) and the number that has been drawn.
   b. Second, draw a slip of paper from the Whole Class or Individual Student jar to determine whether to evaluate the behavior of the entire class or an individual student in terms of the slip of paper that has been drawn from the Behavior jar.
   c. If you draw an "Individual Student" slip, draw a slip from the Names jar. Consult the checklist to determine if that student has met the selected criterion for that behavior during the interval. If that student has met the criterion for that target behavior, announce the target behavior and the criterion and permit that student to draw a slip of paper from the Rewards jar. If the individual student did not meet the criterion, tell the class they have failed to meet the criterion and return the slips of papers to their respective jars without announcing the name of the student. *Example:* If you draw a "Noncompliance–5" slip of paper from the Behavior jar and an "Individual Student" slip of paper from the Whole Class or Individual Student jar, the student whose name has been drawn must have received no more than 5 checks for noncompliance during that interval to meet the criterion.
   d. If you draw a "Whole Class" slip, consult the checklist to determine if the class as a whole has met the selected criterion for that behavior during the interval. If the class has met the criterion, announce the criterion and select a student to draw a slip of paper from the Rewards jar. If not, state that the class has failed to meet the criterion and return the slips of papers to their respective jars without announcing the specifics of the contingency you have drawn. *Example:* If you draw an "All–15" slip of paper, there must be no more than 15 marks on the checklist for the class to meet the criterion.

Notes

1. In the original study, the version with all components randomized (Variation 2) was implemented after the first version (randomized reinforcers only) and appeared to be slightly more effective.

2. According to the authors, the teacher prompt during the interval (see Implementation #3) is a critical component in intervention effectiveness.

3. In the case of students who continue to exhibit unacceptable levels of inappropriate behavior, the checklist can provide information for use in parent–teacher conferences, functional behavioral assessments, and/or behavior support plans.

Source

Kelshaw-Levering, K., Sterling-Turner, H. E., Henry, J. R., & Skinner, C. H. (2000). Randomized interdependent group contingencies: Group reinforcement with a twist. *Psychology in the Schools, 37,* 523–533. Copyright 2000 by John Wiley & Sons, Inc. Adapted by permission.

THE RESPONSE COST RAFFLE

Overview

The response cost procedure involves removing a specific amount of positive reinforcement—usually in the form of a token—contingent upon an act of undesirable behavior. This simple but innovative intervention combines response cost with a classroom raffle system to reduce disruptive behavior. Moreover, removing "raffle tickets" for lack of progress on classroom assignments and emphasizing to students that they must complete classroom tasks can have positive effects on academic productivity. One of the most usable behavioral strategies in this book, it requires very little teacher training, takes only a few minutes to prepare each day, and is highly acceptable to teachers and students alike. In a study with four junior high school students with behavior problems who were receiving part-time services in a special education resource room, the raffle was highly effective in increasing appropriate behavior and academic performance and decreasing disruptive behavior. Here the strategy has been adapted for classwide use. Two variations are presented, including a team-based version that incorporates peer influence for positive behavior and the original version for use with individual students or a small target group.

Purpose

To decrease disruptive behavior and increase academic productivity with a response cost procedure and a classroom lottery.

Materials

1. *Reinforcement Menus,* one per student (optional).
2. "Raffle prize list," consisting of a posterboard chart with a list of rewards or "raffle prizes."
3. "Target behavior chart," consisting of a posterboard chart listing four or five target negative behaviors and alternative positive behaviors, such as:
   a. *Don't* call out. *Do* raise your hand.
   b. *Don't* fail to follow directions. *Do* follow directions the first time they are given.
   c. *Don't* get up without permission. *Do* stay in your seat unless you have permission to get up.
   d. *Don't* use inappropriate language. *Do* use kind and polite words.
4. "Raffle tickets," consisting of slips of paper, five per student per intervention period.
5. "Raffle ticket box," consisting of a shoe box with a top.
6. Tape.
7. "Raffle prizes," consisting of small individual rewards, such as miniature candy bars, bubble gum, homework passes, fast food certificates, and inexpensive school supplies.
8. Slips of colored construction paper, five per student table, with a different color for each table (see Variation 2).
9. Plastic or paper cups, one per student table (see Variation 2).

Observation (Select One or Both)

1. Using a *Group Event Recording Form,* record the frequency of three or four disruptive behaviors that occur during a selected instructional period for the entire class or a group of target students for 4 to 7 days. For example, record the frequency of the following behaviors: (a) calling out, (b) being out of seat, (c) arguing with the teacher or a classmate, and (d) failing to follow teacher directions the first time they are given.
2. Calculate the average percentage of classwork completed by the entire class during a selected instructional period for 5 to 10 days by calculating the percentage completion rate for each student, summing those rates, and then dividing by the total number of students.

Intervention Steps

Introduction and Training

1. Explain to students that they will have a chance to participate in a classroom raffle and win prizes by earning points for good behavior during a selected instructional period.
2. Display the raffle prize list and discuss the individual prizes with the students. Also review a set of group prizes that will be available if you draw a "group" ticket from the box (see Implementation #5), such as a video or DVD, 15 minutes of free time, extra recess, etc. Alternately, distribute copies of a *Reinforcement Menu* and help the class select a set of prizes from among the reinforcers you have listed. List these rewards on the chart and post it at the front of the classroom.
3. Display the target behavior chart. Using *Say, Show, Check: Teaching Classroom Procedures,* demonstrate the target negative behaviors that you wish to decrease (calling out, failing to follow directions, etc.) and the positive behaviors you wish to increase (raising a hand to speak, following directions when first given, etc.).
4. Display the slips of paper and explain that they represent raffle tickets. Tell the class that everyone will receive five tickets at the beginning of the period. Any time that a student displays a target negative behavior during the period, you will remove a ticket from that student's desk. Any remaining tickets will be placed in the raffle ticket box. On Friday, you will hold a drawing, and the student whose slip of paper is drawn will be able to select a reward from the rewards list. Remind the class that students who are able to retain more tickets during the week have a better chance of winning the raffle and receiving a prize.
5. Demonstrate how students should behave when a raffle ticket is removed. Explain that if students argue or respond negatively to ticket removal, they will lose more tickets. Guide several students through a role play of ticket removal to ensure that everyone understands the behavioral expectations.

Implementation

1. At the beginning of the intervention period, give each student five raffle tickets. Have students write their names on the tickets and tape the tickets to the front edge of their desks.
2. Remind students that they are playing the game to help them get more out of the lesson. Whenever a student engages in a negative target behavior, briefly state what the behavior violation is, remove the ticket, and continue with the lesson.

    Example: "Ronnice, you didn't follow directions, so you lose a ticket."
3. If a student argues or responds negatively to the removal of a ticket, quietly remove another ticket. Do this as long as the student responds inappropriately. If the student continues to behave inappropriately and has no tickets left, deliver a preplanned negative consequence, such as taking away recess for that day or requiring the student to complete a *Debriefing* form (see *Debriefing: Helping Students Solve Their Own Behavior Problems*).
4. Five minutes before the end of the period, collect all tickets remaining on students' desks.

Write "group" on two of the tickets and tell the students that the entire class will win a prize if one of these tickets is chosen. Place all of the tickets in the raffle ticket box.

5. On Friday of each week, conduct the raffle by drawing one ticket from the box and declaring the winner. Have the winner select a prize from the list of available rewards. If the class is large, you may wish to draw two tickets and award two prizes.

6. If a group ticket is drawn, the winning student selects from the list of whole-class prizes, such as a classroom game, popcorn party, music time, free time, or a video.

7. Discard the rest of the tickets and begin the raffle procedure again the following Monday during the selected instructional period.

8. As behavior improves, gradually raise the criterion by reducing the number of tickets students receive during each intervention period.

Evaluation (Select One or Both)

1. Compare the frequency of disruptive behaviors during the selected instructional period for the entire class or the group of target students before and after implementation.

2. Compare the average percentage of classwork completed by the entire class during the selected instructional period before and after implementation.

Variations

Variation 1: Individual or Small-Group Variation

1. To implement the raffle with an individual student or a small group of target students, use *Reinforcement Menus* to help students select their own rewards.

2. Using a different color of paper for each student's tickets, tape the tickets to the front of the student's desk or slip them inside the subject area folder or notebook, with half of each ticket showing. Remove a ticket for each rule infraction as described above.

3. At the end of the intervention period, collect any remaining tickets and place them in the raffle ticket box. Conduct the drawing as unobtrusively as possible at the end of the week and deliver the prize as the student is leaving for the day.

4. If a student is displaying very high negative behavior rates, conduct the raffle on a daily rather than a weekly basis initially to enhance motivation. As behavior improves, gradually increase the reward delivery interval from daily to weekly.

Variation 2: Team-Based Variation

1. Divide the class into teams, based on seating arrangements. For students seated at tables or desk clusters, place a plastic or paper cup containing five colored tickets on each table or on one of the desks, with a different color for each group. Use different colors to prevent students from taking other teams' tickets to replace their own.

2. Remove a ticket for each incident of negative behavior as described above.

3. At the end of the intervention period, place all remaining tickets in the raffle ticket box and add two tickets of a different color to serve as group tickets. Taking care not to look at the box so as to avoid seeing the ticket colors, draw a ticket.

4. Deliver a reward to all members of the team whose ticket is drawn or to the entire class, if one of the group tickets is drawn.

Notes

1. For this intervention to be effective, teachers must consequate inappropriate behavior immediately (i.e., remove a ticket for an infraction as soon as the infraction occurs). In the original study, researchers observed that teachers were inconsistent in consequation and often removed tickets only for blatant rule violations.

2. Although the researchers did not report negative student reactions to the withdrawal of tickets, negative student responses were occasionally observed during field testing. During training, and thereafter as needed, model appropriate responses to ticket removal and review the consequences for inappropriate reactions.

3. During field testing, some teachers expressed concern about publicly posting examples of negative behavior. In that case, substitute a chart of the classroom rules, stated in positive terms, for the target behavior chart.

Source

Proctor, M. A., & Morgan, D. (1991). Effectiveness of a response cost raffle procedure on the disruptive classroom behavior of adolescents with behavior problems. *School Psychology Review, 20,* 97–109. Copyright 1991 by the National Association of School Psychologists. Adapted by permission.

POSITIVE PEER REPORTING

Overview

Students who provoke other students or fail to cooperate with their classmates during instruction and group activities are at risk for poor peer relationships and other negative academic and social outcomes. Moreover, efforts to deal with these students can be time-consuming and stressful for teachers, reducing instructional time and creating a negative classroom environment. *Positive Peer Reporting* (PPR) is a strategy that targets not only students who engage in negative interactions with their peers but also socially rejected students. Students earn points toward group rewards by praising their classmates' prosocial behaviors during brief daily compliment sessions, thereby giving individuals with poor social skills an incentive to display appropriate behavior in order to gain positive peer attention and nontargeted students an incentive to focus on the positive rather than negative aspects of their classmates' behavior. PPR has been demonstrated to be effective in improving the social interactions, peer acceptance, and social involvement of socially rejected or isolated elementary and middle school students in regular education, special education, and residential settings. Moreover, PPR helps to create a positive classroom atmosphere that encourages cooperation and promotes learning. Two variations are presented: (1) a version with a randomization component to enhance motivation to observe and report prosocial behavior and (2) a version with a cumulative-point reward system.

Purpose

To enhance prosocial behavior and positive peer relationships and reduce inappropriate social behaviors by systematically encouraging and reinforcing peer compliments.

Materials

1. "Points chart," consisting of a posterboard chart displaying the number of points needed to earn the group reward and the number of points earned per day; if desired, make a bar graph in the form of a thermometer and color in the points earned each day with a different colored marker.

2. "Compliments chart," consisting of a posterboard chart listing the steps in providing compliments and examples, as follows:

Four Steps in Giving Compliments:

   a. Look at the person.
   b. Smile.
   c. Report something positive the person did or said during the day.
   d. Then make a positive comment, such as, "Good job!" or "Way to go!"

Examples of Compliments:

   a. Phoebe told me my new headband looked nice.
   b. Kevin gave me a pencil to borrow when I couldn't find mine.
   c. Joy had a great idea during our group project.
   d. Mario helped me log on during computer time.
3. Glass or see-through plastic jar, labeled "Honey Pot" and cotton balls (optional, see Variation 2).

Observation (Select One or Both)

Option 1

1. Using a *Group Event Recording Form,* record the number of negative and positive social interactions displayed by the entire class or a group of target students during recess, a major transition (such as packing up at the end of the day), or an instructional period that includes classwide discussions or cooperative learning activities.
   a. *Negative social interactions* are defined as incidents of negative verbal behavior (e.g., arguing, teasing, yelling), negative physical behavior (e.g., hitting, pushing, taking materials), or any other unfriendly or uncooperative behavior.
   b. *Positive social interactions* are defined as incidents of appropriate peer–peer interactions, including working or playing cooperatively, giving or offering assistance, talking or listening in a pleasant manner, or any other friendly or cooperative interaction.
2. Conduct these observations during the targeted period for 4 to 7 days. If desired, use these data to help set a criterion for the number of points (compliments) needed to earn the reward (see Intervention Steps/Introduction and Training #4).

Option 2

1. Create a sociometric rating scale by writing student names in alphabetical order on a sheet of paper, with a 5-point Likert-type scale (1 = not at all, 2 = a little, 3 = some, 4 = a lot, 5 = very much) beside each name.
2. Distribute copies of the rating scale and ask students to circle the number that best describes how much they would like to work on a project with each of their classmates (for younger students, ask how much they would like to play with each of their classmates).
3. Collect the completed scales and calculate the average score for each student. Use these data to help identify the group of target students.

Intervention Steps

Introduction and Training

1. Tell the students that they are going to have an opportunity to help create a friendlier classroom atmosphere and earn group rewards by participating in a new activity. Each day, three or four students (or an appropriate number, based on class size) will have a chance to be the class "stars," and everyone will have a chance to praise the stars' friendly and help-

ful behavior that has contributed to making the classroom a good place to learn and have fun.

2. Using the compliments chart, conduct a 20-minute training session in which you teach students how to give compliments. Provide examples and nonexamples of compliments, have students offer their own examples, and give praise and corrective feedback as needed. For example, if students give vague praise ("I want to compliment Allison. She was nice today"), ask, "What nice things did you see Allison do?"

3. Tell students that during the "star time" (e.g., at the end of the morning instructional period, during afternoon homeroom period, during circle/advisory time), you will review the list of stars for the day and invite other students to raise their hands to offer compliments about each of those students.

4. Explain that if you call on a student and he or she is able to offer a sincere, appropriate compliment about one of the class stars, the class will earn a point toward a group reward (e.g., classroom game, special snack, popcorn party, video, music time, extra recess). Set a criterion for the number of points required to earn the reward, using data obtained during the observation period, if desired.

Implementation

1. At the beginning of the day or intervention period, select two or three students at random, as well as one or two of the target students.

2. Announce the list of names, remind the students that they will be asked to provide compliments for each star at the end of the intervention period, and write the names in alphabetical order on the chalkboard.

3. At the end of the intervention period, ask students to raise their hand if they have an appropriate compliment for the first student on the list. Use group rather than individual prompts to encourage praise statements.

   > *Example:* "Would anyone else like to say anything?", not "Does anyone else have a compliment for Maria?"

4. Once the first student has received two or three appropriate compliments, give that star an opportunity to praise another star, if desired. Then move to the next name on the list.

5. After all of the stars have received compliments, tally the number of appropriate compliments and add that number of points to the points chart. The PPR session should last between 5 and 7 minutes.

6. Deliver the reward when the criterion has been reached. Praise the students for their positive and cooperative behavior and begin a new points chart.

Evaluation (Select One or Both)

Option 1

1. Compare the number of positive and negative social interactions for the entire class or the group of target students during recess, the selected transition, or the selected instructional period before and after implementation.

Option 2

1. Compare average sociometric ratings for the group of target students before and after implementation.

Variations

Variation 1: Positive Peer Reporting with Mystery Stars

1. On selected days, tell the students that they will need to observe each other's friendly and helpful behaviors very carefully that day because you will not be announcing the names of the stars until the end of the intervention period or the end of the school day. At the end of the intervention period or day, announce the names of the stars, write their names on the chalkboard, and conduct the PPR session as described above.

Variation 2: Positive Peer Reporting with a "Honey Pot"

1. During PPR sessions, place a cotton ball ("honey") in a jar ("Honey Pot") for each appropriate compliment. When the Honey Pot is full of honey (i.e., the jar is full of cotton balls), deliver the reward.

Notes

1. Do not place the same names on the list every day, even for the most rejected students, because this may embarrass them and lead to greater ostracism by the rest of the class.
2. If a student offers a sarcastic remark rather than a compliment, tell that individual that you will not award points for any comments that may be embarrassing or hurtful to a fellow student, even if they are presented as a compliment. Follow up by talking with the student privately about the purpose of the peer compliments and helping the student formulate appropriate compliments for the next PPR session. If the problem persists, deliver a consequence (e.g., loss of recess) and have the student complete a *Debriefing* form (see *Debriefing: Helping Students Solve Their Own Behavior Problems*).
3. During field testing, teachers observed that some students occasionally reacted negatively (by pouting, arguing, etc.) when their names were not on the daily list of stars, especially during the initial stages of implementation. To address this problem, remind students prior to the announcement of the star list that everyone will have a chance to be a star for the day and model appropriate responses during the star list posting.

Source

Moroz, K. B., & Jones, K. M. (2002). The effects of positive peer reporting on children's social involvement. *School Psychology Review, 31*, 235–245. Copyright 2002 by the National Association of School Psychologists. Adapted by permission.

DECREASING INAPPROPRIATE VERBALIZATIONS WITH A PEER-MONITORED SELF-MANAGEMENT PROGRAM

Overview

Inappropriate verbalizations, such as calling out, talking to peers, and making noises, can be a serious impediment to ongoing instruction. Moreover, unwanted verbalizations often lead to other off-task behaviors and more serious problem behavior, such as student-to-student aggression. In this strategy, students work collaboratively to monitor and evaluate their own verbalizations in the context of a group contingency to reduce inappropriate verbalizations. First implemented in a third-grade classroom that included four students diagnosed with ADHD, the intervention substantially decreased talking out in all four target students, along with their matched controls. In the original study, students also recorded their behavior on individual self-monitoring forms so that researchers could assess the number of inappropriate verbalizations per student, as well as differences between student self-monitoring and teacher monitoring. Because the individual self-monitoring component increases intervention complexity and did not appear to enhance self-monitoring accuracy, it is included here as a variation. A variation with an additional contingency to encourage accurate self-monitoring is also presented.

Purpose

To reduce inappropriate verbalizations and classroom rule infractions by using a peer-monitored self-management procedure with a group contingency.

Materials

1. Posterboard chart listing the class rules, such as:
   a. Talk only when you have permission from the teacher.
   b. Use polite and kind words when talking with others.
   c. Follow all teacher instructions the first time they are given.
   d. Do your work so others can do their work.
2. "Group behavior charts," consisting of 9" × 12" sheets of laminated construction paper divided into three sections (one-half green, one-fourth blue, and one-fourth red), one chart per table or desk cluster.
3. Circles of black laminated construction paper, the size of a 50-cent piece, attached to group behavior charts with Velcro tabs, five circles per chart (or a number reflecting data collected during the observation period).
4. *Reinforcement Menus,* one per student (optional).
5. Paper bag containing small tangible reinforcers, such as stickers, wrapped candy, and inexpensive school supplies (optional).
6. "Individual behavior charts," consisting of 8½" × 11" sheets of paper, with two columns, labeled "I caught myself!" and "Teacher moved my dot," respectively, one per student (optional, see Variation 1).

Observation (Select One or Both)

Option 1

1. Using a sheet of paper attached to a clipboard, record the number of inappropriate verbalizations for the entire class or a target group of students during a selected instructional period. *Inappropriate verbalizations* are defined as student verbalizations made without teacher permission, such as calling out, making noises, or talking to peers.
2. Conduct these observations for 4 to 7 days. If desired, use these data to determine the criterion for the maximum of inappropriate verbalizations allowed for the groups to obtain the reward (i.e., the number of circles on each chart).

Option 2

1. Using a *Classwide Scanning Form* with a 3- or 5-minute interval, scan the room at the end of each interval, starting with the front of the room and ending with the back, and tally the number of students in each of the following behavior categories:
   a. *Appropriate classroom behavior,* defined as behavior that does not interfere with ongoing instruction or the learning of other students and does not include any inappropriate behavior as defined below.

    b. *Inappropriate classroom behavior*, defined as talking without permission, getting out of seat without permission, making noises, or any other verbal or motor behavior that disrupts ongoing instruction or the on-task behavior of other students.
2. Conduct these observations for 30 to 45 minutes for 4 to 7 days.

Intervention Steps

Introduction and Training

1. This intervention requires students to be seated in groups of four or five. If the classroom has individual desks rather than tables, arrange desks in clusters of four. Be sure to disperse the most talkative and disruptive students among the groups.
2. Explain to the students that they will be playing a game that will help remind them to work quietly without talking out and disturbing others.
3. Using *Say, Show, Check: Teaching Classroom Procedures* and the rules chart, review the classroom rules and provide examples and nonexamples of the target behavior (talking without permission). Conduct role plays and provide corrective feedback until you are certain that students understand when talking is permitted and when it is not.
4. Place one chart with the black circles in the green section in the middle of each table or desk cluster within easy reach of each group member. Explain that if a student forgets the rule and talks out (or breaks another of the regular classroom rules), that student must move one dot from the green section to the blue section. If the student fails to do so, a group member should remind him or her. After 10 seconds, you will move the dot to the red section yourself.
5. Caution the class that you will not tolerate any negative behavior toward students who are responsible for having a dot moved. Tell the class that if you observe any negative behavior directed toward a student who has caused the group to have a dot moved, you will move another dot for that group.
6. Tell students that all groups with at least one dot left in the green section of their chart at the end of the intervention period will receive a reward. Explain that you will provide time for a brief daily meeting to give group members an opportunity to brainstorm strategies for earning the reward. If desired, have students select a group name.
7. If desired, distribute the *Reinforcement Menus* and help students identify rewards that each group would like to earn. Alternatively, describe the available activity rewards (game time, free time, extra recess, etc.) or tangible rewards (wrapped candy, decorated pencils, erasers, etc.).
8. Conduct a demonstration in which you model moving a dot and reacting appropriately. Then have students work with their groups to practice the self-monitoring process, including responding to members whose behavior results in dots being moved.

Implementation

1. For the first 5 minutes of each intervention period, have each group conduct a meeting to discuss its performance on the previous day (e.g., "What did we do well? What can we do better? How can we help each other if someone is having a bad day?").
2. During the intervention period, monitor the groups to ensure that students are moving their dots from the green section into the blue section when they make inappropriate verbalizations or break other classroom rules. If a student makes an inappropriate verbalization and no one in the group moves the dot to the blue section within 10 seconds, go over to that group and move the dot to the red section yourself without comment. If any group members argue or display a negative reaction, quietly move another dot.
3. At the end of the intervention period, circulate to determine which groups have at least one dot remaining in the green section and to evaluate the difference between student and teacher monitoring (the difference between the number of dots placed in the blue and the red sections, respectively). Deliver the reward to winning groups or record the names of the winning groups on the chalkboard and deliver the reward at the end of the day.

Evaluation (Select One or Both)

Option 1

1. Compare the frequency of inappropriate verbalizations for the entire class or the group of target students during the selected instructional period before and after implementation.

Option 2

1. Compare the classwide percentages of students exhibiting appropriate and inappropriate classroom behavior during the selected instructional period before and after implementation.

Variations

Variation 1: Group Plus Individual Self-Monitoring

1. Distribute individual behavior sheets to students along with the group charts at the beginning of the intervention period. Tell students that they are responsible not only for monitoring and recording talk-outs as a team but also for recording their own talk-outs.
2. Instruct students to put a check in the appropriate column for every inappropriate verbalization they make, depending on whether they or you first observe a talk-out. That is, they should put a check in the "I caught myself" column when they observe that they talked out and a check in the "Teacher moved my dot" column when you have to move the dot for them.
3. Collect the sheets at the end of each intervention period for use in monitoring inappropriate verbalization rates for individual students and groups and evaluating the accuracy of student self-monitoring.
4. Fade the individual behavior sheets as inappropriate verbalizations decrease and student self-monitoring becomes more accurate.

Variation 2: Self-Monitoring Accuracy-Based Group Contingency

1. To encourage accurate self-monitoring, require teams to have only one dot in the red section in order to receive the reward, even if they have only one dot or none in the blue section. During the original study, researchers found that students did not always monitor their own performance accurately. In fact, there was no measurable difference between the number of times the teacher moved the dots and the number of times students "caught themselves."

Notes

1. Although the original study did not report any negative peer interactions when group dots were moved, peer harassment is a potential side effect of any interdependent group contingency. To minimize this possibility, stress team cooperation, model appropriate responses to the moving of dots, and remove additional dots if a group displays negative behavior toward a member who must move a dot.
2. This intervention is also ideal for targeting negative peer-to-peer verbalizations, such as derogatory remarks, arguing, or teasing.

Source

Davies, S., & Witte, R. (2000). Self-management and peer-monitoring within a group contingency to decrease uncontrolled verbalizations of children with attention-deficit/hyperactivity disorder. *Psychology in the Schools, 37*, 135–147. Copyright 2000 by John Wiley & Sons, Inc. Adapted by permission.

A MULTICOMPONENT INTERVENTION
TO REDUCE DISRUPTIVE BEHAVIOR

Overview

Aggressive, defiant, and disruptive students reduce opportunities to learn for themselves and their fellow students. The more time teachers must spend dealing with disruptive behavior, the greater the impact on student achievement. Interventions targeting disruptive behavior should not only be effective in reducing the problem behaviors, but also time-efficient and capable of being easily integrated into the daily classroom routine. This highly usable intervention combines public posting of classroom rules with a response cost token economy and unpredictable rewards. After students accumulate a predetermined number of points within the token economy, they earn access to a "mystery motivator," a reward or description of a reward placed in an envelope and publicly displayed. Originally implemented with three second graders with behavior disorders, the strategy produced an immediate, pronounced decrease in disruptive behaviors for all three students. Moreover, disruptive behavior rates for target students were consistently lower than rates for a peer control group during the intervention period and a 3-week follow-up phase. The teacher reported that the intervention was easy to implement, and the target students awarded it high satisfaction ratings. Here the strategy is adapted for classwide application with an interdependent group contingency. Two variations are also presented: the original version targeting individual students and a team-based version.

Purpose

To reduce disruptive behavior with a multicomponent intervention consisting of publicly posted classroom rules, a token economy with response cost, and mystery motivators.

Materials

1. Posterboard chart listing the class rules, such as:
    a. Do what the teacher tells you to do.
    b. Stay in your seat unless the teacher gives you permission to leave it.
    c. Keep your eyes on the teacher or your work during instruction.
    d. Talk only when you have been called on after raising your hand.
2. "Points chart," consisting of a chart drawn on the chalkboard, with one column for each day of the week; for Variation 2, divide each column into two, and label the columns "Team 1" and "Team 2."
3. "Mystery Motivator Envelope," consisting of a large manila envelope with a large question mark drawn on it (for Variation 1, one envelope per target student).
4. Index cards listing activity rewards, such as extra recess, indoor games, and music time, or describing access to small tangible rewards, such as "candy for everyone" to indicate that each student may have a piece of wrapped candy.
5. Small tangible rewards, such as stickers, wrapped candy, bubble gum, pencils, and sports cards (optional, see Variation 1).
6. *Reinforcement Menus,* one per student (optional).
7. Red marking pen (optional, see Variation 1).

Observation (Select One or More)

Option 1

1. Using a *Group Event Recording Form,* tally the number of disruptive behaviors for the entire class or a group of target students during the selected instructional period. *Disruptive behav-*

iors are defined as failing to follow teacher directions, getting out of seat without permission, talking out or making noises, playing with nonlesson materials, or any other behavior interfering with instruction.
2. Conduct these observations for 30 to 45 minutes for 4 to 7 days.

Option 2

1. Using a *Group Interval Recording Form* with a 15-second interval, code the behavior of each student in the class or each target student in turn during the selected instructional period as on-task (+) or disruptive (–), beginning at the left side of the room. Place a minus (–) if the student being observed displays one or more disruptive behaviors during the interval, as defined above.
2. Conduct these observations for 30 to 45 minutes for 4 to 7 days.

Option 3

1. Using a sheet of paper attached to a clipboard, record the number of classroom rule infractions during a selected instructional period for the entire class or a target group of students for 4 to 7 days.

Intervention Steps

Introduction and Training

1. Tell the class that they will have an opportunity to earn rewards for following the classroom rules and helping everyone get the most out of instruction during a selected period or intervention interval, such as the morning instructional block.
2. Using the rules chart and *Say, Show, Check: Teaching Classroom Procedures*, review the classroom rules. Post the rules chart where it is visible to everyone.
3. Display the index cards and the Mystery Motivator Envelope, and place one card in the envelope. Explain to the students that they will have an opportunity to earn the reward written on the card if they follow the class rules during the entire period. Place the envelope on your desk where all students can see it.
4. Review the available rewards, or, if desired, distribute copies of a *Reinforcement Menu* and guide the students in selecting a set of rewards.
5. Referring to the points chart on the chalkboard, explain that you will award one point for every 15 minutes (or some other interval) that students follow all the rules. Explain that you will erase a point if any student breaks a rule and/or displays inappropriate behavior at any time. Caution the class that you will deduct an additional point if a student argues or displays inappropriate behavior in response to point removal.
6. Explain that if there are five points remaining at the end of the intervention period, you will select a student to open the Mystery Motivator Envelope and identify the reward written on the card.

Implementation

1. At the beginning of the intervention period, place one of the index cards in the Mystery Motivator Envelope. To increase the suspense, have the students watch while you shuffle the cards and randomly select a card to be placed in the envelope.
2. Place a check on the chalkboard for each 15 minutes (or the predetermined reinforcement interval) that there are no rule infractions and praise students for their good behavior. *Example*: "Great job, class! You earned your point!"

3. If a student breaks a rule, calmly state the student's name and the rule infraction, and erase one point. If the student argues, complains, or responds in some other negative way, deduct another point.

4. At the end of the intervention period, review the point totals on the chalkboard. If there are at least five points remaining, praise the class and permit a randomly selected student to open the Mystery Motivator Envelope and read what is written on the index card. Deliver the reward to the class immediately or at the end of the day.

5. As behavior improves, gradually increase the length of the interval and the number of points needed to earn the reward. Then substitute praise for tangible reinforcers and deduct 5 minutes of recess time for each rule infraction or incident of disruptive behavior.

Evaluation (Select One or More)

Option 1

1. Compare the frequency of disruptive behaviors for the entire class or the target group of students during the selected instructional period before and after implementation.

Option 2

1. Compare the rates of on-task and disruptive behaviors for the entire class or the target group of students during the selected instructional period before and after implementation.

Option 3

1. Compare the number of rule infractions committed by the entire class or the target group of students during the selected instructional period before and after implementation.

Variations

Variation 1: Individual or Small-Group Variation

1. Using a *Reinforcement Menu,* help each target student select a set of possible rewards. Write the name of each target student and a question mark on a manila envelope. Place a small reward or an index card describing an activity reward (e.g., extra computer time, first to line up for lunch, lunch with the teacher) in each envelope and place the envelopes on your desk.

2. Tape an index card to the top of the desk of each target student. Explain to the target students that if they retain at least five points at the end of the intervention period, they will receive the reward in the envelope.

3. During the intervention period, use a red marking pen to mark a point on the index card of each target student who follows the rules for the prescribed interval. If a student breaks a rule, deduct one point.

4. At the end of the period or school day, deliver the reward in the envelope to target students who have retained at least five points. Activity and social rewards can be delivered on the following day when time permits.

5. As behavior improves, require the target students to earn more points over a longer period of time in order to earn a reward.

Variation 2: Team-Based Variation

1. Divide the class into two teams, based on seating arrangements. Make sure that disruptive students are distributed approximately equally across the two teams.

2. Place an index card describing an identical small tangible reward or activity reward in each of two manila envelopes, and place the envelopes in a prominent position on your desk.
3. Record points on the chalkboard at the prescribed interval for teams that are following the classroom rules, and deduct one point from team scores for every rule infraction by a team member, as described above.
4. Tally points at the end of the intervention period and deliver the reward to any team(s) with at least five points. If both teams win, a more valued group activity reward can be delivered.
5. As behavior improves, require teams to meet the criterion on 4 out of 5 days and deliver the reward on Friday.

Notes

1. It is important for students to accrue points for positive behavior as rapidly as possible when the intervention is first implemented. If the class accumulates too many penalty points in the beginning, students may become discouraged and stop attempting to behave positively. To avoid this possible pitfall, begin each intervention period with a brief review of the classroom rules and the potential rewards to enhance students' awareness of the target behaviors and increase anticipation of the reward. Similarly, keep reinforcement intervals relatively short (10–15 minutes) during initial implementation.
2. If a student deliberately misbehaves so as to prevent the class or team from winning, place that student on an independent (i.e., individual) contingency.

Source

Mottram, L. M., Bray, M. A., Kehle, T. J., Broudy, M., & Jenson, W. R. (2002). A classroom-based intervention to reduce disruptive behavior. *Journal of Applied School Psychology, 19,* 65–74. Copyright 2002 by The Haworth Press. Adapted by permission.

Interventions to Improve Behavior in Nonclassroom Settings

Although numerous interventions have been developed to address disruptive and aggressive behavior in classroom settings, the majority of problem behaviors, including bullying and injurious behavior, occur in nonclassroom settings, such as playgrounds, school corridors, cafeterias, restrooms, and buses (Craig, Pepler, & Atlas, 2000; Olweus, 1993). In these environments, which are characterized by large numbers of students, limited adult supervision, and increased opportunities for student-to-student interactions, high rates of discipline problems can occur, with as many as eight problem behaviors per minute (Colvin et al., 1997; Sugai & Horner, 2002). Until quite recently, there was a paucity of interventions targeting nonclassroom settings, compared with classroom-based strategies. With the increased focus on school safety as the result of a series of tragic school shootings and the growing recognition that managing behavior in nonclassroom settings is critical to maintaining an orderly school environment, however, more interventions directed at noninstructional settings are appearing in the literature. Because by definition nonclassroom settings are shared by more than one student group during the school day, these strategies typically focus on the entire student body rather than on individual classrooms or individual students (e.g., Lewis, Sugai, & Colvin, 1998; Scott, 2001). Of the five interventions in this section, four were originally implemented as schoolwide positive behavior support (PBS) strategies, and the fifth can be readily adapted for schoolwide implementation.

SCHOOLWIDE POSITIVE BEHAVIOR SUPPORT

Positive behavior support (PBS) is a general term describing a function-based approach designed to assist students with challenging behaviors in developing and using prosocial behavior. Consistent with an ecological approach to problem solving, PBS models focus on modifying not only student behavior but also environmental variables such as the physical setting, task demands, curriculum, instructional pace, and reinforcement systems. PBS has two major emphases: (1) building prosocial competencies rather than merely reducing problem behavior (i.e., a focus on proactive interventions), and (2) direct instruction as a central intervention component (Lewis, Newcomer, Trussell, & Richter, 2006; Sugai & Horner, 2002). To assess the impact of the behavioral interventions and practices, PBS approaches incorporate data-based decision making using functional behavioral assessment (FBA) and ongoing monitoring. IDEA 2004 has endorsed PBS as the recommended form of intervention for dealing with challenging behavior in children with disabilities (34 C.F.R. § 300.324[a][2][i]).

Originally developed to assist individual students with developmental disabilities, PBS has been expanded to schoolwide models that provide a continuum of support to enhance the behavior and social competence of all students (Lewis et al., 2006; Lewis & Sugai, 1999). Schoolwide PBS procedures are typically implemented in the context of a three-tier model in which the intensity of behavior support is matched to students' behavioral needs. In the first tier, universal interventions are implemented to teach all students prosocial skills and reduce disruptive behavior, with components such as schoolwide discipline plans, classroom rules and procedures, effective instruction, and social skills classroom lessons (Gresham, 2004; Scott, Nelson, & Liaupsin, 2001). In the second tier, targeted interventions are provided to students who are unresponsive to the universal preventive and proactive interventions and are at risk for more serious problem behaviors. These small-group and/or individually focused strategies may include conflict resolution training, daily check-in and check-out procedures, behavior contracts, self-management interventions, remedial academic programs, and increased home–school collaboration (Gresham, 2004). Research suggests that approximately 5 to 15% of students will require support beyond the universal level and that those students typically present with both academic and behavioral needs (Gresham, 2004; Sugai, Horner, et al., 2000; Sugai, Sprague, et al., 2000). A third level of intensive, individual, functionally based interventions will be required for the small percentage of students (1 to 7%) who do not respond to universal or targeted group interventions and display chronic patterns of aggressive or disruptive behavior, as well as academic problems (Lewis & Sugai, 1999; Office of Special Education Programs, 2007; Sugai & Horner, 2002). Such third-tier interventions include individualized academic support, targeted social skills training, and individualized behavior support plans designed not only to reduce students' disruptive behaviors but also help them increase their adaptive skills. At this level, support may include special education services, and the involvement of community agencies (O'Shaughnessy, Lane, Gresham, & Beebe-Frankenberger, 2003). Gresham (2004) estimates that although these students make up only 1 to 7% of a school's population, they account for 40 to 50% of behavioral disruptions.

Schoolwide PBS systems typically include five major components: (1) schoolwide expectations for appropriate behavior, (2) explicit teaching of behavioral expectations to all students, (3) rewards for meeting behavioral standards, (4) consequences for inappropriate behavior, and (5) continuous data collection and review for decision-making and accountability purposes (Sugai & Horner, 2002; Horner et al., 2004). A growing body of evidence indicates that schoolwide PBS programs are associated with significant decreases in discipline problems and concomitant improvement in school climate and academic performance across a variety of student populations and school settings, including urban inner-city schools (Lassen, Steele, & Sailor, 2006; Lewis, Powers, Kelk, & Newcomer, 2002; Luiselli, Putnam, Handler, &

Feinberg, 2005; McCurdy et al., 2003). Recently, Horner and his colleagues (Horner et al., 2004) have developed the *Schoolwide Evaluation Tool* (SET) to assess and evaluate the critical features of a PBS system as implemented in a school over time. The SET consists of a survey that involves collecting information from multiple sources, including a review of permanent products (such as the school discipline handbook), direct observations, and staff and student interviews. The SET and related implementation materials can be downloaded from *http://www.pbis.org/tools/htm.*

BEHAVIOR AND SOCIAL COMPETENCE INTERVENTIONS FOR NONCLASSROOM SETTINGS

The interventions in this section are designed to promote positive behavior and prevent inappropriate behavior in nonclassroom settings, including hallways, playgrounds, gymnasiums, and buses. Two interventions target behavior during hallway transitions. School hallways and major transitions, such as from the playground to the classroom, from inside to outside of the building, or from the classroom to the cafeteria, are prime settings for problem behavior. Helping students to behave appropriately during these transitions is critical because serious problem behaviors, such as vandalism, theft, and fighting, often arise in these settings, which typically have few adult supervisors but a high density of students. Hallway transition behavior also affects students' opportunities to learn because teachers must spend time settling students down at the beginning of class after transitions accompanied by inappropriate behavior (Colvin et al., 1997). *Improving Behavior in Transition Settings with Active Supervision and Precorrection: A Schoolwide Intervention* targets three problematic transitions: (1) entering the school building at the start of the school day, (2) leaving the classroom and moving to the cafeteria, and (3) leaving the classroom and exiting from the building at the end of the day. Transition supervisors are trained to use two empirically validated behavioral strategies: (1) *precorrection,* reminding students of the expected behaviors before they enter transition areas, and (2) *active supervision,* moving around, scanning for problems, and interacting with students. Unlike the majority of strategies targeting disruptive behavior, the training component of this intervention focuses on school staff rather than students and includes a regular brief precorrection delivered by the principal.

The second transition intervention focuses on hallway noise. Although hallway noise may seem less important as a target compared with problem behaviors such as aggression and noncompliance, corridor noise can exert a pervasive negative impact on a school's social climate and interfere with ongoing instruction. In *Reducing Hallway Noise with Sound Level Monitoring and Group Contingencies: A Schoolwide Intervention,* school staff learn to apply a simple set of guidelines based on the principles of positive behavior support (PBS), including modeling, guided practice, and performance feedback, to reduce hallway noise to acceptable levels. Although researchers used a sound level meter in the original study, the strategy can also be implemented by means of a simple qualitative rating scale completed by hall supervisors.

PRECORRECTION AND ACTIVE SUPERVISION: KEY SCHOOLWIDE POSITIVE BEHAVIOR STRATEGIES

Precorrection and active supervision are two key components that are frequently combined in interventions targeting nonclassroom behavior, especially schoolwide strategies (Sugai et al., 2002). A *precorrection* is an instructional prompt presented before students enter a setting that may be the occasion for problem behavior or a setting previously associated with problem behavior. Precorrections include verbal prompts, such as rule reminders or descriptions of the desired behavior; nonverbal prompts, such as gestures or demonstrations of the appropriate behavior; or verbal and visual reminders of rewards available for the targeted prosocial behavior (Colvin, Sugai, & Patching, 1993; De Pry & Sugai, 2002). For example, if students have difficulty transitioning from the classroom to the playground, a precorrection may consist of a role play in which students practice walking quietly in the hall.

Active supervision consists of a set of behaviors performed by supervising intervention agents to prevent problem behavior and promote rule-following behavior. Active supervision includes three basic components: (1) moving around the supervision area, (2) visually scanning for appropriate and inappropriate behavior, and (3) interacting with as many students as possible to make prosocial contacts, such as delivering precorrections, having brief conversations, and praising appropriate behavior (Lewis, Freebairn, & Taylor, 2000; Sugai & Horner, 2002). Interventions combining precorrection and active supervision have been successful in reducing problem behavior in a variety of nonclassroom contexts, including room-to-room transitions (Colvin et al., 1997), the playground (Lewis et al., 1998), and the cafeteria (Lewis, Colvin, & Sugai, 2000), as well as in classroom settings (De Pry & Sugai, 2002).

One intervention targets student behavior on school buses. Managing students' bus-riding behavior is a perennial concern of educators, parents, and bus drivers alike (National Highway Traffic Safety Administration, 1998; Hirsch, Lewis-Palmer, Sugai, & Schnacker, 2004; Schantl, 1991). Maneuvering a large vehicle, often in difficult traffic conditions, while simultaneously maintaining a safe and orderly environment for a group of students of different ages and grades presents a unique set of challenges. Perhaps because of the complexities involved in the successful execution of this task, very few empirically validated interventions targeting disruptive and unsafe bus behavior have appeared in the literature. In contrast to reactive approaches to bus management, such as installing surveillance cameras or conducting disciplinary meetings, *Improving Bus-Riding Behavior with a Schoolwide Intervention* takes a proactive approach, with training for students and bus drivers, faculty–driver collaboration, and social and material incentives for positive student behavior.

Two interventions target student behavior in physical activity settings, including the playground and the gymnasium. Although recess is a potential context for promoting social competence and problem-solving skills, especially for children with disruptive behavior problems (Jarrett et al., 1998; Pellegrini & Byorklund, 1997; Ridgway, Northup, Pellegrini, LaRue, & Hightshoe, 2003), it can also serve as a setting for bullying and victimization, which occur much more frequently on the playground than in the classroom (Craig et al., 2000). Students in inner-city schools may be especially vulnerable to bullying and aggression on the playground because their schools often lack adequate numbers of trained staff and sufficient resources in the form of age-appropriate play equipment (Leff, Power, Costigan, & Manz, 2003). Managing recess behavior can be more difficult than managing classroom behavior because recess periods are typically scheduled for more than one class at a time and playground supervisors may not be the staff members who are most familiar with the children. *Loop the Loop: A Schoolwide Group Contingency Program to Improve Playground Behavior* is a multifaceted intervention that includes several validated components, including direct instruction in the desired behaviors, guided practice in the target setting, and both positive and negative contingencies.

As with recess periods, physical education classes provide opportunities for increased freedom of movement and physical contact among students. As a result, they are often the setting for off-task, noncompliant, or disruptive behavior (Goyette et al., 2000; Sharpe, Brown, & Crider, 1995; Sharpe & Crider, 1996). *Promoting Good Sportsmanship in Physical Education Classes with the Good Behavior Game Plus Merit* encourages appropriate behavior in this setting with a variation of the *Good Behavior Game* intervention presented earlier in this chapter. With its combination of direct instruction, positive team competition, and group-oriented rewards, the strategy is ideally suited for implementation in physical education settings.

CROSS-REFERENCE: For a proactive intervention targeting room-to-room transitions that can be implemented on a classroom or schoolwide basis, see the *Timely Transitions Game: Reducing Room-to-Room Transition Time* in Chapter 3.

IMPROVING BEHAVIOR IN TRANSITION SETTINGS WITH ACTIVE SUPERVISION AND PRECORRECTION: A SCHOOLWIDE INTERVENTION

Overview

Room-to-room transitions, such as leaving the classroom to go to the lunchroom or entering or leaving the school building, are frequent settings for problem behavior. Moreover, if problem behavior occurs during these transitions, it is likely to spill over into the next setting, reducing valuable instructional time. This schoolwide intervention uses two antecedent-based strategies—active supervision and precorrection—to target three critical transitions: (1) entering the school building at the beginning of the day, (2) leaving the classroom and entering the cafeteria, and (3) leaving the classroom and exiting from the school building at the end of the day. Supervisors remind students of the expected behaviors before they enter transition areas (precorrection) and move around, visually scan the areas, and interact with students during transitions (active supervision). This intervention requires a single training session for teachers and supervisors, along with a few reminders at staff meetings, and no supplementary materials or resources. In the original study, conducted in an elementary school with 475 students in kindergarten through grade 5, the intervention resulted in a dramatic reduction in the frequency of problem behavior in all three transition settings.

Purpose

To reduce problem behavior during major transitions by means of a schoolwide effective transition program.

Materials

1. Posterboard charts, one per classroom, one in the hall near the main door, and one near the cafeteria (optional), labeled "How to Make a Great Transition" and listing the transition rules, such as:
   a. Walk when you enter and leave the school and in the hall.
   b. Keep your hands and feet to yourself.
   c. Use a quiet voice.

Observation (Select One or Both)

1. Calculate the number of office disciplinary referrals (ODRs) for inappropriate behavior during beginning-of-day, lunchtime, and end-of-day transitions for the entire student body or for students in selected grades for the previous month or the school year to date.
2. Using a *Group Event Recording Form,* record the number of problem behaviors displayed by students during one or more targeted transitions for 4 to 7 days. *Problem behaviors* are defined as running, pushing, shouting, hitting, yelling, entering prohibited areas (e.g., gardens and shrubbery areas), and failing to follow supervisor instructions.

Intervention Steps

Introduction and Training

FACULTY TRAINING

1. During a whole-faculty meeting, have staff members identify major problem behaviors exhibited by students in the targeted transitions and the appropriate behaviors students are expected to display in those settings. Include all teaching staff and transition area supervisors in the meeting. If supervisors are not available during faculty meeting times, conduct another training meeting.
2. Define *precorrections* as reminders of transition rules. Explain that precorrections or rule reminders help prevent disruptions from occurring by letting students know exactly what behaviors are expected in the transition settings.
3. Ask all staff to deliver three rule reminders to students just before they enter the transition areas: (a) walk, (b) keep your hands and feet to yourself, and (c) use a quiet voice.
4. Model delivery of rule reminders.

   > *Example*: "OK, students, I want you to remember our three rules for leaving the classroom to go home: walk, keep your hands and feet to yourself, and use a quiet voice."

5. Define the three supervisor behaviors that constitute *active supervision* as follows:
   a. *Move around*: Vary your position physically, avoid standing in one place, and remain standing.
   b. *Look around*: Visually scan all areas, especially distant areas.
   c. *Interact with the students*: Greet students by smiling or waving; chat briefly with students about items of interest; gesture to indicate appropriate behavior; comment on good behavior; inform students when they are breaking the rules; praise students who are following the rules; avoid long conversations with individual students.
6. If a student breaks a rule, state the rule that was broken and send the student back to the starting point to begin the transition again.
7. Conduct role plays to show examples and nonexamples of each active supervision component. *Example:* To demonstrate moving around, have two supervisors move constantly around an area of the room. *Nonexample:* Have one supervisor sit down and chat with another supervisor.

STUDENT TRAINING (OPTIONAL)

1. Have teachers use the transition rules charts to discuss appropriate transition behaviors with students during the homeroom or advisory period. Have teachers select students to role-play appropriate transition behaviors and provide praise and corrective feedback as needed.

Implementation

1. At the beginning of the school day, have supervisors direct students to line up at the front doors of the building and remind them of the three transition rules before they are allowed to enter the school. Continue this strategy for the entering-school transition.
2. On a daily basis for the first week and on an intermittent basis for the next 2 weeks, have the principal make the following announcement over the public address system prior to the beginning of the first lunch period: "Excuse me, teachers. I would like you to remind students of the three rules for going to the cafeteria." Near the end of the school day, have the principal make the following announcement: "Excuse me, teachers. I would like you to remind students of the three rules for leaving the school." Have the principal continue to make the announcements on the schedule described above.

3. Have classroom teachers remind students of the three rules just prior to exiting the classroom to go to the cafeteria and just prior to leaving for the day, after the principal's requests.
4. Have teachers continue these reminders even when the principal does not make the announcements.
5. Provide brief (3–5 minute) reminders about active supervision behaviors and precorrections at staff meetings twice a month or more, if needed.

Evaluation (Select One or Both)

1. Compare the number of ODRs for inappropriate behavior during the targeted transitions before and after implementation.
2. Compare the number of problem behaviors displayed by students during one or more targeted transitions before and after implementation.

Notes

1. In the original study, the only direct student training consisted of brief rule reminders by teachers prior to going to the cafeteria and prior to leaving at the end of the day. The optional rule review in classrooms is presented here as an additional precorrection procedure.
2. The researchers determined that activeness of supervisor behaviors was more important than the number of supervisors in reducing inappropriate behavior during implementation. The number of supervisory staff, which varied from one to six, was unrelated to improvement in student transition behaviors.

Source

Colvin, G., Sugai, G., Good, R. H., III, & Young-Yon, L. (1997). Using active supervision and precorrection to improve transition behaviors in an elementary school. *School Psychology Quarterly, 12,* 344–363. Copyright 1997 by The Guilford Press. Adapted by permission.

REDUCING HALLWAY NOISE WITH SOUND LEVEL MONITORING AND GROUP CONTINGENCIES: A SCHOOLWIDE INTERVENTION

Overview

Noise in school hallways during transitions is a perennial problem for teachers and administrators and can be accompanied by disruptive behavior fueled by peer attention. Excessive hallway noise not only interferes with ongoing instruction in classrooms not transitioning but also decreases the quality of a school's social climate. This schoolwide intervention targets transitions to and from the lunchroom with a combination of student-directed components (active teaching, peer modeling, guided practice, and group rewards) and environmental modifications (manipulating hall lights). Implemented in a rural middle school with 525 students in grades 6 through 8, the intervention resulted in a substantial reduction in the level and variability of noise during lunchtime transitions compared with the previous strategy of verbal reminders and detentions. Hall monitors and teachers also observed peer social support for appropriate behavior, with students prompting their classmates to be quiet when they entered the hallway. The faculty continued the intervention into the following year, during which both new and returning students maintained low levels of hallway noise. In the original study, researchers used a sound level meter to assess noise levels. In this adaptation, qualitative ratings of noise levels have been substituted, with the sound level meter version included as a variation. A variation designed for implementation by individual classroom teachers is also presented.

Purpose

To reduce excessive hallway noise and encourage appropriate behavior during lunchtime transitions with a schoolwide intervention package.

Materials

1. Sound level meter (optional, see Observation #3 and Note #3).
2. Rating scale with indices of noise (optional, see Observation #1).

Observation (Select One or More)

1. Create a noise level rating scale with ratings ranging from 1 (very low) to 5 (very high). Using the scale, rate the perceived level of hallway noise during one or more targeted transitions for 4 to 7 days. If desired, graph the ratings.
2. Using a sheet of paper attached to a clipboard, record the number of verbal reminders (e.g., "Walk quietly, Don't yell, Don't push," etc.) delivered by teachers or hall monitors to students during one or more targeted transitions for 4 to 7 days.
3. Using a sound level meter, assess peak noise levels at five 1-minute intervals during one or more targeted transitions and use the median (middle) level as a noise index. Conduct these assessments for 4 to 7 days.

Intervention Steps

Introduction and Training

FACULTY TRAINING

1. At a whole-faculty meeting, obtain a consensus as to appropriate hall behavior and acceptable noise levels for students during the targeted transition(s).
2. Demonstrate the sound level meter or distribute copies of the noise level rating scale and explain the intervention procedures as described below.

STUDENT TRAINING

1. Adjust the school schedule temporarily to allow a 7-minute training session for each lunch period. If another transition is targeted (e.g., entering or exiting the school), have teachers conduct a training session in their classrooms close to the time of the selected transition.
2. During the training session, review appropriate hallway behavior, such as moving quickly and quietly, keeping from talking or talking very quietly, not disturbing other classrooms that are still working, and following teacher and staff instructions.
3. Ask for volunteers or select a small group of students to serve as peer models. Coach the students in demonstrating appropriate noise levels (silence or quiet talking) versus inappropriate levels of noise while walking in the hall.
4. If possible, reduce hall lighting or add a blinking light to provide a visual contrast for times when quiet is required. Teach students a motto to help them remember the rules, such as "Lights low, voices go" or "When you see the light, lips stay tight."
5. Have the student volunteers demonstrate walking through the hall and emitting appropriate and inappropriate levels of noise. Have the rest of the students observe and rate the behavior of the peer models as appropriate or inappropriate with a "thumbs up" or "thumbs down" signal.

6. Tell students that they will receive 5 minutes of extra lunchtime for every 3 days with acceptable levels of noise during lunchtime transitions.
7. Later that day, have each teacher conduct a practice lunchtime transition (or other targeted transition) and provide praise and corrective feedback as needed.

Implementation

1. Have a designated staff member evaluate noise levels using the rating scale or sound meter during the lunchtime transition or the targeted transition. Alternately, assign one teacher or hall monitor to conduct the noise ratings.
2. Announce on the intercom system at the conclusion of each lunchtime transition if the students in that lunch period have met the noise level criterion. If another transition is targeted, make the announcement at the end of the school day. Praise the students if they have met the criterion and encourage them to try harder the next day if they failed to do so.
3. When a lunch period group has made quiet hallway transitions for 3 consecutive days, award the extra lunchtime to the classes in that group.
4. Conduct a follow-up whole-faculty meeting 1 week after initial implementation to monitor effectiveness and make modifications as needed.
5. Gradually fade the visual signal as students become successful in making quiet, disruption-free transitions.

Evaluation (Select One or More)

1. Compare noise ratings during the targeted transitions before and after implementation.
2. Compare the number of verbal reminders made to students during the targeted transitions before and after implementation.
3. Compare median noise levels during the targeted transitions before and after implementation.

Variation: Individual Classroom Version

1. To implement with a single classroom group, flip the classroom lights on and off to signal the beginning of the lunch room transition and carry the rating scale during the transition period to record noise levels.
2. If desired, create a bar graph on the chalkboard to record the occasions on which students earn the extra lunchtime reward. Provide a group activity reward, such as a popcorn or ice cream party after lunch, when the class has earned the reward for a specified number of days.

Notes

1. The extra lunchtime reinforcer is designed to provide the same reward that supports excessive noise in the hallway, that is, peer attention.
2. Sound level monitors beginning at about $60.00 are available from a variety of sources, including *http://www.reliabilitycheck.com* and *http://www.testequipmentdept.com*.

Source

Kartub, D. T., Taylor-Greene, S., March, R. E., & Horner, R. H. (2000). Reducing hallway noise: A systems approach. *Journal of Positive Behavior Interventions, 2,* 179–182. Copyright 2000 by PRO-ED, Inc. Adapted by permission.

IMPROVING BUS-RIDING BEHAVIOR
WITH A SCHOOLWIDE INTERVENTION

Overview

Disruptive behavior on the school bus can create a dangerous situation by distracting the driver or leading to student-to-student aggression. Student conflicts that arise during bus rides can also spill over into the classroom, fueling additional disruption and interfering with instruction. This schoolwide intervention targets bus-riding behavior with training for students in bus rules, training for drivers in rewarding appropriate student behavior, and a weekly lottery available to students receiving good behavior cards from bus drivers. Originally implemented in an elementary school serving 624 students in kindergarten through grade 5 in a high-poverty urban setting, the strategy was highly successful in decreasing disruptive bus behaviors, as measured by bus discipline referrals and bus suspensions. Moreover, these positive outcomes were maintained during a follow-up period, with school personnel assuming full responsibility for implementation without ongoing consultation.

Purpose

To improve bus-riding behavior with explicit instruction for students, training for bus drivers, and a schoolwide lottery for students displaying good bus-riding behavior.

Materials

1. "Safe Bus Riding Chart," consisting of a posterboard displaying schoolwide bus rules and consequences, one per classroom, such as:

Rules for Safe Bus Riding

    a. Stay in your seat while the bus is moving.
    b. Keep hands and objects inside at all times.
    c. Do not eat on the bus.
    d. Follow the driver's instructions at all times.
    e. Be respectful of the driver, other students, and school property.
    f. Use appropriate language.

Consequences

    a. Failure to follow any of the bus rules = office referral.
    b. Endangering the safety of other students or staff, interfering with the operation of the bus, or accumulating __ (predetermined number of) office disciplinary referrals = bus suspension.
2. "Catch-Them-Being-Good" cards, consisting of 3" × 5" index cards or slips of paper with space for recording instances of positive student bus behavior (see Figure 5.2 on p. 364).
3. Rewards, such as fast food certificates, CDs, school supplies, candy bars, etc.

Observation (Select One or Both)

1. Calculate the number of office disciplinary referrals for inappropriate bus behavior for the previous month or marking period.
2. Calculate the number of bus suspensions for the previous month or marking period.

Intervention Steps

Introduction and Training

FACULTY TRAINING

1. During a whole-faculty meeting that includes bus driver representatives, develop a list of safe bus-riding behaviors and consequences for failure to follow the rules. Use the list of rules and consequences to prepare one Safe Bus Riding Chart for each classroom.
2. Review procedures for rewarding positive student behavior with the "Catch-Them-Being-Good" (CTBG) cards and the weekly lottery system as described below.
3. Discuss the types of prizes that students would value and teachers would find acceptable and arrange to obtain or purchase them (see Note 1). Also, develop a list of activity privileges, such as extra gym time, an extended lunch period, early lunchtime release, lunch off campus, 15 minutes of basketball practice with the coach, etc.

STUDENT TRAINING

1. Teachers use the charts to discuss the safe bus-riding behaviors with students during the homeroom or advisory period. Teachers select students to demonstrate appropriate behavior during role plays and provide praise and corrective feedback as needed.
2. Teachers display the "Catch-Them-Being-Good" (CTBG) cards and explain the schoolwide lottery system as follows:
   a. Bus drivers will be observing students to "catch them being good," that is, to catch students who are following the bus-riding rules.
   b. Each day, drivers will award CTBG cards to students who are following the safe bus-riding rules.
   c. Students receiving cards will turn them in to their teachers, who will enter them into a weekly school lottery.
   d. Each Friday, the principal (or some designated staff member) will draw five cards (or some appropriate number, based on the total student population) and announce the winners over the intercom. In addition, the school bus with the fewest office referrals and suspensions will be recognized as "bus of the week."

BUS DRIVER TRAINING

1. Conduct a training session with all drivers during which you review how to monitor students during transportation and how to provide positive reinforcement by "catching students being good."
2. Display the CTBG cards and explain that drivers are to give the cards to students who are displaying appropriate or exemplary behavior.
3. Collaborate with the drivers to determine a specific number of CTBG cards to be awarded each day (such as one or two cards per bus), depending on the number of buses and students.

Implementation

1. Initiate the intervention on a Monday, if possible. Have teachers hand in the CTBG cards for their homerooms or advisories to the designated staff member on Friday.
2. Conduct the drawing and announce the winners, including the bus of the week.
3. Designate a staff member with bus supervisory responsibility to provide brief updates to bus drivers on student bus behavior and review any problems or concerns. Have the staff member distribute additional CTBG cards during these updates.

4. Provide opportunities for bus representatives to attend faculty meetings periodically to enhance collaboration between school staff and drivers in supporting safe bus behavior.

Evaluation (Select One or Both)

1. Compare the number of office disciplinary referrals for inappropriate bus behavior before and after implementation.
2. Compare the number of bus suspensions before and after implementation.

Variation: Bus of the Year

1. Maintain a record of which buses earn the bus of the week award and acknowledge a bus of the year during the final week of school. If desired, post a notice or plaque in the school main hall identifying the number and driver of the winning bus.

Notes

1. In the original study, local merchants donated the majority of tangible prizes, and school-sponsored activity privileges were scheduled during school hours.
2. The researchers noted that surveillance cameras, which had been installed in all of the buses to monitor student activity, were permanently removed during the intervention period.

Source

Putnam, R. F., Handler, M. W., Ramirez-Platt, C. M., & Luiselli, J. K. (2003). Improving student bus-riding behavior through a whole-school intervention. *Journal of Applied Behavior Analysis, 36*, 583–590. Copyright 2003 by the Society for the Experimental Analysis of Behavior. Adapted by permission.

Bus number: _____   Date: _____

Name of student: _____
Grade: _____

What was the positive behavior?

_____
_____
_____

_____
Driver signature

FIGURE 5.2. Catch-Them-Being-Good card for *Improving Bus-Riding Behavior with a Schoolwide Intervention.* Adapted from Putnam, Handler, Ramirez-Platt, and Luiselli (2003). Copyright 2003 by the Society for the Experimental Analysis of Behavior. Adapted by permission.

LOOP THE LOOP: A SCHOOLWIDE INTERVENTION TO REDUCE PROBLEM BEHAVIOR ON THE PLAYGROUND

Overview

Although recess is an activity that occurs daily or several times a week for most students at the elementary level, problems often occur because of the large numbers of students, too few or inadequately trained supervisors, and the inherent difficulty in monitoring a large, unstructured environment. Rules and routines may also vary from supervisor to supervisor, exacerbating the problem because students are unsure of expectations for behavior or consequences for misbehavior. This schoolwide intervention combines classroom instruction and playground practice in appropriate recess behavior, a time-out procedure, and rewards for classrooms displaying appropriate behavior. Implemented in an elementary school of 450 students with a 50% turnover rate and a high percentage of pupils from impoverished backgrounds, the strategy was effective in reducing the frequency of problem behavior across all three targeted recess periods. The strategy can also be implemented with a subset of classrooms or grades that share a common playground time or on an individual classroom basis when the teacher also serves as the recess supervisor.

Purpose

To reduce inappropriate and aggressive behavior on the playground with social skills lessons, guided practice, active monitoring and supervision, and group incentives.

Materials

1. Lessons in playground social skills and games, one lesson per targeted game, activity, and behavior (see Preparation below).
2. "Good Behavior Coupons," consisting of wrist-size brightly colored elastic loops, 20 to 30 loops per playground supervisor per recess period (depending on the number of students on the playground at one time).
3. Cans or jars, one per classroom.
4. Posterboard chart listing playground rules, one per classroom (optional).
5. Small edible rewards, such as wrapped candy (optional).

Observation (Select One or More)

Option 1

1. Calculate the number of office disciplinary referrals for recess rule infractions for the previous month.

Option 2

1. Using a sheet of paper attached to a clipboard, tally the number of disruptive behaviors demonstrated by students during one or more recess periods for 4 to 7 days. *Disruptive behaviors* are defined as aggressive actions against others (e.g., hitting, pushing, kicking); misuse of equipment (e.g., jumping off the top of climbing equipment, throwing kick balls at others, etc.); and disrupting ongoing games (e.g., grabbing the ball, jumping into line, making verbal or physical threats, arguing).
2. If desired, calculate the rate of disruptive behaviors per minute by dividing the total number of disruptive behaviors per period by the number of minutes in the period. For example, if 45 disruptive behaviors occur during a 20-minute recess period, the rate of disruptive behaviors is 2.25 per minute.

Option 3

1. Using a sheet of paper attached to a clipboard, record the number of time-outs served by students during one or more recess periods for 4 to 7 days. A *time-out* is defined as 5 minutes of standing in a designated time-out location on the playground for a recess rule infraction.

Intervention Steps

Preparation

1. In collaboration with physical education teachers and the schoolwide behavior support team or intervention assistance team, develop a set of brief lessons addressing rules and routines for playground games, such as basketball, four square, kickball, jump rope, and soccer. Lessons should include (a) a definition of the rule, (b) examples of the rule, and (c) modeling of the expected behavior. Lessons should be no more than 20 to 30 minutes each.
2. Develop three additional lessons addressing the following playground social skills: (a) how to join a game, (b) how to win and lose a game, and (c) how to line up to reenter the building when the bell rings.

Introduction and Training

FACULTY TRAINING

1. Conduct a whole-faculty meeting, including paraprofessionals involved in playground supervision, in which the staff develops schoolwide rules for playground behavior, such as:
   a. Keep your hands and feet to yourself.
   b. Use equipment appropriately.
   c. Follow the rules for joining games (wait in line or ask).
   d. Use appropriate language.
   e. Show respect for everyone.
   f. Do what the recess supervisors tell you to do, the first time they tell you.
2. Designate a location on the playground to serve as a time-out area, such as a corner or portion of the playground fence marked with tape or chalk.
3. After the social skills lessons have been developed, conduct another whole-faculty meeting to review the lessons and demonstrate sample lessons.

PLAYGROUND SUPERVISOR TRAINING

1. Conduct two training sessions with all faculty and staff playground supervisors to include one 15-minute meeting and one 10-minute follow-up meeting. Training should focus on three supervisor behaviors: (a) moving around the playground area; (b) scanning the entire playground area; and (c) interacting with students to have brief, pleasant conversations, deliver rule reminders, and award Good Behavior Coupons as described below.
2. If needed, include training in organizing and supervising common playground games.

STUDENT TRAINING

1. Teachers introduce the intervention to the students by reviewing the playground behavior rules, using a chart listing the rules, if desired. Teachers model the appropriate behaviors for each rule and have students practice them in the classroom.
2. After the classroom rule review, teachers conduct a playground practice in which they again model appropriate behavior for each rule and have students participate in role plays of appropriate behavior for various games and playground situations.

3. Over the next 2 weeks, teachers deliver the series of social skills lessons in their classrooms. In addition, teachers review and practice the skills with their students at least twice on the playground during nonrecess periods.

Implementation

1. For the first few weeks, teachers conduct a brief review of playground rules before each recess period.
2. During recess periods, playground supervisors organize and supervise group games and activities as needed and review the specific rules briefly with students beforehand.
3. During the recess period, playground supervisors provide specific praise and distribute Good Behavior Coupons to students who are following the behavior rules and exhibiting the targeted social skills.

> *Example*: "Trent, you're doing a great job taking turns in kickball. You've earned a coupon!"

Students can place the loops on their wrists to avoid losing them.

4. If a student breaks a rule, the supervisor delivers a warning.

> *Example*: "Ayesha, one of our playground rules is, *Show respect for everyone.* That means no pushing. This is a warning."

5. If the student breaks the rule again, the supervisor sends the student to the designated time-out area for a 5-minute time-out.
6. If a student exhibits aggression or unsafe behavior, no warning is given and the student serves a 5-minute time-out before being allowed to resume playing.
7. When the students return to the classroom, they place their loops in the can on the teacher's desk. As students place the loops in the can, the teacher asks them why they earned the loop and delivers additional praise. Teachers keep a running total of the number of coupons earned on the chalkboard.
8. When the can is full (or the class has earned a specified number of coupons), the class receives a reward, such as a pizza party, an extra recess period, or a video or DVD with popcorn. If desired, teachers may offer a choice of rewards and let the class vote.

Evaluation (Select One or More)

Option 1

1. Compare the number of office disciplinary referrals for recess infractions before and after implementation.

Option 2

1. Compare the number of disruptive behaviors and/or rate of disruptive behaviors per minute during the targeted recess periods before and after implementation.

Option 3

1. Compare the number of time-outs served by one or more classes during the targeted recess periods before and after implementation.

Notes

1. Encourage supervisors to organize cooperative games rather than having students organize their own games or play randomly. Participation in cooperative games at recess is associ-

ated with decreases in aggressive behaviors compared with participation in competitive games (Heck, Collins, & Peterson, 2001).

2. Regardless of whether implementation is on a schoolwide, grade/classroom cluster, or individual classroom basis, training all personnel serving as supervisors for a specific playground period and providing performance feedback during initial implementation is essential to the success of this intervention.

3. Although the original study did not provide for a backup time-out procedure, field testing indicates that some kind of negative consequence is important in maintaining appropriate playground behavior, even in the context of a token reinforcement program.

4. The strategy can be easily adapted to target appropriate lunchroom behavior if student seating is based on classroom assignment.

Source

Lewis, T. J., Powers, L. J., Kelk, M. J., & Newcomer, L. L. (2002). Reducing problem behaviors on the playground: An investigation of the application of schoolwide positive behavior supports. *Psychology in the Schools, 39,* 181–190. Copyright 2002 by John Wiley & Sons, Inc. Adapted by permission.

PROMOTING SPORTSMANSHIP IN PHYSICAL EDUCATION CLASSES WITH THE GOOD BEHAVIOR GAME PLUS MERIT

Overview

Although physical education classes provide an ideal context for helping students to acquire important social competencies, such as the principles of fair play and good sportsmanship, they also provide opportunities for inappropriate behavior, such as verbal and physical aggression, noncompliance, and attention seeking. This variation of the *Good Behavior Game Plus Merit* is designed to reduce inappropriate behavior and encourage prosocial behavior in the context of playing games. The intervention consists of four components: (1) daily goal setting by the teacher, (2) public posting of student performance, (3) a daily special activity for teams meeting the goal, and (4) an end-of-unit activity for teams consistently meeting the goal. To encourage students to be supportive of each other, teams compete not against each other but against a daily criterion, with all teams meeting the criterion receiving access to reinforcement. First conducted in three physical education classes with fourth-, fifth-, and sixth-grade students during a volleyball unit, the strategy produced immediate reductions in inappropriate behavior and concomitant increases in appropriate social behavior.

Purpose

To promote appropriate social behaviors, especially those related to game playing, using public posting and a group contingency with response cost.

Materials

1. Posterboard chart listing the rules for physical education class, such as:
   a. Follow the teacher's directions.
   b. Line up promptly when you are called.
   c. Use equipment safely.
   d. Do your best to participate in every activity.
   e. Play so that everyone can have fun.

2. Portable chalkboard or whiteboard divided into columns, one column per team, and labeled "Team 1," "Team 2," etc. (or labeled with student-selected team names).
3. Colored chalk or dry erase markers, one color per team (optional).
4. "Points sheet," consisting of a sheet of paper attached to a clipboard divided into columns, one column per team and labeled as described above.
5. Colored tags or badges to distinguish between teams, one set per team (optional, see Variation).

Observation (Select One or Both)

Option 1

1. Using a sheet of paper attached to a clipboard or a *Group Event Recording Form*, tally the number of appropriate and inappropriate social behaviors and false acts that occur during a 30- to 45-minute observation or during the entire physical education period for 4 to 7 days.
   a. *Appropriate social behaviors* are defined as (1) physical contacts or gestures that are supportive or responses to good play (e.g., pat on the back, high five, handshake, thumbs up, raising hands in the air, or clapping hands); and (2) encouraging and supportive verbal statements (e.g., "You can do it," "Good job," "Nice try," "Way to go").
   b. *Inappropriate social behaviors* are defined as (1) physical contact that is combative in nature (e.g., pushing, hitting) or behavior that interferes with the ongoing activity (e.g., damaging equipment, using equipment inappropriately, leaving the game or refusing to participate); (2) discouraging or offensive gestural behavior (e.g., making faces or clapping hands after a poor performance); and (3) discouraging or offensive verbal statements (e.g., ridiculing others, arguing, laughing at others' mistakes, or telling others to "shut up").
   c. *False acts* are defined as appropriate social behaviors emitted in the absence of any play for the purpose of earning points (e.g., saying, "Great job!" to a student during a break in the game and in the proximity of the teacher).
2. If desired, calculate a classwide daily average number of appropriate behaviors by dividing the number of appropriate behaviors by the number of observation days and use this number to set the first daily criterion for winning (see Intervention Steps, Implementation #1 below).

Option 2

1. Using a sheet of paper attached to a clipboard, record the number of reprimands delivered during a 30- to 45-minute observational period or during the entire physical education period. Conduct these observations for 4 to 7 days.

Intervention Steps

Preparation

1. Divide the class into teams of five to six students, depending on the current activity schedule. Be sure to divide disruptive and aggressive students among the teams. Schedule game play so that teams play against each other on a rotated schedule.

Introduction and Training

1. Explain to the students that they will be playing a game designed to help them remember to be good sports so that everyone can have more fun in physical education class.
2. Display the poster listing the rules for behavior during physical education class and review them with the students, including a discussion of the rationale for each rule.
3. Display the chalkboard or whiteboard with the team names and the clipboard. Explain that

you will be awarding points to each team when its members demonstrate good sportsmanship and removing points from the team score if you observe inappropriate behavior.

4. Explain that only genuine instances of good sportsmanship can earn points. Give examples of "false acts" as defined above and explain that you will deduct points for any false acts by team members because these behaviors do not involve good sportsmanship.

5. Announce the teams and, if desired, permit students to select a team name and write it on the points chart. Explain that the winning team(s) will receive 3 minutes of extra game play or a special activity at the end of each lesson.

6. Remind students that being a good loser is part of good sportsmanship. Explain that if any student displays inappropriate behavior in response to not achieving the daily goal, you will deduct a point from that team's total the next day.

7. Conduct a brief game to serve as a classwide practice during which you award points for appropriate behavior and provide feedback and redirection as needed.

Implementation

1. At the beginning of each class, announce the daily criterion. For example, begin with a criterion that is 10 times the class average for appropriate social behaviors prior to intervention (see Observation, Option 1). Thereafter, require teams to meet or exceed the previous day's performance.

2. Record pluses for appropriate behavior and minuses for inappropriate behavior under team columns on the points sheet during game playing. Record a minus if a student commits a false act.

3. During scheduled breaks in the game, select a student from each team to record points awarded for appropriate behavior and/or deducted for inappropriate behavior on the chalkboard or whiteboard under the team name. If desired, have the teams record their points in different colored chalk or markers to discourage cheating.

4. At the end of the game period, have students total their team scores. Announce the winner(s) (teams meeting the criterion) and deliver the special activity reward. Teams not meeting the criterion do not receive the special game time and must sit quietly on the sidelines.

5. After the first day of the intervention, teams must meet or exceed the previous day's performance (or another criterion established in the event that teams earned an exceptionally large number of points on the previous day).

6. At the end of the unit, provide a special lunchtime game for the two teams in the class that met the daily criterion most frequently (or for more teams, if equal).

7. Rotate team membership throughout the year so that students have an opportunity to be on teams with all of their classmates.

8. Gradually fade the public posting of team points to occur only once, at the end of the game period.

Evaluation (Select One or Both)

Option 1

1. Compare the number of appropriate and inappropriate social behaviors and false acts and/or the classwide daily average number of appropriate behaviors during the physical education period before and after implementation.

Option 2

1. Compare the number of reprimands delivered during the physical education period before and after implementation.

Variation: Whole-Group Version

1. For physical education classes that primarily involve whole-class activities rather than team-based games, divide the class into two teams for use in awarding points. Have students wear colored tags or badges during the activities so that you can distinguish the members of each team and award points as described above.

Notes

1. Contrary to the researchers' prediction, the intervention had no effect on students' volleyball skills.
2. Allowing students to select team names fosters team spirit and facilitates praising or reprimanding the teams.

Source

Patrick, C. A., Ward, P., & Crouch, D. W. (1998). Effects of holding students accountable for social behaviors during volleyball games in elementary physical education. *Journal of Teaching in Physical Education, 17,* 143–156. Copyright 1998 by Human Kinetics Publishers, Inc. Adapted by permission.

PRINT RESOURCES

Crone, D. A., & Horner, R. H. (2003). *Building positive behavior support systems in schools: Functional behavioral assessment.* New York: Guilford Press.

    This book presents a comprehensive model for conducting functional behavioral assessments (FBAs) and FBA-based interventions with students with chronic or severe problem behavior, including developing schoolwide behavior support teams to guide the assessment and intervention process. A variety of reproducible forms are provided, including FBA interview and observation forms and consumer satisfaction surveys for parents, students, and teachers.

Crone, D. A., Horner, R. H., & Hawken, L. S. (2004). *Responding to problem behavior in schools: The Behavior Education Program.* New York: Guilford Press.

    This text describes the Behavior Education Program, a research-based intervention program for elementary and middle school students who fail to meet disciplinary standards but do not require the highest level of behavior support. Designed to accommodate up to 30 students, the program combines daily behavior feedback, positive attention from adults, and home–school collaboration. Forms for implementation are included, including daily progress reports and student handouts.

WEBSITES

Association for Positive Behavior Support
http://www.apbsinternational.org

    The Association for Positive Behavior Support is dedicated to the advancement of positive behavior support and publishes the *Journal of Positive Behavior Interventions.* Among the many resources are the Online Academy Positive Behavior Support Modules developed through a grant from the U.S. Department of Education and available free to trainers and individuals.

Center for Effective Collaboration and Practice
http://cecp.air.org/center.asp

    Part of the American Institutes for Research (AIR), this project focuses on fostering the development and the adjustment of children with or at risk of developing serious emotional disturbance. The website includes numerous resources and links related to effective practices.

Kentucky Behavior Home Page
http://www.state.ky.us/agencies/behave/bi/bi.html

A collaborative effort of the Kentucky Department of Education and the Department of Special Education and Rehabilitation Counseling at the University of Kentucky, the Behavior Home Page provides resources for teachers, parents, and other professionals working with children with challenging behaviors. Among the resources are a Teacher's Encyclopedia of Behavior Management, a guide to time-out procedures, and functional behavioral assessment and behavior intervention plan resources.

National Technical Assistance Center on Positive Behavioral Interventions and Support
http://www.pbis.org

Established by the U.S. Department of Education's Office of Special Education Programs, the center provides information and technical assistance for identifying, adapting, and implementing effective schoolwide disciplinary practices. An online library provides links to numerous resources to support implementation, including the Schoolwide Evaluation Tool (SET). SET materials can be downloaded free of charge, other than a $25.00 fee for printing the implementation manual.

APPENDIX 5.1. Summary Characteristics of Behavior Interventions

Intervention	Description	Comments
Interventions to Improve Behavior and Social Competence in the Classroom		
The Good Behavior Game	Intraclass teams compete for rewards and privileges for meeting behavior standards.	To prevent students from becoming discouraged, make sure that students earn the reward early in the implementation process.
The Good Behavior Game Plus Merit	This version of the Good Behavior Game includes a restitution component in which students can earn bonus points for exemplary behavior or academic productivity.	This highly effective and usable intervention lends itself to numerous variations and can have immediate and dramatic effects on classroom behavior.
Three Steps to Self-Managed Behavior	Students monitor their own academic productivity and behavior to earn points for their team.	The teacher–student matching process can be streamlined via a dependent group contingency in which the teacher reviews only one student self-monitoring form per team.
Reducing Disruptive Behavior with Randomized Group Contingencies	This strategy randomizes rewards and reinforcement criteria in a group contingency system to motivate positive behavior.	Increasing the number of randomized contingency components increases the time needed for preparation and reward delivery but can also enhance motivation.
The Response Cost Raffle	Students lose "raffle tickets" for rule infractions, with remaining tickets placed in a weekly drawing for individual or team-based prizes.	This strategy can be easily adapted to a team-based, small-group, or individualized format.
Positive Peer Reporting	Students earn points toward group rewards for reporting the prosocial behaviors of their isolated and rejected classmates.	To enhance students' motivation to observe their peers' positive behaviors, alternate the original version with the two variations, the first of which makes compliment recipients unpredictable ("mystery stars") and the second of which adds a visual feedback component (a "honey pot").
Decreasing Inappropriate Verbalizations with a Peer-Monitored Self-Management Program	Students move colored dots on a chart to record undesired target behaviors in their own small-group setting and earn rewards.	Implementing the variation in which teams are required to have only one dot in the red section (i.e., one teacher-moved dot) to earn a reward is recommended to promote accurate self-monitoring.
A Multicomponent Intervention to Reduce Disruptive Behavior	Students earn points toward a "Mystery Motivator"—a reward concealed in an envelope on the teacher's desk—by avoiding rule infractions for specific intervals.	Keep reinforcement intervals short (10 to 15 minutes) during initial implementation to ensure that students have an opportunity to earn the reward and do not become discouraged.
Interventions to Improve Behavior and Social Competence in Nonclassroom Settings		
Improving Behavior in Transition Settings with Active Supervision and Precorrection: A Schoolwide Intervention	Supervisors prompt students to use expected behaviors prior to entering transition areas and follow up with monitoring and prosocial interactions.	Follow up to ensure that supervisors are engaging in brief positive interactions with students in addition to delivering rule reminders and reprimands to enhance student cooperation and maintain a positive atmosphere during transitions.
Reducing Hallway Noise with Sound Level Monitoring and Group Contingencies: A Schoolwide Intervention	Students learn to make quiet lunchtime transitions with peer modeling, practice, and group incentives.	This intervention can be used to target any nonclassroom transition during which large numbers of students are together in the hallway.

(continued)

373

Intervention	Description	Comments
Improving Bus-Riding Behavior with a Schoolwide Intervention	Students become eligible to participate in a weekly school raffle by earning cards for appropriate bus-riding behavior.	For maximum effectiveness, this intervention requires continuing collaboration among administrative, teaching, and transportation staff to monitor progress and problem solve as needed.
Loop the Loop: A Schoolwide Group Contingency Program to Improve Playground Behavior	Students earn coupons for appropriate recess behavior that can be traded for a reward when the class has accumulated a specific number.	Explicit training and follow-up observation with performance feedback for playground supervisors are essential to the success of this intervention, which requires active supervision, prompt reinforcement delivery, and the application of backup time-out procedures.
Promoting Good Sportsmanship in Physical Education Classes with the Good Behavior Game Plus Merit	In this team-based strategy, students earn points toward special group activities for displaying sportsman-like conduct.	This intervention works equally well for implementation on the playground.

CHAPTER 6

Interventions to Improve Outcomes for Preschool Children

Within the past decade, federal and state initiatives have led to an exponential increase in programs designed to promote children's school readiness, with states spending nearly 1 billion dollars on preschool education (Barnett, Hustedt, Hawkinson, & Robin, 2006) and as many as 43 states currently offering prekindergarten programs (Early et al., 2005). In 2005, 57% of preprimary children ages 3–5 were attending center-based early childhood care and education programs, including 43% of 3-year-olds (National Center for Education Statistics, 2007a). IDEA 2004 permits school districts to use up to 15% of their federal funds to develop and implement early intervention services, including training for teachers in scientifically based academic instruction and behavioral interventions for children who require additional academic and behavioral support but have not been identified as needing special education (20 U.S.C. § 1413[f][1][2]). The growth in early childhood educational programs has also been fueled by concerns related to the rising numbers of young children entering day care and preschool settings with multiple risk factors and the recognition that early intervention is most effective in changing children's developmental trajectories (Good Start Grow Smart Initiative, 2002; VanDerHeyden & Snyder, 2006). Currently, 43% of children under the age of 6 live in low-income households, and 22% live in households below the poverty line (less than $20,000 for a family of four in 2006), and the proportion is rising. Between 2000 and 2005, the percentage of children in low-income families increased by 11%, and the percentage living below the poverty level increased by 16% (National Center for Children in Poverty, 2006). In addition, the preschool population includes a growing number of children who have been identified with special needs even before school entry (Early et al., 2005). With the move toward full inclusion in the field of early childhood special education, preschool teachers are encountering more children with developmental delays, challenging behaviors, and other significant learning and behavioral needs. In a large national sample of kindergarten teachers, respondents reported that 16% of the children in their classrooms had serious difficulty making the transition to kindergarten. In addition, up to 46% of teachers reported that half or more of their students had specific learning-related problems, such as difficulty following directions, academic skill deficiencies, and difficulty working independently (Rimm-Kaufman, Pianta, & Cox, 2000).

The importance of high-quality early educational programs, especially for children from at-risk backgrounds, is documented by a large body of evidence attesting to the powerful and long-term effects of classroom practices in early childhood environments on children's cognitive and social competence (e.g., Burchinal & Cryer, 2003, Burchinal et al., 2002; Magnuson, Ruhm, & Waldfogel, 2007). Unfortunately, not all young children are being served by high-quality programs. According to two major studies of state-funded prekindergarten programs by the National Center for Early Development and Learning (NCEDL; Early et al., 2005), many preschoolers, especially those from low-income families, are enrolled in low-quality programs. Although the prekindergarten classrooms in the NCEDL studies typically had a warm, inviting atmosphere, instructional quality was highly variable and often poor. On average, children were not engaged in meaningful learning or play activities nearly half of the time (42%), with nearly a quarter (22%) of the time occupied by transitions and routines, such as waiting between activities, standing in line, and toileting. Adult–child interactions were infrequent and when they did occur, they were not at a level that would support the development of higher order language or thinking skills. Especially alarming was the finding that the poorest quality classrooms were also those serving the highest proportion of at-risk children, including children living in poverty, children from minority backgrounds, and children in families with lower levels of parental education—precisely the children who were most in need of high-quality educational experiences (LoCasale-Crouch et al., 2007; Pianta et al., 2005).

Evaluating the Effectiveness of Preschool Interventions

Evaluation methods for the interventions in this chapter include measures of the classroom environment and student performance that are both valid and practical in preschool settings. As in the rest of this text, the emphasis is on documenting performance and behavior on a classwide basis, but most of the evaluation strategies are also suitable for assessing the performance of a single student or a group of target students. Measures are tailored to intervention domain and specific target, such as the time required to complete classroom transitions for proactive interventions, verbal production and picture naming measures for language interventions, and rates of on-task behavior and compliance for behavioral interventions. To reflect the briefer durations of typical preschool activity periods compared with instructional periods at higher grade levels, suggested observation sessions have been reduced from the 30- to 45-minute period provided in the previous chapters to intervals ranging from 15 to 30 minutes. In addition, information on three widely used measures of preschool classroom environmental quality is presented below. Information on a set of general outcome measures (GOMs) for assessing language development is presented in the section on language interventions.

CLASSROOM ENVIRONMENT MEASURES: ASSESSING THE QUALITY OF PRESCHOOL CLASSROOMS

Several observational instruments have recently been developed to assess the quality of preschool classroom environments. Three of the most widely used measures are described below, each of which focuses on somewhat different aspects of classroom quality. The first two measures were used in the NCEDL studies discussed above.

Classroom Assessment Scoring System (CLASS; Pianta, La Paro, & Hamre, 2006; *http:// www.classobservation.com*). Designed for classrooms from prekindergarten (pre-K) through grade 3, the CLASS focuses on instructional quality and the nature and quality of teacher–child interactions. Eleven dimensions (12 at the pre-K level) are rated on 7-point scales and grouped to yield three global scores: (1) Emotional Support (consisting of Positive Climate, Negative Climate, Teacher Sensitivity, and Regard for Student Perspectives subscales); (2) Classroom Organization (consisting of Behavior Management, Productivity, and Instructional Learning Formats subscales); and (3) Instructional Support (consisting of Concept Development, Quality of Feedback, Language Modeling, and Literacy Focus [pre-K only] subscales). Another dimension—Student Outcome—is rated on a Student Engagement subscale.

The Early Childhood Environment Rating Scale—Revised Edition (ECERS-R; Harms, Clifford, & Cryer, 1998; *http://www.fpg.unc.edu/~ecers/*). Designed to assess programs for children in preschool and kindergarten, the ECERS-R evaluates the instructional and physical features of the classroom, as well as teacher–student interactions and the learning climate. The scale consists of 43 items, rated from 1 to 7, which are organized into seven subscales: (1) Space and Furnishings, (2) Personal Care Routines, (3) Language-Reasoning, (4) Activities, (5) Interactions, (6) Program Structure, and (7) Parents and Staff.

Early Language and Literacy Classroom Observation (ELLCO; Smith, Dickinson, Sangeorge, & Anastasopoulos, 2002; *http://www.brookespublishing.com*). Designed for prekindergarten through grade 3 classrooms, the ELLCO focuses on literacy and language aspects of the learning environment. It is comprised of three components: (1) the Literacy Environment Checklist, designed to provide a quick inventory of literacy-related items, consisting of 24 items divided into five categories (Book Area, Book Selection, Book Use, Writing Materials, and Writing Around the Room); (2) the Classroom Observation, consisting of 14 items rated from 1 to 5 and divided into two categories (General Classroom Environment and Language, Literacy, and Curriculum), and a Teacher Interview to clarify aspects of the observation; and (3) the Literacy Activities Rating Scale, consisting of 9 questions divided into two categories (Book Reading and Writing).

Proactive Classroom Management Interventions for Preschoolers

Preschool classrooms are often the setting in which children have their first experiences interacting with adults and peers in a structured environment (Hiralall & Martens, 1998). Preschool teachers must not only provide an age-appropriate curriculum addressing multiple aspects of children's development but also teach children the behaviors needed for successful adjustment to their new setting, such as following directions, moving from one activity to another, participating in groups, and working independently. Numerous studies have documented that teachers' instructional and behavior management practices have a powerful influence on preschool children's task engagement and opportunities to learn (e.g., McEnvoy et al., 1991; Zanolli, Daggett, & Pestine, 1995) and continue to exert significant effects on children's academic performance over time (Gilliam & Zigler, 2000; National Institute of Child Health and Human Development Early Child Care Research Network, 2000; Peisner-Feinberg et al., 2001). Especially in the preschool years, misbehavior may occur because children have not been taught the appropriate behaviors for the situation or have not been provided with sufficient opportunities to practice and receive reinforcement for the desired behaviors. Proactive interventions that explicitly teach rules and routines can enhance appropriate social interactions and reduce disruptive behavior and play a key role in helping to prepare children for successful functioning in elementary school settings (Barnett et al., 1999; McEnvoy et al., 1991). Implementing proactive strategies is especially important to maximize learning opportunities for children from high-poverty and inner-city environments, who are more likely to enter school with less well developed social skills and to be at risk for problem behavior (Anthony, Anthony, Morrel, & Acosta, 2005; Duncan & Brooks-Gunn, 2000).

Validated on preschool populations, the interventions in this section target two key features of classroom management in early childhood educational settings: (1) within-class transitions and (2) small-group instruction. Both strategies are designed not only to increase teachers' ability to manage children's behavior but also to build children's capacity to regulate their own behavior in these two critical contexts. The ability to perform within-classroom transitions successfully is a key competency for preschool children. In-class transitions can occupy large amounts of time in early childhood environments—as much of 20 to 30% of the school day (Carta et al., 1990; Early et al., 2005)—and are often associated with problem behavior, especially for preschoolers with developmental delays or behavior disorders (Connell, Carta, & Baer, 1993; Sainato, 1990). Ineffective transitions not only reduce the amount of time children can engage in learning activities but also limit access to inclusive educational settings for children with challenging behaviors (Dooley, Wilczenski, & Torem, 2001). In contrast, explicitly teaching transition skills not only increases all children's opportunities to learn in the preschool environment but also builds important social competencies, such as self-monitoring and self-regulation, which are essential to success in kindergarten (McClelland, Acock, & Morrison, 2006). *Promoting Independent In-Class Transitions with Self-Assessment and Contingent Praise* is a multicomponent strategy that uses an innovative classwide self-management procedure to target in-class transitions. Components include explicit instruction in appropriate transition behaviors, a group-oriented self-assessment, and contingent praise based on the match between teacher and child ratings. The strategy is effective not only in reducing transition times but also in decreasing disruptive and noncompliant behavior during free play and small-group instructional activities (Miller, Strain, Boyd, Jazynka, & McFetridge, 1993).

CROSS-REFERENCE: *Red Light/Green Light*, a strategy targeting disruptive behavior presented later in this chapter, includes a variation that encourages quick and quiet in-class transitions.

Because small-group instruction is a primary delivery system for supplementary instruction in multi-tier RTI models, learning to listen attentively and respond appropriately in small-group settings is a keystone competency for preschool children. Unfortunately, teachers often have difficulty managing small-group instructional formats, so that children do not always obtain the maximum benefit from targeted instruction (Miller et al., 1993). Although teachers may be trained in the use of certain behavior management strategies, such as praise and redirection, they may not have learned how to apply the strategies sequentially during an instructional activity to keep students on task. Moreover, teachers often rely on lengthy verbal directions when attempting to teach a task to children and fail to include the kinds of modeling and guided practice needed for successful completion. *Six Steps to Effective Small-Group Instruction* presents a managerial sequence designed to guide teachers' interactions with students through an activity from beginning to end, thus maximizing opportunities for child learning and minimizing opportunities for disruption. Key components include demanded eye contact, step-by-step directions and modeling for each step of the task, contingent praise for on-task students, and redirectives with additional modeling for off-task students.

CROSS-REFERENCE: Chapter 3 includes three proactive interventions that are especially useful in preschool settings. *Sit and Watch: Teaching Prosocial Behaviors* combines a nonexclusionary time-out procedure with choice making and peer observation to help children regulate their own behavior. *Say Show Check: Teaching Classroom Procedures* is a keystone intervention for teaching classroom routines and can be used as a framework for training students in the procedures for virtually all of the strategies in this book. *Six Steps to Speedy Transitions*, which teaches transitioning skills in a game-like format, includes a simplified variation for preschoolers.

PROMOTING INDEPENDENT IN-CLASS TRANSITIONS WITH SELF-ASSESSMENT AND CONTINGENT PRAISE

Overview

Transitions from one activity to another occupy a significant proportion of the time in preschool classrooms—as much as 30% of the day. This innovative self-management intervention package is designed not only to minimize the amount of time spent on in-class transitions but also to increase students' ability to perform transitions independently, a critical skill for all preschoolers, especially those in early childhood special education environments who will be moving into inclusive classrooms. Unlike many self-management procedures that involve time-consuming one-to-one matches between teacher and student, this intervention requires only one structured teacher–student interaction—a choral-response-based self-assessment—so that learning time is minimally disrupted. In a study with three classrooms of preschoolers with developmental delays, the duration of targeted transitions significantly decreased across all three classrooms. Moreover, all three randomly selected target students demonstrated significant increases in appropriate transition behaviors and accompanying decreases in competing behavior and teacher prompting, with behavioral gains maintained after the strategy was withdrawn. The intervention has also been demonstrated to increase on-task behavior and compliance in free play and small-group instructional settings. A variation with an individual matching procedure for children who do not respond to the classwide self-assessment is also presented.

Purpose

To reduce the duration of in-class transition times and promote independent transition skills with explicit instruction, self-assessment, and contingent praise.

Materials

1. "Good Behavior Chart," consisting of a posterboard chart with photographs of students in the classroom modeling transition behaviors for a targeted transition, such as:
   a. Starting to clean up (represented by a picture of a student with a hand on the light switch).
   b. Putting materials where they belong (represented by a picture of a student placing a toy on a shelf).
   c. Coming to the carpet for circle time (represented by a picture of a student sitting on a rug).
   d. Listening quietly (represented by a child sitting with mouth closed).
2. Sheet of paper with a list of student names down the left-hand side and a column on the right-hand side for recording a plus or minus (optional).
3. Hand stamps or stickers (optional).
4. Additional charts depicting appropriate behaviors for other transitions or activities, such as free play (with photographs of students using materials appropriately in solitary or small-

group play) or small-group instruction (with photographs of students listening attentively and participating actively; optional).

Observation (Select One or More)

Option 1

1. Using a sheet of paper attached to a clipboard, record the number of teacher prompts and reprimands delivered during one or more selected in-class transitions for a group of target students or the entire class for 4 to 7 days.

Option 2

1. Using a list of student names attached to a clipboard, record a plus (+) for appropriate transition behavior or a minus (–) for inappropriate transition behavior for each student during the targeted in-class transition(s), as defined below:
   a. *Appropriate transition behavior* is defined as behavior related to the transition, such as picking up toys, moving to the next activity, getting in line, sitting or standing quietly, and waiting for directions.
   b. *Inappropriate transition behavior* is defined as any behavior that interferes with the transition, such as continuing to play after the cue to clean up or move to another activity has been given, interfering with others cleaning up or transitioning, wandering around the classroom, and failing to comply with a teacher directive.
2. Calculate the classwide percentage of students with appropriate transition behavior by dividing the number of pluses by the number of students in the class.
3. Conduct these observations during the targeted transition(s) for 4 to 7 days.

Option 3

1. Using a stopwatch or watch with a second hand and a sheet of paper attached to a clipboard, record in minutes and seconds the interval from the time that you give the cue for one or more selected in-class transitions to the time that all students have completed the transition.
2. Conduct these observations during one or more in-class transitions for 4 to 7 days.

Intervention Steps

Introduction and Training

1. Select a problematic in-class transition, such as the transition between cleaning up from free play and getting ready for the opening circle time.
2. Tell the children that they are going to learn to how to make transitions quickly and quietly so that everyone can learn more and have more fun at school.
3. Using the Good Behavior Chart, teach appropriate behaviors for the targeted transition as follows:
   a. Select a student to flash the lights and say, "It's time to clean up and come to the carpet for circle time."
   b. Using *Say Show Check: Teaching Classroom Procedures,* discuss appropriate and inappropriate examples of transitioning.

      Example: "Does starting to clean up when told mean that when we flash the light and say, 'It's time to clean up,' we can keep on playing? No. We stop playing and put our things away, don't we?"

   c. First model and then lead students in practicing the appropriate transition behaviors, such as putting toys away, moving to the circle, and sitting on the carpet and waiting quietly for directions.

4. Teach the self-assessment procedure by having students raise their hands or give a thumbs-up/thumbs-down to indicate whether they think they have displayed appropriate transition behaviors.

5. Guide a student through a demonstration of each of the targeted transition skills and the self-assessment procedure. Then conduct a classwide practice and provide feedback on behavior and self-assessment accuracy as needed.

Implementation

1. Prior to the targeted transition, use the Good Behavior Chart to review the rules for transitioning and remind students of the behaviors they will be self-monitoring.

2. During the transition, provide praise for appropriate behavior. If desired, use the list of student names to record a plus (+) for appropriate transition behaviors and a minus (–) for inappropriate transition behaviors so that you can refer to it during the teacher–student matching process.

3. After the students have completed the transition and are ready for the next activity, display the Good Behavior Chart and ask the children to indicate by raising their hands above their heads or giving a thumbs-up if they thought they performed the targeted behaviors during the previous transition. If you have used the checklist to record transition behavior, refer to it at this time to evaluate the accuracy of student self-ratings.

4. During teacher–student matching, provide praise for appropriate behavior and accurate self-assessment.

> *Example:* "Heather, you have your hand in the air. I agree, you did a great job of putting your toys away and coming quickly to circle time."

If desired, also give a sticker or hand stamp to each child who made a successful transition and self-assessed accurately.

5. Provide corrective feedback for inappropriate transition behavior and/or inaccurate self-assessment.

> *Example:* "Devon, you have a thumbs-up, but I don't agree. I saw you playing with toys after you were told to come to the carpet. Let's work harder on that next time."

6. After students are making the targeted transition successfully, fade the self-assessment procedure to twice a week and then to once a week.

7. If desired, use the procedure to target another transition or another setting, such as free play or small-group instruction, using a chart with pictured rules appropriate for that context.

Evaluation (Select One or More)

Option 1

1. Compare the number of prompts and reprimands delivered to the group of target students or the entire class during the selected in-class transition(s) before and after implementation.

Option 2

1. Compare the percentages of students with appropriate and inappropriate transition behavior for the selected in-class transition(s) before and after implementation.

Option 3

1. Compare the amount of time required to complete the selected in-class transition(s) before and after implementation.

Variation: Individual Self-Assessment Format

1. If a student fails to respond to the group self-assessment procedure, conduct a brief (30-second) individual assessment after the targeted transition by asking the student if he or she displayed the appropriate behaviors.

> *Example:* "Tanya, did you start to clean up when the lights flashed? Show me a thumbs-up or thumbs-down."

2. Provide praise for successful performance and accurate self-assessment or corrective feedback as needed. Then continue with the group self-assessment procedure as described above.

Notes

1. Although hand raising makes it easier to see each child's self-rating, teachers in the Miller et al. study (1993) observed that children enjoyed making the thumbs-up/thumbs-down gesture and used it to rate their own performance and that of their peers in nontargeted situations. If you use the thumbs-up/thumbs-down format, teach students to raise their hands above their heads when making the signal and keep them up until you have matched their self-rating.
2. For classrooms served by a teacher and an instructional assistant, divide the class into two groups and conduct the self-assessment procedure simultaneously in two sections of the room.

Sources

Connell, M. C., Carta, J. J., Lutz, S., Randall, C., & Wilson, J. (1993). Building independence during in-class transitions: Teaching in-class transition skills to preschoolers with developmental delays through choral-response-based self-assessment and contingent praise. *Education and Treatment of Children, 16,* 160–174. Copyright 1993 by West Virginia University. Adapted by permission.

Miller, L. J., Strain, P. S., Boyd, K., Jarzynka, J., & McFetridge, M. (1993). The effects of classwide self-assessment on preschool children's engagement in transition, free play, and small-group instruction. *Early Education and Development, 4,* 162–181. Copyright 1993 by Taylor & Francis (*www.informaworld.com*). Adapted by permission.

SIX STEPS TO EFFECTIVE SMALL-GROUP INSTRUCTION

Overview

Learning how to listen and respond appropriately during small-group instruction is a keystone competency for preschool children. Unfortunately, teachers often rely on lengthy verbal directions and fail to include modeling and guided practice when attempting to teach children a learning activity. Moreover, although teachers may be trained in the use of isolated behavior management strategies, such as praise and redirection, they may not have learned how to apply the strategies throughout an instructional activity to maintain attention and ensure task completion. As a result, students have low levels of engagement during learning activities and require constant prompting to pay attention and sustain effort on tasks. This five-step sequence of managerial and instructional strategies, which includes demanded eye contact, step-by-step directions, modeling, praise, and redirectives, structures teachers' interactions to help children successfully complete an activity. Time limits are given for each step in the sequence to ensure a brisk instructional pace. In the original study with four teachers in two day care classrooms and a total of 14 target students with behavior problems, the direct instruction sequence was associated not only in significant increases in attention to instruction and time on task for all of the target children but also with more positive teacher–student interactions.

Purpose

To promote active student engagement and task completion during small-group activities with a structured instructional and managerial sequence.

Materials

None.

Observation (Select One or Both)

Option 1

1. Using a *Group Interval Recording Form* with a 10-second interval, glance at each student participating in a small-group instructional setting and record the student's behavior at that instant as on-task (+) or off-task (–) as defined below.
   a. *On-task behavior* is defined as having one's head and eyes oriented toward the teacher while the teacher is talking, actively working on the assigned task, or having head and eyes oriented toward the task.
   b. *Off-task behavior* is defined as looking around the room, being out of seat, playing with objects unrelated to the task, arguing with classmates, or any other behavior not related to the activity.
2. Conduct these observations for 15 to 20 minutes during a small-group instructional period for a group of target students or the entire class for 4 to 7 days. If you observe the entire class, rotate observations from group to group.

Option 2

1. Using a sheet of paper attached to a clipboard, record the number of redirectives and reprimands delivered to a group of target students after instructions for a small-group activity have been given. *Redirectives* and *reprimands* are defined as statements used to modify or correct a child's behavior once instructions have been given.
2. Conduct these observations for 15 to 20 minutes during a small-group instructional period for 4 to 7 days.

Intervention Steps

Step 1: Demand eye contact and attention. (1 minute)

1. Begin the activity by asking for eye contact and attention. Include a "teaser" statement to heighten children's interest in the activity.

> *Example:* "Look at me and listen. Our activity today is making a holiday card. We are going to learn to make something very special that you can take home to show your family!"

Step 2: Model the steps in the task. (4–5 minutes)

1. Be sure the children are looking at you while you deliver clear oral directions for the activity in a step-by-step format. After you give each direction, model the relevant step.

   Example: "The first thing you have to do is to cut out the card. Now, look at me and watch how I do it." [Demonstrate cutting out the card.]

2. If any of the children in the group are not paying attention, demand eye contact.

   Example: "Ross, look at me and listen."

3. Repeat this format for every step in the task.

Step 3: Provide individual praise to appropriately behaving students. (2 minutes)

1. Deliver specific individual praise to each child who is behaving appropriately. Praise statements should include the child's name and the appropriate action he or she is performing.

   Example: "Anne, you are doing a wonderful job gluing sparkles on your card."

Step 4: Provide individual corrective feedback as needed. (3 minutes)

1. If any children are off-task, demand eye contact and redirect that child individually with a single directive statement.

   Example: "Stefan, look at me, stop playing with the glitter, and please cut out your card."

2. If necessary, provide additional modeling or instruction.

   Example: "Stefan, watch me while I cut out the card."

   Once the off-task child begins to engage in appropriate behavior, deliver praise as described above.

Step 5: Provide additional individual praise to on-task students. (2 minutes)

1. Deliver individual praise to each child who is on-task, as described in Step 3.

Step 6: Redirect off-task students as needed. (3 minutes)

1. As needed, provide individual redirection to any child who is off-task, as indicated in Step 4. Provide praise once the child begins to engage in on-task behavior.

Evaluation (Select One or Both)

Option 1

1. Compare the percentages of on-task and off-task behavior during small-group instruction for the target students or the entire class before and after implementation.

Option 2

1. Compare the number of redirectives and reprimands delivered to the entire class or the target students during small-group instruction before and after implementation.

Note

1. Praise statements should be delivered briskly in order to maintain an appropriate instructional pace and prevent other students from becoming off-task. As students' task engagement increases, praise statements can be shortened.

Source

Hiralall, A. S., & Martens, B. K. (1998). Teaching classroom management skills to preschool staff: The effects of scripted instructional sequences on teacher and student behavior. *School Psychology Quarterly, 13*, 94–115. Copyright 1998 by The Guilford Press. Adapted by permission.

Interventions to Enhance Language Skills for Preschoolers

Language competence plays a critical role in children's socialization, interactions with others, and ability to access their educational experiences. Unfortunately, a substantial number of children are entering kindergarten with low levels of the oral language skills that are critical to future academic success (Lonigan & Whitehurst, 1998; Whitehurst et al., 1999). Hart and Risley (1992, 1995) have documented the profound differences in the quantity and quality of language experiences for young children from different socioeconomic (SES) levels. Hart and Risley estimate that by age 3, the spoken vocabularies of children of families living in urban poverty are only half the size of the vocabularies of children in middle-class families (500 vs. 1,100 unique words). Moreover, children in higher SES families hear many more questions (up to 45% of parent utterances) and more repetitions and elaborations of their own topics (up to 5% of parent utterances) compared with children in lower SES families, where a significant portion of parent utterances (up to 20%) consist of prohibitions. There are also tremendous disparities in children's picture book reading experiences and access to resources for literacy development across SES levels. Adams (1990, p. 85) has estimated that children from low-income families enter first grade with an average of only 25 hours of one-on-one picture book reading, compared with an average of 1,000–1,700 hours of picture book reading for the typical middle-class child. In addition, researchers (Neuman, 1999; Neuman & Celano, 2001) have documented striking differences between low-income and middle-income families in terms of the quality and quantity of print resources. In a study of four neighborhoods in the same city (two low-income and two middle-income neighborhoods), Neuman and Celano (2001) found inequities at all levels of analysis, including signage, public places for reading, and the number and quality of books in childcare centers, school libraries, and public libraries.

COMMUNICATIVE COMPETENCE AND ACADEMIC AND SOCIAL DEVELOPMENT

Children with poorly developed oral language skills are at high risk for negative outcomes in academic and social domains. Although the exact nature of the relationship is unclear, behavior problems are common among children with language difficulties (Qi & Kaiser, 2003; Tomblin, Zhang, Buckwalter, & Catts, 2000), and preschoolers with language impairments are at significantly greater risk for behavior disorders (Beitchman et al., 2001; Benasich, Curtiss, & Tallal, 1993; McCabe, 2005). Language difficulties place children at risk for academic problems and learning disabilities, even after controlling for intelligence (Catts, Fey, Zhang, & Tomblin, 1999; Larrivee & Catts, 1999; Lewis, Freebairn, & Taylor, 2000), as well as for a range of social, emotional, and behavioral problems, especially in the case of boys (Brownlie et al., 2004). Despite the importance of oral language skills in helping children make a successful transition to kindergarten, many at-risk preschoolers are not receiving the kinds of language-enhancing experiences they need. In the NICEDL study cited above, most classrooms offered a poor instructional climate for promoting language and literacy development, with children spending only 7% of their time in teacher-directed language development activities (Early et al., 2005).

THE IGDIS: MEASURING LANGUAGE AND EARLY LITERACY DEVELOPMENT FOR PRESCHOOLERS

The *Individual Growth* and *Development Indicators* (IGDIs) are general outcome measures (GOMs) designed to assess progress toward important developmental outcomes for children ages 30–66 months. Developed by teams of researchers at the University of Minnesota's Early Childhood Research Institute on Measuring Growth and Development, the IGDIs are intended not only to measure growth over time but also to assess the effects of interventions for individual children and groups of students (McConnell, McEnvoy, & Priest, 2002; McConnell, Priest, Davis, & McEnvoy, 2002). Like other GOMS, such as the DIBELS measures (*http://www.dibels.uoregon.edu*), IGDIS are designed to be quick, easy to use, and capable of being administered frequently. Currently, three IGDIs have been validated for preschoolers—one measuring expressive language (Picture Naming) and two measuring phonological awareness (Rhyming and Alliteration). The three measures are described below.

Picture Naming. The child is presented with a series of photographs or line drawings of objects typically found in preschoolers' environments and asked to name as many pictures as quickly as possible. The score is the number of pictures named correctly in 1 minute.

Rhyming. The child is presented with a series of cards, each of which has a picture on the top of the card and three pictures on the bottom. The examiner points to and says the name of each picture, and the child is asked to point to the picture that rhymes with ("sounds the same as") the top picture. The score is the number of rhymes correctly identified in 2 minutes.

Alliteration. The child is presented with a series of cards, each of which has a picture on the top of the card and three pictures on the bottom. The child is asked to point to the picture on the bottom that begins with the same sound as the picture on the top, and the score is the number of alliterations identified correctly in 2 minutes.

Although predictive validity studies are not yet available, the IGDIs appear to be sensitive to growth over time and are positively correlated with norm-referenced tests of preschool language skills (see Missall & McConnell, 2004, for a summary of reliability and validity evidence). Moreover, the IGDIs can help teachers determine whether children as individuals or groups are making adequate progress toward expected goals, especially when the results are presented graphically (Phaneuf & Silberglitt, 2003). The three measures, including administration and scoring procedures and student record sheets, can be downloaded free of charge from the Get It, Got It, Go website (*http://ggg.umn.edu*).

STORYBOOK READING INTERVENTIONS

Reading aloud to children is a common practice in preschool classrooms. Although shared storybook reading can enhance children's vocabulary, print awareness skills, and background knowledge (see Coyne et al., 2004, for a review), many preschoolers have limited access to adult-directed book reading. In the recent NCEDL studies (Early et al., 2005), prekindergarten children spent on average only 5% of their time being read to by an adult. Moreover, storybook reading is not equally effective for all children. Children with smaller initial vocabularies are less likely to acquire new words with typical storybook reading activities than their classmates with larger initial vocabularies (Robbins & Ehri, 1994; Sénéchal, Thomas, & Monker, 1995). As a result, traditional storybook activities are likely to expand rather than reduce the vocabulary gap between at-risk children and their more advantaged classmates (Penno, Wilkinson, & Moore, 2002).

This section includes two interventions that use shared picture book reading to accelerate language and early literacy skills in preschoolers, especially those who have had limited exposure to books and exhibit underdeveloped literacy and language skills. *Enhancing Emergent Literacy Skills with Dialogic Reading* consists of a series of procedures, termed *dialogic reading*, designed to increase children's involvement in the book reading experience. Unlike typical shared reading, in which the adult is the active reader and the child is the passive listener, dialogic reading engages the child in an active dialogue about the content and pictures in a book. Originally developed by Whitehurst and his colleagues (Whitehurst et al., 1988) as a parent–child language-enhancement strategy, dialogic reading has been successfully extended to teacher-led dialogic reading in day care and preschool settings with child–teacher ratios of 5 to 1 (Whitehurst, Arnold, et al., 1994; Lonigan & Whitehurst, 1998) and 8 to 1 (Hargrave & Sénéchal, 2000). One of the most studied of all preschool interventions, dialogic reading is associated with significant improvement in language skills, especially expressive language, for children from families at every socioeconomic level, including middle-class children (Whitehurst et al., 1988), low-income preschoolers (Arnold, Lonigan, Whitehurst, & Epstein, 1992; Whitehurst, Epstein, et al., 1994), educationally at-risk children (Taverne & Sheridan, 1995), English language learners (Valdez-Menchaca & Whitehurst, 1992), and children with language delays (Dale, Crain-Thoreson, Notari-Syverson, & Cole, 1996). Moreover, dialogic reading is superior to traditional storybook reading in accelerating children's language skills (Arnold et al., 1994; Hargrave & Sénéchal, 2000; Whitehurst et al., 1988).

The second intervention also uses interactive book reading procedures to maximize children's opportunities to learn vocabulary from classroom read-alouds. *Building Vocabulary Skills with Interactive Book Reading* is a theme-based strategy that combines shared book reading with story props and extension activities to provide multiple opportunities for children to hear and use the vocabulary words presented in the books. A unique component of this intervention is the use of center time activities linked to story content to reinforce storybook vocabulary. Interactive book reading experiences that include additional explanations of target vocabulary words are associated with larger gains in receptive and expressive language than traditional read-aloud sessions (Brabham & Lynch-Brown, 2002; Penno et al., 2002; Wasik & Bond, 2001).

ENHANCING EMERGENT LITERACY SKILLS WITH DIALOGIC READING

Overview

In the typical picture book reading in preschool classrooms, the teacher reads while the children listen. In dialogic reading, the teacher assumes the role of an active listener, asking specific types of questions and encouraging children's responses to the book so that the children become the storytellers. As the dialogue progresses, the teacher encourages more linguistically complex responses by expanding children's utterances and posing more challenging questions. The acronyms CROWD and PEER are used to help teachers remember the interactional reading strategies. Dialogic reading has a significant positive impact on children's oral language abilities and emergent literacy skills across a wide variety of preschool populations, including English language learners, children with language delays, and educationally at-risk children, and is superior to regular parent- or teacher-led book reading. For best results, dialogic reading should be conducted for about 10 minutes per day, three to five times a week, with groups of no more than eight children. Because some studies indicate that the effects on language development are nearly doubled when children participate in dialogic reading at home and at school, a parent-led version is included as a variation.

Purpose

To improve oral language and emergent literacy skills through a structured picture book reading procedure that involves children as active participants in the reading process.

Materials

1. Attractive illustrated books appropriate for preschoolers, selected according to the following criteria:
    a. Books should contain colorful, attractive illustrations so that the story can be told through the illustrations alone and without having to rely completely on the text.
    b. Books should include vocabulary in the illustrations and text that is potentially novel to the children.
    c. Books should be relatively short in order to increase reader–child interactions.
    d. Books should be appropriate for the entire age range of children in the classroom.
    e. Books should not consist of rhyme or word books, which tend to limit the range of questions that can be asked.
    f. Books should not be specific to particular holidays (e.g., Christmas books in March).
    g. Books should not have been previously shared with children in the classroom.

Observation (Select One or More)

Option 1

1. Read through an unfamiliar book with a group of target students. After reading the book, return to the beginning and ask open-ended questions of each child in turn as you proceed through the book a second time.

    Example: "Mary Anne, tell me about this page."

2. As each child responds, tally on a sheet of paper the number of words or the number of different nouns produced.
3. Calculate an average verbal production score for the target group by summing individual scores and dividing by the number of children in the group.

Option 2

1. Administer the Picture Naming task on the *Individual Growth and Development Indicators* (IGDIs) to a group of target students or to the entire class.
2. If desired, calculate a group or classwide average by summing individual scores and dividing by the number of children in the group or class.

Option 3

1. Create a list of 20 nouns from the first 10 books you will be using during dialogic reading sessions. Make photocopies (color, if possible) of pictures of the 20 nouns from the books.

2. Show the 20 pictures to a group of target students or to the entire class in a one-to-one assessment setting and ask each child to label them.
3. Record a picture naming percent-accuracy score for each student assessed. If you test the entire class, calculate a classwide picture naming percent-accuracy score by summing the total number of pictures accurately named and dividing by the number of children in the class.

Intervention Steps

Preparation

1. Select a picture book, using the criteria listed above.
2. Divide the class into groups of five to eight students. If you share dialogic reading with another person (see Note 1), you can provide daily 10-minute sessions for every student in a class of 20 children (with a ratio of 1 reader to 5 children), for a total of 20 minutes of dialogic reading per school day.

Implementation

1. Have the group sit next to you so that all the children can see the book. Introduce the picture book by displaying the cover and asking the children what they think the book will be about.
2. Have children take turns responding to questions but have the entire group repeat new vocabulary words and phrases. Don't let one child dominate the session, and don't let children interrupt each other.
3. Follow correct answers by asking children to say more or by asking another question. Provide assistance in answering when needed. Convey encouragement for children's responses and your own interest and enthusiasm for the story and the reading process.
4. As you read through the book with the group, ask CROWN questions and use PEER strategies, as follows:

CROWN QUESTION TYPES

    a. *Completion prompts:* Questions that require children to provide a missing word to complete a sentence. *Example:* "When they went outside to play, they put on their _____."
    b. *Recall prompts:* Questions that require children to remember events in the story. *Example:* "Can you remember some of the games that the children played?"
    c. *Open-ended prompts:* Statements that encourage children to respond to the story in their own words. *Example:* "Now it's your turn to tell what's happening on this page. Let's start with Miguel. Miguel, tell us what's happening here."
    d. *Wh-prompts:* Who, what, where, which, and why questions. *Example:* "Where did the children go to play after school?"
    e. Distancing prompts: Questions that require children to relate the story content to their own experiences. *Example:* "Has anyone ever gone to a park like Lorenzo and Maria did?"

PEER STRATEGIES

    a. *Prompt:* Prompt children to label objects in the book and talk about the story. *Example:* "Who knows the name for this kind of animal?"
    b. *Evaluate:* Evaluate children's responses by praising correct responses and offering alternative object labels or providing answers for incorrect responses. *Example:*

        TEACHER: "What did Sammy decide to do after school?"

        CHILD: "Baseball!"

> TEACHER: "Well, Sammy might have wanted to play baseball, but remember that he ended up playing soccer with Mike."

c. *Expand:* Expand children's verbalizations by repeating what they have said and adding information. *Example:*

> TEACHER: "What is happening in this picture?"
>
> CHILD: "He wet!"
>
> TEACHER: "That's right, Anna, the boy is soaking wet because he got caught in the rain."

d. *Repeat:* Encourage children to repeat the expanded utterances. *Example:*

> TEACHER: "What kind of animal is this?"
>
> CHILD: "Doggie!"
>
> TEACHER: "Yes, that's a dog. That kind of dog is called a *beagle*. Let's all say 'beagle!'"
>
> CHILDREN: "Beagle!"

5. During the course of the week, read each book twice to each group.

Evaluation (Select One or More)

Option 1

1. Compare the average verbal production score for the target group of children before and after implementation.

Option 2

1. Compare IGDI Picture Naming average scores for the entire class or the group of target students before and after implementation.

Option 3

1. Compare picture naming percent-accuracy scores for the books for the target group of the entire class before and after implementation.

Variation: Parent-Led Dialogic Reading

1. To train parents in dialogic reading, plan for a 1-hour session, with 30 minutes for demonstration and discussion and 30 minutes for parents to practice the strategies, either with their own children or with other parents in role-play situations. For parent-led dialogic reading, a one-to-one reading format replaces the small-group format, but the basic approach, CROWN questions, and PEER strategies are identical.
2. After the training session, provide parents with a picture book each Monday afternoon. Ask parents to read the book to their child for a minimum of 10 minutes at least five times during the week and to return the book the following Monday. Provide another book every week during the course of the intervention.
3. Because there is some evidence that video-based parent training may be more effective than traditional direct training methods (Arnold et al., 1994), consider videotaping an adult implementing the intervention with a child for use in the parent training session. As always, be sure to obtain signed consent not only from the adult participant but also parental consent for the child to participate in the videotaped session and for the videotape to be used for training purposes.

Notes

1. Dialogic reading can be delivered by trained paraprofessionals, parent or community volunteers, or secondary level students with appropriate monitoring and supervision.
2. Practicing the techniques with a consultant or fellow teacher prior to implementation is very helpful in developing effective dialogic reading skills.

Sources

Hargrave, A. C., & Sénéchal, M. (2000). A book reading intervention with preschool children who have limited vocabularies: The benefits of regular reading and dialogic reading. *Early Childhood Research Quarterly, 15,* 75–90. Copyright 2000 by Elsevier Science, Ltd., Oxford, England. Adapted by permission.

Zevenbergen, A. A., & Whitehurst, G. J. (2003). Dialogic reading: A shared picture book reading intervention for preschoolers. In A. Van Kleeck, S. A. Stahl, & E. B. Bauer (Eds.), *On reading books to children: Parents and teachers* (pp. 177–200). Mahwah, NJ: Erlbaum. Copyright 2003 by Lawrence Erlbaum Associates, Inc. Adapted by permission.

Additional Resources

Read Together, Talk Together (Pearson Early Learning, 2002), a commercially published version of dialogic reading, is available at *http://www.pearsonearlylearning.com*. There are two kits—one for ages 2 and 3 and one for ages 4 to 5—each of which includes 20 books, teacher/parent notes for each book, a program handbook, a teacher training video, and a parent training video.

BUILDING VOCABULARY SKILLS WITH INTERACTIVE BOOK READING

Overview

Shared picture book reading provides opportunities for enhancing early literacy and language development by introducing children to new vocabulary, print conventions and functions, and the syntactic structure of language. For many young children living in poverty, out-of-home environments are the primary place where they experience shared reading. This intervention adapts one-to-one book reading strategies validated in home settings to a whole-group classroom format to enhance the vocabulary skills of children with limited book exposure and underdeveloped literacy and language skills. Presented in a 4-day instructional sequence, the strategy has three key elements: (1) presenting target vocabulary words multiple times and in multiple contexts, (2) providing concrete representations of target words, and (3) using reading strategies that emphasize open-ended questioning and dialoguing. A unique component of this intervention is the use of center time activities linked to story content to reinforce vocabulary. In the original study, conducted in eight classrooms of 4-year-olds from low-income families in a Title I early learning center, children in the intervention classrooms scored significantly better than children in control classrooms on a standardized receptive vocabulary test and on receptive and expressive book vocabulary measures.

Purpose

To promote preschoolers' vocabulary development by combining interactive book reading with multiple opportunities to hear and use target vocabulary in a meaningful context.

Materials

1. Age-appropriate picture books related to common preschool themes, such as "gardening," "welcome to school," "clothing," and "the seasons," and containing similar vocabulary words, two books per theme.
2. "Story prop box," consisting of a box containing objects representing the target vocabulary words, one set of objects per theme; for example, for books related to a gardening theme, objects could include seeds; a miniature shovel, rake, and garden hose; plastic flowers; a carrot; an ear of corn; and plastic insects.
3. List of target vocabulary words selected from the books; target words should be common words that are likely to be unfamiliar to the children but are necessary for understanding the stories.
4. Picture cards depicting target vocabulary words (see Note 3).
5. One large blank book or sheets of paper on a flipchart.
6. Small blank books, one per student (optional).
7. Materials for center time activities related to the target vocabulary (see Preparation).

Observation (Select One or Both)

Option 1

1. Using a sheet of paper attached to a clipboard, show each child in a target group or in the entire class one picture at a time from the picture card set and ask him or her to name the object in the picture.
2. Calculate a picture naming percent-accuracy score for each child by tallying the number of correct responses and dividing by the total number of pictures presented.
3. If desired, calculate a group or classwide median (middle) picture naming percent-accuracy score.

Option 2

1. Display the first set of story props to a group of target children or every child in the class, one at a time, and ask each child to name the objects (to measure expressive vocabulary). Alternatively, display the box with all of the objects in it, name each object, and ask the child to locate it in the box (to measure receptive vocabulary). Using a sheet of paper attached to a clipboard, record the number and percentage of objects named and/or recognized correctly by each child.

Intervention Steps

Preparation

1. Using the picture cards, make a big book of pictures of the target vocabulary words in the two theme-related books or attach the pictures to sheets of paper on a flipchart. If desired, make the same book in a smaller form, one book per child.
2. Develop one or more center time activities related to the vocabulary and concepts in the books. For example, for a garden theme, activities could include arts and crafts (e.g., painting a garden picture or making a paper plate garden), science activities (e.g., planting carrot seeds), and cooking activities (e.g., making a vegetable platter for snack time).

Implementation

1. This intervention requires reading one of the two theme-related books twice and the second book once, according to the following schedule:

Day 1: Have the children identify the story props and read the first book using the interactive reading strategies described below. Between interactive reading sessions, place the story props in an area of the classroom where the children can play and interact with them.

Day 2: Have children identify the story props and read the same book again. Then have children work in small groups in center activities related to the vocabulary.

Day 3: Read the second book and have children label the props.

Day 4: Have children work in small groups in center activities related to the vocabulary. Read the big book containing pictures of vocabulary words and engage the children in a discussion of the words. If you have created small versions of the big book for students, have them follow along in their books as you "read."

2. When reading the books, use the following interactive reading procedures:

BEFORE READING

a. After a child names an object, ask what he or she can do with the object. Introduce the target vocabulary by holding up a story prop and asking, "What is this?" or "What do you call this?" Provide praise for accurate naming and give the correct label if the children are unable to identify an object.

b. Then ask open-ended questions about the object, such as,

"What can I do with this ___?" or "Tell me what you know about this ___."

Provide praise or corrective feedback as needed. Continue the naming and discussion until all the story props have been presented.

c. Introduce the first of the two books as follows:

"Today we are going to read a book about [theme of book]. The name of the book is [title] by [author(s)]. In this book, we will find many of the words for the objects we have just seen. Let's look at the cover of the book to see what we think the book is about. What does it look like this book is about?" (Select three or four children to make predictions about the book.)

DURING READING

a. During reading, ask open-ended questions that promote discussion and involve the children in the story.

Examples: "Tell me more about what is happening on this page." "What do you think will happen next?" "Why do you think [character] did that?" "How did [character] feel about ... "

b. As children respond, refer to the objects in the prop box as appropriate.

AFTER READING

a. After reading, review the story by asking reflection questions.

Examples: "Let's think about the story we just read. How did the boy decide what he would plant?" "What part of the book did you like the best?" "Tell me why you think the boy was so sure the carrot would grow."

b. Make connections between the vocabulary and concepts in the story and the center activity.

Example: "The boy watched his plants grow just like we have been watching our plants grow. Our plants are growing because we watered them and put them in the sun. Now you will have a chance during center time to plant some more seeds."

Evaluation (Select One or Both)

Option 1

1. Compare picture naming percent-accuracy scores for the target children or the entire class before and after implementation. If desired, compare the group or classwide median picture naming percent-accuracy score before and after implementation.

Option 2

1. Compare the percentage of objects named and/or recognized correctly by the group of target children or the entire class before and after implementation.

Notes

1. In the original study, classroom size ranged from 12 to 15 children.
2. To maximize children's ability to attend to the book reading sessions, use *Say, Show, Check: Teaching Classroom Procedures* to demonstrate appropriate listening and participation skills (e.g., raise your hand to speak, listen to others when they are talking) prior to implementation. Conduct periodic reviews at the beginning of sessions as needed.
3. Picture libraries are available from many educational publishers and can often be found in preschool and elementary school media centers.

Source

Wasik, B. A., & Bond, M. A. (2001). Beyond the pages of a book: Interactive book reading and language development in preschool classrooms. *Journal of Educational Psychology, 93,* 243–250. Copyright 2001 by the American Psychological Association. Adapted by permission.

Interventions to Improve Behavior and Enhance Social Competence in Preschoolers

Today's preschool teachers report that disruptive behavior is the greatest problem they face in the classroom (Dunlap et al., 2003). Researchers and educators alike have observed that an increasing number of children with challenging behaviors are participating in early childhood educational settings. As defined by Smith and Fox (2003), *challenging behavior* in young children refers to "any repeated pattern of behavior, or perception of behavior, that interferes with or is at risk of interfering with optimal learning or engagement in pro-social interactions with peers and adults" (p. 6). Challenging behaviors include physical and verbal aggression, prolonged tantrums, disruptive motoric or vocal responding (e.g., stereotypic behaviors, screaming), noncompliance, destruction of property, self-injury, and withdrawal. Although the factors contributing to the increase in aggressive and disruptive behaviors among young children continue to be debated, approximately 10 to 15% of typically developing preschoolers have mild to moderate behavior problems (Campbell, 1995), with higher rates among children living in poverty (Qi & Kaiser, 2003). In a survey of Head Start and community preschool childcare centers, teachers reported that about 10% of children in their classrooms exhibited daily or higher rates of antisocial aggressive behaviors, with boys displaying aggressive behaviors much more frequently than girls (Kupersmidt, Bryant, & Willoughby, 2000). Similarly, data from the Early Childhood Longitudinal Study indicate that 10% of kindergartners display problem behaviors on school entry, such as arguing, fighting, and getting angry easily (West, Denton, & Germino-Hausken, 2000).

The importance of early intervention with preschool children who are at risk for or are already displaying behavior problems has been underscored in light of a growing body of research documenting the stability of aggressive and disruptive behavior in preschoolers and the negative developmental and educational outcomes associated with early problem behavior (Campbell, 2002; Lavigne et al., 1998; McNeil, Capage, Bahl, & Blanc, 1999). Without effective intervention, challenging behaviors can jeopardize children's opportunities to participate in early educational settings. A recent national study of 3,898 prekindergarten classrooms representing all of the 52 state-funded prekindergarten systems operating in 40 states reported that 6.67 preschoolers were expelled per 1,000 enrolled, 3.2 times the rate for K–12 students. Expulsion rates were highest for older preschoolers and African American children, and boys were four and a half times more likely to be expelled than girls (Gilliam, 2005).

Inappropriate behaviors, such as defiance, noncompliance, and aggression, are highly disruptive to preschool learning environments, limit children's opportunities to participate in instructional activities, impair teacher–student relationships, and can lead to early school failure and other negative developmental and educational outcomes (Killu, Sainato, Davis, Ospelt, & Paul, 1998; Powell, Dunlap, & Fox, 2006). Given the stability of disruptive and aggressive behavior and the greater likelihood of successful intervention with younger versus older children, it is essential to intervene as early as possible before antisocial behavior patterns become entrenched and resistant to treatment (Dishion et al., 1991; Patterson et al., 1992). Researchers and practitioners have identified a set of core early social skills, including the ability to comply with teacher directions, cooperate with peers, and manage frustration, that are strong predictors of a successful transition to kindergarten and early academic achievement (Hemmeter, Ostrosky, & Fox, 2006; McClelland et al., 2006; Powell et al., 2006). Interventions targeting social competence are especially important for preschoolers from low-income families, who are at greater risk for developing behavior problems, compared with the general population (see Qi & Kaiser, 2003, for a review).

Although parent and family training programs can be effective in reducing aggression in young children (McNeil et al., 1999; Pade, Taube, Aalborg, & Reiser, 2006; Reid, Webster-Stratton, & Baydar, 2004), such programs are typically delivered by specially trained therapists in clinic rather than school settings and are both time- and labor-intensive. Moreover, even when successful outcomes are obtained, newly learned skills may not generalize to the classroom setting. A promising alternative that is consistent with an ecological perspective is to embed social skills interventions in general education programs. Given the increasing numbers of preschoolers with challenging behaviors, programs integrated into the regular curriculum are not only more efficient than developing individual behavior support plans for each target child but also have the potential for more durable outcomes than pull-out programs because the targeted skills are practiced and reinforced in naturalistic contexts (Vaughn et al., 2003).

PRESCHOOL BEHAVIORAL AND SOCIAL COMPETENCE INTERVENTIONS

This section includes three interventions designed to reduce aggressive and noncompliant behavior and enhance social competence in preschoolers. *Improving Compliance with Precision Requests and a Time-Out Ribbon* is a multifaceted intervention that includes both proactive components (precision requests) and reductive components (response cost). First implemented in clinic settings to interrupt coercive patterns between parents and children (Forehand & McMahon, 1981; Neville & Jenson, 1984), *precision requests* (also called *precision commands*), have been successfully used to improve compliance for children with developmental disabilities in home and childcare settings (Mackay et al., 2001). Here, precision commands are combined with a time-out ribbon procedure, in which students wear a ribbon or some other object signaling that they are eligible for reinforcement. If a student misbehaves or fails to comply with teacher directives, the ribbon is removed and reinforcement is unavailable for a specific period of time. Once the student has earned back the ribbon, he or she is again eligible for reinforcement. In addition to the individual time-out ribbon strategy, a group-oriented version has also been validated (Salend & Gordon, 1987).

Empirically based interventions for young children with ADHD are very rare, and even fewer have been implemented in community-based preschool settings. In *Button, Button, Who's Got the Button? Reducing Disruptive Behavior with Response Cost,* a developmentally appropriate response cost procedure is applied on a classwide basis to encourage appropriate behavior and compliance. *Response cost*—the withdrawal of points or tokens contingent on inappropriate behavior—has been validated as an effective strategy for reducing aggressive and disruptive behavior in preschoolers (e.g., Conyers et al., 2004; Reynolds & Kelley, 1997). The third intervention targeting disruptive behavior in preschoolers was developed during field testing. *Red Light/Green Light*—a variation of the *Good Behavior Game* (GBG)—targets problem behavior with group incentives and a game-like format. This version of the GBG provides continuous visual feedback in the form of a "stoplight" that signals the level of student compliance with classroom rules and access to rewards. Teachers rate the strategy as highly effective in reducing disruptive behavior and very easy to implement, and children enjoy describing themselves as "being on green."

CROSS-REFERENCE: For another proactive intervention incorporating precision requests, see *Delivering Effective Commands* in Chapter 3. The *Good Behavior Game* (GBG) and the *Good Behavior Game Plus Merit*—a GBG variation that permits students to earn back points lost for poor behavior by means of academic productivity or exemplary behavior—are presented in Chapter 5.

IMPROVING COMPLIANCE WITH PRECISION REQUESTS AND A TIME-OUT RIBBON PROCEDURE

Overview

Learning to comply with adult directives is an important social competency for preschoolers and is essential to children's success in school. This simple intervention package promotes compliance with a combination of precision requests and a time-out ribbon procedure in the form of a happy face chart. Happy face cards signaling the availability of reinforcement are posted beside children's names as long as they comply with teacher requests and are removed for failure to comply, with a brief in-class time-out as a backup contingency. In the original study, conducted in a self-contained preschool special education classroom, the combination of precision requests and the time-out ribbon procedure dramatically improved compliance for a target student and was more effective than the time-out ribbon alone. Although all seven students in the classroom received reinforcement each time they complied with a teacher request, reward delivery is delayed in this adaptation until the end of an activity to increase usability and enhance maintenance of appropriate behaviors by lengthening the schedule of reinforcement. A variation for implementation with individual target children is also included.

Purpose

To improve compliance and reduce disruptive behavior by means of precision requests and a time-out ribbon procedure.

Materials

1. "Classroom Rules Chart," consisting of a posterboard listing the classroom rules, with a picture representing each rule, such as:
   a. Do what you are told, the first time you are told.
   b. Do your best on all your work.
   c. Be kind and helpful to others.
   d. Keep your hands and feet to yourself.
2. "Happy Face Chart," consisting of a posterboard chart listing student names, with a happy face card or sticker attached to the chart beside each name.
3. Small tangible reinforcers, such as stickers and hand stamps, or small edible rewards, such as pretzels, marshmallows, jelly beans, and wrapped candy.

Observation (Select One or Both)

Option 1

1. Using a sheet of paper attached to a clipboard, tally the number of reprimands delivered to a target group of students or the entire class during a selected activity period for 4 to 7 days.

Option 2

1. Using a sheet of paper attached to a clipboard, record the number of teacher requests delivered during a selected activity period to a group of target students or the entire class. For each request, record a plus (+) if the student complies within 5 seconds and a minus (–) if the student fails to comply within 5 seconds.
2. Calculate group or classwide compliance rates by dividing the number of teacher requests by the number of times students complied with teacher directives within 5 seconds and multiply the result by 100. *Example*: If there are 30 teacher requests, and students comply within 5 seconds on 15 of the 30 occasions, the compliance rate is 50%.
3. Conduct these observations for 20 to 30 minutes during the selected activity period for 4 to 7 days.

Intervention Steps

Introduction and Training

1. Display the Happy Face Chart and explain to the students that they will be able to earn a reward at the end of an activity (e.g., free play, small-group instruction, and circle time) as long as they follow your directions. The happy face cards will be posted beside their names as long as they follow your directions to let them know that they are able to earn rewards. Post the chart at the front of the classroom where it is visible and accessible to all students.
2. Move a chair to the periphery of classroom activity but not so far away that you cannot easily monitor a student seated in it. Explain to the class that this is the time-out chair. If a student does not follow directions, the student will need to sit in the time-out chair and observe the other children following directions. Be sure that the chair is turned toward, not away from, classroom activities.

Implementation

1. At the beginning of the day, review the classroom rules, using specific examples and modeling appropriate compliance behaviors for each rule. Also point out the Happy Face Chart and encourage the students to follow directions so that they can keep their happy face cards and be eligible for rewards.
2. If a student does not comply with a request, tell the student to take down his or her happy face from the chart or take it down yourself.
3. Then move close to the student, obtain eye contact, if possible, and make the request again, beginning with the prompt "Please." Make the request in the form of a statement and use a firm but quiet tone.

    Example: "Juan, please put the toy away and get in line."
4. If the student complies with the request within 5 seconds, provide praise, referring to the act of compliance or the specific requested behavior.

    Examples: "Very good, Juan, you followed directions about getting in line quickly!"
    "Juan, thank you for getting in line and helping us get to recess on time."

    Restore the happy face card to the chart or let the student put it back.
5. If the student does not comply within 5 seconds, repeat the request using the prompt "*You need to...*"

    Example: "Juan, you need to put the toy away and get in line right now."

    Use the same distance, eye contact, and tone of voice as in the first request.
6. If the student complies with this request within 5 seconds, praise the student and restore the happy face card as in Step 4. If the student still does not comply within 5 to 10 seconds of the second request, send him or her to the time-out chair for 4 minutes.
7. Repeat this process until the student complies, but do not interact with the student during the time-out period.
8. At the end of the activity, deliver rewards to students whose happy face cards are displayed on the Happy Face Chart and praise them for following your directions. Tell students who did not earn a reward that they will have a chance to follow directions and earn a reward during the next activity or intervention period.
9. Restore happy face cards for all students to the chart at the beginning of each activity or intervention period. Gradually lengthen the intervention period and replace tangible rewards with social rewards (e.g., lead the class in applauding their own good behavior, giving a class cheer or thumbs up).

Evaluation (Select One or Both)

Option 1

1. Compare the number of reprimands delivered to the target group of students or the entire class during the selected activity period before and after implementation.

Option 2

1. Compare group or classwide compliance rates during the selected activity period before and after implementation.

Variation: Individualized Time-Out Ribbons

1. For implementation with one student or a small group of students, give each target student a small adhesive happy face sticker to wear at the beginning of each activity. Remove stickers for noncompliance and restore them for compliance as described above for the happy face cards.

2. At the end of the activity period, deliver a small reward to target students still wearing their stickers. As student compliance improves, lengthen the interval between reward delivery (e.g., successful completion of two activities) and substitute social rewards.

Note

1. At the beginning of the original investigation, each student wore a time-out ribbon to indicate eligibility for reinforcement. After 3 days, however, researchers judged that the students did not enjoy wearing the ribbons, and the happy face card system was substituted.

Source

Yeager, C., & McLaughlin, T. F. (1995). The use of a time-out ribbon and precision requests to improve child compliance in the classroom: A case study. *Child and Family Behavior Therapy, 17,* 1–9. Copyright 1995 by The Haworth Press. Adapted by permission.

BUTTON, BUTTON, WHO'S GOT THE BUTTON? REDUCING DISRUPTIVE BEHAVIOR WITH RESPONSE COST

Overview

Inattentiveness, impulsivity, or excessive activity in young children can limit their own opportunities to learn and those of their classmates in preschool settings. This intervention is designed to increase on-task behavior and reduce off-task and disruptive behavior in preschoolers with a developmentally appropriate version of response cost. Buttons posted beside each child's name on a chart are removed for each rule infraction, with rewards available if children retain a specific number of buttons at the end of each activity. Implemented in three general education preschool classrooms with four preschoolers with ADHD, the response cost intervention was associated with marked reductions in disruptive behavior among the targeted students to a level commensurate with that of their peers, as measured by behavioral observations and teacher ratings at the end of treatment and at a 2- or 3-week follow-up. Teachers and students alike judged the intervention to be highly acceptable, and teachers continued to use the strategy after the investigation was withdrawn. Two variations are provided, one substituting an interdependent group contingency for individual rewards and one targeting transitions.

Purpose

To increase on-task behavior and reduce inattentive and disruptive behavior in preschoolers with a response cost procedure.

Materials

1. "Happy Face Chart," consisting of a posterboard chart with space or slots for posting student name cards; write each student's name on the chart or cards; the chart should be large enough to display five small Velcro buttons and one large Velcro button beside each student's name for each activity or intervention period during the day.
2. Five small Velcro buttons and three large Velcro buttons per student per activity or intervention period.
3. Circles of green construction paper and tape, 10 small circles and 1 large circle per activity or intervention period (optional, see Variation).

4. "Surprise Box," consisting of a cardboard box containing small rewards, such as wrapped candy, colored pencils, action figures, small toys, stickers, etc.
5. "Classroom Rules Chart," consisting of a posterboard chart listing the classroom rules, with a drawing or photograph of a student to illustrate each rule, such as:
   a. Stay in the activity area.
   b. Keep your hands and feet to yourself.
   c. Listen quietly when the teacher is talking.
   d. Finish your work.
   e. Raise your hand to talk during circle and meeting time.

Observation (Select One or Both)

Option 1

1. Using a *Group Event Recording Form,* record the number of inappropriate social behaviors during an activity period. *Inappropriate social behaviors* are defined as engaging in negative verbal or physical interactions with adults and/or peers, off-task behavior (looking away from the activity or the teacher for at least 3 seconds), disobeying classroom rules, and displaying tantrums (yelling, kicking, and/or sulking after interacting with an adult or peer).
2. Conduct these observations for a group of target students or the entire class for 20 to 30 minutes during a selected activity period for 4 to 7 days. If you are implementing the variation, use these data to help determine the classwide criterion for reinforcement.

Option 2

1. Using a sheet of paper attached to a clipboard, record the number of time-outs served by the entire class or a group of target students during a selected activity or the morning or afternoon session for 4 to 7 days. A *time-out* is defined as 3 minutes of sitting in a time-out chair or in the time-out area as a consequence for disruptive behavior.

Intervention Steps

Introduction and Training

1. Post the Happy Face Chart at the front of the classroom. Explain to the students that they will have a chance to see how well they are behaving in school every day. They will also have a chance to pick a prize from the Surprise Box if they remember to follow the rules for good behavior.
2. Using the Classroom Rules Chart, review behavior expectations for the class. Help the students provide examples and nonexamples of the expected behaviors. Also model appropriate behavior in response to the removal of a button for a rule infraction.
3. Point out the Velcro buttons on the Happy Face Chart to the students and explain that the buttons will help them follow the classroom rules so that everyone can have fun at school. Tell them that they will lose a small button if they break a rule. If they have three small buttons left at the end of the activity, they will earn a large button. Everyone with three big buttons at the end of the school day will be able to draw a prize from the Surprise Box.

Implementation

1. If a student breaks one of the rules, remove one of the small buttons from the chart next to the child's name, and state the reason for the removal.

   Example: "Jason, you lost a button for not listening to my directions."

2. At the end of the activity, review the chart with the class to determine which students have enough buttons (three) to retain the large button on the chart. Remove the large button for any students with fewer than three buttons left and encourage them to try harder during the next activity.

3. At the end of the day, allow students who have retained three large buttons on the chart to draw a prize from the Surprise Box. Encourage those who did not meet the criterion to try harder the next day.

Evaluation (Select One or Both)

Option 1

1. Compare the frequency of inappropriate social behaviors for the target students or the entire class during the selected activity period before and after implementation.

Option 2

1. Compare the number of time-outs served by the target group or the entire class during the selected activity period or the morning or afternoon session before and after implementation.

Variation: Interdependent Group Contingency Response Cost

1. At the beginning of each activity period, tape 10 small green ("GO") circles (or some other number based on the observational data) and three large circles on the wall where all students can see them.

2. Inform the class of the criterion for reinforcement (the number of circles that must remain at the end of the activity period), and remove one small circle for each rule infraction.

3. If the specified number of circles remain at the end of the activity, praise the class and indicate that they have retained their "GO" button (a large green circle). If the class has not met the criterion, remove the large circle and encourage them to do better during the next activity.

4. Continue this procedure for each activity and leave the large circles posted on the wall when students meet the criterion. Deliver a reward to each student if three large circles remain at the end of the day.

Notes

1. Establishing clear, specific rules for instructional activities and reviewing them with students at the beginning of each school day and/or prior to each activity are essential to the success of this intervention.

2. In the original study, an individual token reinforcement system in which students earned buttons for following the rules was also effective in reducing disruptive behavior. Teachers indicated that it was difficult to observe and consequate positive behaviors on a consistent basis, however, and preferred the response cost procedure.

Source

McGoey, K. E., & DuPaul, G. J. (2000). Token reinforcement and response cost procedures: Reducing the disruptive behavior of preschool children with attention-deficit/hyperactivity disorder. *School Psychology Quarterly, 15,* 330–343. Copyright 2000 by The Guilford Press. Adapted by permission.

RED LIGHT/GREEN LIGHT

Overview

For young children, the ability to adjust to classroom behavior standards and expectations, such as following teacher directives, relating positively to peers, attending to instruction, and managing negative emotions, is essential to future school success. This adaptation of the *Good Behavior Game* provides continuous visual cues and immediate performance feedback in the context of a group-oriented contingency to encourage appropriate academic and social behavior. Providing visual signals for behavior is especially helpful for young children, who often have difficulty attending to oral directions. Moreover, the ongoing visual feedback encourages children to monitor and regulate their own behavior. Field testing indicates that this strategy is easy to implement and is effective in increasing on-task behavior and academic productivity and reducing off-task and disruptive behavior in prekindergarten and early primary grade classrooms. Two variations are presented, one targeting transitions and one with classwide rather than team-based contingencies for maximum usability.

Purpose

To reduce off-task and disruptive behavior by combining a visual feedback system for appropriate classroom behavior with team-based rewards.

Materials

1. Posterboard chart with a list of classroom rules, such as:
   a. Listen when the teacher is talking.
   b. Stay in your seat or area unless you have permission to move.
   c. Be kind and helpful to others.
   d. Use inside voices during center time.
   e. Do what the teacher tells you to do, the first time you are told.
2. "Stoplights," consisting of posterboard or flannel cutouts in the shape of a stoplight, with three vertical circles to which paper or flannel circles can be affixed and labeled with team names or numbers, one stoplight per team (one stoplight for Variation 2).
3. Red, yellow, and green flannel or paper circles with tape, three sets per team (one set for Variation 2).
4. "Team badges," consisting of colored adhesive tags, color-coded by team, one badge per student.
5. Stickers, hand stamps, "good day" certificates, or "victory tags," consisting of circles of brightly colored construction paper with or without "winner" or gold star stickers and hung around the neck with yarn.

Observation (Select One or More)

Option 1

1. Using a *Group Interval Recording Form* and beginning at the left side of the room, glance at each student every 10 seconds and record that student's behavior at that instant as on-task, off-task, or disruptive as defined below. When you have rated all the students, begin again at the left side of the room.
   a. *On-task behavior* is defined as working on the task at hand, looking at the teacher during instruction, and any other behavior relevant to the lesson or activity.
   b. *Off-task behavior* is defined as sitting without having appropriate materials at hand, playing with nonlesson materials, failing to look at the teacher during instruction, or failing to begin an activity or task after directions have been given.

c. *Disruptive behavior* is defined as calling out, being out of seat without permission, verbal or physical aggression, failing to comply with teacher directives, and any other behavior interfering with instruction or the on-task behavior of another student.

2. Conduct these observations for 20 to 30 minutes during a selected instructional period for 4 to 7 days.

Option 2

1. Using a *Group Event Recording Form,* tally the number of disruptive behaviors during one or more instructional periods for the entire class or a group of target students for 3 to 5 days. *Disruptive behaviors* are defined as verbal or physical aggression, noncompliance, or any other behaviors that interfere with instruction or the on-task behavior of other students.

Option 3

1. Using a list of student names attached to a clipboard, tally the number of times you issue a directive and a student fails to comply within 5 seconds of the directive during a selected activity or instructional period.

2. Conduct these observations for 20 to 30 minutes for a group of target students or the entire class for 4 to 7 days.

Intervention Steps

Introduction and Training

1. Select a time for implementation, such as center time or an instructional period when students are especially unproductive and disruptive.

2. Divide the class into two or more teams. If the students are seated at tables, use tables as teams. Be sure to distribute the most disruptive students and male and female students among teams. Help each team select a name, if desired, and have each student wear a team badge so that you can easily identify team membership as students move from one activity to another.

3. Explain to the students that they will be playing a game during that period to help everyone get the most out of the activity or lesson.

4. Using *Say Show Check: Teaching Classroom Procedures,* display the list of classroom rules and review each rule.

5. Explain that you will be observing the teams and using the stoplights to show them how well they are following the rules during the activity, as follows:

   a. Teams following the rules receive a green light ("GO"), indicating that they should continue their good behavior.

   b. Teams that break a rule receive a yellow light ("WARNING"), indicating that they are being warned to stop the inappropriate behavior.

   c. Teams that continue to break a rule after a warning or display any aggressive behaviors receive a red light ("STOP").

   d. Teams ending the rating period on green are winners. All teams can win or lose.

6. Display the stoplights and demonstrate the use of the circles to rate student behavior. Model appropriate student responses to changing the circles from green to yellow or yellow to red.

Implementation

1. At the beginning of the intervention period, attach a green circle to each stoplight.

2. Every 20 to 30 minutes or at the end of each activity, rate each team's behavior by attaching a circle to the team's stoplight. Briefly state why each team is receiving that particular rating. If the rating is unchanged from the previous rating interval, state why the rating is the same.

3. If a team member displays any aggressive or highly disruptive behavior before the regular rating time, immediately change that team's rating to red. Also, if any team member responds inappropriately (argues, sulks, etc.) when you change a rating from green to yellow, immediately change that team's rating to red.
4. Deliver rewards to any teams ending the intervention period on green. As behavior improves, increase the length of the interval between rewards until you are delivering rewards at the end of the morning and/or afternoon session or at the end of the school day.

Evaluation (Select One or More)

Option 1

1. Compare the percentages of on-task, off-task, and disruptive behavior during the selected period before and after implementation.

Option 2

1. Compare the frequency of disruptive behaviors for the entire class or for the target students during the selected period(s) before and after implementation.

Option 3

1. Compare noncompliance rates for the target students or the entire class during the selected period before and after implementation.

Variations

Variation 1: Red Light/Green Light for Transitions

1. To encourage rapid, orderly transitions between activities, add a rule about transitions (e.g., "Make quick and quiet transitions") and rate teams on transition-related behaviors as well.

Variation 2: Classwide Red Light/Green Light

1. Implement the strategy as a classwide intervention and use only one stoplight. Rate behavior every 20 to 30 minutes (or once per activity) as described above and deliver an individual reward to each student or a group activity-based reward, such as music time or a classroom game, if the class ends the rating period on green.

Notes

1. Victory tags are especially valued as reinforcers by young children and make practical rewards because they can be reused.
2. In the case of a persistently noncompliant or aggressive child who does not respond to the team or group format, make an individual stoplight for the child to wear (similar to a victory tag), in effect, making the student a team of one.

Source

Barrish, H. H., Saunders, M., & Wolf, M. M. (1969). Good behavior game: Effects of individual contingencies for group consequences on disruptive behavior in a classroom. *Journal of Applied Behavior Analysis, 2,* 119–124. Copyright 1969 by the Society for the Experimental Analysis of Behavior. Adapted by permission.

PRINT RESOURCES

Barnett, D. W., Bell, S. H., & Carey, K. T. (1999). *Designing preschool interventions: A practitioner's guide.* New York: Guilford Press.

Written from an ecobehavioral perspective, this book presents a framework for designing individualized interventions for children ages 2 to 5 with learning or behavior difficulties. Emphasis is placed on evidence-based interventions that can be used in natural settings with individuals or small groups of children.

Gimpel, G. A., & Holland, M. L. (2003). *Emotional and behavioral problems of young children: Effective intervention in the preschool and kindergarten years.* New York: Guilford Press.

This highly usable book provides information and resources for addressing common emotional and behavioral problems in young children (ages 3–6). Topics include assessing mental health issues, treating externalizing and internalizing problems, and working with young children who have been abused. More than 30 reproducible parent handouts and other clinical tools are included.

VanDerHeyden, A., Snyder, P., & Hojnoski, R. (Eds.). (2006). Integrating frameworks from early childhood intervention and school psychology to accelerate growth for all young children [Special series]. *School Psychology Review, 35*(4).

This special series includes articles addressing critical components of response-to-intervention (RTI) approaches with young children, including barriers to effective implementation and decision making, progress monitoring tools for quantifying child outcomes, strategies for helping children with extremely challenging behaviors, models for differentiating academic from language deficits, and multi-tiered behavioral intervention programs.

WEBSITES

Center for Evidence-Based Practice: Young Children with Challenging Behavior
http://challengingbehavior.fmhi.usf.edu

Funded by the U.S. Department of Education's Office of Special Education Programs, the center focuses on developing a database on evidence-based practices to address the needs of young children who are displaying, or are at risk for, problem behavior.

Get It Got It Go!
http://ggg.umn.edu

Funded by the U.S. Department of Education and part of the Center for Early Education Development at the University of Minnesota, Get It Got It Go! provides a free online management system to help practitioners learn to use the *Individual Growth and Development Indicators* (IGDIs), download the IGDI measures, and manage children's scores, including generating graphical progress reports. The site also offers links to resources for preschool teachers, including a lesson bank and fund of language and early literacy activities (*http://ggg.umn.edu/go/go_teacherideas.html*).

Get Ready to Read
http://getreadytoread.org

Launched by the National Center for Learning Disabilities in 2001, Get Ready to Read is a nationwide campaign to provide early childhood care providers and parents with an understanding of the skills and knowledge 4-year-old children need in order to be ready to learn to read in kindergarten. The site offers a 20-item research-based screening instrument assessing print knowledge, emergent writing, and linguistic awareness.

National Center for Early Development and Learning
http://www.ncedl.org

The National Center for Early Development and Learning (NCEDL) is an early childhood research project sponsored by the U.S. Department of Education's Institute for Educational Sciences (IES). NCEDL focuses on enhancing the cognitive, social, and emotional development of children from birth through age 8 and provides an online journal.

Recognition and Response

http://www.recognitionandresponse.org

Managed by the National Center for Learning Disabilities, the Recognition and Response system provides information on the use of the RTI approach with preschoolers and is designed to help parents and teachers respond to learning difficulties in young children who may be at risk for learning disabilities before they are referred for formal assessment and placement in special education. Current efforts include the development of an observational assessment called the *Recognition and Response Observation and Rating System* (RRORS) for use with other screening and progress monitoring measures.

APPENDIX 6.1. Summary Characteristics of Interventions for Preschoolers

Intervention	Description	Comments
Proactive Interventions		
Promoting Independent In-Class Transitions with Self-Assessment and Contingent Praise	Students learn to transition from one activity to another with direct instruction and a group-oriented self-assessment procedure.	This intervention is also effective in reducing disruptive and noncompliant behavior during small-group instructional activities and free play.
Six Steps to Effective Small-Group Instruction	Teachers use a structured managerial sequence to promote engagement and task completion in small-group settings.	Although providing praise and redirection (as needed) for each student is critical to the success of this strategy, teachers must deliver verbal comments contingently and briskly to maintain the flow of the activity and the attention of all of the children in the group.
Interventions to Enhance Language Skills		
Enhancing Emergent Literacy Skills with Dialogic Reading	Using specific prompts and types of questions, teachers engage children in an active dialogue about the content and pictures in a book.	Originally developed for use by parents and caregivers, this intervention is especially effective in enhancing language skills when it is implemented in both home and school settings.
Building Vocabulary Skills with Interactive Book Reading	This strategy combines shared book reading with props and center-time activities linked to story content to reinforce story book vocabulary.	Because this strategy provides multiple opportunities for children to hear and use new vocabulary, it is especially helpful for children with limited language and literacy experiences.
Interventions to Promote Positive Behavior and Social Competence		
Improving Compliance with Precision Requests and a Time-Out Ribbon	This strategy combines effective command sequences with a time-out ribbon procedure in the form of a happy face chart signaling the availability of reinforcement for each child.	This strategy can be implemented with one or a few students by having target students wear a small happy face sticker that is removed for noncompliance and restored for compliance and at the beginning of a new activity.
Button, Button, Who's Got the Button? Reducing Disruptive Behavior with Response Cost	Buttons on a chart are removed for rule infractions, with rewards for each child retaining a specified number of buttons at the end of each activity.	The variation with an interdependent group contingency (i.e., one set of buttons for the entire class) is easier to implement than the original independent group contingency but is not appropriate if the class includes one or more students with high levels of disruptive or noncompliant behavior.
Red Light/Green Light	This variation of the Good Behavior Game uses a "stoplight" to provide students with visual feedback about their behavior and access to rewards.	If the class includes one or more very noncompliant and disruptive children who do not respond to the group-oriented procedures, provide them with an individual "stoplight" that can be hung on yarn around the neck.

References

Abbott, M., Walton, C., Tapia, Y., & Greenwood, C. R. (1999). Research to practice: A "blueprint" for closing the gap in local schools. *Exceptional Children, 65,* 339–352.

Abramowitz, A. J., Eckstrand, D., O'Leary, S. G., & Dulcan, M. K. (1992). ADHD children's responses to stimulant medication and two intensities of a behavioral intervention. *Behavior Modification, 16,* 193–203.

Abramowitz, A. J., & O'Leary, S. G. (1990). Effectiveness of delayed punishment in an applied setting. *Behavior Therapy, 21,* 231–239.

Abramowitz, A. J., O'Leary, S. G., & Futtersak, M. W. (1988). The relative impact of long and short reprimands on children's off-task behavior in the classroom. *Behavior Therapy, 19,* 243–247.

Acker, M. M., & O'Leary, S. G. (1987). Effects of reprimands and praise on appropriate behavior in the classroom. *Journal of Abnormal Child Psychology, 15,* 549–557.

Adams, M. J. (1990). *Beginning to read: Thinking and learning about print.* Cambridge, MA: MIT Press.

Agostin, T. M., & Bain, S. K. (1997). Predicting early school success with developmental and social skill screeners. *Psychology in the Schools, 34,* 219–228.

Agran, M., Blanchard, C., Wehmeyer, M., & Hughes, C. (2001). Teaching students to self-regulate their behavior: The differential effects of student- vs. teacher-delivered reinforcement. *Research in Developmental Disabilities, 22,* 319–332.

Akin-Little, K. A., Eckert, T. L., Lovett, B. J., & Little, S. G. (2004). Extrinsic reinforcement in the classroom: Bribery or best practice. *School Psychology Review, 33,* 344–362.

Alber, S. R., Heward, W. L., & Hippler, B. J. (1999). Teaching middle school students with learning disabilities to recruit positive teacher attention. *Exceptional Children, 65,* 253–270.

Alderman, G. L., & Nix, M. (1997). Teachers' intervention preferences related to explanations for behavior problems, severity of the problem, and teacher experience. *Behavioral Disorders, 22,* 87–95.

Alexander, K. L., Entwisle, D. R., & Dauber, S. L. (1993). First-grade classroom behavior: Its short- and long-term consequences for school performance. *Child Development, 64,* 801–814.

Allen, S. J., & Blackston, A. R. (2003). Training preservice teachers in collaborative problem-solving: An investigation of the impact on teacher and student behavior change in real-world settings. *School Psychology Quarterly, 18,* 22–51.

Allinder, R. M., Dunse, L., Brunken, C. D., & Obermiller-Krolikowski, H. J. (2001). Improving fluency in at-risk readers and students with learning disabilities. *Remedial and Special Education, 22,* 48–54.

Allinder, R. M., & Oats, R. G. (1997). Effects of acceptability on teachers' implementation of curriculum-based measurement and student achievement in mathematics computation. *Remedial and Special Education, 18,* 113–120.

Al Otaiba, S., & Fuchs, D. (2002). Characteristics of children who are unresponsive to early literacy intervention: A review of the literature. *Remedial and Special Education, 23,* 300–316.

Alvermann, D. E., O'Brien, D. G., & Dillon, D. R. (1990). What teachers do when they say they're having discussions of content area reading assignments: A qualitative analysis. *Reading Research Quarterly, 25,* 296–322.

American Psychiatric Association. (2000). *Diagnostic and statistical manual of mental disorders* (4th ed., text rev.). Washington, DC: Author.

American Psychological Association. (2002). *Ethical principles of psychologists and code of conduct. American Psychologist, 57,* 1060–1073. Available online at *http:///www.apa.org/ethics/code2002. html.*

Anderson, A. R., Christenson, S. L., Sinclair, M. F., & Lehr, C. A. (2004). Check & connect: The importance of relationships for promoting engagement with school. *Journal of School Psychology, 42,* 95–113.

Anderson, R. C., Spiro, R. J., & Anderson, M. C. (1978). Schemata as scaffolding for the representation of information in connected discourse. *American Educational Research Journal, 15,* 433–440.

Ang, R. P., & Hughes, J. N. (2002). Differential effects of skills training with antisocial youth based on group composition: A meta-analytic investigation. *School Psychology Review, 31,* 164–185.

Anthony, B. J., Anthony, L. G., Morrel, T. M., & Acosta, M. (2005). Evidence for social and behavior problems in low-income, urban preschoolers: Effects of site, classroom, and teacher. *Journal of Youth and Adolescence, 34,* 31–39.

Archer, A. L., Gleason, M. M., & Vachon, V. L. (2003). Decoding and fluency: Foundation skills for struggling older readers. *Learning Disability Quarterly, 26,* 89–101.

Ardoin, S. P., Witt, J. C., Suldo, S. M., Connell, J. E., Koenig, J. L., Resetar, J. L., et al. (2004). Examining the incremental benefits of administering a maze and three versus one curriculum-based reading probes when conducting universal screening. *School Psychology Review, 33,* 218–233.

Armbruster, B. B., & Anderson, T. H. (1988). On selecting "considerate" content area textbooks. *Remedial and Special Education, 9,* 47–52.

Armbruster, B. B., & Ostertag, J. (1993). Questions in elementary science and social studies textbooks. In B. K. Britton, A. Woodward, & M. R. Binkley (Eds.), *Learning from textbooks: Theory and practice* (pp. 69–94). Hillsdale, NJ: Erlbaum.

Armendariz, F., & Umbreit, J. (1999). Using active responding to reduce disruptive behavior in a general education classroom. *Journal of Positive Behavioral Interventions, 1,* 152–158.

Arnold, D. H., Lonigan, C. J., Whitehurst, G. J., & Epstein, J. N. (1994). Accelerating language development through picture book reading: Replication and extension to a videotape training format. *Journal of Educational Psychology, 86,* 235–243.

Arnold, D. H., McWilliams, L., & Arnold, E. H. (1998). Teacher discipline and child misbehavior in day care: Untangling causality with correlational data. *Developmental Psychology, 34,* 276–287.

Artiles, A. J., Trent, S. C., & Kuan, L. (1997). Learning disabilities empirical research on ethnic minority students: An analysis of 22 years of studies published in selected refereed journals. *Learning Disabilities Research and Practice, 12,* 82–91.

Athanasiou, M. S., Geil, M., Hazel, C. E., & Copeland, E. P. (2002). A look inside school-based consultation: A qualitative study of the beliefs and practices of school psychologists and teachers. *School Psychology Quarterly, 17,* 258–298.

Babyak, A. E., Koorland, M., & Mathes, P. G. (2000). The effects of story mapping instruction on the reading comprehension of students with behavioral disorders. *Behavioral Disorders, 25,* 239–258.

Bahl, A. B., McNeil, C. B., Cleavenger, C. J., Blanc, H. M., & Bennett, G. M. (2000). Evaluation of a whole-classroom approach for the management of disruptive behavior. *Proven Practice, 2(2),* 62–71.

Bahr, M. W. (1994). The status and impact of prereferral interventions: "We need a better way to determine success." *Psychology in the Schools, 31,* 309–318.

Bahr, M. W., Fuchs, D., Fuchs, L. S., Fernstrom, P., & Stecker, P. M. (1993). Effectiveness of student versus teacher monitoring during prereferral intervention. *Exceptionality, 4,* 17–30.

Bahr, M. W., & Kovaleski, J. F. (Eds.). (2006a). Current status of problem-solving consultation teams [Special series]. *Remedial and Special Education, 27(1 & 3).*

Bahr, M. W., & Kovaleski, J. F. (2006b). The need for problem-solving teams: Introduction to the special issue. *Remedial and Special Education, 27,* 2–5.

Bahr, M. W., Walker, K., Hampton, E. M., Buddle, B. S., Freeman, T., Ruschman, N., et al. (2006). Creative problem solving for general education intervention teams: A two-year evaluation study. *Remedial and Special Education, 27,* 27–41.

Bahr, M. W., Whitten, E., Dieker, L., Kocarek, C. E., & Manson, D. (1999). A comparison of school-based intervention teams: Implications for educational and legal reform. *Exceptional Children, 66,* 67–83.

Baker, L. (2003). The role of parents in motivating struggling readers. *Reading and Writing Quarterly, 19,* 87–106.

Baker, L., Scher, D., & Machler, K. (1997). Home and family influences on motivation for reading. *Educational Psychologist, 32,* 69–82.

Baker, S., Gersten, R., & Graham, S. (2003). Teaching expressive writing to students with learning disabilities: Research-based applications and examples. *Journal of Learning Disabilities, 36,* 109–123.

Baker, S., Gersten, R., & Grossen, B. (2002). Interventions for students with reading comprehension problems. In M. R. Shinn, H. M. Walker, & G. Stoner (Eds.), *Interventions for academic and behavior problems II: Preventive and remedial approaches* (pp. 731–754). Bethesda, MD: National Association of School Psychologists.

Baker, S., Gersten, R., & Lee, D. (2002). A synthesis of empirical research on teaching mathematics to low-achieving students. *Elementary School Journal, 103,* 51–73.

Baker, S. K., Gersten, R., & Scanlon, S. (2002). Procedural facilitators and cognitive strategies: Tools for unraveling the mysteries of comprehension and the writing process, and for providing meaningful access to the general curriculum. *Learning Disabilities Research and Practice, 17,* 65–77.

Baker, S. K., Simmons, D. C., & Kame'enui, E. J. (1998). Vocabulary acquisition: Research bases. In D. C. Simmons & E. J. Kame'enui (Eds.), *What reading research tells us about children with diverse learning needs: Bases and basics* (pp. 183–217). Mahwah, NJ: Erlbaum.

Ball, E. W., & Blachman, B. A. (1991). Does phoneme awareness training in kindergarten make a difference in early word recognition and developmental spelling? *Reading Research Quarterly, 26,* 49–66.

Barbetta, P. M., Heron, T. E., & Heward, W. L. (1993). Effects of active student response during error correction on the acquisition, maintenance, and generalization of sight words by students with developmental disabilities. *Journal of Applied Behavior Analysis, 26,* 111–119.

Barkley, R. (1987). *Defiant children: A clinician's manual for parent training.* New York: Guilford Press.

Barnett, D. (2002). Best practices in early intervention. In A. Thomas & J. Grimes (Eds.), *Best practices in school psychology IV* (Vol. 2, pp. 1247–1262). Bethesda, MD: National Association of School Psychologists.

Barnett, D. W., Bauer, A. M., Ehrhardt, K. E., Lentz, F. E., & Stollar, S. A. (1996). Keystone targets for change: Planning for widespread positive consequences. *School Psychology Quarterly, 11,* 95–117.

Barnett, D. W., Bell, S. H., Bauer, A., Lentz, F. E. Jr., Petrelli, S., Air, A., et al. (1997). The Early Childhood Intervention Project: Building capacity for service delivery. *School Psychology Quarterly, 12,* 293–315.

Barnett, D. W., Bell, S. H., & Carey, K. T. (1999). *Designing preschool interventions: A practitioner's guide.* New York: Guilford Press.

Barnett, D. W., Collins, R., Coulter, C., Curtis, M. J., Ehrhardt, K., Glaser, A., et al. (1995). Ethnic validity and school psychology: Concepts and practices associated with cross-cultural professional competence. *Journal of School Psychology, 33,* 219–234.

Barnett, D. W., Daly, E. J. III, Jones, K. M., & Lentz, F. E. (2004). Response to intervention: Empirically based special service decisions from single-case designs of increasing and decreasing intensity. *Journal of Special Education, 38,* 66–79.

Barnett, D. W., Petipon, A. E., Bell, S. H., Gilkey, C. M., Smith, J. J., Stone, C. J., et al. (1999). Evaluating early intervention: Accountability methods for service delivery innovations. *Remedial and Special Education, 33,* 177–188.

Barnett, W. S., Hustedt, J. T., Hawkinson, L. E., & Robin, K. B. (2006). *The state of preschool 2006: State preschool yearbook.* New Brunswick, NJ: National Institute for Early Education Research, State University at Rutgers. Retrieved March 12, 2007, from *http://www.nieer.org.*

Barrish, H. H., Saunders, M., & Wolf, M. M. (1969). Good behavior game: Effects of individual contingencies for group consequences on disruptive behavior in a classroom. *Journal of Applied Behavior Analysis, 2,* 119–124.

Barth, J. M., Dunlap, S. T., Dane, H., Lochman, J. E., & Wells, K. C. (2004). Classroom environment influences on aggression, peer relations, and academic focus. *Journal of School Psychology, 42,* 115–133.

Bates, S. L. (2005). Evidence-based family–school interventions with preschool children. *School Psychology Quarterly, 20,* 352–370.

Battistich, V., Solomon, D., Watson, M., & Schaps, E. (1997). Caring school communities. *Educational Psychologist, 32*(3), 137–151.

Baumann, J. F., & Bergeron, B. S. (1993). Story map instruction using children's literature: Effects on first graders' comprehension of central narrative elements. *Journal of Reading Behavior, 25,* 407–437.

Baumann, J. F., Hoffman, J. V., Duffy-Hester, A. M., & Ro, J. M. (2000). The First R yesterday and today: U.S. elementary reading instruction practices reported by teachers and administrators. *Reading Research Quarterly, 35,* 338–377.

Beal, C. R., Garrod, A. C., & Bonitatibus, G. J. (1990). Fostering children's revision skills through training in comprehension monitoring. *Journal of Educational Psychology, 82,* 275–280.

Beaman, R., & Wheldall, K. (2000). Teachers' use of approval and disapproval in the classroom. *Educational Psychology, 20,* 431–446.

Bear, D. R., Invernizzi, M., Templeton, S., & Johnston, F. (2004). *Words their way: Word study for phonics, vocabulary, and spelling instruction* (3rd ed.). Upper Saddle River, NJ: Prentice-Hall.

Beck, I., & McKeown, M. (1991). Conditions of vocabulary acquisition. In R. Barr, M. Kamil, P. Mosenthal, & P. D. Pearson (Eds.), *Handbook of reading research* (Vol. 2, pp. 789–814). New York: Longman.

Beitchman, J. H., Wilson, B., Johnson, C. J., Atkinson, L., Young, A., Adlaf, E., et al. (2001). Fourteen-year follow-up of speech/language-impaired and control children: Psychiatric outcome. *Journal of the American Academy of Child and Adolescent Psychiatry, 40,* 75–82.

Bell, S. H., & Barnett, D. W. (1999). Peer micronorms in the assessment of young children: Methodological review and examples. *Topics in Early Childhood Special Education, 19,* 112–122.

Benasich, A. A., Curtiss, S., & Tallal, P. (1993). Language, learning, and behavioral disturbances in childhood: A longitudinal perspective. *Journal of the American Academy of Child and Adolescent Psychiatry, 32,* 585–594.

Bennett, K. J., Brown, K. S., Boyle, M., Racine, Y., & Offord, D. R. (2003). Does low reading achievement at school entry cause conduct problems? *Social Science and Medicine, 56,* 2443–2448.

Bennett, K. J., Lipman, E. L., Brown, S., Racine, Y., Boyle, M. N., & Offord, D. R. (1999). Predicting conduct problems: Can high-risk children be identified in kindergarten and grade 1? *Journal of Consulting and Clinical Psychology, 67,* 470–480.

Bennett, S. N., & Blundell, D. (1983). Quantity and quality of work in rows and classroom groups. *Educational Psychology, 3,* 93–105.

Bentum, K. E., & Aaron, P. G. (2003). Does reading instruction in learning disability resource rooms really work? A longitudinal study. *Reading Psychology, 24,* 361–382.

Berkowitz, M. J., & Martens, B. K. (2001). Assessing teachers' and students' preferences for school-based reinforcers: Agreement across method and different effort requirements. *Journal of Developmental and Physical Disabilities, 13,* 373–387.

Berninger, V., Abbott, R., Rogan, L., Reed, L., Abbott, S., Brooks, A., et al. (1998). Teaching spelling to children with specific learning disabilities: The mind's ear and eye beats the computer or pencil. *Learning Disability Quarterly, 21,* 106–122.

Best, R. M., Rowe, M., Ozuru, Y., & McNamara, D. S. (2005). Deep-level comprehension of science texts: The role of the reader and the text. *Topics in Language Disorders, 25,* 65–83.

Beyda, S. D., Zentall, S. S., & Ferko, D. J. K. (2002). The relationship between teacher practices and the task-appropriate and social behavior of students with behavioral disorders. *Behavioral Disorders, 27,* 236–255.

Bhattacharya, A., & Ehri, L. C. (2004). Graphosyllabic analysis helps adolescent struggling readers read and spell words. *Journal of Learning Disabilities, 37,* 331–348.

Biemiller, A. (2003). Vocabulary: Needed if more children are to read well. *Reading Psychology, 24,* 323–325.

Biemiller, A., & Slonim, N. (2001). Estimating root word vocabulary growth in normative and advantaged populations: Evidence for a common sequence of vocabulary acquisition. *Journal of Educational Psychology, 93,* 498–520.

Birch, S. H., & Ladd, G. W. (1997). The teacher–child relationship and children's early school adjustment. *Journal of School Psychology, 35,* 61–79.

Birch, S. H., & Ladd, G. W. (1998). Children's interpersonal behaviors and the teacher–child relationship. *Developmental Psychology, 34,* 934–946.

Birsh, J. R. (Ed.). (1999). *Multisensory teaching of basic language skills.* Baltimore: Brookes.

Blum, R. W., & Libbey, H. P. (Eds.). (2004). School connectedness: Strengthening health and education outcomes for teenagers [Special issue]. *Journal of School Health, 74*(7).

Boardman, A. G., Arguelles, M. E., Vaughn, S., Hughes, M. T., & Klingner, J. (2005). Special education teachers' views of research-based practices. *Journal of Special Education, 39,* 168–180.

Bohn, C. M., Roehrig, A. D., & Pressley, M. (2004). The first days of school in the classrooms of two more effective and four less effective primary-grades teachers. *Elementary School Journal, 104,* 269–287.

Boulineau, T., Fore, C. III, Hagan-Burke, S., & Burke, M. D. (2004). Use of story-mapping to increase the story-grammar text comprehension of elementary students with learning disabilities. *Learning Disability Quarterly, 27,* 105–121.

Bowers, F. E., McGinnis, J. C., Ervin, R. A., & Friman, P. C. (1999). Merging research and practice: The example of positive peer reporting applied to social rejection. *Education and Treatment of Children, 22,* 218–228.

Bowers, F. E., Woods, D. W., Carlyon, W. D., & Friman, P. C. (2000). Using positive peer reporting to improve the social interactions and acceptance of socially isolated adolescents in residential care: A systematic replication. *Journal of Applied Behavior Analysis, 33,* 239–242.

Boyle, J. R. (1996). The effects of a cognitive mapping strategy on the literal and inferential comprehension of students with mild disabilities. *Learning Disability Quarterly, 19,* 86–98.

Brabham, E. G., & Lynch-Brown, C. (2002). Effects of teachers' reading-aloud styles on vocabulary acquisition and comprehension of students in the early elementary grades. *Journal of Educational Psychology, 94,* 465–473.

Bradley, R., Danielson, L., & Hallahan, D. P. (Eds.). (2002). *The identification of learning disabilities: Research to practice.* Mahwah, NJ: Erlbaum.

Bradley-Klug, K. L., Shapiro, E. S., Lutz, J. G., & DuPaul, G. J. (1998). Evaluation of oral reading rate as a curriculum-based measure within literature-based curriculum. *Journal of School Psychology, 36,* 183–197.

Bramlett, R. K., Murphy, J. J., Johnson, J., & Wallingsford, L. (2002). Contemporary practices in school psychology: A national survey of roles and referral problems. *Psychology in the Schools, 39,* 327–335.

Brantley, D. C., & Webster, R. E. (1993). Use of an independent group contingency management system in a regular classroom setting. *Psychology in the Schools, 30,* 60–66.

Brigham, F. J., Scruggs, T. E., & Mastropieri, M. A. (1992). Teacher enthusiasm in learning disabilities classrooms: Effects on learning and behavior. *Learning Disabilities Research and Practice, 7,* 68–73.

Broidy, L. M., Nagin, D. S., Tremblay, R. E., Bates, J. E., Brame, B., Dodge, K. A., et al. (2003). Developmental trajectories of childhood disruptive behaviors and adolescent delinquency: A six-site, cross-national study. *Developmental Psychology, 39,* 222–245.

Brooks, D. M. (1985). The teacher's communicative competence: The first day of school. *Theory into Practice, 24,* 63–70.

Brophy-Herb, H. E., Lee, R. E., Nievar, M. A., & Stollak, G. (2007). Preschoolers' social competence: Relations to family characteristics, teacher behaviors and classroom climate. *Journal of Applied Developmental Psychology, 28,* 134–148.

Broughton, S. F., & Hester, J. R. (1993). Effects of administrative and community support on teacher acceptance of classroom interventions. *Journal of Educational and Psychological Consultation, 4,* 169–177.

Broussard, C., & Northup, J. (1997). Peer interventions for disruptive classroom behavior. *School Psychology Quarterly, 12,* 65–76.

Brownlie, E. B., Beitchman, J. H., Escobar, M., Young, A., Atkinson, L., Johnson, C., et al. (2004). Early language impairment and young adult delinquent and aggressive behavior. *Journal of Abnormal Child Psychology, 32,* 453–467.

Bru, E., Stephens, P., & Torsheim, T. (2002). Students' perceptions of class management and reports of their own misbehavior. *Journal of School Psychology, 40,* 287–307.

Bryan, T., Burstein, K., & Bryan, J. (2001). Students with learning disabilities: Homework problems and promising practices. *Educational Psychologist, 36,* 167–180.

Bryant, D. P., Goodwin, J., Bryant, B. R., & Higgins, K. (2003). Vocabulary instruction for students with learning disabilities: A review of the research. *Learning Disability Quarterly, 26,* 117–128.

Bryant, D. P., Ugel, N., Thompson, S., & Hamff, A. (1999). Instructional strategies for content-area reading instruction. *Intervention in School and Clinic, 34,* 293–302.

Bryant, D. P., Vaughn, S., Linan-Thompson, S., Ugle, N., Hamff, A., & Hougen, M. (2000). Reading outcomes for students with and without reading disabilities in general education middle-school content area classes. *Learning Disability Quarterly, 23,* 24–38.

Buck, G. H., Polloway, E. A., Smith-Thomas, A., & Cook, K. W. (2003). Prereferral intervention processes: A survey of state practices. *Exceptional Children, 69,* 349–360.

Bullis, M., Walker, H. M., & Sprague, J. R. (2001). A promise unfulfilled: Social skills training with at-risk and antisocial children and youth. *Exceptionality, 9,* 67–90.

Burchinal, M. R., & Cryer, D. (2003). Diversity, child care quality and developmental outcomes. *Early Childhood Research Quarterly, 18,* 401–426.

Burchinal, M. R., Peisner-Feinberg, E., Pianta, R., & Howes, C. (2002). Development of academic skills from preschool through second grade: Family and classroom predictors of developmental trajectories. *Journal of School Psychology, 40,* 415–436.

Burks, M. (2004). Effects of ClassWide Peer Tutoring on the number of words spelled correctly by students with LD. *Intervention in School and Clinic, 39,* 301–304.

Burnett, P. C. (2001). Teacher praise and feedback and students' perceptions of the classroom environment. *Educational Psychology, 22,* 1–16.

Burns, M. K. (1999). Effectiveness of special education personnel in the intervention assistance team model. *Journal of Educational Research, 92,* 354–356.

Burns, M. K., & Symington, T. (2002). A meta-analysis of prereferral intervention teams: Student and systemic outcomes. *Journal of School Psychology, 40,* 437–447.

Burns, M. K., VanDerHeyden, A. M., & Jiban, C. L. (2006). Assessing the instructional level for mathematics: A comparison of methods. *School Psychology Review, 15,* 401–418.

Bursuck, W. D., Harniss, M. K., Epstein, M. H., Polloway, E. A., Jayanthi, M., & Wissinger, L. M. (1999). Solving communication problems about homework: Recommendations of special education teachers. *Learning Disabilities Research and Practice, 14,* 149–158.

Busch, T. W., & Espin, C. A. (2003). Using curriculum-based measurement to prevent failure and assess learning in the content areas. *Assessment for Effective Intervention, 28,* 49–58.

Byrne, B., & Fielding-Barnsley, R. (1991). Evaluation of a program to teach phonemic awareness to young children. *Journal of Educational Psychology, 83,* 451–455.

Caccamise, D., & Snyder, L. (2005). Theory and pedagogical practices of text comprehension. *Topics in Language Disorders, 25,* 5–20.

Calhoon, M. B. (2005). Effects of a peer-mediated phonological skill and reading comprehension program on reading skill acquisition for middle school students with reading disabilities. *Journal of Learning Disabilities, 38,* 424–433.

Calhoon, M. B., Al Otaiba, S., Greenberg, D., King, A., & Avalos, A. (2006). Improving reading skills in predominantly Hispanic Title 1 first-grade classrooms: The promise of peer-assisted learning strategies. *Learning Disabilities Research and Practice, 21,* 261–272.

Callahan, K., Rademacher, J. A., & Hildreth, B. L. (1998). The effect of parent participation in strategies to improve the homework performance of students who are at risk. *Remedial and Special Education, 19,* 131–141.

Cameron, C. E., Connor, C. M., & Morrison, F. J. (2005). Effects of variation in teacher organization on classroom functioning. *Journal of School Psychology, 43,* 61–86.

Cameron, C. E., Pierce, W. D., Banko, K. M., & Gear, A. (2005). Achievement-based rewards and intrinsic motivation: A test of cognitive mediators. *Journal of Educational Psychology, 97,* 641–655.

Cameron, J., & Pierce, W. D. (1994). Reinforcement, reward, and intrinsic motivation: A meta-analysis. *Review of Educational Research, 64,* 363–423.

Cameron, J., & Pierce, W. D. (1996). The debate about rewards and intrinsic motivation: Protests and accusations do not alter the results. *Review of Educational Research, 66,* 39–51.

Campbell, R. (1994). The teacher response to children's miscues of substitution. *Journal of Research in Reading, 17,* 147–154.

Campbell, S. B. (1995). Behavior problems in preschool children: A review of recent research. *Journal of Child Psychology and Psychiatry, 36,* 113–149.

Campbell, S. B. (2002). *Behavior problems in preschool children: Clinical and developmental issues.* New York: Guilford Press.

Campbell, S., & Skinner, C. H. (2004). Combining explicit timing with an interdependent group contingency program to decrease transition times: An investigation of the timely transitions game. *Journal of Applied School Psychology, 20,* 11–27.

Cancelli, A. S., Harris, A. M., Friedman, D. L., & Yoshida, R. K. (1993). Type of instruction and the relationship of classroom behavior to achievement among learning disabled children. *Journal of Classroom Interaction, 28,* 13–19.

Carlos, M. S., August, D., McLaughlin, B., Snow, C. E., Dressler, C., Lippmann, D. N., et al. (2004). Closing the gap: Addressing the vocabulary needs of English-language learners in bilingual and mainstream classrooms. *Reading Research Quarterly, 39,* 188–215.

Carr, E. G., Horner, R. H., Turnbull, A. P., Marquis, J. G., McLaughlin, D. M., McAtee, M. L., et al. (1999). *Positive behavior support for people with developmental disabilities: A research synthesis.* Washington, DC: American Association on Mental Retardation. (ERIC Document Reproduction Service No. ED 439580)

Carr, E. G., Taylor, J. C., & Robinson, S. (1991). The effects of severe behavior problems in children on the teaching behavior of adults. *Journal of Applied Behavior Analysis, 24,* 523–535.

Carr, J. E., Coriaty, S., Wilder, D. A., Gaunt, B. T., Dozier, C. L., Britton, L. N., et al. (2000). A review of "noncontingent" reinforcement as treatment for the aberrant behavior of individuals with developmental disabilities. *Research in Developmental Disabilities, 21,* 377–391.

Carrington, P., Lehrer, P. M., & Wittenstrom, K. (1997). A children's self-monitoring system for reducing homework-related problems: Parent efficacy ratings. *Child and Family Behavior Therapy, 19,* 1–22.

Carta, J. J., Atwater, J. B., Schwartz, J. S., & Miller, P. A. (1990). Applications of ecobehavioral analysis to the study of transitions across early education settings. *Education and Treatment of Children, 13,* 298–316.

Carter, K., & Doyle, W. (2006). Classroom management in early childhood and elementary classrooms. In C. M. Evertson & C. S. Weinstein (Eds.), *Handbook of classroom management: Research, practice, and contemporary issues* (pp. 373–406). Mahwah, NJ: Erlbaum.

Case, L. P., Harris, K. R., & Graham, S. (1992). Improving the mathematical problem-solving skills of students with learning disabilities: Self-regulated strategy development. *Journal of Special Education, 26,* 1–19.

Case, L. P., Speece, D. L., & Molloy, D. E. (2003). The validity of a response-to-instruction paradigm to identify reading disabilities: A longitudinal analysis of individual differences and contextual factors. *School Psychology Review, 32,* 557–582.

Cashwell, T. H., Skinner, C. H., & Smith, E. S. (2001). Increasing second-grade students' reports of peers' prosocial behaviors via direct instruction, group reinforcement, and progress feedback: A replication and extension. *Education and Treatment of Children, 24,* 161–175.

Cassel, J., & Reid, R. (1996). Use of a self-regulated strategy intervention to improve word problem-solving skills of students with mild disabilities. *Journal of Behavioral Education, 6,* 153–172.

Catts, H. W., Fey, M. E., Zhang, X., & Tomblin, J. B. (1999). Language basis of reading and reading disabilities: Evidence from a longitudinal investigation. *Scientific Studies of Reading, 3,* 331–361.

Catts, H. W., & Kamhi, A. G. (Eds.). (1999). *Language and reading disabilities.* Needham Heights, MA: Allyn & Bacon.

Cavanaugh, R. A., Heward, W., & Donelson, F. (1996). Effects of response cards during lesson closure on the academic performance of secondary students in an earth science course. *Journal of Applied Behavior Analysis, 29,* 403–406.

Cawley, J. F., Parmar, R. S., Yan, W., & Miller, J. H. (1998). Arithmetic computation performance of students with learning disabilities: Implications for curriculum. *Learning Disabilities Research and Practice, 13,* 68–74.

Chafouleas, S. M., Martens, B. K., Dobson, R. L., Weinstein, K. S., & Gardner, K. B. (2004). Fluent reading as the improvement of stimulus control:

Additive effects of performance-based interventions to repeated reading on students' reading and error rates. *Journal of Behavioral Education, 13,* 67–81.

Chalfant, J. C., & Pysh, M. V. (1989). Teacher assistance teams: Five descriptive studies on 96 teams. *Remedial and Special Education, 10,* 49–58.

Chalfant, J. C., Pysh, M. V., & Moultrie, R. (1979). Teacher assistance teams: A model for within-building problem solving. *Learning Disability Quarterly, 2,* 85–96.

Chalk, K., & Bizo, L. A. (2004). Specific praise improves on-task behaviour and numeracy enjoyment: A study of year four pupils engaged in the numeracy hour. *Educational Psychology in Practice, 20,* 335–351.

Chall, J. S. (1983). *Stages of reading development.* New York: McGraw-Hill.

Chall, J. S., Jacobs, V. A., & Baldwin, L. E. (1990). *The reading crisis: Why poor children fall behind.* Cambridge, MA: Harvard University Press.

Chard, D. J., Clarke, B., Baker, S., Otterstedt, J., Braun, D., & Katz, R. (2005). Using measures of number sense to screen for difficulties in mathematics: Preliminary findings. *Assessment for Effective Intervention, 30,* 3–14.

Chard, D. J., Simmons, D. C., & Kame'enui, E. J. (1998). Word recognition: Research bases. In D. C. Simmons & E. J. Kame'enui (Eds.), *What reading research tells us about children with diverse learning needs: Bases and basics* (pp. 141–167). Mahwah, NJ: Erlbaum.

Chard, D. J., Vaughn, S., & Tyler, B. (2002). A synthesis of research on effective interventions for building reading fluency with elementary students with learning disabilities. *Journal of Learning Disabilities, 35,* 386–406.

Christenson, S. L., Carlson, C., & Valdez, C. R. (2002). Evidence-based interventions in school psychology: Opportunities, challenges, and cautions. *School Psychology Quarterly, 17,* 466–474.

Christie, C. A., & Schuster, J. W. (2003). The effects of using response cards on student participation, academic achievement, and on-task behavior during whole-class, math instruction. *Journal of Behavioral Education, 12,* 147–165.

Clarke, B., & Shinn, M. R. (2004). A preliminary investigation into the identification and development of early mathematics curriculum-based measurement. *School Psychology Review, 33,* 234–248.

Clay, M. M. (1993). *Reading recovery: A guidebook for teachers in training.* Portsmouth, NH: Heinemann.

Cohen, J. (1988). *Statistical power analysis for the behavioral sciences* (2nd ed.). Hillsdale, NJ: Erlbaum.

Coie, J. D., Lochman, J. E., Terry, R., & Hyman, C. (1992). Predicting early adolescent disorders from childhood aggression and peer rejection. *Journal of Consulting and Clinical Psychology, 60,* 783–792.

Colvin, G., & Lazar, M. (1997). *The effective elementary classroom: Managing for success.* Longmont, CO: Sopris West.

Colvin, G., Sugai, G., Good, R. H. III, & Young-Yon, L. (1997). Using active supervision and precorrection to improve transition behaviors in an elementary school. *School Psychology Quarterly, 12,* 344–363.

Colvin, G., Sugai, G., & Patching, B. (1993). Precorrection: An instructional approach for managing predictable problem behaviors. *Intervention in School and Clinic, 28,* 143–150.

Conduct Problems Prevention Research Group. (1999). Initial impact of the Fast Track prevention trial for conduct problems: II. Classroom effects. *Journal of Consulting and Clinical Psychology, 67,* 648–657.

Conley, C. M., Derby, K. M., Roberts-Gwinn, M., Weber, K. P., & McLaughlin, T. F. (2004). An analysis of initial acquisition and maintenance of sight words following picture matching and copy, cover, and compare teaching methods. *Journal of Applied Behavior Analysis, 37,* 339–350.

Connell, M. C., Carta, J. J., & Baer, D. M. (1993). Programming generalization of in-class transition skills: Teaching preschoolers with developmental delays to self-assess and recruit contingent teacher praise. *Journal of Applied Behavior Analysis, 26,* 345–352.

Connell, M. C., Carta, J. J., Lutz, S., Randall, C., & Wilson, J. (1993). Building independence during in-class transitions: Teaching in-class transition skills to preschoolers with developmental delays through choral-response-based self-assessment and contingent praise. *Education and Treatment of Children, 16,* 160–174.

Conoley, J. C., & Conoley, C. W. (1992). *School consultation: Practice and training* (2nd ed.). Boston: Allyn & Bacon.

Conyers, C., Miltenberger, R., Maki, A., Barenz, R., Jurgens, M., Sailer, A., et al. (2004). A comparison of response cost and differential reinforcement of other behavior to reduce disruptive behavior in a preschool classroom. *Journal of Applied Behavior Analysis, 37,* 411–415.

Cooper, D. H., & Speece, D. L. (1990). Maintaining at-risk children in regular education settings: Initial effects of individual differences and classroom environments. *Exceptional Children, 57,* 117–182.

Cooper, H., Lindsay, J. J., Nye, B., & Greathouse, C. (1998). Relationships among attitudes about homework, amount of homework assigned and completed, and student achievement. *Journal of Educational Psychology, 90,* 70–83.

Cooper, H., & Nye, B. (1994). Homework for students with learning disabilities: The implications of research for policy and practice. *Journal of Learning Disabilities, 27,* 470–479.

Cooper, H., & Valentine, J. C. (2001). Using research to answer practical questions about homework. *Educational Psychologist, 36,* 143–153.

Cooper, H., Valentine, J. C., & Charlton, K. (2000). The methodology of meta-analysis. In R. Gersten, E. P. Schiller, & S. Vaughn (Eds.), *Contemporary special education research: Syntheses of the knowledge base on critical instructional issues* (pp. 263–280). Mahwah, NJ: Erlbaum.

Cornoldi, C., & Oakhill, J. (Eds.). (1996). *Reading comprehension difficulties: Processes and intervention.* Mahwah, NJ: Erlbaum.

Cothran, D. J., Kulinna, P. H., & Garrahy, D. A. (2003). "This is kind of giving a secret away ... ": Students' perspectives on effective class management. *Teaching and Teacher Education, 19,* 435–444.

Courson-Krause, P. S., Marchand-Martella, N., Martella, R. C., & Schmitt, B. (1997). Reducing negative comments through self-monitoring and contingency contracting. *International Journal of Special Education, 12,* 42–50.

Cowan, R. J., & Sheridan, S. M. (2003). Investigating the acceptability of behavioral interventions in applied conjoint behavioral consultation: Moving from analog conditions to naturalistic settings. *School Psychology Quarterly, 18,* 1–21.

Cox, D. D. (2005). Evidence-based interventions using home–school collaboration. *School Psychology Quarterly, 20,* 473–497.

Coyne, J. D., Simmons, D. C., & Kame'enui, E. J. (2004). Vocabulary instruction for young children at risk of experiencing reading difficulties: Teaching word meanings through shared storybook reading. In J. F. Baumann & E. J. Kame'enui (Eds.), *Vocabulary instruction: Research to practice* (pp. 41–58). New York: Guilford Press.

Craft, M. A., Alber, S. R., & Heward, W. L. (1998). Teaching elementary students with developmental disabilities to recruit teacher attention in a general education classroom: Effects on teacher praise and academic productivity. *Journal of Applied Behavior Analysis, 28,* 399–415.

Craig, W. M., Pepler, D., & Atlas, R. (2000). Observations of bullying in the playground and in the classroom. *School Psychology International, 21,* 22–36.

Crone, D. A., & Horner, R. H. (2003). *Building positive behavior support systems in schools: Functional behavioral assessment.* New York: Guilford Press.

Crone, D. A., Horner, R. H., & Hawken, L. S. (2004). *Responding to problem behavior in schools: The Behavior Education Program.* New York: Guilford Press.

Cunningham, A. E., Perry, K. E., Stanovich, K. E., & Stanovich, P. J. (2004). Disciplinary knowledge of K–3 teachers and their knowledge calibration in the domain of early literacy. *Annals of Dyslexia, 54,* 139–167.

Cunningham, A. E., & Stanovich, K. E. (1997). Early reading acquisition and its relation to reading experience and ability 10 years later. *Developmental Psychology, 33,* 934–945.

Cunningham, A. E., & Stanovich, K. E. (1998). What reading does for the mind. *American Educator, 22,* 8–15.

Dale, P. S., Crain-Thoreson, C., Notari-Syverson, A., & Cole, K. (1996). Parent–child book reading as an intervention technique for young children with language delays. *Topics in Early Childhood Special Education, 16,* 213–235.

Dalton, T., Martella, R. C., & Marchand-Martella, N. E. (1999). The effects of a self-management program in reducing off-task behavior. *Journal of Behavioral Education, 9,* 157–176.

Daly, E. J., Chafouleas, S., & Skinner, C. H. (2005). *Interventions for reading problems: Designing and evaluating effective strategies.* New York: Guilford Press.

Daly, E. J. III, Andersen, M., Gortmaker, V., & Turner, A. (2006). Using experimental analysis to identify reading fluency interventions: Connecting the dots. *Behavior Analyst Today, 7,* 133–150.

Daly, E. J. III, & Martens, B. K. (1994). A comparison of three interventions for increasing oral reading performance: Application of the instructional hierarchy. *Journal of Applied Behavior Analysis, 27,* 459–469.

Daly, E. J. III, Martens, B. K., Dool, E. J., & Hintze, J. M. (1998). Using brief functional analysis to select interventions for oral reading. *Journal of Behavioral Education, 8,* 203–218.

Daly, E. J. III, Martens, B. K., Hamler, K. R., Dool, E. J., & Eckert, T. L. (1999). A brief experimental analysis for identifying instructional components needed to improve oral reading fluency. *Journal of Applied Behavior Analysis, 32,* 83–94.

Daly, E. J. III, Murdoch, A., Lillenstein, L., Webber, L., & Lentz, F. E. (2002). An examination of methods for testing treatments: Conducting brief experimental analyses of the effects of instructional components on oral reading fluency. *Education and Treatment of Children, 25,* 288–316.

Daly, E. J. III, Persampieri, M., McCurdy, M., & Gortmaker, V. (2005). Generating reading interventions through experimental analysis of academic skills: Demonstration and empirical evaluation. *School Psychology Review, 34,* 395–414.

Daly, E. J. III, Witt, J. C., Martens, B. K., & Dool, E. J. (1997). A model for conducting a functional analysis of academic performance problems. *School Psychology Review, 26,* 554–574.

D'Anna, C. A., Zechmeister, E. B., & Hall, J. W. (1991). Toward a meaningful definition of vocabulary size. *Journal of Reading Behavior, 23,* 109–122.

Danoff, B., Harris, K. R., & Graham, S. (1993). Incorporating strategy instruction within the writing process in the regular classroom: Effects on the writing of students with and without learning disabilities. *Journal of Reading Behavior, 25,* 295–322.

Darch, C. B., & Kame'enui, E. J. (2004). *Instructional classroom management: A proactive approach to behavior management* (2nd ed.). Upper Saddle River, NJ: Pearson Education.

Darch, C. B., Kim, S., Johnson, S., & James, H. (2000). The strategic spelling skills of students with learning disabilities: The results of two studies. *Journal of Instructional Psychology, 27,* 15–26.

Darveaux, D. X. (1984). The good behavior game plus merit: Controlling disruptive behavior and improving student motivation. *School Psychology Review, 13,* 510–514.

Davies, S., & Witte, R. (2000). Self-management and peer-monitoring within a group contingency to decrease uncontrolled verbalizations of children with attention-deficit/hyperactivity disorder. *Psychology in the Schools, 37,* 135–147.

Davis, C. A., & Fox, J. (1999). Evaluating environmental arrangement as setting events: Review and implications for measurement. *Journal of Behavioral Education, 9,* 77–96.

Davis, C. A., & Reichle, J. E. (2002). High-probability requests and a preferred item as a distractor: Increasing successful transitions in children with behavior problems. *Education and Treatment of Children, 23,* 423–440.

Deci, E. L., Koestner, R., & Ryan, R. M. (1999). A meta-analytic review of experiments examining the effects of extrinsic rewards on intrinsic motivation. *Psychological Bulletin, 125,* 627–668.

Deci, E. L., & Ryan, R. M. (1987). The support of autonomy and the control of behavior. *Journal of Personality and Social Psychology, 53,* 1024–1037.

Decker, D. M., Dona, D. P., & Christenson, S. L. (2007). Behaviorally at-risk African American students: The importance of student–teacher relationships for student outcomes. *Journal of School Psychology, 45,* 83–109.

De La Paz, S. (1997). Strategy instruction in planning: Teaching students with learning disabilities to compose persuasive and expository essays. *Learning Disability Quarterly, 20,* 227–248.

De La Paz, S. (1999). Self-regulated strategy instruction in regular education settings: Improving outcomes for students with and without learning disabilities. *Learning Disabilities Research and Practice, 14,* 92–106.

De La Paz, S., & Graham, S. (1997). Strategy instruction in planning: Effects on the writing performance and behavior of students with learning difficulties. *Exceptional Children, 63,* 167–181.

De La Paz, S., & Graham, S. (2002). Explicitly teaching strategies, skills, and knowledge: Writing instruction in the classroom. *Journal of Educational Psychology, 94,* 687–698.

De La Paz, S., & MacArthur, C. (2000). Knowing the how and why of history: Expectations for secondary students with and without learning disabilities. *Learning Disability Quarterly, 26,* 142–154.

De La Paz, S., Owen, B., Harris, K. R., & Graham, S. (2000). Riding Elvis' motorcycle: Using self-regulated strategy development to PLAN and WRITE for a state writing exam. *Learning Disabilities Research and Practice, 15,* 101–109.

De La Paz, S., Swanson, P. N., & Graham, S. (1998). The contribution of executive control to the revising by students with writing and learning difficulties. *Journal of Educational Psychology, 90,* 448–460.

Delquadri, J., Greenwood, C. R., Whorton, D., Carta, J. J., & Hall, R. V. (1986). Classwide peer tutoring. *Exceptional Children, 52,* 535–542.

De Martini-Scully, D., Bray, M. A., & Kehle, T. J. (2000). A packaged intervention to reduce disruptive behaviors in general education students. *Psychology in the Schools, 37,* 149–156.

Deno, S. L. (1985). Curriculum-based measurement: The emerging alternative. *Exceptional Children, 52,* 219–232.

Deno, S. L. (1986). Formative evaluation of individual student programs: A new role for school psychologists. *School Psychology Review, 15,* 358–374.

Deno, S. L. (2003). Developments in curriculum-based measurement. *Journal of Special Education, 37,* 184–192.

Deno, S. L., Fuchs, L. S., Marston, D., & Shin, J. (2001). Using curriculum-based measurement to establish growth standards for students with learning disabilities. *School Psychology Review, 30,* 507–524.

Deno, S. L., & Mirkin, P. K. (1977). *Data-based program modification: A manual.* Reston, VA: Council for Exceptional Children.

De Pry, R. L., & Sugai, G. (2002). The effect of active supervision and pre-correction on minor behavioral incidents in a sixth grade general education classroom. *Journal of Behavioral Education, 11,* 255–267.

Deshler, D. D., Schumaker, J. B., Lenz, B. K., Bulgren, J. A., Hock, M. F., Knight, J., et al. (2001). Ensuring content-area learning by secondary students with learning disabilities. *Learning Disabilities Research and Practice, 16,* 96–108.

Dimino, J., Gersten, R., Carnine, D., & Blake, G. (1990). Story grammar: An approach for promoting at-risk secondary students' comprehension of literature. *Elementary School Journal, 91,* 19–22.

DiPerna, J. C., & Elliott, S. N. (2002). Promoting academic enablers to improve student performance: An introduction to the mini-series. *School Psychology Quarterly, 31,* 293–297.

Dishion, T. J., Nelson, S. E., Winter, C. E., & Bullock, B. M. (2004). Adolescent friendship as a dynamic system: Entropy and deviance in the etiology and course of male antisocial behavior. *Journal of Abnormal Child Psychology, 32,* 651–663.

Dishion, T. J., Patterson, G. R., Stoolmiller, M., & Skinner, M. L. (1991). Family, school, and behavioral antecedents to early adolescent involvement with antisocial peers. *Developmental Psychology, 27,* 172–180.

Dishion, T. J., Spracklen, K. M., Andrews, D. W., & Patterson, G. R. (1996). Deviancy training in male adolescent friendships. *Behavior Therapy, 27,* 373–390.

Dolan, L. J., Kellam, S. G., Brown, C. H., Werthamer-Larsson, L., Rebok, G. W., Mayer, L. S., et al. (1993). The short-term impact of two classroom-based preventive interventions on aggressive and shy behaviors and poor achievement. *Journal of Applied Developmental Psychology, 14,* 317–345.

Doll, B., Haack, K., Kosse, S., Osterloh, M., & Seimers, E. (2005). The dilemma of pragmatics: Why schools don't use quality team consultation practices. *Journal of Educational and Psychological Consultation, 16,* 127–155.

Donovan, M. S., & Cross, C. T. (2002). *Minority students in special and gifted education.* Washington, DC: National Academy Press.

Dooley, P., Wilczenski, F. L., & Torem, C. (2001). Using an activity schedule to smooth school transitions. *Journal of Positive Behavior Interventions, 3,* 57–61.

Doughty, S. S., & Anderson, C. M. (2006). Effects of noncontingent reinforcement and functional communication training on problem behavior and mands. *Education and Treatment of Children, 29,* 23–50.

Doyle, W. (2006). Classroom management in early childhood and elementary classrooms. In C. M. Evertson & C. S. Weinstein (Eds.), *Handbook of classroom management: Research, practice, and contemporary issues* (pp. 97–125). Mahwah, NJ: Erlbaum.

Duke, N. K. (2000). 3.6 minutes per day: The scarcity of informational texts in first grade. *Reading Research Quarterly, 35,* 202–224.

Duncan, G. J., & Brooks-Gunn, J. (2000). Family poverty, welfare reform, and child development. *Child Development, 71,* 188–196.

Dunlap, G., Clarke, S., Jackson, M., Wright, S., Ramos, E., & Brinson, S. (1995). Self-monitoring of classroom behaviors with students exhibiting emotional and behavioral challenges. *School Psychology Quarterly, 10,* 165–177.

Dunst, C. J., Trivett, C. M., & Cutspec, P. A. (2002). Toward an operational definition of evidence-based practice. *Centerscope, 1*(1), 1–10.

DuPaul, G. J., & Eckert, T. L. (1994). The effects of social skills curricula: Now you see them, now you don't. *School Psychology Quarterly, 9,* 113–132.

Durlak, J. A. (2002). Evaluating evidence-based interventions in school psychology. *School Psychology Quarterly, 17,* 475–482.

Duvall, S. F., Delquadri, J. C., Elliott, M., & Hall, R. V. (1992). Parent-tutoring procedures: Experimental analysis and validation of generalization in oral reading across passages, settings, and time. *Journal of Behavioral Education, 2,* 281–303.

Duvall, S. F., Delquadri, J. C., & Hall, R. V. (1996). *Parents as reading tutors.* Longmont, CO: Sopris West (*http://www.sopriswest.com*).

Dweck, C. S. (2002). Messages that motivate: How praise molds students' beliefs, motivation, and performance (in surprising ways). In J. Aronson (Ed.), *Improving academic achievement: Impact of psychological factors in education* (pp. 38–60). New York: Academic Press.

Early, D., Barbarin, O., Bryant, D., Burchinal, M., Chang, F., Clifford, R., et al. (2005). *Pre-kindergarten in eleven states: NCEDL's multi-state study of pre-kindergarten and study of state-wide early education programs (SWEEP): Preliminary descriptive report.* Chapel Hill: University of North Carolina, Frank Porter Graham Child Development Institute, National Center for Early Development and Learning. Retrieved November 27, 2006, from *http://www.fpg.unc.edu/~NCEDL/.*

Eckert, T. L., Ardoin, S. P., Daisey, D. M., & Scarola, M. D. (2000). Empirically evaluating the effectiveness of reading interventions: The use of brief experimental analysis and single case design. *Psychology in the Schools, 37,* 463–473.

Eckert, T. L., Ardoin, S. P., Daly, E. J. III, & Martens, B. M. (2002). Improving oral reading fluency: A brief experimental analysis of combining an antecedent intervention with consequences. *Journal of Applied Behavior Analysis, 35,* 271–281.

Eckert, T. L., Dunn, E., & Ardoin, S. (2006). The effects of alternate forms of performance feedback on elementary-aged students' oral reading fluency. *Journal of Behavioral Education, 15,* 148–161.

Eckert, T. L., & Hintze, J. M. (2000). Behavioral conceptions and applications of acceptability: Issues related to service delivery and research methodology. *School Psychology Quarterly, 15,* 123–148.

Eddy, J. M., Reid, J. B., & Curry, V. (2002). The etiology of youth antisocial behavior, delinquency, and violence and a public health approach to prevention. In M. R. Shinn, H. M. Walker, & G. Stoner (Eds.), *Interventions for academic and behavior problems II: Preventive and remedial approaches* (pp. 27–51). Bethesda, MD: National Association of School Psychologists.

Egeland, B., Kalkoske, M., Gottesman, N., & Erickson, M. F. (1990). Preschool behavior problems:

Stability and factors accounting for change. *Journal of Child Psychology and Psychiatry, 31,* 891–909.

Egeland, B., Pianta, R., & Ogawa, J. (1996). Early behavior problems: Pathways to mental disorders in adolescence. *Development and Psychopathology, 8,* 735–749.

Ehrhardt, K. E., Barnett, D. W., Lentz, F. E., Stollar, S. A., & Reifin, L. H. (1996). Innovative methodology in ecological consultation: Use of scripts to promote treatment acceptability and integrity. *School Psychology Quarterly, 11,* 49–168.

Ehri, L. C. (1995). Phases of development in learning to read words by sight. *Journal of Research in Reading, 18,* 116–125.

Eilam, B. (2001). Primary strategies for promoting homework performance. *American Educational Research Journal, 38,* 691–725.

Eisenberger, R., Rhoades, L., & Cameron, J. (1999). Does pay for performance increase or decrease perceived self-determination and intrinsic motivation? *Journal of Personality and Social Psychology, 77,* 1026–1040.

Eisenhower, A. S., Baker, B. L., & Blacher, J. (2007). Early student–teacher relationships of children with and without intellectual disability: Contributions of behavioral, social, and self-regulatory competence. *Journal of School Psychology, 45,* 363–384.

Elbaum, B., Vaughn, S., Hughes, M., & Moody, S. W. (1999). Grouping practices and reading outcomes for students with disabilities. *Exceptional Children, 65,* 399–415.

Elbaum, B., Vaughn, S., Hughes, M., & Moody, S. W., & Schumm, J. S. (2000). How reading outcomes of students with disabilities are related to instructional grouping formats. In R. Gersten, E. P. Schiller, & S. Vaughn (Eds.), *Contemporary special education research: Syntheses of the knowledge base on critical instructional issues* (pp. 105–135). Mahwah, NJ: Erlbaum.

Elias, M. J., & Dilworth, J. E. (2003). Ecological/developmental theory, context-based best practice, and school-based action research: Cornerstones of school psychology training and policy. *Journal of School Psychology, 41,* 293–297.

Elkonin, D. B. (1973). U.S.S.R. In J. Downing (Ed.), *Comparative reading* (pp. 551–579). New York: Macmillan.

Elliott, S. N. (1988). Acceptability of behavioral treatments: Review of variables that influence treatment selection. *Professional Psychology: Research and Practice, 19,* 68–80.

Elliott, S. N., & Treuting, M. V. (1991). The Behavior Intervention Rating Scale: Development and validation of a pretreatment acceptability and effectiveness measure. *Journal of School Psychology, 29,* 43–51.

Elliott, S. N., Turco, T. L., & Gresham, F. M. (1987).

Consumers' and clients' pretreatment acceptability ratings of classroom group contingencies. *Journal of School Psychology, 25,* 145–153.

Elliott, S. N., Witt, J. C., Kratochwill, T. R., & Stoiber, K. C. (2002). Selecting and evaluating classroom interventions. In M. R. Shinn, H. M. Walker, & G. Stoner (Eds.), *Interventions for academic and behavior problems II: Preventive and remedial approaches* (pp. 243–294). Bethesda, MD: National Association of School Psychologists.

Embry, D. D. (2002). The Good Behavior Game: A best practice candidate as a universal behavioral vaccine. *Clinical Child and Family Psychology Review, 5,* 273–297.

Emmer, E. T., Evertson, C. M., & Worsham, M. E. (2006). *Classroom management for middle and high school teachers* (7th ed.). Boston: Allyn & Bacon.

Emmer, E. T., & Gerwels, M. C. (2006). Classroom management in middle and high school classrooms. In C. M. Evertson & C. S. Weinstein (Eds.), *Handbook of classroom management: Research, practice, and contemporary issues* (pp. 407–437). Mahwah, NJ: Erlbaum.

Emmer, E. T., & Hickman, J. (1991). Teacher efficacy in classroom management and discipline. *Educational and Psychological Measurement, 51,* 755–765.

Englert, C. S., Raphael, T. E., Anderson, L. M., Anthony, H. M., & Stevens, D. D. (1991). Making writing strategies and self-talk visible: Writing instruction in regular and special education classrooms. *American Educational Research Journal, 28,* 337–372.

Epstein, M. H., Munk, D., Bursuck, W. D., Polloway, E. A., & Jayanthi, M. (1999). Strategies for improving home–school communication about homework for students with disabilities: Perceptions of general educators. *Journal of Special Education, 33,* 166–176.

Erchul, W. P., & Martens, B. K. (2002). *School consultation: Conceptual and empirical bases of practice* (2nd ed.). New York: Kluwer Academic/Plenum.

Ervin, R. A., Johnston, E. S., & Friman, P. C. (1998). Positive peer reporting to improve the social interactions of a socially rejected girl. *Proven Practice: Prevention and Remediation Solutions of School Problems, 1,* 17–21.

Ervin, R. A., Miller, P. M., & Friman, P. C. (1996). Feed the hungry bee: Using positive peer reports to improve the social interactions and acceptance of a socially rejected girl in residential care. *Journal of Applied Behavior Analysis, 29,* 251–253.

Espin, C. A., Busch, T. W., Shin, J., & Kruschwitz, R. (2001). Curriculum-based measurement in the content areas: Validity of vocabulary-matching as an indicator of performance in social studies.

Learning Disabilities Research and Practice, 16, 142–151.

Espin, C. A., & Deno, S. L. (1989). The effects of modeling and prompting feedback strategies on sight word reading of students labeled learning disabled. *Education and Treatment of Children, 12,* 219–231.

Espin, C. A., & Foegen, A. (1996). Validity of general outcome measures for predicting secondary students' performance on content-area tasks. *Exceptional Children, 62,* 497–514.

Espin, C. A., Scierka, B. J., Skare, S., & Halverson, N. (1999). Criterion-related validity of curriculum-based measures in writing for secondary school students. *Reading and Writing Quarterly, 14,* 5–27.

Espin, C. A., Shin, J., & Busch, T. W. (2005). Curriculum-based measurement in the content areas: Vocabulary matching as an indicator of progress in social studies learning. *Journal of Learning Disabilities, 38,* 353–363.

Espin, C. A., Shin, J., Deno, S. L., Skare, S., Robinson, S., & Benner, B. (2000). Identifying indicators of written expression proficiency for middle school students. *Journal of Special Education, 34,* 140–153.

Espin, C. A., & Tindal, G. (1998). Curriculum-based measurement for secondary students. In M. R. Shinn (Ed.), *Advanced applications of curriculum-based measurement* (pp. 214–253). New York: Guilford Press.

Everett, G. E., Olmi, D. J., Edwards, R. P., & Tingstrom, D. H. (2005). The contributions of eye contact and contingent praise to effective instruction delivery in compliance training. *Education and Treatment of Children, 28,* 48–62.

Evertson, C. M. (1985). Training teachers in classroom management: An experimental study in secondary school classrooms. *Journal of Educational Research, 79,* 51–58.

Evertson, C. M. (1989). Improving elementary classroom management: A school-based training program for beginning the year. *Journal of Educational Research, 83,* 82–90.

Evertson, C. M., & Emmer, E. T. (1982). Effective management at the beginning of the school year in junior high classes. *Journal of Educational Psychology, 74,* 485–498.

Evertson, C. M., Emmer, E. T., & Worsham, M. E. (2006). *Classroom management for elementary teachers* (7th ed.). Boston: Allyn & Bacon.

Evertson, C. M., & Weinstein, C. S. (Eds.). (2006). *Handbook of classroom management: Research, practice, and contemporary issues.* Mahwah, NJ: Erlbaum.

Fairbanks, L. D., & Stinnett, T. A. (1997). Effects of professional group membership, intervention type, and diagnostic label on treatment acceptability. *Psychology in the Schools, 34,* 329–335.

Falk, K. B., & Wehby, J. H. (2001). The effects of

peer-assisted learning strategies on the beginning reading skills of young children with emotional or behavioral disorders. *Behavioral Disorders, 26,* 344–359.

Family Educational Rights and Privacy Act of 1974 (Pub. L. No. 93–380). (1974).

Fantuzzo, J. W., Davis, G. Y., & Ginsburg, M. D. (1995). Effects of parent involvement in isolation or in combination with peer tutoring on student self-concept and mathematics achievement. *Journal of Educational Psychology, 87,* 272–281.

Fantuzzo, J. W., King, J. A., & Heller, L. R. (1992). Effects of reciprocal peer tutoring on mathematics and school adjustment: A component analysis. *Journal of Educational Psychology, 84,* 331–339.

Fantuzzo, J. W., & Polite, K. (1990). School-based self-management interventions with elementary school children: A component analysis. *School Psychology Quarterly, 5,* 180–198.

Fantuzzo, J. W., King, J. A., & Heller, L. R. (1992). Effects of reciprocal peer tutoring on mathematics and school adjustment: A component analysis. *Journal of Educational Psychology, 84,* 331–339.

Fiala, C. L., & Sheridan, S. M. (2003). Parent involvement and reading: Using curriculum-based measurement to assess the effects of paired reading. *Psychology in the Schools, 40,* 613–626.

Figueroa, R. A., & Newsome, P. (2006). The diagnosis of LD in English learners: Is it nondiscriminatory? *Journal of Learning Disabilities, 39,* 206–214.

Filcheck, H. A., McNeil, C. B., Greco, L. A., & Bernard, R. S. (2004). Using a whole-class token economy and coaching of teacher skills in a preschool classroom to manage disruptive behavior. *Psychology in the Schools, 41,* 351–361.

Fishbein, J. E., & Wasik, B. H. (1981). Effect of the Good Behavior Game on disruptive library behavior. *Journal of Applied Behavior Analysis, 14,* 89–93.

Fleece, L., O'Brien, T., & Drabman, R. (1981). The use of a contingent observation procedure to reduce disruptive behavior in a preschool child. *Journal of Clinical Child Psychology, 10,* 128–130.

Fleischner, J. E., & Manheimer, M. A. (1997). Math interventions for students with learning disabilities: Myths and realities. *School Psychology Review, 26,* 397–413.

Fletcher, J. M., Coulter, W. A., Reschly, D. J., & Vaughn, S. (2004). Alternative approaches to the definition and identification of learning disabilities: Some questions and answers. *Annals of Dyslexia, 54,* 304–331.

Fletcher, J. M., Francis, D. J., Shaywitz, S. E., Lyon, G. R., Foorman, B. R., Stuebing, K., et al. (1998). Intelligent testing and the discrepancy model for children with learning disabilities. *Learning Disabilities Research and Practice, 13,* 186–203.

Fletcher, J. M., Lyon, G. R., Barnes, M., Stuebing,

K. K., Francis, D. J., Olson, R. K., et al. (2002). Classification of learning disabilities: An evidence-based evaluation. In R. Bradley, L. Danielson, & D. P. Hallahan (Eds.), *Identification of learning disabilities: Research to practice* (pp. 185–250). Mahwah, NJ: Erlbaum.

Flugum, K. R., & Reschly, D. J. (1994). Prereferral interventions: Quality indices and outcomes. *Journal of School Psychology, 32,* 1–14.

Foorman, B. R., & Torgesen, J. (2001). Critical elements of classroom and small-group instruction promote reading success in all children. *Learning Disabilities Research and Practice, 16,* 203–212.

Ford, A. D., Olmi, D. J., Edwards, R. P., & Tingstrom, D. H. (2001). The sequential introduction of compliance training components with elementary-aged children in general education classroom settings. *School Psychology Quarterly, 16,* 142–157.

Forehand, R. L., & McMahon, R. J. (1981). *Helping the noncompliant child: A clinician's guide to parent training.* New York: Guilford Press.

Forehand, R., & Wierson, M. (1993). The role of developmental factors in planning behavioral interventions for children: Disruptive behavior as an example. *Behavior Therapy, 24,* 117–141.

Forness, S., Kavale, K., Blum, I., & Lloyd, J. (1997). A mega-analysis of meta-analyses: What works in special education and related services. *Teaching Exceptional Children, 29,* 4–9.

Fresch, M. J. (2003). A national survey of spelling instruction: Investigating teachers' beliefs and practice. *Journal of Literacy Research, 35,* 819–848.

Friedman, D. L., Cancelli, A. A., & Yoshida, R. K. (1988). Academic engagement of elementary school children with learning disabilities. *Journal of School Psychology, 26,* 327–340.

Fuchs, D., & Deshler, D. D. (2007). What we need to know about responsiveness to intervention (and shouldn't be afraid to ask). *Learning Disabilities Research and Practice, 22,* 129–136.

Fuchs, D., & Fuchs, L. S. (1996). Consultation as a technology and the politics of school reform. *Remedial and Special Education, 17,* 386–392.

Fuchs, D., & Fuchs, L. S. (2005). Peer-assisted learning strategies: Promoting word recognition, fluency, and reading comprehension in young children. *Journal of Special Education, 39,* 34–44.

Fuchs, D., & Fuchs, L. S. (Eds.). (2007). Responsiveness to intervention [Special issue]. *Teaching Exceptional Children, 39*(5).

Fuchs, D., Fuchs, L. S., & Bahr, M. W. (1990). Mainstream assistance teams: A scientific basis for the art of consultation. *Exceptional Children, 57,* 128–139.

Fuchs, D., Fuchs, L. S., & Burish, P. (2000). Peer-assisted learning strategies: An evidence-based practice to promote reading achievement. *Learning Disabilities Research and Practice, 15,* 85–91.

Fuchs, D., Fuchs, L. S., Harris, A. H., & Roberts, P. H. (1996). Bridging the research-to-practice gap with mainstream assistance teams: A cautionary tale. *School Psychology Quarterly, 11,* 244–266.

Fuchs, D., Fuchs, L. S., Mathes, P. G., & Simmons, D. G. (1997). Peer-assisted learning strategies: Making classrooms more responsive to diversity. *American Educational Research Journal, 34,* 174–206.

Fuchs, D., Fuchs, L. S., Thompson, A., Al Otaiba, S., Yen, L., Yang, N. J., et al. (2002). Exploring the importance of reading programs for kindergartners with disabilities in mainstream classrooms. *Exceptional Children, 68,* 295–311.

Fuchs, D., Fuchs, L. S., Thompson, A., Swenson, E., Yen, L., Al Otaiba, S., et al. (2001). Peer-assisted learning strategies in reading: Extensions for kindergarten, first grade, and high school. *Remedial and Special Education, 22,* 15–21.

Fuchs, D., Mock, D., Morgan, P. L., & Young, C. L. (2003). Responsiveness-to-intervention: Definitions, evidence, and implications for the learning disabilities construct. *Learning Disabilities Research and Practice, 18,* 157–171.

Fuchs, L. S., & Deno, S. L. (1994). Must instructionally useful performance assessment be based in the curriculum? *Exceptional Children, 61,* 15–24.

Fuchs, L. S., Fuchs, D., & Compton, D. L. (2004). Monitoring early reading development in first grade: Word identification fluency versus nonsense word fluency. *Exceptional Children, 71,* 7–21.

Fuchs, L. S., Fuchs, D., Hamlett, C. L., & Allinder, R. M. (1991). The contribution of skills analysis to curriculum-based measurement in spelling. *Exceptional Children, 57,* 443–452.

Fuchs, L. S., Fuchs, D., Hamlett, C. L., Walz, L., & Germann, G. (1993). Formative evaluation of academic progress: How much growth can we expect? *School Psychology Review, 22,* 27–48.

Fuchs, L. S., Fuchs, D., Hosp, M. K., & Jenkins, J. R. (2001). Oral reading fluency as an indicator of reading competence: A theoretical, empirical, and historical analysis. *Scientific Studies of Reading, 5,* 239–256.

Fuchs, L. S., Fuchs, D., Karns, K., Hamlett, C. L., & Katzaroff, M. (1999). Mathematics performance assessment in the classroom: Effects on teacher planning and student learning. *American Educational Research Journal, 36,* 609–646.

Fuchs, L. S., Fuchs, D., & Kazdan, S. (1999). Effects of peer-assisted learning strategies on high school students with serious reading problems. *Remedial and Special Education, 20,* 309–318.

Fuchs, L. S., Fuchs, D., Yazdian, L., & Powell, S. R. (2002). Enhancing first-grade children's mathematical development with peer-assisted learning strategies. *School Psychology Review, 31,* 529–539.

Fulk, B. M., & Stormont-Spurgin, M. (1995). Spelling interventions for students with disabilities: A review. *Journal of Special Education, 28,* 488–513.

Furrer, C., & Skinner, E. (2003). Sense of relatedness as a factor in children's academic engagement and performance. *Journal of Educational Psychology, 95,* 148–162.

Gajria, M., & Salend, S. J. (1995). Homework practices of students with and without learning disabilities: A comparison. *Journal of Learning Disabilities, 28,* 291–296.

Gajria, M., & Salvia, J. (1992). The effects of summarization instruction on text comprehension of students with learning disabilities. *Exceptional Children, 58,* 508–516.

Gansle, K. A., Noell, G. H., VanDerHeyden, A. M., Naquin, G. M., & Slider, N. J. (2002). Moving beyond total words written: The reliability, criterion validity, and time cost of alternate measures for curriculum-based measurement in writing. *School Psychology Review, 31,* 477–497.

Garcia, S. B., & Ortiz, A. A. (2006). Preventing disproportionate representation: Culturally and linguistically responsive prereferral interventions. *Teaching Exceptional Children, 38,* 64–68.

Gardill, M. C., & Jitendra, A. K. (1999). Advanced story map instruction: Effects on the reading comprehension of students with learning disabilities. *Journal of Special Education, 33,* 2–17, 28.

Gardner, R. III. (1990). Life space interviewing: It can be effective, but don't. . . . *Behavioral Disorders, 15,* 111–119.

Gardner, R. III, Heward, W. L., & Grossi, T. A. (1994). Effects of response cards on student participation and academic achievement: A systematic replication with inner-city students during whole-class science instruction. *Journal of Applied Behavior Analysis, 27,* 63–71.

Gartin, B. C., & Murdick, N. L. (2001). A new IDEA mandate. *Remedial and Special Education, 22,* 344–349.

Geary, D. C., Hamson, C. O., & Hoard, M. K. (2000). Numerical and arithmetical cognition: A longitudinal study of process and concept deficits in children with learning disability. *Journal of Experimental Child Psychology, 77,* 236–263.

Gerber, M., Jimenez, T., Leafstedt, J., Villaruz, J., Richards, C., & English J. (2004). English reading effects of small-group intensive intervention in Spanish for K–1 English learners. *Learning Disabilities Research and Practice, 19,* 239–251.

Gersten, R., & Baker, S. (2000a). The professional knowledge base on instructional practices that support cognitive growth for English-language learners. In R. Gersten, E. P. Schiller, & S. Vaughn (Eds.), *Contemporary special education research: Syntheses of the knowledge base on critical instructional issues* (pp. 31–79). Mahwah, NJ: Erlbaum.

Gersten, R., & Baker, S. (2000b). What we know about effective instructional practices for English-language learners. *Exceptional Children, 66,* 454–470.

Gersten, R., & Baker, S. (2001). Teaching expressive writing to students with learning disabilities. *Elementary School Journal, 101,* 251–272.

Gersten, R., Chard, D., & Baker, S. (2000). Factors enhancing sustained use of research-based instructional practices. *Journal of Learning Disabilities, 33,* 445–457.

Gersten, R., Fuchs, L. S., Williams, J. P., & Baker, S. (2001). Teaching reading comprehension strategies to students with learning disabilities: A review of the literature. *Review of Educational Research, 71,* 279–320.

Gettinger, M. (1988). Methods of proactive classroom management. *School Psychology Review, 17,* 227–242.

Gettinger, M., & Seibert, J. K. (2002). Best practices in increasing academic learning time. In A. Thomas & J. Grimes (Eds.), *Best practices in school psychology IV* (Vol. 1, pp. 773–787). Bethesda, MD: National Association of School Psychologists.

Giebelhaus, C. R. (1994). The mechanical third ear device: A student teaching supervision alternative. *Journal of Teacher Education, 45,* 365–373.

Gilliam, W. S. (2005). *Prekindergarteners left behind: Expulsion rates in state prekindergarten systems.* New Haven, CT: Yale University Child Study Center.

Gilliam, W. S., & Zigler, E. F. (2000). A critical meta-analysis of all evaluations of state-funded preschool from 1977 to 1998: Implications for policy, service delivery and program evaluation. *Early Childhood Research Quarterly, 15,* 441–473.

Gillingham, A., & Stillman, B. (1997). *The Gillingham manual: Remedial training for children with specific disability in reading, writing, and penmanship* (8th ed.). Cambridge, MA: Educators Publishing Service.

Gimpel, G. A., & Holland, M. L. (2003). *Emotional and behavioral problems of young children: Effective intervention in the preschool and kindergarten years.* New York: Guilford Press.

Ginsburg-Block, M., & Fantuzzo, J. (1997). Reciprocal peer tutoring: An analysis of training and experience. *School Psychology Quarterly, 12,* 134–149.

Godfrey, S. A., Grisham-Brown, J., Schuster, J. W., & Hemmeter, M. L. (2003). The effects of three techniques on student participation with preschool children with attending problems. *Education and Treatment of Children, 26,* 255–272.

Good, R. H., & Kaminski, R. A. (Eds.). (2002). *Dynamic Indicators of Basic Early Literacy Skills–Sixth Edition.* Eugene, OR: Institute for the Development of Educational Achievement. Available online at *http://dibels.uoregon.edu/*.

Good, R. H., Simmons, D. C., & Kame'enui, E. J. (2001). The importance and decision-making utility of a continuum of fluency-based indicators of foundational reading skills for third-grade high-stakes outcomes. *Scientific Studies of Reading, 5,* 257–288.

Good Start Grow Smart Initiative. (2002). *Good Start, Grow Smart: The Bush administration's early childhood initiative.* Retrieved February 8, 2007, from *http://www.whitehouse.gov/infocus/earlychildhood/toc.html.*

Gordon, J., Vaughn, S., & Schumm, J. S. (1993). Spelling interventions: A review of literature and implications for instruction for students with learning disabilities. *Learning Disabilities Research and Practice, 8,* 15–181.

Gough, P. B. (1996). How children learn to read and why they fail. *Annals of Dyslexia, 46,* 3–20.

Goyette, R., Dore, R., & Dion, E. (2000). Pupils' misbehaviors and the reactions and causal attributions of physical education student teachers: A sequential analysis. *Journal of Teaching in Physical Education, 20,* 3–14.

Graden, J. L. (1989). Redefining "prereferral" intervention as intervention assistance: Collaboration between general and special education. *Exceptional Children, 56,* 227–231.

Graden, J. L., Casey, A., & Bonstrom, O. (1985). Implementing a prereferral intervention system: Part II. The data. *Exceptional Children, 51,* 487–496.

Graden, J. L., Casey, A., & Christenson, S. L. (1985). Implementing a prereferral intervention system: Part I. The model. *Exceptional Children, 51,* 377–384.

Graham, S. (1990). The role of production factors in learning disabled students' compositions. *Journal of Educational Psychology, 82,* 781–791.

Graham, S. (1999). Handwriting and spelling instruction for students with learning disabilities: A review. *Learning Disability Quarterly, 22,* 78–98.

Graham, S., Berninger, V. W., Abbott, R. D., Abbott, S. P., & Whitaker, D. (1997). Role of mechanics in composing of elementary school students: A new methodological approach. *Journal of Educational Psychology, 89,* 170–182.

Graham, S., & Harris, K. R. (1989). A component analysis of cognitive strategy instruction: Effects on learning disabled students' compositions. *Exceptional Children, 56,* 201–214.

Graham, S., & Harris, K. R. (1997). It can be taught, but it does not develop naturally: Myths and realities in writing instruction. *School Psychology Review, 26,* 414–424.

Graham, S., & Harris, K. R. (2002). The road less traveled: Prevention and intervention in written language. In K. G. Butler & E. R. Silliman (Eds.), *Speaking, reading, and writing in children with language learning disabilities: New paradigms in research and practice* (pp. 199–217). Mahwah, NJ: Erlbaum.

Graham, S., & Harris, K. R. (2003). Students with learning disabilities and the process of writing: A meta-analysis of SRSD studies. In H. L. Swanson, K. R. Harris, & S. Graham (Eds.), *Handbook of learning disabilities* (pp. 383–402). New York: Guilford Press.

Graham, S., & Harris, K. R. (2006a). Improving the writing performance of young struggling writers: Theoretical and programmatic research from the Center on Accelerating Student Learning. *Journal of Special Education, 39,* 19–33.

Graham, S., & Harris, K. R. (2006b). Preventing writing difficulties: Providing additional handwriting and spelling instruction to at-risk children in first grade. *Teaching Exceptional Children, 38*(5), 64–66.

Graham, S., Harris, K. R., & Fink-Chorzempa, B. (2002). Contribution of spelling instruction to the spelling, writing, and reading of poor spellers. *Journal of Educational Psychology, 94,* 669–686.

Graham, S., Harris, K. R., Fink-Chorzempa, B., & MacArthur, C. (2003). Primary grade teachers' instructional adaptations for struggling writers: A national survey. *Journal of Educational Psychology, 95,* 279–292.

Graham, S., Harris, K. R., & Larsen, L. (2001). Prevention and intervention of writing difficulties for students with learning disabilities. *Learning Disabilities Research and Practice, 16,* 74–84.

Graham, S., Harris, K. R., & Loynachan, C. (1993). The basic spelling vocabulary list. *Journal of Educational Research, 86,* 363–368.

Graham, S., Harris, K. R., & Loynachan, C. (1994). The spelling for writing list. *Journal of Learning Disabilities, 27,* 210–214.

Graham, S., Harris, K. R., & MacArthur, C. A. (1993). Improving the writing of students with learning problems: Self-regulated strategy development. *School Psychology Review, 22,* 656–670.

Graham, S., Harris, K. R., MacArthur, C. A., & Schwartz, S. (1991). Writing and writing instruction for students with learning disabilities: Review of a research program. *Learning Disability Quarterly, 14,* 89–114.

Graham, S., Harris, K. R., & Troia, G. A. (2000). Self-regulated strategy development revisited: Teaching writing strategies to struggling writers. *Topics in Language Disorders, 20*(4), 1–14.

Graham, S., & Perin, D. (2007). *Writing next: Effective strategies to improve writing of adolescents in middle and high schools—A report to Carnegie Corporation of New York.* Washington, DC: Alliance for Excellent Education. Retrieved March 3, 2007, from *http://www.all4ed.org.*

Gravois, T. A., & Rosenfield, S. (2006). Impact of instructional consultation teams on the disproportionate referral and placement of minority students in special education. *Remedial and Special Education, 27,* 42–52.

Gray, C. L., Gutkin, T. B., & Riley, T. R. (2001). Acceptability of rewards among high school teachers, parents, students, and administrators: Ecological implications for consultation at the high school level. *Journal of Educational and Psychological Consultation, 13,* 185–217.

Greenwood, C. R. (1991). Longitudinal analysis of time, engagement, and achievement in at-risk versus non-risk students. *Exceptional Children, 57,* 521–535.

Greenwood, C. R., Arreaga-Mayer, C., & Carta, J. J. (1994). Identification and translation of effective teacher-developed instructional procedures for general practice. *Remedial and Special Education, 15,* 140–151.

Greenwood, C. R., Arreaga-Mayer, C., Utley, C. A., Gavin, K. M., & Terry, B. J. (2001). ClassWide Peer Tutoring Management System: Applications with elementary-level English language learners. *Remedial and Special Education, 22,* 34–47.

Greenwood, C. R., Carta, J. J., Kamps, D., & Delquadri, J. (1997). *Ecobehavioral Assessment Systems Software (EBASS Version 3.0): Practitioners manual.* Kansas City: Juniper Gardens Children's Project, University of Kansas.

Greenwood, C. R., Carta, J. J., Kamps, D., Terry, B., & Delquadri, J. (1994). Development and validation of standard classroom observation systems for school practitioners: Ecobehavioral Assessment Systems Software (EBASS). *Exceptional Children, 61,* 197–210.

Greenwood, C. R., & Delquadri, J. (1995). Class-Wide Peer Tutoring and the prevention of school failure. *Preventing School Failure, 39*(4), 21–25.

Greenwood, C. R., Delquadri, J. C., & Hall, R. V. (1989). Longitudinal effects of classwide peer tutoring. *Journal of Educational Psychology, 81,* 371–383.

Greenwood, C. R., Delquadri, J., & Hall, R. V. (1997). *Together we can: ClassWide Peer Tutoring for basic academic skills.* Longmont, CO: Sopris West.

Greenwood, C. R., Horton, B. T., & Utley, C. A. (2002). Academic engagement: Current perspectives on research and practice. *School Psychology Review, 31,* 328–349.

Greenwood, C. R., Maheady, L., & Delquadri, J. (2002). Classwide peer tutoring programs. In M. A. Shinn, H. M. Walker, & G. Stoner (Eds.), *Interventions for academic and behavior problems II: Preventive and remedial approaches.* Bethesda, MD: National Association of School Psychologists.

Greenwood, C. R., Terry, B., Utley, C. A., Montagna, D., & Walker, D. (1993). Achievement, placement, and services: Middle school benefits of ClassWide Peer Tutoring used at the elementary school. *School Psychology Review, 22,* 497–516.

Gresham, F. M. (1989). Assessment of treatment integrity in school consultation and prereferral intervention. *School Psychology Review, 18,* 37–50.

Gresham, F. M. (1992). Social skills and learning disabilities: Causal, concomitant, or correlational? *School Psychology Review, 21,* 348–360.

Gresham, F. M. (1997). Social competence and students with behavior disorders: Where we've been, where we are, and where we should go. *Education and Treatment of Children, 20,* 233–249.

Gresham, F. M. (1998). Social skills training: Should we raze, remodel, or rebuild? *Behavioral Disorders, 24,* 19–25.

Gresham, F. M. (2002a). Responsiveness to intervention: An alternative approach to the identification of learning disabilities. In R. Bradley, L. Danielson, & D. P. Hallahan (Eds.), *Identification of learning disabilities: Research to practice* (pp. 467–519). Mahwah, NJ: Erlbaum.

Gresham, F. M. (2002b). Teaching social skills to high-risk children and youth: Preventive and remedial strategies. In M. R. Shinn, H. M. Walker, & G. Stoner (Eds.), *Interventions for academic and behavior problems II: Preventive and remedial approaches* (pp. 403–432). Bethesda, MD: National Association of School Psychologists.

Gresham, F. M. (2004). Current status and future directions of school-based behavioral interventions. *School Psychology Review, 33,* 326–343.

Gresham, F. M., & Elliott, S. N. (1990). *Social Skills Rating System.* Bloomington, MN: Pearson Assessments.

Gresham, F. M., Gansle, K. A., & Noell, G. H. (1993). Treatment integrity in applied behavior analysis with children. *Journal of Applied Behavior Analysis, 26,* 257–263.

Gresham, F. M., Gansle, K. A., Noell, G. H., Cohen, S., & Rosenblum, S. (1993). Treatment integrity of school-based behavioral intervention studies: 1980–1990. *School Psychology Review, 22,* 254–272.

Gresham, F. M., & Lopez, M. F. (1996). Social validation: A unifying concept for school-based consultation research and practice. *School Psychology Quarterly, 11,* 204–227.

Gresham, F. M., & MacMillan, D. L. (1997). Social competence and affective characteristics of students with mild disabilities. *Review of Educational Research, 67,* 377–415.

Gresham, F. M., MacMillan, D. L., Beebe-Frankenberger, M. E., & Bocian, K. M. (2000). Treatment integrity in learning disabilities intervention research: Do we really know how treatments are implemented? *Learning Disabilities Research and Practice, 15,* 198–205.

Guastello, E. F., Beasley, T. M., & Sinatra, R. C. (2000). Concept mapping effects on science content comprehension of low-achieving inner-city seventh graders. *Remedial and Special Education, 21,* 356–365.

Gumpel, T. P. (2007). Are social competence difficulties caused by performance or acquisition deficits?

The importance of self-regulatory mechanisms. *Psychology in the Schools, 44,* 351–372.

Gumpel, T. P., & David, S. (2000). Exploring the efficacy of self-regularity training as a possible alternative to social skills training. *Behavioral Disorders, 25,* 131–141.

Gumpel, T. P., & Golan, H. (2000). Teaching game-playing social skills using a self-monitoring treatment package. *Psychology in the Schools, 37,* 253–261.

Gunn, B., Biglan, A., Smolkowski, K., & Ary, D. (2000). The efficacy of supplemental instruction in decoding skills for Hispanic and non-Hispanic students in early elementary school. *Journal of Special Education, 34,* 90–103.

Gunter, P. L., Hummel, J. H., & Conroy, M. A. (1998). Increasing correct academic responding: An effective intervention strategy to decrease behavior problems. *Effective School Practices, 17,* 55–62.

Gunter, P. L., Reffel, J. M., Barnett, C. A., Lee, J. M., & Patrick, J. (2004). Academic response rates in elementary-school classrooms. *Education and Treatment of Children, 27,* 105–113.

Gurney, D., Gersten, R., Dimino, J., & Carnine, D. (1990). Story grammar: Effective literature instruction for high school students with learning disabilities. *Journal of Learning Disabilities, 23,* 335–342, 348.

Guthrie, J. T., & Davis, M. H. (2003). Motivating struggling readers in middle school through an engagement model of classroom practice. *Reading and Writing Quarterly: Overcoming Learning Difficulties, 19,* 59–85.

Gutkin, T. B. (Ed.). (2002). Evidence-based interventions in school psychology: The state of the art and future directions [Special issue]. *School Psychology Quarterly, 17*(4).

Gutkin, T. B., & Curtis, M. J. (1999). School-based consultation theory and practice: The art and science of indirect service delivery. In C. R. Reynolds & T. B. Gutkin (Eds.), *Handbook of school psychology* (3rd ed., pp. 598–637). New York: Wiley.

Gutkin, T. B., Henning-Stout, M., & Piersel, W. C. (1988). Impact of a districtwide behavioral consultation prereferral intervention service on patterns of school psychological service delivery. *Professional School Psychology, 3,* 301–308.

Gutkin, T. B., & Nemeth, C. (1997). Selected factors impacting decision making in prereferral intervention and other school-based teams: Exploring the intersection between school and social psychology. *Journal of School Psychology, 35,* 195–216.

Haagar, D., & Windmueller, M. P. (2001). Early reading intervention for English language learners at-risk for learning disabilities: Student and teacher outcomes in an urban school. *Learning Disability Quarterly, 24,* 235–250.

Hamlet, C. C., Axelrod, S., & Kuerschener, S. (1984). Eye contact as an antecedent to compliant behavior. *Journal of Applied Behavior Analysis, 17,* 553–557.

Hamre, B. K., & Pianta, R. C. (2001). Early teacher–child relationships and the trajectory of children's school outcomes through eighth grade. *Child Development, 72,* 625–638.

Hargrave, A. C., & Sénéchal, M. (2000). A book reading intervention with preschool children who have limited vocabularies: The benefits of regular reading and dialogic reading. *Early Childhood Research Quarterly, 15,* 75–90.

Harmon, J. M., Hedrick, W. B., & Fox, E. A. (2000). A content analysis of vocabulary instruction in social studies textbooks for grades 4–8. *Elementary School Journal, 100,* 253–272.

Harms, T., Clifford, R. M., & Cryer, D. (1998). *The Early Childhood Environment Rating Scale* (rev. ed.). New York: Teachers College Press.

Harniss, M. K., Epstein, M. H., Bursuck, W. D., Nelson, J., & Jayanthi, M. (2001). Resolving homework-related communication problems: Recommendations of parents of children with and without disabilities. *Reading and Writing Quarterly: Overcoming Learning Difficulties, 17,* 205–225.

Harris, A. J., & Jacobson, M. D. (1972). *Basic elementary reading vocabularies.* New York: Macmillan.

Harris, K. R., & Graham, S. (1999). Programmatic intervention research: Illustrations from the evolution of self-regulated strategy development. *Learning Disability Quarterly, 17,* 251–262.

Hart, B., & Risley, T. R. (1992). American parenting of language-learning children: Persisting differences in family–child interactions observed in natural home environments. *Developmental Psychology, 28,* 1096–1105.

Hart, B., & Risley, T. R. (1995). *Meaningful differences in the everyday experience of young American children.* Baltimore: Brookes.

Hartman, J. M., & Fuller, M. L. (1997). The development of curriculum-based measurement norms in literature-based classrooms. *Journal of School Psychology, 35,* 351–375.

Hasbrouck, J. E. (1997). Mediated peer coaching for training preservice teachers. *Journal of Special Education, 31,* 251–271.

Hasbrouck, J. E., & Christen, M. H. (1997). Providing peer coaching in inclusive classrooms: A tool for consulting teachers. *Intervention in School and Clinic, 32,* 172–177.

Hasbrouck, J., & Tindal, G. A. (2006). Oral reading fluency norms: A valuable assessment tool for reading teachers. *Reading Teacher, 59,* 636–639.

Hayeck, R. A. (1987). The teacher assistance team: A pre-referral support system. *Focus on Exceptional Children, 20,* 1–7.

Heller, L. R., & Fantuzzo, J. W. (1993). Reciprocal peer tutoring and parent partnership: Does parent involvement make a difference? *School Psychology Review, 22,* 517–534.

Helmke, A., & Schrader, F. W. (1988). Successful student practice during seatwork: Efficient management and active supervision not enough. *Journal of Educational Research, 82,* 70–75.

Hemmeter, M. L., Ostrosky, M., & Fox, L. (2006). Social and emotional foundations for early learning: A conceptual model for intervention. *School Psychology Review, 35,* 583–601.

Hennessey, B. A. (2007). Promoting social competence in school-aged children: The effects of the Open Circle Program. *Journal of School Psychology, 45,* 349–360.

Heron, T. E., Martz, S. A., & Margolis, H. (1996). Ethical and legal issues in consultation. *Remedial and Special Education, 17,* 377–385.

Heubusch, J. D., & Lloyd, J. W. (1998). Corrective feedback in oral reading. *Journal of Behavioral Education, 8,* 63–79.

Heward, W. L., Gardner, R., Cavanaugh, R. A., Courson, F. H., Grossi, T. A., & Barbetta, P. M. (1996). Everybody participates in this class: Using response cards to increase active student response. *Teaching Exceptional Children, 28*(2), 4–11.

Hinshaw, S. P. (1992a). Academic underachievement, attention deficits, and aggression: Comorbidity and implications for intervention. *Journal of Consulting and Clinical Psychology, 60,* 893–903.

Hinshaw, S. P. (1992b). Externalizing behavior problems and academic underachievement in childhood and adolescence: Causal relationships and underlying mechanisms. *Psychological Bulletin, 111,* 127–155.

Hintze, J. M., Callahan, J. E., Matthews, W. J., Williams, S. A. S., & Tobin, K. G. (2002). Oral reading fluency and prediction of reading comprehension in African American and Caucasian elementary school children. *School Psychology Review, 31,* 477–497.

Hintze, J. M., & Christ, T. J. (2004). An examination of variability as a function of passage variance in CBM progress monitoring. *School Psychology Review, 33,* 204–217.

Hintze, J. M., Shapiro, E. S., & Lutz, J. G. (1994). The effects of curriculum on the sensitivity of curriculum-based measurement in reading. *Journal of Special Education, 28,* 188–202.

Hiralall, A. S., & Martens, B. K. (1998). Teaching classroom management skills to preschool staff: The effects of scripted instructional sequences on teacher and student behavior. *School Psychology Quarterly, 13,* 94–115.

Hirsch, E. D. (2003). Reading comprehension requires knowledge—of words and the world: Scientific insights into the fourth-grade slump and the nation's stagnant comprehension scores. *American Educator, 27,* 10–22, 28, 29, 44, 48.

Hirsch, E. J., Lewis-Palmer, T., Sugai, G., & Schnacker, L. (2004). Using school bus discipline referral data in decision making: Two case studies. *Preventing School Failure, 48*(4), 4–9.

Hoff, K. E., & DuPaul, G. J. (1998). Reducing disruptive behavior in general education classrooms: The use of self-management strategies. *School Psychology Review, 27,* 290–303.

Hoff, K. E., & Robinson, S. L. (2002). Best practices in peer-mediated interventions. In A. Thomas & J. Grimes (Eds.), *Best practices in school psychology IV* (Vol. 2, pp. 1555–1567). Bethesda, MD: National Association of School Psychologists.

Hoffman, J., Roser, N., & Battle, J. (1993). Reading aloud in classrooms: From the modal toward a model. *Reading Teacher, 46,* 496–503.

Homan, S. P., Klesius, J. P., & Hite, C. (1993). Effects of repeated readings and nonrepetitive strategies on students' fluency and comprehension. *Journal of Educational Research, 87,* 94–99.

Hook, C. L., & DuPaul, G. J. (1999). Parent tutoring for students with attention-deficit/hyperactivity disorder: Effects on reading performance at home and school. *School Psychology Review, 28,* 60–75.

Horner, R. H., Todd, A. W., Lewis-Palmer, T., Irvin, L. K., Sugai, G., & Boland, J. P. (2004). The School-wide Evaluation Tool (SET): A research instrument for assessing school-wide positive behavior support. *Journal of Positive Behavior Interventions, 6,* 3–12.

Hosp, J. L., & Reschly, D. J. (2003). Referral rates for intervention or assessment: A meta-analysis of racial differences. *Journal of Special Education, 37,* 67–80.

Hosp, M. K., Hosp, J. L., & Howell, K. W. (2007). *The ABCs of CBM: A practical guide to curriculum-based measurement.* New York: Guilford Press.

Houghton, S., Wheldall, K., Jukes, R., & Sharpe, A. (1990). The effects of limited private reprimands and increased private praise on classroom behaviour in four British secondary school classes. *British Journal of Educational Psychology, 60,* 255–265.

Houlihan, D., & Jones, R. N. (1990). Exploring the reinforcement of compliance with "do" and "don't" requests and the side effects: A partial replication and extension. *Psychological Reports, 67,* 439–448.

Howes, C. (2000). Social-emotional classroom climate in child care, child–teacher relationships and children's second grade peer relations. *Social Development, 9,* 191–204.

Hubbert, E. R., Weber, K. P., & McLaughlin, T. (2000). A comparison of Copy, Cover, & Compare and a traditional spelling intervention for an adolescent with a conduct disorder. *Child and Family Behavior Therapy, 22,* 55–68.

Hughes, C. A., Ruhl, K. L., Schumaker, J. B., & Deshler, D. D. (2002). Effects of instruction in an assignment completion strategy on the homework performance of students with learning disabilities in general education class. *Learning Disabilities Research and Practice, 17,* 1–18.

Hughes, J. N. (2002). Authoritative teaching: Tipping the balance in favor of school versus peer effects. *Journal of School Psychology, 40,* 485–492.

Hughes, J. N., Cavell, T. A., & Jackson, T. (1999). Influence of the teacher–student relationship on childhood conduct problems: A prospective study. *Journal of Clinical Child Psychology, 28,* 173–184.

Hughes, J. N., Cavell, T. A, & Willson, V. (2001). Further support for the developmental significance of the quality of the teacher–student relationship. *Journal of School Psychology, 39,* 289–301.

Idol, L. (1987a). A critical thinking map to improve content area comprehension of poor readers. *Remedial and Special Education, 8*(4), 28–40.

Idol, L. (1987b). Group story mapping: A comprehension strategy for both skilled and unskilled readers. *Journal of Learning Disabilities, 20,* 196–205.

Idol, L., & Croll, V. J. (1987). Story-mapping training as a means of improving reading comprehension. *Learning Disability Quarterly, 10,* 214–229.

Individuals with Disabilities Education Act of 2004, Pub. L. No. 108–446.

Invernizzi, M., & Hayes, L. (2004). Developmental-spelling research: A systematic imperative. *Reading Research Quarterly, 39,* 216–228.

Ishii-Jordan, S. R. (2000). Behavioral interventions used with diverse students. *Behavioral Disorders, 25,* 299–309.

Iverson, A. M. (2002). Best practices in problem-solving team structure and process. In A. Thomas & J. Grimes (Eds.), *Best practices in school psychology IV* (Vol. 1, pp. 657–669). Bethesda, MD: National Association of School Psychologists.

Jackson, H. B., & Neel, R. S. (2006). Observing mathematics: Do students with EBD have access to standards-based mathematics instruction? *Education and Treatment of Children, 29,* 593–614.

Jacob, S., & Hartshorne, T. S. (2006). *Ethics and law for school psychologists* (5th ed.). New York: Wiley.

Jarrett, O. S., Maxwell, D. M., Dickerson, C., Hoge, P., Davies, G., & Gwen, Y. (1998). Impact of recess on classroom behavior: Group effects and individual differences. *Journal of Educational Research, 92,* 121–126.

Jenkins, J. R., Fuchs, L. S., van den Broek, P., Espin, C., & Deno, S. L. (2003). Accuracy and fluency in list and context reading of skilled and RD groups: Absolute and relative performance levels. *Learning Disabilities Research and Practice, 18,* 237–245.

Jenkins, J. R., & Jewell, M. (1993). Examining the validity of two measures for formative teaching: Reading aloud and maze. *Exceptional Children, 59,* 421–432.

Jewell, J., & Maleki, C. K. (2005). The utility of CBM written language indices: An investigation of production-dependent, production-independent, and accurate-production scores. *School Psychology Review, 34,* 27–44.

Jitendra, A., DiPipi, C. J., & Perron-Jones, N. (2002). An exploratory study of scheme-based word-problem-solving instruction for middle school students with learning disabilities: An emphasis on conceptual and procedural understanding. *Journal of Special Education, 36,* 23–38.

Jitendra, A. K., Griffin, C., Deatline-Buchman, A., DiPipi-Hoy, C., Sczesniak, E., Sokol, N. G., et al. (2005). Adherence to mathematics professional standards and instructional design criteria for problem-solving in mathematics. *Exceptional Children, 71,* 319–338.

Jitendra, A. K., Hoff, K., & Beck, M. M. (1999). Teaching middle school students with learning disabilities to solve word problems using a schema-based approach. *Remedial and Special Education, 20,* 50–64.

Jitendra, A. K., Hoppes, M. K., & Xin, Y. P. (2000). Enhancing main idea comprehension for students with learning problems. *Journal of Special Education, 34,* 127–139.

Jitendra, A. K., Salmento, M. M., & Haydt, L. A. (1999). A case analysis of fourth-grade subtraction instruction in basal mathematics programs: Adherence to important instructional design criteria. *Learning Disabilities Research and Practice, 14,* 69–79.

Johnson, L., Graham, S., & Harris, K. R. (1997). The effects of goal setting and self-instruction on learning a reading comprehension strategy: A study of students with learning disabilities. *Journal of Learning Disabilities, 30,* 80–91.

Johnson, T. C., Stoner, G., & Green, S. K. (1996). Demonstrating the experimenting society model with classwide behavior management interventions. *School Psychology Review, 25,* 199–214.

Johnston, F. R. (2001). Exploring classroom teachers' spelling practices and beliefs. *Reading Research and Instruction, 40,* 143–156.

Jones, K. M., & Wickstrom, K. F. (2002). Done in sixty seconds: Further analysis of the brief assessment model for academic problems. *School Psychology Review, 31,* 544–568.

Jones, K. M., Wickstrom, K. F., & Friman, P. C. (1997). The effects of observational feedback on treatment integrity in school-based behavioral consultation. *School Psychology Quarterly, 12,* 316–326.

Jones, K. M., Young, M. M., & Friman, P. C. (2000). Increasing peer praise of socially rejected delinquent youth: Effects on cooperation and acceptance. *School Psychology Quarterly, 15,* 30–39.

Jones, M. G. (1990). Action zone theory, target students, and science classroom interactions. *Journal of Research in Science Teaching, 27,* 651–660.

Jones, V. (2006). How do teachers learn to be effective classroom managers? In C. M. Evertson & C. S. Weinstein (Eds.), *Handbook of classroom management: Research, practice, and contemporary issues* (pp. 897–907). Mahwah, NJ: Erlbaum.

Joseph, L. M. (1998–1999). Word boxes help children with learning disabilities identify and spell words. *Reading Teacher, 52,* 348–356.

Joseph, L. M. (2000a). Developing first-graders' phonemic awareness, word identification and spelling: A comparison of two contemporary phonic instructional approaches. *Reading Research and Instruction, 39,* 160–169.

Joseph, L. M. (2000b). Using word boxes as a large group phonics approach in a first grade classroom. *Reading Horizons, 41,* 117–127.

Joseph, L. M. (2002). Facilitating word recognition and spelling using word boxes and word sort phonic procedures. *School Psychology Review, 31,* 122–129.

Kahle, A. L., & Kelley, M. L. (1994). Children's homework problems: A comparison of goal-setting and parent training. *Behavior Therapy, 25,* 275–290.

Kahng, S., & Iwata, B. A. (1998). Computerized systems for collecting real-time observational data. *Journal of Applied Behavior Analysis, 31,* 253–261.

Kame'enui, E. J., & Simmons, D. C. (Eds.). (2001). The role of fluency in reading competence, assessment, and instruction: Fluency at the intersection of accuracy and speed [Special issue]. *Scientific Studies of Reading, 5*(1).

Kamins, M. L., & Dweck, C. S. (1999). Person versus process praise and criticism: Implications for contingent self-worth and coping. *Developmental Psychology, 35,* 835–847.

Kaminski, R. A., & Good, R. H. (1996). Toward a technology for assessing basic early literacy skills. *School Psychology Review, 25,* 215–227.

Kamps, D., Greenwood, C. R., & Leonard, B. (1991). Ecobehavioral assessment in classrooms serving children with autism and developmental disabilities. In R. J. Prinz (Ed.), *Advances in behavioral assessment of children and families* (pp. 203–237). New York: Jessica Kingsley.

Kartub, D. T., Taylor-Greene, S., March, R. E., & Horner, R. H. (2000). Reducing hallway noise: A systems approach. *Journal of Positive Behavior Interventions, 2,* 179–182.

Kavale, K. A., & Forness, S. R. (1999). Effectiveness of special education. In T. B. Gutkin & C. R. Reynolds (Eds.), *The handbook of school psychology* (3rd ed., pp. 984–1024). New York: Wiley.

Kehle, T. J., Madaus, M. M., Baratta, V. S., & Bray, M. A. (1998). Augmented self-modeling as a treatment for children with selective mutism. *Journal of School Psychology, 36,* 247–260.

Keith, T. Z., Diamond-Hallam, C., & Fine, J. G. (2004). Longitudinal effects of in-school and out-of-school homework on high school grades. *School Psychology Quarterly, 19,* 187–211.

Kellam, S. G., Ling, X., Merisca, R., Brown, C. H., & Ialongo, N. (1998). The effect of the level of aggression in the first grade classroom on the course and malleability of aggressive behavior into middle school. *Development and Psychopathology, 10,* 165–185.

Kellam, S. G., Rebok, G. W., Ialongo, N. S., & Mayer, L. S. (1994). The course and malleability of aggressive behavior from early first grade into middle school: Results of a developmental epidemiology-based preventive trial. *Journal of Child Psychology and Psychiatry, 35,* 259–281.

Kelshaw-Levering, K., Sterling-Turner, H. E., Henry, J. R., & Skinner, C. H. (2000). Randomized interdependent group contingencies: Group reinforcement with a twist. *Psychology in the Schools, 37,* 523–533.

Kern, L., Dunlap, G., Childs, K. E., & Clarke, S. (1994). Use of a classwide self-management program to improve the behavior of students with emotional and behavioral disorders. *Education and Treatment of Children, 17,* 445–458.

Killu, K., Sainato, D. M., Davis, C. A., Ospelt, H., & Paul, J. N. (1998). Effects of high-probability request sequences on preschoolers' compliance and disruptive behavior. *Journal of Behavioral Education, 8,* 347–368.

Kim, A., Vaughn, S., Wanzek, J., & Wei, S. (2004). Graphic organizers and their effects on the reading comprehension of students with LD: A synthesis of research. *Journal of Learning Disabilities, 37,* 105–118.

Klem, A. M., & Connell, J. P. (2004). Relationships matter: Linking teacher support to student engagement and achievement. *Journal of School Health, 74,* 262–273.

Klingner, J. K., Ahwee, S., Pilonieta, P., & Menendez, R. (2003). Barriers and facilitators in scaling up research-based practices. *Exceptional Children, 69,* 411–429.

Klingner, J. K., & Artiles, A. J. (2006). English language learners struggling to learn to read: Emerging scholarship on linguistic differences and learning disabilities. *Journal of Learning Disabilities, 39,* 386–389.

Klingner, J. K., & Harry, B. (2006). The special education referral and decision-making process for English language learners: Child study team meetings and placement conferences. *Elementary School Journal, 108,* 2247–2281.

Klingner, J. K., & Vaughn, S. (1996). Reciprocal teaching of reading comprehension strategies for students with learning disabilities who use English as a second language. *Elementary School Journal, 96,* 275–293.

Klingner, J. K., Vaughn, S., Arguelles, M. E., Hughes,

M. T., & Leftwich, S. A. (1999). Collaborative strategic reading: "Real-world" lessons from classroom teachers. *Remedial and Special Education, 25,* 291–302.

Klingner, J. K., Vaughn, S., Hughes, M. T., & Arguelles, M. E. (1999). Sustaining research-based practices in reading: A 3-year follow-up. *Remedial and Special Education, 20,* 262–274, 287.

Klingner, J. K., Vaughn, S., & Schumm, J. S. (1998). Collaborative strategic reading during social studies in heterogeneous fourth-grade classrooms. *Elementary School Journal, 99,* 3–22.

Kohn, A. (1993). *Punished by rewards: The trouble with gold stars, incentive plans, A's, praise, and other bribes.* New York: Houghton Mifflin.

Kohn, A. (1996). By all available means: Cameron and Pierce's defense of extrinsic motivators. *Review of Educational Research, 66,* 1–4.

Kovaleski, J. F. (2002). Best practices in operating pre-referral intervention teams. In A. Thomas & J. Grimes (Eds.), *Best practices in school psychology IV* (Vol. 1, pp. 645–655). Bethesda, MD: National Association of School Psychologists.

Kovaleski, J. F., Gickling, E. E., Morrow, H., & Swank, P. R. (1999). High versus low implementation of instructional support teams: A case for maintaining program fidelity. *Remedial and Special Education, 20,* 170–183.

Kovaleski, J. F., Tucker, J., & Stevens, L. (1996). Bridging special and regular education: The Pennsylvania Initiative. *Educational Leadership, 53*(5), 44–47.

Kratochwill, T. R., Elliott, S. N., & Callan-Stoiber, K. (2002). Best practices in school-based problem-solving consultation. In A. Thomas & J. Grimes (Eds.), *Best practices in school psychology IV* (Vol. 1, pp. 583–608). Bethesda, MD: National Association of School Psychologists.

Kratochwill, T. R., & Shernoff, E. S. (2004). Evidence-based practice: Promoting evidence-based interventions in school psychology. *School Psychology Quarterly, 18,* 389–408.

Kratochwill, T. R., & Stoiber, K. C. (2000a). Diversifying theory and science: Expanding the boundaries of empirically supported interventions in school psychology. *Journal of School Psychology, 38,* 349–358.

Kratochwill, T. R., & Stoiber, K. C. (2000b). Empirically supported interventions and school psychology: Conceptual and practical issues—Part II. *School Psychology Quarterly, 15,* 233–253.

Kratochwill, T. R., & Stoiber, K. C. (2002). Evidence-based interventions in school psychology: Conceptual foundations of the *Procedural and Coding Manual* of Division 16 and the Society for the Study of School Psychology Task Force. *School Psychology Quarterly, 17,* 341–389.

Kroesbergen, E. H., & Van Luit, J. E. H. (2003). Mathematics interventions for children with special educational needs: A meta-analysis. *Remedial and Special Education, 24,* 97–114.

Kruger, L. J., Struzziero, J., Watts, R., & Vacca, D. (1995). The relationship between organizational support and satisfaction with teacher assistance teams. *Remedial and Special Education, 16,* 203–211.

Kupersmidt, J. B., Bryant, D., & Willoughby, M. T. (2002). Prevalence of aggressive behaviors among preschoolers in Head Start and community care programs. *Behavioral Disorders, 26,* 42–52.

Lacourse, E., Cote, S., Nagin, D. S., Vitaro, F., Brendgan, M., & Tremblay, R. E. (2002). A longitudinal-experimental approach to testing theories of antisocial behavior development. *Development and Psychopathology, 14,* 909–924.

Ladd, G. W., & Burgess, K. B. (2001). Do relational risks and protective factors moderate the linkages between childhood aggression and early psychological and school adjustment? *Child Development, 72,* 1579–1601.

LaFleur, L., Witt, J. C., Naquin, G., Harwell, V., & Gilbertson, D. M. (1998). Use of coaching to enhance proactive classroom management by improvement of student transitioning between classroom activities. *Effective School Practices, 17,* 70–82.

Lalli, J. S., Kates, K., & Casey, S. D. (1999). Response covariation: The relationship between correct academic responding and problem behavior. *Behavior Modification, 23,* 339–357.

Lane, K. L. (1999). Young students at risk for antisocial behavior: The utility of academic and social skills interventions. *Journal of Emotional and Behavioral Disorders, 7,* 211–223.

Lane, K. L., Beebe-Frankenberger, M. E., Lambros, K. M., & Pierson, M. (2001). Designing effective interventions for children at-risk for antisocial behavior: An integrated model of components necessary for making valid inferences. *Psychology in the Schools, 38,* 365–379.

Lane, K. L., Givner, C. C., & Pierson, M. R. (2005). Teacher expectations of student behavior: Social skills necessary for success in elementary school classrooms. *Journal of Special Education, 38,* 104–110.

Lane, K. L., Mahdavi, J. N., & Borthwick-Duffy, S. (2003). Teacher perceptions of the prereferral intervention process: A call for assistance with school-based interventions. *Preventing School Failure, 47,* 148–155.

Lane, K. L., & Menzies, H. M. (2003). A school-wide intervention with primary and secondary levels of support for elementary students: Outcomes and considerations. *Education and Treatment of Children, 26,* 431–451.

Lane, K. L., O'Shaughnessy, T. E., Lambros, K. M., Gresham, F. M., & Beebe-Frankenberger, M. E. (2001). The efficacy of phonological awareness training with first-grade students who have behavior problems and reading difficulties. *Journal of Emotional and Behavioral Disorders, 9,* 219–231.

Lane, K. L., Wehby, J. H., Menzies, H. M., Gregg, R. M., Doukos, G. L., & Munton, S. M. (2002). Early literacy instruction for first-grade students at-risk for antisocial behavior. *Education and Treatment of Children, 25,* 438–458.

La Paro, K. M., & Pianta, R. C. (2000). Predicting children's competence in the early school years: A meta-analytic review. *Review of Educational Research, 70,* 443–484.

Larrivee, L. S., & Catts, H. W. (1999). Early reading achievement in children with expressive phonological disorders. *American Journal of Speech–Language Pathology, 8,* 118–128.

Lassen, S. R., Steele, M. M., & Sailor, W. (2006). The relationship of school-wide positive behavior support to academic achievement in an urban middle school. *Psychology in the Schools, 43,* 701–712.

Lavigne, J. V., Arend, R., Rosenbaum, D., Binns, H. J., Christoffel, K. K., & Gibbons, R. D. (1998). Psychiatric disorders with onset in the preschool years: 1. Stability of diagnoses. *Journal of the American Academy of Child and Adolescent Psychiatry, 37,* 1246–1254.

Law, M., & Kratochwill, T. R. (1993). Paired reading: An evaluation of a parent tutorial program. *School Psychology International, 14,* 119–147.

Learning Disabilities Roundtable. (2002). *Specific learning disabilities: Finding common ground.* Washington, DC: U.S. Department of Education, Office of Special Education Programs, Office of Innovation and Development.

Lebzelter, S., & Nowacek, E. J. (1999). Reading strategies for secondary students with mild disabilities. *Intervention in School and Clinic, 34,* 212–219.

Lee, M. J., & Tingstrom, D. H. (1994). A group math intervention: The modification of Cover, Copy, and Compare for group application. *Psychology in the Schools, 31,* 133–145.

Leff, S. S., & Lakin, R. (2005). Playground-based observational systems: A review and implications for practitioners and researchers. *School Psychology Review, 34,* 475–489.

Leff, S. S., Power, T. J., Costigan, T. E., & Manz, P. H. (2003). Assessing the climate of the playground and lunchroom: Implications for bullying prevention programming. *School Psychology Review, 32,* 418–430.

Lembke, E., Deno, S. L., & Hall, K. (2003). Identifying an indicator of growth in early writing proficiency for elementary school students. *Assessment for Effective Intervention, 28,* 23–36.

Lentz, F. E. Jr., Allen, S. J., & Ehrhardt, K. E. (1996). The conceptual elements of strong interventions in school settings. *School Psychology Quarterly, 11,* 118–136.

Lenz, B. K., & Hughes, C. A. (1990). A word identification strategy for adolescents with learning disabilities. *Journal of Learning Disabilities, 23,* 149–158, 163.

Lepper, M. R., Keavney, M., & Drake, M. (1996). Intrinsic motivation and extrinsic rewards: A commentary on Cameron and Pierce's meta-analysis. *Review of Educational Research, 66,* 5–32.

Leslie, L., & Caldwell, J. (2006). *Qualitative Reading Inventory* (4th ed.). New York: Pearson Education.

Levy, B. A., Nicholls, A., & Kohen, D. (1993). Repeated reading: Process benefits for good and poor readers. *Journal of Experimental Child Psychology, 56,* 303–327.

Levy, S., & Vaughn, S. (2002). An observational study of teachers' reading instruction of students with emotional or behavioral disorders. *Behavioral Disorders, 27,* 215–235.

Lewis, B. A., Freebairn, L. A., & Taylor, H. G. (2000). Academic outcomes in children with histories of speech sound disorders. *Journal of Communication Disorders, 33,* 11–30.

Lewis, R. (2001). Classroom discipline and student responsibility: The students' view. *Teaching and Teacher Education, 17,* 307–319.

Lewis, T. J., Colvin, G., & Sugai, G. (2000). The effects of pre-correction and active supervision on the recess behavior of elementary school students. *Education and Treatment of Children, 23,* 109–121.

Lewis, T. J., Newcomer, L. L., Trussell, R., & Richter, M. (2006). Schoolwide positive behavior support: Building systems to develop and maintain appropriate social behavior. In C. M. Evertson & C. S. Weinstein (Eds.), *Handbook of classroom management: Research, practice, and contemporary issues* (pp. 833–854). Mahwah, NJ: Erlbaum.

Lewis, T. J., Powers, L. J., Kelk, M. J., & Newcomer, L. L. (2002). Reducing problem behaviors on the playground: An investigation of the application of schoolwide positive behavior supports. *Psychology in the Schools, 39,* 181–190.

Lewis, T. J., & Sugai, G. (1999). Effective behavior support: A systems approach to proactive schoolwide management. *Focus on Exceptional Children, 31*(6), 1–24.

Lewis, T. J., Sugai, G., & Colvin, G. (1998). Reducing problem behavior through a school-wide system of effective behavioral support: Investigation of a school-wide social skills training program and contextual interventions. *School Psychology Review, 27,* 446–459.

Lindo, E. J. (2006). The African American presence in reading intervention experiments. *Remedial and Special Education, 27,* 148–153.

Little, E., Hudson, A., & Wilks, R. (2002). The efficacy of written teacher advice (tip sheets) for managing classroom behaviour problems. *Educational Psychology, 22,* 251–266.

Lo, Y., Loe, S. A., & Cartledge, C. (2002). The effects

of social skills instruction on the social behaviors of students at risk for emotional or behavioral disorders. *Behavioral Disorders, 27,* 371–385.

LoCasale-Crouch, J., Konold, T., Pianta, R., Howes, C., Burchinal, M., Bryant, D., et al. (2007). Observed classroom quality profiles in state-funded pre-kindergarten programs and associations with teacher, program, and classroom characteristics. *Early Childhood Research Quarterly, 22,* 3–17.

Loeber, R., & Stouthamer-Loeber, M. (1998). Development of juvenile aggression and violence: Some common misconceptions and controversies. *American Psychologist, 53,* 242–252.

Logan, K. R., Bakeman, R., & Keefe, E. B. (1997). Effects of instructional variables on engaged behavior of students with disabilities in general education classrooms. *Exceptional Children, 63,* 481–498.

Lonigan, C. J., & Whitehurst, G. J. (1998). Relative efficacy of parent and teacher involvement in a shared-reading intervention for preschool children from low-income backgrounds. *Early Childhood Research Quarterly, 13,* 263–290.

Lou, Y., Abrami, P. C., & Spence, J. C. (2000). Effects of within-class grouping on student achievement: An exploratory model. *Journal of Educational Research, 94,* 101–113.

Luiselli, J. K., Putnam, R. F., Handler, M. W., & Feinberg, A. B. (2005). Whole-school positive behaviour support: Effects on student discipline problems and academic performance. *Educational Psychology, 25,* 183–198.

Lyon, G. R. (1996). Learning disabilities. *The Future of Children: Special Education for Students with Disabilities, 6,* 54–76.

Lyon, G. R., Fletcher, J. M., Shaywitz, S. E., Shaywitz, B. A., Torgesen, J. K., Wood, F. B., et al. (2001). Rethinking learning disabilities. In C. E. Finn Jr., A. J. Rotherham, & C. R. Hokanson Jr. (Eds.), *Rethinking special education for a new century* (pp. 259–287). Washington, DC: Thomas B. Fordham Foundation.

Maag, J. W. (2001). Rewarded by punishment: Reflections on the disuse of positive reinforcement in schools. *Exceptional Children, 67,* 173–186.

Maccini, P., & Hughes, C. A. (1997). Mathematics interventions for adolescents with learning disabilities. *Learning Disabilities Research and Practice, 12,* 168–176.

Mace, F. C., & Heller, M. (1990). A comparison of exclusion time-out and contingent observation for reducing severe disruptive behavior in a 7-year-old boy. *Child and Family Behavior Therapy, 12,* 57–68.

Mackay, S., McLaughlin, T. F., Weber, K., & Derby, K. M. (2001). The use of precision requests to decrease noncompliance in the home and neighborhood: A case study. *Child and Family Behavior Therapy, 23,* 43–52.

Madaus, M. M. R., Kehle, T. J., Madaus, J., & Bray, M. A. (2003). Mystery motivator as an intervention to promote homework completion and accuracy. *School Psychology International, 24,* 369–377.

Magnuson, K. A., Ruhm, C., & Waldfogel, J. (2007). The persistence of preschool effects: Do subsequent classroom experiences matter? *Early Childhood Research Quarterly, 22,* 18–38.

Maleki, C. K., & Elliott, S. N. (2002). Children's social behaviors as predictors of academic achievement: A longitudinal analysis. *School Psychology Quarterly, 17,* 1–23.

Maleki, C. K., & Jewell, J. (2003). Developmental, gender, and practical considerations in scoring: Curriculum-based measurement writing probes. *Psychology in the Schools, 40,* 379–390.

Malone, B. G., & Tietjens, C. L. (2000). Re-examination of classroom rules: The need for clarity and specified behavior. *Special Services in the Schools, 16,* 159–170.

Malone, L. D., & Mastropieri, M. A. (1992). Reading comprehension instruction: Summarization and self-monitoring training for students with learning disabilities. *Exceptional Children, 58,* 270–279.

Malone, R. A., & McLaughlin, T. F. (1997). The effects of reciprocal peer tutoring with a group contingency on quiz performance in vocabulary with seventh- and eighth-grade students. *Behavioral Interventions, 12,* 27–40.

Marcus, B. A., & Vollmer, T. R. (1996). Combining noncontingent reinforcement and differential reinforcement schedules as treatment for aberrant behavior. *Journal of Applied Behavior Analysis, 29,* 43–51.

Margolis, H., & McCabe, P. P. (1997). Homework challenges for students with reading and writing problems: Suggestions for effective practice. *Journal of Educational and Psychological Consultation, 8,* 41–74.

Marks, E. S. (1995). *Entry strategies for school consultation.* New York: Guilford Press.

Marston, D. B. (1989). A curriculum-based measurement approach to assessing academic performance: What it is and why do it. In M. R. Shinn (Ed.), *Curriculum-based measurement: Assessing special children* (pp. 18–78). New York: Guilford Press.

Marston, D., Deno, S. L., Kim, D., Diment, K., & Rogers, D. (1995). Comparison of reading intervention approaches for students with mild disabilities. *Exceptional Children, 62,* 20–37.

Martella, R. C., Leonard, I. J., Marchand-Martella, N., & Agran, M. (1993). Self-monitoring negative statements. *Journal of Behavioral Education, 3,* 77–86.

Martens, B. K., & Hiralall, A. S. (1997). Scripted sequences of teacher interaction: A versatile, low-impact procedure for increasing appropriate behavior in a nursery school. *Behavior Modification, 21,* 308–323.

Martens, B. K., Hiralall, A. S., & Bradley, T. A. (1997). A note to teacher: Improving student behavior through goal setting and feedback. *School Psychology Quarterly, 12,* 33–41.

Martens, B. K., & Witt, J. C. (2004). Competence, persistence and success: The positive psychology of behavioral skill instruction. *Psychology in the Schools, 41,* 19–30.

Martens, B. K., Witt, J. C., Elliott, S. N., & Darveaux, D. X. (1985). Teacher judgments concerning the acceptability of school-based interventions. *Professional Psychology: Research and Practice, 16,* 191–198.

Martens, B. K., Witt, J. C., Daly, E. J. III, & Vollmer, T. R. (1999). Behavior analysis: Theory and practice in educational settings. In C. R. Reynolds & T. B. Gutkin (Eds.), *Handbook of school psychology* (3rd ed., pp. 638–663). New York: Wiley.

Marzano, R. J., Pickering, D. J., & Pollack, J. E. (2001). *Classroom instruction that works: Research-based strategies for increasing student achievement.* Alexandria, VA: Association for Supervision and Curriculum Development.

Marx, A., Fuhrer, U., & Hartig, T. (1999). Effects of classroom seating arrangements on children's question-asking. *Learning Environments Research, 2,* 249–263.

Mason, L. H. (2004). Explicit self-regulated strategy development versus reciprocal questioning: Effect on expository reading comprehension among struggling readers. *Journal of Educational Psychology, 96,* 283–296.

Mason, L. H., Harris, K. R., & Graham, S. (2002). Every child has a story to tell: Self-regulated strategy development for story writing. *Education and Treatment of Children, 25,* 496–506.

Mastropieri, M. A., & Scruggs, T. E. (1997). Best practices in promoting reading comprehension in students with learning disabilities: 1976 to 1996. *Remedial and Special Education, 18,* 197–213.

Mastropieri, M. A., Scruggs, T. E., & Magnusen, M. (1999). Reading comprehension instruction for secondary students: Challenges for struggling students and teachers. *Learning Disability Quarterly, 26,* 103–116.

Mastropieri, M. A., Scruggs, T. E., Spencer, V., & Fontana, J. (2003). Promoting success in high school world history: Peer tutoring versus guided notes. *Learning Disabilities Research and Practice, 18,* 52–65.

Mathes, P. G., Fuchs, D., & Fuchs, L. S. (1997). Cooperative story mapping. *Remedial and Special Education, 18,* 20–27.

Mathes, P. G., Fuchs, D., Fuchs, L. S., Henley, A. M., & Sanders, A. (1994). Increasing strategic reading practice with Peabody Classwide Peer Tutoring. *Learning Disabilities Research and Practice, 9,* 44–48.

Matheson, A. S., & Shriver, M. D. (2005). Training teachers to give effective commands: Effects on student compliance and academic behaviors. *School Psychology Review, 34,* 202–219.

Mathur, S. R., Kavale, K. A., Quinn, M. M., Forness, S. R., & Rutherford, R. B. (1998). Social skills interventions with students with emotional and behavioral problems: A quantitative synthesis of single-subject research. *Behavioral Disorders, 23,* 193–201.

Mathur, S. R., & Rutherford, R. B. (1996). Is social skills training effective for students with emotional or behavioral problems? Research issues and needs. *Behavioral Disorders, 22,* 21–28.

Matsumura, K. C., Patthey-Chavez, G. G., Valdés, R., & Garnier, H. (2002). Teacher feedback, writing assignment quality, and third-grade students' revision in lower- and higher-achieving urban schools. *Elementary School Journal, 103,* 3–25.

McAuley, S. M., & McLaughlin, T. F. (1992). Comparison of Add-A-Word and Compuspell Programs with low-achieving students. *Journal of Educational Research, 85,* 362–369.

McCabe, P. C. (2005). Social and behavioral correlates of preschoolers with specific language impairment. *Psychology in the Schools, 42,* 373–387.

McCandliss, B., Beck, I. L., Sandak, R., & Perfetti, C. (2003). Focusing attention on decoding for children with poor reading skills: Design and preliminary tests of the word building intervention. *Scientific Studies of Reading, 7,* 75–104.

McClelland, M. M., Acock, A. C., & Morrison, F. J. (2006). The impact of kindergarten learning-related skills on academic trajectories at the end of elementary school. *Early Childhood Research Quarterly, 21,* 471–490.

McClelland, M. M., Morrison, F. J., & Holmes, D. L. (2000). Children at risk for early academic problems: The role of learning-related social skills. *Early Childhood Research Quarterly, 15,* 307–329.

McCloskey, D., & Athanasiou, M. S. (2000). Assessment and intervention practices with second-language learners among school psychologists. *Psychology in the Schools, 37,* 209–225.

McConnell, M. E., McEnvoy, M. A., & Priest, J. S. (2002). "Growing" measures for monitoring progress in early childhood education: A research and development process for individual growth and development indicators. *Assessment for Effective Intervention, 27,* 3–14.

McConnell, M. E., Priest, J. S., Davis, S. D., & McEnvoy, M. A. (2002). Best practices in measuring growth and development in preschool children. In A. Thomas & J. Grimes (Eds.), *Best practices in school psychology IV* (Vol. 2, pp. 1231–1246). Bethesda, MD: National Association of School Psychologists.

McCurdy, B. L., Mannella, M. C., & Eldridge,

N. (2003). Positive behavior support in urban schools: Can we prevent the escalation of antisocial behavior? *Journal of Positive Behavioral Interventions, 5,* 158–170.

McCutchen, D., Abbott, R. D., Green, L. B., Beretvas, S. N., Cox, S., Potter, N. S., et al. (2002). Beginning literacy: Links among teacher knowledge, teacher practice, and student learning. *Journal of Learning Disabilities, 35,* 69–86.

McDonnell, J., Thorson, N., Allen, C., & Mathot-Buckner, C. (2000). The effects of partner learning during spelling for students with severe disabilities and their peers. *Journal of Behavioral Education, 10,* 107–121.

McDougal, J. L., Clonan, S. M., & Martens, B. K. (2000). Using organizational change procedures to promote the acceptability of prereferral intervention services: The School-Based Intervention Team Project. *School Psychology Quarterly, 15,* 149–171.

McEnvoy, M. A., Fox, J. J., & Rosenberg, M. S. (1991). Organizing preschool environments: Suggestions for enhancing the development/learning of preschool children with handicaps. *Topics in Early Childhood Special Education, 11*(2), 18–28.

McGill-Franzen, A., & Allington, R. L. (1991). Every child's right: Literacy. *Reading Teacher, 45,* 86–90.

McGinnis, J. C., Frederick, B. P., & Edwards, R. (1995). Enhancing classroom management through proactive rules and procedures. *Psychology in the Schools, 32,* 220–224.

McGlinchey, M. T., & Hixson, M. D. (2004). Using curriculum-based measurement to predict performance on state assessments in reading. *School Psychology Review, 33,* 193–203.

McGoey, K. E., & DuPaul, G. J. (2000). Token reinforcement and response cost procedures: Reducing the disruptive behavior of preschool children with attention-deficit/hyperactivity disorder. *School Psychology Quarterly, 15,* 330–343.

McIntosh, K., Horner, R. H., Chard, D. J., Boland, J. B., & Good, R. H. (2006). The use of reading and behavior screening measures to predict response to school-wide positive behavior support: A longitudinal analysis. *School Psychology Review, 35,* 275–291.

McIntyre, T. C., & Brulle, A. R. (1989). The effectiveness of various types of teacher directions with students labeled behavior disordered. *Academic Therapy, 25,* 123–131.

McLaughlin, T. F., Reiter, S. M., Mabee, W. S., & Byram, B. J. (1991). An analysis and replication of the Add-A-Word Spelling Program with mildly handicapped middle school students. *Journal of Behavioral Education, 1,* 413–426.

McNamara, K. (2002). Best practices in promotion of social competence in schools. In A. Thomas & J. Grimes (Eds.), *Best practices in school psy-chology IV* (Vol. 2, pp. 911–927). Bethesda, MD: National Association of School Psychologists.

McNamara, K. M., & Hollinger, C. L. (1997). Intervention-based assessment: Rates of evaluation and eligibility for specific learning disability classification. *Psychological Reports, 81,* 620–622.

McNamara, K. M., & Hollinger, C. L. (2003). Intervention-based assessment: Evaluation rates and eligibility findings. *Exceptional Children, 69*(2), 181–193.

McNamara, K. M., Telzrow, C., & DeLamatre, J. (1999). Parent reactions to implementation of intervention-based assessment. *Journal of Educational and Psychological Consultation, 10,* 343–362.

McNeil, C. B., Capage, L. C., Bahl, A., & Blanc, H. (1999). Importance of early intervention for disruptive behavior problems: Comparison of treatment and waitlist-control group. *Early Education and Development, 10,* 162–181.

Meehan, B. T., Hughes, J. N., & Cavell, T. A. (2003). Teacher–student relationships as compensatory resources for aggressive children. *Child Development, 74,* 1145–1157.

Menlo, A., & Johnson, M. C. (1971). The use of percentage gain as a means toward the assessment of individual achievement. *California Journal of Educational Research, 22,* 193–201.

Merrell, K. W., Johnson, E. R., Merz, J. M., & Ring, E. N. (1992). Social competence of students with mild handicaps and low achievement: A comparative study. *School Psychology Review, 21,* 125–137.

Meyer, M. S. (2000). The ability-achievement discrepancy: Does it contribute to an understanding of learning disabilities? *Educational Psychology Review, 12,* 315–337.

Meyer, M. S., & Felton, R. H. (1999). Repeated reading to enhance fluency: Old approaches and new directions. *Annals of Dyslexia, 49,* 283–306.

Meyers, B., Valentino, C. T., Meyers, J., Boretti, M., & Brent, D. (1996). Implementing prereferral intervention teams as an approach to school-based consultation in an urban school setting. *Journal of Educational and Psychological Consultation, 7,* 119–149.

Miller, B. V., & Kratochwill, T. R. (1996). An evaluation of the paired reading program using competency-based training. *School Psychology International, 17,* 269–291.

Miller, D. L., & Kelley, M. L. (1994). The use of goal setting and contingency contracting for improving children's homework performance. *Journal of Applied Behavior Analysis, 27,* 73–84.

Miller, L. J., Strain, P. S., Boyd, K., Jarzynka, J., & McFetrideg, M. (1993). The effects of classwide self-assessment on preschool children's engagement in transition, free play, and small-group instruction. *Early Education and Development, 4,* 162–181.

Missall, K. N., & McConnell, S. R. (2004). *Psycho-metric characteristics of individual growth and development indicators: Picture naming, rhyming, and alliteration.* University of Minnesota, Center for Early Education and Development, Minneapolis, MN. Retrieved March 7, 2006, from *http://ggg.umn.edu/techreports/ecri_report8.html*.

Mitchem, K. J., Young, K. R., West, R. P., & Benyo, J. (2001). CWPASM: A classwide peer-assisted self-management program for general education classrooms. *Education and Treatment of Children, 24,* 111–140.

Moats, L. C. (1995). *Spelling: Development, disability, and instruction.* Baltimore: York Press.

Moats, L. C. (2001). When older students can't read. *Educational Leadership, 58,* 36–40.

Montague, M. (1997). Cognitive strategy instruction in mathematics for students with learning disabilities. *Journal of Learning Disabilities, 30,* 164–177.

Moody, S. W., Vaughn, S., Hughes, M. T., & Fischer, M. (2000). Reading instruction in the resource room: Set up for failure. *Exceptional Children, 66,* 305–316.

Moody, S. W., Vaughn, S., & Schumm, J. S. (1997). Instructional grouping for reading. *Remedial and Special Education, 18,* 347–356.

Mooney, P., Ryan, J. B., Uhing, J. B., Reid, R., & Epstein, M. H. (2005). A review of self-management interventions targeting academic outcomes for students with emotional and behavioral disorders. *Journal of Behavioral Education, 14,* 203–221.

Moore, L. A., Waguespack, A. M., Wickstrom, K. F., Witt, J. C., & Gaydos, G. R. (1994). Mystery motivator: An effective and time-efficient intervention. *School Psychology Review, 23,* 106–118.

Moroz, K. B., & Jones, K. M (2002). The effects of positive peer reporting on children's social involvement. *School Psychology Review, 31,* 235–245.

Morris, D., Blanton, L., Blanton, W. E., & Perney, J. (1995). Spelling achievement in six classrooms. *Elementary School Journal, 96,* 145–162.

Morrow, L. M., Reutzel, D. R., & Casey, H. (2006). Organization and management of language arts teaching: Classroom environments, grouping practices and exemplary instruction. In C. M. Evertson & C. S. Weinstein (Eds.), *Handbook of classroom management: Research, practice, and contemporary issues* (pp. 559–581). Mahwah, NJ: Erlbaum.

Mortenson, B. P., & Witt, J. C. (1998). The use of weekly performance feedback to increase teacher implementation of a prereferral academic intervention. *School Psychology Review, 27,* 613–627.

Mortweet, S. L., Utley, C. A., Walker, D., Dawson, H. L., Delquadri, J. C., Reddy, S. S., et al. (1999). Classwide peer tutoring: Teaching students with mild mental retardation in inclusive classrooms. *Exceptional Children, 65,* 524–536.

Mottram, L. M., Bray, M. A., Kehle, T. J., Broudy, M., & Jenson, W. R. (2002). A classroom-based intervention to reduce disruptive behavior. *Journal of Applied School Psychology, 19,* 65–74.

Mueller, C. M., & Dweck, C. S. (1998). Praise for intelligence can undermine children's motivation for performance. *Journal of Personality and Social Psychology, 75,* 33–52.

Murphy, K. A., Theodore, L. A., Aloiso, D., Alric-Edwards, J. M., & Hughes, T. L. (2007). Interdependent group contingency and mystery motivators to reduce preschool disruptive behavior. *Psychology in the Schools, 44,* 53–63.

Murray, C., & Greenberg, M. T. (2001). Relationships with teachers and bonds with school: Social emotional adjustment correlates for children with and without disabilities. *Psychology in the Schools, 38,* 25–41.

Musser, E. H., Bray, M. A., Kehle, T. J., & Jenson, W. R. (2001). Reducing disruptive behaviors in students with serious emotional disturbance. *School Psychology Review, 30,* 294–304.

Muyskens, P., & Ysseldyke, J. E. (1998). Student academic responding time as a function of classroom ecology and time of day. *Journal of Special Education, 31,* 411–424.

Myers, V. M., & Kline, C. E. (2002). Secondary school intervention assistance teams: Can they be effective? *High School Journal, 85*(2), 33–42.

Myles, B. S., Simpson, R. L., & Ormsbee, C. K. (1996). Teachers' perceptions of the effectiveness of preassessment for students with behavior and learning problems. *Preventing School Failure, 41,* 14–19.

Narayan, J. S., Heward, W. L., Gardner, R. III, Courson, F. H., & Omness, C. K. (1990). Using response cards to increase student participation in an elementary classroom. *Journal of Applied Behavior Analysis, 23,* 483–490.

Nastasi, B. K., & Truscott, S. D. (2000). Acceptability research in school psychology: Current trends and future directions. *School Psychology Quarterly, 15,* 117–122.

National Association of School Psychologists. (2000). *Professional conduct manual:* Bethesda, MD: Author. Available online at *http://www.naspweb.org*.

National Center for Children in Poverty. (2006). *Basic facts about low-income children: Birth to age 6.* New York: Columbia University Mailman School of Public Health, National Center for Children in Poverty. Retrieved November 26, 2006, from *http://www.nccp.org/pub_ycp06b.html*.

National Center for Education Statistics. (2003). *The nation's report card: Writing 2002* (NCES 2003-529). Washington, DC: U.S. Department of Education. Retrieved May 23, 2005, from *http://nces.ed.gov/nationsreportcard/writing/*.

National Center for Education Statistics. (2004a). *Highlights from the trends in international mathematics and science study (TIMSS) 2003* (NCES

2005-005). Washington, DC: U.S. Department of Education. Retrieved August 15, 2006, from *http://nces.ed.gov/timss/*.

National Center for Education Statistics. (2004b). *NAEP 2004 trends in academic progress: Three decades of student performance in reading and mathematics* (NCES 2005-464). Washington, DC: U.S. Department of Education. Retrieved May 15, 2006, from *http://nces.ed.gov/pubsearch/pubsinfo.asp?pubid=2005464*.

National Center for Education Statistics. (2005). *The nation's report card: Reading 2005* (NCES 2006-451). Washington, DC: U.S. Department of Education. Retrieved April 14, 2006, from *http://nces.ed.gov/nationsreportcard/reading/*.

National Center for Education Statistics. (2006a). *The nation's report card: Mathematics 2005* (NCES 2006-453). Washington, DC: National Center for Educational Statistics. Retrieved May 17, 2007, from *http://nces.ed.gov/nationsreportcard/pdf/main2005/2006453.pdf*.

National Center for Education Statistics. (2006b). *The nation's report card: Science 2005* (NCES 2006-466). Washington, DC: U.S. Department of Education. Retrieved May 13, 2006, from *http://nces.ed.gov/nationsreportcard/science/*.

National Center for Education Statistics. (2007a). *The condition of education 2007* (NCES 2007-064). Washington, DC: U.S. Department of Education, Institute of Education Sciences. Retrieved June 1, 2007, from *http://nces.ed.gov/programs/coe/*.

National Center for Education Statistics. (2007b). *The nation's report card: Civics 2006* (NCES 2007-476). Washington, DC: National Center for Educational Statistics. Retrieved May 17, 2007, from *http://nces.ed.gov/nationsreportcard/ushistory*.

National Center for Education Statistics. (2007c). *The nation's report card: 12th-grade reading and math–2005* (NCES 2007-468). Washington, DC: U.S. Department of Education. Retrieved February 24, 2007, from *http://nces.ed.gov/nationsreportcard/pdf/main2005/2007468.pdf*.

National Center for Education Statistics. (2007d). *The nation's report card: U.S. History 2006* (NCES 2007-474). Washington, DC: National Center for Educational Statistics. Retrieved May 17, 2007, from *http://nces.ed.gov/nationsreportcard/ushistory*.

National Commission on Writing. (2003). *The neglected R: The need for a writing revolution.* Washington, DC: U.S. Department of Education. Retrieved March 3, 2007, from *http://www.writingcommission.org/report*.

National Commission on Writing. (2004). *Writing: A ticket to work … or a ticket out: A survey of business leaders.* Washington, DC: U.S. Department of Education. Retrieved March 3, 2007, from *http://www.writingcommission.org*.

National Commission on Writing. (2005). *Writing: A powerful message from state government.* Washington, DC: U.S. Department of Education. Retrieved March 3, 2007, from *http://www.writingcommission.org*.

National Commission on Writing. (2006). *Writing and school reform.* Washington, DC: U.S. Department of Education. Retrieved March 3, 2007, from *http://www.writingcommission.org*.

National Council of Teachers of Mathematics (NCTM). (2000). *Principles and standards in school mathematics.* Reston, VA: Author.

National Council of Teachers of Mathematics (NCTM). (2006). *Curriculum focal points for prekindergarten through grade 8 mathematics: A quest for coherence.* Reston, VA: Author.

National Highway Traffic Safety Administration. (1998). *School bus safety: Safe passage for America's children* (Report No. DOT-HS-808-755). Washington, DC: Author. (ERIC Document Reproduction Service ED 437 736)

National Institute of Child Health and Human Development Early Child Care Research Network. (2000). The relation of child care to cognitive and language development. *Child Development, 71,* 960–980.

National Reading Panel. (2000). *Report of the National Reading Panel: Teaching children to read: An evidence-based assessment of the scientific research literature on reading and its implications for reading instructions: Reports of the subgroups.* Bethesda, MD: National Institutes of Health, National Institute of Child Health and Human Development.

National Research Council, Mathematics Learning Study Committee, Center for Education, Division of Behavioral and Social Sciences and Education. (2001). In J. Kilpatrick, J. Swafford, & B. Findell (Eds.), *Adding it up: Helping children learn mathematics.* Washington, DC: National Academy Press.

Neef, N. A., Shafer, M. S., Engel, A. L., Cataldo, M. F., & Parrish, J. M. (1983). The class specific effects of compliance training with "do" and "don't" requests: Analogue analysis and classroom application. *Journal of Applied Behavior Analysis, 16,* 81–99.

Nelson, J. M., & Machek, G. R. (2007). A survey of training, practice, and competence in reading assessment and intervention. *School Psychology Review, 36,* 311–327.

Nelson, J. R., Benner, G. J., & Gonzalez, J. (2003). Learner characteristics that influence the treatment effectiveness of early literacy interventions. *Learning Disabilities Research and Practice, 18,* 255–267.

Nelson, J. R., & Roberts, M. L. (2000). Ongoing reciprocal teacher–student interactions involving disruptive behaviors in general education classrooms. *Journal of Emotional and Behavioral Disorders, 8,* 27–37.

Nelson, J. R., Smith, D. J., & Dodd, J. M. (1992). The effects of teaching a summary skills strategy to students identified as learning disabled on their comprehension of science text. *Education and Treatment of Children, 15,* 228–243.

Neville, M. H., & Jenson, W. R. (1984). Precision commands and the "Sure I Will" program: A quick and efficient compliance training sequence. *Child and Family Behavior Therapy, 6,* 61–65.

Neufeld, B., & Roper, D. (2003). *Coaching: A strategy for developing instructional capacity: Promises and practicalities.* Washington, DC: Aspen Institute Program on Education/Providence, RI: Annenberg Institute for School Reform. Retrieved June 1, 2007, from *http://www.annenberginstitute.org/images/Coaching.pdf.*

Neuman, S. B. (1999). Books make a difference: A study of access to literacy. *Reading Research Quarterly, 34,* 286–311.

Neuman, S. B., & Celano, D. (2001). Access to print in low-income and middle-income communities: An ecological study of four neighborhoods. *Reading Research Quarterly, 36,* 8–26.

No Child Left Behind Act of 2001, 20 U.S.C. § 6301 *et seq.*

Noell, G. H., Duhon, G. J., Gatti, S. L., & Connell, J. E. (2002). Consultation, follow-up, and implementation of behavior management interventions in general education. *School Psychology Review, 31,* 217–234.

Noell, G. H., Freeland, J. T., Witt, J. C., & Gansle, K. A. (2001). Using brief assessments to identify effective interventions for individual students. *Journal of School Psychology, 39,* 335–355.

Noell, G. H., & Witt, J. C. (1999). When does consultation lead to intervention implementation?: Critical issues for research and practice. *Journal of Special Education, 33,* 29–35.

Noell, G. H., Witt, J. C., Gilbertson, D. N., Ranier, D. D., & Freeland, J. T. (1997). Increasing teacher intervention implementation in general education settings through consultation and performance feedback. *School Psychology Quarterly, 12,* 77–88.

Noell, G. H., Witt, J. C., LaFleur, L. H., Mortenson, B. P., Ranier, D. D., & LeVelle, J. (2000). Increasing intervention implementation in general education following consultation: A comparison of two follow-up strategies. *Journal of Applied Behavior Analysis, 33,* 271–284.

Noell, G. H., Witt, J. C., Slider, N. J., Connell, J. E., Gatti, S. L., Williams, K. L., et al. (2005). Treatment implementation following behavioral consultation in schools: A comparison of three follow-up strategies. *School Psychology Review, 34,* 87–106.

Northup, J. (2000). Further evaluation of the accuracy of reinforcer surveys: A systematic replication. *Journal of Applied Behavior Analysis, 33,* 335–338.

Northup, J., George, T., Jones, K., Broussard, C., & Vollmer, T. (1996). A comparison of reinforcer assessment methods: The utility of verbal and pictorial choice procedures. *Journal of Applied Behavior Analysis, 29,* 201–212.

Northup, J., Wacker, D. P., Berg, W. K., Kelly, L., Sasso, G., & De Raad, A. (1994). The treatment of severe behavior problems in school settings using a technical assistance model. *Journal of Applied Behavior Analysis, 27,* 33–47.

Nowacek, E. J., McKinney, J. D., & Hallahan, D. P. (1990). Instructional behaviors of more and less effective beginning regular and special educators. *Exceptional Children, 57,* 140–149.

Nowicki, E. A. (2003). A meta-analysis of the social competence of children with learning disabilities compared to classmates of low and average to high achievement. *Learning Disability Quarterly, 26,* 171–188.

Nucci, L. (2006). Classroom management for moral and social development. In C. M. Evertson & C. S. Weinstein (Eds.), *Handbook of classroom management: Research, practice, and contemporary issues* (pp. 711–731). Mahwah, NJ: Erlbaum.

O'Connor, R. E., Bell, K. M., Harty, K. R., Larkin, L. K., Sackor, S. M., & Zigmond, H. (2002). Teaching reading to poor readers in the intermediate grades: A comparison of text difficulty. *Journal of Educational Psychology, 94,* 474–485.

O'Donnell, P., Weber, K. P., & McLaughlin, T. F. (2003). Improving correct and error rate and reading comprehension using key words and previewing: A case report with a language minority student. *Education and Treatment of Children, 26,* 237–254.

Office of Special Education Programs: Technical Assistance Center on Positive Behavioral Interventions and Supports. (2007). School-wide PBS. Retrieved August 19, 2007, from *http://www.pbis.org/schoolwide.htm.*

Olive, M. L., & Liu, Y.-J. (2005). Social validity of parent and teacher implemented assessment-based interventions for challenging behavior. *Educational Psychology, 25,* 305–312.

Olweus, D. (1993). *Bullying at school: What we know and what we can do.* Cambridge, UK: Blackwell.

Olympia, D. E., Sheridan, S. M., Jenson, W. R., & Andrews, D. (1994). Using student-managed interventions to increase homework completion and accuracy. *Journal of Applied Behavior Analysis, 27,* 85–99.

Ortiz, A. A., Wilkinson, C. Y., Robertson-Courtney, P., & Kushner, M. I. (2006). Considerations in implementing intervention assistance teams to support English language learners. *Remedial and Special Education, 27,* 53–63.

Ortiz, S. O., & Flanagan, D. P. (2002). Best practices in working with culturally diverse children and families. In A. Thomas & J. Grimes (Eds.),

Best practices in school psychology IV (Vol. 1, pp. 337–351). Bethesda, MD: National Association of School Psychologists.

O'Shaughnessy, T. E., Lane, K. L., Gresham, F. M., & Beebe-Frankenberger, M. E. (2003). Children placed at risk for learning and behavioral difficulties: Implementing a school-wide system of early identification and intervention. *Journal of Special Education, 24,* 27–35.

O'Shea, L. J., Sindelar, P. T., & O'Shea, D. J. (1985). The effects of repeated readings and attentional cues on reading fluency and comprehension. *Journal of Reading Behavior, 17,* 129–142.

Otero, J., León, J. A., & Graesser, A. C. (Eds.). (2002). *The psychology of science text comprehension.* Mahwah, NJ: Erlbaum.

Pade, H., Taube, D. O., Aalborg, A. E., & Reiser, P. J. (2006). An immediate and long-term study of a temperament and parent–child interaction therapy based community program for preschoolers with behavior problems. *Child and Family Behavior Therapy, 28,* 1–28.

Paine, S. C., Radicchi, J., Rosellini, L. C., Deutchman, L., & Darch, C. B. (1983). *Structuring your classroom for academic success* (pp. 123–127). Champaign, IL: Research Press.

Palincsar, A. S., & Brown, A. L. (1984). The reciprocal teaching of comprehension-fostering and comprehension-monitoring activities. *Cognition and Instruction, 1,* 117–175.

Palincsar, A. S., & Klenk, L. (1992). Fostering literacy learning in supportive contexts. *Journal of Learning Disabilities, 25,* 211–225, 229.

Parker, R., Tindal, G., & Hasbrouck, J. (1991). Countable indices of writing quality: Their suitability for screening-eligibility decisions. *Exceptionality, 2,* 1–17.

Parmar, S., Deluca, C. B., & Janczak, T. M. (1994). Investigations into the relationship between science and language abilities of students with mild disabilities. *Remedial and Special Education, 15,* 117–126.

Patrick, C. A., Ward, P., & Crouch, D. W. (1998). Effects of holding students accountable for social behaviors during volleyball games in elementary physical education. *Journal of Teaching in Physical Education, 17,* 143–156.

Patterson, G. R., Reid, J. B., & Dishion, T. J. (1992). *A social interactional approach: Vol. 4. Antisocial boys.* Eugene, OR: Castalia.

Paxton, R. J. (1999). A deafening silence: History textbooks and the students who read them. *Review of Educational Research, 69,* 315–339.

Peisner-Feinberg, E. S., Burchinal, M. R., Clifford, R. M., Culkin, M. L., Howes, C., Kagan, S. L., et al. (2001). The relation of preschool child-care quality to children's cognitive and social developmental trajectories through second grade. *Child Development, 72,* 1534–1553.

Pelco, L. E., & Reed-Victor, E. (2007). Self-regulation and learning-related social skills: Intervention ideas for elementary school students. *Preventing School Failure, 51,* 36–42.

Pellegrini, A. D., & Byorklund, D. F. (1997). The role of recess in children's cognitive performance. *Educational Psychologist, 32,* 35–40.

Pellegrino, J. W., & Goldman, S. R. (1987). Information processing and elementary mathematics. *Journal of Learning Disabilities, 20,* 23–32, 57.

Penno, J. F., Wilkinson, I. A. G., & Moore, D. W. (2002). Vocabulary acquisition from teacher explanation and repeated listening to stories: Do they overcome the Matthew effect? *Journal of Educational Psychology, 94,* 23–33.

Perfetti, C. A. (1992). The representation problem in reading acquisition. In P. B. Gough, L. C. Ehri, & R. Treiman (Eds.), *Reading acquisition* (pp. 145–174). Hillsdale, NJ: Erlbaum.

Perry, K. E., Donohue, K. M., & Weinstein, R. S. (2007). Teaching practices and the promotion of achievement and adjustment in first grade. *Journal of School Psychology, 45,* 269–292.

Persampieri, M., Gortmaker, V., Daly, E. J. III, Sheridan, S. M., & McCurdy, M. (2006). Promoting parent use of empirically supported reading interventions: Two experimental investigations of child outcomes. *Behavioral Interventions, 21,* 31–57.

Pfiffner, L. J., Rosén, L. A., & O'Leary, S. G. (1985). The efficacy of an all-positive approach to classroom management. *Journal of Applied Behavior Analysis, 18,* 257–261.

Phaneuf, R. L., & Silbberglitt, B. (2003). Tracking preschoolers' language and preliteracy development using a general outcome measurement system. *Topics in Early Childhood Special Education, 23,* 114–123.

Pianta, R. C. (1999). *Enhancing relationships between children and teachers.* Washington, DC: American Psychological Association.

Pianta, R. C. (2006). Classroom management and relationships between children and teachers: Implications for research and practice. In C. M. Evertson & C. S. Weinstein (Eds.), *Handbook of classroom management: Research, practice, and contemporary issues* (pp. 685–709). Mahwah, NJ: Erlbaum.

Pianta, R. C., Hamre, B., & Stuhlman, M. W. (2003). Relationships between teachers and children. In W. M. Reynolds & G. E. Miller (Eds.), *Handbook of psychology: Educational psychology* (Vol. 7, pp. 199–234). New York: Wiley.

Pianta, R. C., Howes, C., Burchinal, M., Bryant, D., Clifford, R., Early, D., et al. (2005). Features of pre-kindergarten programs, classrooms, and teacher: Do they predict observed classroom quality and child–teacher interactions? *Applied Developmental Science, 9,* 144–159.

Pianta, R. C., La Paro, K. M., Payne, C., Cox, M. J., & Bradley, R. (2002). The relation of kindergarten classroom environment to teacher, family, and school characteristics and child outcomes. *The Elementary School Journal, 102,* 225–238.

Pianta, R. C., La Paro, K. M., & Hamre, B. K. (2006). *Classroom Assessment Scoring System (CLASS) manual: Preschool (Pre-K) version.* Charlottesville, VA: Center for Advanced Study of Teaching and Learning.

Pianta, R. C., Steinberg, M. S., & Rollins, K. B. (1995). The first two years of school: Teacher–child relationships and deflections in children's classroom adjustment. *Development and Psychopathology, 7,* 295–312.

Poglinco, S. M., Bach, A. J., Hovde, K., Rosenblum, S., Saunders, M., & Supovitz, J. A. (2003). *The heart of the matter: The coaching model in America's choice schools.* Philadelphia: Consortium for Policy Research in Education, University of Pennsylvania. Retrieved May 13, 2007, from *http:// www.cpre.org.*

Popkin, J., & Skinner, C. H. (2003). Enhancing academic performance in a classroom serving students with serious emotional disturbance: Interdependent group contingencies with randomly selected components. *School Psychology Review, 32,* 282–295.

Porterfield, J. K., Herbert-Jackson, E., & Risley, T. R. (1976). Contingent observation: An effective and acceptable procedure for reducing disruptive behavior of young children in a group setting. *Journal of Applied Behavior Analysis, 9,* 55–64.

Powell, D., Dunlap, G., & Fox, L. (2006). Prevention and intervention for the challenging behaviors of toddlers and preschoolers. *Infants and Young Children, 19,* 25–35.

Pratt-Struthers, J. P., Bartalamay, H., Williams, R. L., & McLaughlin, T. F. (1989). Effects of the Add-A-Word Spelling Program on spelling accuracy during creative writing: A replication across two classrooms. *British Columbia Journal of Special Education, 13,* 151–158.

Pratt-Struthers, J. P., Struthers, T. B., & Williams, R. L. (1983). The effects of the Add-A-Word Spelling Program on spelling accuracy during creative writing. *Education and Treatment of Children, 6,* 277–283.

Prawat, R. S., & Anderson, A. L. H. (1994). The affective experiences of children during mathematics. *Journal of Mathematical Behavior, 13,* 201–222.

Pressley, M., Wharton-McDonald, R., Allington, R., Block, C. C., Morrow, L., Tracey D., et al. (2001). A study of effective first-grade literacy instruction. *Scientific Studies of Reading, 5,* 35–58.

Pressley, M., Yokoi, L., Rankin, J., Wharton-McDonald, R., & Mistretta, J. (1997). A survey of the instructional practices of grade 5 teachers nominated as effective in promoting literacy. *Scientific Studies of Reading, 1,* 145–160.

Proctor, M. A., & Morgan, D. (1991). Effectiveness of a response cost raffle procedure on the disruptive classroom behavior of adolescents with behavior problems. *School Psychology Review, 20,* 97–109.

Putnam, R. F., Handler, M. W., Ramirez-Platt, C. M., & Luiselli, J. K. (2003). Improving student bus-riding behavior through a whole-school intervention. *Journal of Applied Behavior Analysis, 36,* 583–590.

Qi, C. H., & Kaiser, A. P. (2003). Behavior problems of preschool children from low-income families: Review of the literature. *Topics in Early Childhood Special Education, 23,* 188–216.

Quinn, M. M., Kavale, K. A., Mathur, S. R., Rutherford, R. B., & Forness, S. R. (1999). A meta-analysis of social skill interventions for students with emotional or behavioral disorders. *Journal of Emotional and Behavioral Disorders, 7,* 54–64.

Rademacher, J. A., Callahan, K., & Pederson-Seelye, V. A. (1998). How do your classroom rules measure up: Guidelines for developing an effective rule management routine. *Intervention in School and Clinic, 33,* 284–289.

Rafoth, M. A., & Foriska, T. (2006). Administrator participation in promoting effective problem-solving teams. *Remedial and Special Education, 22,* 75–88.

Randolph, J. J. (2007). Meta-analysis of the research on response cards: Effects on test achievement, quiz achievement, participation, and off-task behavior. *Journal of Positive Behavioral Interventions, 9,* 113–128.

Raphael, T. E., & Englert, C. S. (1990). Writing and reading: Partners in constructing meaning. *Reading Teacher, 43,* 388–400.

Rapport, M. D., Murphy, H. A., & Bailey, J. S. (1982). Ritalin vs. response cost in the control of hyperactive children: A within-subject comparison. *Journal of Applied Behavior Analysis, 15,* 205–216.

Rashotte, C. A., MacPhee, K., & Torgesen, J. K. (2001). The effectiveness of a group reading instruction program with poor readers in multiple grades. *Learning Disability Quarterly, 24,* 119–134.

Rasinski, T. V. (1990). Effects of repeated reading and listening-while-reading on reading fluency. *Journal of Educational Research, 83,* 147–150.

Rathvon, N. (1996). *The unmotivated child: Helping your underachiever become a successful student.* New York: Simon & Schuster.

Rathvon, N. (1999). *Effective school interventions: Enhancing academic achievement and social competence.* New York: Guilford Press.

Rathvon, N. (2004a). Academic interventions. In C. Spielberger (Ed. in Chief), *Encyclopedia of applied psychology* (pp. 9–20). San Diego, CA: Academic Press.

Rathvon, N. (2004b). *Early reading assessment: A practitioner's handbook*. New York: Guilford Press.

Reid, M. J., Webster-Stratton, C., & Baydar, N. (2004). Halting the development of conduct problems in Head Start children: The effects of parent training. *Journal of Clinical Child and Adolescent Psychology, 33*, 279–291.

Reid, R., & Nelson, J. R. (2002). The utility, acceptability, and practicality of functional behavioral assessment for students with high-incidence problem behavior. *Remedial and Special Education, 23*, 15–23.

Reitman, D. (1998). Punished by misunderstanding: A critical evaluation of Kohn's *Punished by Rewards* and its implications for behavioral interventions with children. *Behavior Analyst, 21*, 143–157.

Renaissance Learning. (2002). *Accelerated Reader: Learning information system for reading and literacy systems*. Wisconsin Rapids, WI: Author.

Reschly, D. J., & Ysseldyke, J. E. (2002). Paradigm shift: The past is not the future. In A. Thomas & J. Grimes (Eds.), *Best practices in school psychology IV* (Vol. 1, pp. 3–20). Bethesda, MD: National Association of School Psychologists.

Reynolds, L. K., & Kelley, M. L. (1997). The efficacy of a response cost-based treatment package for managing aggressive behavior in preschoolers. *Behavior Modification, 21*, 216–230.

Reys, B. J., Dingman, S., Sutter, A., & Teuscher, D. (2005). *Development of state-level mathematics curriculum documents: Report of a survey*. Columbia: University of Missouri, Center for the Study of Mathematics Curriculum. Retrieved January 2, 2007, from *http://www.mathcurriculum-center.org/recourses/ASSMReport.pdf*.

Rhoades, M. M., & Kratochwill, T. R. (1998). Parent training and consultation: An analysis of a homework intervention program. *School Psychology Quarterly, 13*, 241–264.

Rhode, G., Jenson, W. R., & Reavis, H. K. (1992). *The tough kid book: Practical classroom management strategies*. Longmont, CO: Sopris West.

Rhymer, K. N., Dittmer, K. I., Skinner, C. H., & Jackson, B. (2000). Effectiveness of a multicomponent treatment for improving mathematics fluency. *School Psychology Quarterly, 15*, 40–51.

Ridgway, A., Northup, J., Pellegrin, A., LaRue, R., & Hightshoe, A. (2003). Effects of recess on the classroom behavior of children with and without attention-deficit hyperactivity disorder. *School Psychology Quarterly, 18*, 253–268.

Riley-Tillman, R. C., Chafouleas, S. M., Eckert, T. L., & Kelleher, C. (2005). Bridging the gap between research and practice: A framework for building research agendas in school psychology. *Psychology in the Schools, 42*, 459–473.

Rimm-Kaufman, S. E., & Chiu, Y.-J. I. (2007). Promoting social and academic competence in the classroom: An intervention study examining the contribution of the responsive classroom approach. *Psychology in the Schools, 44*, 397–413.

Rimm-Kaufman, S. E., Fan, X., Chiu, Y.-J., & You, W. (2007). The contribution of the responsive classroom approach on children's academic achievement: Results from a three year longitudinal study. *Journal of School Psychology, 45*, 401–421.

Rimm-Kaufman, S. E., Pianta, R. C., & Cox, M. J. (2000). Teachers' judgments of problems in the transition to kindergarten. *Early Childhood Research Quarterly, 15*, 147–166.

Robbins, C., & Ehri, L. C. (1994). Reading storybooks to kindergartners helps them learn new vocabulary words. *Journal of Educational Psychology, 86*, 54–64.

Robbins, J. R., & Gutkin, T. B. (1994). Consultee and client remedial and preventive outcomes following consultation: Some mixed empirical results and directions for future researchers. *Journal of Educational and Psychological Consultation, 5*, 149–167.

Rohrbeck, C. A., Ginsburg-Block, M. D., Fantuzzo, J. W., & Miller, T. R. (2003). Peer-assisted learning interventions with elementary school students: A meta-analytic review. *Journal of Educational Psychology, 95*, 240–257.

Rose, L. C., & Gallup, A. M. (2006). The 38th annual Phi Delta Kappa/Gallup Poll of the public's attitudes toward the public schools. *Phi Delta Kappan, 88*, 41–53.

Rose, T. L., & Sherry, L. (1984). Relative effects of two previewing procedures on LD adolescents' oral reading performance. *Learning Disability Quarterly, 7*, 39–44.

Rosén, L. A., O'Leary, S. G., Joyce, S. A., Conway, G., & Pfiffner, L. J. (1984). The importance of prudent negative consequences for maintaining the appropriate behavior of hyperactive students. *Journal of Abnormal Child Psychology, 12*, 581–604.

Rosén, L. A., Taylor, L. A., O'Leary, S. G., & Sanderson, W. (1990). A survey of classroom management practices. *Journal of School Psychology, 28*, 257–269.

Rosenberg, M. S. (1986). Maximizing the effectiveness of structured classroom management programs: Implementing rule-review procedures with disruptive and distractible students. *Behavioral Disorders, 11*, 239–248.

Rosenfield, P., Lambert, N. M., & Black, A. (1985). Desk arrangement effects on pupil classroom behavior. *Journal of Educational Psychology, 77*, 101–108.

Rosenfield, S. A., & Gravois, T. A. (1996). *Instructional consultation teams: Collaborating for change*. New York: Guilford Press.

Rosenfield, S., Lambert, N. M., & Black, A. (1985). Desk arrangement effects on pupil classroom behavior. *Journal of Educational Psychology, 77,* 101–108.

Roth, J. L., Brooks-Gunn, J., Linver, M. R., & Hofferth, S. L. (2003). What happens during the school day?: Time diaries from a national sample of elementary school teachers. *Teachers College Record, 105,* 317–343.

Rousseau, M. K., & Tam, B. K. (1991). The efficacy of previewing and discussion of key words on the oral reading proficiency of bilingual learners with speech and language impairments. *Education and Treatment of Children, 14,* 199–209.

Rousseau, M. K., Tam, B. K., & Ramnarain, R. (1993). Increasing reading proficiency of language-minority students with speech and language impairments. *Education and Treatment of Children, 16,* 254–271.

Rubinson, F. (2002). Lessons learned from implementing problem-solving teams in urban high schools. *Journal of Educational and Psychological Consultation, 13,* 185–217.

Sáenz, L. M., & Fuchs, L. S. (2002). Peer-assisted learning strategies in reading: Extensions for kindergarten, first grade, and high school. *Remedial and Special Education, 23,* 31–41.

Safran, S. P., & Safran, J. S. (1996). Intervention assistance programs and prereferral teams: Directions for the twenty-first century. *Remedial and Special Education, 17,* 363–369.

Saft, E. W., & Pianta, R. C. (2001). Teachers' perceptions of their relationships with students: Effects of child age, gender, and ethnicity of teachers and children. *School Psychology Quarterly, 16,* 125–141.

Sainato, D. M. (1990). Classroom transitions: Organizing environments to promote independent performance in preschool children with disabilities. *Education and Treatment of Children, 13,* 288–297.

Salend, S. J., & Gordon, B. D. (1987). A group-oriented timeout ribbon procedure. *Behavioral Disorders 12,* 131–137.

Salend, S. J., & Henry, K. (1981). Response cost in mainstreamed settings. *Journal of School Psychology, 19,* 242–249.

Salend, S. J., Reynolds, C. J., & Coyle, E. M. (1989). Individualizing the Good Behavior Game across type and frequency of behavior with emotionally disturbed adolescents. *Behavior Modification, 13,* 108–126.

Samuels, S. J. (1979). The method of repeated readings. *Reading Teacher, 32,* 403–408.

Scardamalia, M., & Bereiter, C. (1986). Research on written composition. In M. C. Wittrock (Ed.), *Handbook on research on teaching* (3rd ed., pp. 778–803). New York: Macmillan.

Schantl, W. (1991). *A bus behavioral modification plan for grades K–5: A practicum report.* Nova Southeastern University. (ERIC Document Reproduction Service ED 335787)

Scheeler, M. C., & Lee, D. L. (2002). Using technology to deliver immediate corrective feedback to preservice teachers. *Journal of Behavioral Education, 11,* 231–241.

Scheeler, M. C., Ruhl, K., & McAfee, J. (2004). Providing performance feedback to teachers: A review. *Young Exceptional Children, 27,* 396–407.

Schermerhorn, P. K., & McLaughlin, T. F. (1997). Effects of the Add-A-Word Spelling Program on test accuracy, grades, and retention of spelling words with fifth and sixth grade regular education students. *Child and Family Behavior Therapy, 19,* 23–35.

Schmidt, W. H., McKnight, C. C., & Raizen, S. A. (1997). *A splintered vision: An investigation of U.S. science and mathematics education.* Dordrecht, The Netherlands: Kluwer Academic.

Schumaker, J. B., Deshler, D. D., & McKnight, P. C. (2002). Ensuring success in the secondary general education curriculum through the use of teaching routines. In M. R. Shinn, H. M. Walker, & G. Stoner (Eds.), *Interventions for academic and behavior problems II: Preventive and remedial approaches* (pp. 791–824). Bethesda, MD: National Association of School Psychologists.

Schumm, J. S., Moody, S. W., & Vaughn, S. (2000). Grouping for reading instruction: Does one size fit all? *Journal of Learning Disabilities, 33,* 477–488.

Scott, T. M. (2001). A schoolwide example of positive behavioral support. *Journal of Positive Behavior Interventions, 3,* 88–94.

Scott, T. M., McIntyre, J., Liaupsin, C., Nelson, C. M., Conroy, M., & Payne, L. D. (2005). An examination of the relation between functional behavior assessment and selected intervention strategies with school-based teams. *Journal of Positive Behavior Interventions, 7,* 205–215.

Scott, T. M., Nelson, C. M., & Liaupsin, C. J. (2001). Effective instruction: The forgotten component in preventing school violence. *Education and Treatment of Children, 24,* 309–322.

Scruggs, T. E., & Mastropieri, M. A. (2003). Science and social studies. In H. L. Swanson, K. R. Harris, & S. Graham (Eds.), *Handbook of learning disabilities* (pp. 364–379). New York: Guilford Press.

Sénéchal, M., Thomas, E., & Monker, J.-A. (1995). Individual differences in 4-year-old children's acquisition of vocabulary during storybook reading. *Journal of Educational Psychology, 87,* 218–229.

Serna, L., Nielson, E., Lambros, K., & Forness, S. (2002). Primary prevention with children at risk for emotional or behavioral disorders: Data on a universal intervention for Head Start classrooms. *Behavioral Disorders, 26,* 70–84.

Sexton, M., Harris, K. R., & Graham, S. (1998). Self-regulated strategy development and the writing process: Effects on essay writing and attributions. *Exceptional Children, 64,* 295–311.

Shapiro, E. S. (2004a). *Academic skills problems: Direct assessment and intervention* (3rd ed.). New York: Guilford Press.

Shapiro, E. S. (2004b). *Academic skills problems workbook* (rev. ed.). New York: Guilford Press.

Shapiro, E. S., Durnan, S. L., Post, E. E., & Levinson, T. S. (2002). Self-monitoring procedures for children and adolescents. In M. R. Shinn, H. M. Walker, & G. Stoner (Eds.), *Interventions for academic and behavior problems II: Preventive and remedial approaches* (pp. 433–454). Bethesda, MD: National Association of School Psychologists.

Shapiro, E. S., Keller, M. A., Lutz, J. G., Santoro, L. E., & Hintze, J. M. (2004). Curriculum-based measures and self-monitoring in assessing children's problems. *Psychological Assessment, 11,* 448–457.

Shapiro, E. S., Keller, M. A., Lutz, J. G., Santoro, L. E., & Hintze, J. M. (2006). Curriculum-based measures and performance on state assessment and standardized tests: Reading and math performance in Pennsylvania. *Journal of Psychoeducational Assessment, 24,* 19–35.

Share, D. L. (1995). Phonological recoding and self-teaching: *Sine qua non* of reading acquisition. *Cognition, 55,* 151–218.

Sharp, S. R., & Skinner, C. H. (2004). Using interdependent group contingencies with randomly selected criteria and paired reading to enhance class-wide reading performance. *Journal of Applied School Psychology, 20,* 29–45.

Sharpe, T., Brown, M., & Crider, K. (1995). The effects of a sportsmanship curriculum on generalized positive social behavior in urban elementary school students. *Journal of Applied Behavior Analysis, 28,* 401–416.

Sharpe, T., & Crider, K. (1996). Description and effects of prosocial instruction in an elementary physical education setting. *Education and Treatment of Children, 19,* 435–457.

Sheridan, S. M. (2000). Considerations of multiculturalism and diversity in behavioral consultation with parents and teachers. *School Psychology Review, 29,* 344–353.

Sheridan, S. M., Eagle, J. W., & Doll, B. (2006). An examination of the efficacy of conjoint behavioral consultation with diverse clients. *School Psychology Quarterly, 21,* 396–417.

Sheridan, S. M., & Gutkin, T. B. (2000). The ecology of school psychology: Examining and changing our paradigm for the 21st century. *School Psychology Review, 29,* 485–502.

Sheridan, S. M., Hungelmann, A., & Maughan, D. P. (1999). A contextualized framework for social skills assessment, intervention, and generalization. *School Psychology Review, 28,* 84–103.

Shin, J., Deno, S. L., & Espin, C. (2000). Technical adequacy of the maze task for curriculum-based measurement of reading growth. *Journal of Special Education, 34,* 164–172.

Shinn, M. R., & Marston, D. (1985). Differentiating mildly handicapped, low-achieving, and regular education students: A curriculum-based approach. *Remedial and Special Education, 6,* 31–38.

Shinn, M. R., Walker, H. M., & Stoner, G. (2002). *Interventions for academic and behavior problems: II. Preventive and remedial approaches.* Bethesda, MD: National Association of School Psychologists.

Shinn, M. R., Ysseldyke, J. E., Deno, S. L., & Tindal, G. A. (1986). A comparison of differences between students labeled as learning disabled and low achieving on measures of classroom performance. *Journal of Learning Disabilities, 19,* 545–552.

Shores, R. E., Gunter, P. L., & Jack, S. L. (1993). Classroom management strategies: Are they setting events for coercion? *Behavioral Disorders, 18,* 92–102.

Shores, R. E., & Wehby, J. H. (1999). Analyzing the classroom social behavior of students with EBD. *Journal of Emotional and Behavioral Disorders, 7,* 194–199.

Silver, R. B., Measelle, J. R., Armstrong, J. M., & Essex, M. J. (2005). Trajectories of classroom externalizing behavior: Contributions of child characteristics, family characteristics, and the teacher–child relationship during the school transition. *Journal of School Psychology, 43,* 39–60.

Simmons, D. C., Fuchs, L. S., Fuchs, D., Mathes, P., & Hodge, J. P. (1995). Effects of explicit teaching and peer tutoring on the reading achievement of learning-disabled and low-performing students in regular classrooms. *Elementary School Journal, 95,* 387–408.

Simmons, D. C., & Kame'enui, E. J. (Eds.) (1998). *What reading research tells us about children with diverse learning needs: Bases and basics.* Mahwah, NJ: Erlbaum.

Sindelar, P. T., Griffin, C. C., Smith, S. W., & Watanabe, A. K. (1992). Prereferral intervention: Encouraging notes on preliminary findings. *Elementary School Journal, 92,* 245–259.

Sindelar, P. T., Monda, L. E., & O'Shea, L. J. (1990). Effects of repeated reading on instructional- and mastery-level readers. *Journal of Educational Research, 83,* 220–226.

Sindelar, P. T., & Stoddard, K. (1991). Teaching reading to mildly disabled students in regular classes. In G. Stoner, M. R. Shinn, & H. M. Walker (Eds.), *Interventions for achievement and behavior problems* (pp. 357–378). Silver Spring, MD: National Association of School Psychologists.

Singer, H., & Donlan, D. (1983). Active comprehension: Problem-solving scheme with question generation for comprehension of complex short stories. *Reading Research Quarterly, 17,* 166–186.

Singh, N. N. (1990). Effects of two error-correction procedures on oral reading errors: Word supply versus sentence repeat. *Behavior Modification, 14,* 188–199.

Skinner, C. H., Adamson, K. L., Woodward, J. R., Jackson, R. R., Atchison, L. A., & Mims, J. W. (1993). A comparison of fast-rate, slow-rate, and silent previewing interventions on reading performance. *Journal of Learning Disabilities, 26,* 674–681.

Skinner, C. H., Belfiore, P. J., & Pierce, N. (1992). Cover, Copy, and Compare: Increasing geography accuracy in students with behavior disorders. *School Psychology Review, 21,* 73–81.

Skinner, C. H., Cashwell, C. S., & Dunn, M. S. (1996). Independent and interdependent group contingencies: Smoothing the rough waters. *Special Services in the Schools, 12,* 61–78.

Skinner, C. H., Cashwell, T. H., & Skinner, A. L. (2000). Increasing tootling: The effects of a peer-monitored group contingency program on students' reports of peers' prosocial behaviors. *Psychology in the Schools, 37,* 263–270.

Skinner, C. H., Cooper, L., & Cole, C. L. (1997). The effects of oral presentation previewing rates on reading performance. *Journal of Applied Behavior Analysis, 30,* 332–333.

Skinner, C. H., McLaughlin, T. F., & Logan, P. (1997). Cover, Copy, and Compare: A self-managed academic intervention effective across skills, students, and settings. *Journal of Behavioral Education, 7,* 295–306.

Skinner, C. H., Skinner, A. L., & Sterling-Turner, H. E. (2002). Best practices in contingency management: Application of individual and group contingencies in educational settings. In A. Thomas & J. Grimes (Eds.), *Best practices in school psychology IV* (Vol. 1, pp. 817–830). Bethesda, MD: National Association of School Psychologists.

Skinner, C. H., Wallace, M. A., & Neddenriep, C. E. (2002). Academic remediation: Educational applications of research on assignment preference and choice. *Child and Family Behavior Therapy, 24,* 51–65.

Skinner, C. H., Williams, R. L., & Neddenriep, C. E. (2004). Using interdependent group-oriented reinforcement to enhance academic performance in general education classrooms. *School Psychology Review, 33,* 384–397.

Slonski-Fowler, K. E., & Truscott, S. D. (2004). General education teachers' perceptions of the prereferral intervention team process. *Journal of Educational and Psychological Consultation, 15,* 1–39.

Smith, B. J., & Fox, L. (2003). *Systems of service delivery: A synthesis of evidence relevant to young children at risk of or who have challenging behavior.* Tampa, FL: University of South Florida, Center for Evidence-Based Practice: Young Children with Challenging Behavior.

Smith, M. W., Dickinson, D. K., Sangeorge, A., & Anastasopoulos, L. (2002). *Users' guide to the Early Language and Literacy Classroom Observation Toolkit, research edition.* Baltimore, MD: Brookes.

Smith, T. J., Dittmer, K. I., & Skinner, C. H. (2002). Enhancing science performance in students with learning disabilities using Cover, Copy, and Compare: A student shows the way. *Psychology in the Schools, 39,* 417–426.

Snow, C. E. (2002). *Reading for understanding: Toward a research and development program in reading comprehension.* Santa Monica, CA: RAND. Retrieved September 8, 2002, from *http://www.rand.org/pubs/authors/s/snow_catherine.html.*

Snow, C. E., Burns, M. S., & Griffin, P. (1998). *Preventing reading difficulties in young children.* Washington, DC: National Academy Press.

Snyder, J., Schrepferman, L., Oeser, J., Patterson, G., Stoolmiller, M., Johnson, K., et al., (2005). Deviance training and association with deviant peers in young children: Occurrence and contribution to early-onset conduct problems. *Development and Psychopathology, 17,* 397–413.

Spear-Swerling, L., & Brucker, P. O. (2003). Teachers' acquisition of knowledge about English word structure. *Annals of Dyslexia, 53,* 72–103.

Spear-Swerling, L., & Brucker, P. O. (2004). Preparing novice teachers to develop basic reading and spelling skills in children. *Annals of Dyslexia, 54,* 332–364.

Speece, D. L., Mills, C., Ritchey, K. D., & Hillman, E. (2003). Initial evidence that letter fluency tasks are valid indicators of early reading skill. *Journal of Special Education, 36,* 223–233.

Speece, D. L., & Ritchey, K. D. (2005). A longitudinal study of the development of oral reading fluency in young children at risk for reading failure. *Journal of Learning Disabilities, 38,* 387–399.

Spencer, V. G., Scruggs, T. E., & Mastropieri, M. A. (2003). Content area learning in middle school social studies classrooms and students with emotional or behavioral disorders: A comparison of strategies. *Behavioral Disorders, 28,* 77–93.

Stading, M., Williams, R. L., & McLaughlin, T. F. (1996). Effects of a copy, cover, and compare procedure on multiplication facts mastery with a third grade girl with learning disabilities in a home setting. *Education and Treatment of Children, 19,* 425–434.

Stage, S. A., & Quiroz, D. R. (1997). A meta-analysis of interventions to decrease disruptive classroom behavior in public education settings. *School Psychology Review, 26,* 333–368.

Stanovich, K. E. (1986). Matthew effects in reading: Some consequences of individual differences in the acquisition of literacy. *Reading Research Quarterly, 21,* 360–407.

Stanovich, K. E. (1991). Changing models of reading and reading acquisition. In L. Rieben & C. A. Perfetti (Eds.), *Learning to read: Basic research and its implications* (pp. 19–32). Hillsdale, NJ: Erlbaum.

Stanovich, K. E. (1993–1994). Romance and reality. *Reading Teacher, 47,* 280–291.

Steege, M., Brown-Chidsey, R., & Mace, F. C. (2002). Best practices in evaluating interventions. In A. Thomas & J. Grimes (Eds.), *Best practices in school psychology IV* (Vol. 1, pp. 517–534). Bethesda, MD: National Association of School Psychologists.

Stein, M., Dixon, R. C., & Isaacson, S. (1994). Effective writing instruction for diverse learners. *School Psychology Review, 23,* 392–405.

Sterling-Turner, H. E., Robinson, S. L., & Wilczynski, S. M. (2001). Functional assessment of distracting and disruptive behaviors in the school setting. *School Psychology Review, 30,* 211–226.

Sterling-Turner, H. E., Watson, T. S., Wildmon, M., Watkins, C., & Little, E. (2001). Investigating the relationship between training type and treatment integrity. *School Psychology Quarterly, 16,* 78–89.

Sternberg, R. J., & Grigorenko, E. L. (2002). Difference scores in the identification of children with learning disabilities: It's time to use a different method. *Journal of School Psychology, 40,* 65–83.

Stewart, L. H., & Kaminski, R. (2002). Best practices in developing local norms for academic problem solving. In A. Thomas & J. Grimes (Eds.), *Best practices in school psychology IV* (Vol. 1, pp. 737–752). Bethesda, MD: National Association of School Psychologists.

Stichter, J., Clarke, S., & Dunlap, G. (2004). An analysis of trends regarding proactive and ecologically valid interventions in applied research. *Education and Treatment of Children, 27,* 86–104.

Stoddard, B., & MacArthur, C. A. (1993). A peer editor strategy: Guiding learning-disabled students in response and revision. *Research in the Teaching of English, 27,* 76–103.

Stoiber, K. C., & Kratochwill, T. R. (2000). Empirically supported interventions and school psychology: Rationale and methodological issues—Part I. *School Psychology Quarterly, 15,* 75–105.

Stoner, G., Scarpati, S. E., Phaneuf, R. L., & Hintze, J. M. (2002). Using curriculum-based measurement to evaluate intervention efficacy. *Child and Family Behavior Therapy, 24,* 101–112.

Stormshak, E. A., Bierman, K. L., Bruschi, C., Dodge, K. A., Coe, J. D., & Conduct Problems Prevention Research Group. (1999). The relation between behavior problems and peer preference in different classroom contexts. *Child Development, 70,* 169–182.

Stough, L. M. (2006). The place of classroom management and standards in teacher education. In C. M. Evertson & C. S. Weinstein (Eds.), *Handbook of classroom management: Research, practice, and contemporary issues* (pp. 909–923). Mahwah, NJ: Erlbaum.

Struthers, J. P., Bartlamay, H., Bell, S., & McLaughlin, T. F. (1994). An analysis of the Add-A-Word Spelling Program and public posting across three categories of children with special needs. *Reading Improvement, 31,* 28–36.

Sugai, G., & Colvin, G. (1997). Debriefing: A transition step for promoting acceptable behavior. *Education and Treatment of Children, 20,* 209–221.

Sugai, G., & Horner, R. H. (2002). The evolution of discipline practices: School-wide positive behavior supports. *Child and Family Behavior Therapy, 24,* 23–50.

Sugai, G., Horner, R. H., Dunlap, G., Hieneman, M., Lewis, T., Nelson, C. M., et al. (2000). Applying positive behavior support and functional behavioral assessment in schools. *Journal of Positive Behavior Interventions, 2,* 131–143.

Sugai, G., Horner, R. H., & Gresham, F. M. (2002). Behaviorally effective school environments. In M. R. Shinn, H. M. Walker, & G. Stoner (Eds.), *Interventions for academic and behavior problems II: Preventive and remedial approaches* (pp. 315–350). Bethesda, MD: National Association of School Psychologists.

Sugai, G., Sprague, J. R., Horner, R. H., & Walker, H. M. (2000). Preventing school violence: The use of office discipline referrals to assess and monitor school-wide discipline interventions. *Journal of Emotional and Behavioral Disorders, 8,* 94–101.

Sullivan, M. A., & O'Leary, S. G. (1990). Maintenance following reward and cost token programs. *Behavior Therapy, 21,* 139–149.

Sulzer-Azaroff, B., & Mayer, G. R. (1991). *Behavior analysis for lasting change.* Fort Worth, TX: Holt, Rinehart & Winston.

Sutherland, K. S., & Wehby, J. H. (2001). Exploring the relationship between increased opportunities to respond to academic requests and the academic and behavioral outcomes of students with EBD: A review. *Remedial and Special Education, 22,* 113–121.

Sutherland, K. S., Wehby, J. H., & Copeland, S. R. (2000). Effect of varying rates of behavior-specific praise on the on-task behavior of students with EBD. *Journal of Emotional and Behavioral Disorders, 8,* 2–8, 26.

Swanson, H. L.. Hoskyn, M., & Lee, C. (1999). *Interventions for students with learning disabilities: A meta-analysis of treatment outcomes.* New York: Guilford Press.

Swiezy, N. B., Matson, J. L., & Box, P. (1992). The Good Behavior Game: A token reinforcement system for preschoolers. *Child and Family Behavior Therapy, 14,* 22–32.

Taverne, A., & Sheridan, S. M. (1995). Parent training in interactive book reading: An investigation of its effects with families at risk. *School Psychology Quarterly, 10,* 41–64.

Taylor, B. M., Pearson, P. D., Clark, K., & Walpole, S. (2000). Effective schools and accomplished teachers: Lessons about primary-grade reading instruction in low-income schools. *Elementary School Journal, 101,* 121–165.

Taylor, L. K., Alber, S. R., & Walker, D. W. (2002). The comparative effects of a modified self-questioning strategy and story mapping on the reading comprehension of elementary students with learning disabilities. *Journal of Behavioral Education, 11,* 69–87.

Telzrow, C. F., McNamara, K., & Hollinger, C. L. (2000). Fidelity of problem-solving implementation and relationship to student performance. *School Psychology Review, 29,* 443–461.

Templeton, S., & Morris, D. (1999). Questions teachers ask about spelling. *Reading Research Quarterly, 34,* 102–112.

Teo, A., Carlson, E., Mathieu, P. J., Egeland, B., & Sroufe, L. A. (1996). A prospective longitudinal study of psychosocial predictors of achievement. *Journal of School Psychology, 34,* 285–306.

Theodore, L. A., Bray, M. A., & Kehle, T. J. (2004). A comparative study of group contingencies and randomized reinforcers to reduce classroom disruptive behavior. *School Psychology Quarterly, 19,* 253–271.

Theodore, L. A., Bray, M. A., Kehle, T. J., & Jenson, W. R. (2001). Randomization of group contingencies and reinforcers to reduce classroom disruptive behavior. *Journal of School Psychology, 39,* 267–277.

Thurber, R. S., Shinn, M. R., & Smolkowski, K. (2002). What is measured in mathematics tests? Construct validity of curriculum-based mathematics measures. *School Psychology Review, 31,* 498–513.

Thurston, L. P., & Dasta, K. (1990). An analysis of in-home parent tutoring procedures: Effects on children's academic behavior at home and in school and on parents' tutoring behaviors. *Remedial and Special Education, 11,* 41–52.

Tilly, W. D. (2002). Best practices in school psychology as a problem-solving enterprise. In A. Thomas & J. Grimes (Eds.), *Best practices in school psychology IV* (Vol. 1, pp. 21–36). Bethesda, MD: National Association of School Psychologists.

Tilly, D. W., Knoster, T. P., & Ikeda, M. J. (2000). Functional behavioral assessment. In C. E. Telzrow & M. Tankersley (Eds.), *IDEA amendments of 1997* (pp. 151–197). Bethesda, MD: National Association of School Psychologists.

Tingstrom, D. H., Edwards, R. P., & Olmi, D. J. (1995). Listening previewing in reading to read: Relative effects on oral reading fluency. *Psychology in the Schools, 32,* 318–327.

Todd, A. W., Horner, R. H., & Sugai, G. (1999). Self-monitoring and self-recruited praise: Effects on problem behavior, academic engagement, and work completion in a typical classroom. *Journal of Positive Behavior Interventions, 1*(2), 66–76.

Tomblin, J. B., Zhang, X., Buckwalter, P., & Catts, H. (2000). The association of reading disability, behavioral disorders, and language impairment among second-grade children. *Journal of Child Psychology and Psychiatry and Allied Disciplines, 41,* 473–482.

Torbeyns, J., Verschaffel, L., & Ghesquière, P. (2004). Strategy development in children with mathematical disabilities: Insights from the choice/no-choice method and the chronological-age/ability-level-match design. *Journal of Learning Disabilities, 37,* 119–131.

Torgesen, J. K. (2000). Individual differences in response to early interventions in reading: The lingering problem of treatment resisters. *Learning Disabilities Research and Practice, 15,* 55–64.

Torgesen, J. K., Alexander, A. W., Wagner, R. K., Rashotte, C. A., Voeller, K. K. S., & Conway, T. (2001). Intensive remedial instruction for children with severe reading disabilities: Immediate and long-term outcomes from two instructional approaches. *Journal of Learning Disabilities, 34,* 33–58, 78.

Torgesen, J. K., & Burgess, S. R. (1998). Consistency of reading-related phonological processes throughout early childhood: Evidence from longitudinal–correlational and instructional studies. In J. L. Metsala & L. C. Ehri (Eds.), *Word recognition in beginning literacy* (pp. 161–188). Mahwah, NJ: Erlbaum.

Torgesen, J. K., Wagner, R. K., Rashotte, C. A., Alexander, A. W., & Conway, T. (1997). Preventive and remedial interventions for children with severe reading disabilities. *Learning Disabilities: A Multidisciplinary Journal, 8,* 51–61.

Torgesen, J. K., Wagner, R. K., Rashotte, C. A., Rose, E., Lindamood, P., Conway, T., et al. (1999). Preventing reading failure in young children with phonological processing disabilities: Group and individual responses to instruction. *Journal of Educational Psychology, 91,* 579–593.

Tournaki, N. (2003). The differential effects of teaching addition through strategy instruction versus drill and practice to students with and without learning disabilities. *Journal of Learning Disabilities, 36,* 449–458.

Tremblay, R. E., Masse, B., Perron, D., Leblanc, M., Schwartzman, A. E., & Ledingham, J. E. (1992). Early disruptive behavior, poor school achievement, delinquent behavior, and delinquent personality: Longitudinal analyses. *Journal of Consulting and Clinical Psychology, 60,* 64–72.

Troia, G. A., Graham, S., & Harris, K. R. (1999). Teaching students with learning disabilities to mindfully plan when writing. *Exceptional Children, 65,* 215–252.

Truscott, S. D., Cohen, C. E., Sams, D. P., Sanborn, K. J., & Frank, A. J. (2005). The current state(s) of prereferral intervention teams: A report from two national surveys. *Remedial and Special Education, 26,* 130–140.

Truscott, S. D., Cosgrove, G., Meyers, J., & Eidle-Barkman, K. A. (2000). The acceptability of organizational consultation with prereferral intervention teams. *School Psychology Quarterly, 15,* 172–206.

Tucker, M., Sigafoos, J., & Bushell, H. (1998). Use of noncontingent reinforcement in the treatment of challenging behavior: A review and clinical guide. *Behavior Modification, 22,* 529–547.

Turco, T. L., & Elliott, S. N. (1986). Assessment of students' acceptability ratings of teacher-initiated interventions for classroom misbehavior. *Journal of School Psychology, 24,* 277–283.

U.S. Department of Education. (2003). *Mathematics and science initiative concept paper.* Retrieved February 28, 2007, from *http://www.ed.gov/rschstat/research/progs/mathscience/concept_paper.pdf.*

U.S. Department of Education, Office of Special Education and Rehabilitative Services. (2002). *A new era: Revitalizing special education for children and their families.* Washington, DC: President's Commission on Excellence in Special Education. Retrieved March 20, 2006, from *www.ed.gov/inits/commissionsboards/whspecialeducation/reports/index.html.*

Utley, C. A., Mortweet, S. L., & Greenwood, C. R. (1997). Peer-mediated instruction and intervention. *Focus on Exceptional Children, 29*(5), 1–24.

Vadasy, P. F., Jenkins, J. R., Antil, L. R., Wayne, S. K., & O'Connor, R. E. (1997). Community-based early reading intervention for at-risk first graders. *Learning Disabilities Research and Practice, 12,* 29–39.

Vadasy, P. F., Jenkins, J. R., Antil, L. R., Phillips, N. B., & Pool, K. (1993). The research-to-practice ball game: Classwide peer tutoring and teacher interest, implementation, and modifications. *Remedial and Special Education, 18,* 143–156.

Valdez-Menchaca, M. C., & Whitehurst, G. J. (1992). Accelerating language development through picture-book reading: A systematic extension to Mexican day care. *Developmental Psychology, 28,* 1106–1114.

Vallecorsa, A. L., & deBettencourt, L. U. (1997). Using a mapping procedure to teach reading and writing skills to middle grade students with learning disabilities. *Education and Treatment of Children, 20,* 173–188.

Valleley, R. J., Evans, J. H., & Allen, K. D. (2002). Parent implementation of an oral reading intervention: A case study. *Child and Family Behavior Therapy, 24*(4), 39–50.

Valleley, R. J., & Shriver, M. D. (2003). An examination of the effects of repeated readings with secondary students. *Journal of Behavioral Education, 12,* 55–76.

Valverde, G. A., & Schmidt, W. M. (1997–1998). Refocusing U.S. math and science education. *Issues in Science and Technology, 14,* 60–66.

Van Acker, R., & Grant, S. H. (1996). Teacher and student behavior as a function of risk for aggression. *Education and Treatment of Children, 19,* 316–334.

VanAuken, T., Chafouleas, S. J., Bradley, T. A., & Martens, B. K. (2002). Using brief experimental analysis to select oral reading interventions: An investigation of treatment utility. *Journal of Behavioral Education, 11,* 165–181.

VanDerHeyden, A. M., & Burns, M. K. (2005). Using curriculum-based assessment and curriculum-based measurement to guide elementary mathematics instruction: Effect on individual and group accountability scores. *Assessment for Effective Intervention, 30,* 15–31.

VanDerHeyden, A. M., & Snyder, P. (2006). Integrating frameworks from early childhood intervention and school psychology to accelerate growth for all young children. *School Psychology Review, 35,* 519–534.

VanDerHeyden, A., Snyder, P., & Hojnoski, R. (Eds.). (2006). Integrating frameworks from early childhood intervention and school psychology to accelerate growth for all young children [Special series]. *School Psychology Review, 35*(4).

Van Houten, R., Nau, P. A., MacKenzie-Keating, S. E., Sameoto, D., & Colavecchia, B. (1982). An analysis of some variables influencing the effectiveness of reprimands. *Journal of Applied Behavior Analysis, 15,* 65–83.

Vaughn, S., & Briggs, K. L. (2003). *Reading in the classroom: Systems for the observation of teaching and learning.* Baltimore: Brookes.

Vaughn, S., Chard, D. J., Bryant, D. P., Coleman, M., Tyler, B., Linan-Thompson, S., et al. (2000). Fluency and comprehension interventions for third-grade students. *Remedial and Special Education, 21,* 325–335.

Vaughn, S., & Coleman, M. (2004). The role of mentoring in promoting use of research-based practices in reading. *Remedial and Special Education, 25,* 25–38.

Vaughn, S., & Fuchs, L. S. (2003). Redefining learning disabilities as inadequate response to instruction: The promise and potential problems. *Learning Disabilities Research and Practice, 18,* 137–146.

Vaughn, S., Gersten, R., & Chard, D. (2000). The underlying message in LD intervention research:

Findings from research syntheses. *Exceptional Children, 67,* 99–114.

Vaughn, S., & Klingner, J. K. (1999). Teaching reading comprehension through collaborative strategic reading. *Intervention in School and Clinic, 34,* 284–292.

Vaughn, S., Levy, S., Coleman, M., & Bos, C. S. (2002). Reading instruction for students with LD and EBD: A synthesis of observational studies. *Journal of Special Education, 36,* 2–13.

Vaughn, S., Linan-Thompson, S., & Hickman, P. (2003). Response to instruction as a means of identifying students with reading/learning disabilities. *Exceptional Children, 69,* 391–409.

Vaughn, S., Moody, S. W., & Schumm, J. S. (1998). Broken promises: Reading instruction in the resource room. *Exceptional Children, 64,* 1211–225.

Vaughn, S., & Schumm, J. S. (1996). Classroom ecologies: Classroom interactions and implications for inclusion of students with learning disabilities. In D. L. Speece & B. K. Keogh (Eds.), *Research on classroom ecologies: Implications for inclusion of children with learning disabilities* (pp. 107–124). Mahwah, NJ: Erlbaum.

Volpe, R. J., DiPerna, J. C., Hintze, J. M., & Shapiro, E. S. (2005). Observing students in classroom settings: A review of seven coding schemes. *School Psychology Review, 34,* 454–474.

VonBrock, M. B., & Elliott, S. N. (1987). Influence of treatment effectiveness information on the acceptability of classroom interventions. *Journal of School Psychology, 25,* 131–144.

von Ravensberg, H., & Tobin, T. J. (2006). *IDEA 2004 final regulations: The reauthorized functional behavioral assessment.* Eugene, OR: University of Oregon, College of Education, Educational and Community Supports. Retrieved March 2, 2007, from *www.uoregon.edu/~hvr/docs/idea04fba.doc.*

Walker, H. M., Steiber, S., Ramsey, E., & O'Neill, R. E. (1991). Longitudinal prediction of the school achievement, adjustment, and delinquency of antisocial versus at-risk boys. *Remedial and Special Education, 12,* 43–51.

Wallace, T., Anderson, A. R., Bartholomay, T., & Hupp, S. (2002). An ecobehavioral examination of high school classrooms that include students with disabilities. *Exceptional Children, 68,* 345–359.

Wang, M. C., Haertel, G. D., & Walberg, H. J. (1993). Toward a knowledge base for school learning. *Review of Educational Research, 63*(3), 249–294.

Wanzek, J., Vaughn, S., Wexler, J., Swanson, E. A., Edmonds, M., & Kim, A-H. (2006). A synthesis of spelling and reading interventions and their effects on the spelling outcomes of students with LD. *Journal of Learning Disabilities, 39,* 528–543.

Wasik, B. A., & Bond, M. A. (2001). Beyond the pages of a book: Interactive book reading and language development in preschool classrooms. *Journal of Educational Psychology, 93,* 243–250.

Watkinson, J. T., & Lee, S. W. (1992). Curriculum-based measures of written expression for learning-disabled and nondisabled students. *Psychology in the Schools, 29,* 184–191.

Watson, T. S., & Kramer, J. J. (1995). Teaching problem solving skills to teachers-in-training: An analogue experimental analysis of three methods. *Journal of Behavioral Education, 5,* 281–293.

Watson, T. S., & Robinson, S. L. (1996). Direct behavioral consultation: An alternative approach to didactic consultation. *School Psychology Quarterly, 11,* 267–278.

Weber, K. P., Killu, K., Derby, K. M., & Barretto, A. (2005). The status of functional behavior assessment (FBA): Adherence to standard practice in FBA methodology. *Psychology in the Schools, 42,* 737–744.

Webster-Stratton, C. (1993). Strategies for helping early school-aged children with oppositional defiant and conduct disorders: The importance of home–school partnerships. *School Psychology Review, 22,* 437–457.

Wehby, J. H., Dodge, K. A., & Valente, E. (1993). School behavior of first grade children identified as at-risk for development of conduct problems. *Behavioral Disorders, 19,* 67–78.

Wehby, J. H., Symons, F. J., Canale, J. A., & Go, F. J. (1998). Teaching practices in classrooms for students with emotional and behavioral disorders: Discrepancies between recommendations and observations. *Behavioral Disorders, 24,* 51–56.

Wehby, J. H., Symons, F. J., & Shores, R. E. (1995). A descriptive analysis of aggressive behavior in classrooms for students with emotional and behavioral disorders. *Behavioral Disorders, 20,* 87–105.

Wehby, J. H., Tally, B. B., & Falk, K. B. (2004). Identifying the relation between the function of student problem behavior and teacher instructional behavior. *Assessment for Effective Intervention, 30,* 41–51.

Weiner, R. K., Sheridan, S. M., & Jenson, W. R. (1998). The effects of conjoint behavioral consultation and a structured homework program on math completion and accuracy in junior high students. *School Psychology Quarterly, 13,* 281–309.

Weinstein, C. S. (2003). *Secondary classroom management: Lessons from research and practice* (2nd ed.). New York: McGraw-Hill.

Weinstein, G., & Cooke, N. L. (1992). The effects of two repeated reading interventions on the generalization of fluency. *Learning Disability Quarterly, 15,* 21–28.

Weissenburger, J. W., & Espin, C. (2005). Curriculum-based measures of writing across grade levels. *Journal of School Psychology, 43,* 153–169.

Welch, M., Brownell, K., & Sheridan, S. M. (1999). What's the score and game plan on teaming in schools? A review of the literature on team teaching and school-based problem-solving teams. *Remedial and Special Education, 20*, 36–49.

Welsh, M., Parke, R. D., Widaman, K., & O'Neil, R. (2001). Linkages between children's social and academic competence: A longitudinal analysis. *Journal of School Psychology, 39*, 463–481.

Wentzel, K. R. (1991). Relations between social competence and academic achievement in early adolescence. *Child Development, 62*, 1066–1078.

Wentzel, K. R. (1993). Does being good make the grade? Social behavior and academic competence in middle school. *Journal of Educational Psychology, 85*, 357–364.

Wentzel, K. R. (1998). Social support and adjustment in middle school: The role of parents, teachers, and peers. *Journal of Educational Psychology, 90*, 202–209.

Wentzel, K. R. (1999). Social-motivational processes and interpersonal relationships: Implications for understanding students' academic success. *Journal of Educational Psychology, 91*, 76–97.

Wentzel, K. R. (2002). Are effective teachers like good parents? Teaching styles and student adjustment in early adolescence. *Child Development, 73*, 287–301.

West, J., Denton, K., & Germino-Hausken, E. (2000). *America's kindergarteners* (NCES 2000-070). Washington, DC: U.S. Department of Education, National Center for Educational Statistics. Retrieved June 3, 2007, from *nces.ed.gov/pubs2000/2000070.pdf*.

Wharton-McDonald, R., Pressley, M., & Hampston, J. M. (1998). Literacy instruction in nine first-grade classrooms: Teacher characteristics and student achievement. *Elementary School Journal, 99*, 101–128.

Wheldall, K., & Lam, Y. (1988). Rows versus tables: II. The effects of two classroom seating arrangements on classroom disruption rate, on-task behaviour and teacher behaviour in three special school classes. *Educational Psychology, 7*, 303–312.

Wheldall, K., Morris, M., Vaughan, P., & Ng, Y. Y. (1981). Rows versus tables: An example of the use of behavioral ecology in two classes of eleven-year-old children. *Educational Psychology, 1*, 171–184.

Whinnery, K. W., & Fuchs, L. S. (1993). Effects of goal and test-taking strategies on the computation performance of students with learning disabilities. *Learning Disabilities Research and Practice, 8*, 204–214.

Whinnery, K. W., Fuchs, L. S., & Fuchs, D. (1991). General, special, and remedial teachers' acceptance of behavioral and instructional strategies for mainstreaming students with mild handicaps. *Remedial and Special Education, 12*, 6–17.

White, A. G., & Bailey, J. S. (1990). Reducing disruptive behaviors of elementary physical education students with sit and watch. *Journal of Applied Behavior Analysis, 23*, 353–359.

Whitehurst, G. J., Arnold, D. S., Epstein, J. N., Angell, A. L., Smith, M., & Fischel, J. (1994). A picture book reading intervention in day care and home for children from low-income families. *Developmental Psychology, 30*, 679–689.

Whitehurst, G. J., Epstein, J. N., Angell, A. L., Payne, A. C., Crone, D. A., & Fischel, J. E. (1994). Outcomes of an emergent literacy intervention in Head Start. *Journal of Educational Psychology, 86*, 542–555.

Whitehurst, G. J., Falco, F. L., Lonigan, C. J., Fischel, J., DeBaryshe, B. D., Valdez-Menchaca, M. C., et al. (1988). Accelerating language development through picture book reading. *Developmental Psychology, 24*, 552–559.

Whitehurst, G. J., Zevenbergen, A. A., Crone, D. A., Schultz, M. D., Velting, O. N., & Fischel, J. E. (1999). Outcomes of an emergent literacy intervention from Head Start through second grade. *Journal of Educational Psychology, 92*, 261–272.

Whitten, E., & Dieker, L. (1995). Intervention assistance teams: A broader vision. *Preventing School Failure, 40*(1), 41–45.

Wickstrom, K. F., Jones, K. M., LaFleur, L. H., & Witt, J. C. (1998). An analysis of treatment integrity in school-based behavioral consultation. *School Psychology Quarterly, 13*, 141–154.

Wickstrom, K. R., & Witt, J. C. (1993). Resistance within school-based consultation. In J. E. Zins, T. R. Kratochwill, & S. N. Elliott (Eds.), *Handbook of consultation services for children: Applications in educational and clinical settings* (pp. 159–178). San Francisco: Jossey-Bass.

Wiley, H. I., & Deno, S. L. (2005). Oral reading and maze measures as predictors of success for English learners on a state standards assessment. *Remedial and Special Education, 26*, 207–214.

Wilkinson, C. Y., Ortiz, A. A., Robertson, P. M., & Kushner, M. L. (2006). English language learners with reading-related LD: Linking data from multiple sources to make eligibility decisions. *Journal of Learning Disabilities, 39*, 129–141.

Wilkinson, L. A. (2005). Bridging the research-to-practice gap in school-based consultation: An example using case studies. *Journal of Educational and Psychological Consultation, 16*, 175–200.

Williams, J. P. (2004). Teaching expository text structure to young at-risk learners: Building the basics of comprehension instruction. *Exceptionality, 12*, 129–144.

Williams, J. P. (2005). Instruction in reading comprehension for primary-grade students: A focus on text structure. *Journal of Special Education, 39*, 6–18.

Wilson, C. P., Gutkin, T. B., Hagen, K. M., & Oats, R. G. (1998). General education teachers' knowledge and self-reported use of classroom interventions for working with difficult-to-teach students: Implications for consultation, prereferral intervention and inclusive services. *School Psychology Quarterly, 13,* 45–62.

Witt, J. C. (1997). Talk is not cheap. *School Psychology Quarterly, 12,* 281–292.

Witt, J. C., & Elliott, S. N. (1982). The response cost lottery: A time efficient and effective classroom intervention. *Journal of School Psychology, 20,* 155–161.

Witt, J. C., & Elliott, S. N. (1985). Acceptability of classroom intervention strategies. In T. R. Kratochwill (Ed.), *Advances in school psychology* (Vol. 4, pp. 251–288). Hillsdale, NJ: Erlbaum.

Witt, J. C., Gresham, F. M., & Noell, G. H. (1996). What's behavioral about behavioral consultation? *Journal of Educational and Psychological Consultation, 7,* 327–344.

Witt, J. C., Noell, G. H., LaFleur, L. H., & Mortenson, B. P. (1997). Teacher use of interventions in general education settings: Measurement and analysis of the independent variable. *Journal of Applied Behavior Analysis, 30,* 693–696.

Witt, J. C., & Robbins, J. R. (1985). Acceptability of reductive interventions for the control of inappropriate child behavior. *Journal of Abnormal Child Psychology, 13,* 59–67.

Witzel, B. S., & Mercer, C. D. (2003). Using rewards to teach students with disabilities: Implications for motivation. *Remedial and Special Education, 24,* 88–96.

Wolf, M. M. (1978). Social validity: The case for subjective measurement or how applied behavior analysis is finding its heart. *Journal of Applied Behavior Analysis, 11,* 203–214.

Wolfe, V. V., Boyd, L. A., & Wolfe, D. A. (1983). Teaching cooperative play to behavior-problem preschool children. *Education and Treatment of Children, 6,* 1–10.

Wolfgang, C. H. (2005). *Solving discipline and classroom management problems: Methods and models for today's teachers* (6th ed.). Hoboken, NJ: Wiley.

Wolfgang, C. H., & Wolfgang, M. E. (1995). *The three faces of discipline for early childhood: Empowering teachers and students* (pp. 223–225). Boston: Allyn & Bacon.

Wood, F. H. (1990). When we talk with children: The life space interview. *Behavioral Disorders, 15,* 110.

Wood, S. J., Murdock, J. Y., Cronin, M. E., Daw-son, N. M., & Kirby, P. C. (1998). Effects of self-monitoring on on-task behaviors of at-risk middle school students. *Journal of Behavioral Education, 8,* 263–279.

Woodward, J. (2004). Mathematics education in the United States: Past to present. *Journal of Learning Disabilities, 37,* 16–31.

Wurtele, S. K., & Drabman, R. S. (1984). "Beat the buzzer" for classroom dawdling: A one-year trial. *Behavior Therapy, 15,* 403–409.

Xin, Y. P., & Jitendra, A. K. (1999). The effects of instruction in solving mathematical word problems for students with learning problems: A meta-analysis. *Journal of Special Education, 32,* 207–225.

Yarbrough, J. L., Skinner, C. H., Lee, Y. J., & Lemmons, C. (2004). Decreasing transition times in a second grade classroom: Scientific support for the timely transitions game. *Journal of Applied School Psychology, 20,* 85–107.

Yeager, C., & McLaughlin, T. F. (1995). The use of a time-out ribbon and precision requests to improve child compliance in the classroom: A case study. *Child and Family Behavior Therapy, 17,* 1–9.

Yeaton, W. H., & Sechrest, L. (1981). Critical dimensions in the choice and maintenance of successful treatment: Strength, integrity, and effectiveness. *Journal of Consulting and Clinical Psychology, 49,* 156–167.

Yell, M. L., Shriner, J. G., & Katsiyannis, A. (2006). Individuals with Disabilities Education Improvement Act of 2004 and IDEA regulations of 2006: Implications for educators, administrators, and teacher trainers. *Focus on Exceptional Children, 39,* 1–24.

Zevenbergen, A. A., & Whitehurst, G. J. (2003). Dialogic reading: A shared picture book reading intervention for preschoolers. In A. Van Kleeck, S. A. Stahl, & E. B. Bauer (Eds.), *On reading books to children: Parents and teachers* (pp. 177–200). Mahwah, NJ: Erlbaum.

Zanolli, K., Daggett, J., & Pestine, H. (1995). The influence of the pace of teacher attention on preschool children's engagement. *Behavior Modification, 19,* 339–356.

Zins, J. E., & Erchul, W. P. (2002). Best practices in school consultation. In A. Thomas & J. Grimes (Eds.), *Best practices in school psychology IV* (Vol. 1, pp. 625–643). Bethesda, MD: National Association of School Psychologists.

Index

"f" following a page number indicates a figure; "t" following a page number indicates a table.